10 5 0 Kilometres 5 10 15
5 0 Miles 5 10
4 centimetres to 10 kilometres (one grid square)
1 kilometre = 0·6214 mile
1 mile = 1·6093 kilometres
SANDY
Potton
Little Shelford
Melbourn
ROYSTON
Ashwell
BALDOCK
LETCHWORTH
SAFFRON WALDEN
STEVENAGE
STANSTED MOUNTFITCHET
London (Stansted) Airport
GREAT DUNMOW
BISHOP'S STORTFORD
Buntingford
SAWBRIDGEWORTH
WARE
HERTFORD
WELWYN GARDEN CITY
HATFIELD
HODDESDON
HARLOW
CHESHUNT
WALTHAM ABBEY
EPPING
CHIPPING ONGAR
POTTERS BAR
ENFIELD
LOUGHTON
BARNET
EAST BARNET
EDGWARE
HENDON
HORNSEY
WALTHAMSTOW
ROMFORD
HORNCHURCH
UPMINSTER
BRENTWOOD
ILFORD
WANSTEAD
LEYTON
STOKE NEWINGTON
HAMPSTEAD

COUNTY
STREET ATLAS

HERTS

OS

COUNTY STREET ATLAS

PHILIP'S

HERTS

COUNTY STREET ATLAS
HERTFORDSHIRE

First Edition published 1986
This Edition published 1990 by

Ordnance Survey
Romsey Road
Maybush
Southampton SO9 4DH

and

George Philip Ltd
59 Grosvenor Street
London W1X 9DA

ISBN 0 540 05597 2 (George Philip)
ISBN 0 319 00229 2 (Ordnance Survey)

To the best of the Publishers' knowledge, the information in this atlas was correct at the time of going to press. No responsibility can be accepted for any errors or their consequences.

The representation in this atlas of a road, track or path is no evidence of the existence of a right of way.

Printed in Great Britain by
Butler & Tanner Ltd, Frome and London

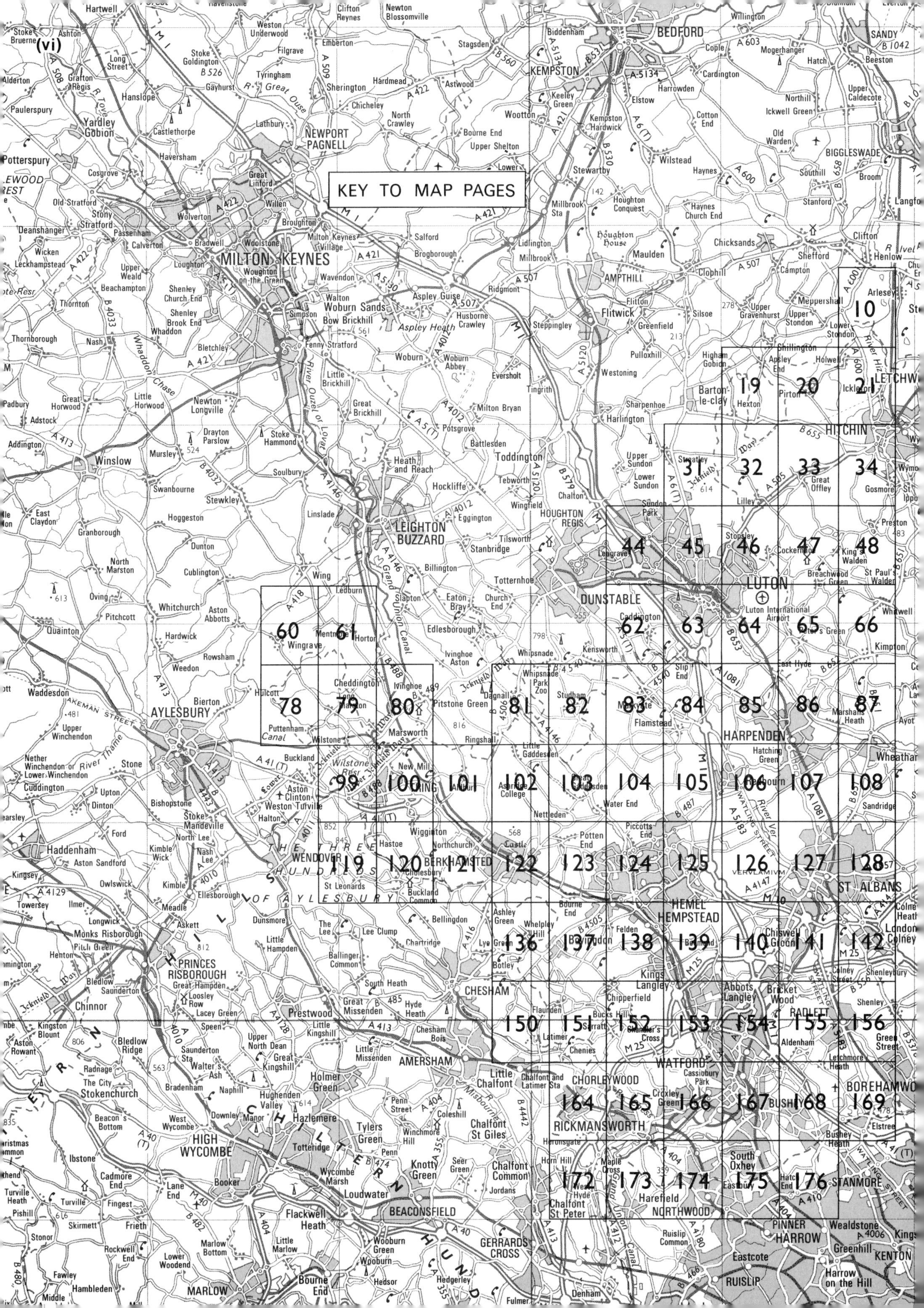
KEY TO MAP PAGES
10
19 20 21
31 32 33 34
44 45 46 47 48
60 61 62 63 64 65 66
78 79 80 81 82 83 84 85 86 87
99 100 101 102 103 104 105 106 107 108
119 120 121 122 123 124 125 126 127 128
136 137 138 139 140 141 142
150 151 152 153 154 155 156
164 165 166 167 168 169
172 173 174 175 176
BEDFORD
KEMPSTON
MILTON KEYNES
NEWPORT PAGNELL
BIGGLESWADE
AMPTHILL
Flitwick
Woburn Sands
LEIGHTON BUZZARD
HOUGHTON REGIS
DUNSTABLE
LUTON
HITCHIN
Toddington
AYLESBURY
HARPENDEN
HEMEL HEMPSTEAD
ST ALBANS
WENDOVER
BERKHAMSTED
CHESHAM
AMERSHAM
PRINCES RISBOROUGH
HIGH WYCOMBE
BEACONSFIELD
GERRARDS CROSS
MARLOW
RICKMANSWORTH
CHORLEYWOOD
WATFORD
NORTHWOOD
RADLETT
BOREHAMWOOD
STANMORE
PINNER
HARROW
RUISLIP
Winslow
Chinnor
Tring
Wing
Shefford
SANDY
LETCHWORTH

Contents

Key map	vi-vii
Administrative map	viii
Street maps	1-177
Index explanation and abbreviations	178
List of towns, villages and rural localities	179
Index	180

key to map symbols

British Rail Station	Motorway and Dual Carriageway
London Transport Station	Main or through road
Private Railway Station	A 27(T) Road numbers (Dept of Transport)
Bus or Coach Station	Gate and obstruction to traffic (restrictions may not apply at all times and to all vehicles)
Police Station (may not be open 24hrs)	Footpath / Bridleway — The representation in this atlas of a road, track or path is no evidence of the existence of a right of way.
Hospital with Casualty Facilities (may not be open 24hrs)	
Post Office	Amb Sta — Ambulance Station
	Coll — College
Place of Worship	FB — Foot Bridge
	F Sta — Fire Station
Important Building	LC — Level Crossing
	Liby — Library
P Parking	Mus — Museum
	Sch — School
120 Adjoining page indicator	TH — Town Hall

The large letters and numbers around the edge of the maps are the referencing system.
An explanation of how to use the system for locating the position of street names appears on page **154**

The small numbers identify the 1 kilometre National Grid lines.

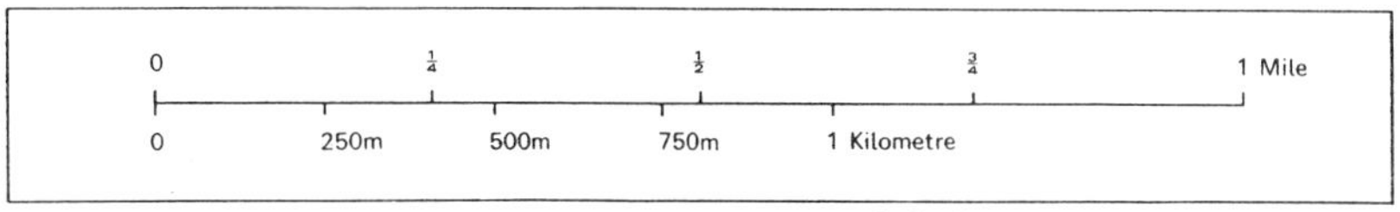

Scale of Maps is 3½ inches to 1 mile (1:18103)

Potton
Sandy
Everton
Cockayne Hatley
East Hatley
Arrington
Wimpole Hall
Croydon
Orwell
New Wimpole
Barrington
Newton
Little Shelford
Babraham
Sawston
Little Abington
Great Abington
Hildersham
Balsham
Sutton
Wrestlingworth
Tadlow
Wendy
Shepreth
Foxton
Thriplow
Whittlesford
Pampisford
Linton
Horseheath
Eyeworth
Whaddon
Meldreth
Fowlmere
Duxford
Hinxton
Bartlow
Guilden Morden
Dunton
Abington Pigotts
Kneesworth
Bassingbourn
Melbourn
Ickleton
Stump Cross
Hadstock
Shudy Camps
Castle Camps
Steeple Morden
Litlington
Great Chesterford
Little Chesterford
Ashdon
Langford
Edworth
Hinxworth
Ashwell
Royston
Heydon
Great Chishill
Little Walden
Church End
Astwick
Henlow
Caldecote
Barley
Chrishall
Elmdon
Strethall
Littlebury
Sewards End
Church End
Newnham
Therfield
Little Chishill
Duddenhoe End
Littlebury Green
Wendons Ambo
Audley End
Saffron Walden
Radwinter
Hempstead
Stotfold
Radwell
Norton
Bygrave
Icknield Way
Kelshall
Reed
Barkway
Langley
Arkesden
Audley End Sta
Wimbish
Great Sampford
Sandon
Baldock
Nuthampstead
Newport
Howlett End
Wimbish Green
Little Sampford
Wallington
Buckland
Mill End
Debden
Letchworth
Clothall
Rushden
Chipping
Wyddial
Anstey
Meesden
Brent Pelham
Clavering
Wicken Bonhunt
Rickling
Widdington
Debden Green
Thaxted
Little Bardfield
Weston
Throcking
Quendon
Willian
Cottered
Berden
Great Wymondley
Hall's Green
Cromer
Buntingford
Hare Street
Great Hormead
Stocking Pelham
Ugley
Henham
Little Wymondley
Graveley
Ardeley
Aspenden
Westmill
Furneux Pelham
East End
Ugley Green
Duton Hill
St Ippollitts
Walkern
Manuden
Broxted
Lindsell
Elsenham
Wood End
Braughing
Patmore Heath
Farnham Green
Stansted Mountfitchet
Great Easton
Preston
Stevenage
Aston End
Benington
Nasty
Puckeridge
Albury
Little Hadham
Farnham
Molehill Green
Butcher's Pasture
Paul's Walden
Langley
Aston
Standon
Birchanger
London (Stansted) Airport
Little Easton
Great Dunmow
Churchend
Old Knebworth
Bragbury End
Dane End
Colliers End
Hadham Ford
Bury Green
Stane Street
Takeley
Whitwell
Knebworth
Datchworth
Watton at Stone
Sacombe
High Cross
Much Hadham
Bishop's Stortford
Thorley
Great Hallingbury
Bacon End
Kimpton
Woolmer Green
Ermine Street
Hadham Cross
Wallbury
Spellbrook
Great Canfield
Codicote
Oakland
Stapleford
Wadesmill
Perry Green
Little Hallingbury
Hatfield Broad Oak
High Roding
Ayot St Lawrence
Burnham Green
Welwyn
Tonwell
Thundridge
Bakers End
Wareside
Widford
Sawbridgeworth
Hatfield Heath
Ayot St Peter
Harmer Green
Tewin
Bramfield
Waterford
Ware
Hunsdon
High Wych
Aythorpe Roding
Leaden Roding
High Easter
The Rodings
Wheathampstead
Welwyn Garden City
Hertford
Great Amwell
Stanstead Abbotts
Eastwick
Harlow
Sheering
Matching Tye
Matching
White Roothing or White Roding
Abbess Roding
Margaret Roding
Good Easter
Mashbury
Stanborough
Hertingfordbury
Hertford Heath
Letty Green
Hailey
Roydon
Potter Street
Matching Green
Little Laver
Beauchamp Roding
Hatfield
R Lea or Lee
Essendon
Bayford
Hoddesdon
Brickendon
Broxbourne
Lower Nazeing
Great Parndon
Foster Street
High Laver
Magdalen Laver
Shellow Bowells
Little Berkhamsted
Epping Green
Woodside
Welham Green
Broadley Common
Nazeing
Hastingwood
Fyfield
Willingale
Moreton
Colney Heath
Wormley West End
Newgate Street
Hammond Street
Wormley
Bumble's Green
Epping Green
Thornwood Common
Bobbingworth
Blake Hall
Norton Mandeville
Cooksmill Green
London Colney
Water End
Brookmans Park
Goff's Oak
Cheshunt
Cobbin's Brook
North Weald Bassett
High Ongar
Loves Green
Norton Heath
South Mimms
Northaw
Cuffley
Epping
Greensted
Chipping Ongar
Nine Ashes
Potters Bar
Waltham Abbey
Upshire
Fiddlers Hamlet
Toot Hill
Blackmore
Mill Green
Ridge
Crews Hill
Waltham Cross
Theydon Bois
Stanford Rivers
Little End
Stondon Massey
Fryerning
Green Street
Wrotham Park
Enfield Chase
Forty Hill
Stapleford Tawney
Kelvedon Hatch
Doddinghurst
Heybridge
High Beach
Navestock Heath
Mountnessing
Hamwood
Monken Hadley
Cockfosters
Enfield
Ponders End
Loughton
Abridge
Navestock Side
Arkley
Barnet
Winchmore Hill
Stapleford Abbotts
Pilgrims Hatch
Elstree
Totteridge
East Barnet
Lambourne
Shenfield
Hutton
Brentwood
Edgware
Mill Hill
Friern Barnet
Finchley
Brook Street
Ingrave
Great Warley
Little Warley
Herongate
Dunton Wayletts
Hendon
Walthamstow
Barkingside
Romford
Kingsbury
Golders Green
Hornsey
Seven Kings
Hornchurch
West Horndon
Kenton
Wanstead
Leyton
Stoke Newington
Hampstead
Ilford
Becontree
Rush Green
Upminster
Cranham
Bulphan
10 5 0 Kilometres 5 10 15
5 0 Miles 5 10
4 centimetres to 10 kilometres (one grid square)
1 kilometre = 0·6214 mile
1 mile = 1·6093 kilometres

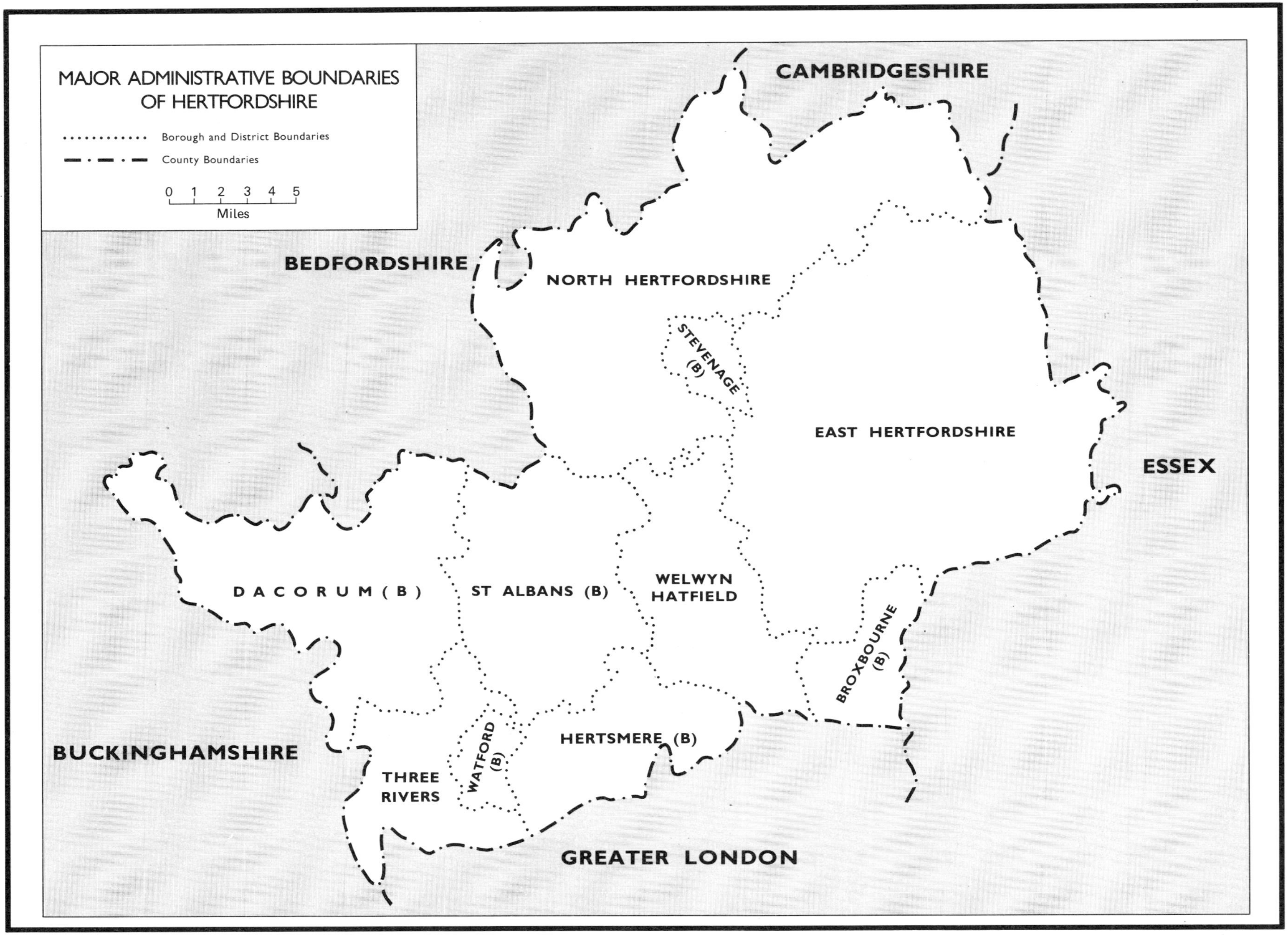
MAJOR ADMINISTRATIVE BOUNDARIES OF HERTFORDSHIRE
Borough and District Boundaries
County Boundaries
0 1 2 3 4 5
Miles
CAMBRIDGESHIRE
BEDFORDSHIRE
ESSEX
BUCKINGHAMSHIRE
GREATER LONDON
NORTH HERTFORDSHIRE
STEVENAGE (B)
EAST HERTFORDSHIRE
DACORUM (B)
ST ALBANS (B)
WELWYN HATFIELD
BROXBOURNE (B)
HERTSMERE (B)
THREE RIVERS
WATFORD (B)

not continued, see key diagram

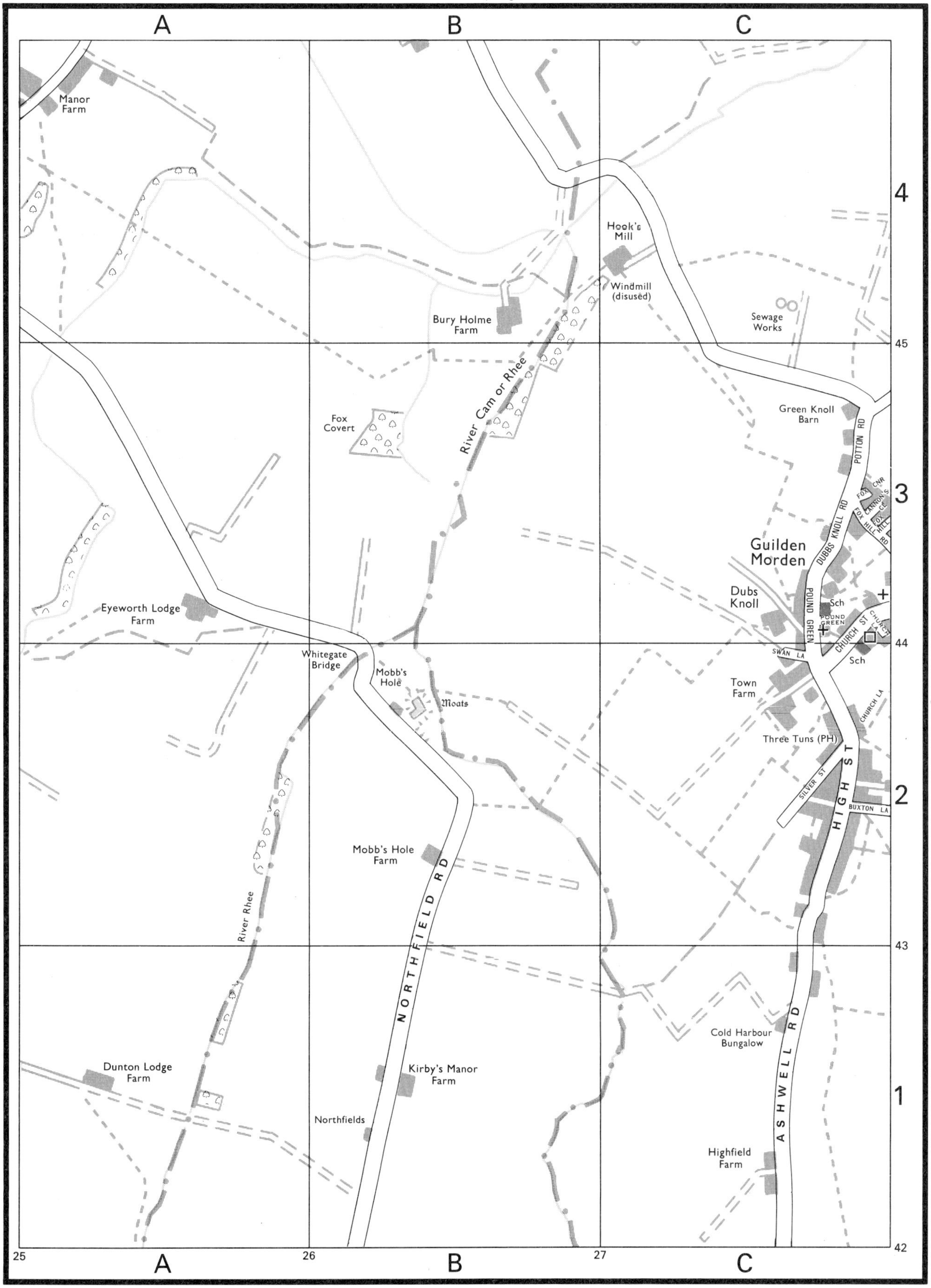

not continued, see key diagram

4

not continued, see key diagram

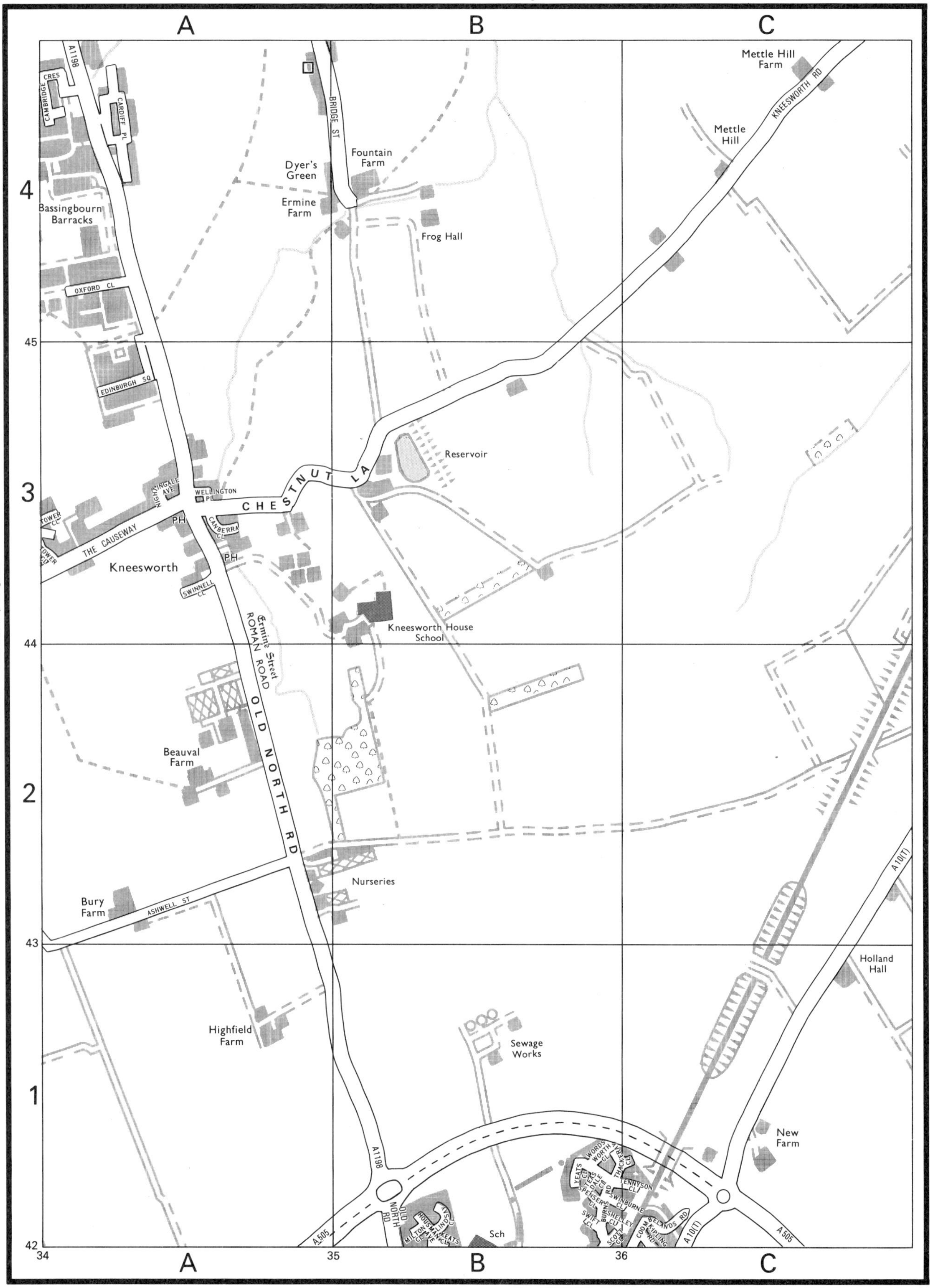

not continued, see key diagram

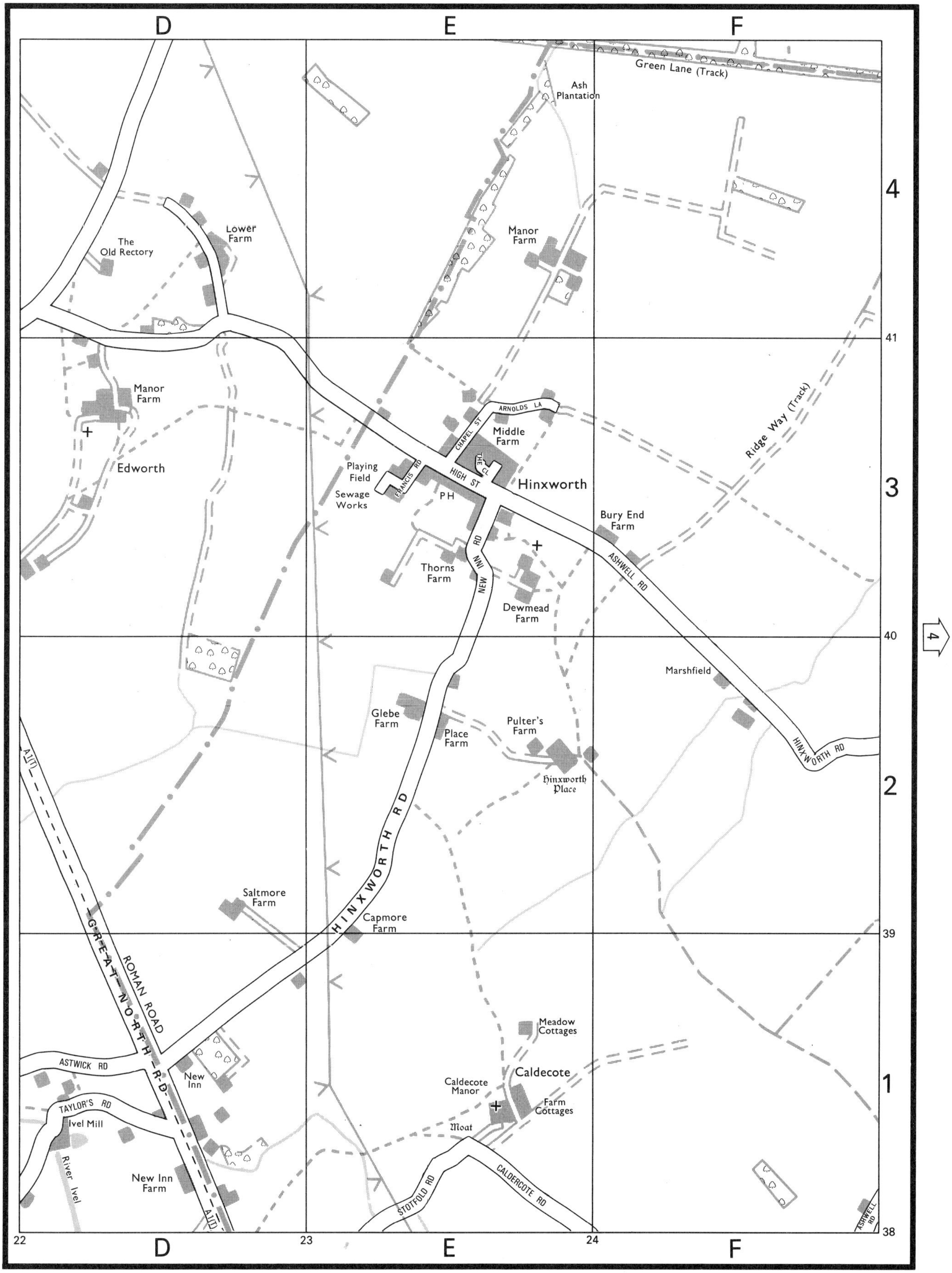

4

12

1

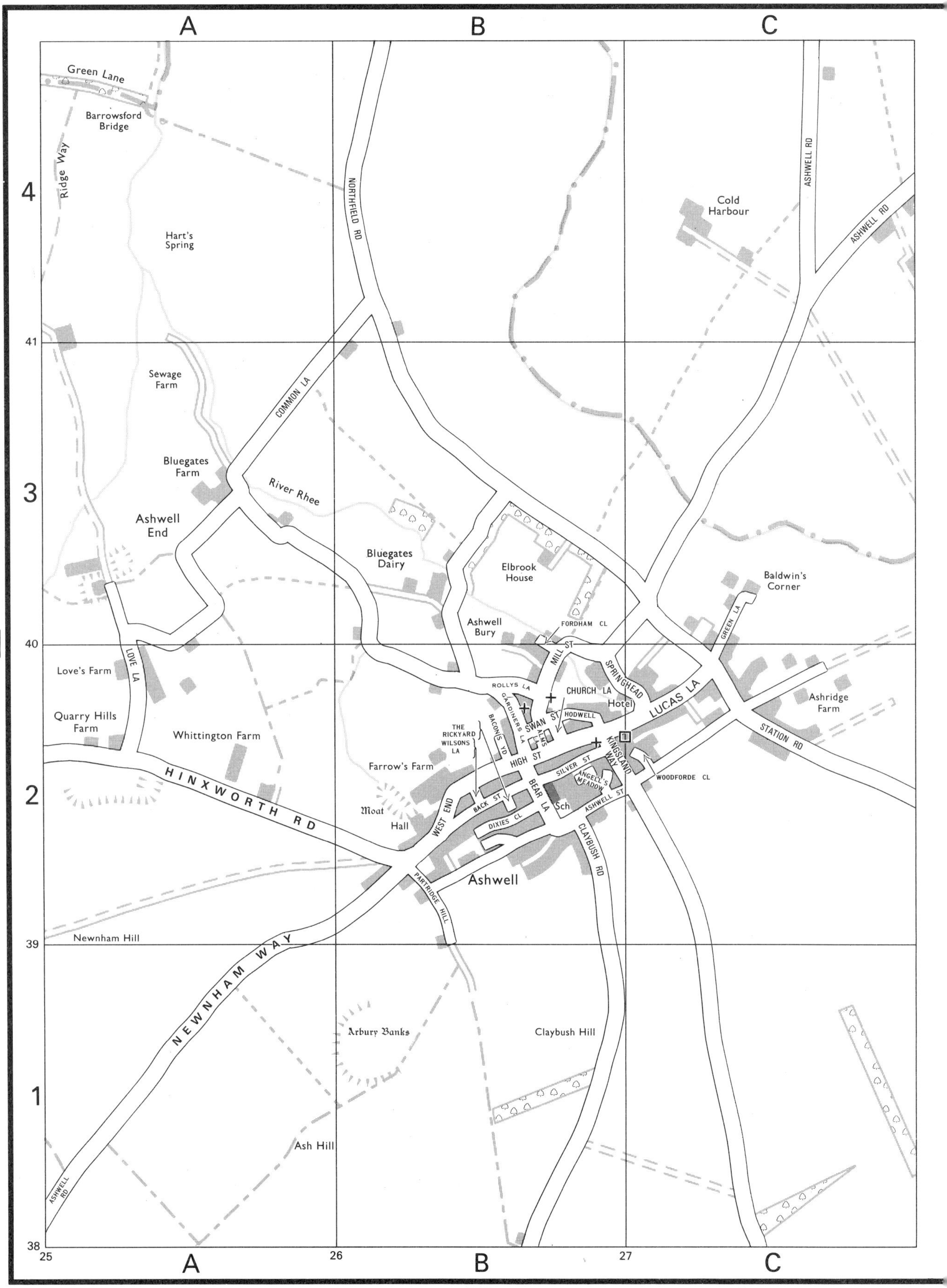
A
B
C
Green Lane
Barrowsford Bridge
Ridge Way
4
Hart's Spring
NORTHFIELD RD
ASHWELL RD
Cold Harbour
ASHWELL RD
41
Sewage Farm
COMMON LA
Bluegates Farm
3
River Rhee
Ashwell End
Bluegates Dairy
Elbrook House
Baldwin's Corner
Ashwell Bury
FORDHAM CL
GREEN LA
40
MILL ST
SPRINGHEAD
Love's Farm
LOVE LA
ROLLYS LA
CHURCH LA
Hotel
LUCAS LA
Ashridge Farm
GARDINERS LA
SWAN ST
HODWELL
Quarry Hills Farm
Whittington Farm
THE RICKYARD
WILSONS LA
BACON'S YD
ALMS LA
KINGSLAND WAY
STATION RD
HIGH ST
SILVER ST
Farrow's Farm
ANGELL'S MEADOW
WOODFORDE CL
HINXWORTH RD
2
BACK ST
BEAR LA
Sch
ASHWELL ST
Moat
WEST END
Hall
DIXIES CL
CLAYBUSH RD
PARTRIDGE HILL
Ashwell
39
Newnham Hill
NEWNHAM WAY
Arbury Banks
Claybush Hill
1
Ash Hill
ASHWELL RD
38
25
26
27

3

13

not continued, see key diagram

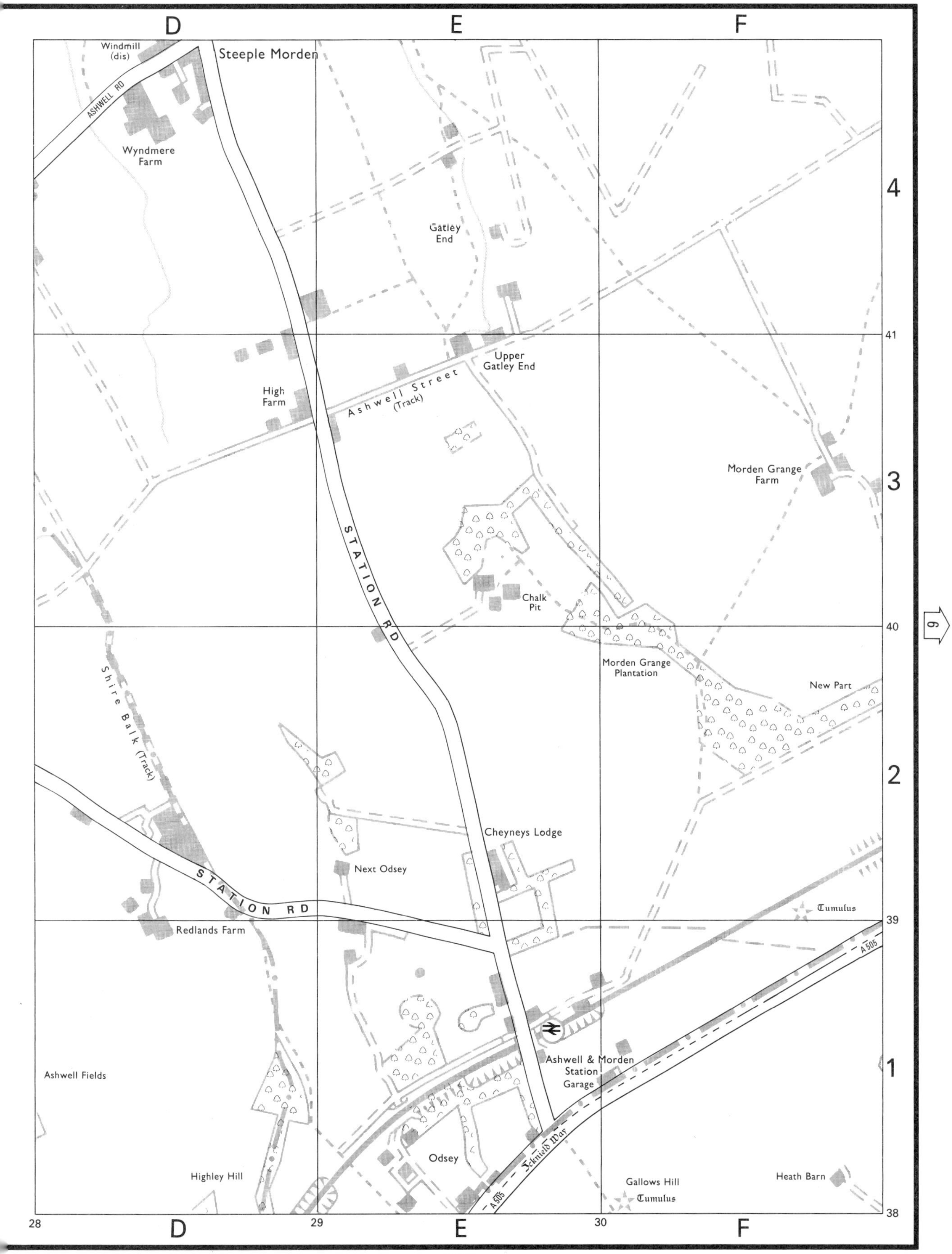

14

not continued, see key diagram

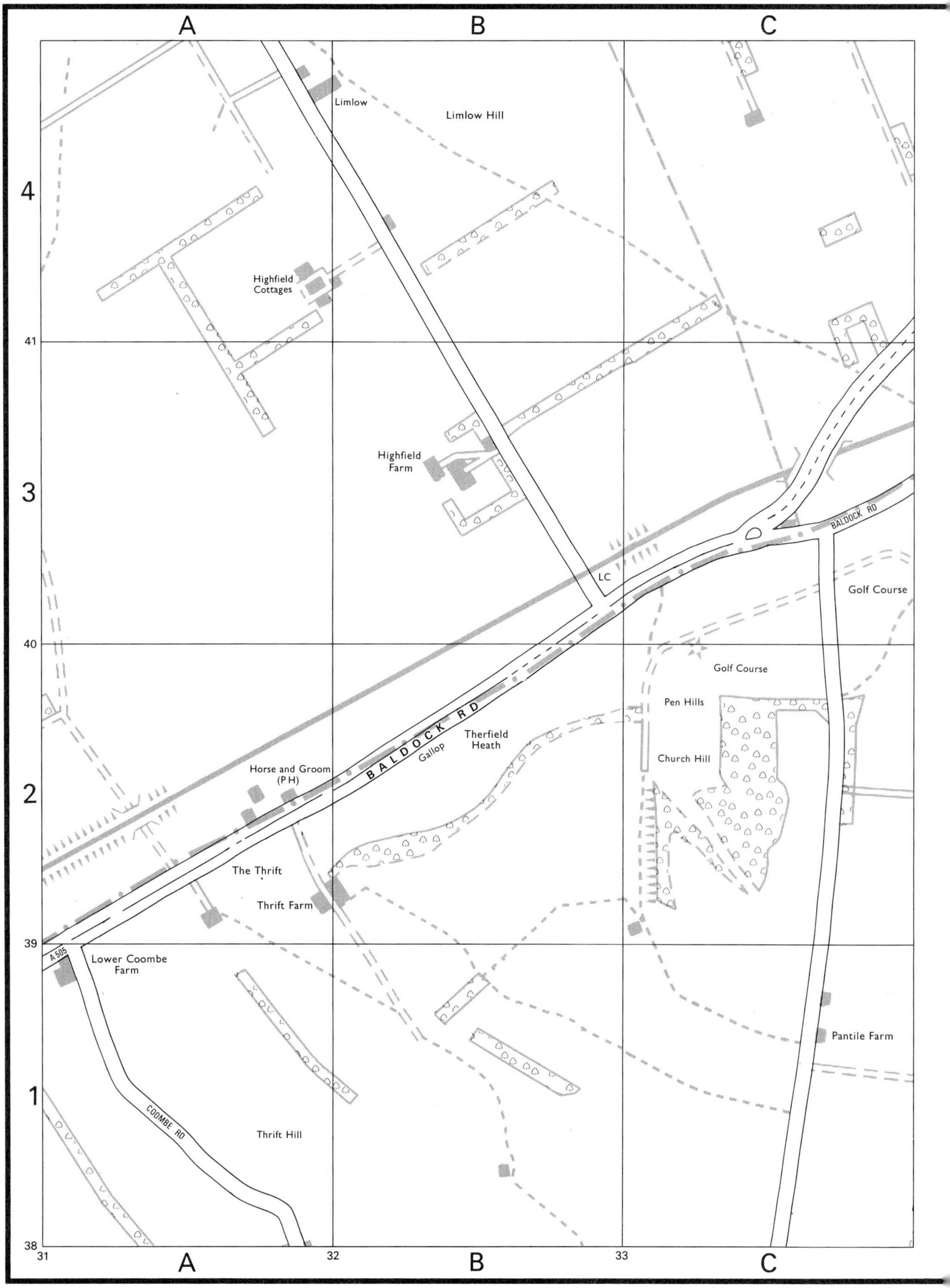

5

15

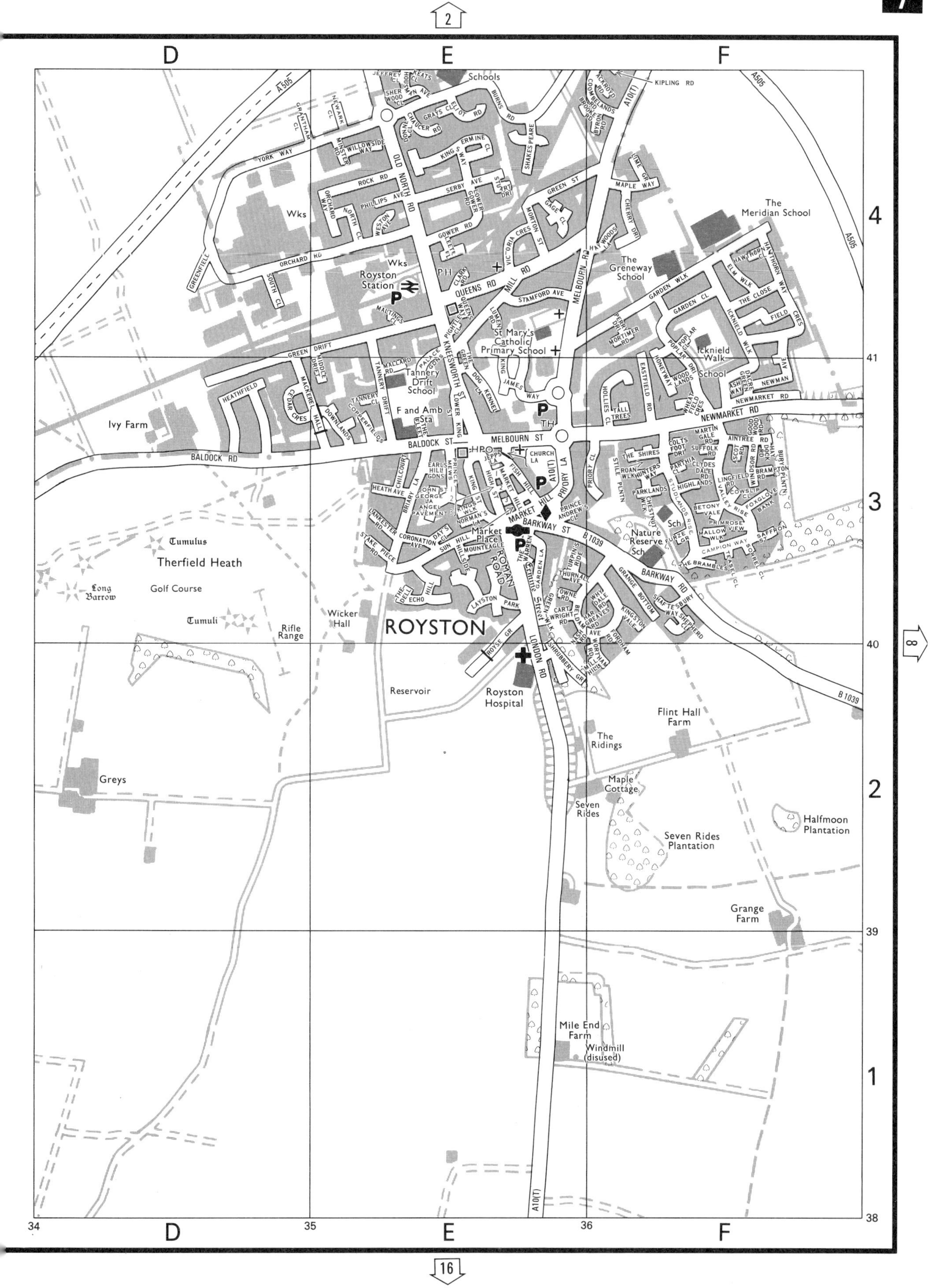
2
16
8
D
E
F
4
3
2
1
41
40
39
38
34
35
36
Schools
KIPLING RD
A505
A10(T)
B1039
The Meridian School
The Greneway School
Wks
Royston Station
St Mary's Catholic Primary School
Icknield Walk School
Tannery Drift School
F and Amb Sta
Ivy Farm
Tumulus
Therfield Heath
Golf Course
Long Barrow
Tumuli
Rifle Range
Wicker Hall
ROYSTON
Market Place
Nature Reserve
Sch
Reservoir
Royston Hospital
Flint Hall Farm
The Ridings
Maple Cottage
Seven Rides
Seven Rides Plantation
Halfmoon Plantation
Grange Farm
Greys
Mile End Farm
Windmill (disused)
YORK WAY
ORCHARD RD
GREEN DRIFT
BALDOCK RD
BALDOCK ST
MELBOURN ST
NEWMARKET RD
BARKWAY ST
BARKWAY RD
QUEENS RD
MILL RD
MELBOURN RD
OLD NORTH RD
KNEESWORTH ST
LONDON RD
ROMAN ROAD
Icknield Street
GREEN ST
GARDEN WLK
STAMFORD AVE
PRIORY LA
MARKET HILL
FISH HILL
HIGH ST
KING ST
SUN HILL
CORONATION AVE
HEATH AVE
LAYSTON PARK
ROYSE GR
GRANGE BOTTOM
SHAFTESBURY WAY
KINGSTON VALE
HEATHFIELD
MACKEREL HALL
DOWNLANDS
COPPERFIELDS
TANNERY DRIFT
CHILCOURT
BRIARY LA
THE SHIRES
CAMPION WAY
THE BRAMBLES
HOLLIES CL
EASTFIELD RD
NEWMAN AVE
THE CLOSE
FIELD CL
HAWTHORN WAY
MAPLE WAY
CHERRY DRI
SERBY AVE
ROCK RD
WILLOWSIDE WAY
PHILLIPS AVE
SHAKESPEARE RD
BURNS RD
ERMINE CL
CHAUCER RD
SOUTH CL
GREENFIELD
NEWARK CL
GRANTHAM CL
ECHO HILL
THE DELL
STAKE PIECE RD
LANKESTER RD

not continued, see key diagram

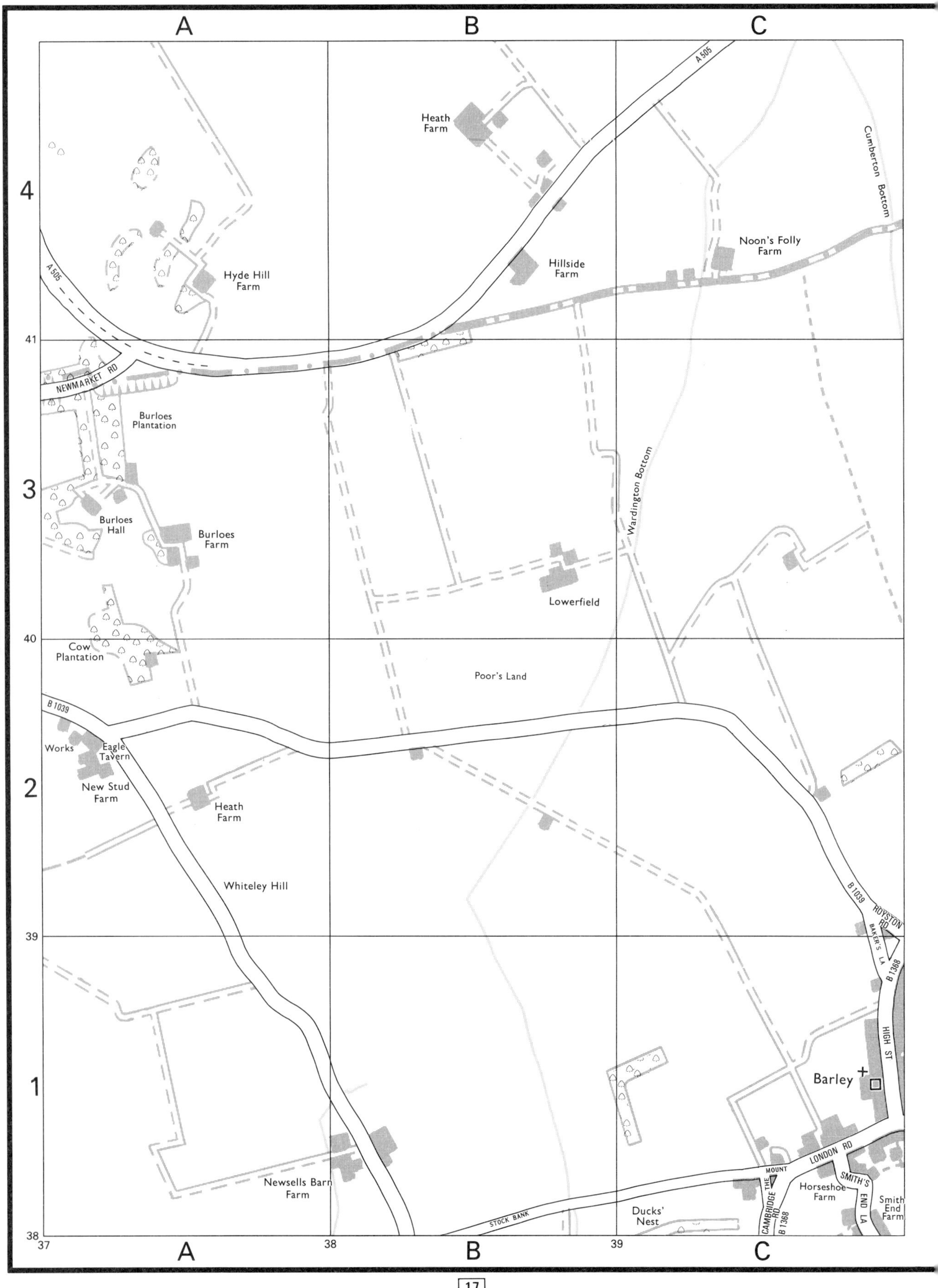

7

17

not continued, see key diagram

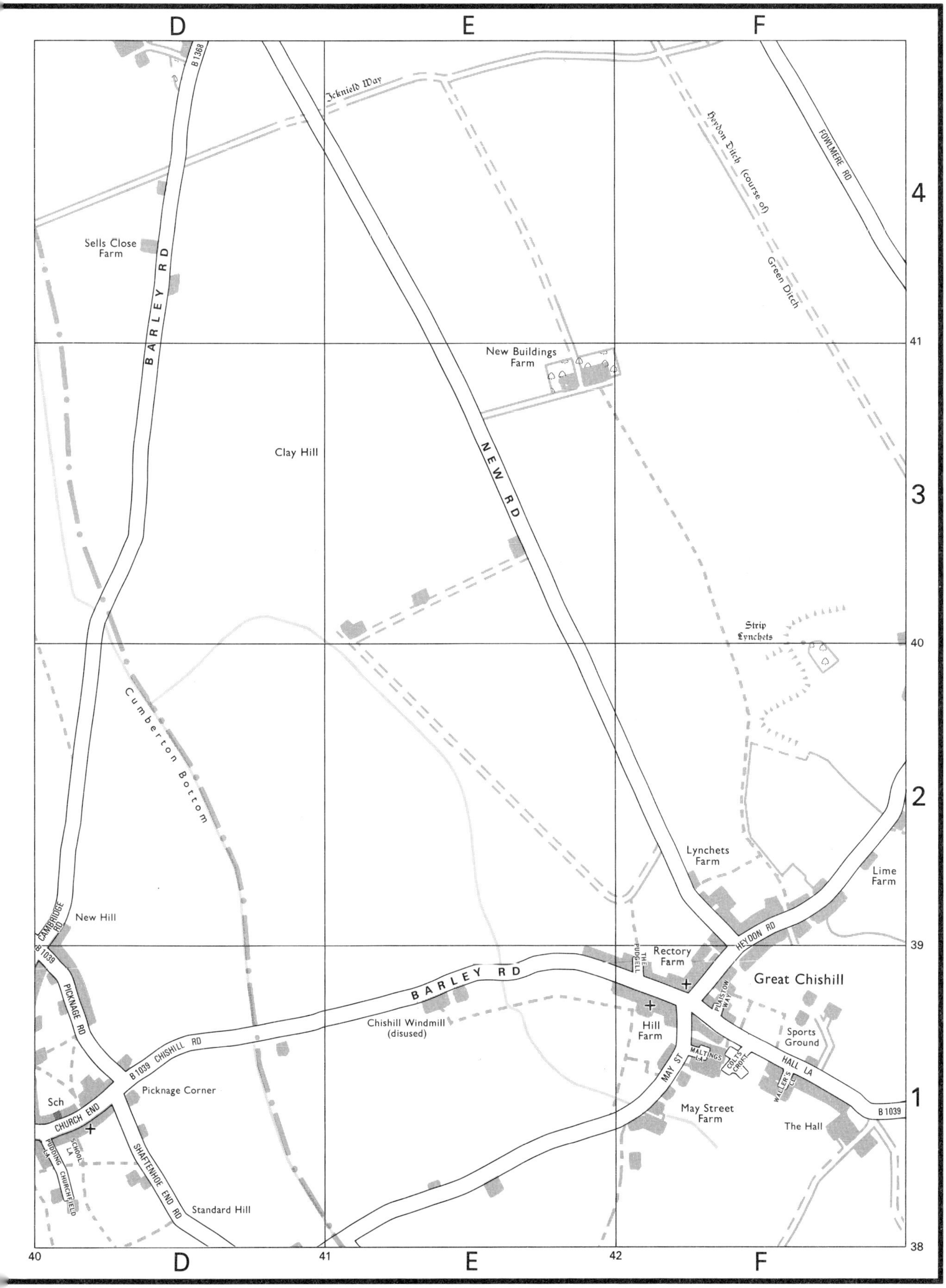

not continued, see key diagram

not continued, see key diagram

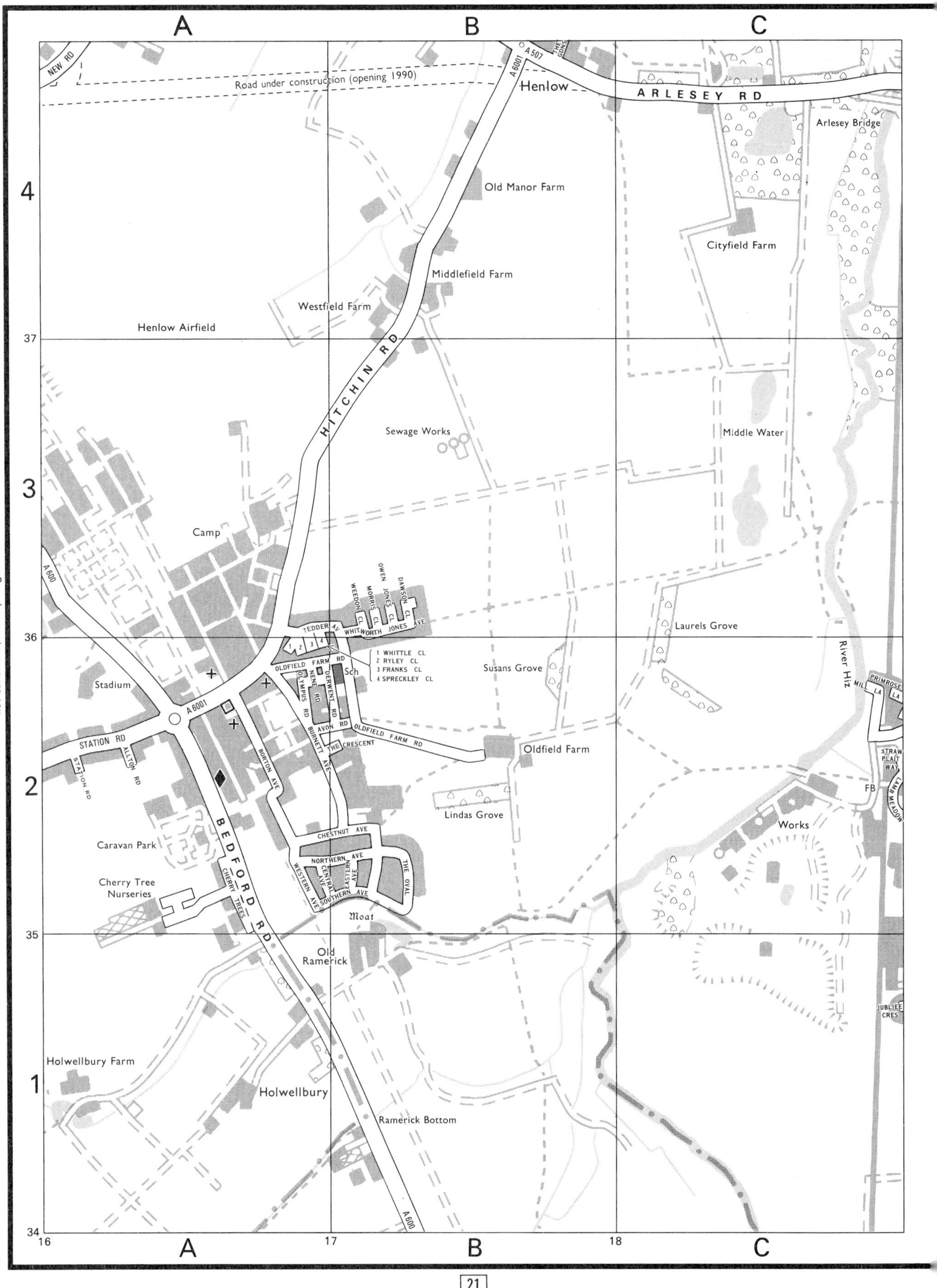

not continued, see key diagram

21

not continued, see key diagram

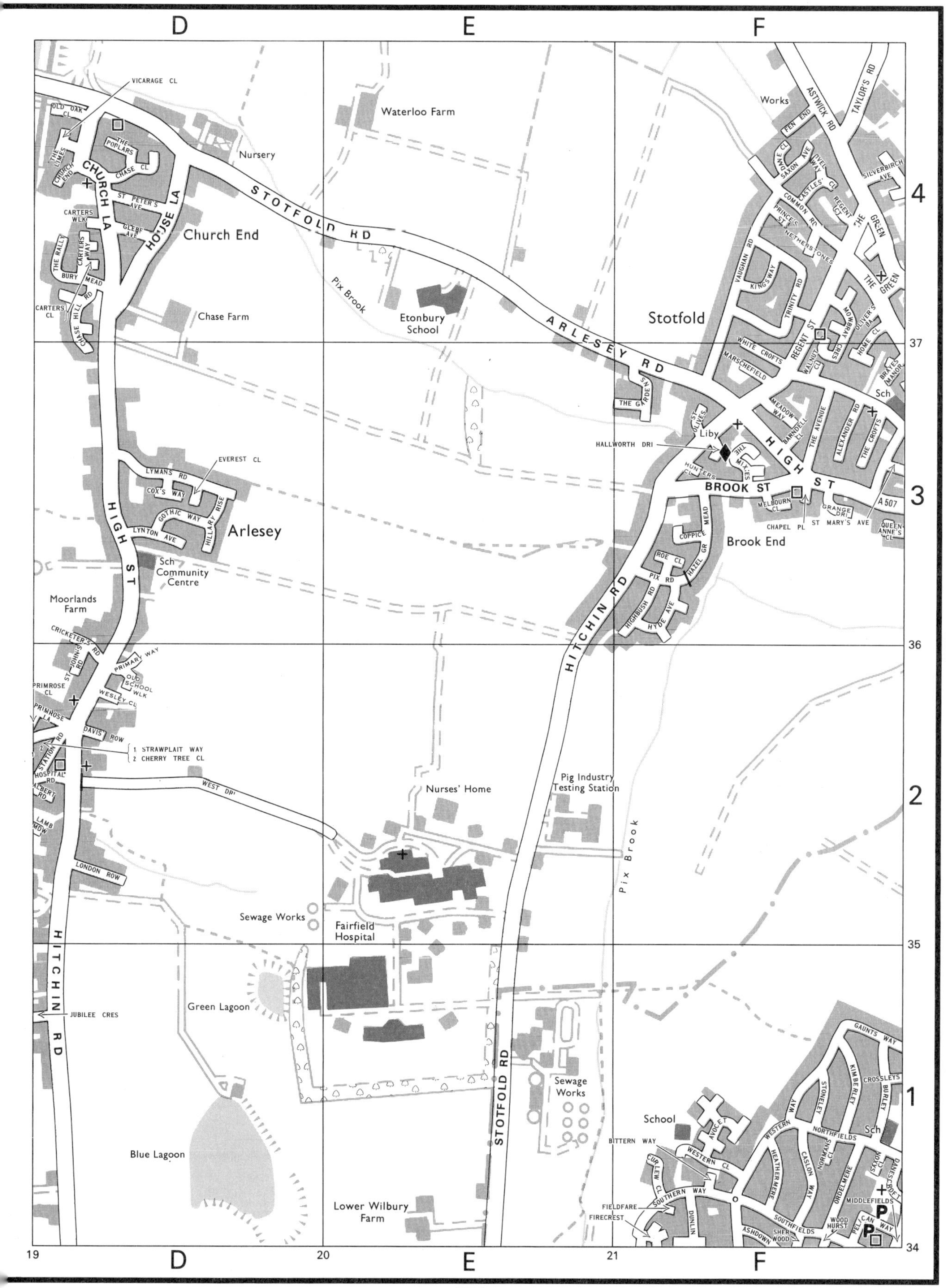

12

22

3

11

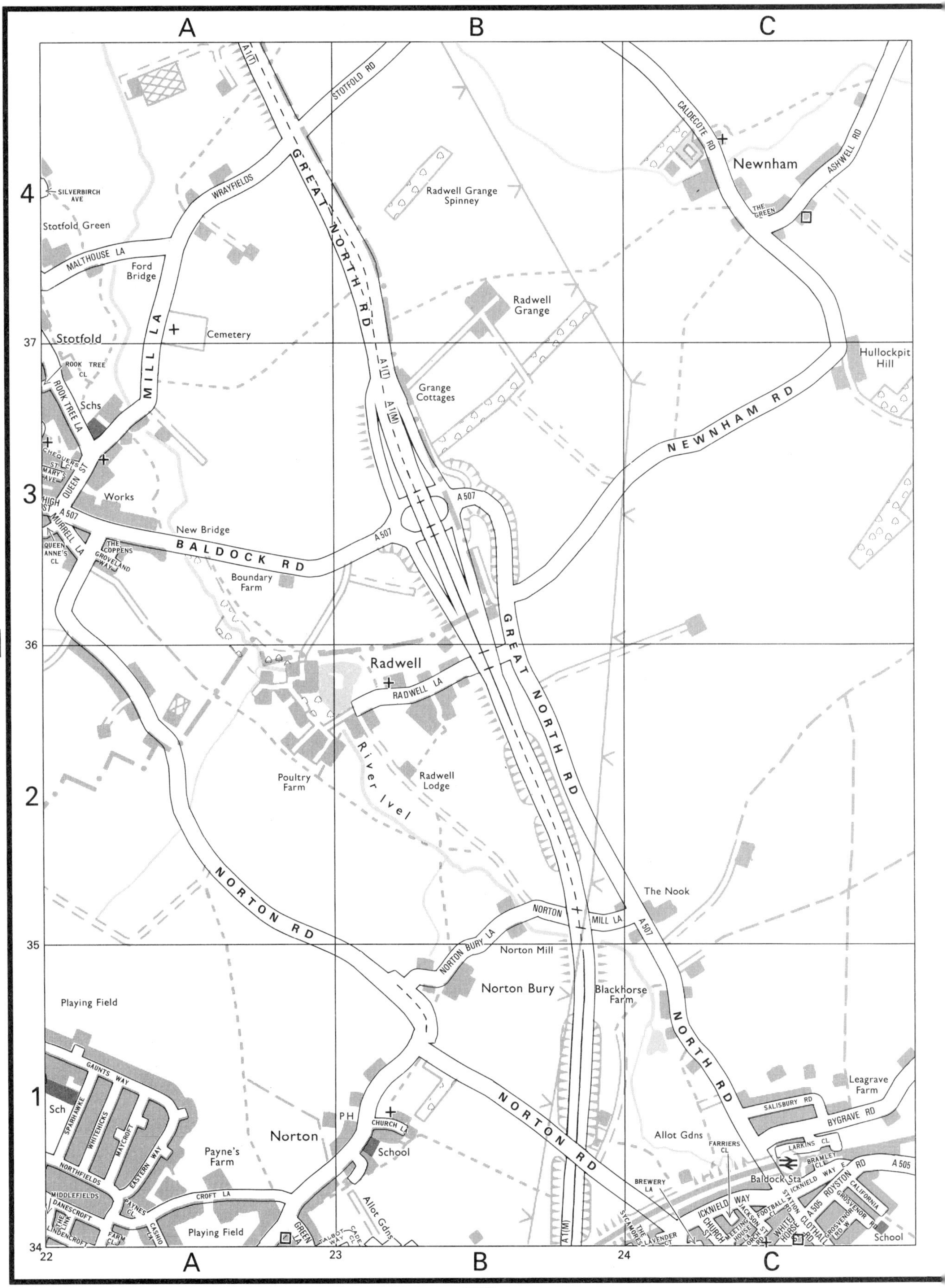
A
B
C
4
3
2
1
37
36
35
34
22
23
24
SILVERBIRCH AVE
Stotfold Green
MALTHOUSE LA
Ford Bridge
WRAYFIELDS
STOTFOLD RD
A1(T)
GREAT NORTH RD
Radwell Grange Spinney
Radwell Grange
CALDECOTE RD
Newnham
ASHWELL RD
THE GREEN
Cemetery
Stotfold
MILL LA
ROOK TREE CL
ROOK TREE LA
Schs
CHEQUERS ST
ST MARY'S AVE
QUEEN ST
HIGH ST
MURRELL LA
QUEEN ANNE'S CL
Works
A 507
New Bridge
THE COPPENS
GROVELAND WAY
BALDOCK RD
Boundary Farm
Grange Cottages
A1(M)
Hullockpit Hill
NEWNHAM RD
Radwell
RADWELL LA
Poultry Farm
River Ivel
Radwell Lodge
The Nook
NORTON RD
NORTON MILL LA
NORTON BURY LA
Norton Mill
Norton Bury
Blackhorse Farm
NORTH RD
Playing Field
GAUNTS WAY
Sch
SPARHAWKE
WHITEHICKS
MAYCROFT
EASTERN WAY
NORTHFIELDS
MIDDLEFIELDS
DANESCROFT
THE LINK
LINDENCROFT
FARM CL
PAYNES CL
CASHIO LA
Payne's Farm
CROFT LA
Norton
PH
CHURCH LA
School
GREEN LA
TALBOT WAY
CADE CL
Allot Gdns
Leagrave Farm
SALISBURY RD
BYGRAVE RD
Allot Gdns
FARRIERS CL
LARKINS CL
BRAMLEY CL
A 505
BREWERY LA
Baldock Sta
ICKNIELD WAY
ICKNIELD WAY E
ROYSTON RD
CALIFORNIA
GROSVENOR RD
GROSVENOR RD W
SYCAMORES
THE LAVENDER CT
CHURCH ST
JACKSON ST
MEETING HOUSE LA
FOOTBALL CL
STATION RD
WHITE HORSE ST
CLOTHALL RD
School

23

4

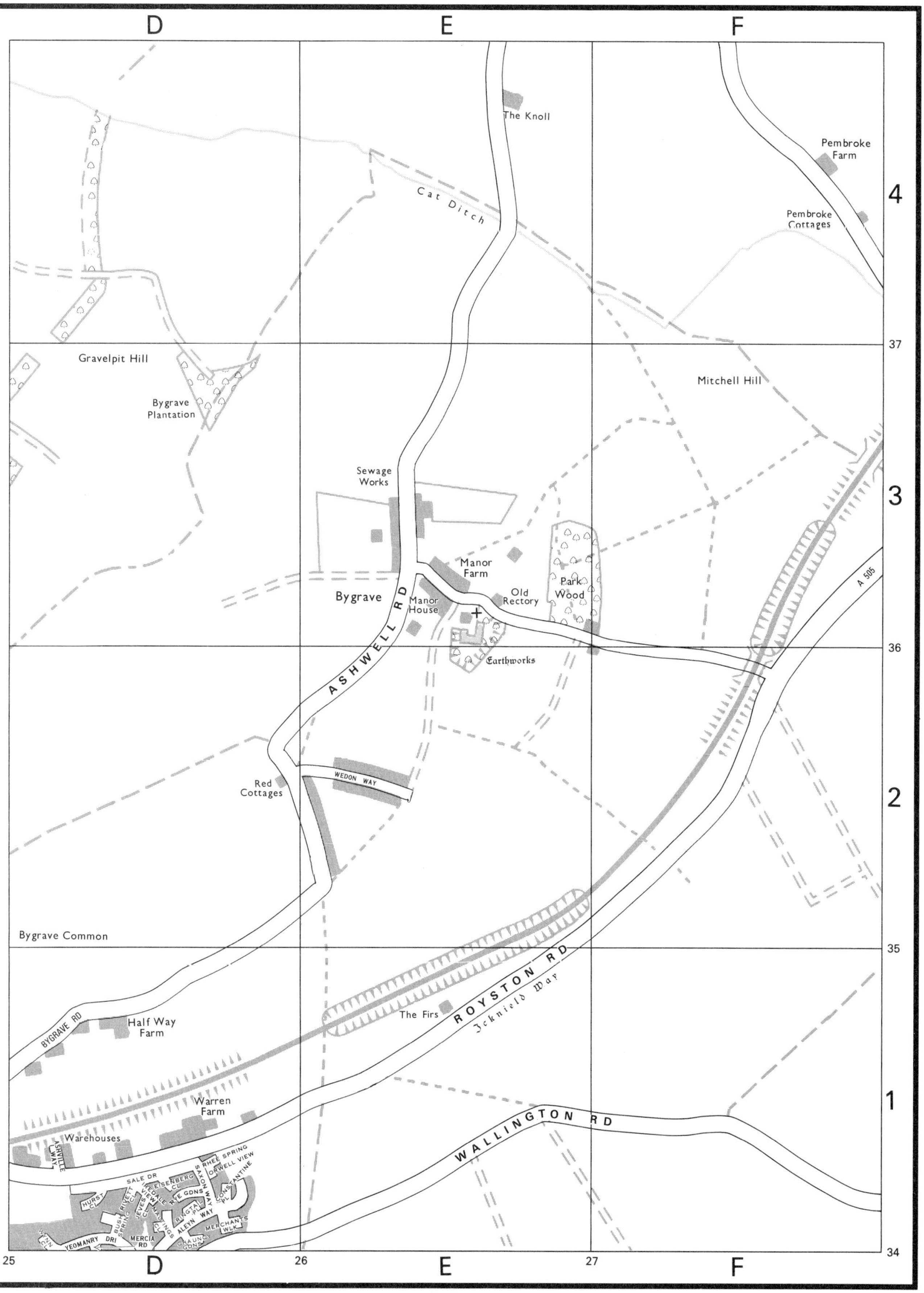

D
E
F
The Knoll
Pembroke Farm
Cat Ditch
Pembroke Cottages
4
37
Gravelpit Hill
Bygrave Plantation
Mitchell Hill
Sewage Works
3
Manor Farm
Bygrave
Manor House
Old Rectory
Park Wood
A 505
ASHWELL RD
Earthworks
36
WEDON WAY
Red Cottages
2
Bygrave Common
35
ROYSTON RD
Icknield Way
The Firs
BYGRAVE RD
Half Way Farm
1
Warren Farm
Warehouses
WALLINGTON RD
ASHVILLE WAY
SALE DR
RHEE SPRING
ORWELL VIEW
HURST CL
YEOMANRY DRI
MERCIA RD
MERCHANTS WLK
ALEYN WAY
25
26
27
34

14

24

5

13

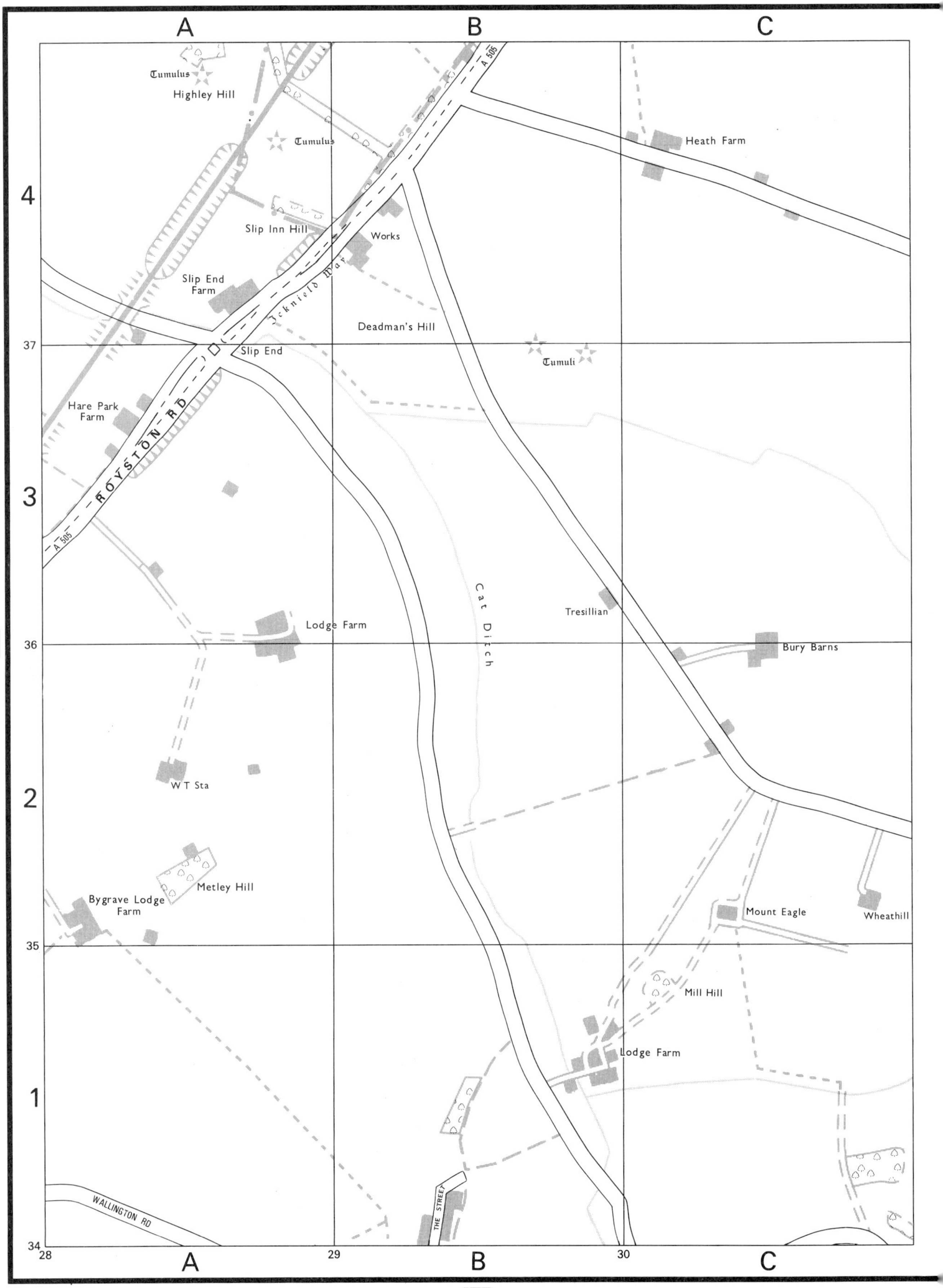
A
B
C
4
3
2
1
37
36
35
34
28
29
30
Tumulus
Highley Hill
Tumulus
Slip Inn Hill
Works
Slip End Farm
Jcknield Way
Deadman's Hill
Slip End
A 505
Heath Farm
Tumuli
Hare Park Farm
ROYSTON RD
A 505
Cat Ditch
Tresillian
Lodge Farm
Bury Barns
W T Sta
Metley Hill
Bygrave Lodge Farm
Mount Eagle
Wheathill
Mill Hill
Lodge Farm
WALLINGTON RD
THE STREET
A
B
C

25

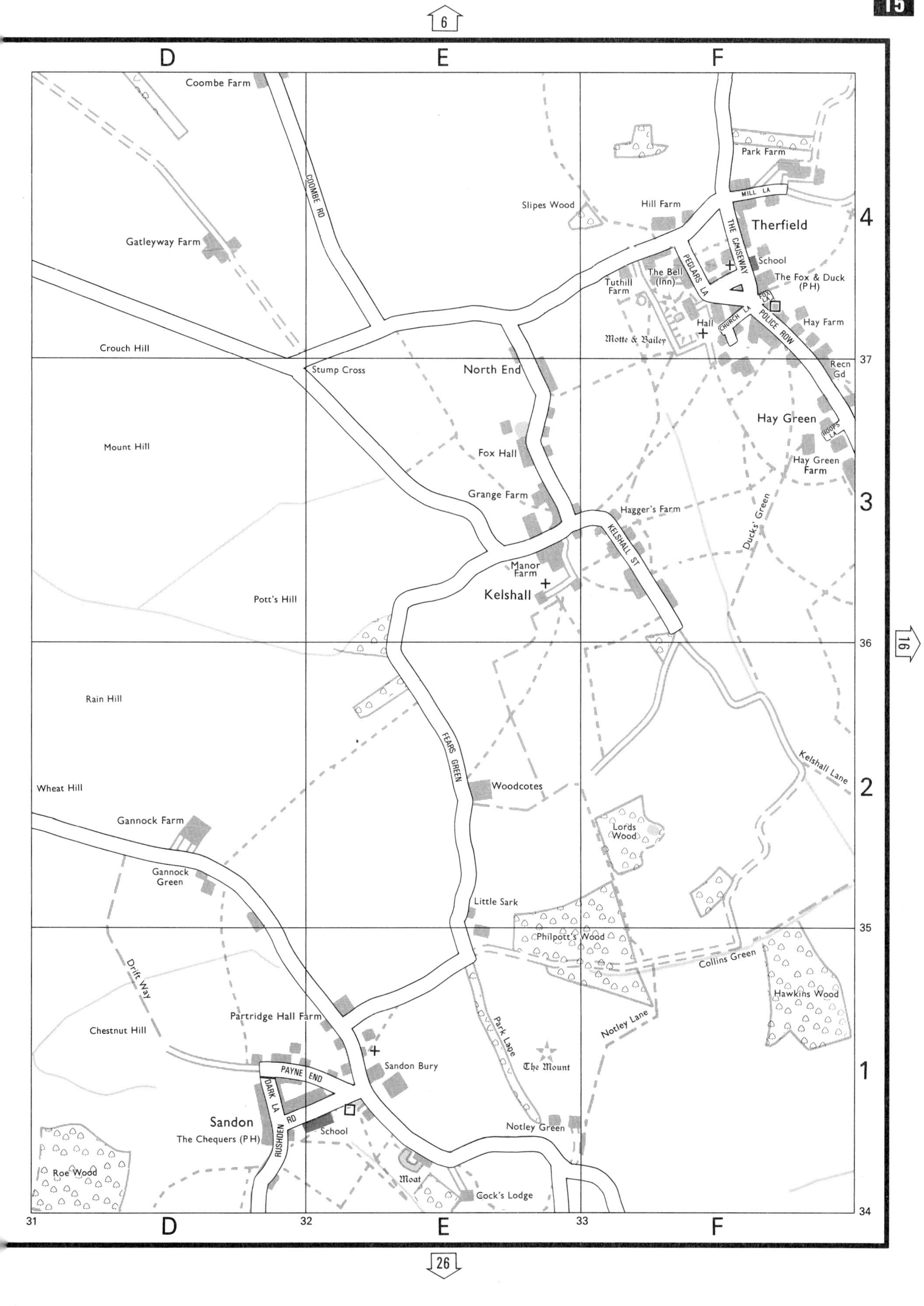
6
D
E
F
Coombe Farm
COOMBE RD
Gatleyway Farm
Slipes Wood
Hill Farm
Park Farm
MILL LA
Therfield
THE CAUSEWAY
School
The Fox & Duck (PH)
The Bell (Inn)
PEDLARS LA
Tuthill Farm
FOX LA
CHURCH LA
POLICE ROW
Hay Farm
Hall
Motte & Bailey
Crouch Hill
Stump Cross
North End
Recn Gd
Hay Green
HOOPS LA
Hay Green Farm
Mount Hill
Fox Hall
Grange Farm
Hagger's Farm
Ducks' Green
KELSHALL ST
Manor Farm
Kelshall
Pott's Hill
Rain Hill
16
FEARS GREEN
Kelshall Lane
Wheat Hill
Woodcotes
Gannock Farm
Lords Wood
Gannock Green
Little Sark
Philpott's Wood
Collins Green
Drift Way
Hawkins Wood
Chestnut Hill
Partridge Hall Farm
Park Lane
Notley Lane
PAYNE END
Sandon Bury
The Mount
DARK LA
RD
Sandon
School
Notley Green
The Chequers (PH)
RUSHDEN
Roe Wood
Moat
Cock's Lodge
4
37
3
36
2
35
1
34
31
32
33
26

7

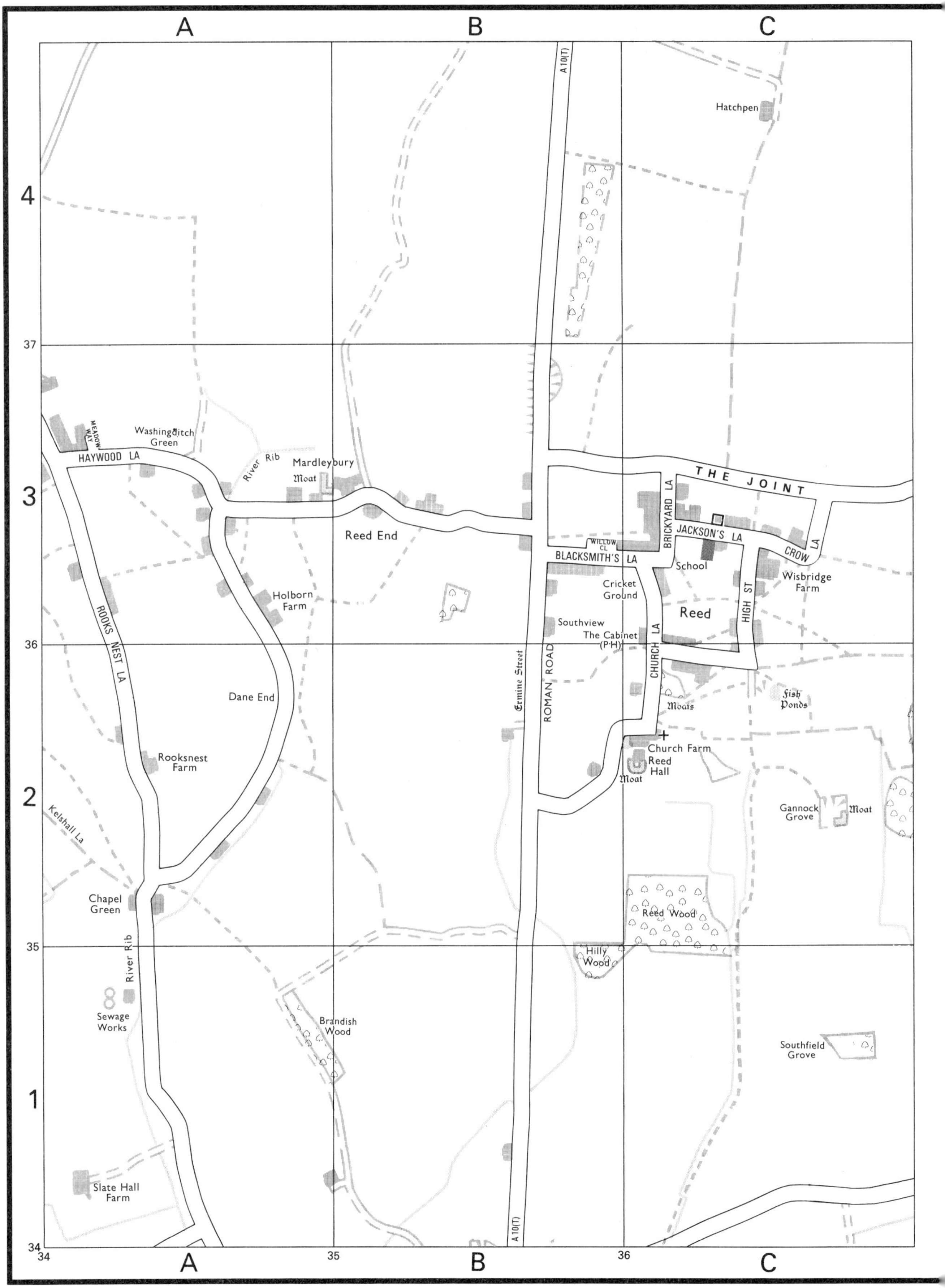
A
B
C
4
3
2
1
37
36
35
34
34
35
36
A
B
C
A10(T)
Hatchpen
MEADOW WAY
Washingditch Green
HAYWOOD LA
River Rib
Mardleybury
Moat
THE JOINT
BRICKYARD LA
JACKSON'S LA
CROW LA
WILLOW CL
BLACKSMITH'S LA
Reed End
School
Wisbridge Farm
Holborn Farm
Cricket Ground
HIGH ST
Reed
ROOKS NEST LA
Southview
The Cabinet (P.H)
CHURCH LA
Ermine Street
ROMAN ROAD
Dane End
Fish Ponds
Moats
Church Farm
Reed Hall
Moat
Rooksnest Farm
Kelshall La
Gannock Grove
Moat
Chapel Green
Reed Wood
Hilly Wood
River Rib
Sewage Works
Brandish Wood
Southfield Grove
Slate Hall Farm
A10(T)

15

27

8

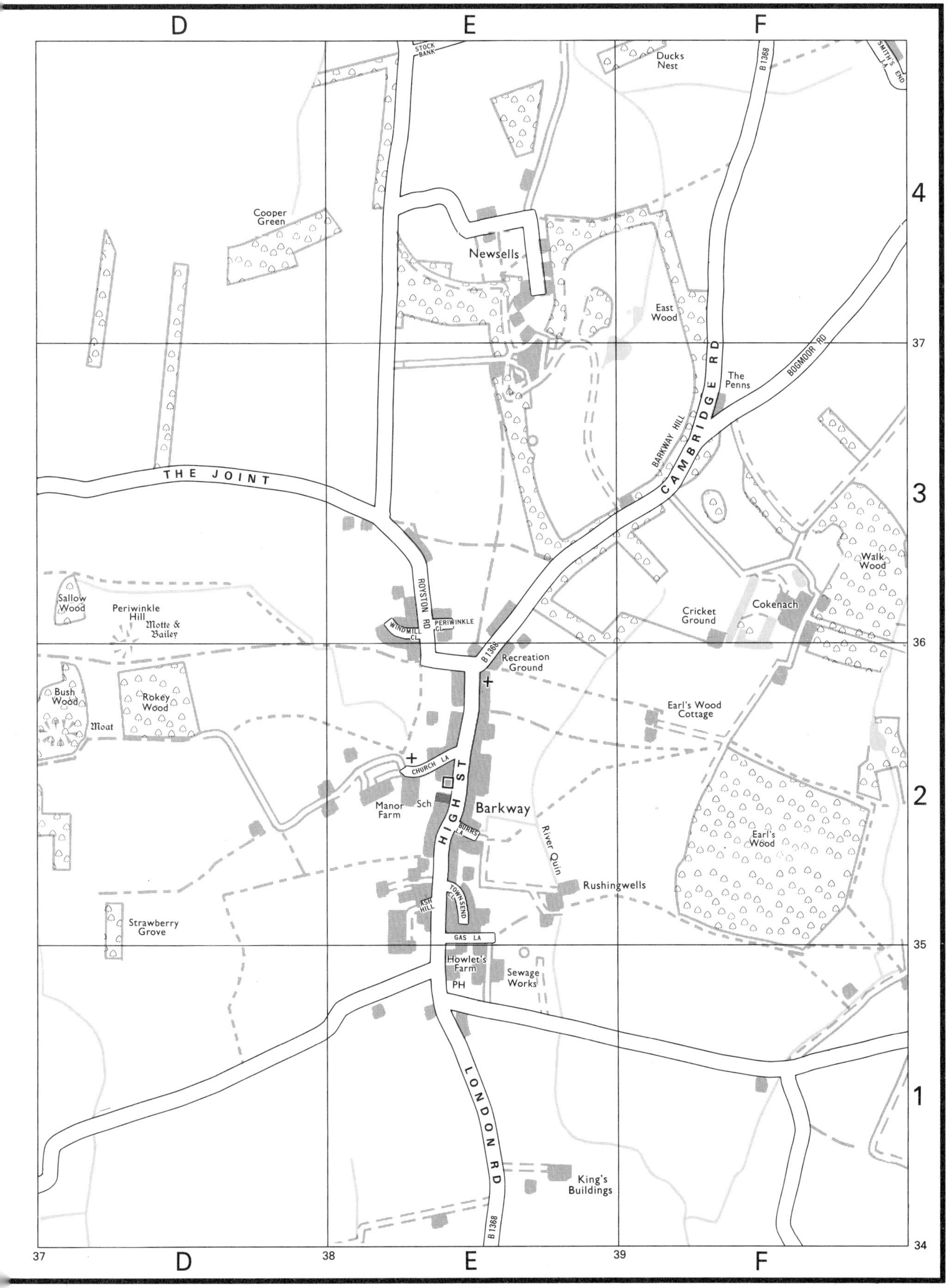
D
E
F
STOCK BANK
Ducks Nest
B 1368
SMITH'S END LA
4
Cooper Green
Newsells
East Wood
37
CAMBRIDGE RD
The Penns
BOGMOOR RD
BARKWAY HILL
THE JOINT
3
Walk Wood
Sallow Wood
Periwinkle Hill
Motte & Bailey
ROYSTON RD
WINDMILL CL
PERIWINKLE CL
Cricket Ground
Cokenach
36
B 1368
Recreation Ground
Bush Wood
Rokey Wood
Moat
Earl's Wood Cottage
CHURCH LA
HIGH ST
Manor Farm
Sch
Barkway
2
BURRS LA
River Quin
Earl's Wood
Rushingwells
ASH HILL
TOWNSEND CL
Strawberry Grove
GAS LA
35
Howlet's Farm
PH
Sewage Works
LONDON RD
1
King's Buildings
B 1368
34
37
38
39

18

28

9

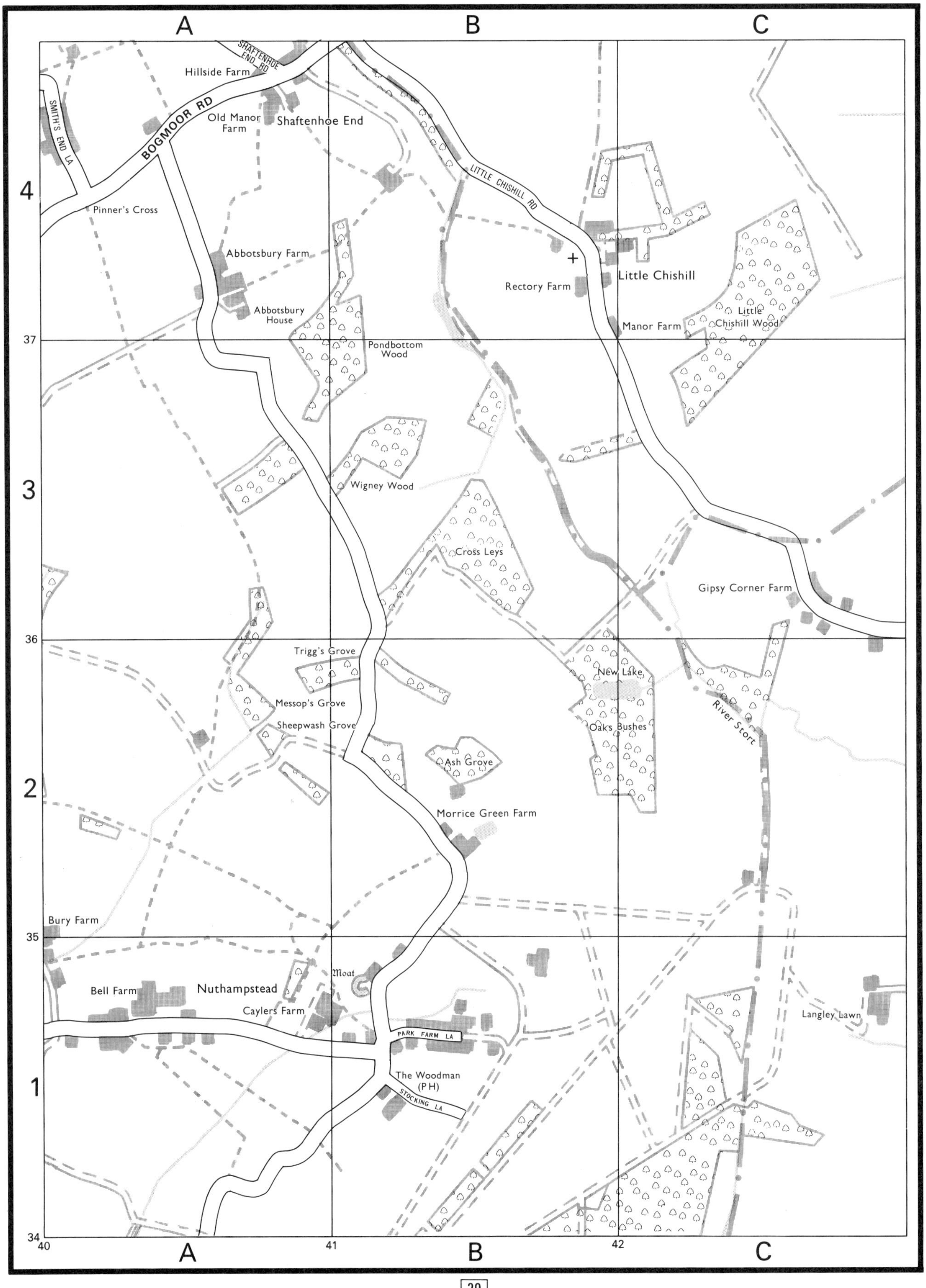
A
B
C
4
3
2
1
37
36
35
34
40
41
42
SHAFTENHOE END RD
Hillside Farm
SMITH'S END LA
BOGMOOR RD
Old Manor Farm
Shaftenhoe End
LITTLE CHISHILL RD
Pinner's Cross
Abbotsbury Farm
Rectory Farm
Little Chishill
Abbotsbury House
Little Chishill Wood
Manor Farm
Pondbottom Wood
Wigney Wood
Cross Leys
Gipsy Corner Farm
Trigg's Grove
New Lake
Messop's Grove
Sheepwash Grove
Oaks Bushes
River Stort
Ash Grove
Morrice Green Farm
Bury Farm
Moat
Bell Farm
Nuthampstead
Caylers Farm
PARK FARM LA
Langley Lawn
The Woodman (PH)
STOCKING LA

17

29

not continued, see key diagram

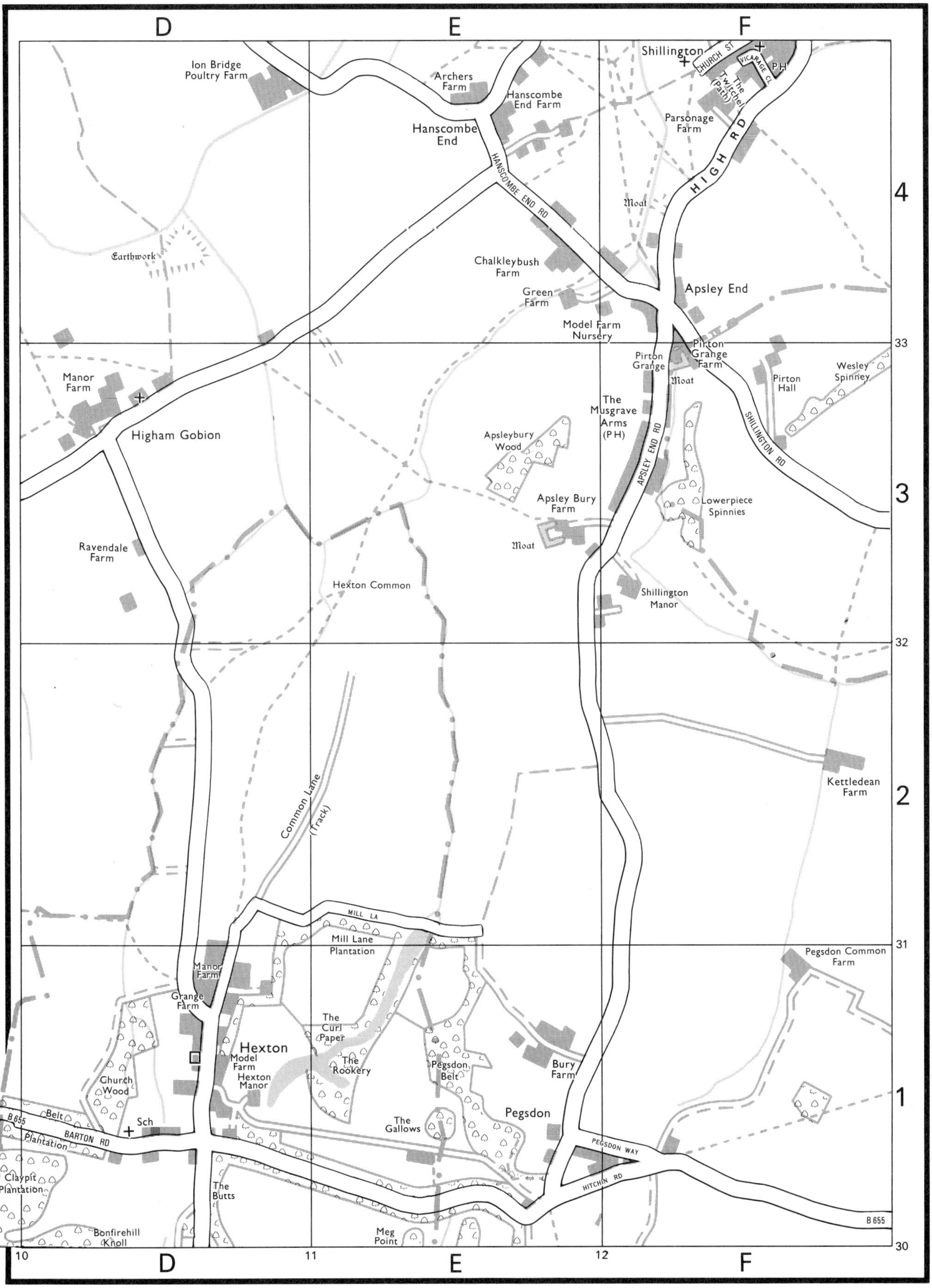

20

32

not continued, see key diagram

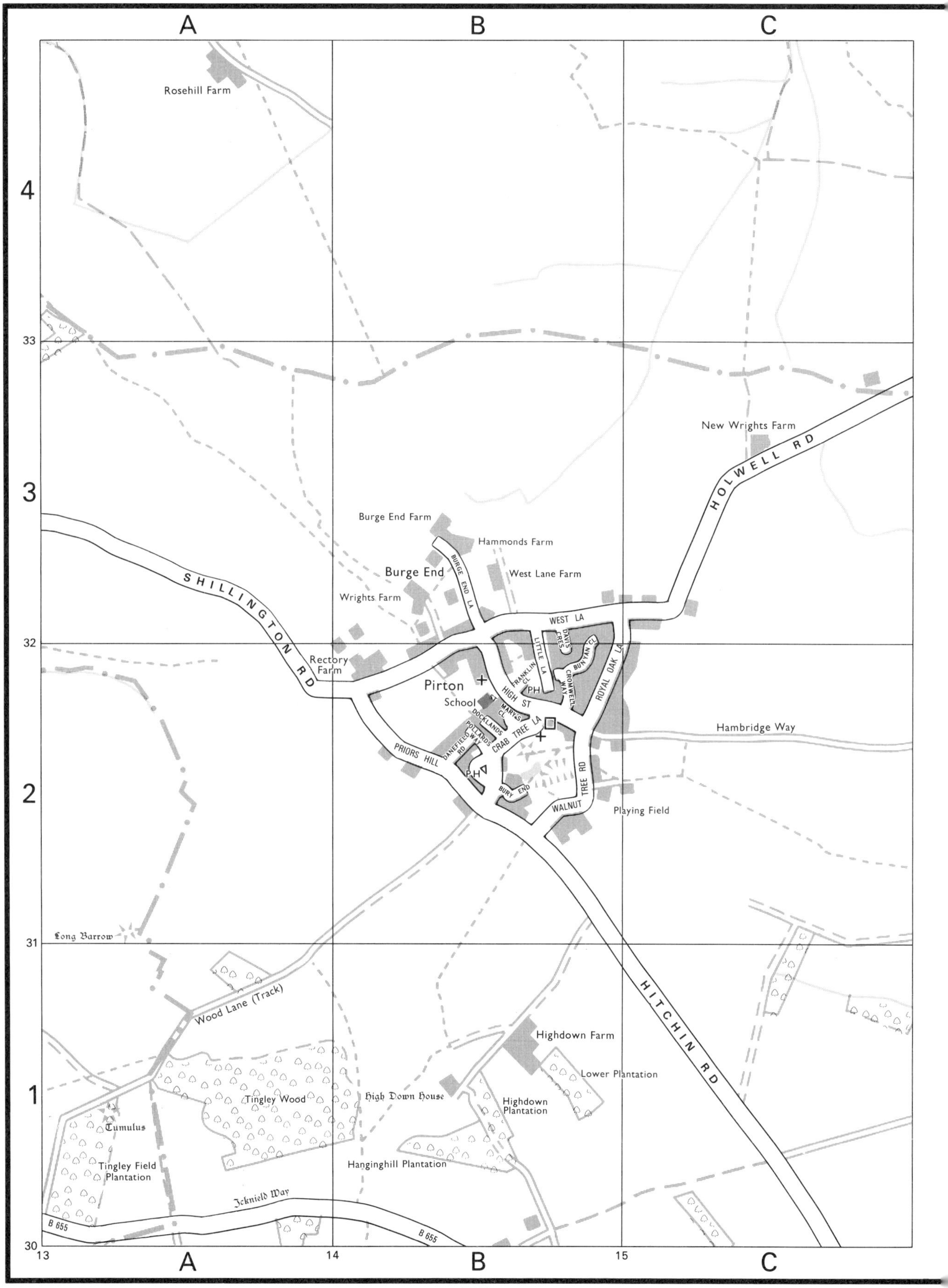

19

33

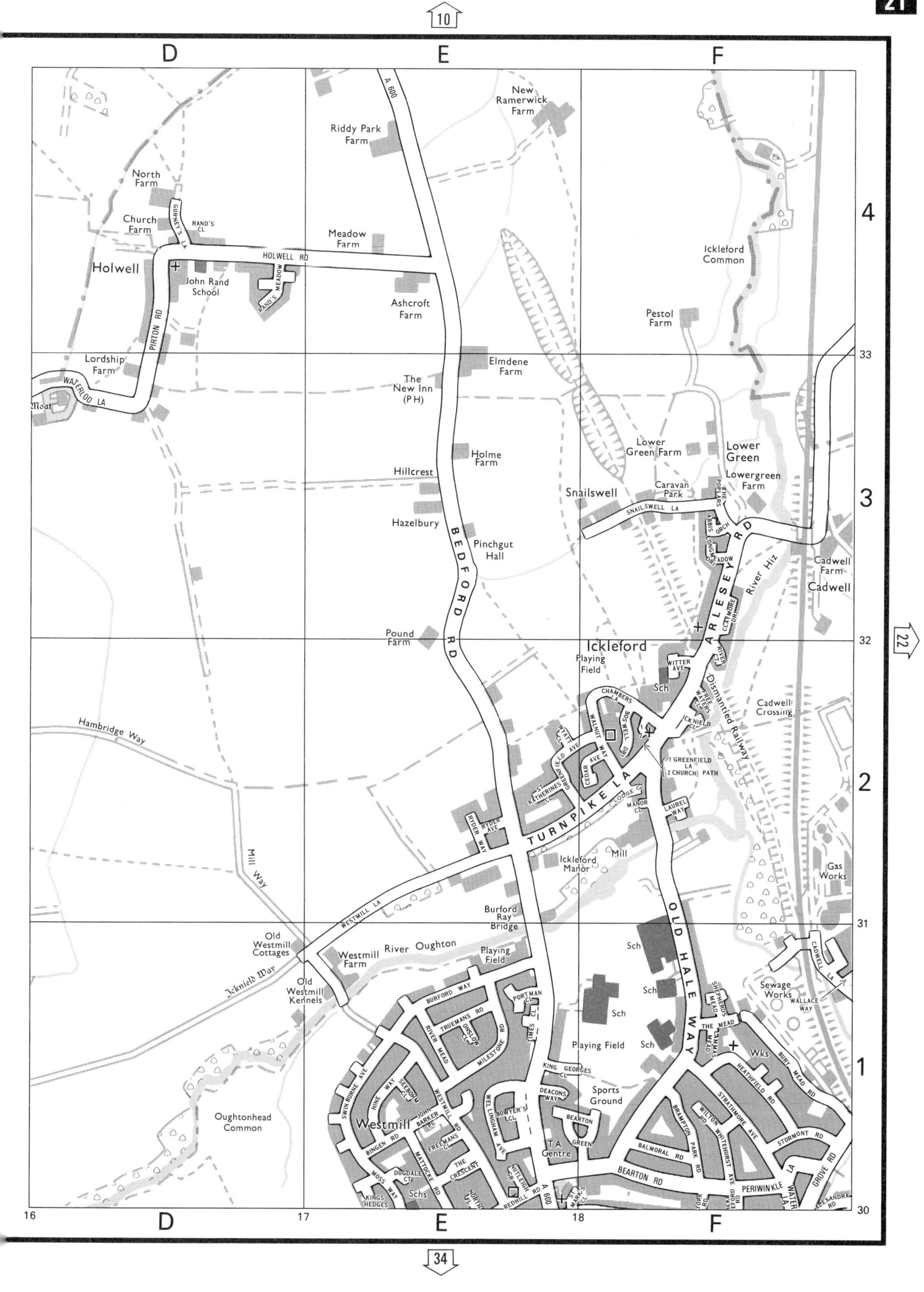
10
D
E
F
4
3
2
1
33
32
31
30
16
17
18
22
34
New Ramerwick Farm
Riddy Park Farm
North Farm
Church Farm
Holwell
Meadow Farm
John Rand School
Ashcroft Farm
Ickleford Common
Pestol Farm
Lordship Farm
Elmdene Farm
The New Inn (PH)
Moat
Holme Farm
Lower Green Farm
Lower Green
Lowergreen Farm
Hillcrest
Snailswell
Caravan Park
Hazelbury
Pinchgut Hall
Cadwell Farm
Cadwell
River Hiz
Pound Farm
Ickleford
Playing Field
Sch
Cadwell Crossing
Dismantled Railway
Hambridge Way
Mill Way
Ickleford Manor
Mill
Gas Works
Burford Ray Bridge
Old Westmill Cottages
Westmill Farm
River Oughton
Playing Field
Icknield Way
Old Westmill Kennels
Sewage Works
Playing Field
Sports Ground
Oughtonhead Common
Westmill
TA Centre
Wks
Schs
A 600
BEDFORD RD
HOLWELL RD
GURNEY'S LA
RAND'S CL
RAND'S MEADOW
PIRTON RD
WATERLOO LA
SNAILSWELL LA
ARLESEY RD
THE POPLARS
ABBIS ORCH
LONGMEADOW DRI
CLAYMORE DRI
RIVER CT
WITTER AVE
CHAMBERS LA
BOSWELL DRI
WALNUT WAY
TREE WATERS CL
ICKNIELD CL
WYATT CL
GREENFIELD AVE
CEDAR AVE
ST KATHERINES CL
1 GREENFIELD LA
2 CHURCH PATH
LODGE CT
MANOR CL
LAUREL WAY
TURNPIKE LA
RYDER WAY
RYDER AVE
WESTMILL LA
OLD HALE WAY
CADWELL LA
WALLACE WAY
SHEPHERDS MEAD
THE MEAD
LAMMAS MEAD
BURY MEAD RD
HEATHFIELD RD
BURFORD WAY
PORTMAN CL
TRUEMANS RD
ONSLOW CL
RIVER MEAD
MILESTONE RD
TIMES CL
KING GEORGES CL
SWINBURNE AVE
HINE WAY
SEEBOHM CL
JOHN BARKER PL
WESTMILL RD
WELLINGHAM AVE
BOWYER'S CL
DEACONS WAY
BEARTON GREEN
BRAMPTON PARK RD
WILTON RD
STRATHMORE AVE
WHITEHURST AVE
STORMONT RD
BINGEN RD
FREEMANS CL
THE CRESCENT
MATTOCKE RD
DUGDALE CT
MOSS WAY
KINGS HEDGES
NORTH PL
WHITLEIGH GR
REDHILL RD
ST MARKS CL
BALMORAL RD
BEARTON RD
ICKLEFORD RD
YORK RD
PERIWINKLE LA
WATER LA
GROVE RD
ALEXANDRA RD

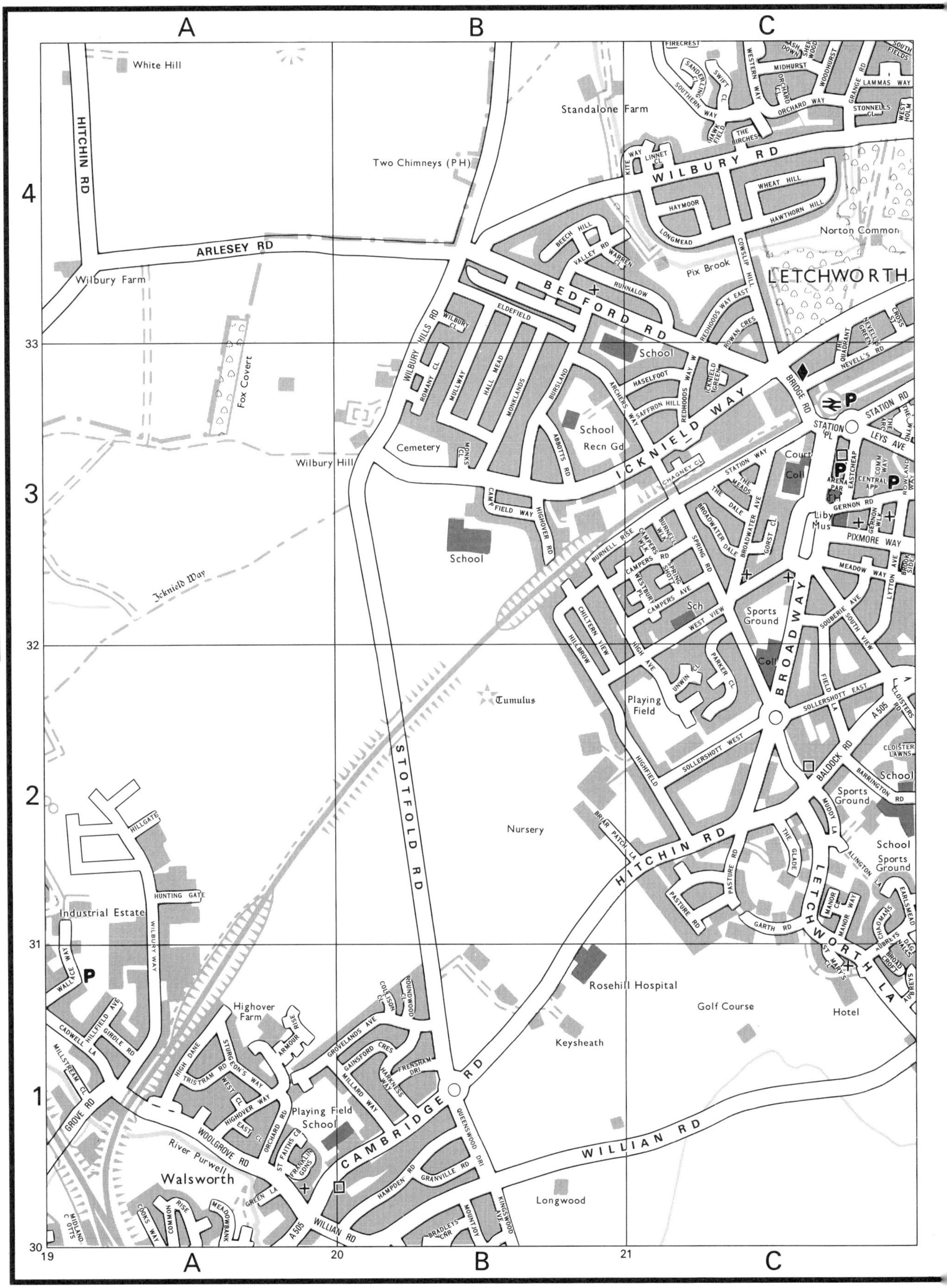
11
35
21
A
B
C
4
3
2
1
33
32
31
30
19
20
21
White Hill
HITCHIN RD
Standalone Farm
Two Chimneys (PH)
WILBURY RD
ARLESEY RD
Wilbury Farm
BEDFORD RD
Fox Covert
LETCHWORTH
Norton Common
Pix Brook
School
School
Recn Gd
Cemetery
Wilbury Hill
ICKNIELD WAY
Icknield Way
School
Tumulus
STOTFOLD RD
Nursery
Playing Field
Sports Ground
BROADWAY
HITCHIN RD
Industrial Estate
Highover Farm
Rosehill Hospital
Golf Course
Keysheath
Hotel
Playing Field
School
Walsworth
River Purwell
CAMBRIDGE RD
WILLIAN RD
Longwood
LETCHWORTH LA
BALDOCK RD
Sports Ground
School
School
Sports Ground
STATION RD
LEYS AVE
PIXMORE WAY
SOLLERSHOTT EAST
SOLLERSHOTT WEST
HIGHFIELD
BRIAR PATCH LA
WILBURY WAY
HUNTING GATE
HILLGATE
CADWELL LA
GROVE RD
WOOLGROVE RD
A505

12

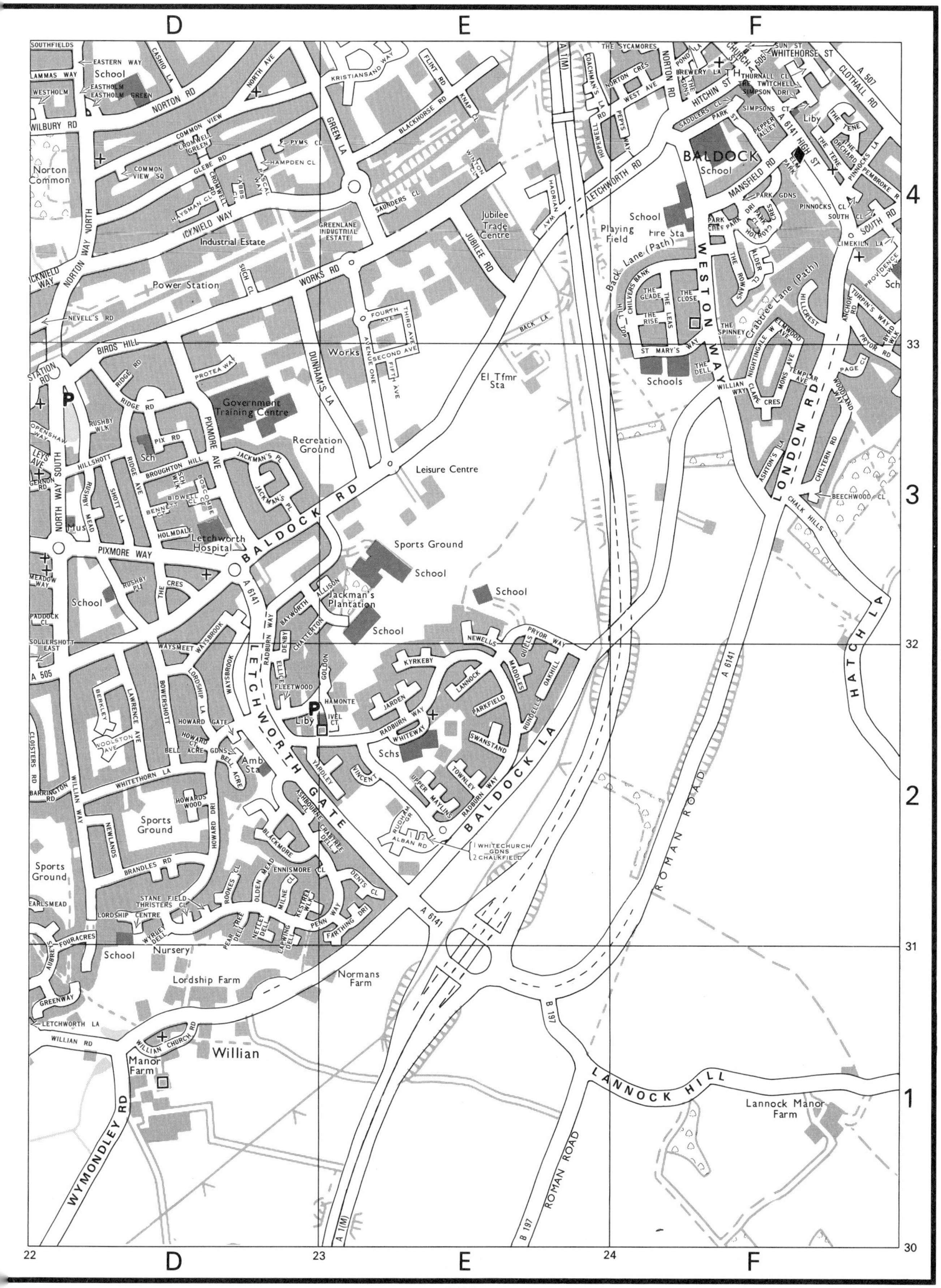
D
E
F
SOUTHFIELDS
EASTERN WAY
LAMMAS WAY
School
EASTHOLM
EASTHOLM GREEN
WESTHOLM
CASHIO LA
NORTH AVE
NORTON RD
WILBURY RD
COMMON VIEW
CROMWELL GREEN
PYMS CL
HAMPDEN CL
GLEBE RD
CROWELL RD
TABBS CL
PASCAL WAY
COMMON VIEW SQ
HAYSMAN CL
ICKNIELD WAY
Norton Common
Industrial Estate
NORTON WAY NORTH
ICKNIELD WAY
Power Station
SUCH CL
NEVELL'S RD
KRISTIANSAND WAY
GREEN LA
FLINT RD
KNAP CL
BLACKHORSE RD
WILTON CL
SAUNDERS CL
GREENLANE INDUSTRIAL ESTATE
WORKS RD
Jubilee Trade Centre
JUBILEE RD
FOURTH AVE
THIRD AVE
SECOND AVE
AVENUE ONE
FIFTH AVE
Works
BACK LA
BIRDS HILL
STATION RD
RIDGE RD
PROTEA WAY
Government Training Centre
DUNHAM'S LA
El Tfmr Sta
RUSHBY WLK
OPENSHAW WAY
PIX RD
PIXMORE AVE
Recreation Ground
Leisure Centre
LEYS AVE
HILLSHOTT
Sch
BROUGHTON HILL
JACKMAN'S PL
GERNON RD
NORTH WAY SOUTH
RUSHBY MEAD
SHOTT LA
RIDGE AVE
SCH WLK
BOSCOMBE CT
BIDWELL CL
BENNETT CT
BALDOCK RD
Mus
HOLMDALE
Letchworth Hospital
Sports Ground
PIXMORE WAY
MEADOW WAY
RUSHBY PL
THE CRES
A 6141
School
Jackman's Plantation
ALLISON
PADDOCK CL
SOLLERSHOTT EAST
WAYSMEET
WAYSBROOK
BAYWORTH
CHATTERTON
RADBURN WAY
School
A 505
BERKLEY
LAWRENCE AVE
BOWERSHOTT
LORDSHIP LA
DENBY
ELLICE
FLEETWOOD
GOLDON
KYRKEBY
NEWELLS
PRYOR WAY
QUILLS
MADDLES
OAKHILL
LANNOCK
HAMONTE
JARDEN
P
Liby
IVEL CT
RADBURN WAY
WHITEWAY
PARKFIELD
RUNDELLS
WOOLSTON AVE
HOWARD GATE
HOWARD CT
BELL ACRE GDNS
Amb Sta
LETCHWORTH GATE
Schs
SWANSTAND
CLOISTERS RD
BARRINGTON RD
WILLIAN WAY
WHITETHORN LA
BELL ACRE
YARDLEY
VINCENT
TOWNLEY
BALDOCK LA
HOWARDS WOOD
Sports Ground
HOWARD DRI
ASHBOURNE CT
UPPER MAYLINS
RADBURN WAY
NEWLANDS
BLACKMORE
CRABTREE DELL
RUDHAM GR
ALBAN RD
1 WHITECHURCH GDNS
2 CHALKFIELD
Sports Ground
BRANDLES RD
ENNISMORE CL
DENTS CL
EARLSMEAD
STANE FIELD
THRISTERS CL
ROOKES CL
OLDEN MEAD
MILNE CL
KESTREL WLK
PENN WAY
LORDSHIP CENTRE
PEAR TREE DELL
NETLEY DELL
LAPWING DELL
FARTHING DRI
A 6141
WYNDLEY DELL
FOURACRES
AUBREYS
School
Nursery
Lordship Farm
Normans Farm
GREENWAY
LETCHWORTH LA
WILLIAN RD
WILLIAN CHURCH RD
Willian
Manor Farm
WYMONDLEY RD
A 1(M)
B 197
ROMAN ROAD
B 197
LANNOCK HILL
Lannock Manor Farm
A 1(M)
THE SYCAMORES
COACHMAN'S LA
NORTON CRES
WEST AVE
NORTON RD
POND LA
BREWERY LA
THE GDNS
CHURCH ST
SUN ST
WHITEHORSE ST
A 505
HITCHIN ST
THURNALL CL
THE TWITCHELL
SIMPSON DRI
CLOTHALL RD
A 507
PEMBERTON RD
PEPYS WAY
SADDLERS CL
PARK ST
SIMPSONS CT
PEPPER ALLEY
A 6141 HIGH ST
Liby
THE TENE
THE ORCHARD
HADRIAN WAY
LETCHWORTH RD
BALDOCK
School
MANSFIELD RD
ELM PARK
PEMBROKE R
PINNOCKS LA
PARK GDNS
PINNOCKS CL
SOUTH RD
School
Playing Field
Fire Sta
PARK CRES
PARK DRI
HOLROYD CRES
LIMEKILN LA
Back Lane (Path)
WESTON WAY
PROVIDENCE WAY
Sch
CHILVERS BANK
THE GLADE
THE LEAS
THE CLOSE
THE ROWANS
ALDER CL
Crabtree Lane (Path)
TURPIN'S WAY
BIRD WLK
HILL TOP
THE RISE
THE SPINNEY
NIGHTINGALE WAY
ELMWOOD
HILLCREST
ANCHOR RD
PRYOR RD
ST MARY'S WAY
THE DELL
Schools
MONS AVE
TEMPLAR AVE
PAGE CL
WOODLAND WAY
WILLIAN WAY
CLARE CRES
LONDON RD
ASHTON'S LA
CHILTERN RD
BEECHWOOD CL
CHALK HILLS
A 6141
HATCH LA
ROMAN ROAD
4
33
3
32
2
31
1
22
23
24
30

24

36

13

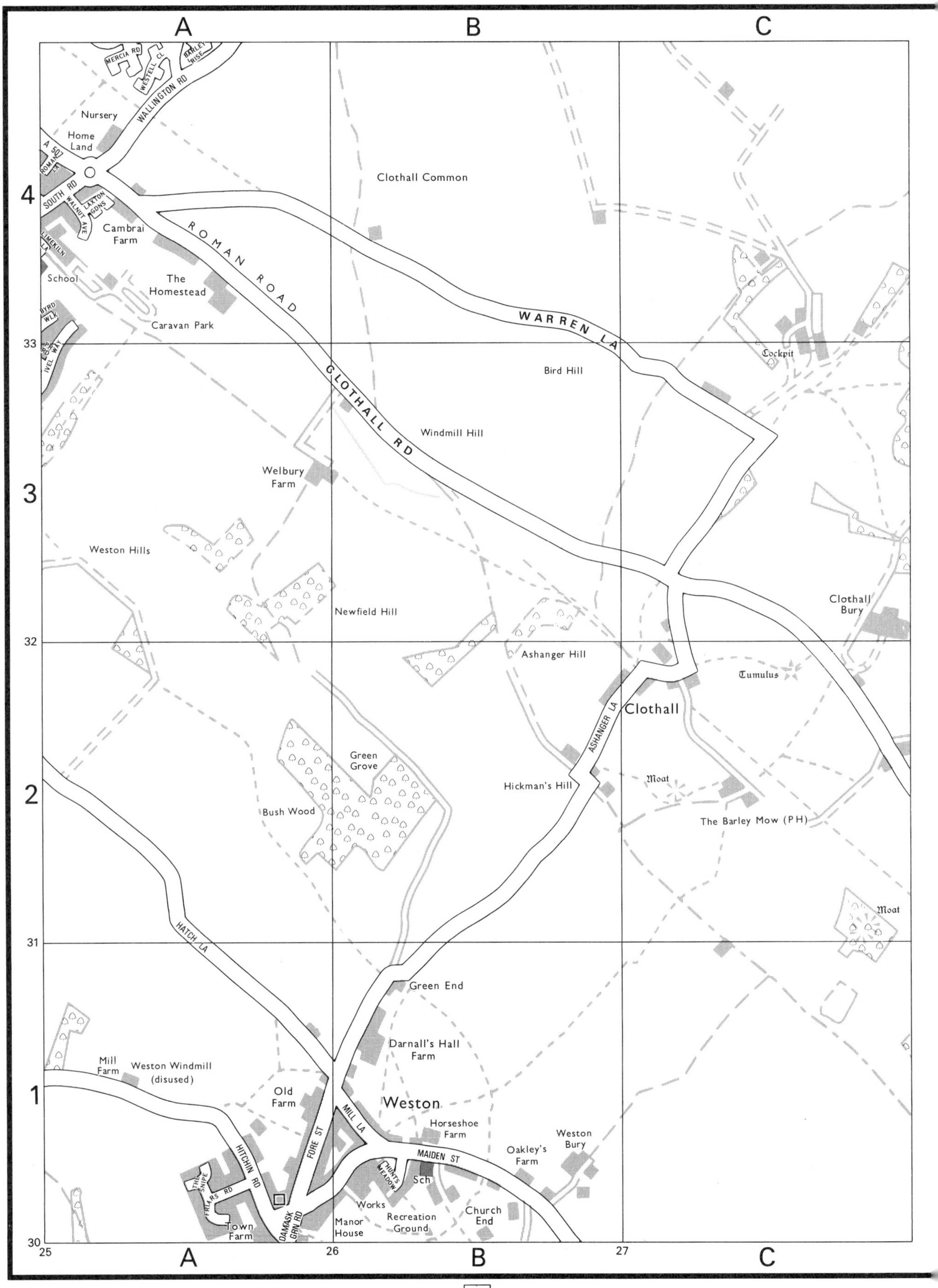
A
B
C
4
3
2
1
33
32
31
30
25
26
27
MERCIA RD
WESTELL CL
BARLEY RISE
WALLINGTON RD
Nursery
Home Land
A 507
ROMAN LA
SOUTH RD
WALNUT AVE
LAXTON GDNS
Cambrai Farm
LIMEKILN LA
School
The Homestead
BYRD WLK
IVEL WAY
Caravan Park
ROMAN ROAD
Clothall Common
WARREN LA
Bird Hill
Cockpit
CLOTHALL RD
Windmill Hill
Welbury Farm
Weston Hills
Newfield Hill
Clothall Bury
Ashanger Hill
Tumulus
ASHANGER LA
Clothall
Green Grove
Bush Wood
Hickman's Hill
Moat
The Barley Mow (PH)
Moat
HATCH LA
Green End
Darnall's Hall Farm
Mill Farm
Weston Windmill (disused)
Old Farm
Weston
MILL LA
Horseshoe Farm
FORE ST
HITCHIN RD
MAIDEN ST
Oakley's Farm
Weston Bury
THE SNIPE
FRIARS RD
HUNTS MEADOW
Sch
Works
Town Farm
DAMASK GRN RD
Manor House
Recreation Ground
Church End

23

37

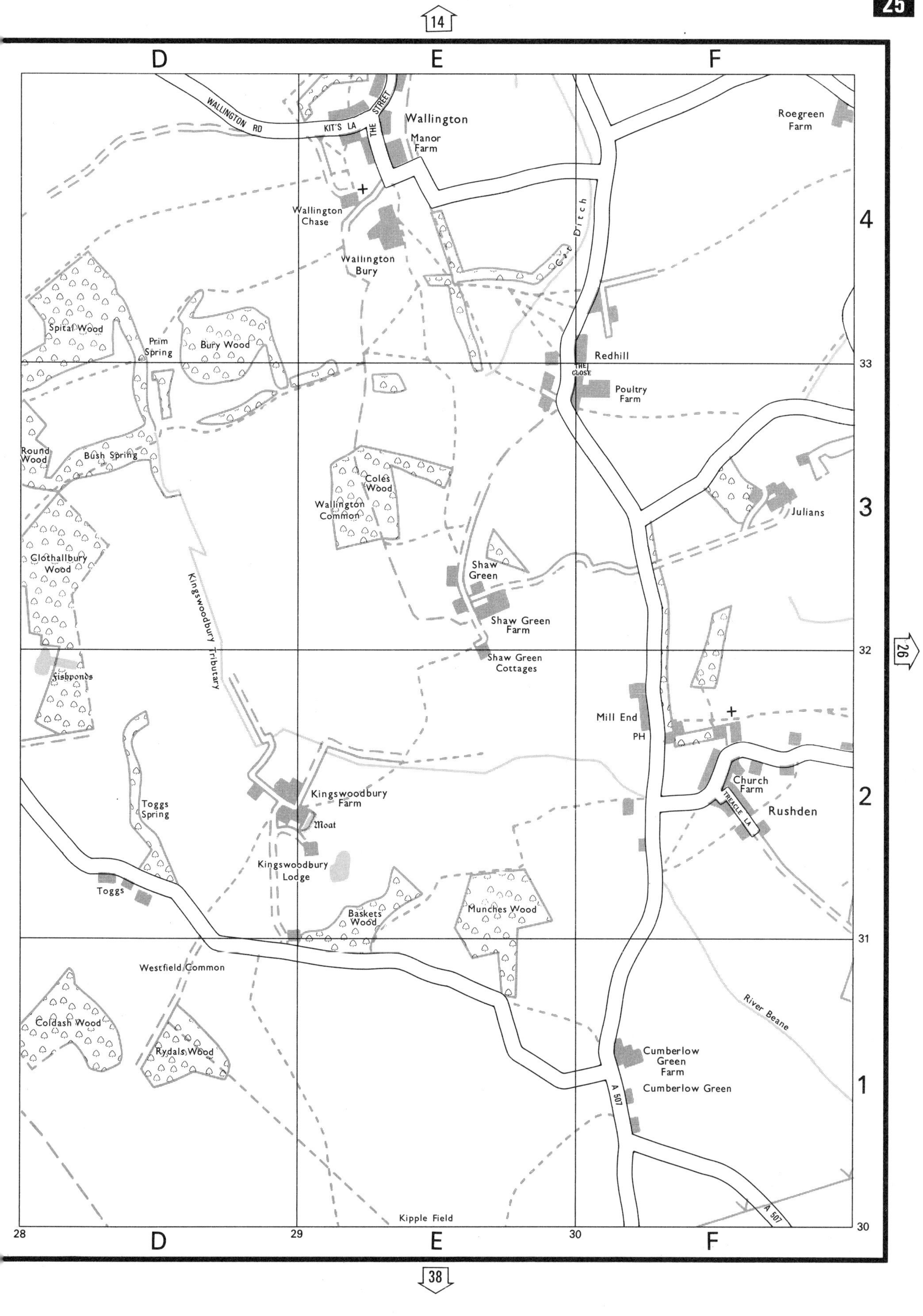
14
D
E
F
WALLINGTON RD
KIT'S LA
THE STREET
THE
Wallington
Manor Farm
Roegreen Farm
Wallington Chase
Wallington Bury
Cat Ditch
4
Spital Wood
Prim Spring
Bury Wood
Redhill
THE CLOSE
33
Poultry Farm
Round Wood
Bush Spring
Coles Wood
Wallington Common
Julians
3
Clothallbury Wood
Shaw Green
Kingswoodbury Tributary
Shaw Green Farm
32
Shaw Green Cottages
26
Fishponds
Mill End
PH
Church Farm
Kingswoodbury Farm
TREACLE LA
Rushden
2
Toggs Spring
Moat
Kingswoodbury Lodge
Toggs
Baskets Wood
Munches Wood
31
Westfield Common
River Beane
Coldash Wood
Cumberlow Green Farm
Rydals Wood
Cumberlow Green
1
A 507
A 507
Kipple Field
28
29
30
30
D
E
F
38

15

25

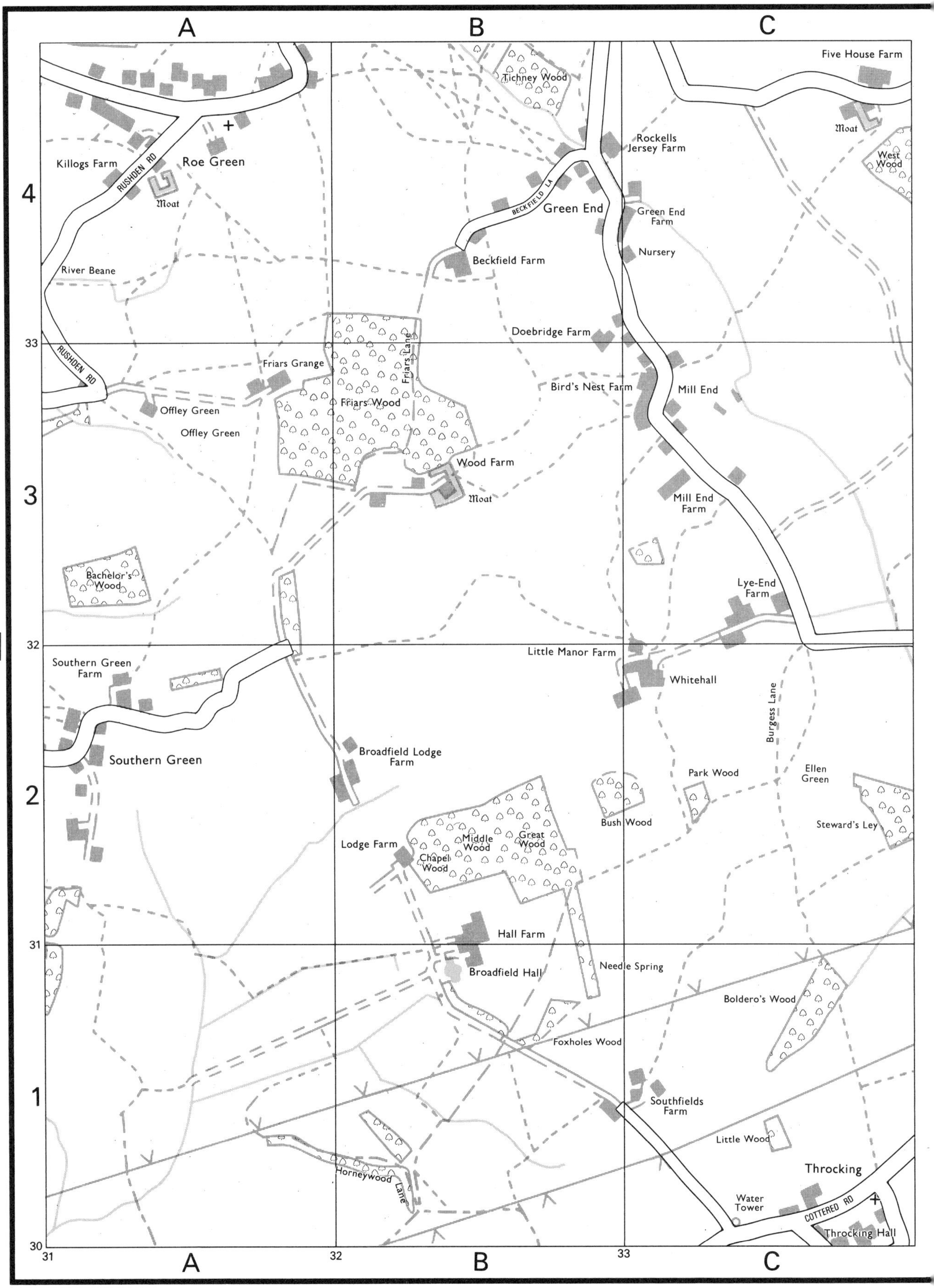
A
B
C
Five House Farm
Tichney Wood
Moat
Rockells
Jersey Farm
West
Wood
Killogs Farm
RUSHDEN RD
Roe Green
Moat
BECKFIELD LA
Green End
Green End
Farm
Nursery
Beckfield Farm
River Beane
Doebridge Farm
RUSHDEN RD
Friars Grange
Friars Lane
Bird's Nest Farm
Mill End
Friars Wood
Offley Green
Offley Green
Wood Farm
Moat
Mill End
Farm
Bachelor's
Wood
Lye-End
Farm
Little Manor Farm
Southern Green
Farm
Whitehall
Burgess Lane
Broadfield Lodge
Farm
Southern Green
Park Wood
Ellen
Green
Bush Wood
Steward's Ley
Lodge Farm
Middle
Wood
Great
Wood
Chapel
Wood
Hall Farm
Broadfield Hall
Needle Spring
Boldero's Wood
Foxholes Wood
Southfields
Farm
Little Wood
Horneywood
Lane
Throcking
Water
Tower
COTTERED RD
Throcking Hall
4
3
2
1
33
32
31
30
31
32
33

39

16

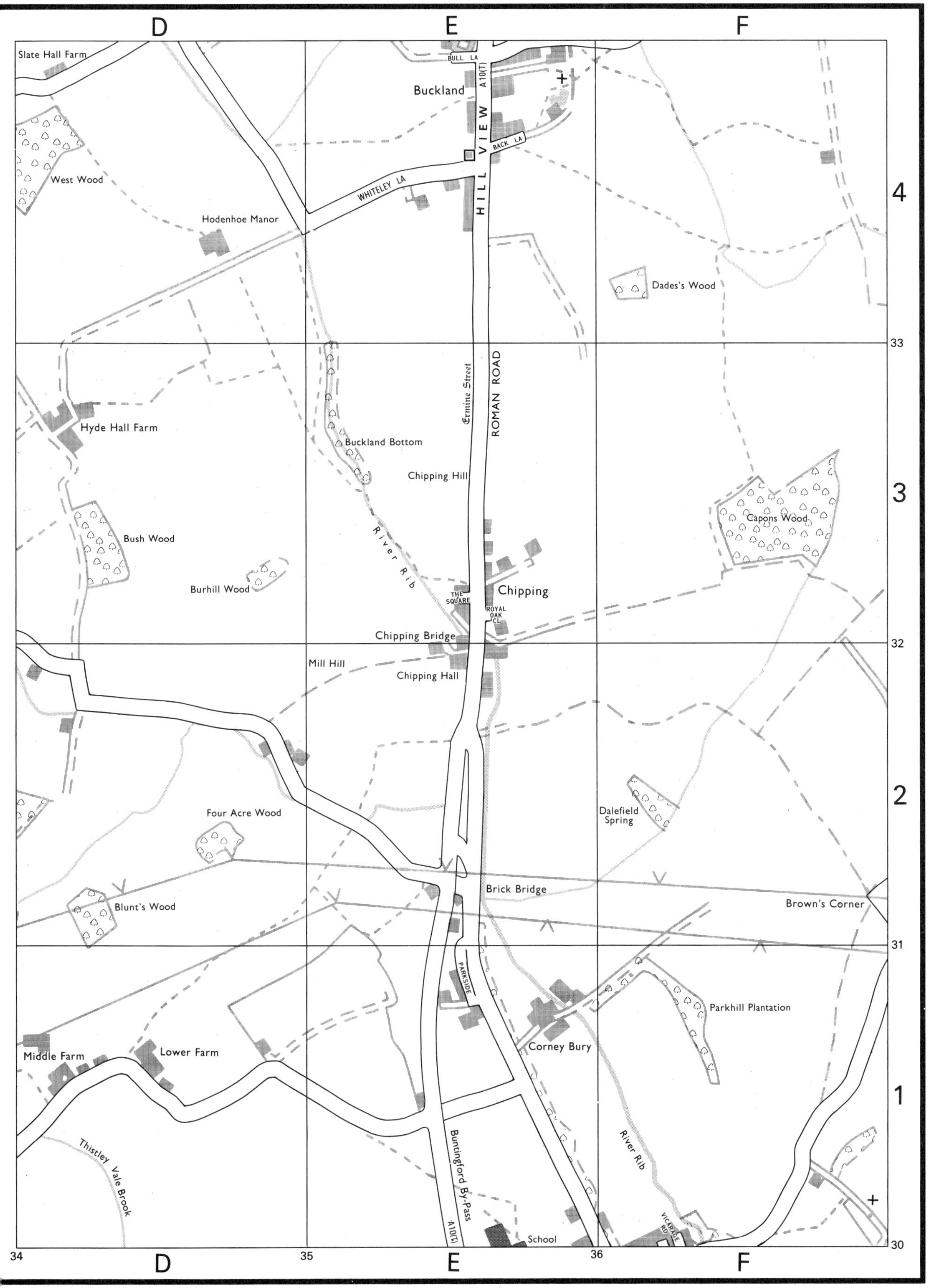
D
E
F
Slate Hall Farm
BULL LA
Buckland
A10(T)
HILL VIEW
BACK LA
WHITELEY LA
West Wood
Hodenhoe Manor
Dades's Wood
4
33
Ermine Street
ROMAN ROAD
Hyde Hall Farm
Buckland Bottom
Chipping Hill
3
Capons Wood
Bush Wood
River Rib
Burhill Wood
THE SQUARE
Chipping
ROYAL OAK CL
Chipping Bridge
32
Mill Hill
Chipping Hall
2
Four Acre Wood
Dalefield Spring
Brick Bridge
Blunt's Wood
Brown's Corner
31
PARKSIDE
Parkhill Plantation
Middle Farm
Lower Farm
Corney Bury
1
Thistley Vale Brook
Buntingford By-Pass
A10(T)
River Rib
VICARAGE RD
School
30
34
35
36
D
E
F

28

40

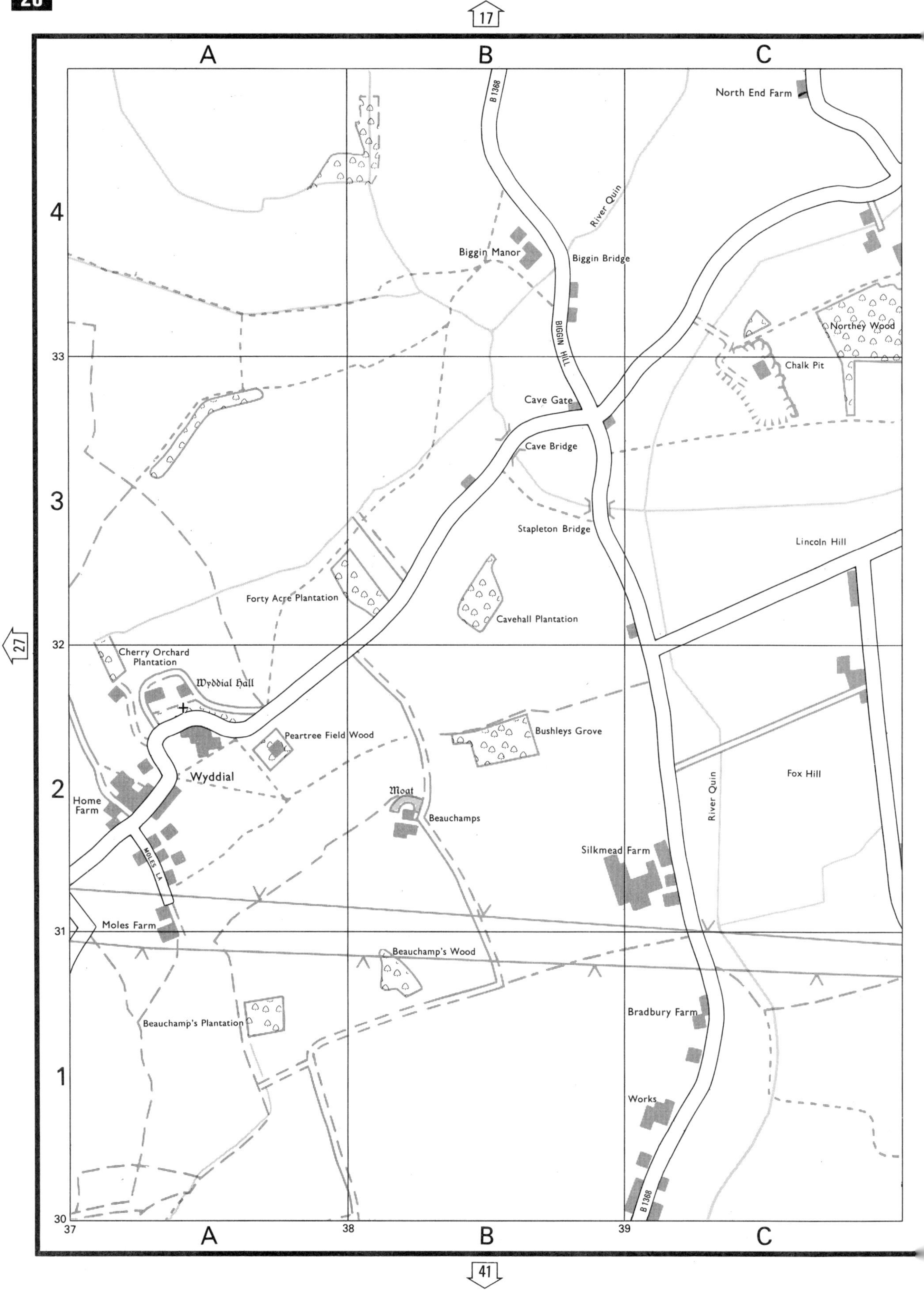
17
A
B
C
4
3
2
1
33
32
31
30
37
38
39
27
41
B 1368
North End Farm
River Quin
Biggin Manor
Biggin Bridge
BIGGIN HILL
Northey Wood
Chalk Pit
Cave Gate
Cave Bridge
Stapleton Bridge
Lincoln Hill
Forty Acre Plantation
Cavehall Plantation
Cherry Orchard Plantation
Wyddial Hall
Peartree Field Wood
Bushleys Grove
Wyddial
Fox Hill
Home Farm
Moat
Beauchamps
MOLES LA
Silkmead Farm
Moles Farm
Beauchamp's Wood
Bradbury Farm
Beauchamp's Plantation
Works

18

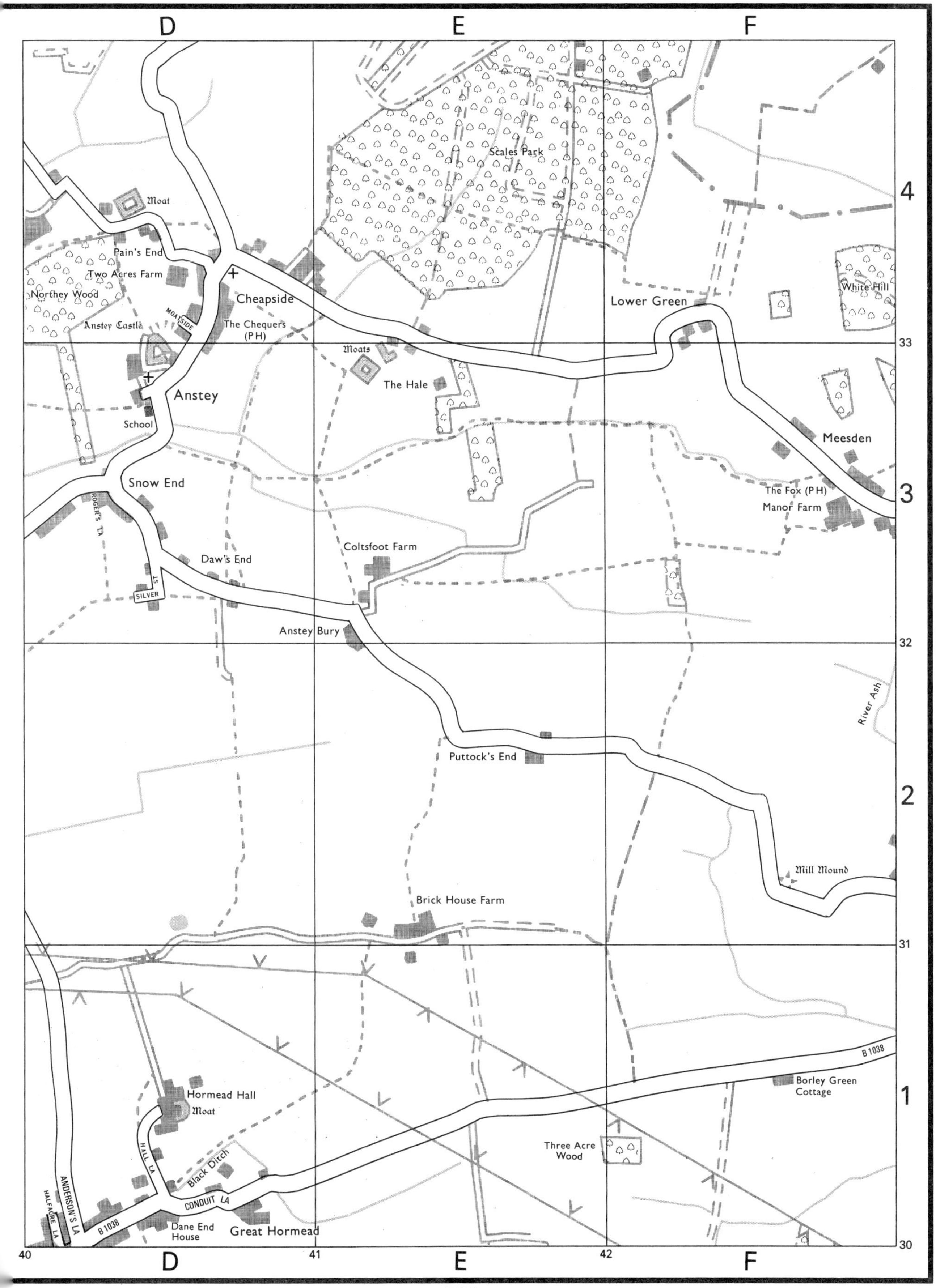
D
E
F
Scales Park
Moat
Pain's End
Two Acres Farm
Northey Wood
Anstey Castle
MOATSIDE
Cheapside
The Chequers (PH)
Lower Green
White Hill
Moats
The Hale
Anstey
School
Meesden
Snow End
The Fox (PH)
Manor Farm
ROGER'S LA
Coltsfoot Farm
Daw's End
SILVER ST
Anstey Bury
River Ash
Puttock's End
Mill Mound
Brick House Farm
B1038
Borley Green Cottage
Hormead Hall
Moat
Three Acre Wood
HALL LA
Black Ditch
ANDERSON'S LA
HALFACRE LA
CONDUIT LA
B1038
Dane End House
Great Hormead
4
33
3
32
2
31
1
30
40
41
42
D
E
F

30

42

not continued, see key diagram

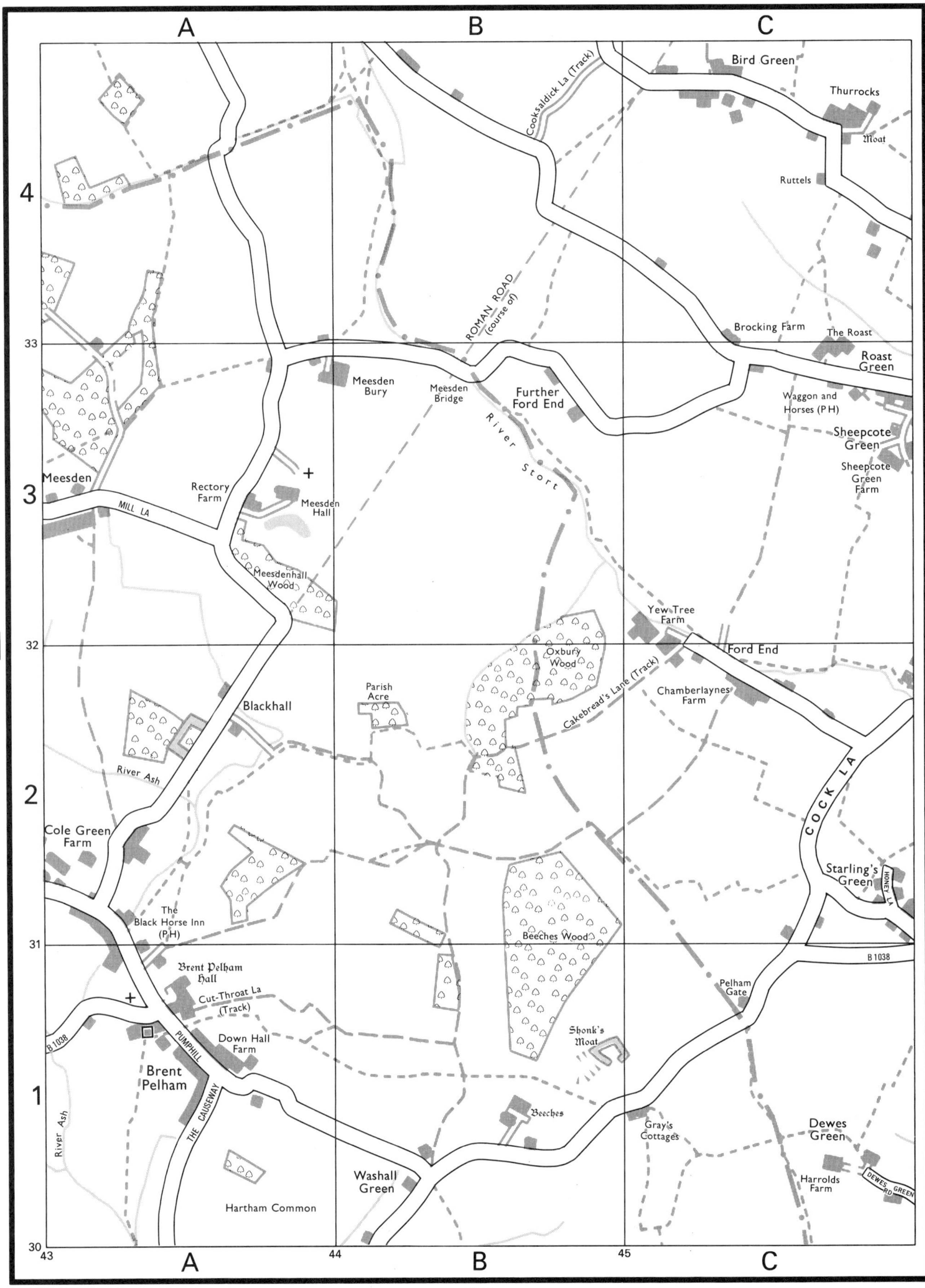

29

43

not continued, see key diagram

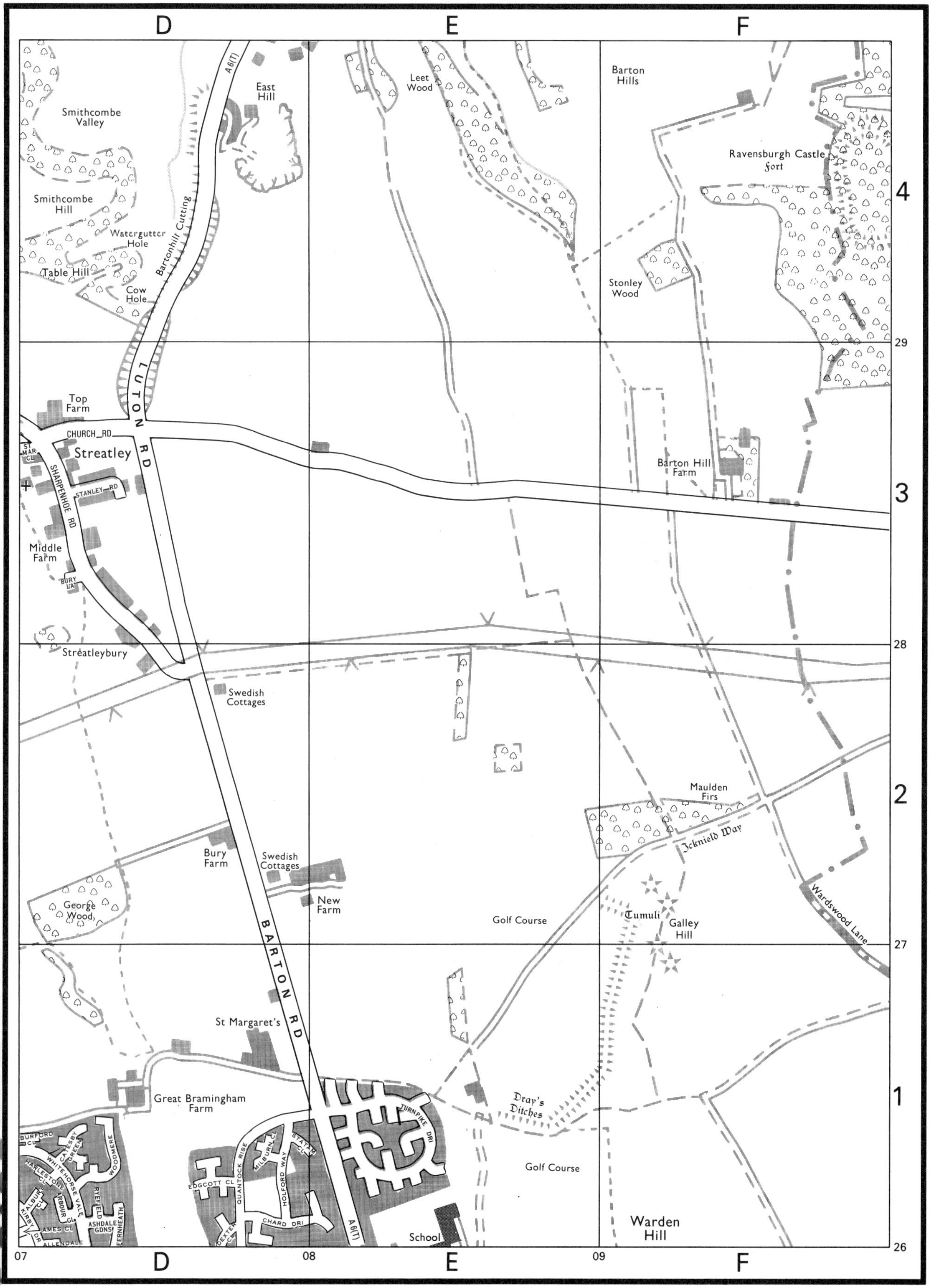

32

45

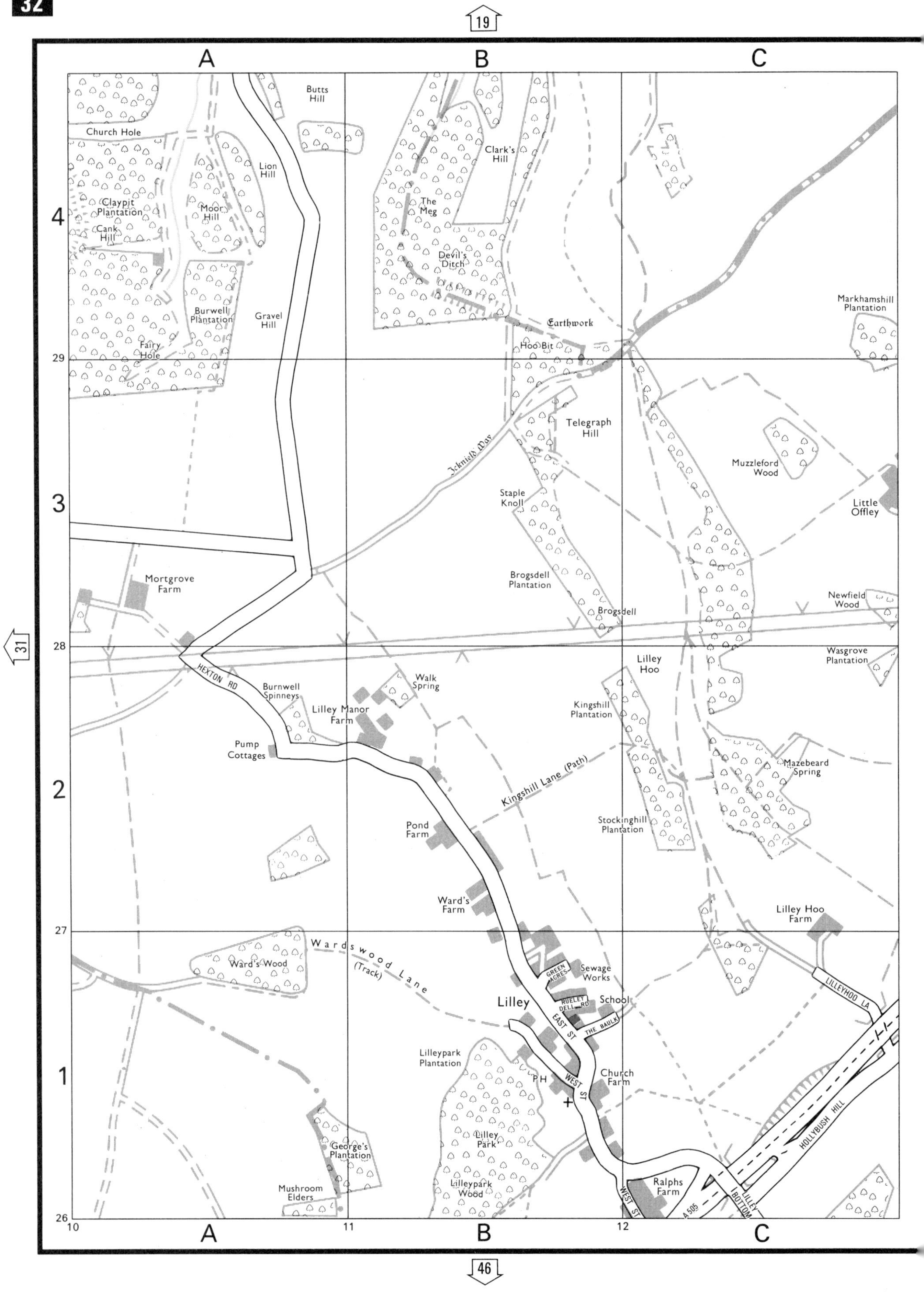

19
A
B
C
4
3
2
1
29
28
27
26
10
11
12
31
46
Church Hole
Butts Hill
Lion Hill
Claypit Plantation
Cank Hill
Moor Hill
Burwell Plantation
Gravel Hill
Fairy Hole
Clark's Hill
The Meg
Devil's Ditch
Earthwork
Hoo Bit
Markhamshill Plantation
Telegraph Hill
Icknield Way
Muzzleford Wood
Little Offley
Staple Knoll
Brogsdell Plantation
Brogsdell
Mortgrove Farm
Newfield Wood
Wasgrove Plantation
Lilley Hoo
HEXTON RD
Burnwell Spinneys
Walk Spring
Lilley Manor Farm
Kingshill Plantation
Pump Cottages
Kingshill Lane (Path)
Mazebeard Spring
Pond Farm
Stockinghill Plantation
Ward's Farm
Lilley Hoo Farm
Wardswood Lane
(Track)
Ward's Wood
GREEN ACRES
Sewage Works
Lilley
RUELEY DELL RD
School
EAST ST
THE BAULK
LILLEYHOO LA
Lilleypark Plantation
PH
WEST ST
Church Farm
HOLLYBUSH HILL
George's Plantation
Lilley Park
Mushroom Elders
Lilleypark Wood
Ralphs Farm
A 505
LILLEY BOTTOM

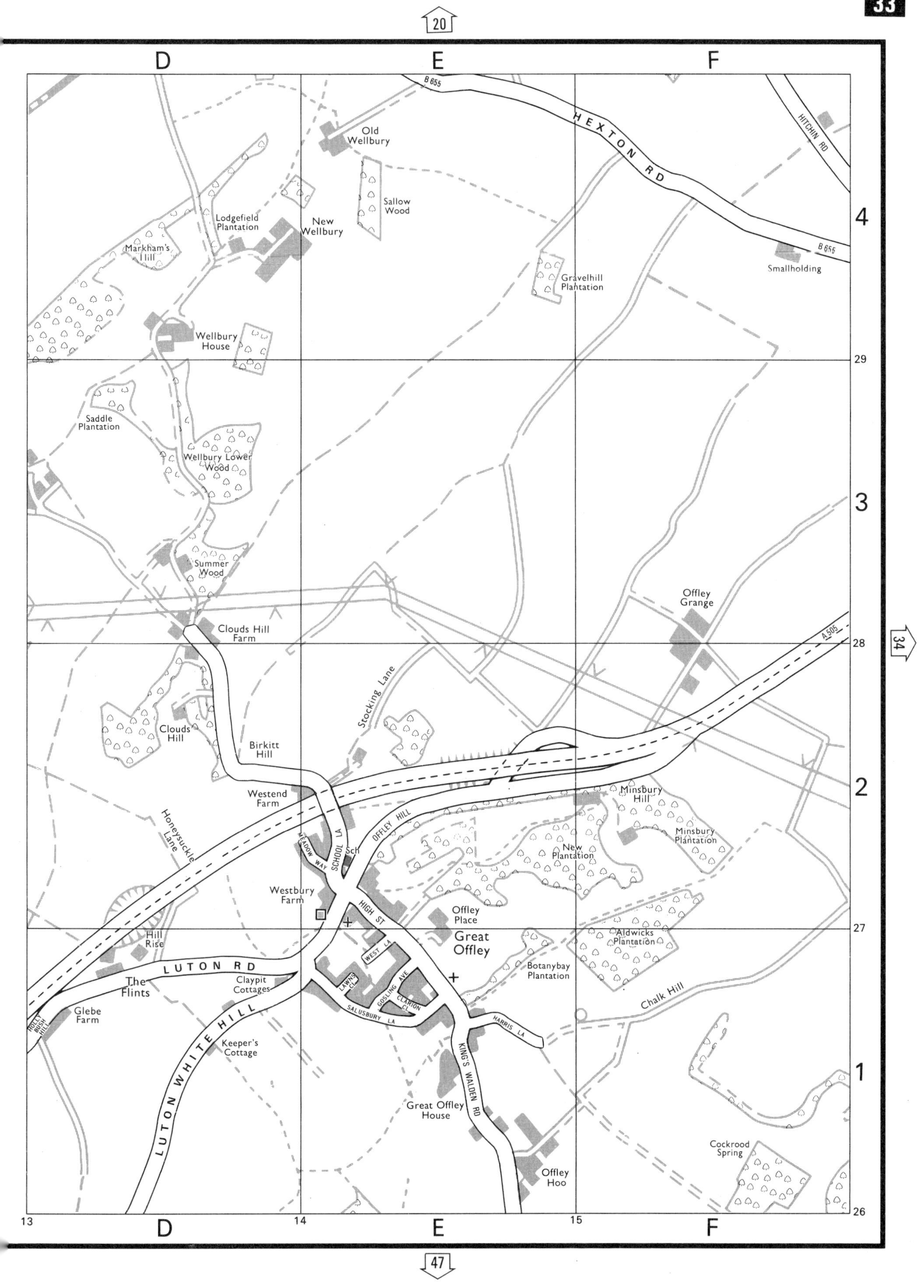
20
D
E
F
B 655
HEXTON RD
HITCHIN RD
Old Wellbury
Sallow Wood
Lodgefield Plantation
New Wellbury
Markham's Hill
Gravelhill Plantation
B 655
Smallholding
Wellbury House
29
Saddle Plantation
Wellbury Lower Wood
3
4
Summer Wood
Offley Grange
Clouds Hill Farm
A 505
28
34
Stocking Lane
Clouds Hill
Birkitt Hill
Westend Farm
Minsbury Hill
2
Honeysuckle Lane
MEADOW WAY
SCHOOL LA
Sch
OFFLEY HILL
Minsbury Plantation
New Plantation
Westbury Farm
HIGH ST
Offley Place
Great Offley
27
Hill Rise
WEST LA
Aldwicks Plantation
Botanybay Plantation
LUTON RD
The Flints
Claypit Cottages
LAWNS CL
GOSLING AVE
CLARION CL
SALUSBURY LA
HARRIS LA
Chalk Hill
HOLLY BUSH HILL
Glebe Farm
LUTON WHITE HILL
Keeper's Cottage
KING'S WALDEN RD
1
Great Offley House
Cockrood Spring
Offley Hoo
26
13
14
15
D
E
F
47

21

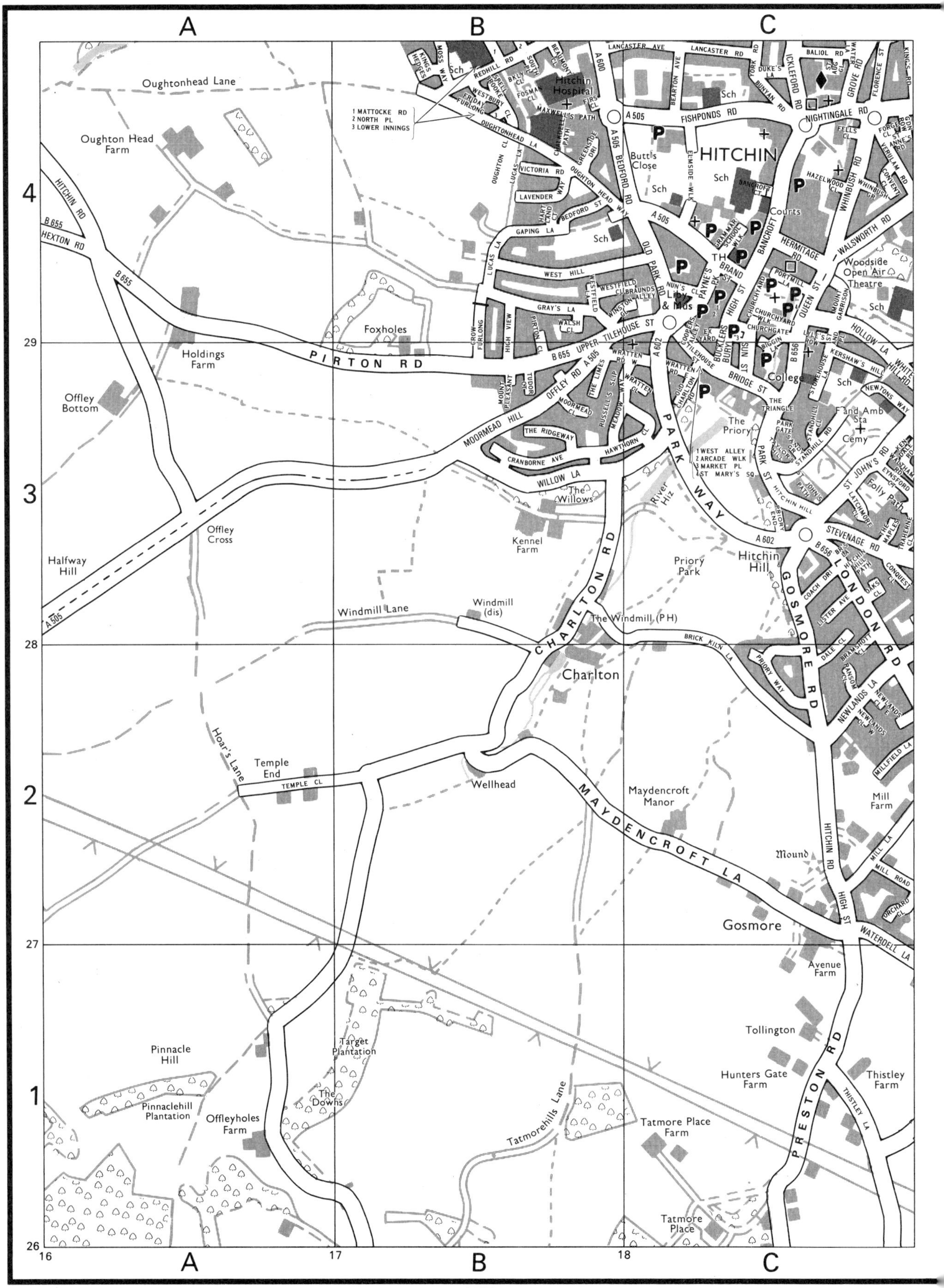

A
B
C
4
3
2
1
29
28
27
26
16
17
18
Oughtonhead Lane
Oughton Head Farm
HITCHIN RD
B 655
HEXTON RD
Holdings Farm
Offley Bottom
PIRTON RD
Foxholes
Offley Cross
Halfway Hill
A 505
Windmill Lane
Windmill (dis)
Hoar's Lane
Temple End
TEMPLE CL
Wellhead
Kennel Farm
The Willows
WILLOW LA
CRANBORNE AVE
THE RIDGEWAY
MOORMEAD HILL
HAWTHORN CL
CHARLTON RD
The Windmill (PH)
Charlton
BRICK KILN LA
MAYDENCROFT LA
Maydencroft Manor
Priory Park
Hitchin Hill
PARK WAY
River Hiz
The Priory
1 WEST ALLEY
2 ARCADE WLK
3 MARKET PL
4 ST MARY'S SQ
1 MATTOCKE RD
2 NORTH PL
3 LOWER INNINGS
Hitchin Hospital
HITCHIN
Butt's Close
Sch
Courts
College
Liby & Mus
FISHPONDS RD
LANCASTER AVE
LANCASTER RD
BEDFORD RD
OLD PARK RD
WEST HILL
GAPING LA
LUCAS LA
OUGHTONHEAD LA
VICTORIA RD
LAVENDER
BEDFORD ST
GRAY'S LA
WALSH CL
UPPER TILEHOUSE ST
B 655
A 602
BANCROFT
HERMITAGE RD
NIGHTINGALE RD
WALSWORTH RD
Woodside Open Air Theatre
HOLLOW LA
QUEEN ST
HIGH ST
BRIDGE ST
THE TRIANGLE
STOREHOUSE LA
Fand Amb Sta
Cemy
ST JOHN'S RD
STEVENAGE RD
GOSMORE RD
LONDON RD
PRIORY WAY
COACH DRI
LISTER AVE
DALE CL
NEWLANDS LA
MILLFIELD LA
Mill Farm
Mound
HITCHIN RD
HIGH ST
WATERDELL LA
Gosmore
Avenue Farm
Tollington
Hunters Gate Farm
Thistley Farm
THISTLEY LA
PRESTON RD
Tatmore Place Farm
Tatmore Place
Tatmorehills Lane
The Downs
Target Plantation
Offleyholes Farm
Pinnacle Hill
Pinnaclehill Plantation

33

48

22

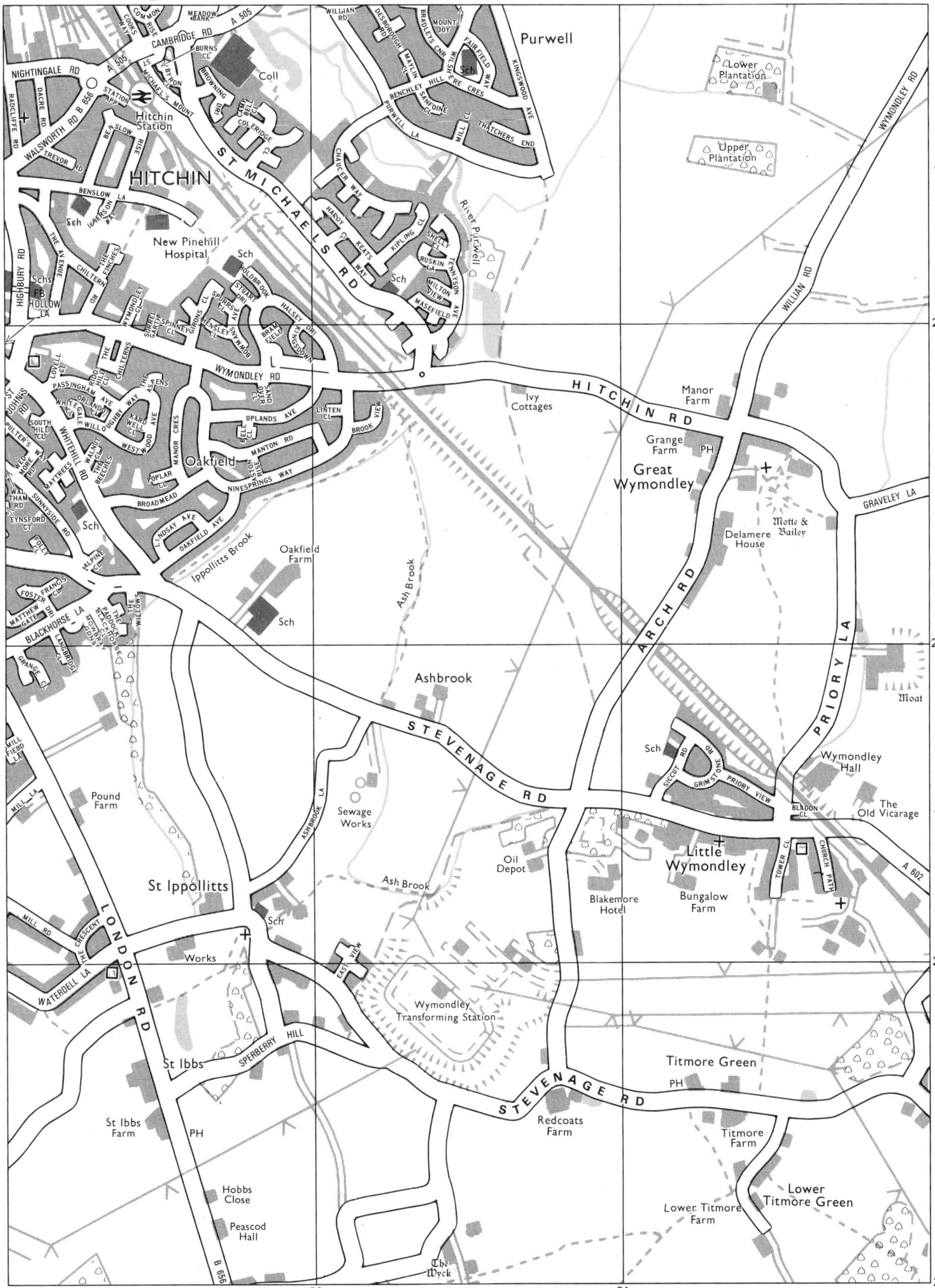
D
E
F
HITCHIN
Hitchin Station
Purwell
Coll
New Pinehill Hospital
Sch
Schs
FB
Lower Plantation
Upper Plantation
WYMONDLEY RD
WILLIAN RD
HITCHIN RD
ST MICHAELS RD
NIGHTINGALE RD
CAMBRIDGE RD
A 505
WALSWORTH RD B 656
TREVOR RD
BENSLOW LA
BENSLOW RISE
HIGHBURY RD
HOLLOW LA
THE AVENUE
CHILTERN RD
River Purwell
CHAUCER WAY
KIPLING CL
TENNYSON AVE
MASEFIELD
PURWELL LA
BENCHLEY HILL
THATCHERS END
KINGSWOOD AVE
FAIRFIELD WAY
MOUNT JOY
DESBOROUGH RD
HALSEY DRI
KINGSDOWN
BRAMFIELD
Ivy Cottages
Manor Farm
Grange Farm
PH
Great Wymondley
Motte & Bailey
Delamere House
GRAVELEY LA
ARCH RD
PRIORY LA
Moat
Oakfield
UPLANDS AVE
MANTON RD
NINESPRINGS WAY
BROADMEAD
WHITEHILL RD
Ippollitts Brook
Oakfield Farm
Ash Brook
Sch
Ashbrook
STEVENAGE RD
Sch
SICCUT RD
GRIMSTONE
PRIORY VIEW
Wymondley Hall
The Old Vicarage
BLADON CL
Little Wymondley
TOWER CL
CHURCH PATH
A 602
Bungalow Farm
Blakemore Hotel
Oil Depot
Sewage Works
ASHBROOK LA
Ash Brook
Pound Farm
St Ippollitts
LONDON RD
MILL RD
WATERDELL LA
THE CRESCENT
Works
Sch
EAST VIEW
Wymondley Transforming Station
SPERBERRY HILL
St Ibbs
Titmore Green
PH
STEVENAGE RD
Redcoats Farm
Titmore Farm
St Ibbs Farm
PH
Hobbs Close
Peascod Hall
B 656
The Wyck
Lower Titmore Farm
Lower Titmore Green
19
20
21
26
27
28
29
1
2
3
4

36

49

23

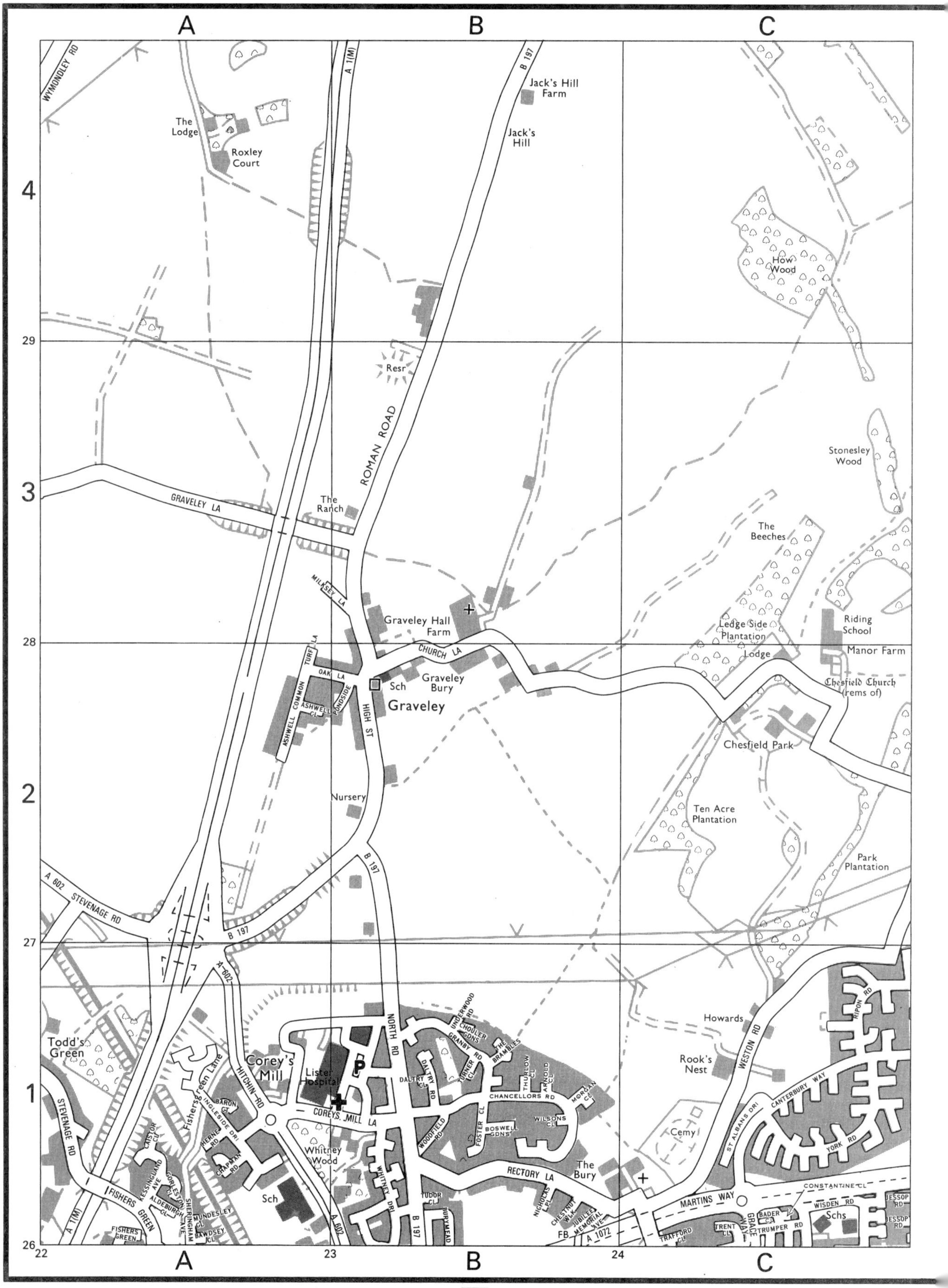
A
B
C
4
3
2
1
29
28
27
26
22
23
24
WYMONDLEY RD
A 1(M)
B 197
Jack's Hill Farm
Jack's Hill
The Lodge
Roxley Court
How Wood
Resr
ROMAN ROAD
Stonesley Wood
GRAVELEY LA
The Ranch
The Beeches
MILKSEY LA
Graveley Hall Farm
Riding School
Ledge Side Plantation
Manor Farm
Lodge
CHURCH LA
TURF LA
OAK LA
Sch
Graveley Bury
Chesfield Church (rems of)
ASHWELL COMMON
ASHWELL CL
PONDSIDE
HIGH ST
Graveley
Chesfield Park
Nursery
Ten Acre Plantation
Park Plantation
A 602
STEVENAGE RD
B 197
A 602
Todd's Green
Corey's Mill
Lister Hospital
NORTH RD
UNDERWOOD RD
CHOULER GDNS
GRANBY RD
THE BRAMBLES
TURNER CL
DALTRY RD
THURLOW CL
ARNOUD CL
MORGAN CL
CHANCELLORS RD
Howards
Rook's Nest
WESTON RD
RIPON RD
CANTERBURY WAY
ST ALBANS DRI
YORK RD
Fishers Green Lane
HITCHIN RD
BARON CT
INGLESIDE DRI
COREYS MILL LA
WOODFIELD RD
FOSTER CL
BOSWELL GDNS
WILSONS CL
Cemy
STEVENAGE RD
CAISTOR CL
HERNE RD
CHAPMAN RD
Whitney Wood
WHITNEY DRI
RECTORY LA
The Bury
KESSINGLAND AVE
GORLESTON CL
SHERINGHAM AVE
ALDEBURGH CL
Sch
TUDOR CL
NICHOLAS PL
MARTINS WAY
CONSTANTINE CL
FISHERS GREEN
MUNDESLEY CL
BAWDSEY CL
A 602
B 197
BURYMEAD
CHESTNUT WLK
JUBILEE MEMORIAL AVE
FB
A 1072
TRAFFORD CL
TRENT CL
GRACE WAY
BADER CL
TRUMPER RD
WISDEN RD
Schs
JESSOP RD
A 1(M)
FISHERS GREEN

35

50

24

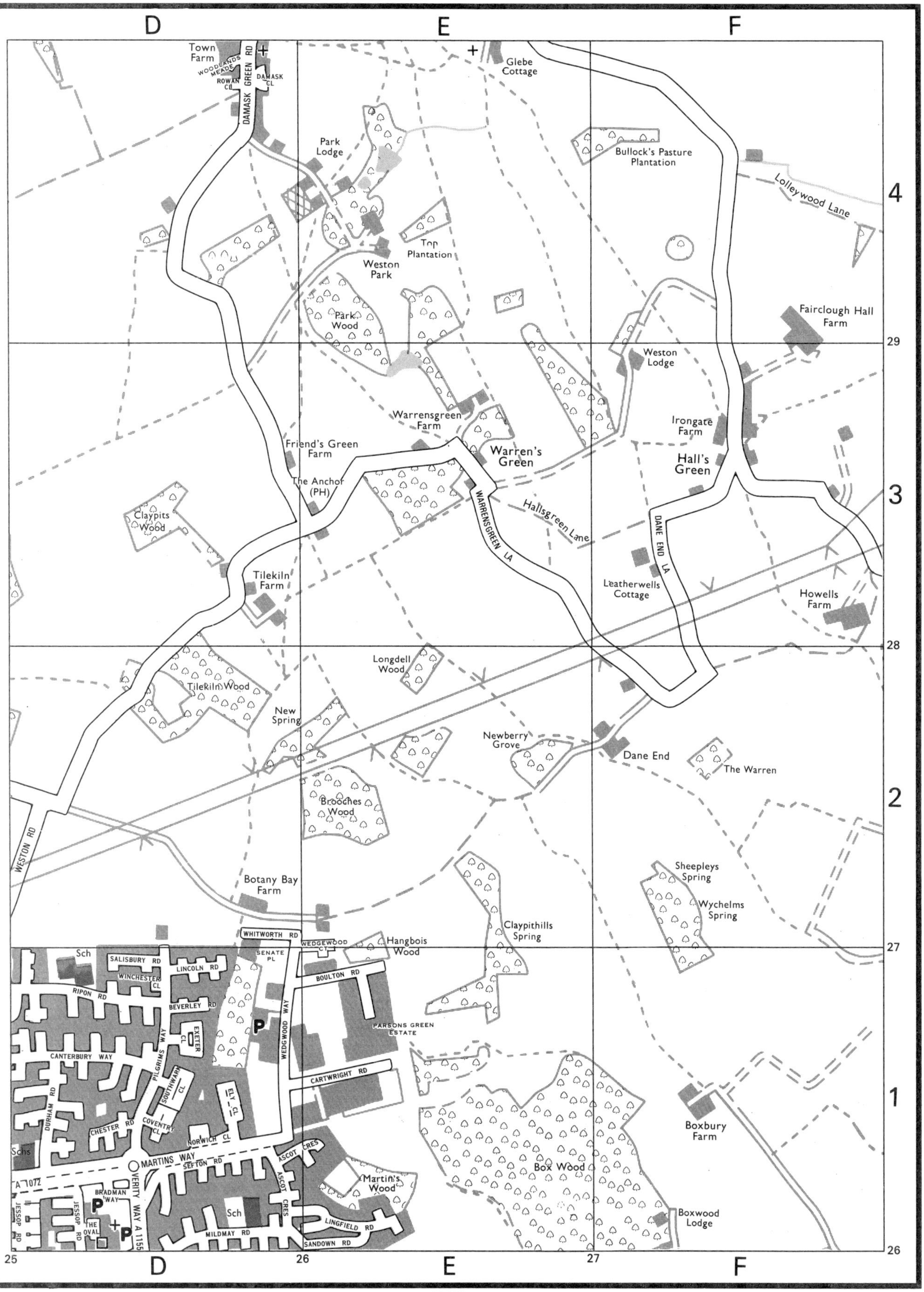
D
E
F
Town Farm
WOODLANDS MEADE
ROWAN CL
DAMASK GREEN RD
DAMASK CL
Glebe Cottage
Park Lodge
Bullock's Pasture Plantation
Lolleywood Lane
4
Top Plantation
Weston Park
Park Wood
Fairclough Hall Farm
29
Weston Lodge
Warrensgreen Farm
Irongate Farm
Friend's Green Farm
Warren's Green
Hall's Green
The Anchor (PH)
Claypits Wood
3
Hallsgreen Lane
WARRENSGREEN LA
DANE END LA
Tilekiln Farm
Leatherwells Cottage
Howells Farm
28
Longdell Wood
Tilekiln Wood
New Spring
Newberry Grove
Dane End
The Warren
2
Brooches Wood
WESTON RD
Sheepleys Spring
Botany Bay Farm
Wychelms Spring
Claypithills Spring
WHITWORTH RD
WEDGEWOOD
Hangbois Wood
27
Sch
SALISBURY RD
LINCOLN RD
SENATE PL
WINCHESTER CL
BOULTON RD
RIPON RD
BEVERLEY RD
EXETER CL
PARSONS GREEN ESTATE
CANTERBURY WAY
PILGRIMS WAY
WEDGWOOD WAY
SOUTHWARK CL
ELY CL
CARTWRIGHT RD
1
DURHAM RD
CHESTER RD
COVENTRY CL
NORWICH CL
Boxbury Farm
Schs
MARTINS WAY
SEFTON RD
ASCOT CRES
A 1072
VERITY WAY A 1155
Martin's Wood
Box Wood
BRADMAN WAY
JESSOP RD
THE OVAL
Sch
LINGFIELD RD
Boxwood Lodge
MILDMAY RD
SANDOWN RD
26
25
26
27
D
E
F

38

51

25

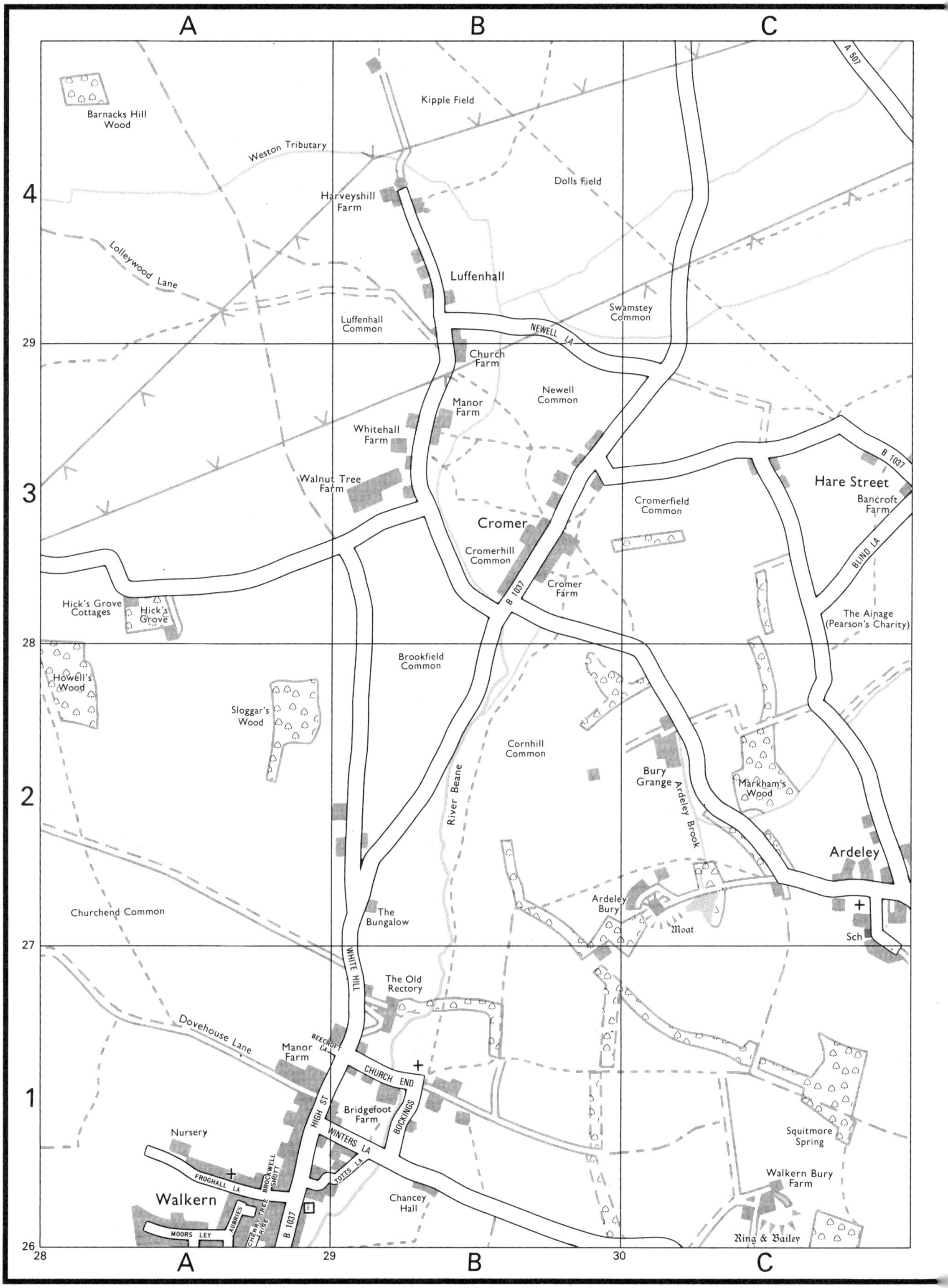
A
B
C
4
3
2
1
29
28
27
26
28
29
30
Barnacks Hill Wood
Kipple Field
Weston Tributary
Harveyshill Farm
Dolls Field
Lolleywood Lane
Luffenhall
Luffenhall Common
Swamstey Common
NEWELL LA
Church Farm
Newell Common
Manor Farm
Whitehall Farm
Walnut Tree Farm
B 1037
Hare Street
Bancroft Farm
Cromerfield Common
Cromer
Cromerhill Common
Cromer Farm
BLIND LA
Hick's Grove Cottages
Hick's Grove
The Ainage (Pearson's Charity)
Brookfield Common
Howell's Wood
Sloggar's Wood
Cornhill Common
Bury Grange
Ardeley Brook
Markham's Wood
River Beane
Ardeley
Churchend Common
The Bungalow
Ardeley Bury
Moat
Sch
WHITE HILL
The Old Rectory
Dovehouse Lane
BEECROFT LA
Manor Farm
CHURCH END
Bridgefoot Farm
HIGH ST
BUCKINGS
WINTERS LA
Nursery
TOTTS LA
BROCKWELL SHOTT
FROGHALL LA
Squitmore Spring
Walkern Bury Farm
Walkern
Chancey Hall
AUBRIES
CHERRY TREE RISE
MOORS LEY
Ring & Bailey
A 507

37

52

26

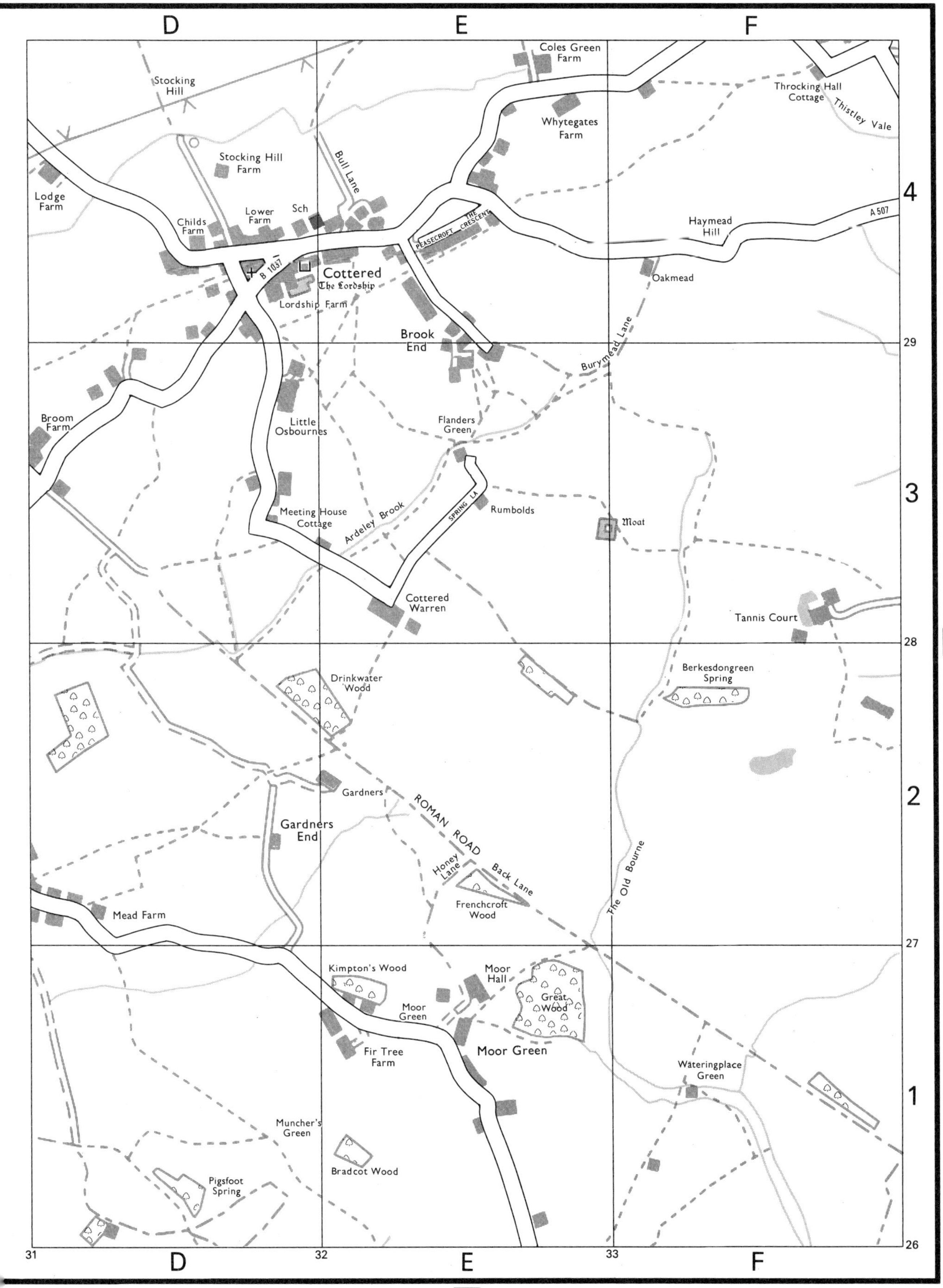
D
E
F
Stocking Hill
Coles Green Farm
Throcking Hall Cottage
Thistley Vale
Whytegates Farm
Stocking Hill Farm
Bull Lane
Lodge Farm
Childs Farm
Lower Farm
Sch
PEASECROFT
THE CRESCENT
Haymead Hill
A 507
4
B 1037
Cottered
The Lordship
Lordship Farm
Oakmead
Burymead Lane
Brook End
29
Broom Farm
Little Osbournes
Flanders Green
3
Meeting House Cottage
Ardeley Brook
SPRING LA
Rumbolds
Moat
Cottered Warren
Tannis Court
28
Drinkwater Wood
Berkesdongreen Spring
Gardners
ROMAN ROAD
2
Gardners End
Honey Lane
Back Lane
The Old Bourne
Frenchcroft Wood
Mead Farm
27
Kimpton's Wood
Moor Hall
Moor Green
Great Wood
Fir Tree Farm
Moor Green
Wateringplace Green
1
Muncher's Green
Pigsfoot Spring
Bradcot Wood
26
31
32
33
D
E
F

40

53

27

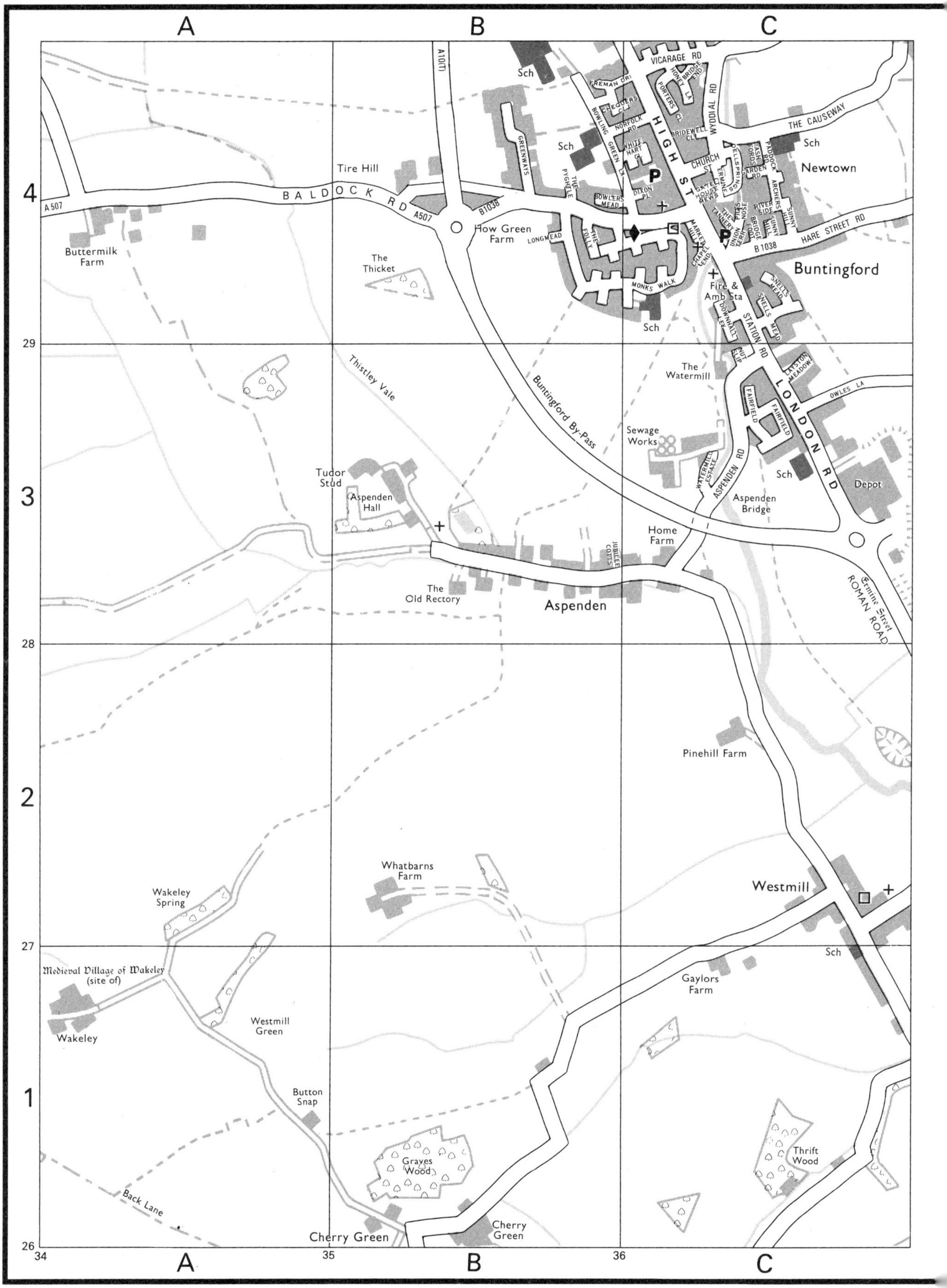
A
B
C
4
3
2
1
29
28
27
26
34
35
36
A507
BALDOCK RD
A10(T)
B1038
Tire Hill
Buttermilk Farm
How Green Farm
The Thicket
LONGMEAD
Sch
GREENWAYS
FREMAN DR
CHEQUERS CL
BOWLING GREEN LA
NORFOLK RD
WHITE HART CL
THE PYGHLE
BOWLERS MEAD
DIXON PL
THE FOLLY
MONKS WALK
VICARAGE RD
HONEY LA
BRIDGE END
PORTERS CL
WYDDIAL RD
HIGH ST
BRIDEWELL CL
CHURCH ST
MARKET HILL
CHAPEL END
THE CAUSEWAY
Newtown
PADDOCK RD
HARE STREET RD
B1038
Buntingford
Fire & Amb Sta
SNELLS MEAD
STATION RD
DOWNHALL LEY
NUT SLIP
LAYSTON MEADOW
OWLES LA
LONDON RD
FAIRFIELD
The Watermill
Sewage Works
WATERMILL ESTATE
ASPENDEN RD
Aspenden Bridge
Depot
Thistley Vale
Buntingford By-Pass
Tudor Stud
Aspenden Hall
Home Farm
JUBILEE COTTS
The Old Rectory
Aspenden
Ermine Street
ROMAN ROAD
Pinehill Farm
Whatbarns Farm
Wakeley Spring
Westmill
Sch
Gaylors Farm
Medieval Village of Wakeley (site of)
Wakeley
Westmill Green
Button Snap
Graves Wood
Back Lane
Cherry Green
Thrift Wood

39

54

28

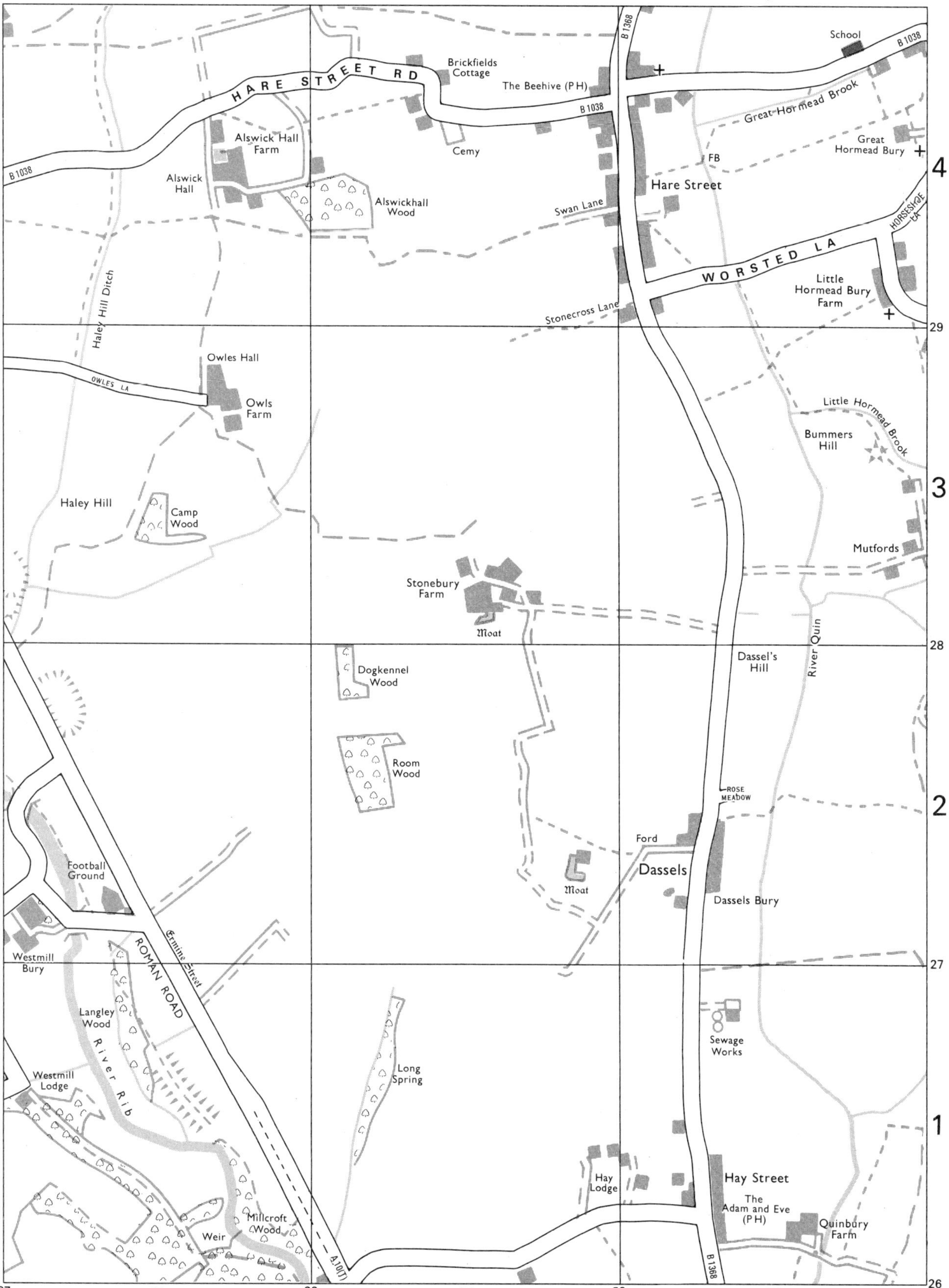
D
E
F
HARE STREET RD
B 1038
B 1368
Brickfields Cottage
The Beehive (PH)
School
Great Hormead Brook
Great Hormead Bury
Alswick Hall Farm
Alswick Hall
Cemy
FB
Hare Street
Alswickhall Wood
Swan Lane
HORSESHOE LA
WORSTED LA
Little Hormead Bury Farm
Stonecross Lane
Haley Hill Ditch
Owles Hall
OWLES LA
Owls Farm
Little Hormead Brook
Bummers Hill
Haley Hill
Camp Wood
Mutfords
Stonebury Farm
Moat
Dogkennel Wood
Dassel's Hill
River Quin
Room Wood
ROSE MEADOW
Ford
Football Ground
Dassels
Moat
Dassels Bury
Westmill Bury
ROMAN ROAD
Ermine Street
Langley Wood
Sewage Works
River Rib
Westmill Lodge
Long Spring
Hay Lodge
Hay Street
The Adam and Eve (PH)
Quinbury Farm
Millcroft Wood
Weir
A10(T)
37
38
39
26
27
28
29
1
2
3
4

42

55

29

41

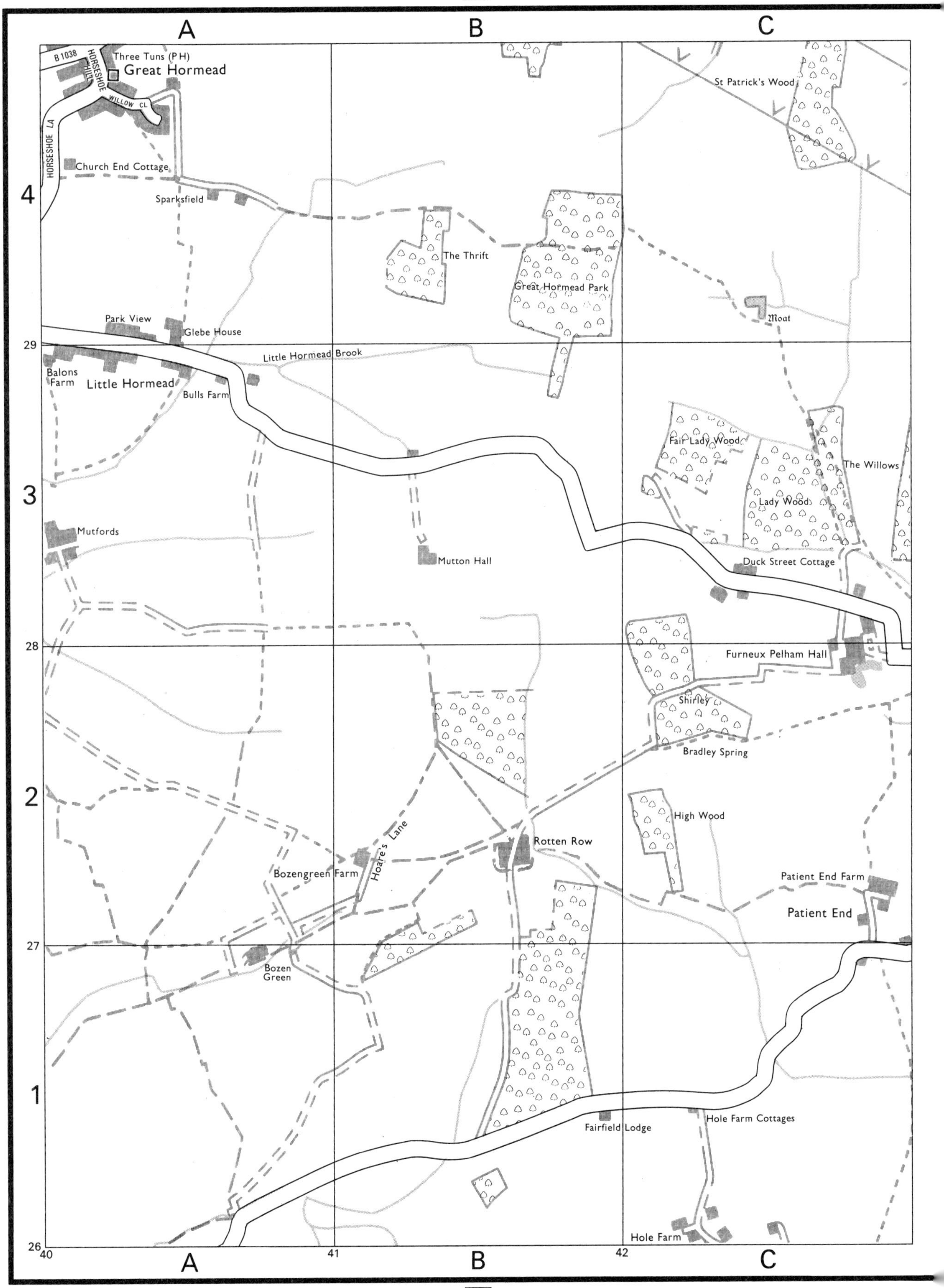
A
B
C
4
3
2
1
29
28
27
26
40
41
42
B 1038
HORSESHOE HILL
Three Tuns (PH)
Great Hormead
WILLOW CL
HORSESHOE LA
Church End Cottage
Sparksfield
St Patrick's Wood
The Thrift
Great Hormead Park
Moat
Park View
Glebe House
Little Hormead Brook
Balons Farm
Little Hormead
Bulls Farm
Fair Lady Wood
The Willows
Lady Wood
Mutfords
Mutton Hall
Duck Street Cottage
Furneux Pelham Hall
Shirley
Bradley Spring
High Wood
Rotten Row
Hoare's Lane
Bozengreen Farm
Patient End Farm
Patient End
Bozen Green
Fairfield Lodge
Hole Farm Cottages
Hole Farm

56

30

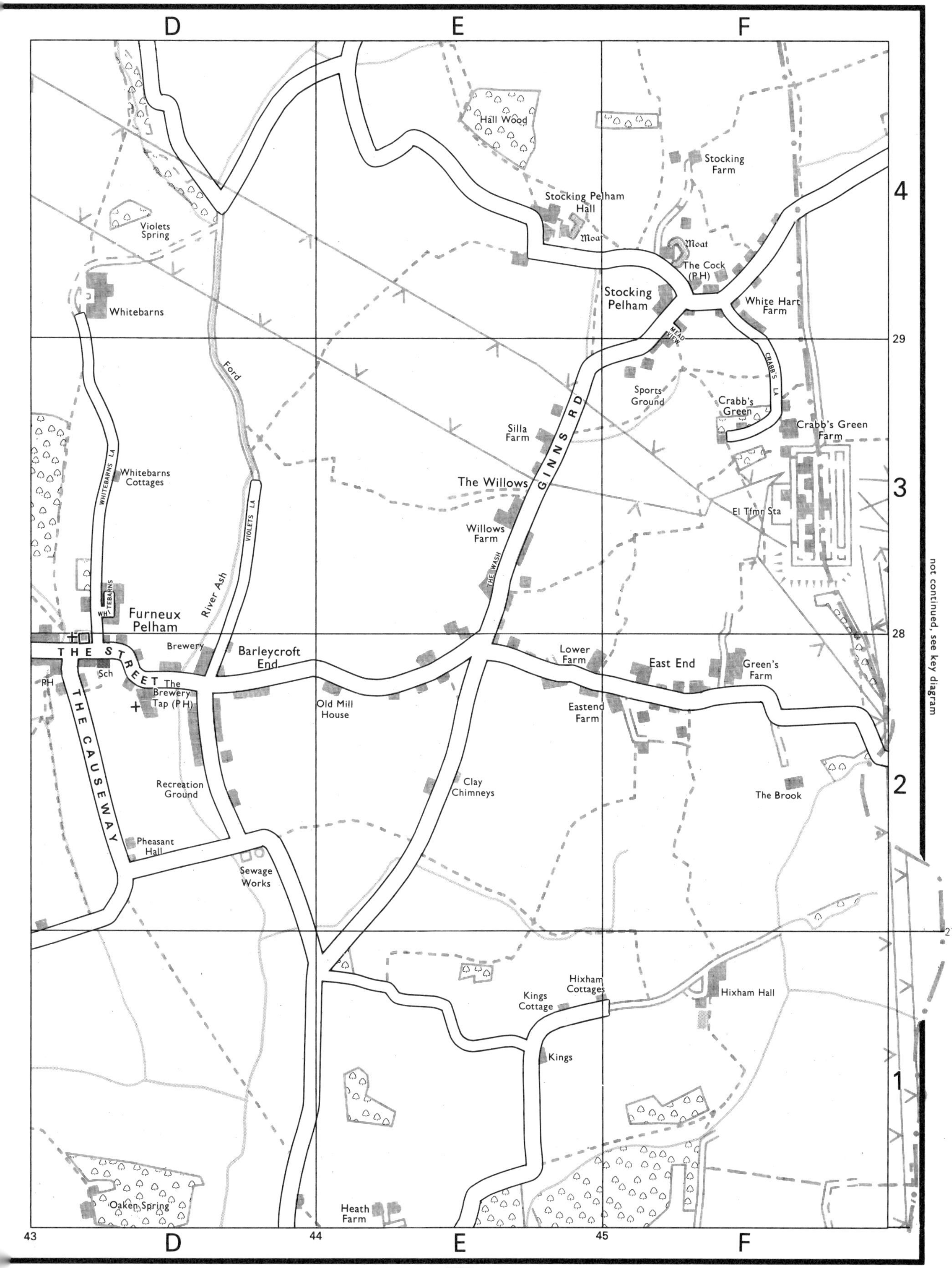

not continued, see key diagram

57

not continued, see key diagram

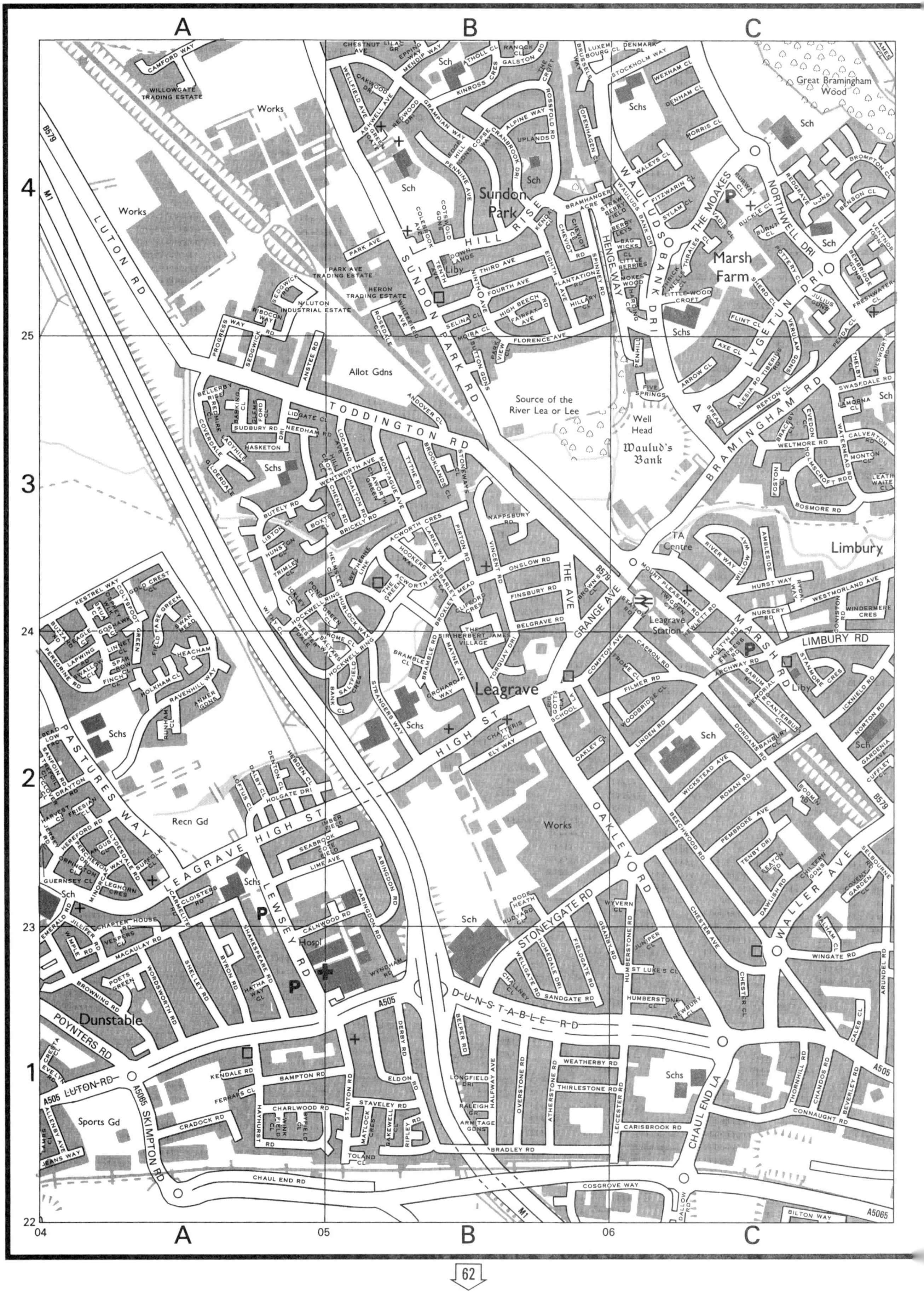

not continued, see key diagram

31

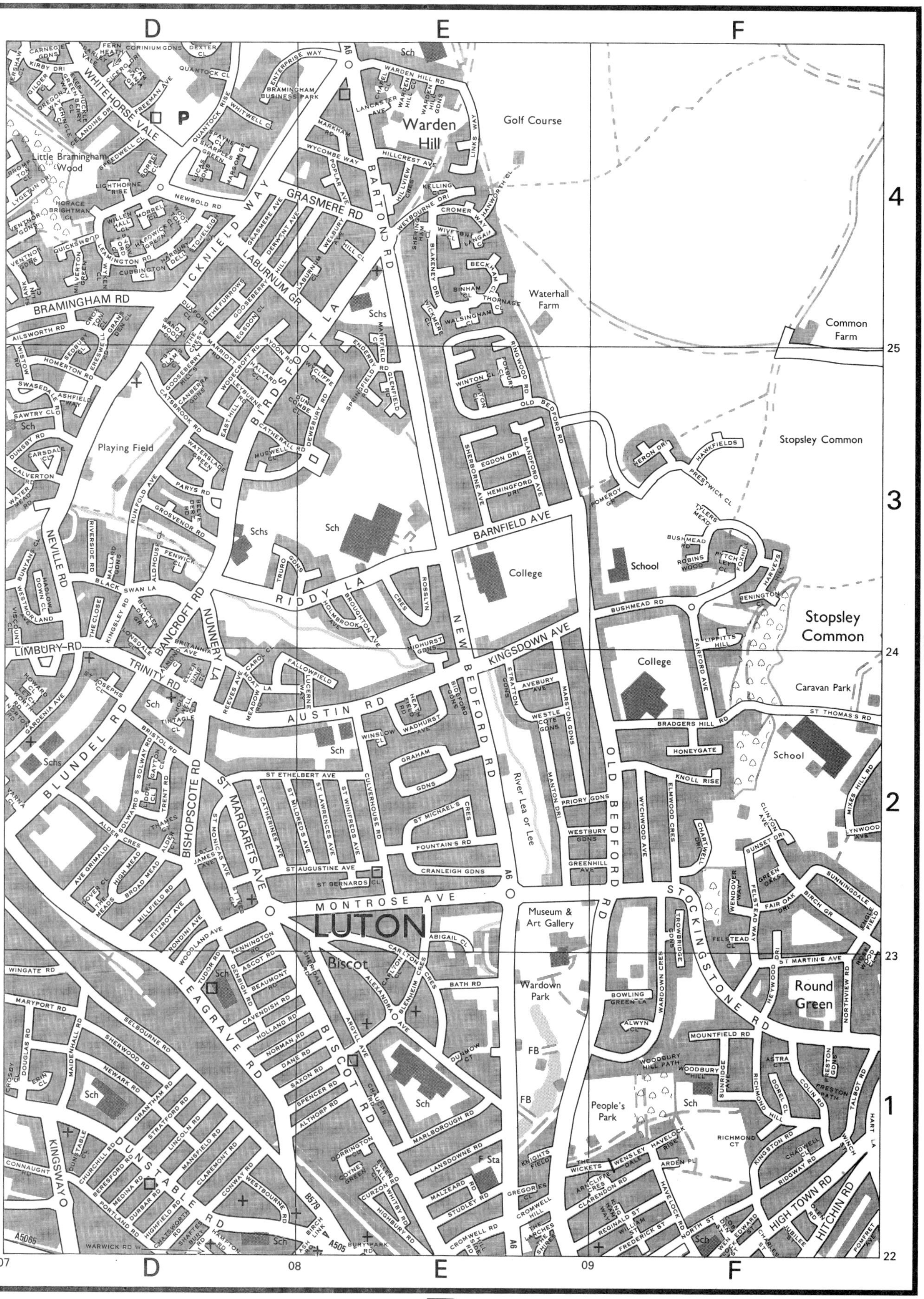
D
E
F
4
3
2
1
25
24
23
22
07
08
09
LUTON
Warden Hill
Golf Course
Waterhall Farm
Common Farm
Stopsley Common
Stopsley Common
Caravan Park
School
College
College
Round Green
Biscot
Museum & Art Gallery
Wardown Park
People's Park
Little Bramingham Wood
Playing Field
River Lea or Lee
Sch
Schs
F Sta
FB
WHITEHORSE VALE
ICKNIELD WAY
GRASMERE RD
BARTON RD
LABURNUM GR
BIRDSFOOT LA
BRAMINGHAM RD
BRAMINGHAM BUSINESS PARK
ENTERPRISE WAY
WARDEN HILL RD
LINKS WAY
HILLCREST AVE
WYCOMBE WAY
NEWBOLD RD
OLD BEDFORD RD
NEW BEDFORD RD
BARNFIELD AVE
RIDDY LA
KINGSDOWN AVE
BUSHMEAD RD
BRADGERS HILL RD
ST THOMAS'S RD
AUSTIN RD
LIMBURY RD
TRINITY RD
BANCROFT RD
NUNNERY LA
NEVILLE RD
BLUNDELL RD
BISHOPSCOTE RD
ST MARGARETS AVE
MONTROSE AVE
LEAGRAVE RD
BISCOT RD
DUNSTABLE RD
KINGSWAY
STOCKINGSTONE RD
HIGH TOWN RD
HITCHIN RD
MARLBOROUGH RD
HAVELOCK RD
CAVENDISH RD
WESTBOURNE RD
SELBOURNE RD
SHERWOOD RD
NEWARK RD
MARYPORT RD
WINGATE RD
CONNAUGHT RD
WARWICK RD
KNOLL RISE
HONEYGATE
MOUNTFIELD RD
RICHMOND HILL
SUNNINGDALE
A6
A505
A5065
B579
46

63

32
45
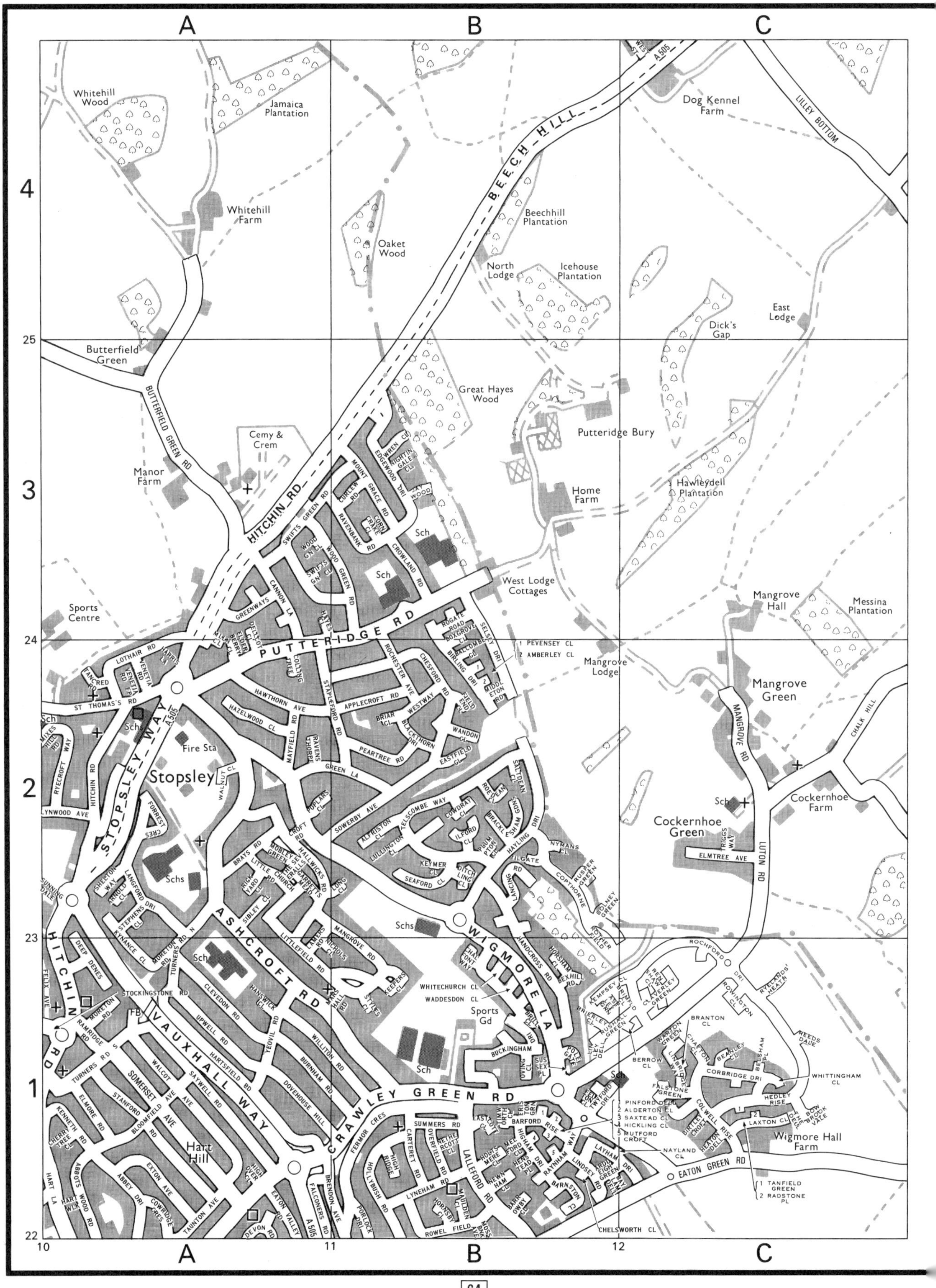
A
B
C
4
3
2
1
25
24
23
22
10
11
12
Whitehill Wood
Jamaica Plantation
Dog Kennel Farm
LILLEY BOTTOM
BEECH HILL
A505
Whitehill Farm
Oaket Wood
Beechhill Plantation
North Lodge
Icehouse Plantation
East Lodge
Dick's Gap
Butterfield Green
BUTTERFIELD GREEN RD
Great Hayes Wood
Putteridge Bury
Cemy & Crem
Manor Farm
Home Farm
Hawleydell Plantation
HITCHIN RD
Sch
West Lodge Cottages
Mangrove Hall
Messina Plantation
Sports Centre
PUTTERIDGE RD
1 PEVENSEY CL
2 AMBERLEY CL
Mangrove Lodge
Mangrove Green
MANGROVE RD
CHALK HILL
Fire Sta
Stopsley
STOPSLEY WAY
Cockernhoe Farm
Cockernhoe Green
ELMTREE AVE
LUTON RD
Schs
WIGMORE LA
ASHCROFT RD
VAUXHALL WAY
HITCHIN RD
ROCHFORD DRI
WHITECHURCH CL
WADDESDON CL
Sports Gd
CRAWLEY GREEN RD
WHITTINGHAM CL
1 PINFORD DELL
2 ALDERTON CL
3 SAXTEAD CL
4 HICKLING CL
5 HUTFORD CROFT
NAYLAND CL
EATON GREEN RD
Wigmore Hall Farm
Hart Hill
1 TANFIELD GREEN
2 RADSTONE PL
CHELSWORTH CL
ROWEL FIELD
A505
64

33

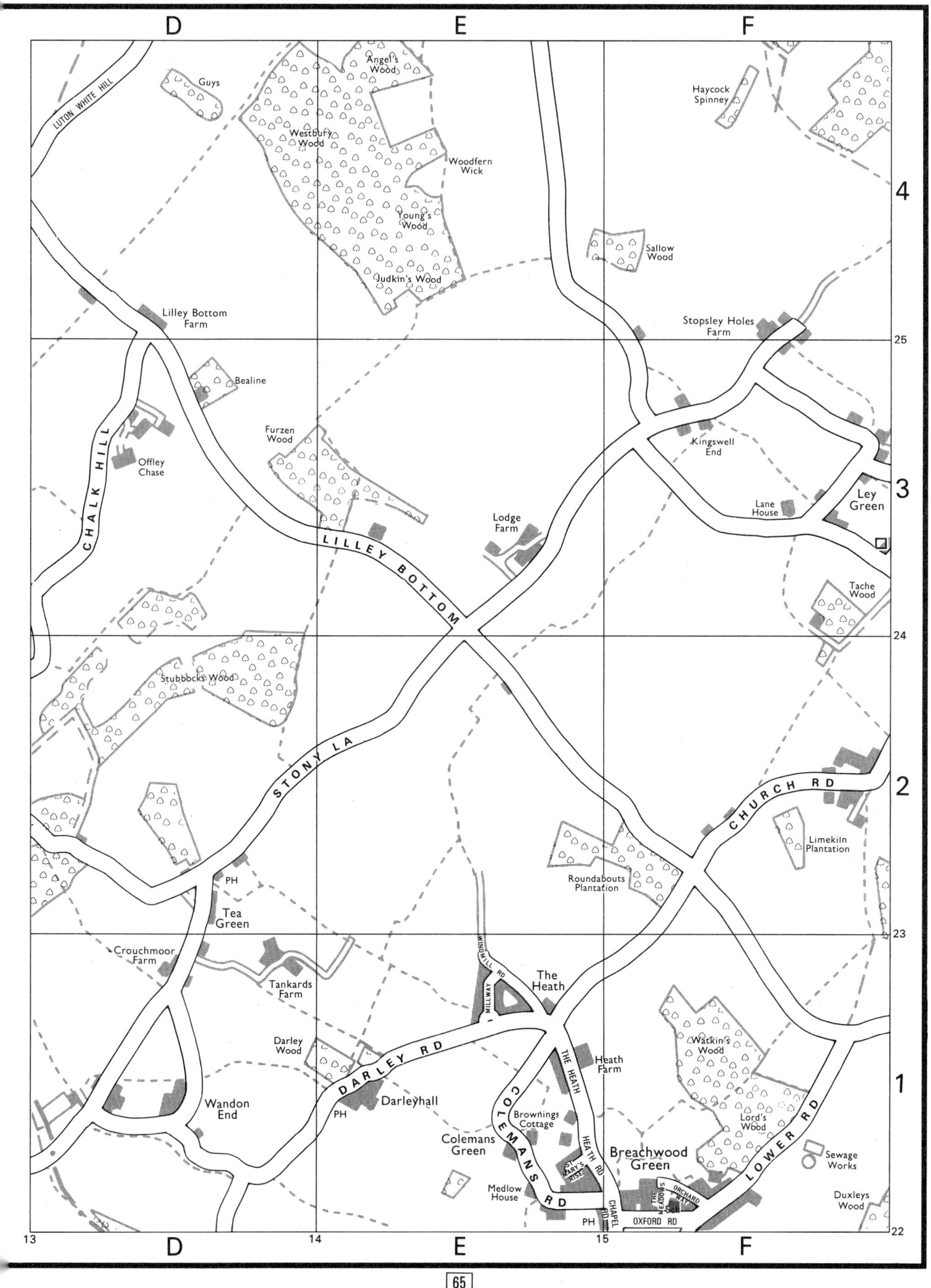
D
E
F
Guys
LUTON WHITE HILL
Angel's Wood
Westbury Wood
Woodfern Wick
Young's Wood
Judkin's Wood
Haycock Spinney
Sallow Wood
4
Lilley Bottom Farm
Stopsley Holes Farm
25
Bealine
Furzen Wood
Kingswell End
CHALK HILL
Offley Chase
3
Ley Green
Lane House
Lodge Farm
LILLEY BOTTOM
Tache Wood
24
Stubbocks Wood
STONY LA
CHURCH RD
2
Limekiln Plantation
Roundabouts Plantation
PH
Tea Green
23
Crouchmoor Farm
Tankards Farm
WINDMILL RD
MILLWAY
The Heath
Darley Wood
DARLEY RD
Heath Farm
Watkin's Wood
1
Wandon End
PH
Darleyhall
THE HEATH
COLEMANS RD
Brownings Cottage
Colemans Green
HEATH RD
Breachwood Green
Lord's Wood
LOWER RD
Sewage Works
ST MARY'S RISE
Medlow House
THE MEADOWS
ORCHARD WAY
Sch
Duxleys Wood
PH
CHAPEL RD
OXFORD RD
13
14
15
22
D
E
F

48

65

34

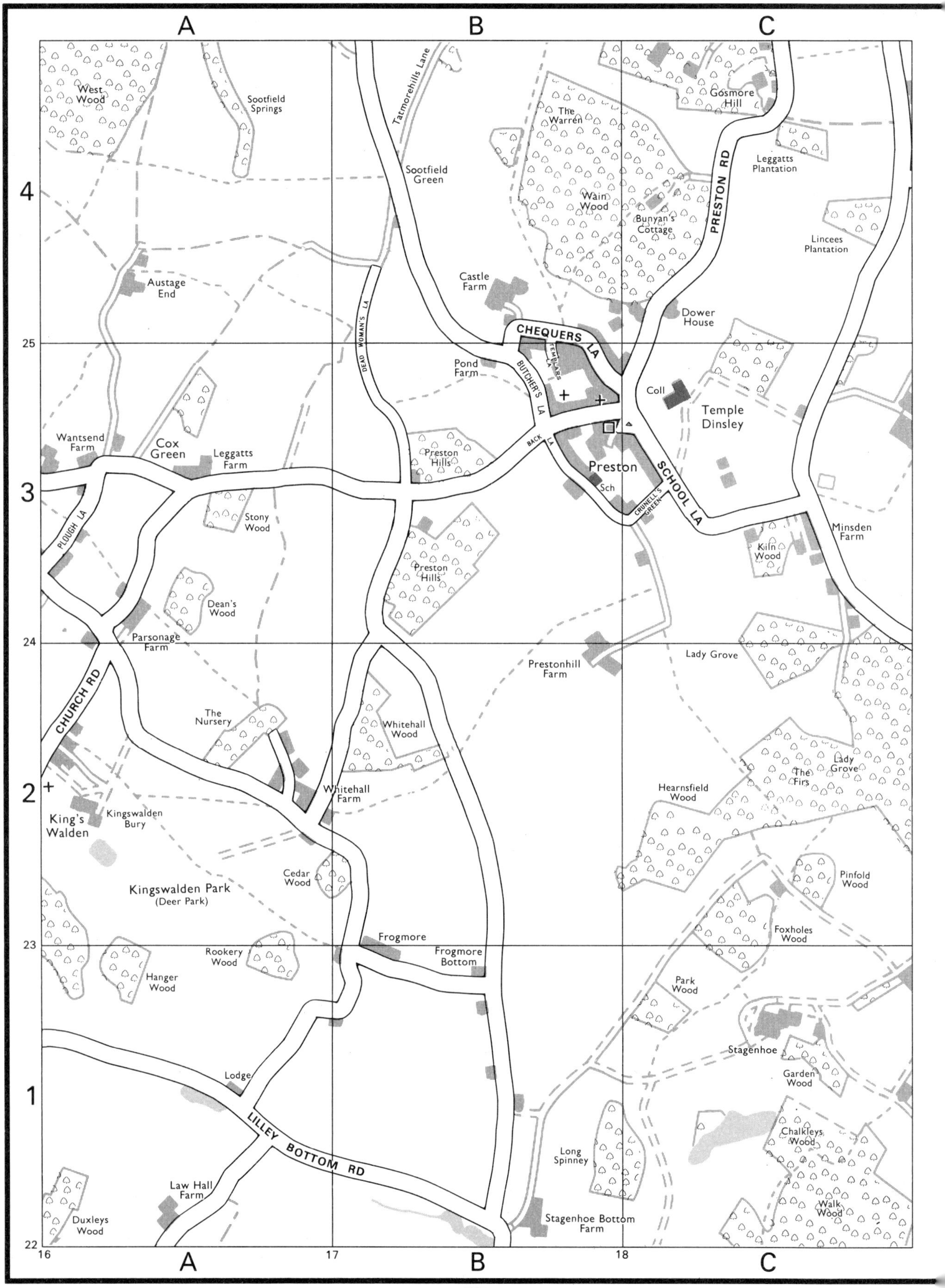
A
B
C
West Wood
Sootfield Springs
Tatmorehills Lane
The Warren
Gosmore Hill
Leggatts Plantation
Sootfield Green
Wain Wood
Bunyan's Cottage
PRESTON RD
Lincees Plantation
Austage End
Castle Farm
Dower House
DEAD WOMAN'S LA
CHEQUERS LA
TEMPLARS LA
Pond Farm
BUTCHER'S LA
Coll
Temple Dinsley
Wantsend Farm
Cox Green
Leggatts Farm
BACK LA
Preston Hills
Preston
Sch
SCHOOL LA
CRUNELL'S GREEN
Stony Wood
PLOUGH LA
Minsden Farm
Kiln Wood
Preston Hills
Dean's Wood
Parsonage Farm
Lady Grove
Prestonhill Farm
CHURCH RD
The Nursery
Whitehall Wood
The Firs
Lady Grove
Hearnsfield Wood
Whitehall Farm
King's Walden
Kingswalden Bury
Cedar Wood
Pinfold Wood
Kingswalden Park
(Deer Park)
Foxholes Wood
Frogmore
Frogmore Bottom
Rookery Wood
Hanger Wood
Park Wood
Stagenhoe
Garden Wood
Lodge
LILLEY BOTTOM RD
Chalkleys Wood
Long Spinney
Law Hall Farm
Walk Wood
Duxleys Wood
Stagenhoe Bottom Farm
4
25
3
24
2
23
1
22
16
17
18

47

66

35

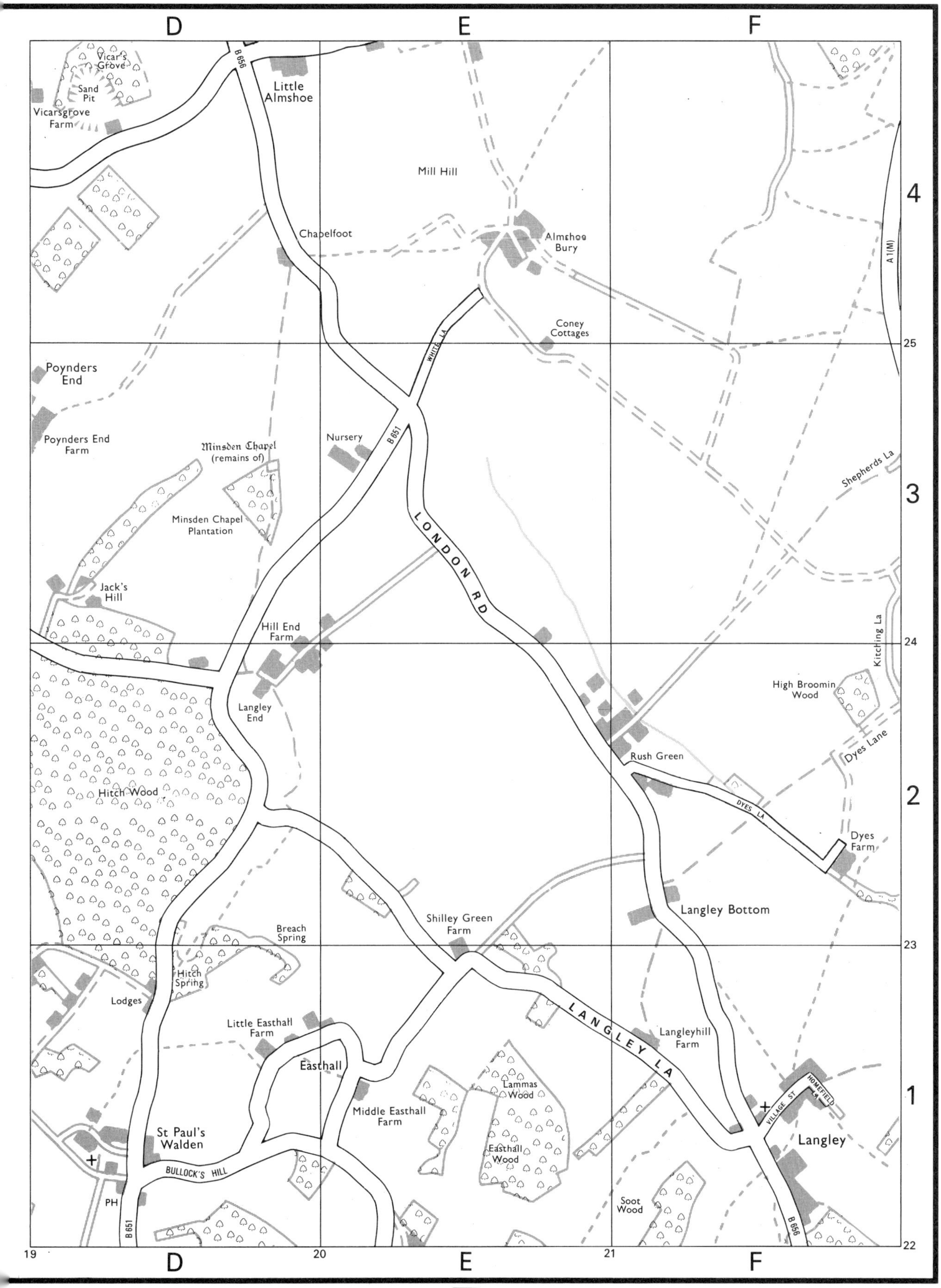

D
E
F
Vicar's Grove
Sand Pit
Vicarsgrove Farm
B 656
Little Almshoe
Mill Hill
Chapelfoot
Almshoe Bury
A1(M)
4
Coney Cottages
WHITE LA
25
Poynders End
Poynders End Farm
Nursery
B 651
Minsden Chapel (remains of)
Minsden Chapel Plantation
Shepherds La
3
LONDON RD
Jack's Hill
Hill End Farm
24
Kitching La
High Broomin Wood
Langley End
Dyes Lane
Rush Green
Hitch Wood
2
DYES LA
Dyes Farm
Langley Bottom
Shilley Green Farm
Breach Spring
23
Hitch Spring
Lodges
LANGLEY LA
Little Easthall Farm
Langleyhill Farm
Easthall
Lammas Wood
1
HOMEFIELD
VILLAGE ST
Middle Easthall Farm
St Paul's Walden
Langley
Easthall Wood
BULLOCK'S HILL
PH
B 651
Soot Wood
B 656
19
20
21
22

50

67

36

49

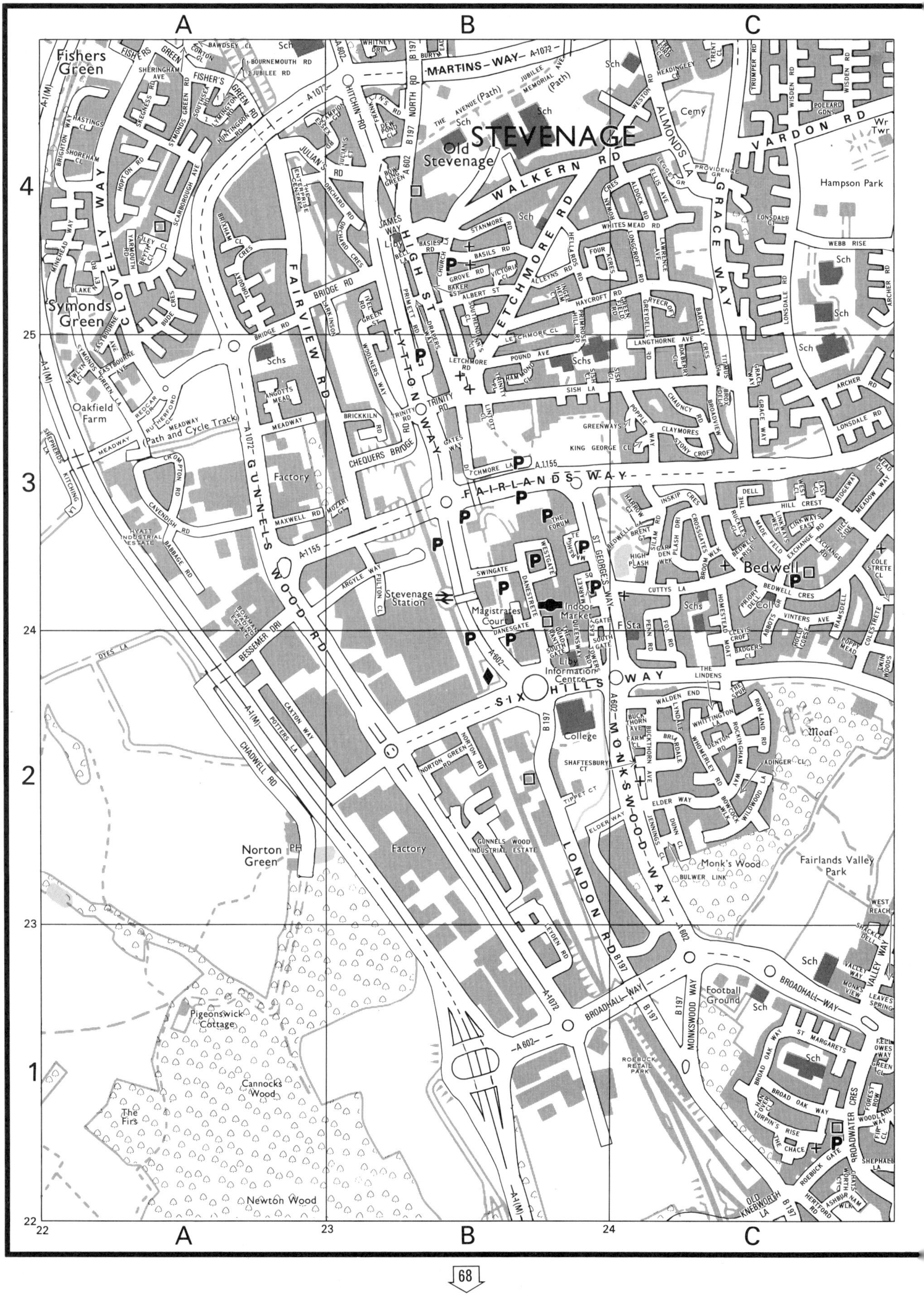
A
B
C
STEVENAGE
Old Stevenage
Fishers Green
Symonds Green
Oakfield Farm
Hampson Park
Bedwell
Norton Green
Pigeonswick Cottage
Cannocks Wood
The Firs
Newton Wood
Monk's Wood
Fairlands Valley Park
Roebuck Retail Park
Football Ground
Stevenage Station
Magistrates Court
Indoor Market
Information Centre
College
Factory
Hyatt Industrial Estate
Bowman Trading Estate
Gunnels Wood Industrial Estate
Moat
Cemy
Wr Twr
MARTINS WAY
WALKERN RD
LETCHMORE RD
HIGH ST
LYTTON WAY
FAIRVIEW RD
GUNNELS WOOD RD
FAIRLANDS WAY
SIX HILLS WAY
MONKSWOOD WAY
LONDON RD
BROADHALL WAY
GRACE WAY
VARDON RD
ALMONDS LA
CLOVELLY WAY
ST GEORGES WAY
CHADWELL RD
BESSEMER DRI
CAXTON WAY
CHEQUERS BRIDGE
ARGYLE WAY
BRIDGE RD
MEADWAY
Path and Cycle Track
CAVENDISH RD
BEDWELL CRES
BROAD OAK WAY
BROADWATER CRES
A-1(M)
A 602
A 1072
A 1155
B 197
4
3
2
1
25
24
23
22
22
23
24

68

37

D
E
F
4
3
2
1
25
24
23
22
26
27
Pin Green
Chells Manor
Chells
Fairlands Valley Park
The Education Centre
Shephall
Poplars
Broadwater
Shephalbury Park
Aston End
Aston
Aston Dene
White Farm
Tatler's Farm
Lord's Farm
Holders
New Wood
Elm Green
Recn Gd
Wr Twr
Bareleigh
Park Farm
Astonbury Farm
Golf Course
Lady's Wood
Ridlins Wood
Aston End Brook
SIX HILLS WAY
SHEPHALL WAY
GRESLEY WAY
FAIRLANDS WAY
WALKERN RD
STEVENAGE RD
BROADHALL WAY
HYDEAN WAY
MOBBSBURY WAY
CHELLS WAY
A1155 VERITY WAY
B 1037
A 602
Lanterns Lane (Path and Cycle Track)
Path and Cycle Track
LONG LA
SHORT LA
TATLERS LA
ASTON END RD
BROOKFIELD LA
BENINGTON RD
STRINGERS LA
ASTON LA
BROADWATER LA
SHEPHALL LA
SHEPHALL GREEN
SHEPHALL GREEN LA
OAKS CROSS
VALLEY WAY
SHEPHALL VIEW
Sch
Schs
P
1 BLACKBERRY MEAD
2 CAMPKIN MEAD
1 EDGEWORTH CL
2 GODDARD END

52

69

38

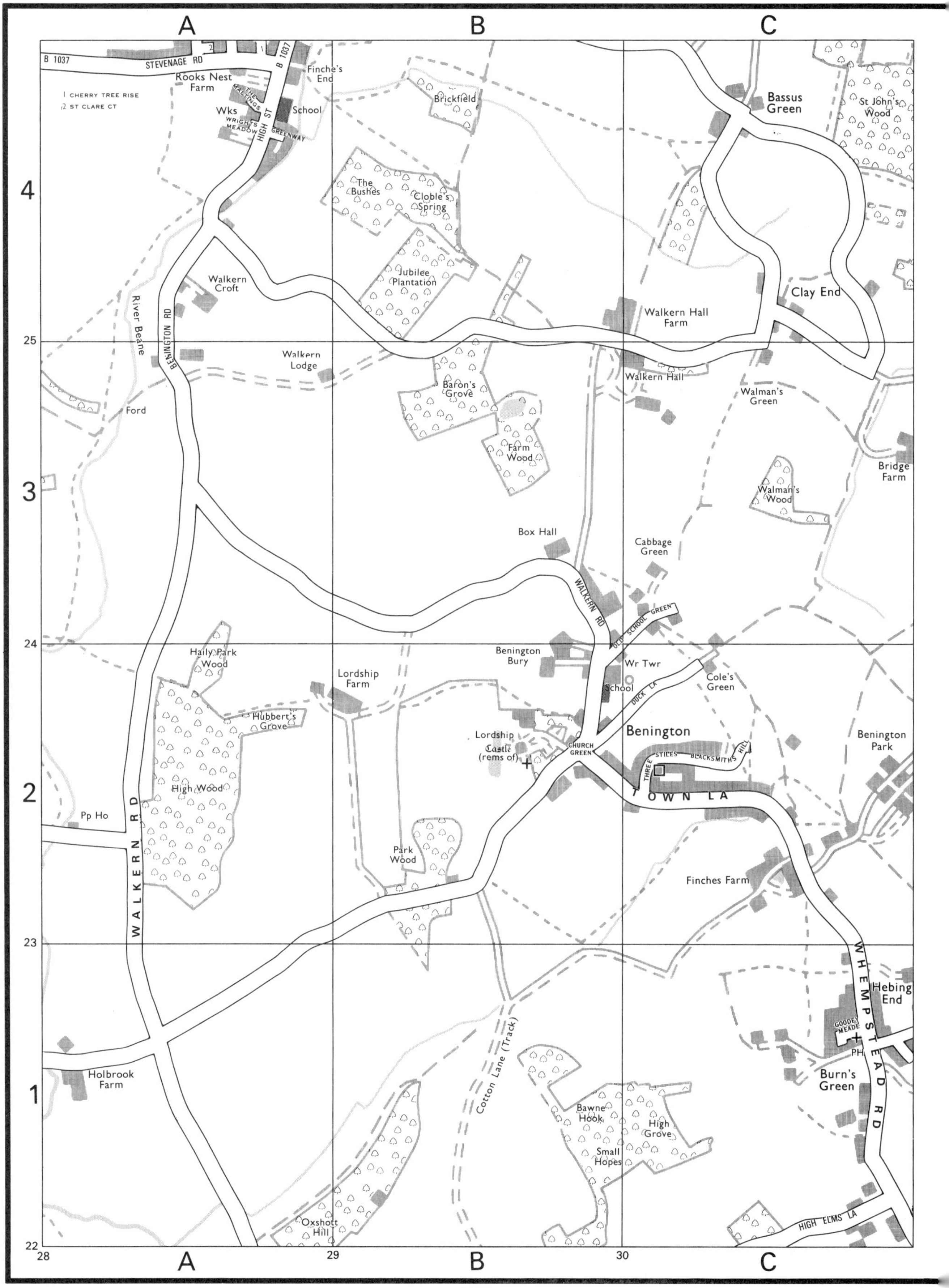
A
B
C
4
3
2
1
25
24
23
22
28
29
30
B 1037
STEVENAGE RD
Rooks Nest Farm
1 CHERRY TREE RISE
2 ST CLARE CT
THE MALTINGS
Wks
WRIGHTS MEADOW
HIGH ST
B 1037
School
GREENWAY
Finche's End
Brickfield
Bassus Green
St John's Wood
The Bushes
Cloble's Spring
Jubilee Plantation
Walkern Croft
Clay End
Walkern Hall Farm
River Beane
BENINGTON RD
Walkern Lodge
Walkern Hall
Baron's Grove
Walman's Green
Ford
Farm Wood
Bridge Farm
Walman's Wood
Box Hall
Cabbage Green
WALKERN RD
OLD SCHOOL GREEN
Haily Park Wood
Benington Bury
Wr Twr
Lordship Farm
School
DUCK LA
Cole's Green
Hubbert's Grove
Lordship Castle (rems of)
CHURCH GREEN
Benington
THREE STILES
BLACKSMITHS HILL
Benington Park
High Wood
TOWN LA
Pp Ho
WALKERN RD
Park Wood
Finches Farm
WHEMPSTEAD RD
Hebing End
GOODEY MEADE
PH
Cotton Lane (Track)
Holbrook Farm
Burn's Green
Bawne Hook
High Grove
Small Hopes
Oxshott Hill
HIGH ELMS LA

51

70

39

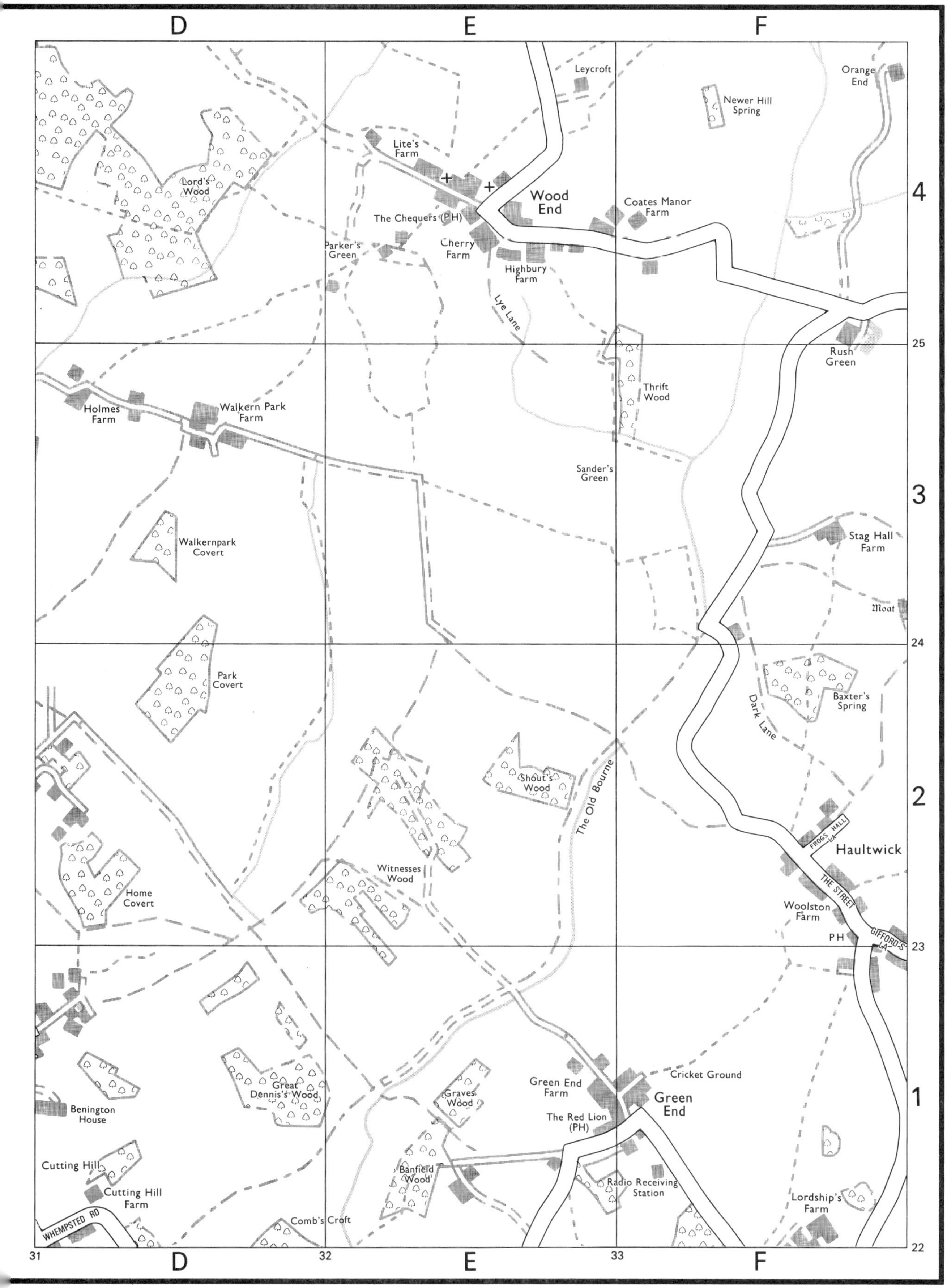

D
E
F
Leycroft
Orange End
Newer Hill Spring
Lite's Farm
Lord's Wood
Wood End
Coates Manor Farm
The Chequers (PH)
Parker's Green
Cherry Farm
Highbury Farm
Lye Lane
Rush Green
Thrift Wood
Holmes Farm
Walkern Park Farm
Sander's Green
Walkernpark Covert
Stag Hall Farm
Moat
Park Covert
Baxter's Spring
Dark Lane
Shout's Wood
The Old Bourne
Frogs Hall La
Haultwick
The Street
Witnesses Wood
Home Covert
Woolston Farm
PH
Gifford's La
Cricket Ground
Green End Farm
Green End
Great Dennis's Wood
Graves Wood
Benington House
The Red Lion (PH)
Cutting Hill
Banfield Wood
Radio Receiving Station
Cutting Hill Farm
Lordship's Farm
Whempsted Rd
Comb's Croft
4
3
2
1
25
24
23
22
31
32
33

54

71

40

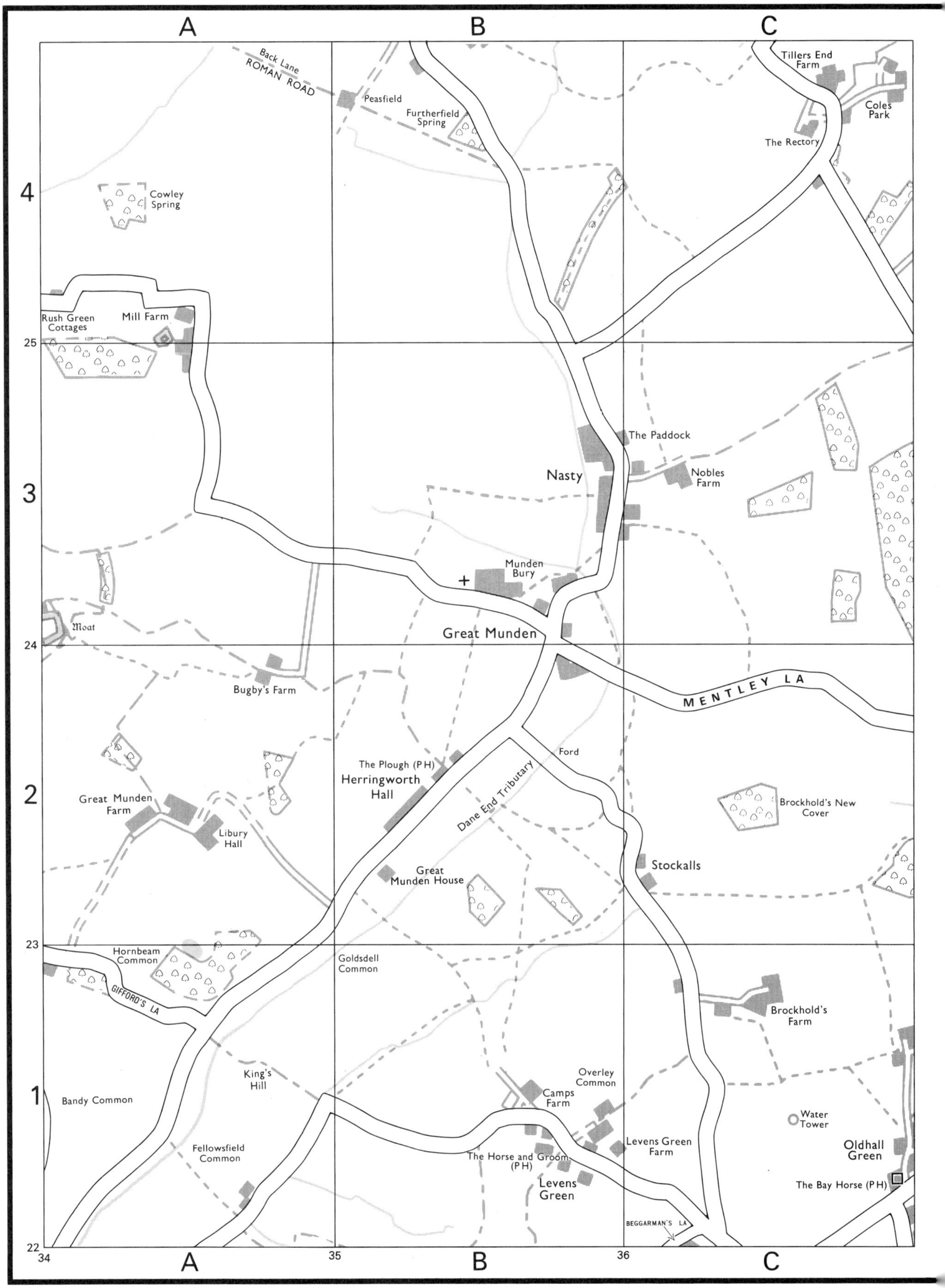
A
B
C
4
3
2
1
25
24
23
22
34
35
36
Back Lane
ROMAN ROAD
Peasfield
Furtherfield Spring
Tillers End Farm
Coles Park
The Rectory
Cowley Spring
Rush Green Cottages
Mill Farm
The Paddock
Nasty
Nobles Farm
Munden Bury
Moat
Great Munden
MENTLEY LA
Bugby's Farm
Ford
The Plough (PH)
Herringworth Hall
Dane End Tributary
Great Munden Farm
Libury Hall
Brockhold's New Cover
Stockalls
Great Munden House
Hornbeam Common
Goldsdell Common
GIFFORD'S LA
Brockhold's Farm
King's Hill
Overley Common
Camps Farm
Bandy Common
Water Tower
Levens Green Farm
Oldhall Green
Fellowsfield Common
The Horse and Groom (PH)
Levens Green
The Bay Horse (PH)
BEGGARMAN'S LA

53

72

41

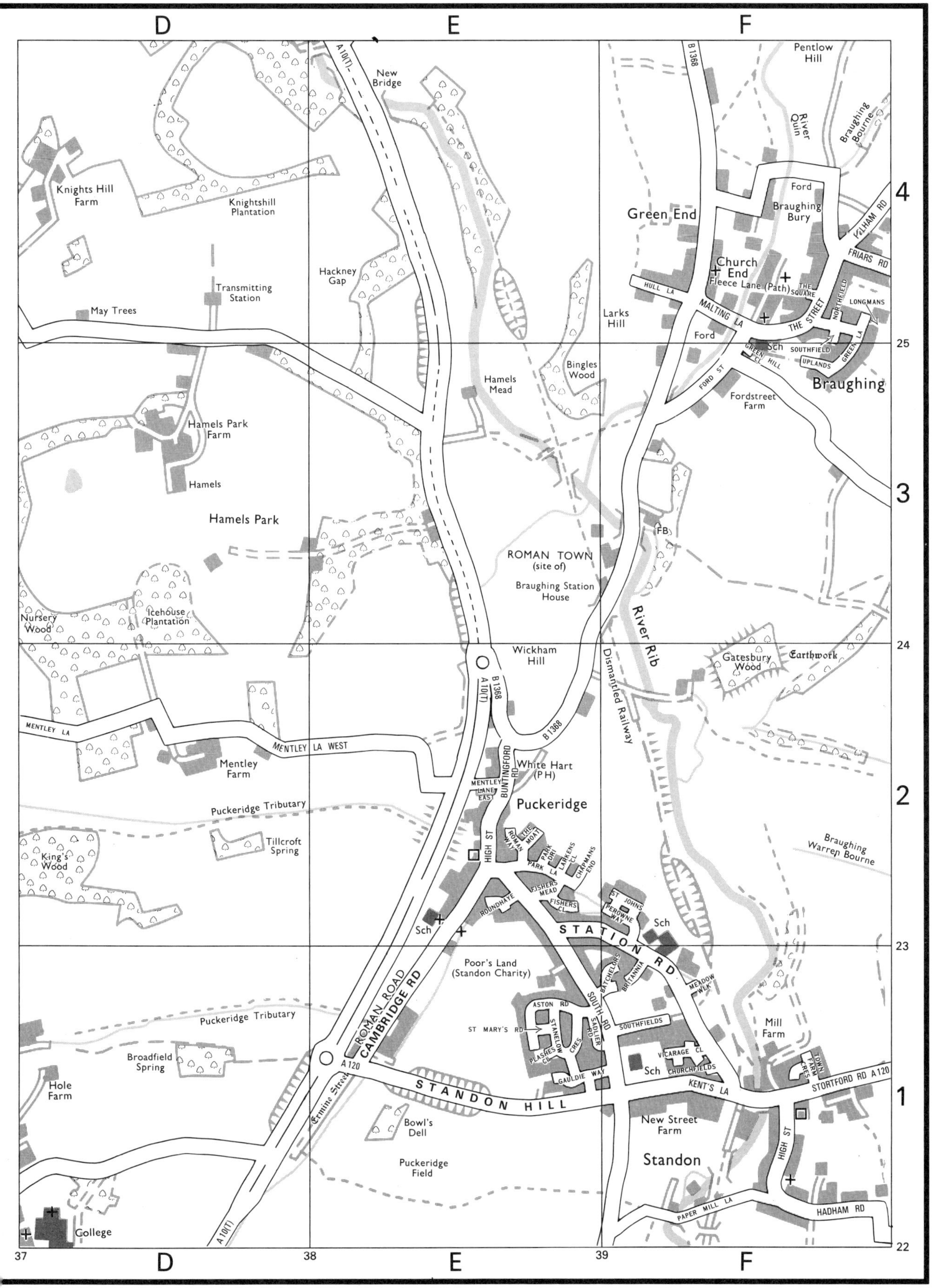
D
E
F
Knights Hill Farm
Knightshill Plantation
New Bridge
A 10(T)
B 1368
Pentlow Hill
River Quin
Braughing Bourne
Ford
Braughing Bury
Green End
Church End
Fleece Lane (Path)
THE SQUARE
HULL LA
MALTING LA
THE STREET
NORTHFIELD
LONGMANS
FRIARS RD
ELLHAM RD
Hackney Gap
Transmitting Station
May Trees
Larks Hill
Ford
Sch
SOUTHFIELD
GREEN LA
UPLANDS
GREEN HILL CL
FORD ST
Braughing
Fordstreet Farm
Bingles Wood
Hamels Mead
Hamels Park Farm
Hamels
Hamels Park
FB
ROMAN TOWN
(site of)
Braughing Station House
River Rib
Nursery Wood
Icehouse Plantation
Wickham Hill
Gatesbury Wood
Earthwork
Dismantled Railway
MENTLEY LA
MENTLEY LA WEST
Mentley Farm
BUNTINGFORD RD
White Hart (PH)
MENTLEY LANE EAST
Puckeridge
Puckeridge Tributary
Tillcroft Spring
King's Wood
HIGH ST
ROMAN WAY
THE MOAT
PARK DRI
LARKENS CL
CHAPMANS END
PARK LA
FISHERS MEAD
FISHERS CL
ROUNDHAYE
ST JOHNS
PEROWNE WAY
Sch
STATION RD
Braughing Warren Bourne
Poor's Land
(Standon Charity)
BATCHELORS
BRITANNIA
MEADOW WLK
ROMAN ROAD
CAMBRIDGE RD
ASTON RD
ST MARY'S RD
STANELOW CRES
SADLIER RD
SOUTH RD
SOUTHFIELDS
Mill Farm
Broadfield Spring
PLASHES CL
GAULDIE WAY
VICARAGE CL
CHURCHFIELDS
Sch
TOWN FARM CRES
A 120
STANDON HILL
KENT'S LA
STORTFORD RD A 120
Hole Farm
Ermine Street
Bowl's Dell
New Street Farm
Standon
HIGH ST
Puckeridge Field
PAPER MILL LA
HADHAM RD
College
A 10(T)
37
38
39
D
E
F
22
23
24
25
1
2
3
4

56

73

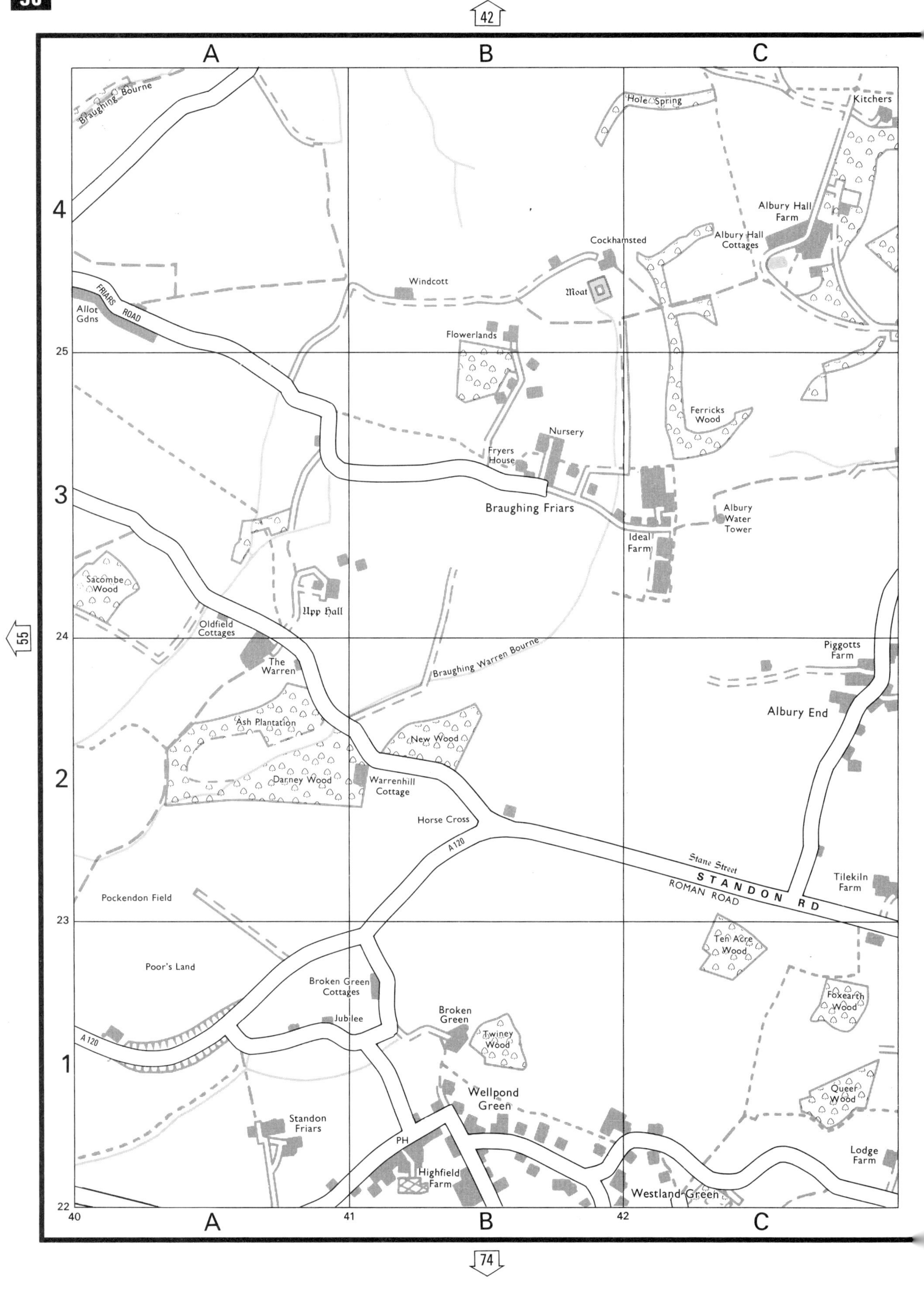
42
A
B
C
4
3
2
1
25
24
23
22
40
41
42
55
74
Braughing Bourne
Hole Spring
Kitchers
Albury Hall Farm
Albury Hall Cottages
Cockhamsted
Moat
Windcott
FRIARS ROAD
Allot Gdns
Flowerlands
Ferricks Wood
Nursery
Fryers House
Braughing Friars
Albury Water Tower
Ideal Farm
Sacombe Wood
Upp Hall
Oldfield Cottages
The Warren
Braughing Warren Bourne
Piggotts Farm
Albury End
Ash Plantation
New Wood
Darney Wood
Warrenhill Cottage
Horse Cross
A 120
Stane Street
STANDON RD
ROMAN ROAD
Tilekiln Farm
Pockendon Field
Ten Acre Wood
Poor's Land
Broken Green Cottages
Jubilee
Broken Green
Twiney Wood
Foxearth Wood
A 120
Wellpond Green
Queer Wood
Standon Friars
PH
Highfield Farm
Westland Green
Lodge Farm

43

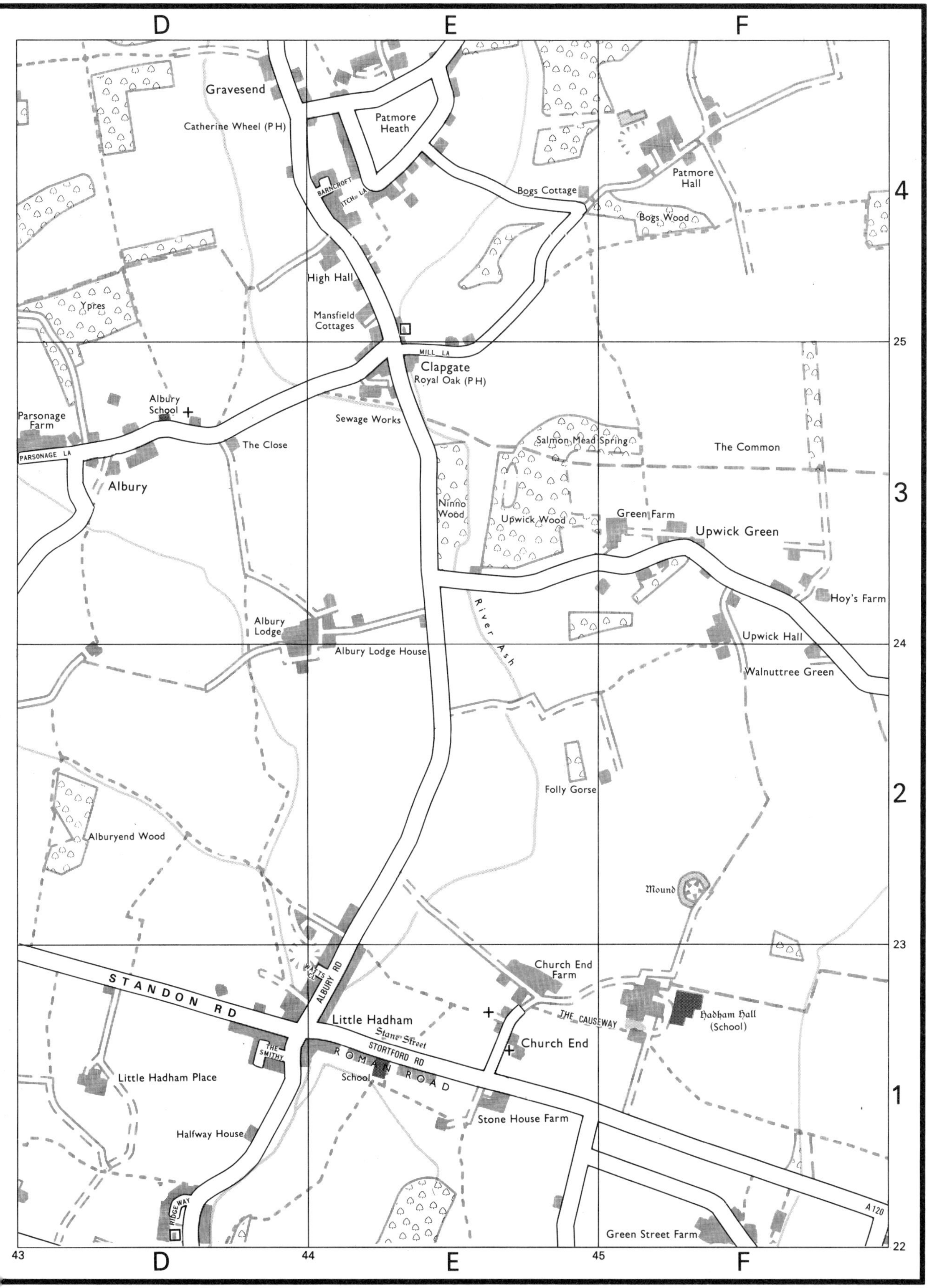
D
E
F
Gravesend
Catherine Wheel (PH)
Patmore Heath
BARNCROFT
ITCH LA
Bogs Cottage
Patmore Hall
Bogs Wood
High Hall
Ypres
Mansfield Cottages
MILL LA
Clapgate
Royal Oak (PH)
Albury School
Parsonage Farm
PARSONAGE LA
Sewage Works
The Close
Salmon Mead Spring
The Common
Albury
Ninno Wood
Upwick Wood
Green Farm
Upwick Green
Hoy's Farm
Albury Lodge
Albury Lodge House
River Ash
Upwick Hall
Walnuttree Green
Folly Gorse
Alburyend Wood
Mound
STANDON RD
WATTS CL
ALBURY RD
Church End Farm
THE CAUSEWAY
Hadham Hall (School)
Little Hadham
Stane Street
STORTFORD RD
ROMAN ROAD
THE SMITHY
Church End
School
Little Hadham Place
Stone House Farm
Halfway House
RIDGEWAY
A120
Green Street Farm
4
25
3
24
2
23
1
22
43
44
45

58

75

not continued, see key diagram

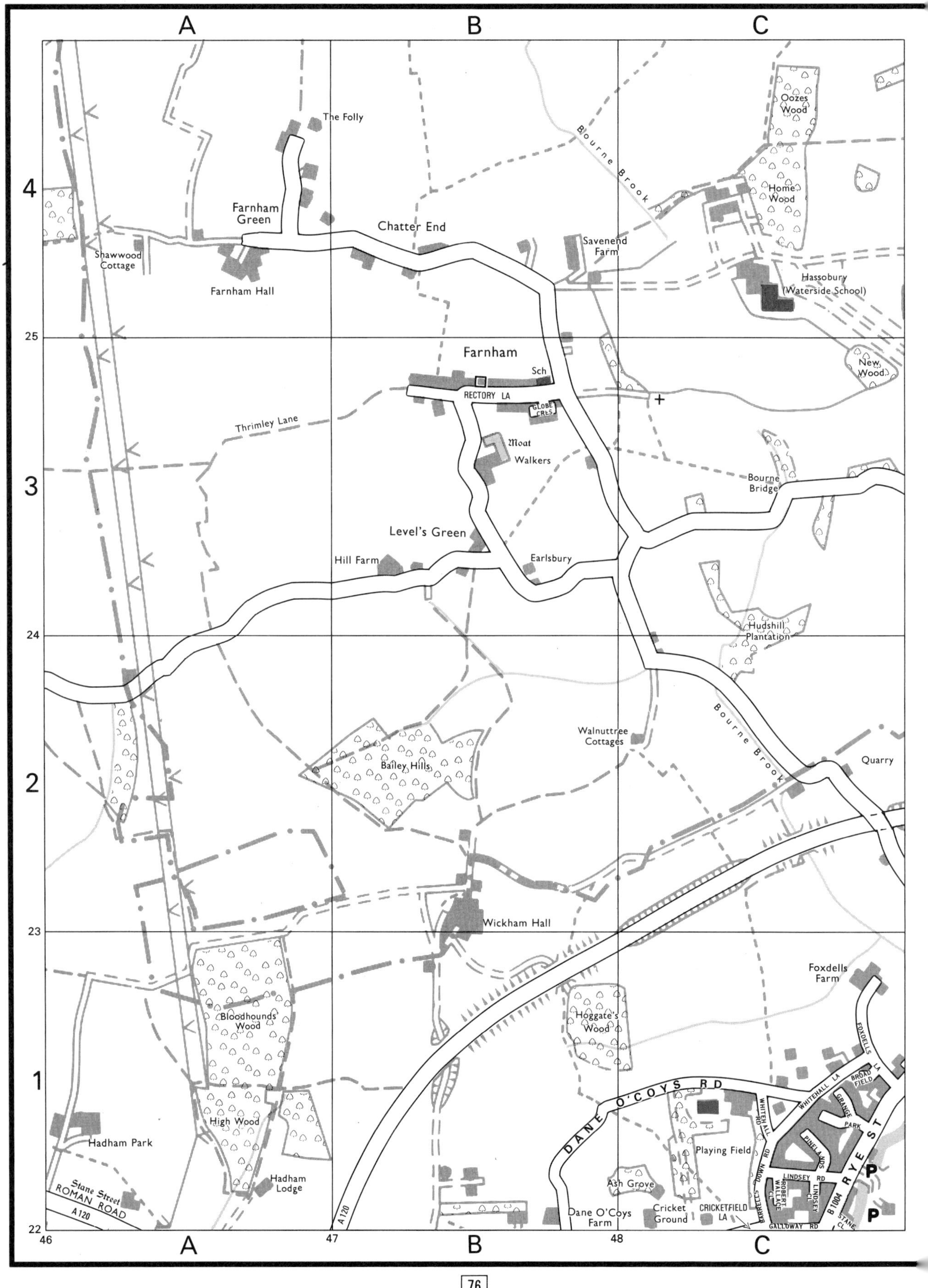

57

76

not continued, see key diagram

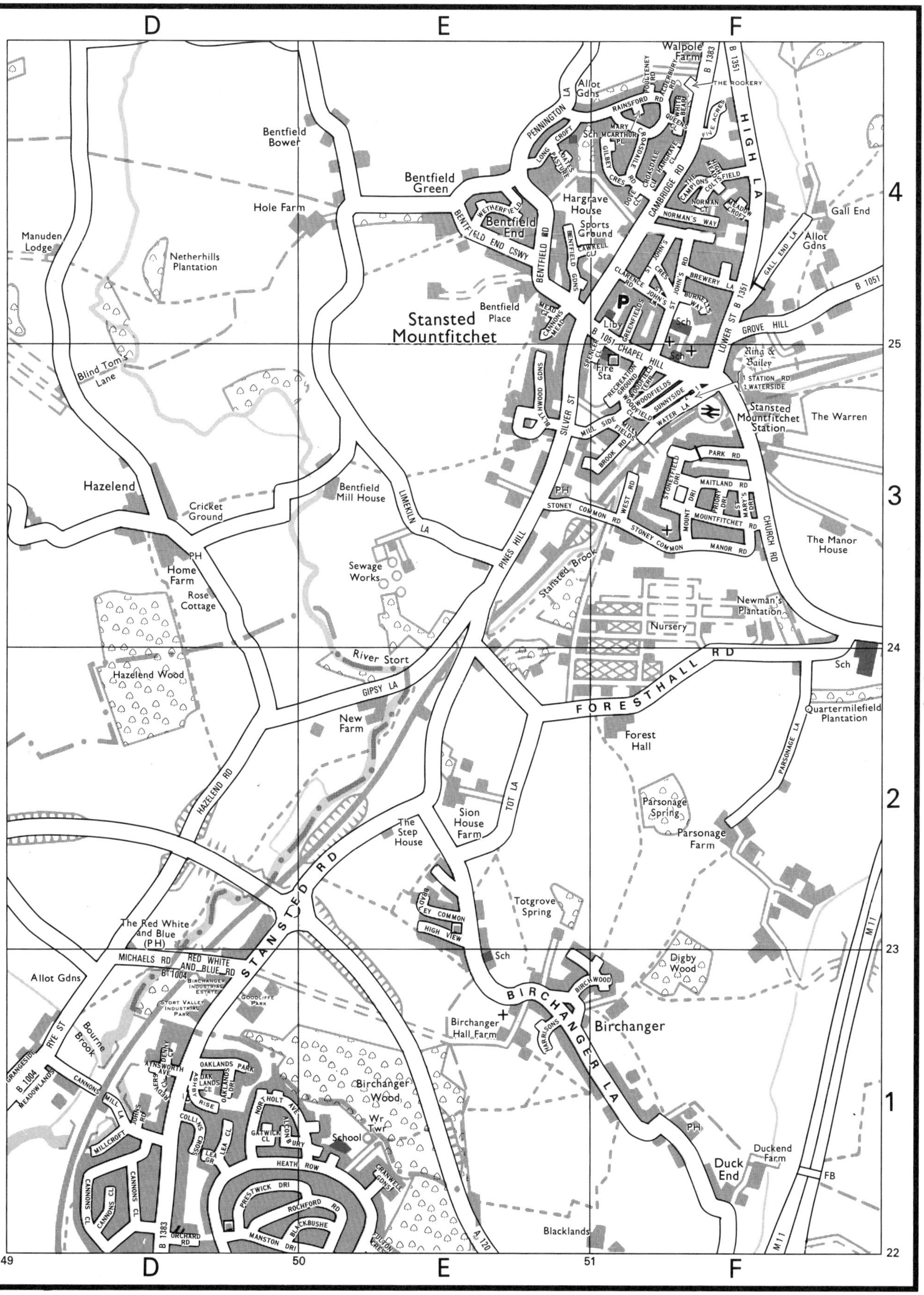

not continued, see key diagram

77

not continued, see key diagram

not continued, see key diagram

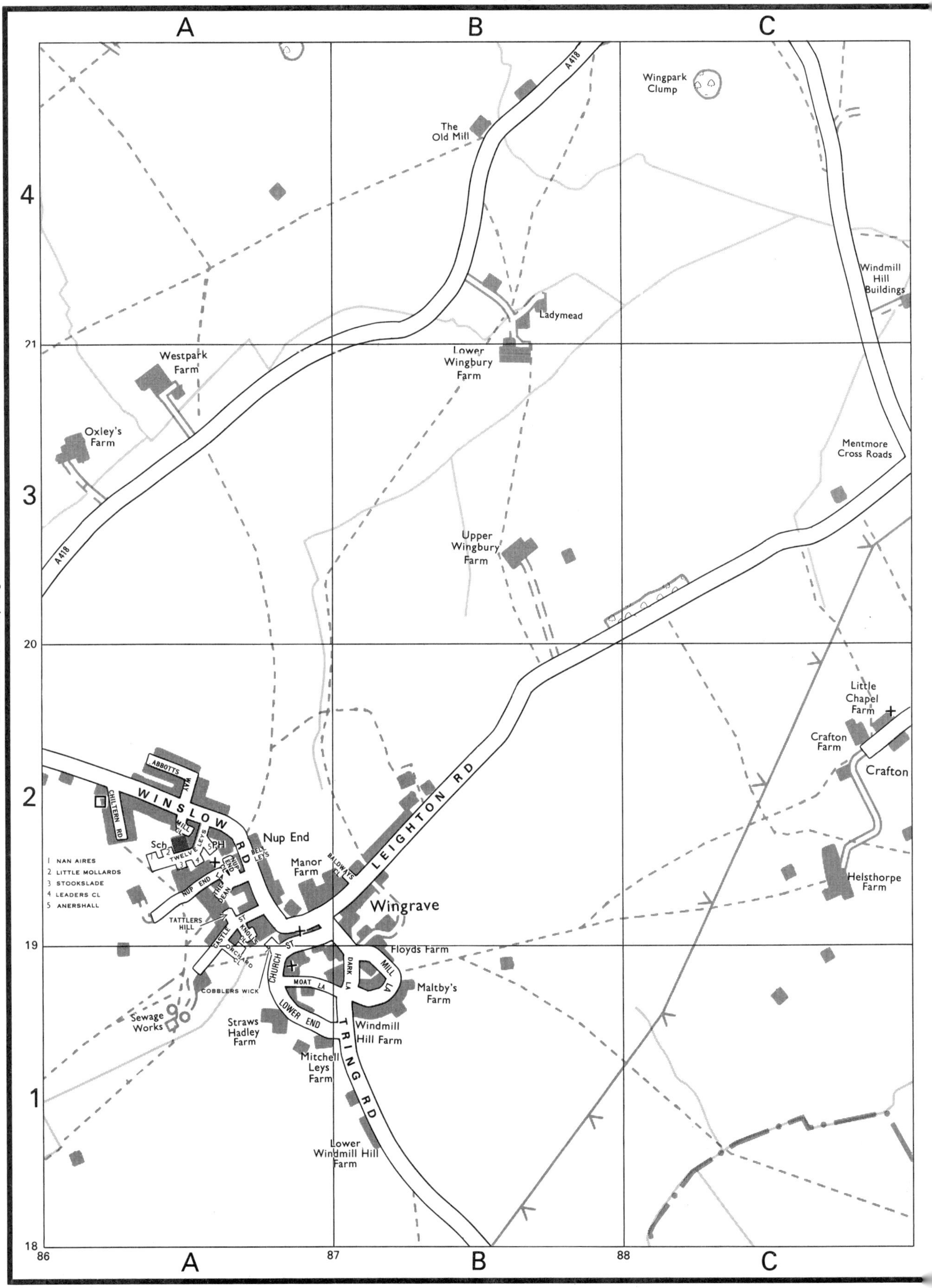

78

not continued, see key diagram

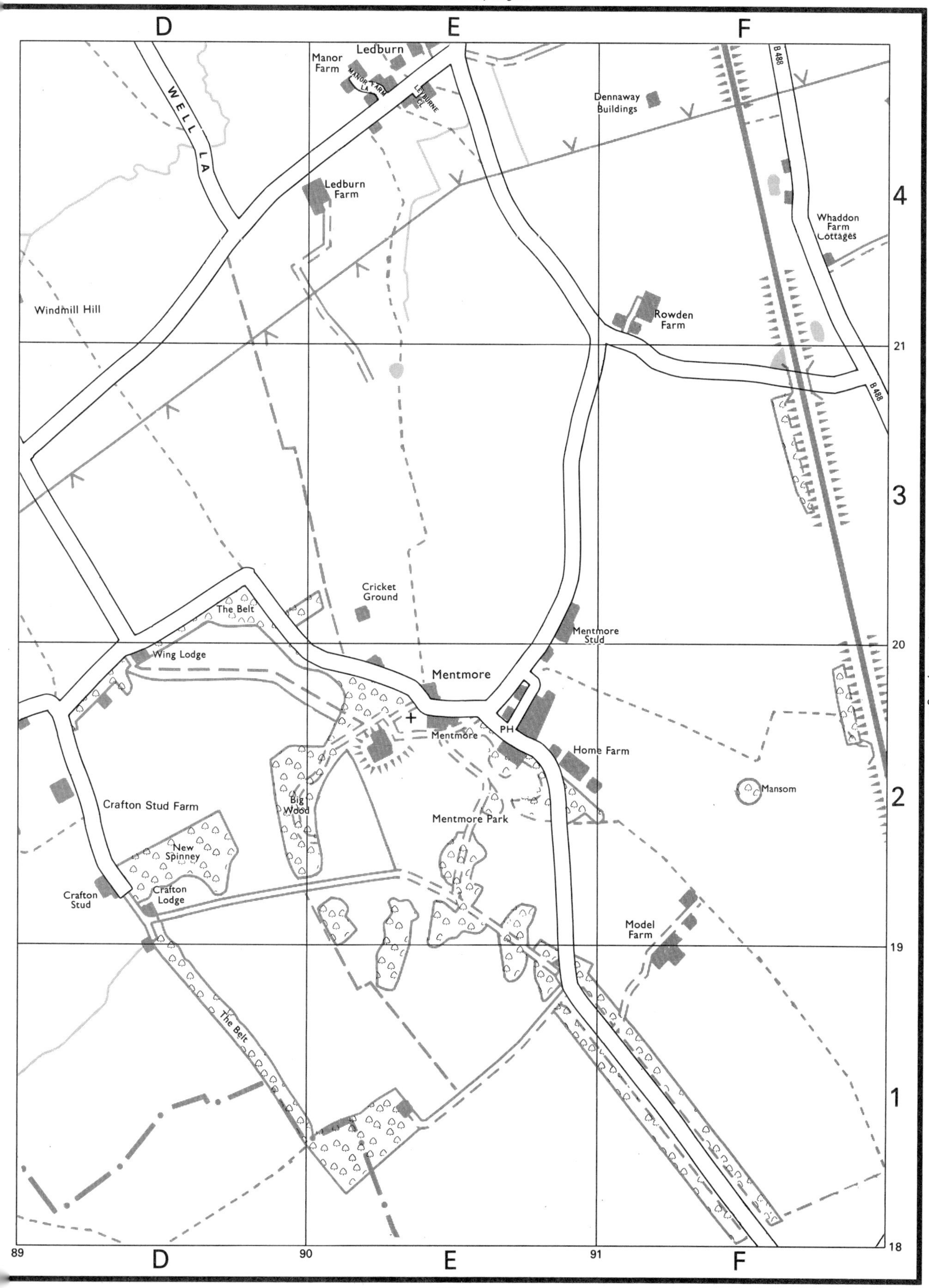

not continued, see key diagram

44

not continued, see key diagram

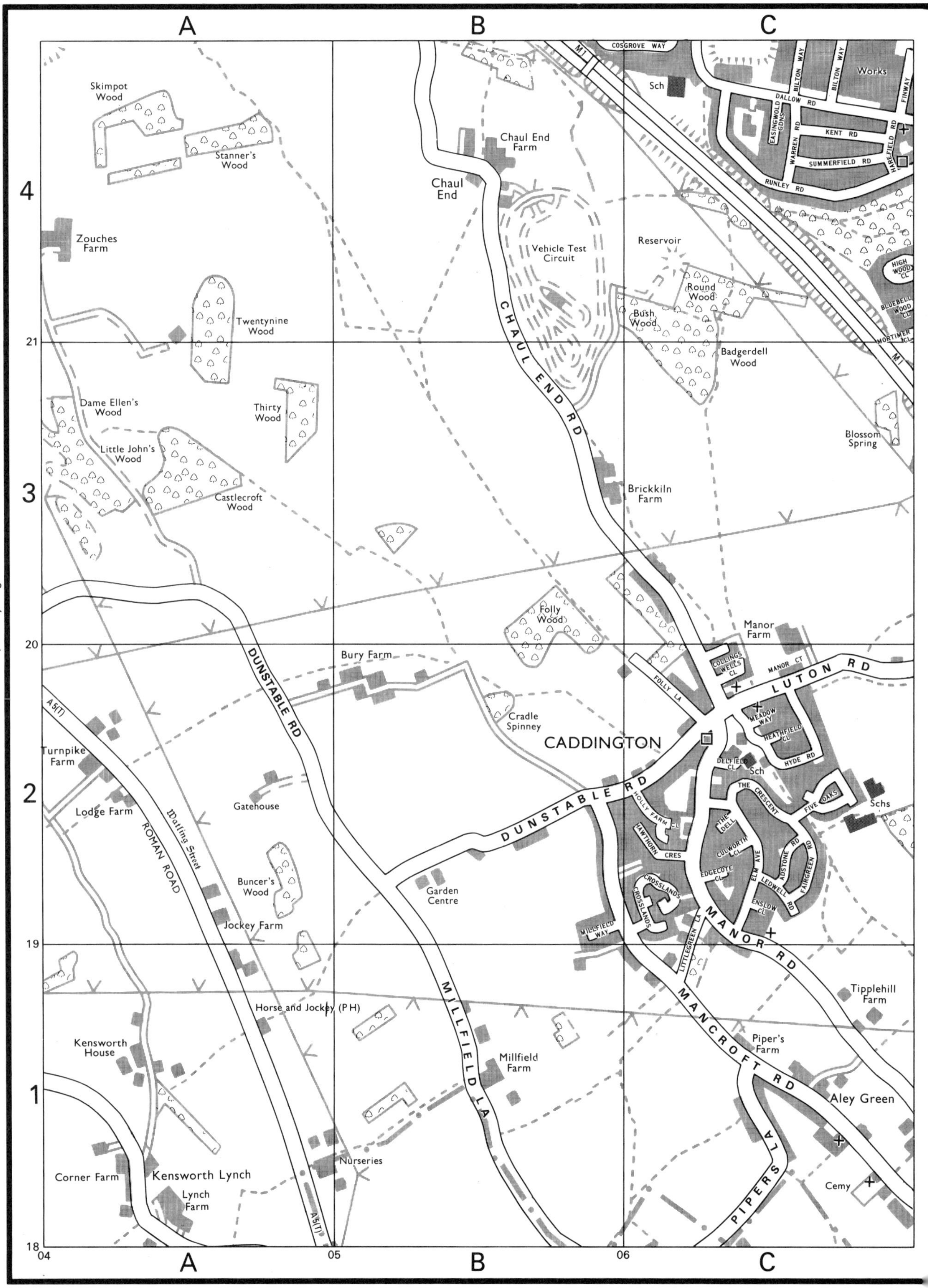

83

45

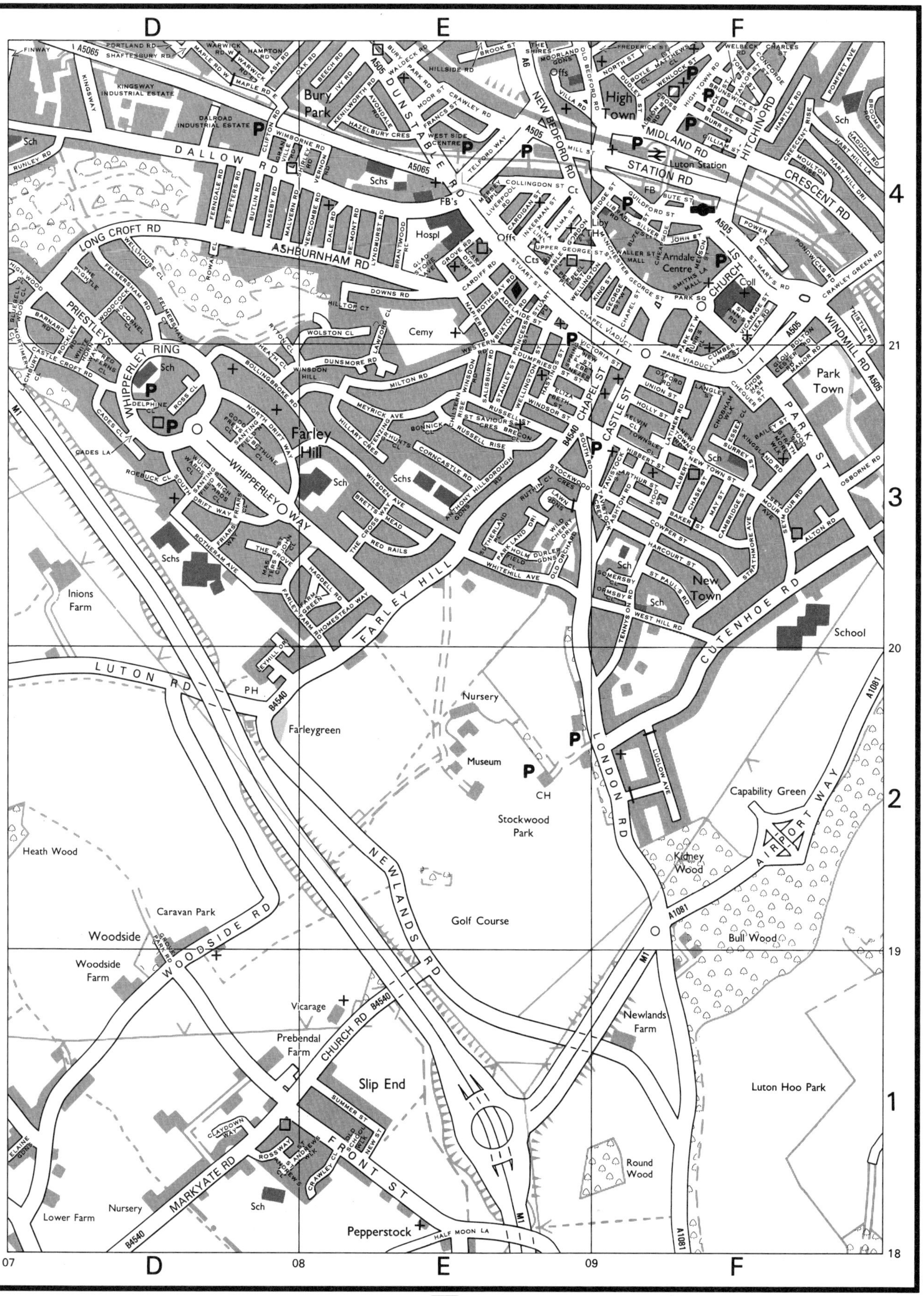
D
E
F
Bury Park
High Town
Luton Station
Farley Hill
Park Town
New Town
Farleygreen
Stockwood Park
Capability Green
Kidney Wood
Bull Wood
Heath Wood
Woodside
Woodside Farm
Inions Farm
Caravan Park
Golf Course
Museum
Nursery
Vicarage
Prebendal Farm
Slip End
Newlands Farm
Luton Hoo Park
Round Wood
Lower Farm
Pepperstock
School
Arndale Centre
KINGSWAY INDUSTRIAL ESTATE
DALROAD INDUSTRIAL ESTATE
DALLOW RD
ASHBURNHAM RD
LONG CROFT RD
WHIPPERLEY RING
WHIPPERLEY WAY
PRIESTLEYS
FARLEY HILL
LUTON RD
WOODSIDE RD
NEWLANDS RD
LONDON RD
AIRPORT WAY
CUTENHOE RD
CRESCENT RD
STATION RD
MIDLAND RD
HITCHIN RD
DUNSTABLE RD
NEW BEDFORD RD
CHAPEL ST
CASTLE ST
PARK ST
WINDMILL RD
CHURCH ST
MILTON RD
MARKYATE RD
CHURCH RD
FRONT ST
HALF MOON LA
LUDLOW AVE
Cemy
Hospl
Sch
Schs
Coll
CH
PH
A505
A5065
A6
B4540
A1081
M1
07
08
09
21
20
19
18
4
3
2
1

D E F

64

84

46

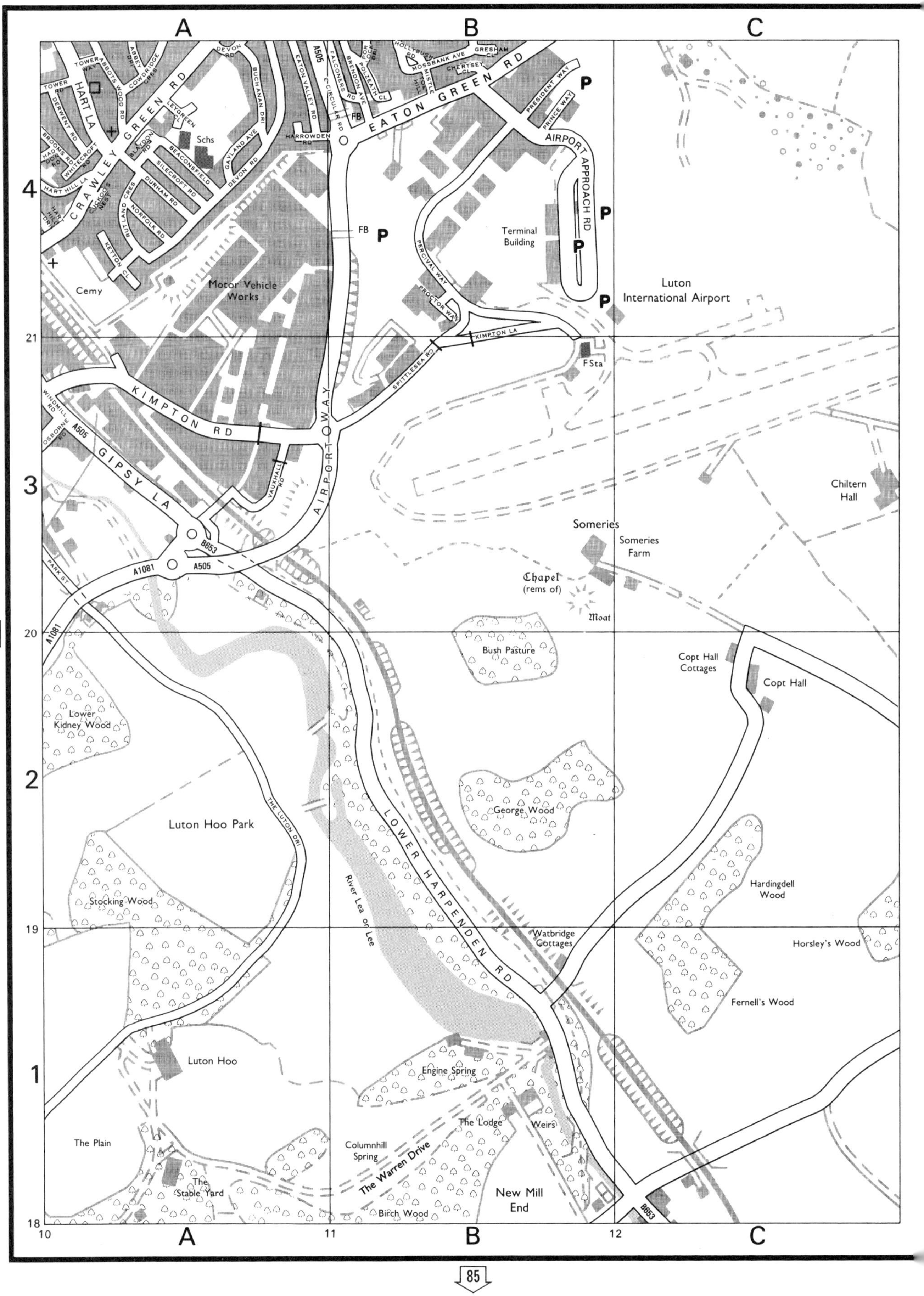
A
B
C
4
3
2
1
21
20
19
18
10
11
12
HART LA
TOWER RD
CRAWLEY GREEN RD
EATON GREEN RD
AIRPORT APPROACH RD
PRESIDENT WAY
PRINCE WAY
Schs
Cemy
Motor Vehicle Works
Terminal Building
Luton International Airport
FB
P
PERCIVAL WAY
PROCTOR WAY
KIMPTON LA
SPITTLESEA RD
F Sta
KIMPTON RD
AIRPORT WAY
VAUXHALL RD
GIPSY LA
A505
B653
A1081
PARK ST
Someries
Someries Farm
Chapel (rems of)
Moat
Chiltern Hall
Bush Pasture
Copt Hall Cottages
Copt Hall
Lower Kidney Wood
George Wood
Luton Hoo Park
THE LUTON DRI
LOWER HARPENDEN RD
River Lea or Lee
Hardingdell Wood
Stocking Wood
Watbridge Cottages
Horsley's Wood
Fernell's Wood
Luton Hoo
Engine Spring
The Lodge
Weirs
The Plain
Columnhill Spring
The Warren Drive
The Stable Yard
New Mill End
Birch Wood

63

85

47

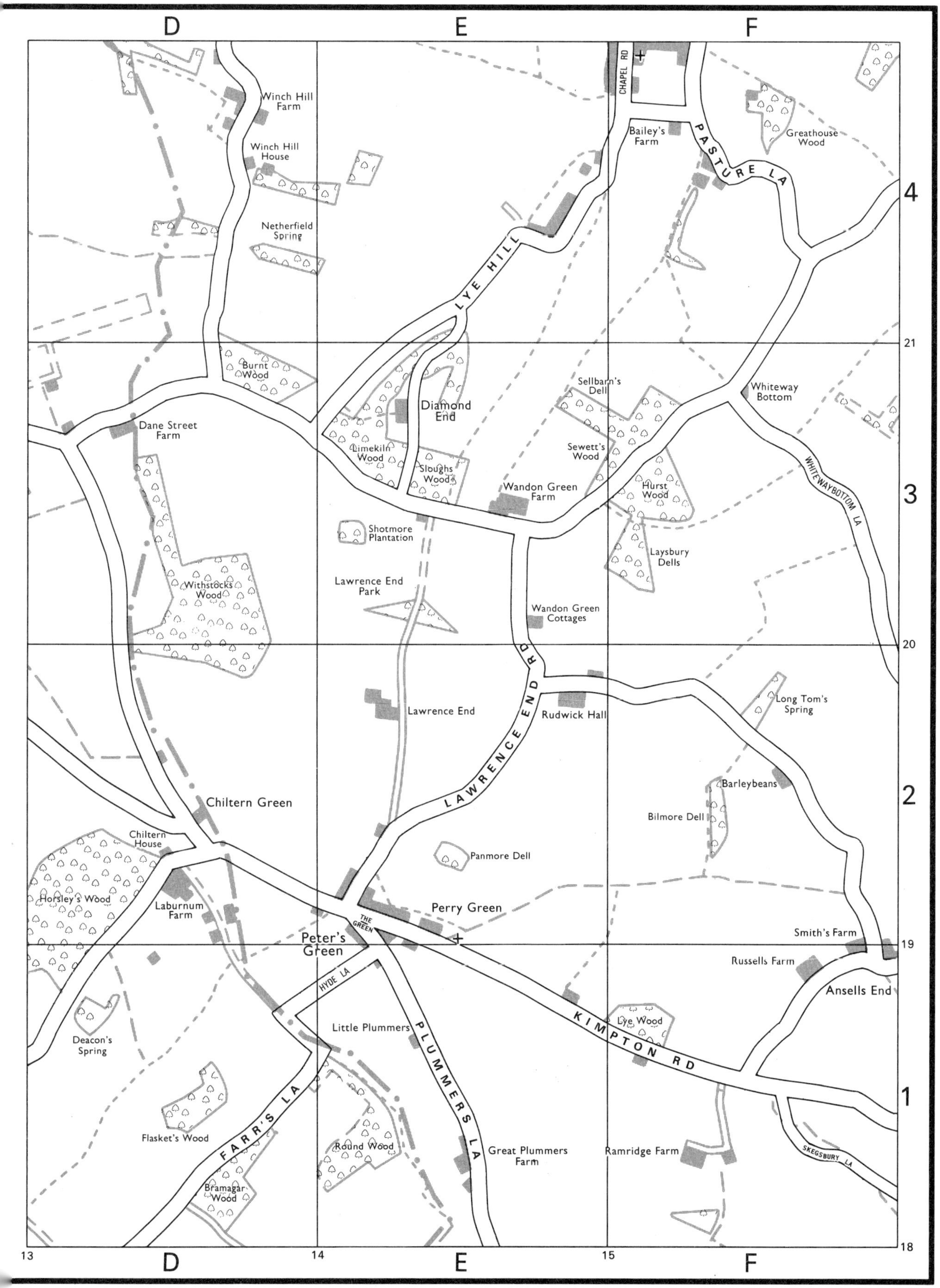
D
E
F
Winch Hill
Farm
Winch Hill
House
Netherfield
Spring
CHAPEL RD
Bailey's
Farm
PASTURE LA
Greathouse
Wood
LYE HILL
4
21
Burnt
Wood
Dane Street
Farm
Diamond
End
Limekiln
Wood
Sloughs
Wood
Sellbarn's
Dell
Sewett's
Wood
Whiteway
Bottom
Wandon Green
Farm
Hurst
Wood
WHITEWAYBOTTOM LA
3
Shotmore
Plantation
Laysbury
Dells
Withstocks
Wood
Lawrence End
Park
Wandon Green
Cottages
20
LAWRENCE END RD
Rudwick Hall
Lawrence End
Long Tom's
Spring
Barleybeans
2
Chiltern Green
Bilmore Dell
Chiltern
House
Panmore Dell
Horsley's Wood
Laburnum
Farm
Perry Green
THE GREEN
Peter's
Green
Smith's Farm
19
Russells Farm
Ansells End
HYDE LA
Little Plummers
Lye Wood
Deacon's
Spring
KIMPTON RD
PLUMMERS LA
1
Flasket's Wood
FARR'S LA
Round Wood
Great Plummers
Farm
Ramridge Farm
SKEGSBURY LA
Bramagar
Wood
18
13
14
15
D
E
F

99

86

48

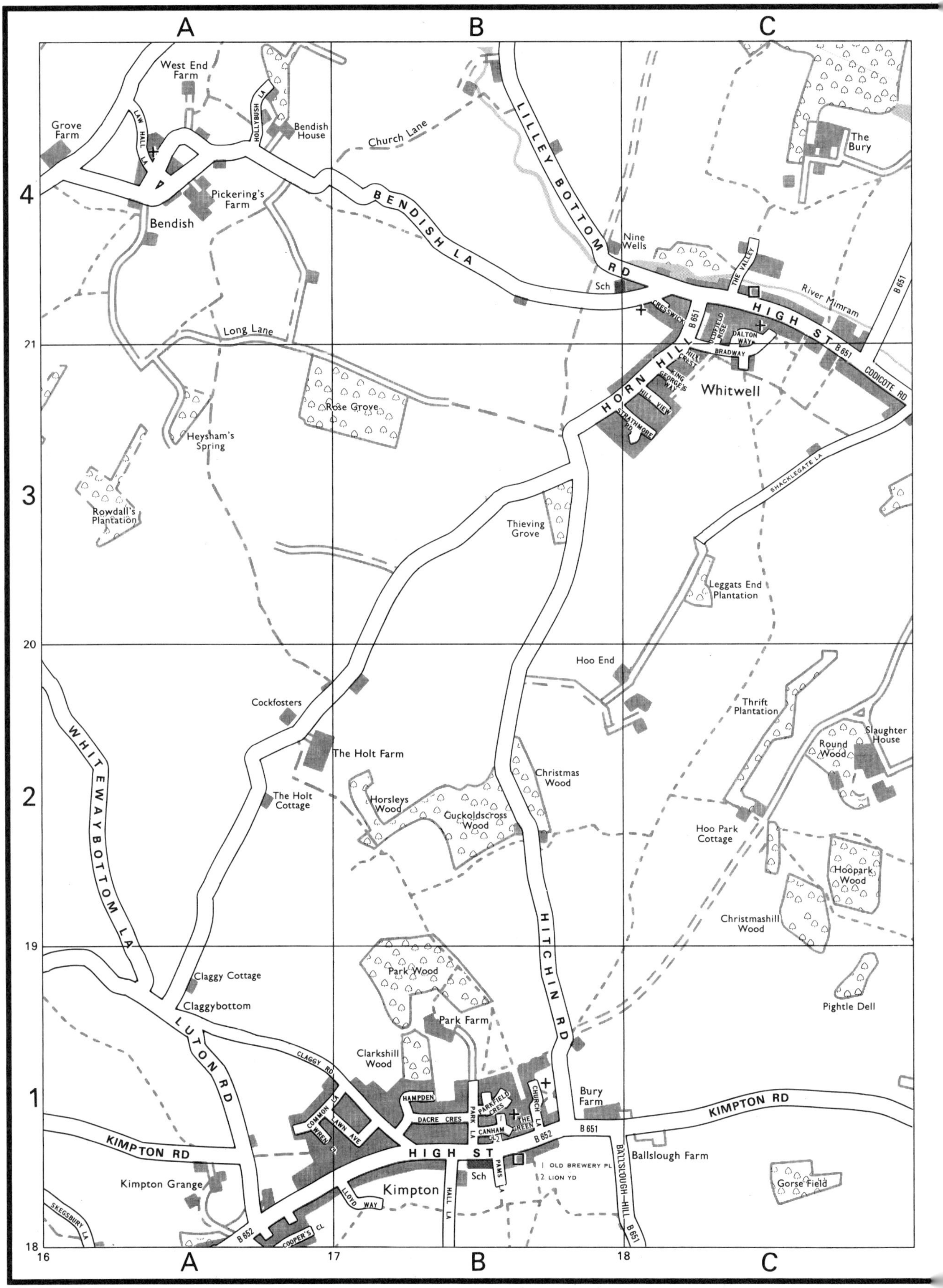
A
B
C
4
3
2
1
21
20
19
18
16
17
18
West End Farm
Grove Farm
LAW HALL LA
HOLLYBUSH LA
Bendish House
Church Lane
Pickering's Farm
Bendish
BENDISH LA
LILLEY BOTTOM RD
The Bury
Nine Wells
Sch
THE VALLEY
River Mimram
B 651
CRESSWICK
OLDFIELD RISE
DALTON WAY
HIGH ST
BRADWAY
HILL CREST
HORN HILL
KING GEORGE'S WAY
HILL VIEW
STRATHMORE RD
Whitwell
CODICOTE RD
Long Lane
Rose Grove
Heysham's Spring
Rowdall's Plantation
Thieving Grove
SHACKLEGATE LA
Leggats End Plantation
Hoo End
Cockfosters
Thrift Plantation
Slaughter House
Round Wood
The Holt Farm
Christmas Wood
WHITEWAYBOTTOM LA
The Holt Cottage
Horsleys Wood
Cuckoldscross Wood
Hoo Park Cottage
Hoopark Wood
Christmashill Wood
HITCHIN RD
Claggy Cottage
Park Wood
Pightle Dell
Claggybottom
LUTON RD
Park Farm
Clarkshill Wood
CLAGGY RD
HAMPDEN
PARKFIELD CRES
CHURCH LA
Bury Farm
KIMPTON RD
COMMON LA
LAWN AVE
DACRE CRES
PARK LA
CANHAM CL
THE GREEN
WREN CL
B 652
B 651
KIMPTON RD
HIGH ST
PAMS LA
Ballslough Farm
1 OLD BREWERY PL
2 LION YD
Kimpton Grange
Kimpton
HALL LA
BALLSLOUGH HILL
Gorse Field
LLOYD WAY
SKEGSBURY LA
COOPER'S CL

65

87

49

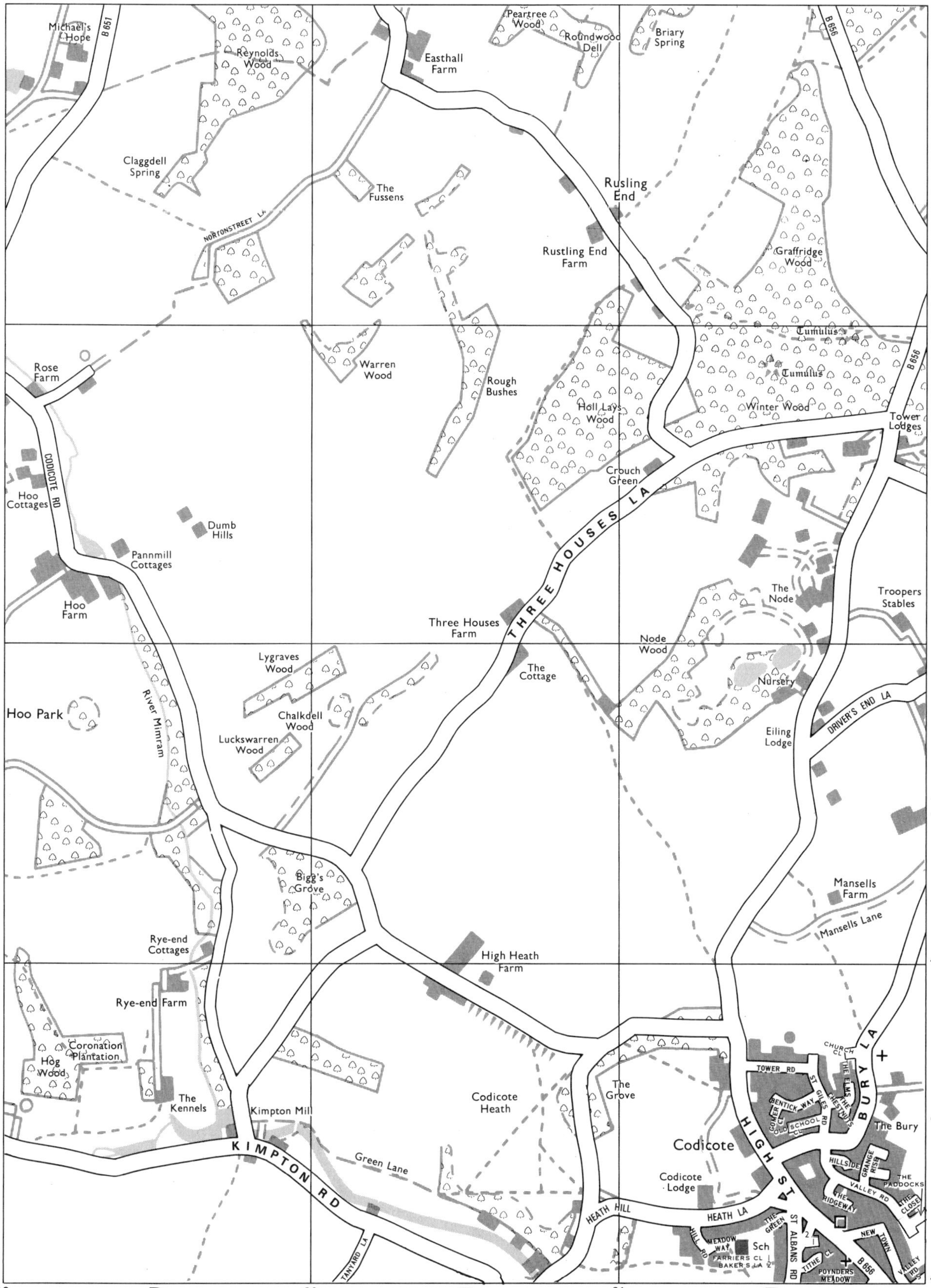
D
E
F
Michael's Hope
B 651
Reynolds Wood
Easthall Farm
Peartree Wood
Roundwood Dell
Briary Spring
B 656
Claggdell Spring
The Fussens
Rusling End
NORTONSTREET LA
Rustling End Farm
Graffridge Wood
4
21
Tumulus
Tumulus
Rose Farm
Warren Wood
Rough Bushes
Holl Lays Wood
Winter Wood
Tower Lodges
CODICOTE RD
Crouch Green
Hoo Cottages
THREE HOUSES LA
3
Dumb Hills
Pannmill Cottages
The Node
Troopers Stables
Hoo Farm
Three Houses Farm
Node Wood
20
Lygraves Wood
The Cottage
Nursery
Hoo Park
River Mimram
Chalkdell Wood
DRIVER'S END LA
Luckswarren Wood
Eiling Lodge
2
Bigg's Grove
Mansells Farm
Mansells Lane
Rye-end Cottages
High Heath Farm
19
Rye-end Farm
CHURCH CL
TOWER RD
BURY LA
THE ELMS
Coronation Plantation
Hog Wood
The Grove
BENTICK WAY
GOWER CL
ST GILES RD
THE CHESTNUTS
OLD SCHOOL CL
The Kennels
Kimpton Mill
Codicote Heath
HIGH ST
The Bury
1
KIMPTON RD
Codicote
HILLSIDE
GRANGE RISE
THE PADDOCKS
Green Lane
Codicote Lodge
VALLEY RD
THE RIDGEWAY
THE CLOSE
HEATH HILL
HEATH LA
THE GREEN
ST ALBANS RD
HILL RD
MEADOW WAY
Sch
NEW TOWN
TANYARD LA
FARRIERS CL
BAKER'S LA
TITHE CL
B 656
POYNDERS MEADOW
VALLEY RD
18
19
D
20
E
21
F

68

88

50

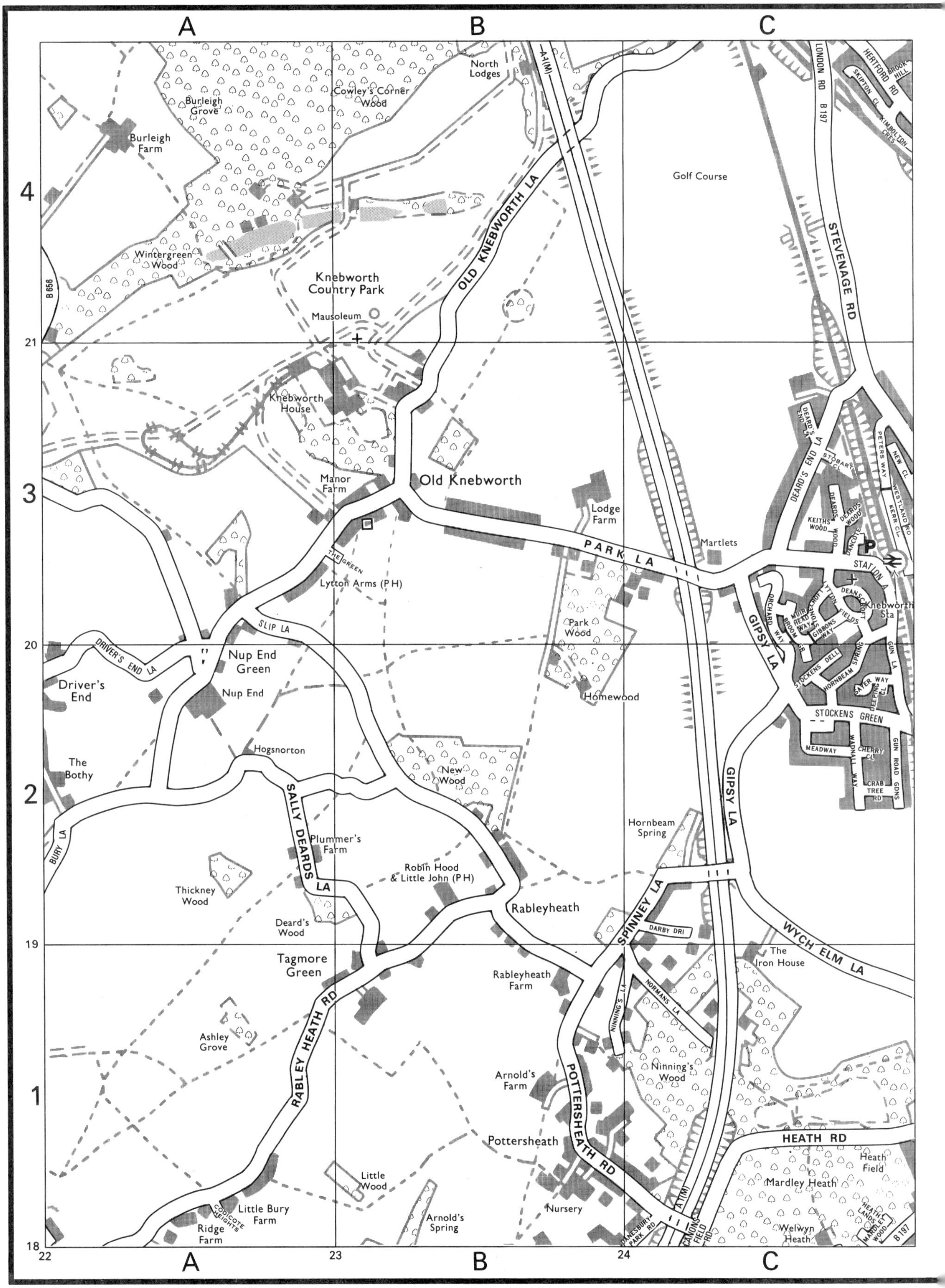
A
B
C
North Lodges
Burleigh Grove
Cowley's Corner Wood
Burleigh Farm
Golf Course
LONDON RD
B 197
HERTFORD RD
BROOK HILL
SKIPTON CL
KIMBOLTON CRES
STEVENAGE RD
OLD KNEBWORTH LA
A1(M)
Wintergreen Wood
B 656
Knebworth Country Park
Mausoleum
Knebworth House
Manor Farm
Old Knebworth
Lodge Farm
THE GREEN
Lytton Arms (PH)
PARK LA
Martlets
DEARD'S END LA
STOBART CL
PETERS WAY
NEW CL
WESTLAND RD
KERR CL
KEITHS WOOD
DEARDS WOOD
DANCOTE
STATION A
Knebworth Sta
ORCHARD WAY
MUIR WAY
ROOKROFT READ WAY
LYTTON FIELDS
DEANSCROFT
GIBBONS WAY
BROOM GR
GIPSY LA
SLIP LA
DRIVER'S END LA
Nup End Green
Park Wood
Driver's End
Nup End
Homewood
STOCKENS DELL
HORNBEAM SPRING
SAYER WAY
DEEPING CL
GUN LA
STOCKENS GREEN
MEADWAY
CHERRY CL
WADNALL WAY
GUN ROAD GDNS
CRAB TREE RD
Hogsnorton
The Bothy
New Wood
SALLY DEARDS LA
Plummer's Farm
BURY LA
Hornbeam Spring
Robin Hood & Little John (PH)
Thickney Wood
Rableyheath
SPINNEY LA
DARBY DRI
Deard's Wood
Tagmore Green
The Iron House
WYCH ELM LA
Rableyheath Farm
NINNING'S LA
NORMANS LA
RABLEY HEATH RD
Ashley Grove
Arnold's Farm
Ninning's Wood
POTTERSHEATH RD
Pottersheath
HEATH RD
Heath Field
Little Wood
Mardley Heath
CODICOTE HEIGHTS
Little Bury Farm
Ridge Farm
Arnold's Spring
Nursery
DANESBURY PARK RD
CANONS FIELD RD
Welwyn Heath
HEATH LANDS
MARDLE WOOD
B 197
4
3
2
1
21
20
19
18
22
23
24

67

89

51

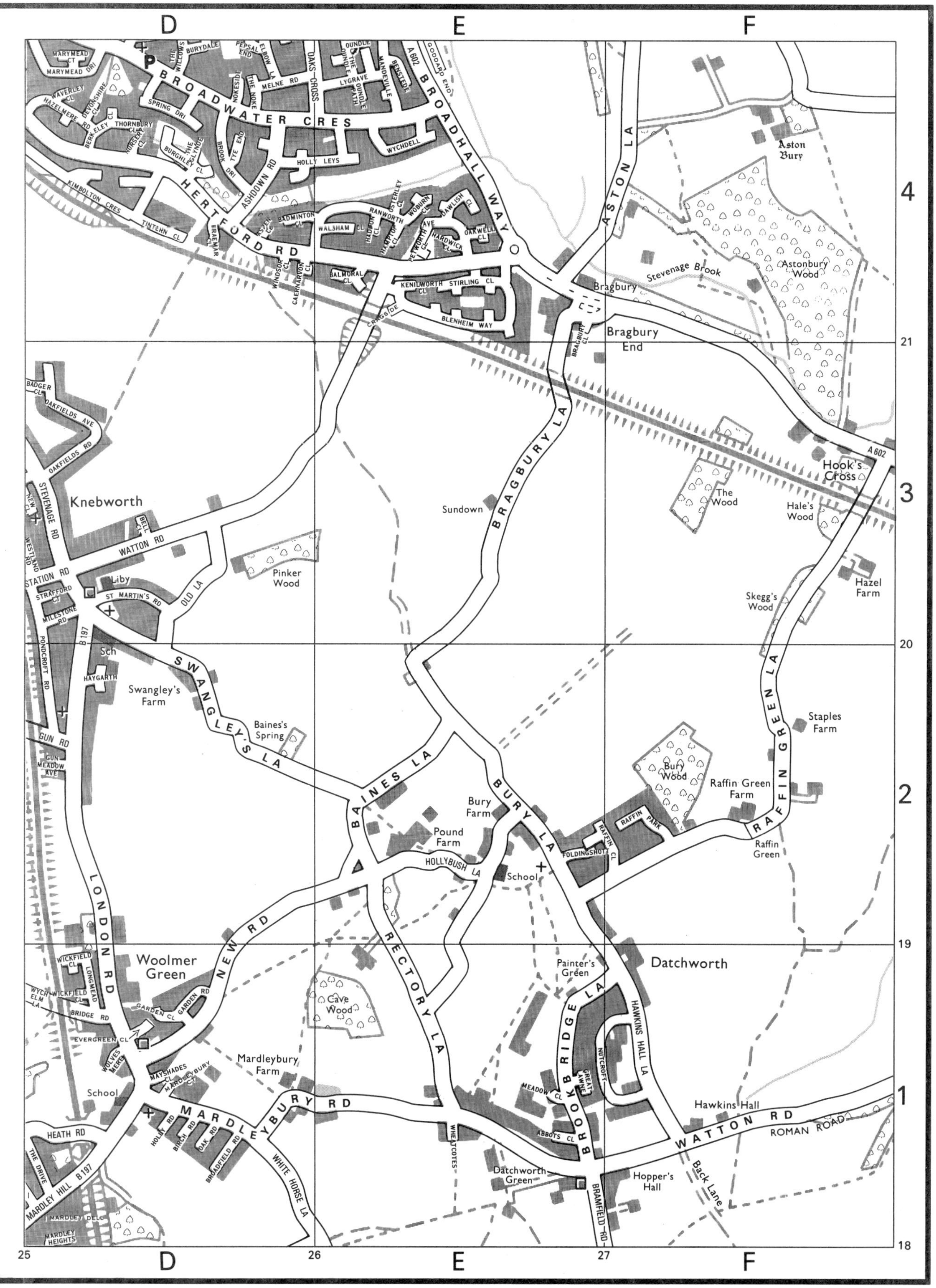
D
E
F
Knebworth
Woolmer Green
Datchworth
Datchworth Green
Bragbury
Bragbury End
Aston Bury
Astonbury Wood
Stevenage Brook
Hook's Cross
Hale's Wood
The Wood
Hazel Farm
Skegg's Wood
Staples Farm
Bury Wood
Raffin Green Farm
Raffin Green
Sundown
Pinker Wood
Swangley's Farm
Baines's Spring
Bury Farm
Pound Farm
School
Painter's Green
Cave Wood
Mardleybury Farm
Hawkins Hall
Hopper's Hall
Liby
Sch
BROADWATER CRES
BROADHALL WAY
HERTFORD RD
ASTON LA
BRAGBURY LA
WATTON RD
STATION RD
SWANGLEY'S LA
BAINES LA
BURY LA
HOLLYBUSH LA
RECTORY LA
NEW RD
LONDON RD
MARDLEYBURY RD
WHITE HORSE LA
RAFFIN GREEN LA
RAFFIN PARK
FOLDINGSHOT
BROOKBRIDGE LA
HAWKINS HALL LA
BRAMFIELD RD
Back Lane
ROMAN ROAD
OLD LA
ST MARTIN'S RD
STEVENAGE RD
OAKFIELDS RD
OAKFIELDS AVE
BADGER CL
GUN RD
GUN MEADOW AVE
HAYGARTH
PONDCROFT RD
MILESTONE RD
STRAFFORD CT
BELL CL
WICKFIELD CL
LONGMEAD
BRIDGE RD
GARDEN RD
GARDEN CL
EVERGREEN CL
HEATH RD
THE DRIVE
MARDLEY HILL B197
MARDLEY DELL
MARDLEY HEIGHTS
HOLLY RD
BIRCH RD
OAK RD
BROADFIELD RD
WHEATCOTES
ABBOTS CL
MEADOW CL
NUTCROFT
KIMBOLTON CRES
TINTERN CL
ASHDOWN RD
WALSHAM CL
BADMINTON CL
KENILWORTH CL
STIRLING CL
BLENHEIM WAY
BALMORAL CL
WINDSOR CL
CAERNARVON CL
OAKWELL CL
DAWLISH CL
WOBURN CL
PETWORTH AVE
HARDWICK CL
RANWORTH CL
HOLLY LEYS
WYCHDELL
MELNE RD
LYGRAVE
MANDEVILLE
BENSTEDE
OAKS CROSS
SPRING DRI
THORNBURY CL
MARYMEAD DRI
MARYMEAD CT
HAZELMERE RD
WAVERLEY CL
DEVONSHIRE CL
BURGHLEY CL
BROOK DRI
TYE END
A 602
B 197
18
19
20
21
3
4
2
1
25
26
27

70

90

52

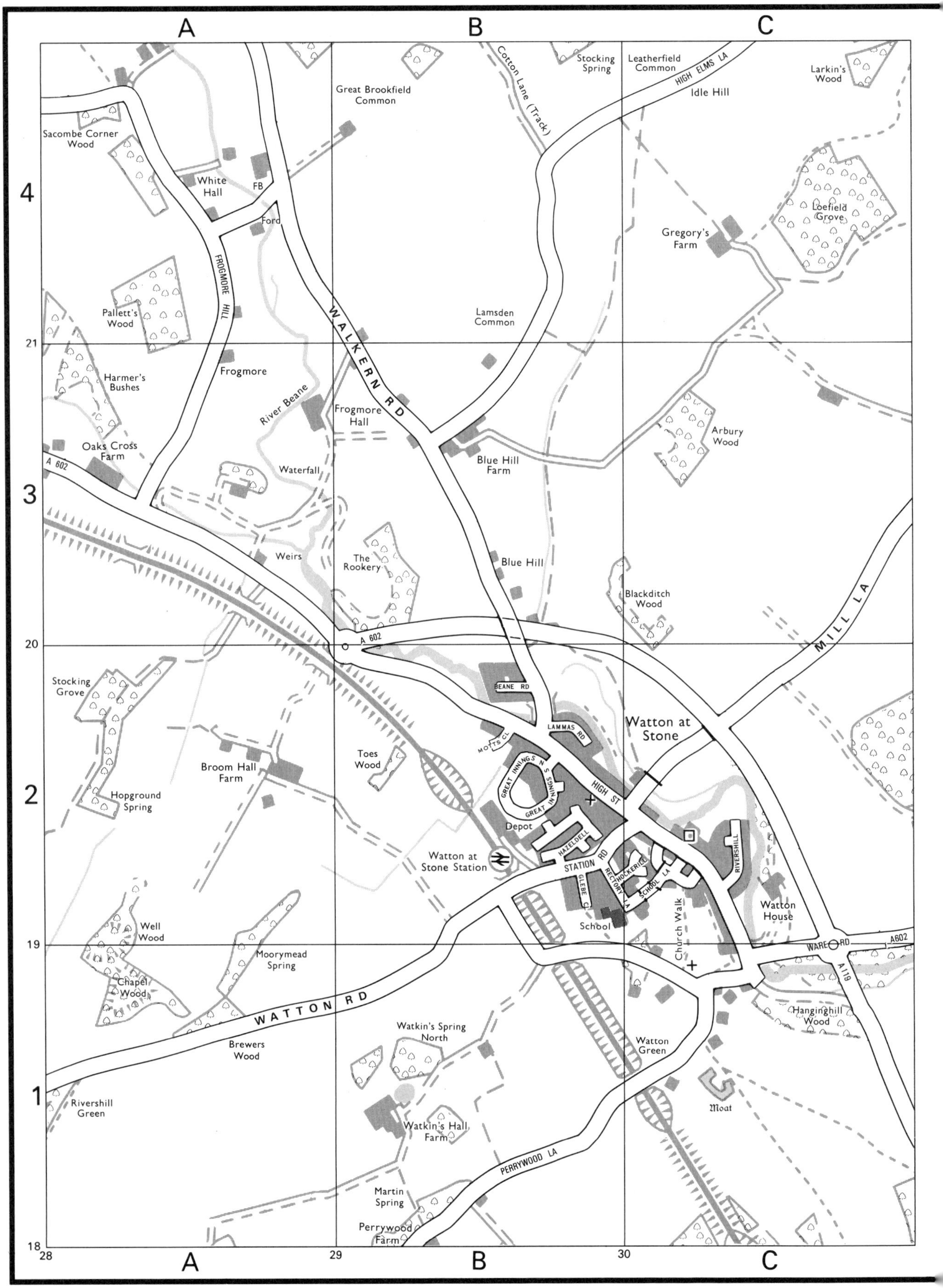
A
B
C
4
3
2
1
21
20
19
18
28
29
30
Stocking Spring
Leatherfield Common
HIGH ELMS LA
Larkin's Wood
Great Brookfield Common
Cotton Lane (Track)
Idle Hill
Sacombe Corner Wood
White Hall
FB
Ford
Loefield Grove
Gregory's Farm
FROGMORE HILL
Pallett's Wood
WALKERN RD
Lamsden Common
Harmer's Bushes
Frogmore
River Beane
Frogmore Hall
Arbury Wood
Oaks Cross Farm
A 602
Waterfall
Blue Hill Farm
Weirs
The Rookery
Blue Hill
Blackditch Wood
A 602
MILL LA
Stocking Grove
BEANE RD
Watton at Stone
LAMMAS RD
MOTTS CL
GREAT INNINGS N
GREAT INNINGS S
Broom Hall Farm
Toes Wood
HIGH ST
Hopground Spring
Depot
HAZELDELL
RIVERSHILL
Watton at Stone Station
STATION RD
GLEBE CL
RECTORY LA
SHOCKERICK
SCHOOL LA
Church Walk
Watton House
School
Well Wood
WARE RD
A602
A119
Moorymead Spring
Chapel Wood
Hanginghill Wood
WATTON RD
Watkin's Spring North
Brewers Wood
Watton Green
Rivershill Green
Moat
Watkin's Hall Farm
PERRYWOOD LA
Martin Spring
Perrywood Farm

69

91

53

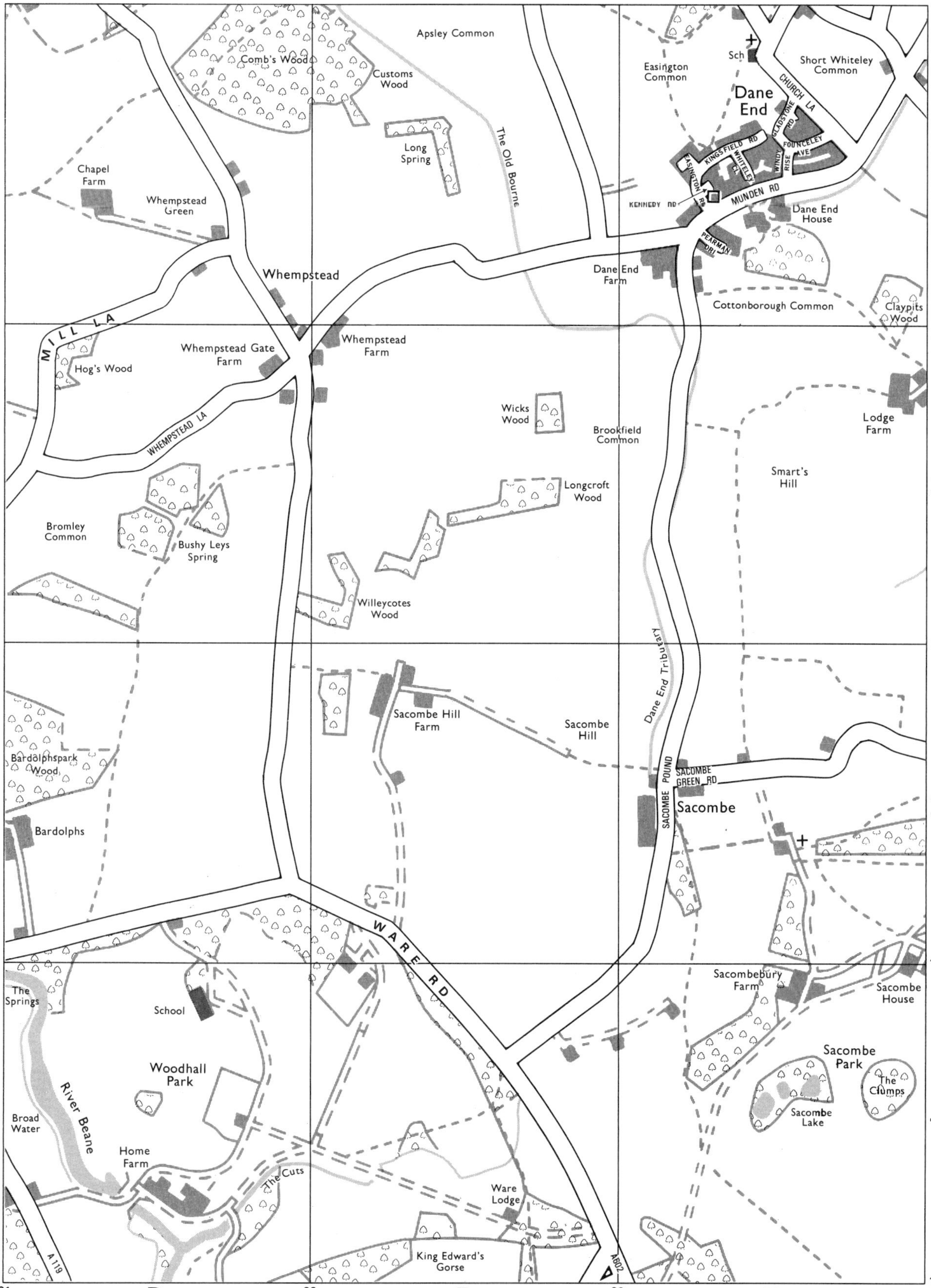
D
E
F
Apsley Common
Comb's Wood
Customs Wood
Long Spring
The Old Bourne
Easington Common
Sch
Dane End
Short Whiteley Common
CHURCH LA
GLADSTONE RD
KINGSFIELD RD
WHITELEY CL
WINDY RISE
FOUNCELEY AVE
EASINGTON RD
KENNEDY RD
MUNDEN RD
Dane End House
PEARMAN DRI
Chapel Farm
Whempstead Green
Whempstead
Dane End Farm
Cottonborough Common
Claypits Wood
MILL LA
Whempstead Gate Farm
Whempstead Farm
Hog's Wood
Wicks Wood
Brookfield Common
Lodge Farm
WHEMPSTEAD LA
Longcroft Wood
Smart's Hill
Bromley Common
Bushy Leys Spring
Willeycotes Wood
Dane End Tributary
Sacombe Hill Farm
Sacombe Hill
Bardolphspark Wood
SACOMBE POUND
SACOMBE GREEN RD
Sacombe
Bardolphs
WARE RD
Sacombebury Farm
Sacombe House
The Springs
School
Sacombe Park
Woodhall Park
River Beane
The Clumps
Sacombe Lake
Broad Water
Home Farm
The Cuts
Ware Lodge
King Edward's Gorse
A119
A602
4
3
2
1
21
20
19
18
31
32
33

72

92

54

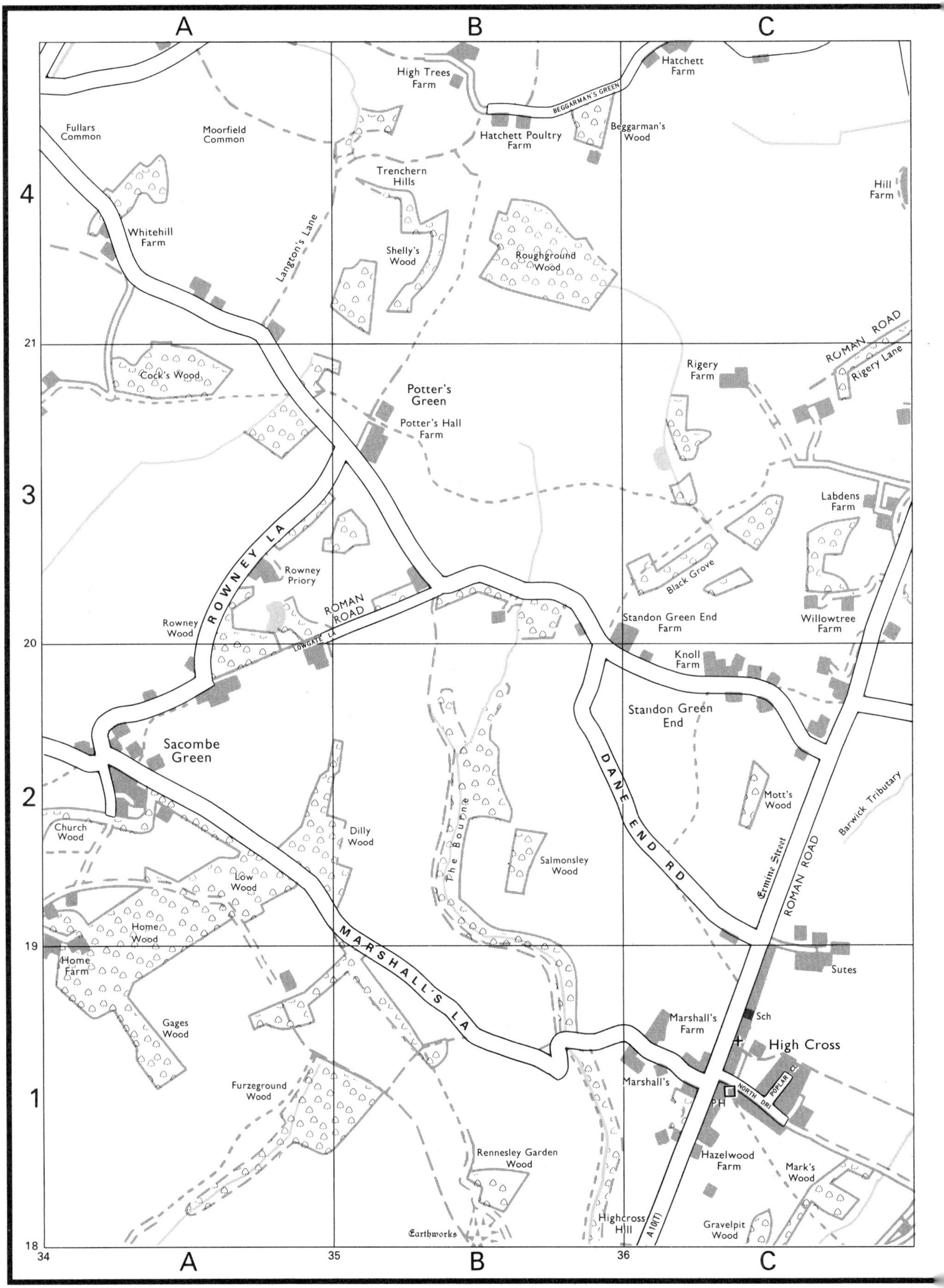
A
B
C
Hatchett Farm
High Trees Farm
BEGGARMAN'S GREEN
Beggarman's Wood
Fullars Common
Moorfield Common
Hatchett Poultry Farm
Trenchern Hills
Hill Farm
4
Whitehill Farm
Langton's Lane
Shelly's Wood
Roughground Wood
21
Cock's Wood
ROMAN ROAD
Rigery Farm
Rigery Lane
Potter's Green
Potter's Hall Farm
3
Labdens Farm
ROWNEY LA
Rowney Priory
Black Grove
ROMAN ROAD
Rowney Wood
Standon Green End Farm
Willowtree Farm
LOWGATE LA
20
Knoll Farm
Standon Green End
Sacombe Green
DANE END RD
Mott's Wood
Barwick Tributary
2
Church Wood
Dilly Wood
The Bourne
Salmonsley Wood
Low Wood
Ermine Street
ROMAN ROAD
Home Wood
19
Home Farm
MARSHALL'S LA
Sutes
Sch
Gages Wood
Marshall's Farm
High Cross
POPLAR CL
NORTH DRI
Marshall's
PH
1
Furzeground Wood
Rennesley Garden Wood
Hazelwood Farm
Mark's Wood
Earthworks
Highcross Hill
A10(T)
Gravelpit Wood
18
34
35
36
A
B
C

71

93

55

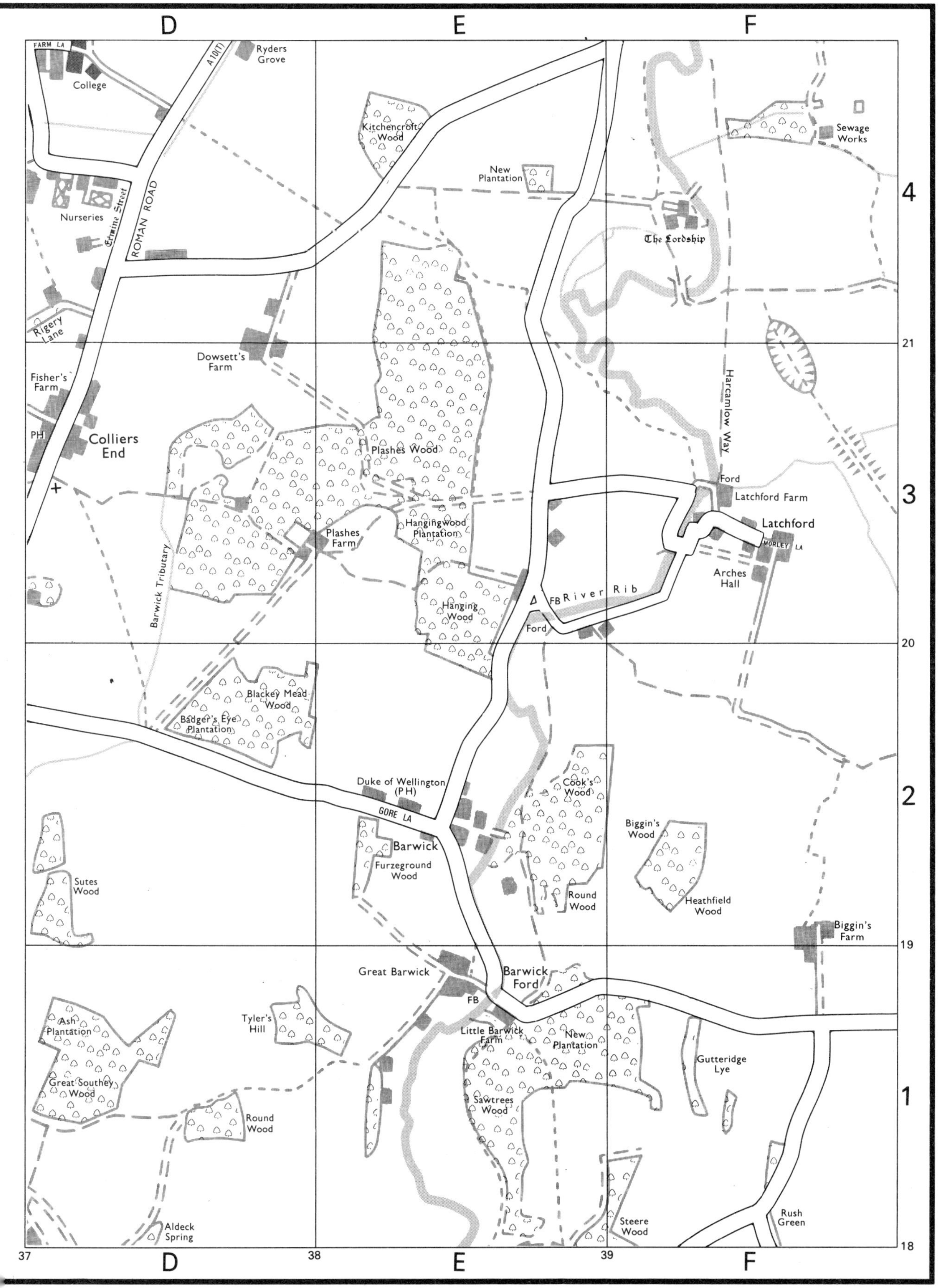
D
E
F
FARM LA
Ryders Grove
A10(T)
College
Kitchencroft Wood
Sewage Works
New Plantation
4
Nurseries
Ermine Street
ROMAN ROAD
The Lordship
Rigery Lane
21
Dowsett's Farm
Fisher's Farm
Harcamlow Way
PH
Colliers End
Plashes Wood
Ford
Latchford Farm
3
Latchford
Plashes Farm
Hangingwood Plantation
MORLEY LA
Arches Hall
Barwick Tributary
FB
River Rib
Hanging Wood
Ford
20
Blackey Mead Wood
Badger's Eye Plantation
Duke of Wellington (PH)
Cook's Wood
2
GORE LA
Barwick
Biggin's Wood
Furzeground Wood
Sutes Wood
Round Wood
Heathfield Wood
Biggin's Farm
19
Great Barwick
Barwick Ford
FB
Tyler's Hill
Ash Plantation
Little Barwick Farm
New Plantation
Gutteridge Lye
Great Southey Wood
1
Sawtrees Wood
Round Wood
Rush Green
Steere Wood
Aldeck Spring
37
38
39
18
D
E
F

74

94

56

73

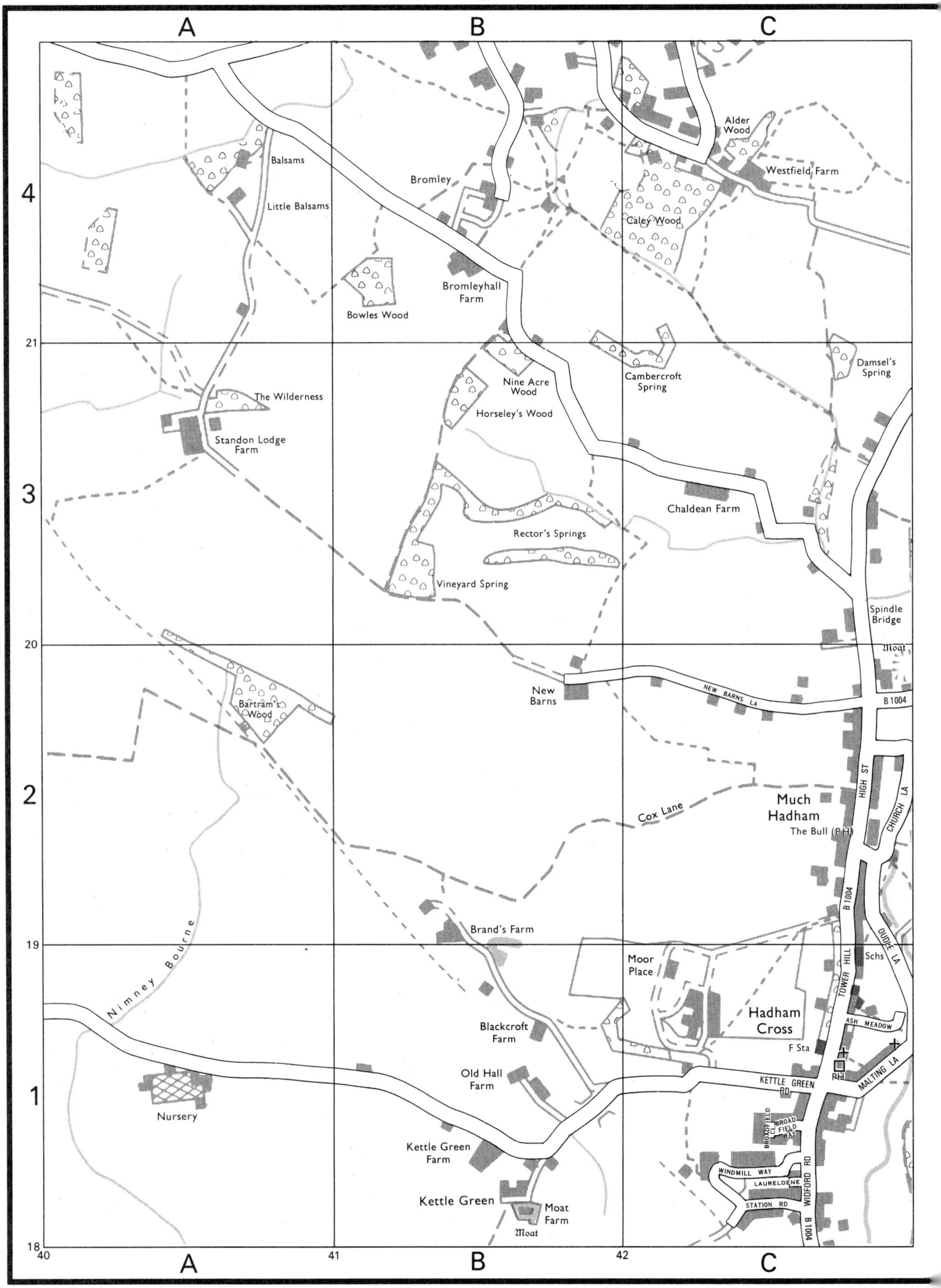
A
B
C
4
3
2
1
21
20
19
18
40
41
42
Balsams
Little Balsams
Bromley
Alder Wood
Westfield Farm
Caley Wood
Bromleyhall Farm
Bowles Wood
Nine Acre Wood
Cambercroft Spring
Damsel's Spring
The Wilderness
Horseley's Wood
Standon Lodge Farm
Chaldean Farm
Rector's Springs
Vineyard Spring
Spindle Bridge
Moat
New Barns
NEW BARNS LA
B 1004
Bartram's Wood
HIGH ST
CHURCH LA
Much Hadham
Cox Lane
The Bull (PH)
B 1004
Nimney Bourne
Brand's Farm
Moor Place
TOWER HILL
Schs
DUDIE LA
Hadham Cross
ASH MEADOW
Blackcroft Farm
F Sta
Old Hall Farm
KETTLE GREEN RD
PH
MALTING LA
Nursery
BROADFIELD CL
BROAD FIELD WAY
Kettle Green Farm
WINDMILL WAY
LAURELDENE
STATION RD
WIDFORD RD
B 1004
Kettle Green
Moat Farm
Moat

95

57

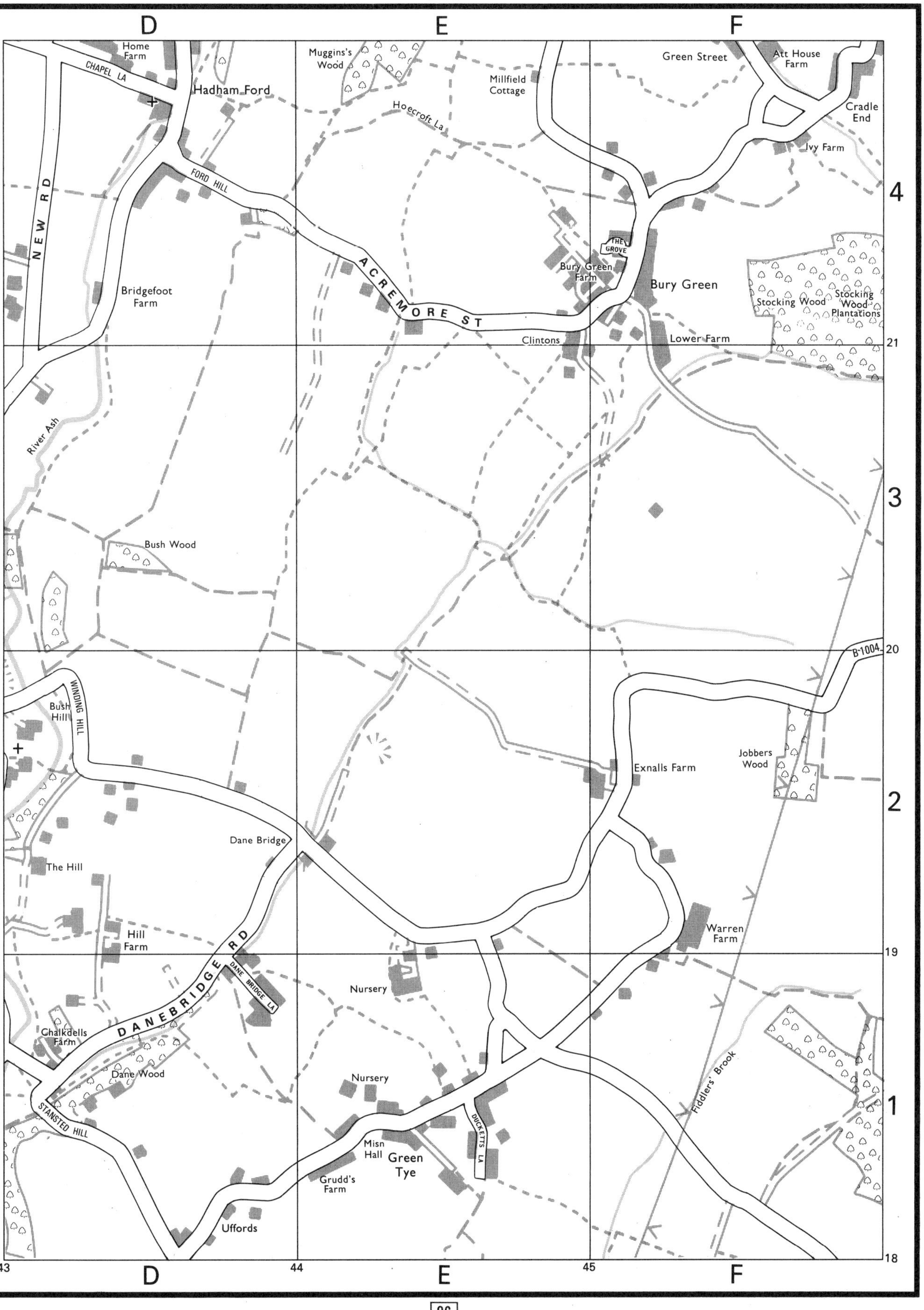
D
E
F
Home Farm
CHAPEL LA
Hadham Ford
Muggins's Wood
Millfield Cottage
Hoecroft La
Green Street
Att House Farm
Cradle End
Ivy Farm
4
NEW RD
FORD HILL
ACREMORE ST
THE GROVE
Bury Green Farm
Bury Green
Bridgefoot Farm
Stocking Wood
Stocking Wood Plantations
Clintons
Lower Farm
21
River Ash
3
Bush Wood
20
B1004
WINDING HILL
Bush Hill
Exnalls Farm
Jobbers Wood
2
Dane Bridge
The Hill
Warren Farm
Hill Farm
DANEBRIDGE RD
DANE BRIDGE LA
19
Nursery
Chalkdells Farm
Dane Wood
Nursery
1
Fiddlers' Brook
STANSTED HILL
DUCKETTS LA
Misn Hall
Green Tye
Grudd's Farm
Uffords
43
44
45
18
D
E
F

76

96

58

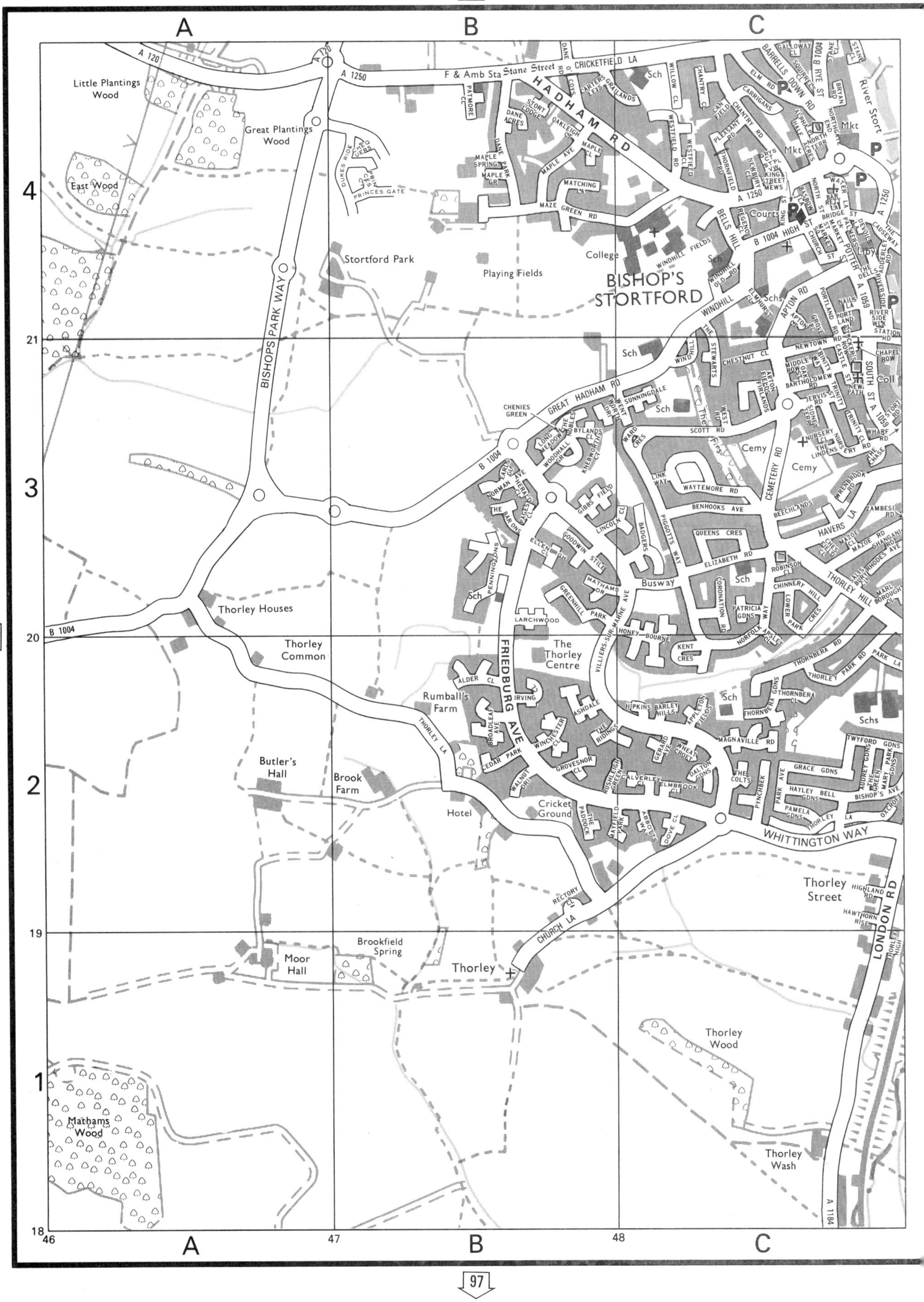
A
B
C
4
3
2
1
21
20
19
18
46
47
48
A 120
A 1250
F & Amb Sta
Stane Street
CRICKETFIELD LA
Little Plantings Wood
Great Plantings Wood
East Wood
HADHAM RD
BARRELLS DOWN RD
B 1004
River Stort
Mkt
College
Stortford Park
Playing Fields
BISHOP'S STORTFORD
BISHOPS PARK WAY
WINDHILL
GREAT HADHAM RD
B 1004
CHENIES GREEN
Sch
Cemy
CEMETERY RD
WAYTEMORE RD
BENHOOKS AVE
QUEENS CRES
ELIZABETH RD
Busway
THORLEY HILL
PIGGOTTS WAY
Thorley Houses
B 1004
Thorley Common
LARCHWOOD
The Thorley Centre
FRIEDBURG AVE
Rumball's Farm
THORLEY LA
Butler's Hall
Brook Farm
Hotel
Cricket Ground
WHITTINGTON WAY
MAGNAVILLE RD
Schs
Thorley Street
LONDON RD
CHURCH LA
RECTORY CL
Moor Hall
Brookfield Spring
Thorley
Thorley Wood
Mathams Wood
Thorley Wash
A 1184
A 1060
Coll
Courts
Lib

75

97

59

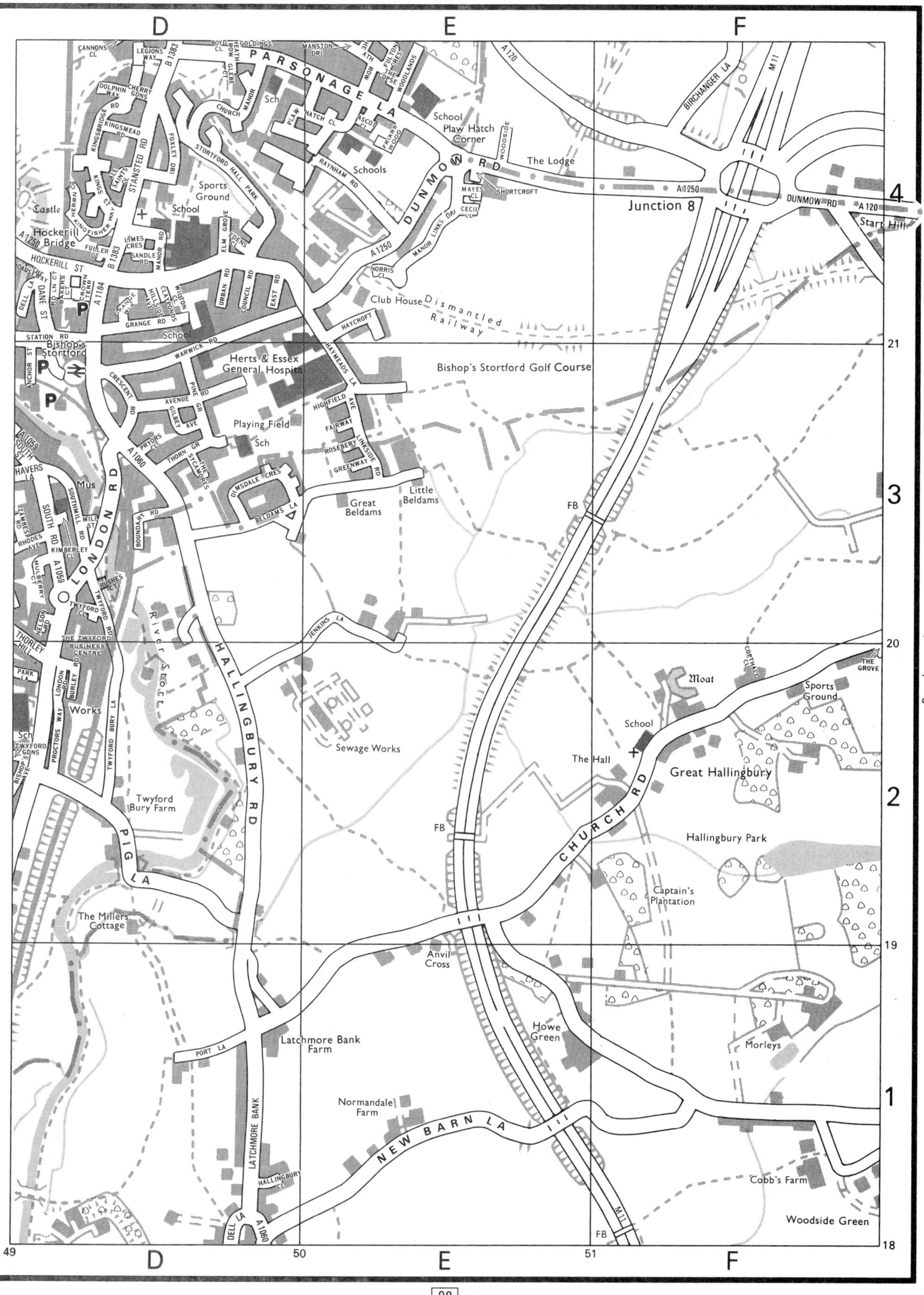

not continued, see key diagram

98

60

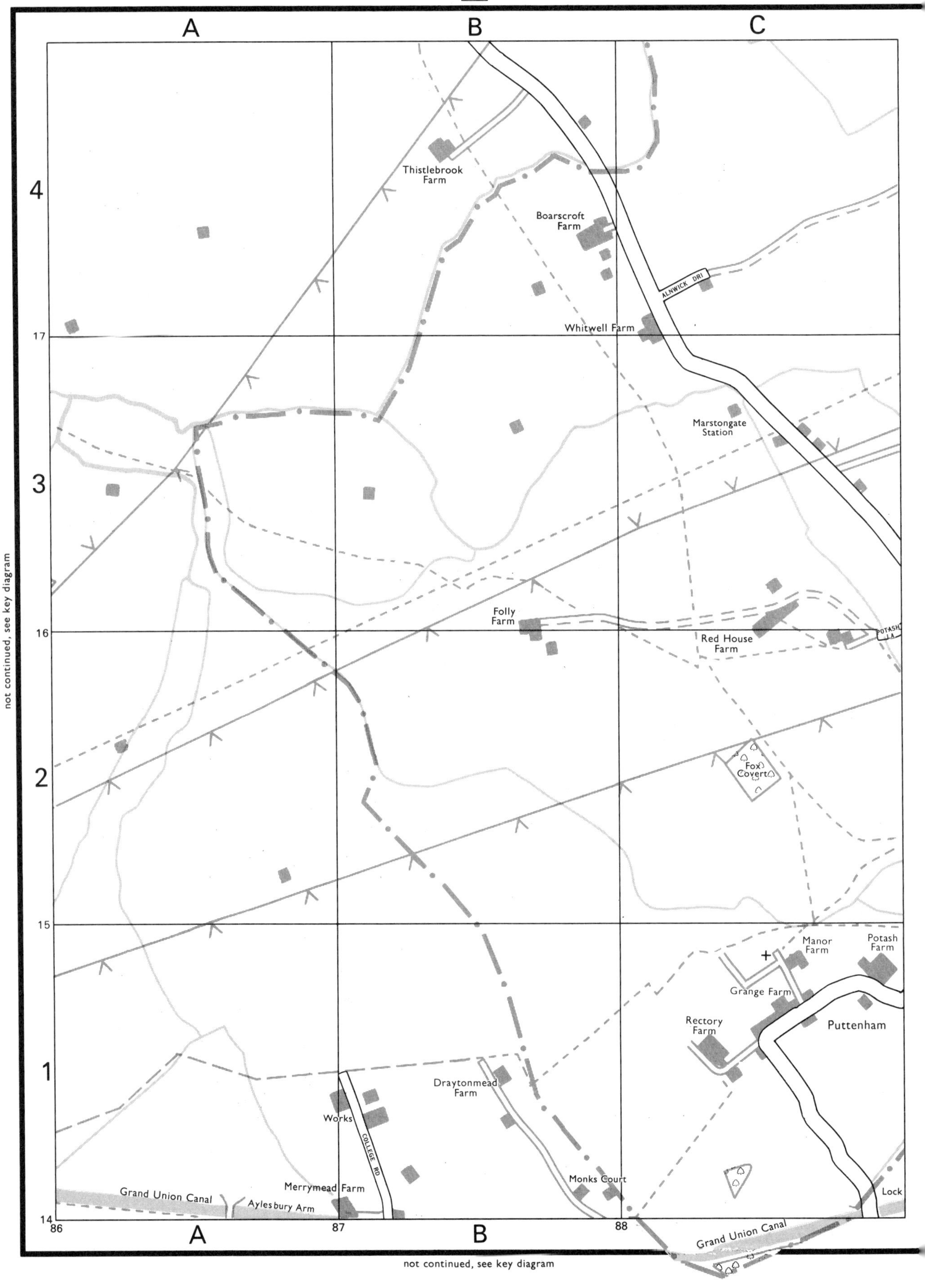

not continued, see key diagram

not continued, see key diagram

61

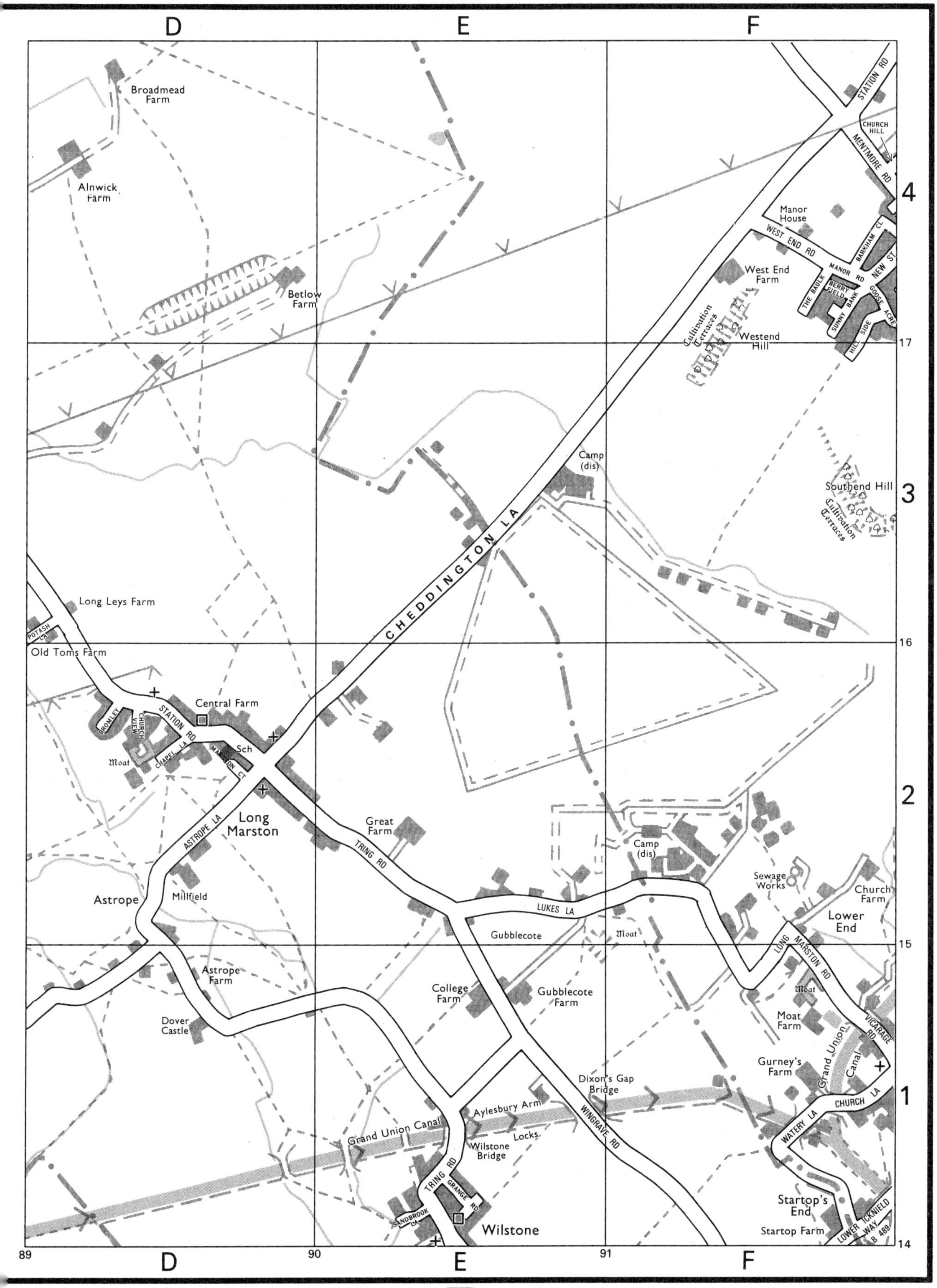

D
E
F
Broadmead Farm
Alnwick Farm
Betlow Farm
West End Farm
Manor House
Westend Hill
Cultivation Terraces
Camp (dis)
Southend Hill
CHEDDINGTON LA
Long Leys Farm
Old Toms Farm
Central Farm
Sch
Moat
Long Marston
Astrope
Millfield
Great Farm
TRING RD
LUKES LA
Gubblecote
Camp (dis)
Sewage Works
Church Farm
Lower End
Astrope Farm
Dover Castle
College Farm
Gubblecote Farm
Moat Farm
Gurney's Farm
Grand Union Canal
Dixon's Gap Bridge
Aylesbury Arm
Locks
Wilstone Bridge
WINGRAVE RD
CHURCH LA
WATERY LA
Startop's End
Startop Farm
Wilstone
STATION RD
CHURCH HILL
MENTMORE RD
WEST END RD
MANOR RD
BARKHAM CL
NEW ST
THE BAULK
BERRY FIELD
SUNNY BANK
GOOSE ACRE
HILL SIDE
POTASH LA
BROMLEY
CHURCH VIEW
CHAPEL LA
MARSTON CT
ASTROPE LA
LONG MARSTON RD
VICARAGE RD
SANDBROOK LA
GRANGE RD
LOWER ICKNIELD WAY
B 489
89
90
91
14
15
16
17
1
2
3
4

80

not continued, see key diagram

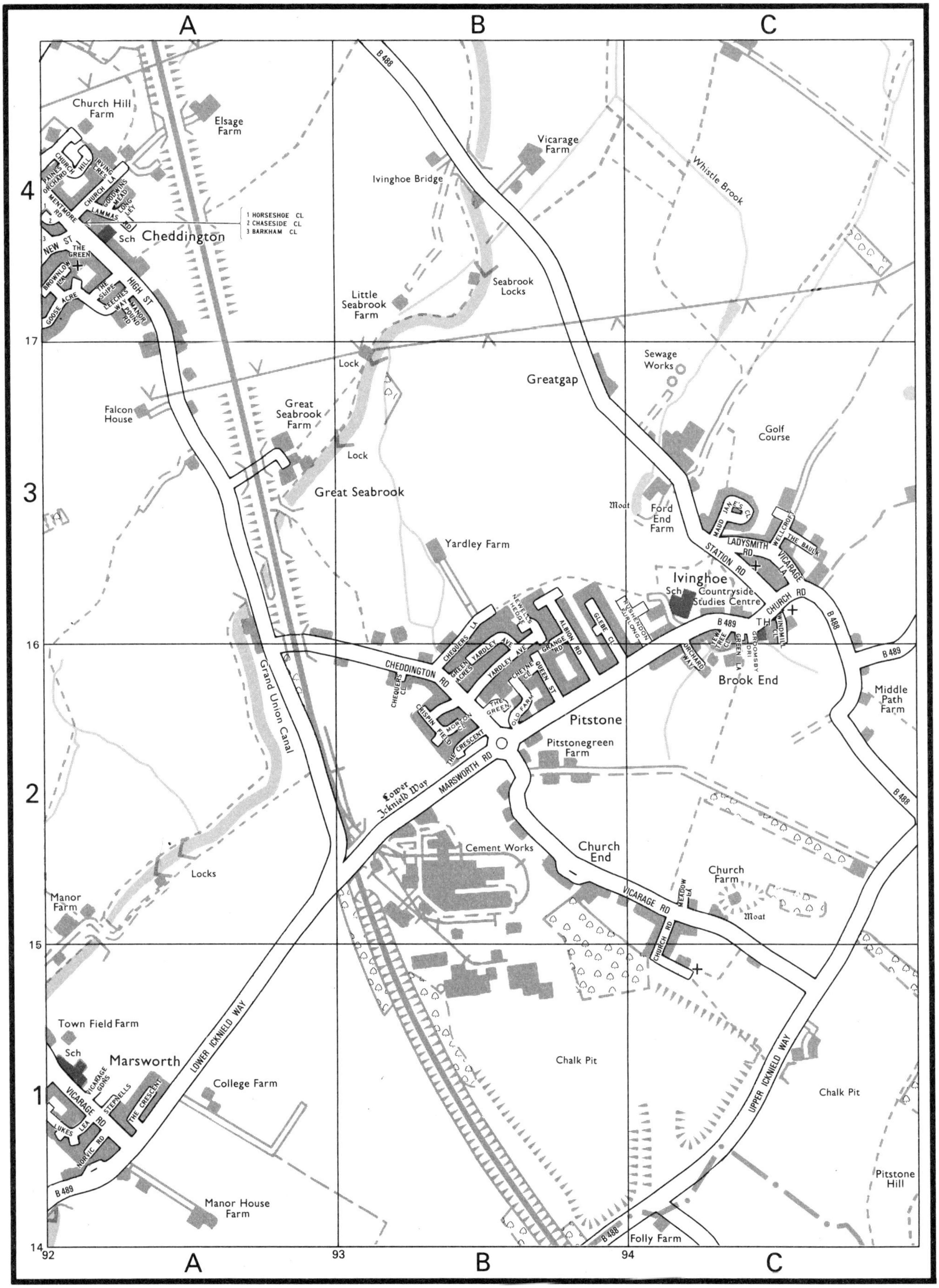

79

100

not continued, see key diagram

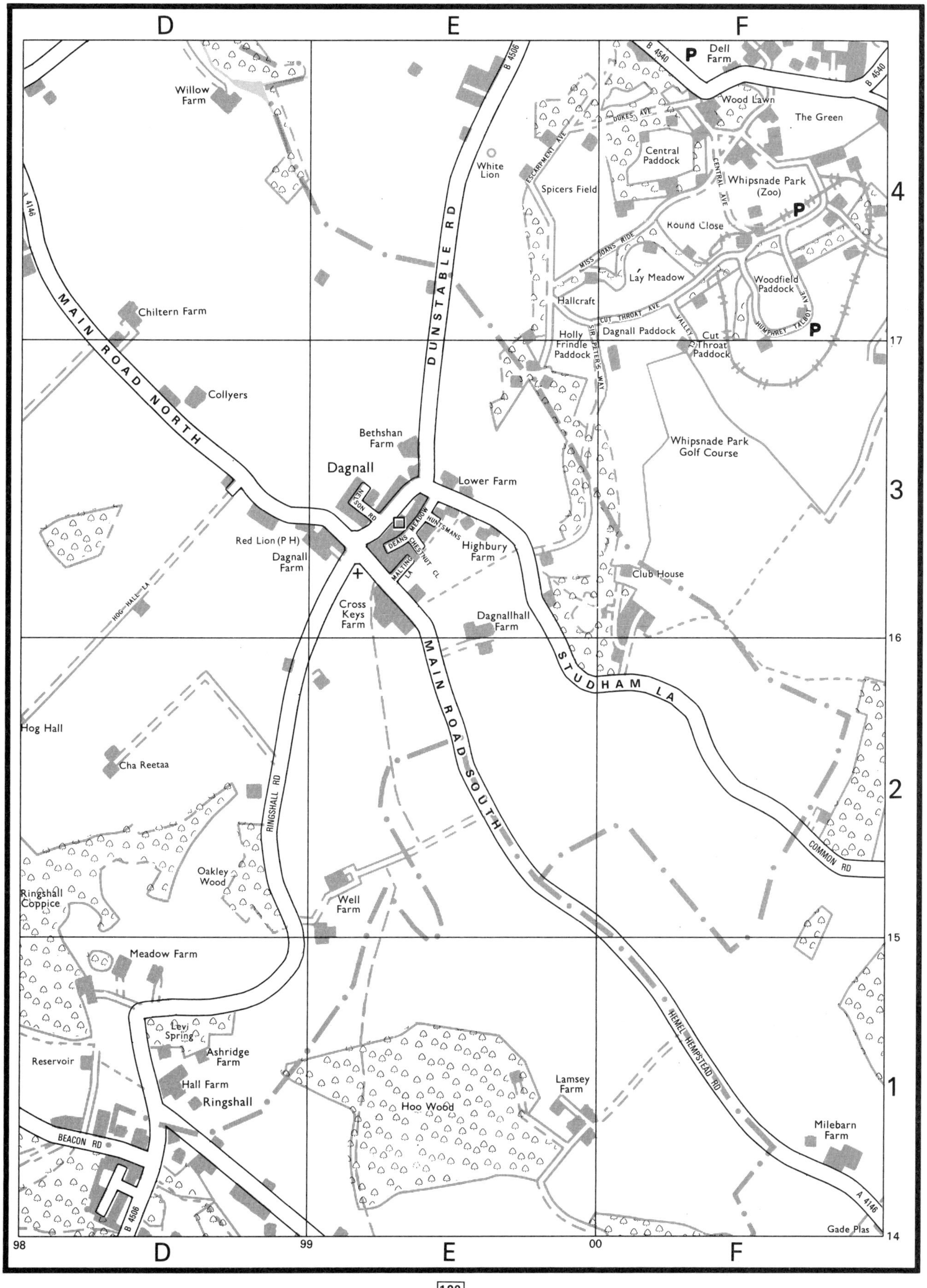

82

102

not continued, see key diagram

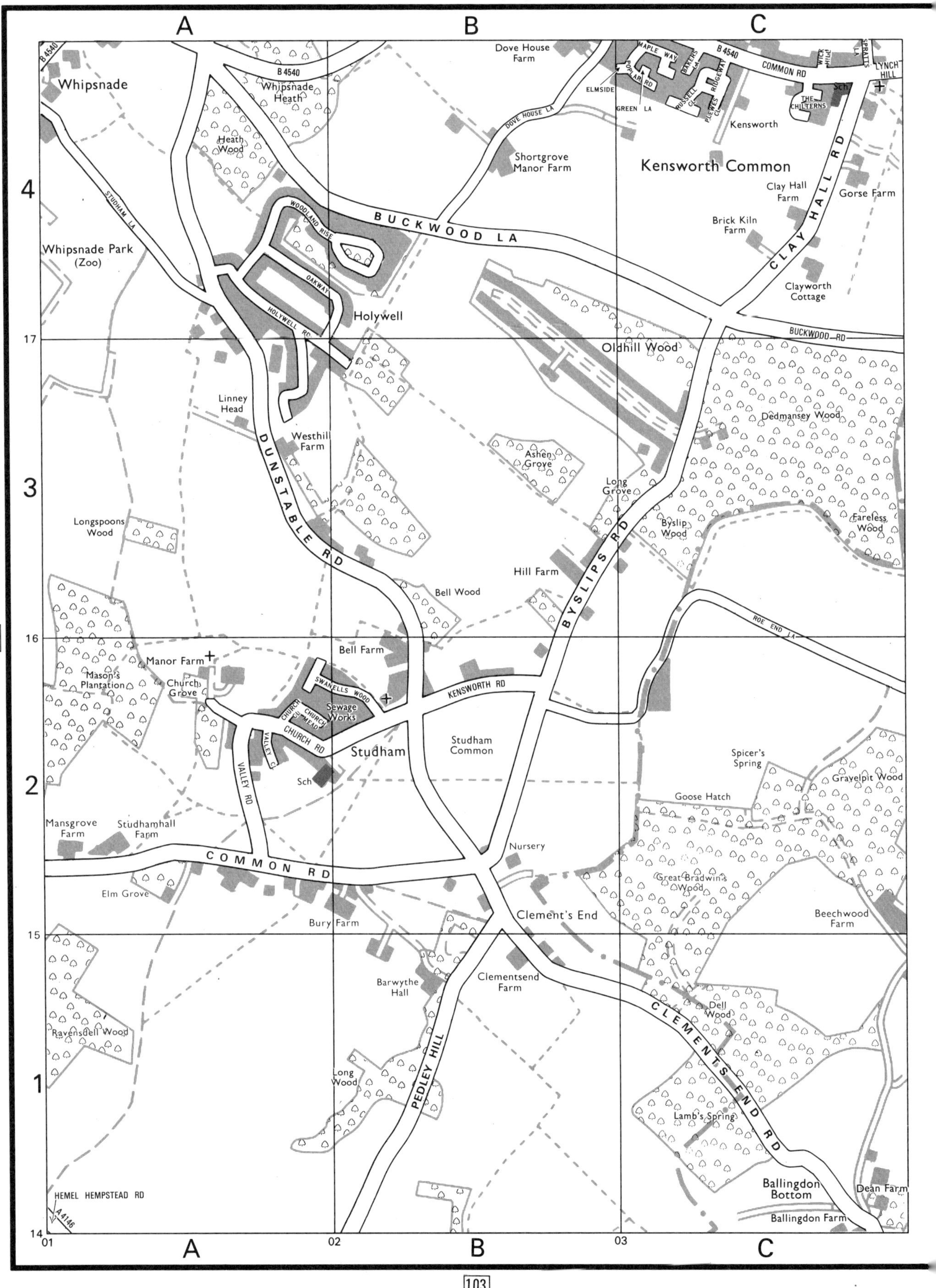

81

62

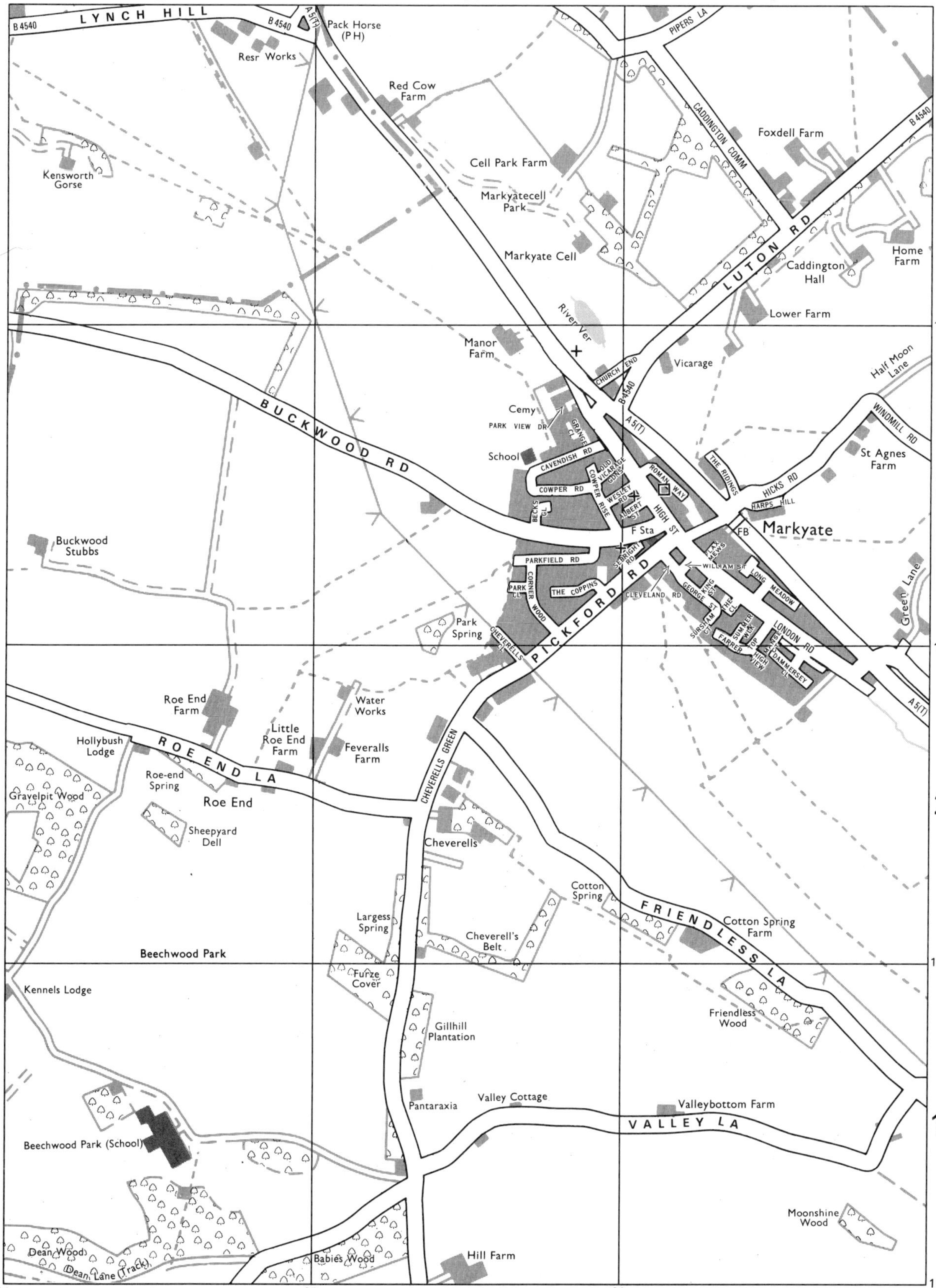
D
E
F
LYNCH HILL
B 4540
A5(T)
Pack Horse (PH)
Resr Works
Red Cow Farm
Kensworth Gorse
Cell Park Farm
Markyatecell Park
Markyate Cell
PIPERS LA
CADDINGTON COMM
Foxdell Farm
B 4540
LUTON RD
Caddington Hall
Home Farm
Lower Farm
River Ver
Manor Farm
CHURCH END
Vicarage
Half Moon Lane
WINDMILL RD
St Agnes Farm
Cemy
PARK VIEW DR
GRANGE CL
School
CAVENDISH RD
COWPER RD
COWPER RISE
OLD VICARAGE GDNS
WESLEY RD
ALBERT ST
ROMAN WAY
HIGH ST
THE RIDINGS
HICKS RD
HARPS HILL
Markyate
FB
F Sta
BUCKWOOD RD
BECKS CL
PARKFIELD RD
SEBRIGHT RD
FLAX MEWS
WILLIAM ST
LONG MEADOW
PARK CL
CORNER WOOD
THE COPPINS
CLEVELAND RD
GEORGE ST
KING ST
THE CL
SURSHAM CT
SUMMER WALK
FARRER TOP
HIGH VIEW
LONDON RD
DAMMERSEY CL
Green Lane
Buckwood Stubbs
Park Spring
CHEVERELLS CL
PICKFORD RD
A5(T)
Roe End Farm
Water Works
Little Roe End Farm
Feveralls Farm
Hollybush Lodge
ROE END LA
Roe-end Spring
Roe End
Gravelpit Wood
Sheepyard Dell
CHEVERELLS GREEN
Cheverells
Cotton Spring
FRIENDLESS LA
Cotton Spring Farm
Largess Spring
Cheverell's Belt
Beechwood Park
Kennels Lodge
Furze Cover
Gillhill Plantation
Friendless Wood
Pantaraxia
Valley Cottage
Valleybottom Farm
VALLEY LA
Beechwood Park (School)
Moonshine Wood
Dean Wood
Dean Lane (Track)
Babies Wood
Hill Farm
4
3
2
1
17
16
15
14
04
05
06

84

104

63

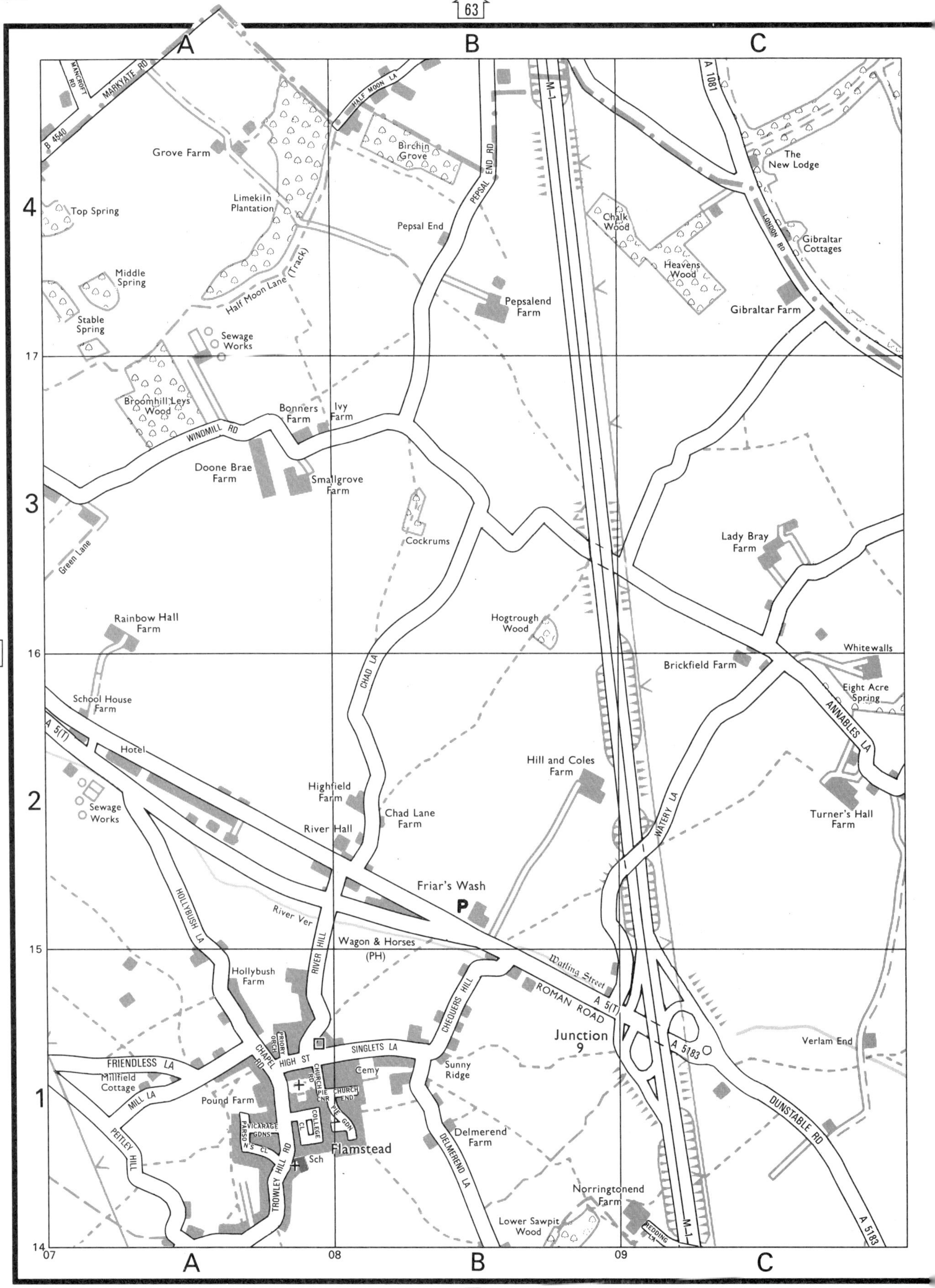
A
B
C
4
3
2
1
17
16
15
14
07
08
09
MANCROFT RD
MARKYATE RD
B 4540
HALF MOON LA
Grove Farm
Birchin Grove
PEPSAL END RD
M-1
A 1081
The New Lodge
Top Spring
Limekiln Plantation
Pepsal End
Chalk Wood
LONDON RD
Gibraltar Cottages
Middle Spring
Half Moon Lane (Track)
Heavens Wood
Pepsalend Farm
Gibraltar Farm
Stable Spring
Sewage Works
Broomhill Leys Wood
Bonners Farm
Ivy Farm
WINDMILL RD
Doone Brae Farm
Smallgrove Farm
Cockrums
Lady Bray Farm
Green Lane
Rainbow Hall Farm
Hogtrough Wood
Whitewalls
Brickfield Farm
CHAD LA
School House Farm
Eight Acre Spring
A 5(T)
ANNABLES LA
Hotel
Hill and Coles Farm
Highfield Farm
Sewage Works
Chad Lane Farm
WATERY LA
Turner's Hall Farm
River Hall
Friar's Wash
P
HOLLYBUSH LA
River Ver
RIVER HILL
Wagon & Horses (PH)
Watling Street
Hollybush Farm
CHEQUERS HILL
ROMAN ROAD
A 5(T)
Junction 9
A 5183
Verlam End
FRIENDLESS LA
CHAPEL RD
PRIORY ORCH
HIGH ST
SINGLETS LA
Millfield Cottage
CHURCH RD
Cemy
Sunny Ridge
MILL LA
PIE CNR
CHURCH END
Pound Farm
PIE GDN
COLLEGE CL
DUNSTABLE RD
VICARAGE GDNS
PARSON'S CL
Flamstead
Delmerend Farm
PEITLEY HILL
Sch
TROWLEY HILL RD
DELMEREND LA
Norringtonend Farm
Lower Sawpit Wood
REDDING LA
M-1
A 5183
07
08
09
A
B
C

83

105

64

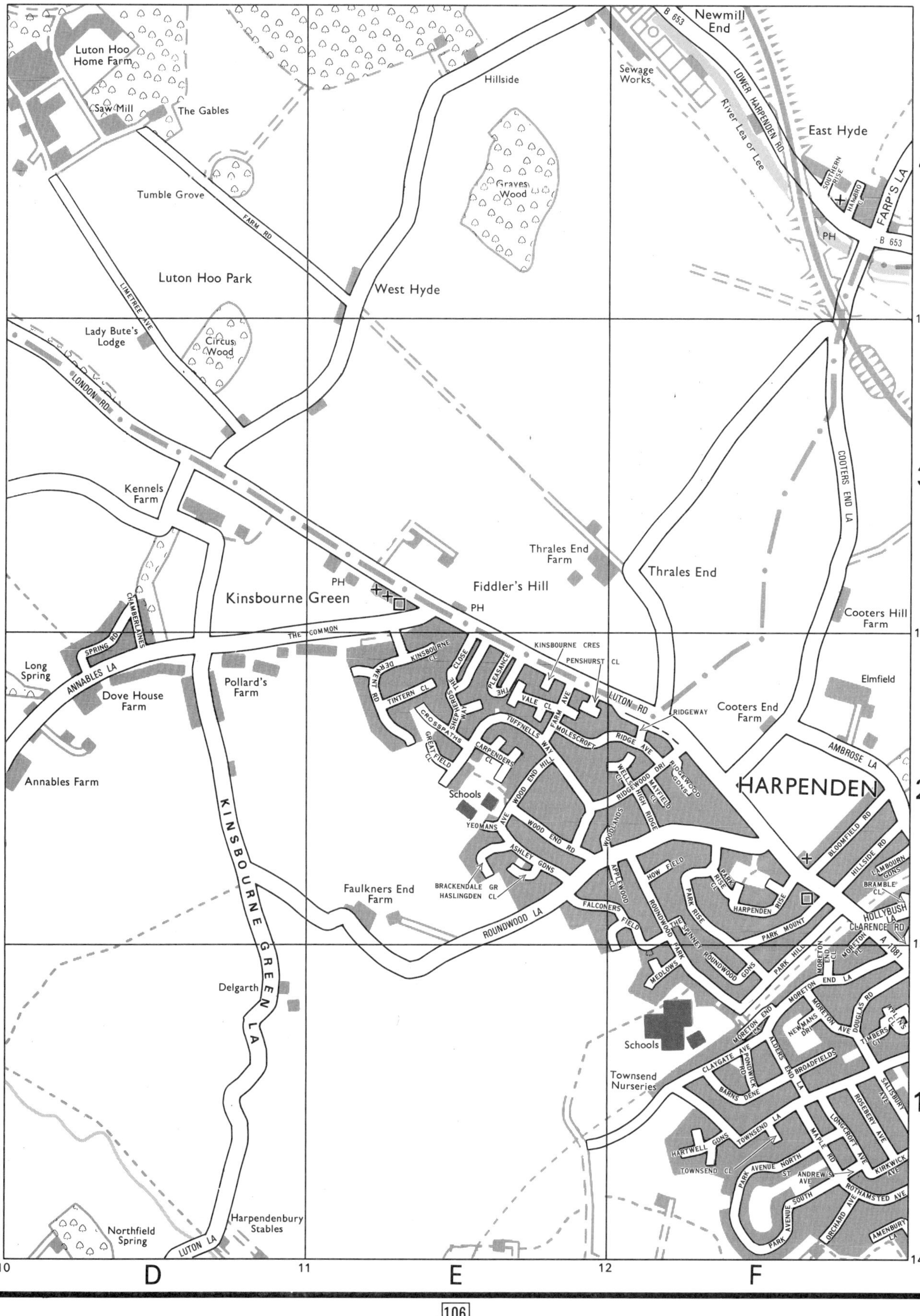
D
E
F
4
3
2
1
17
16
15
14
10
11
12
Luton Hoo
Home Farm
Saw Mill
The Gables
Tumble Grove
FARM RD
Luton Hoo Park
LIMETREE AVE
Lady Bute's
Lodge
Circus
Wood
LONDON RD
Hillside
Graves
Wood
West Hyde
Newmill
End
B 653
Sewage
Works
LOWER HARPENDEN RD
River Lea or Lee
East Hyde
SOUTHERN RISE
HAMBRO PL
FARP'S LA
PH
Kennels
Farm
Thrales End
Farm
Thrales End
COOTERS END LA
Fiddler's Hill
PH
Kinsbourne Green
CHAMBERLAINES
SPRING RD
THE COMMON
Long
Spring
ANNABLES LA
Dove House
Farm
Pollard's
Farm
Annables Farm
KINSBOURNE GREEN LA
Cooters Hill
Farm
Elmfield
Cooters End
Farm
AMBROSE LA
KINSBOURNE CRES
PENSHURST CL
LUTON RD
RIDGEWAY
DERWENT RD
KINSBOURNE CL
TINTERN CL
THE CLOSE
SHEPHERDS WAY
THE PLEASANCE
VALE CL
FARM AVE
CROSSPATHS
GREAT FIELD CL
CARPENDERS CL
TUFFNELLS WAY
MOLESCROFT
RIDGE AVE
WELLSWOOD CL
RIDGEWOOD DRI
MAYFIELD CL
RIDGEWOOD GDNS
HARPENDEN
Schools
WOOD END HILL
YEOMANS AVE
WOOD END RD
HIGH RIDGE
WOODLANDS
BLOOMFIELD RD
HILLSIDE RD
LAMBOURN GDNS
BRAMBLE CL
ASHLEY GDNS
BRACKENDALE GR
HASLINGDEN CL
APPLEWOOD CL
HOW FIELD
PARK RISE CL
PARK RISE
HARPENDEN RISE
HOLLYBUSH LA
CLARENCE RD
Faulkners End
Farm
ROUNDWOOD LA
FALCONERS FIELD
ROUNDWOOD PARK
THE SPINNEY
PARK MOUNT
MORETON PL
A 1081
MEDLOWS
ROUNDWOOD GDNS
PARK HILL
MORETON END CL
MORETON END LA
Delgarth
Schools
MORETON END
NEWMANS DRI
MORETON AVE
DOUGLAS RD
TIMBERS CT
CLAYGATE AVE
PONDWICK RD
ALDERS END LA
BROADFIELDS
SALISBURY AVE
Townsend
Nurseries
BARNS DENE
ROSEBERY AVE
HARTWELL GDNS
TOWNSEND LA
LONGCROFT AVE
MAPLE RD
TOWNSEND CL
PARK AVENUE NORTH
ST ANDREW'S AVE
KIRKWICK AVE
ROTHAMSTED AVE
PARK AVENUE SOUTH
ORCHARD AVE
AMENBURY LA
Northfield
Spring
LUTON LA
Harpendenbury
Stables

98

106

65

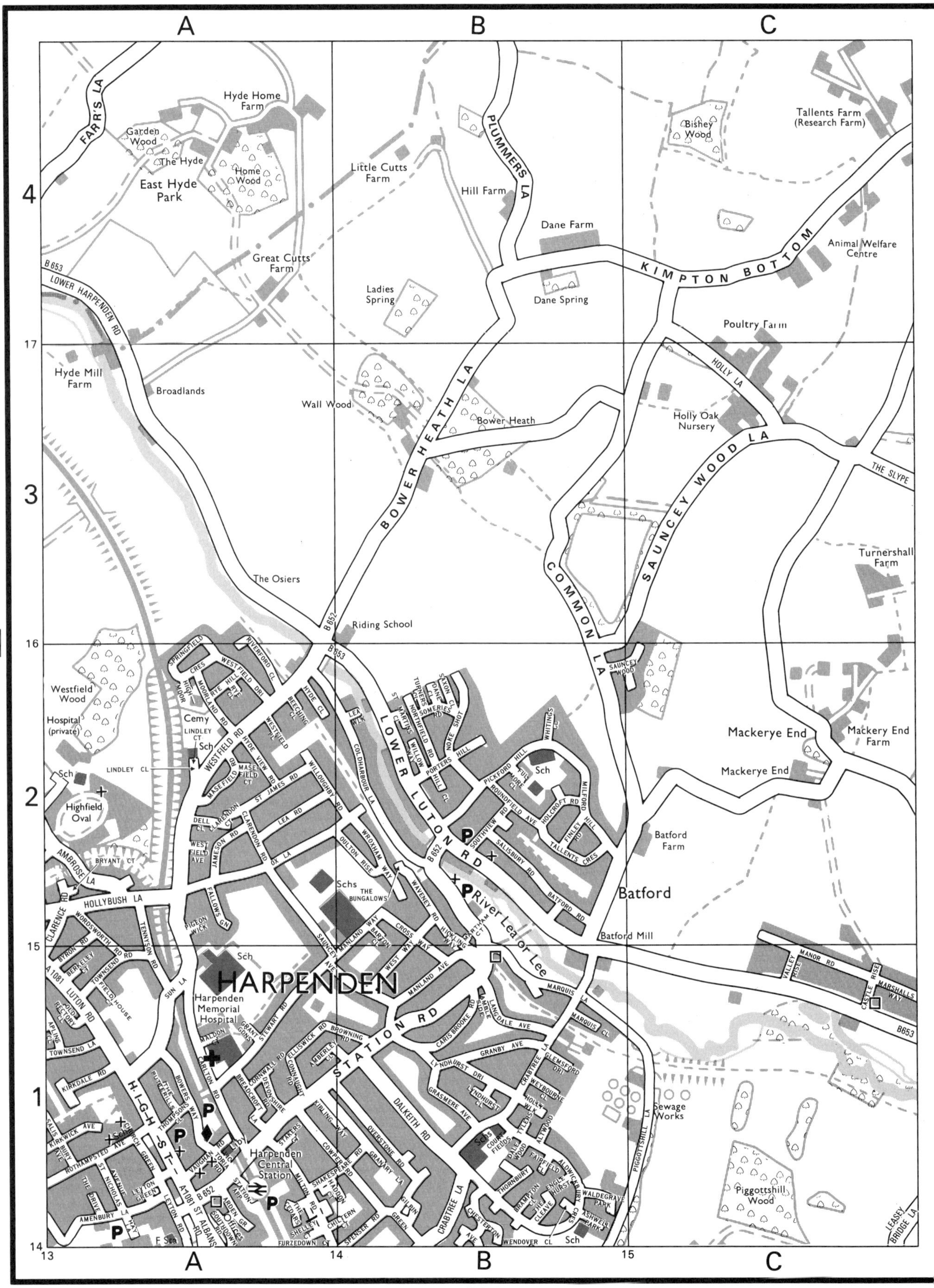
A
B
C
4
3
2
1
17
16
15
14
13
14
15
Hyde Home Farm
Garden Wood
The Hyde
Home Wood
East Hyde Park
FARR'S LA
Little Cutts Farm
Hill Farm
PLUMMERS LA
Bishey Wood
Tallents Farm (Research Farm)
Dane Farm
Animal Welfare Centre
KIMPTON BOTTOM
Great Cutts Farm
B 653
LOWER HARPENDEN RD
Ladies Spring
Dane Spring
Poultry Farm
Hyde Mill Farm
Broadlands
Wall Wood
Bower Heath
BOWER HEATH LA
HOLLY LA
Holly Oak Nursery
SAUNCEY WOOD LA
THE SLYPE
COMMON LA
Turnershall Farm
The Osiers
Riding School
B 652
Westfield Wood
Hospital (private)
Cemy
Sch
Highfield Oval
Mackerye End
Mackery End Farm
Batford Farm
Batford
Batford Mill
LOWER LUTON RD
River Lea or Lee
HARPENDEN
Harpenden Memorial Hospital
STATION RD
HIGH ST
Harpenden Central Station
Schs
Sewage Works
Piggottshill Wood
PIGGOTTSHILL LA
LEASEY BRIDGE LA
MANOR RD
VALLEY RISE
CASTLE RISE
MARSHALLS WAY
B653
A 1081
LUTON RD
SUN LA
HOLLYBUSH LA
AMBROSE LA
CLARENCE RD
WESTFIELD RD
ST JAMES RD
WILLOUGHBY RD
LEA RD
OX LA
COLDHARBOUR LA
WROXHAM WAY
WAVENEY RD
MARQUIS LA
LANGDALE AVE
GRANBY AVE
CRABTREE LA
DALKEITH RD
OVERSTONE RD
SALISBURY RD
TALLENTS CRES
ROUNDFIELD AVE
MILFORD HILL
BATFORD RD
KIRKDALE RD
TOWNSEND LA
ROTHAMSTED AVE
AMENBURY LA
ST NICHOLAS AVENUE
THE DRIVE
KIRKWICK AVE
BOWERS WAY
THOMPSONS CL
CARLTON RD
CORNWALL RD
DEVONSHIRE
BROWNING RD
CARISBROOKE RD
LYNDHURST DRI
GRASMERE AVE
COWPER RD
SHAKESPEARE RD
SPENSER RD
MILTON RD
CHILTERN RD
FURZEDOWN CT
WENDOVER CL
CHESTERTON AVE
WALDEGRAVE PARK
ASHWELL PARK
THORNBURY
BRAMPTON CL
THE CLEAVE
ALLWOOD
GLEMSFORD DRI
WEYBOURNE
TENNYSON RD
WORDSWORTH RD
BYRON RD
BERKELEY
LINDLEY CL
LINDLEY CT
BRYANT CT
PIGEON WICK
FALLOWS GN
JAMESON RD
CLARENDON RD
MASEFIELD RD
HYDE VIEW RD
HYDE CL
BEECHING CL
WESTFIELD DRI
RIVERFORD CL
SPRINGFIELD CRES
MOORLAND RD
RYE HILL
PORTERS HILL
NOKE SHOT
NORTHFIELD RD
SOMERIES RD
TURNERS CL
PICKFORD HILL
HOLCROFT RD
FINLEY RD
SOUTHVIEW RD
MANLAND WAY
MANLAND AVE
WEST WAY
CROSS WAY
OULTON RISE
THE BUNGALOWS
SAUNCEY AVE
STEWART RD
GRANT GDNS
MALDON CT
ELLISWICK RD
AMBERLEY CL
CONNAUGHT RD
BREADCROFT LA
KIRLING WAY
GRANARY LA
GILPIN GREEN
ARDEN GR
SOUTHDOWN RD
ST ALBANS RD
LEYTON RD
LEYTON GREEN
VAUGHAN RD
VICTORIA RD
STATION APP
F Sta

85

66

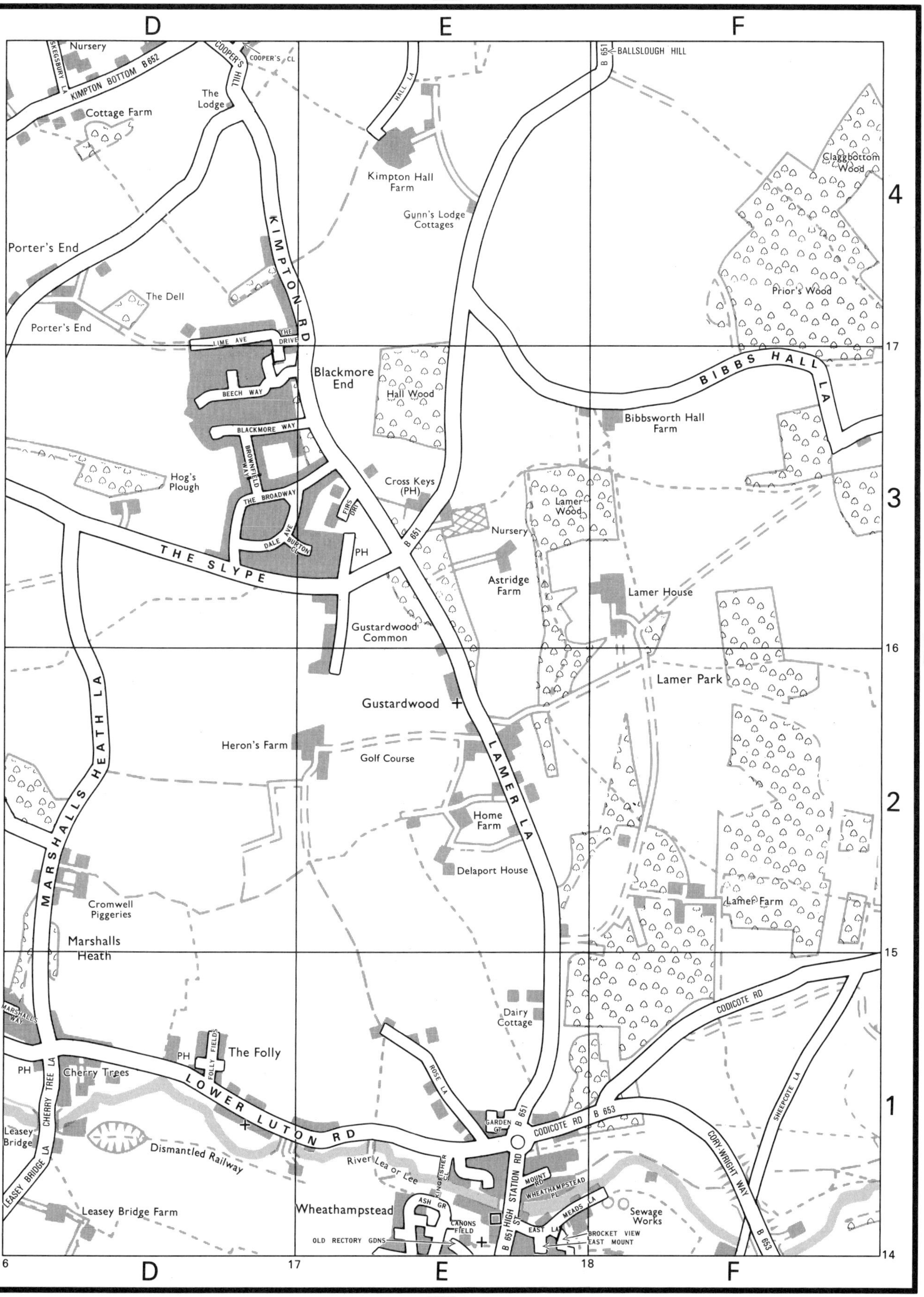
D
E
F
Nursery
SKEGSBURY LA
KIMPTON BOTTOM B652
COOPER'S HILL
COOPER'S CL
B 651
BALLSLOUGH HILL
HALL LA
Cottage Farm
The Lodge
Kimpton Hall Farm
Gunn's Lodge Cottages
Claggbottom Wood
4
KIMPTON RD
Porter's End
The Dell
Porter's End
Prior's Wood
LIME AVE
THE DRIVE
17
BIBBS HALL LA
Blackmore End
Hall Wood
BEECH WAY
BLACKMORE WAY
Bibbsworth Hall Farm
BROWNFIELD WAY
Hog's Plough
THE BROADWAY
Cross Keys (PH)
FIRS DRI
Lamer Wood
3
B 651
Nursery
DALE AVE
BURTON CL
PH
THE SLYPE
Astridge Farm
Lamer House
Gustardwood Common
16
Lamer Park
MARSHALLS HEATH LA
Gustardwood
Heron's Farm
Golf Course
LAMER LA
2
Home Farm
Delaport House
Cromwell Piggeries
Lamer Farm
Marshalls Heath
15
CODICOTE RD
Dairy Cottage
MARSHALLS WAY
PH
FOLLY FIELDS
The Folly
PH
Cherry Trees
CHERRY TREE LA
ROSE LA
SHEEPCOTE LA
LOWER LUTON RD
1
GARDEN CT
B 651
CODICOTE RD
B 653
CORY-WRIGHT WAY
Leasey Bridge
Dismantled Railway
River Lea or Lee
KINGSFISHER CL
HIGH ST
STATION RD
MOUNT RD
WHEATHAMPSTEAD PL
MEADS LA
LEASEY BRIDGE LA
Leasey Bridge Farm
Wheathampstead
ASH GR
CANONS FIELD
Sewage Works
OLD RECTORY GDNS
B 651
EAST LA
BROCKET VIEW
EAST MOUNT
B 653
14
16
17
18
D
E
F
88

108

67

87

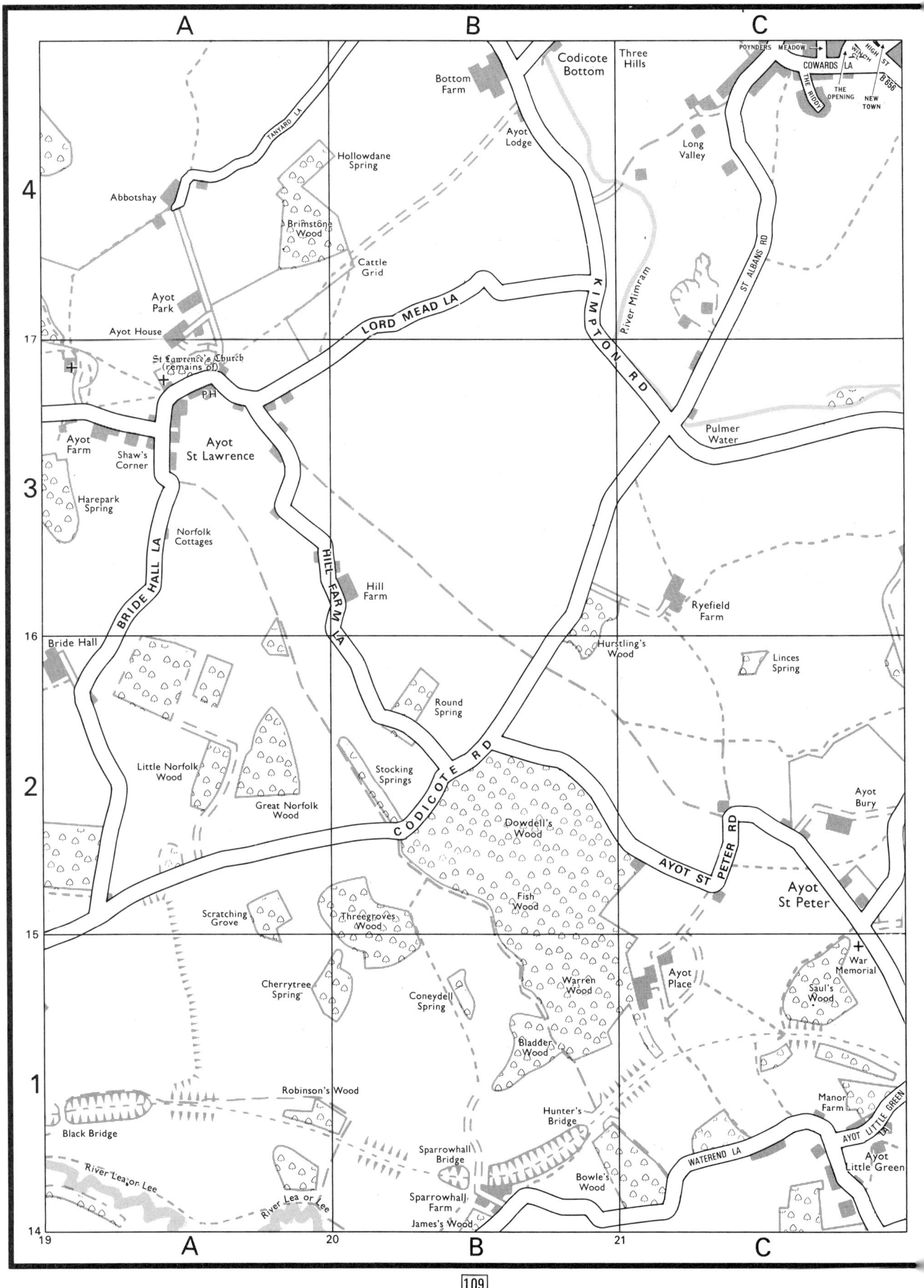
A
B
C
4
3
2
1
17
16
15
14
19
20
21
POYNDERS MEADOW
COWARDS LA
HIGH ST
B 656
THE RIDDY
THE OPENING
NEW TOWN
Codicote Bottom
Three Hills
Bottom Farm
Ayot Lodge
TANYARD LA
Hollowdane Spring
Long Valley
Abbotshay
Brimstone Wood
Cattle Grid
ST ALBANS RD
River Mimram
Ayot Park
LORD MEAD LA
KIMPTON RD
Ayot House
St Lawrence's Church (remains of)
PH
Ayot Farm
Shaw's Corner
Ayot St Lawrence
Pulmer Water
Harepark Spring
Norfolk Cottages
BRIDE HALL LA
HILL FARM LA
Hill Farm
Ryefield Farm
Bride Hall
Hurstling's Wood
Linces Spring
Round Spring
CODICOTE RD
Little Norfolk Wood
Great Norfolk Wood
Stocking Springs
Dowdell's Wood
Ayot Bury
AYOT ST PETER RD
Ayot St Peter
Fish Wood
Scratching Grove
Threegroves Wood
War Memorial
Ayot Place
Cherrytree Spring
Coneydell Spring
Warren Wood
Saul's Wood
Bladder Wood
Robinson's Wood
Hunter's Bridge
Manor Farm
AYOT LITTLE GREEN LA
Black Bridge
Sparrowhall Bridge
WATEREND LA
Ayot Little Green
River Lea or Lee
Bowle's Wood
Sparrowhall Farm
James's Wood

109

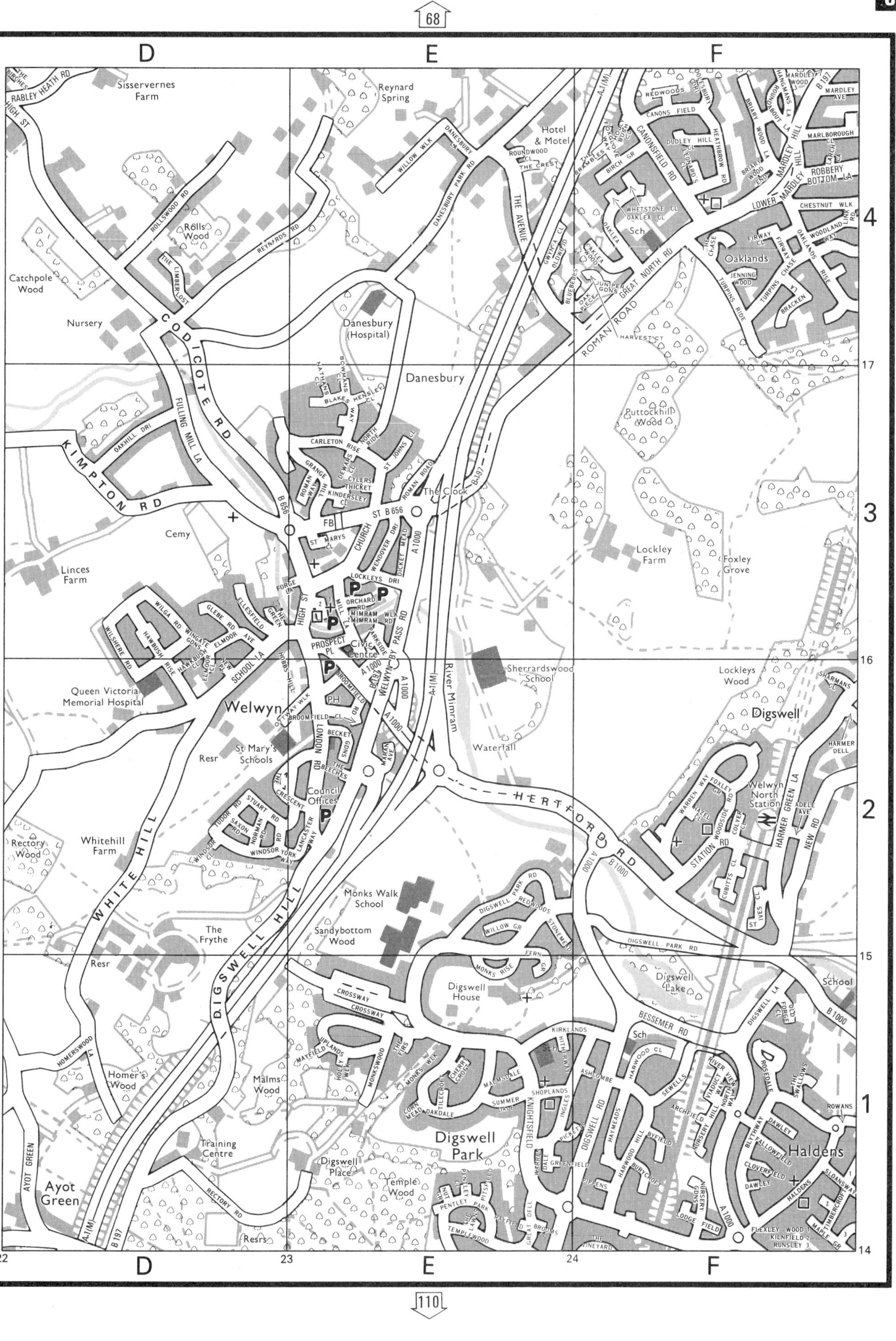
68
D
E
F
Sisservernes Farm
Reynard Spring
Hotel & Motel
Rolls Wood
Catchpole Wood
Nursery
Danesbury (Hospital)
Danesbury
Oaklands
Puttockhill Wood
The Clock
Cemy
Lockley Farm
Foxley Grove
Linces Farm
Queen Victoria Memorial Hospital
Welwyn
Sherrardswood School
Lockleys Wood
Digswell
St Mary's Schools
Resr
Waterfall
Welwyn North Station
Council Offices
Whitehill Farm
Rectory Wood
Monks Walk School
The Frythe
Sandybottom Wood
Digswell Lake
Digswell House
School
Homer's Wood
Malms Wood
Digswell Park
Haldens
Training Centre
Digswell Place
Temple Wood
Ayot Green
Resrs
CODICOTE RD
KIMPTON RD
WHITE HILL
DIGSWELL HILL
HERTFORD RD
GREAT NORTH RD
ROMAN ROAD
THE AVENUE
DANESBURY PARK RD
DIGSWELL RD
BESSEMER RD
DIGSWELL PARK RD
LONDON RD
HIGH ST
WELWYN BY PASS RD
A1(M)
A1000
B656
B197
B1000
4
3
2
1
17
16
15
14
22
23
24
90
110

69

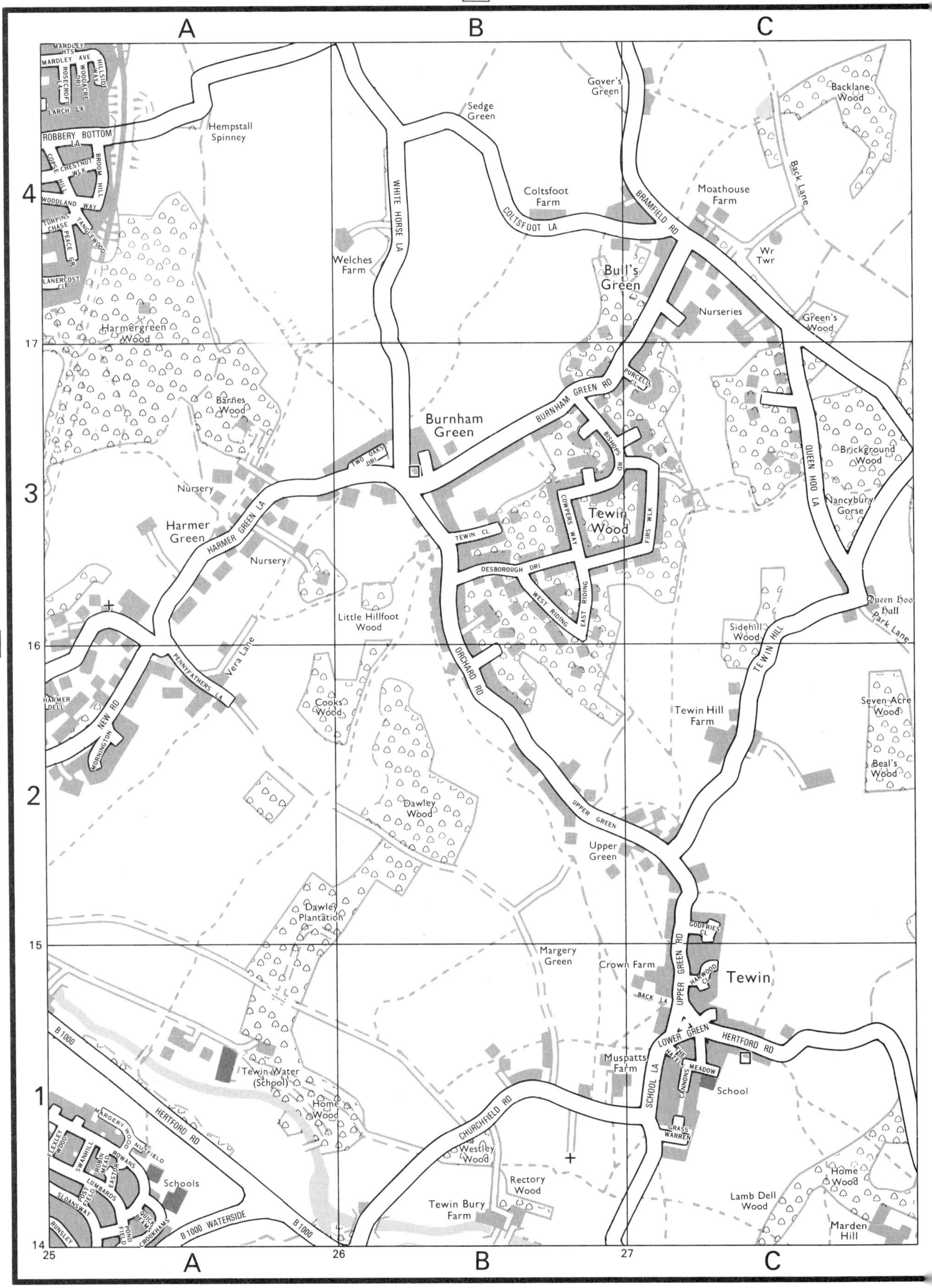
A
B
C
Hempstall Spinney
Sedge Green
Gover's Green
Backlane Wood
Coltsfoot Farm
Moathouse Farm
WHITE HORSE LA
COLTSFOOT LA
BRAMFIELD RD
Back Lane
Welches Farm
Wr Twr
Bull's Green
Nurseries
Green's Wood
Harmergreen Wood
Barnes Wood
Burnham Green
BURNHAM GREEN RD
PURCELL CL
BISHOPS RD
Brickground Wood
QUEEN HOO LA
TWO OAKS DRI
Nursery
Harmer Green
HARMER GREEN LA
Tewin Wood
COWPERS WAY
FIRS WLK
TEWIN CL
Nancybury Gorse
DESBOROUGH DRI
Nursery
WEST RIDING
EAST RIDING
Little Hillfoot Wood
Queen Hoo Hall
Park Lane
Sidehill Wood
TEWIN HILL
PENNYFATHERS LA
Vera Lane
ORCHARD RD
HARMER DELL
NEW RD
MORNINGTON
Cooks Wood
Tewin Hill Farm
Seven Acre Wood
Beal's Wood
Dawley Wood
UPPER GREEN
Upper Green
Dawley Plantation
GODFRIES CL
Margery Green
Crown Farm
UPPER GREEN RD
HARWOOD CL
Tewin
BACK LA
B 1000
LOWER GREEN
HERTFORD RD
THE HAYES
MEADOW
Muspatts Farm
SCHOOL LA
CANNONS
Tewin Water (School)
School
Home Wood
GRASS WARREN
HERTFORD RD
CHURCHFIELD RD
MARGERY WOOD
NUTFIELD
FLEXLEY WOOD
SWANHILL
ROBIN MEAD
ROWANS
EASTOR
Westley Wood
Schools
Home Wood
Lamb Dell Wood
Rectory Wood
POSTFIELD
LUMBARDS
SLOANSWAY
QUICKBEAMS
POND FIELD
CROOKHAMS
RUNSLEY
B 1000 WATERSIDE
B 1000
Tewin Bury Farm
Marden Hill
MARDLEY HTS
MARDLEY AVE
WOODACRE DRI
HILLSIDE WAY
ROSECROFT LA
LARCH LA
ROBBERY BOTTOM LA
CORSE HILL
CHESTNUT WLK
BROOM HILL
WOODLAND WAY
TURPINS CHASE
TANGLEWOOD
PEACE GR
LANERCOST CL
4
3
2
1
17
16
15
14
25
26
27
A
B
C

89

111

70

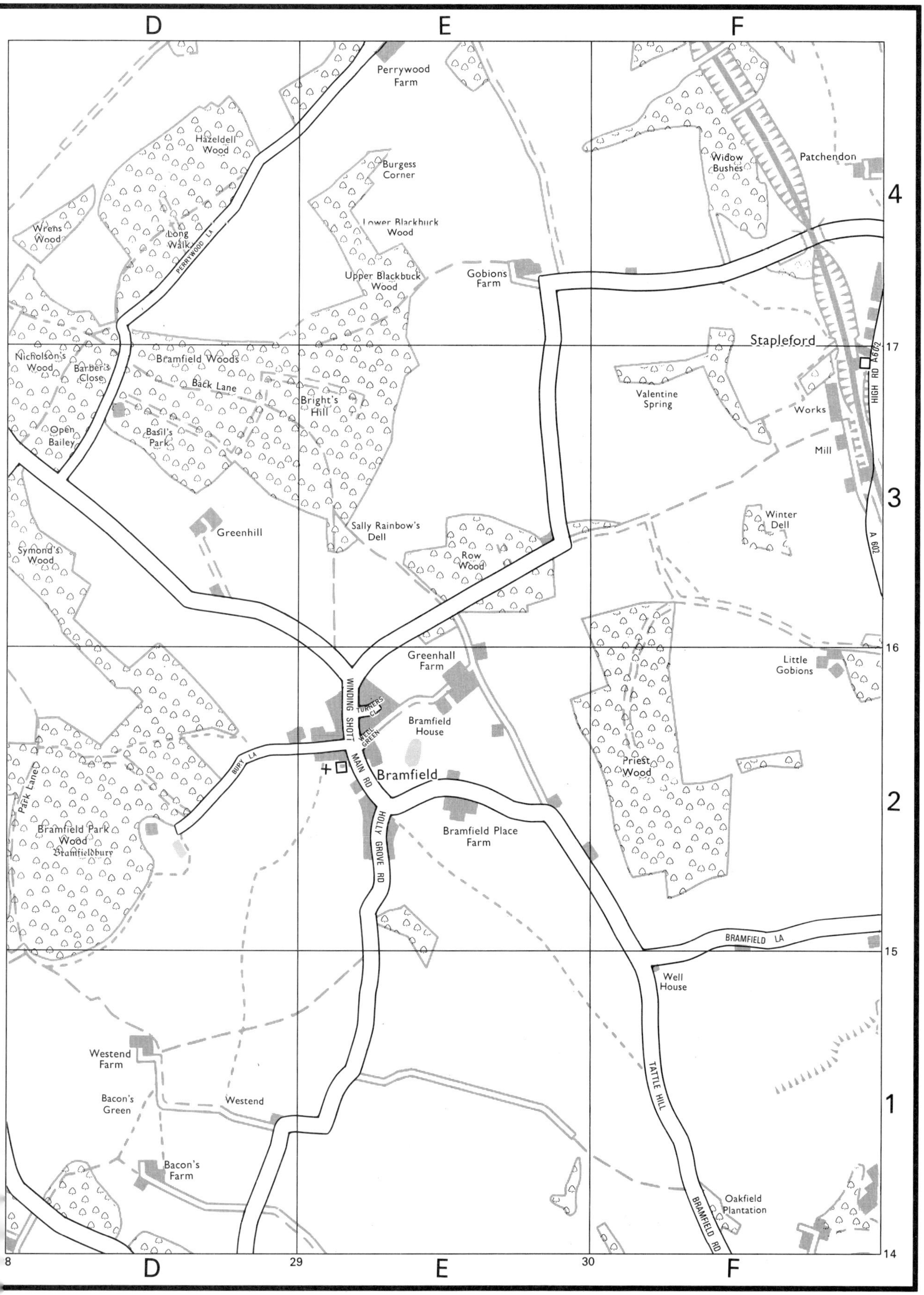
D
E
F
Perrywood Farm
Hazeldell Wood
Burgess Corner
Lower Blackbuck Wood
Wrens Wood
Long Walk
PERRYWOOD LA
Upper Blackbuck Wood
Gobions Farm
Widow Bushes
Patchendon
Stapleford
HIGH RD
A602
Nicholson's Wood
Barber's Close
Bramfield Woods
Back Lane
Bright's Hill
Open Bailey
Basil's Park
Valentine Spring
Works
Mill
Greenhill
Sally Rainbow's Dell
Winter Dell
Symond's Wood
Row Wood
A 602
Greenhall Farm
Little Gobions
WINDING SHOTT
TURNERS CL
WELL GREEN
Bramfield House
BURY LA
MAIN RD
Bramfield
Priest Wood
Park Lane
Bramfield Park Wood
Bramfieldbury
HOLLY GROVE RD
Bramfield Place Farm
BRAMFIELD LA
Well House
Westend Farm
Bacon's Green
Westend
TATTLE HILL
Bacon's Farm
Oakfield Plantation
BRAMFIELD RD
4
3
2
1
17
16
15
14
8
29
30
D
E
F

92

112

71

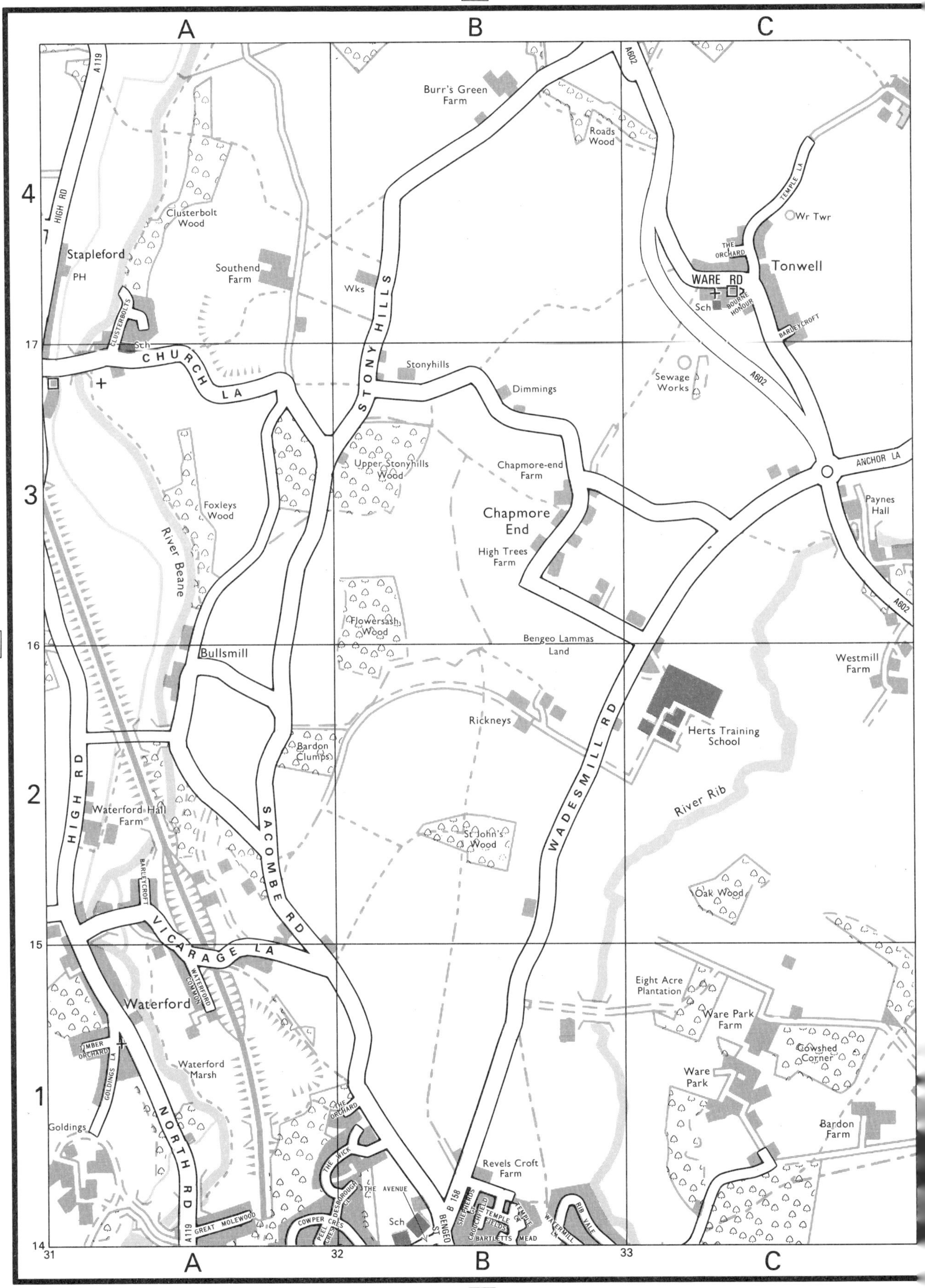
A
B
C
Burr's Green Farm
Roads Wood
A602
A119
HIGH RD
4
Clusterbolt Wood
Stapleford
PH
Southend Farm
Wks
STONY HILLS
TEMPLE LA
Wr Twr
THE ORCHARD
Tonwell
WARE RD
Sch
BOURNE HONOUR
BARLEYCROFT
CLUSTERBOLTS
Sch
17
CHURCH LA
Stonyhills
Dimmings
Sewage Works
A602
Upper Stonyhills Wood
Chapmore-end Farm
ANCHOR LA
3
Foxleys Wood
Chapmore End
Paynes Hall
High Trees Farm
River Beane
Flowersash Wood
16
Bullsmill
Bengeo Lammas Land
Westmill Farm
Rickneys
Herts Training School
WADESMILL RD
HIGH RD
Bardon Clumps
2
Waterford Hall Farm
SACOMBE RD
St John's Wood
River Rib
BARLEYCROFT
Oak Wood
15
VICARAGE LA
WATERFORD COMMON
Waterford
Eight Acre Plantation
Ware Park Farm
TIMBER ORCHARD
Waterford Marsh
Cowshed Corner
GOLDINGS LA
Ware Park
1
NORTH RD
THE ORCHARD
Bardon Farm
Goldings
THE WICK
DESBOROUGH CL
THE AVENUE
Revels Croft Farm
B 158
SHEPHERDS CT
CROUCHFIELD
TEMPLE FIELDS
TEMPLE CL
WATERMILL LN
RIB VALE
COWPER CRES
PEEL CRES
Sch
BENGEO ST
BARTLETTS MEAD
GREAT MOLEWOOD
A119
14
31
32
33
A
B
C

91

113

72

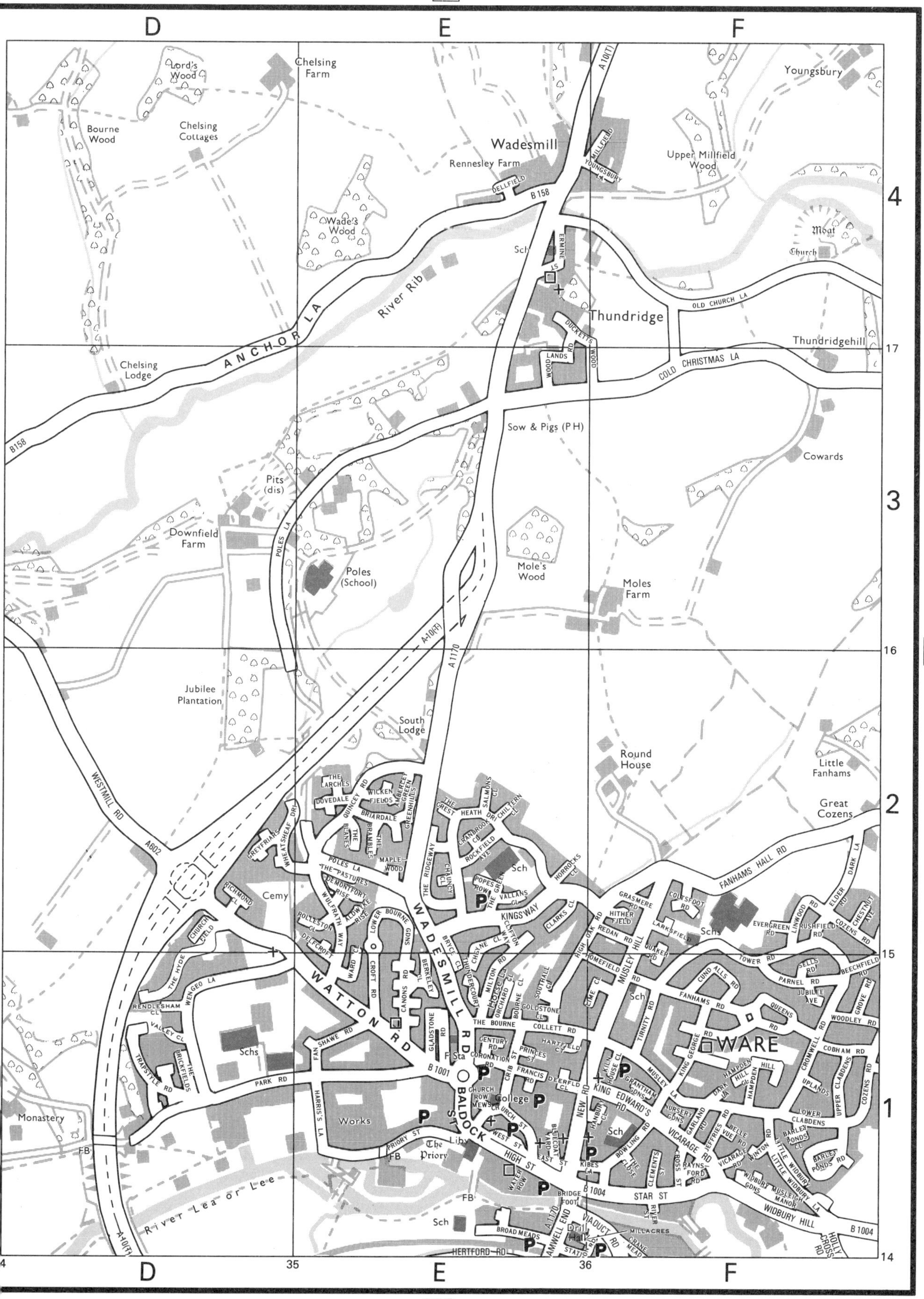

D
E
F
4
3
2
1
17
16
15
14
35
36
Chelsing Farm
Lord's Wood
Bourne Wood
Chelsing Cottages
Wadesmill
Rennesley Farm
DELLFIELD
B 158
A 10(T)
MILLFIELD
YOUNGSBURY LA
Youngsbury
Upper Millfield Wood
Wade's Wood
Moat
Church
ERMINE ST
Sch
River Rib
ANCHOR LA
Thundridge
OLD CHURCH LA
DUCKETTS WOOD
WOOD LANDS
Thundridgehill
COLD CHRISTMAS LA
Chelsing Lodge
B158
Sow & Pigs (PH)
Cowards
Pits (dis)
Downfield Farm
POLES LA
Poles (School)
Mole's Wood
Moles Farm
A 10(T)
A 1170
Jubilee Plantation
South Lodge
Round House
Little Fanhams
Great Cozens
WESTMILL RD
A602
FANHAMS HALL RD
DARK LA
Cemy
Sch
Schs
WADESMILL RD
WATTON RD
KINGS WAY
HIGH OAK RD
MUSLEY HILL
WARE
F Sta
B 1001
BALDOCK ST
College
Works
PARK RD
Monastery
FB
The Priory
Liby
HIGH ST
B 1004
STAR ST
WIDBURY HILL
River Lea or Lee
HERTFORD RD
BROAD MEADS
AMWELL END
VIADUCT RD
Drill Hall
HOLLY CROSS RD
A10(T)

94

114

73
93

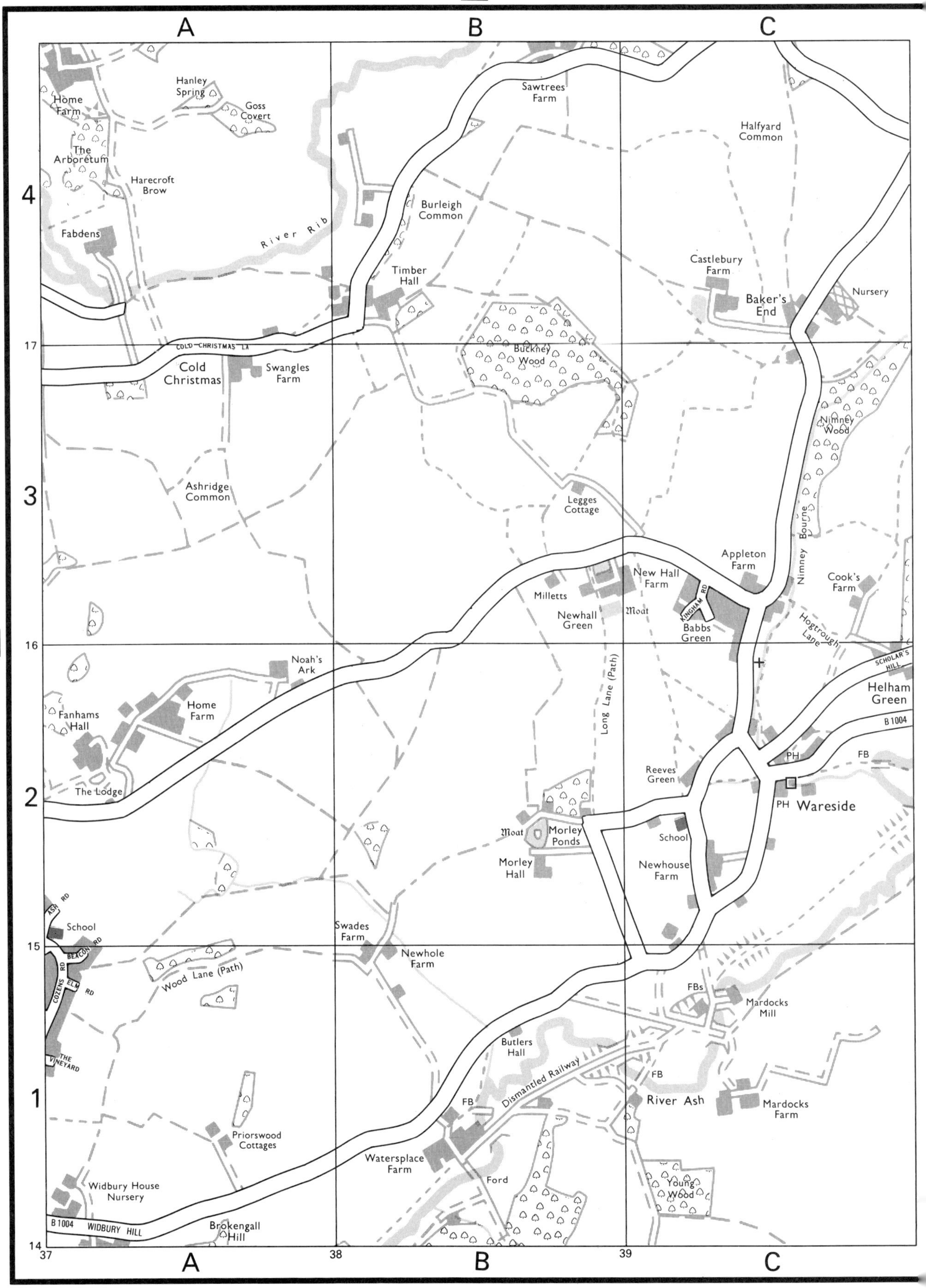
A
B
C
4
3
2
1
17
16
15
14
37
38
39
Home Farm
Hanley Spring
Goss Covert
The Arboretum
Harecroft Brow
Fabdens
River Rib
Sawtrees Farm
Halfyard Common
Burleigh Common
Timber Hall
Castlebury Farm
Baker's End
Nursery
COLD CHRISTMAS LA
Cold Christmas
Swangles Farm
Buckney Wood
Nimney Wood
Ashridge Common
Legges Cottage
Nimney Bourne
Appleton Farm
Cook's Farm
New Hall Farm
Milletts
KINGHAM RD
Newhall Green
Moat
Babbs Green
Hogtrough Lane
SCHOLAR'S HILL
Helham Green
B 1004
Noah's Ark
Home Farm
Fanhams Hall
Long Lane (Path)
PH
FB
Reeves Green
The Lodge
Wareside
Moat
Morley Ponds
School
Morley Hall
Newhouse Farm
ASH RD
School
Swades Farm
BEACON RD
Newhole Farm
COZENS RD
ELM RD
Wood Lane (Path)
FBs
Mardocks Mill
THE VINEYARD
Butlers Hall
Dismantled Railway
FB
River Ash
Mardocks Farm
Priorswood Cottages
Watersplace Farm
Ford
Young Wood
Widbury House Nursery
B 1004
WIDBURY HILL
Brokengall Hill

115

74

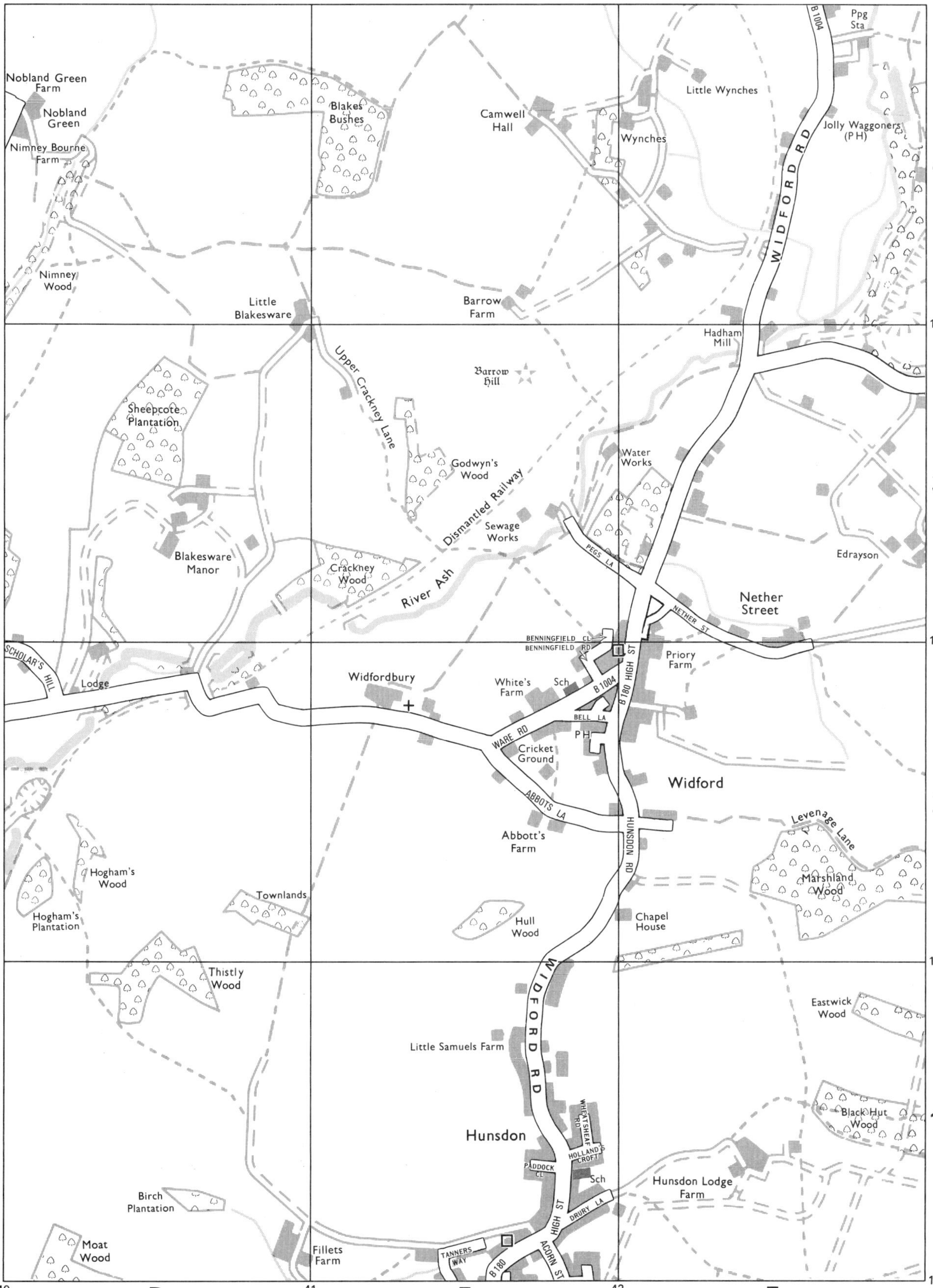
D
E
F
Nobland Green Farm
Nobland Green
Nimney Bourne Farm
Nimney Wood
Blakes Bushes
Camwell Hall
Little Wynches
Ppg Sta
B 1004
Wynches
Jolly Waggoners (PH)
WIDFORD RD
4
Little Blakesware
Barrow Farm
17
Hadham Mill
Upper Crackney Lane
Barrow Hill
Sheepcote Plantation
Godwyn's Wood
Water Works
Dismantled Railway
3
Sewage Works
Blakesware Manor
Crackney Wood
PEGS LA
Edrayson
River Ash
Nether Street
NETHER ST
BENNINGFIELD CL
BENNINGFIELD RD
16
SCHOLAR'S HILL
Lodge
Widfordbury
White's Farm
Sch
B 1004
B 180 HIGH ST
Priory Farm
WARE RD
BELL LA
PH
Cricket Ground
Widford
ABBOTS LA
HUNSDON RD
2
Abbott's Farm
Levenage Lane
Hogham's Wood
Marshland Wood
Townlands
Hogham's Plantation
Hull Wood
Chapel House
Thistly Wood
15
WIDFORD RD
Eastwick Wood
Little Samuels Farm
WHEATSHEAF RD
1
Black Hut Wood
Hunsdon
HOLLAND CROFT
PADDOCK CL
Sch
Hunsdon Lodge Farm
Birch Plantation
HIGH ST
DRURY LA
Moat Wood
Fillets Farm
TANNERS WAY
ACORN ST
B 180
14
40
41
42
D
E
F

96

116

75

95

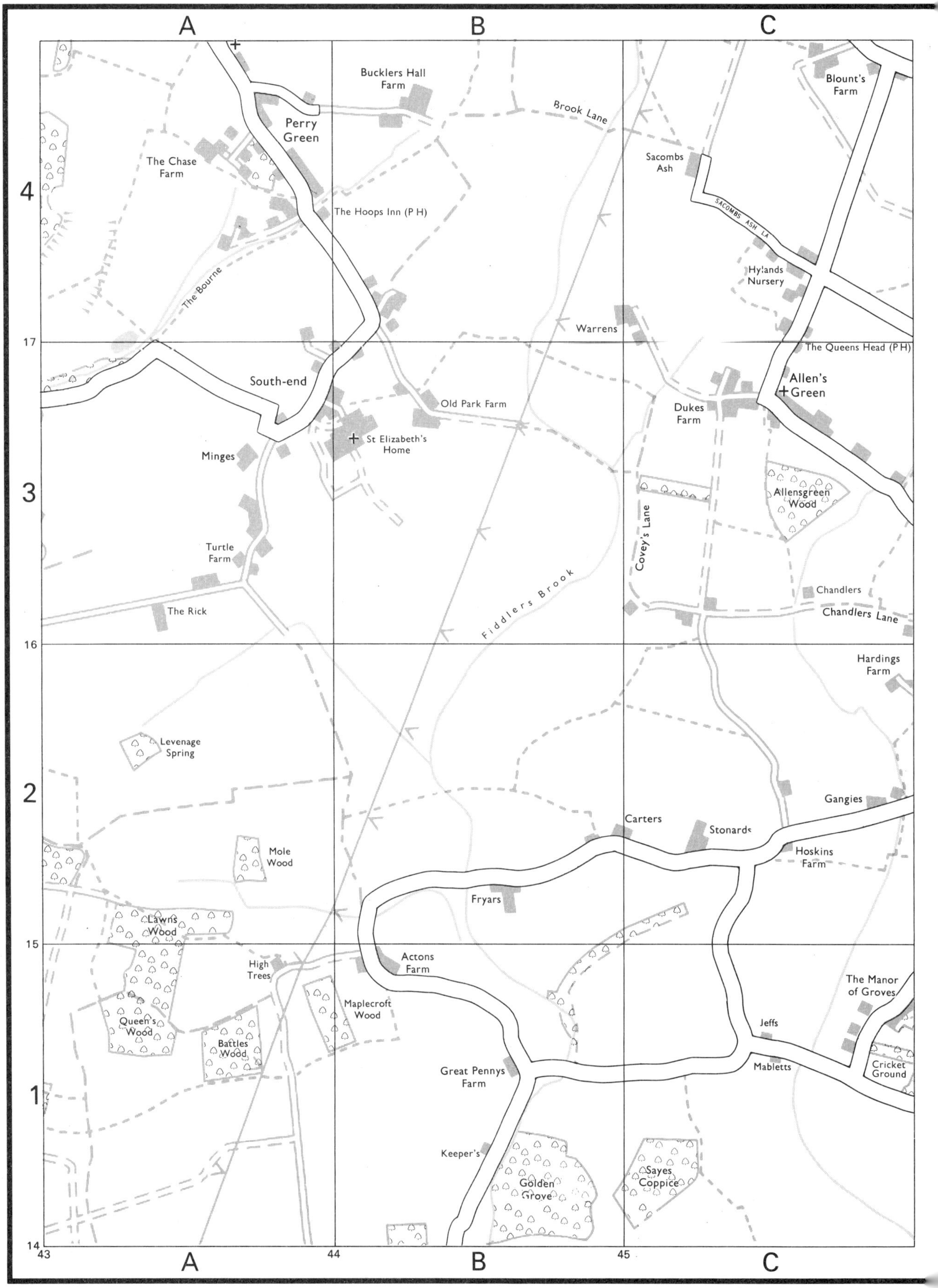

A
B
C
4
3
2
1
17
16
15
14
43
44
45
Bucklers Hall Farm
Brook Lane
Blount's Farm
Perry Green
The Chase Farm
Sacombs Ash
SACOMBS ASH LA
The Hoops Inn (P H)
Hylands Nursery
The Bourne
Warrens
The Queens Head (P H)
South-end
Allen's Green
Old Park Farm
Dukes Farm
St Elizabeth's Home
Minges
Allensgreen Wood
Covey's Lane
Turtle Farm
Fiddlers Brook
Chandlers
The Rick
Chandlers Lane
Hardings Farm
Levenage Spring
Gangies
Carters
Stonards
Mole Wood
Hoskins Farm
Fryars
Lawns Wood
High Trees
Actons Farm
The Manor of Groves
Maplecroft Wood
Queen's Wood
Jeffs
Battles Wood
Great Pennys Farm
Mabletts
Cricket Ground
Keeper's
Sayes Coppice
Golden Grove

117

76

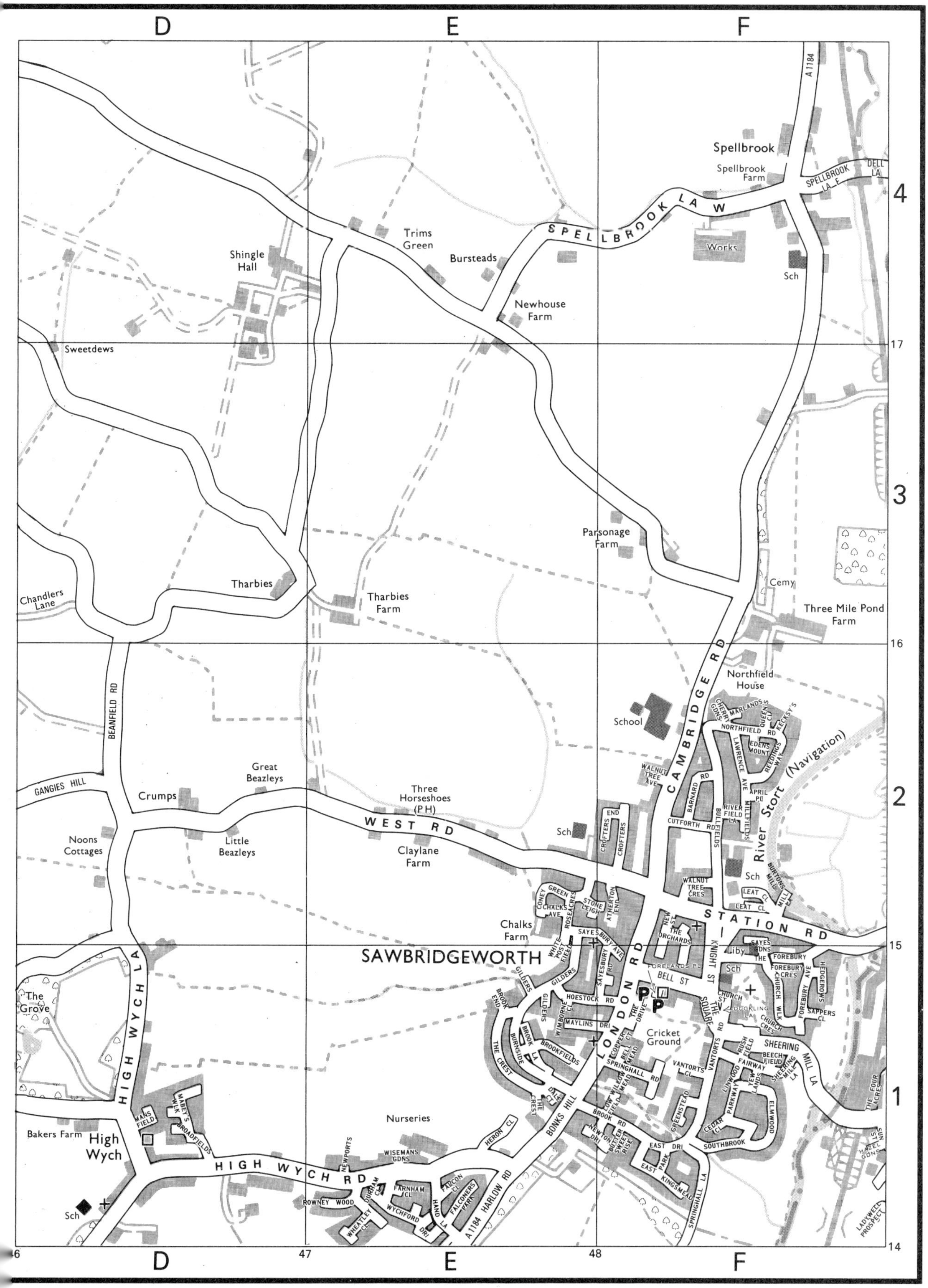
D
E
F
4
3
2
1
17
16
15
14
46
47
48
Spellbrook
Spellbrook Farm
SPELLBROOK LA E
DELL LA
A1184
SPELLBROOK LA W
Works
Sch
Trims Green
Bursteads
Newhouse Farm
Shingle Hall
Sweetdews
Parsonage Farm
Cemy
Three Mile Pond Farm
Tharbies
Tharbies Farm
Chandlers Lane
Northfield House
School
CAMBRIDGE RD
BEANFIELD RD
GANGIES HILL
Crumps
Great Beazleys
Three Horseshoes (PH)
WEST RD
Little Beazleys
Noons Cottages
Claylane Farm
River Stort (Navigation)
STATION RD
Chalks Farm
SAWBRIDGEWORTH
The Grove
HIGH WYCH LA
Cricket Ground
SHEERING MILL LA
Nurseries
Bakers Farm
High Wych
HIGH WYCH RD
A1184 HARLOW RD
BONKS HILL
LONDON RD
KNIGHT ST
BELL ST
Liby
Sch
SPRINGHALL LA
THE FOUR ACRES
LADYWELL PROSPECT

96

118

77

97

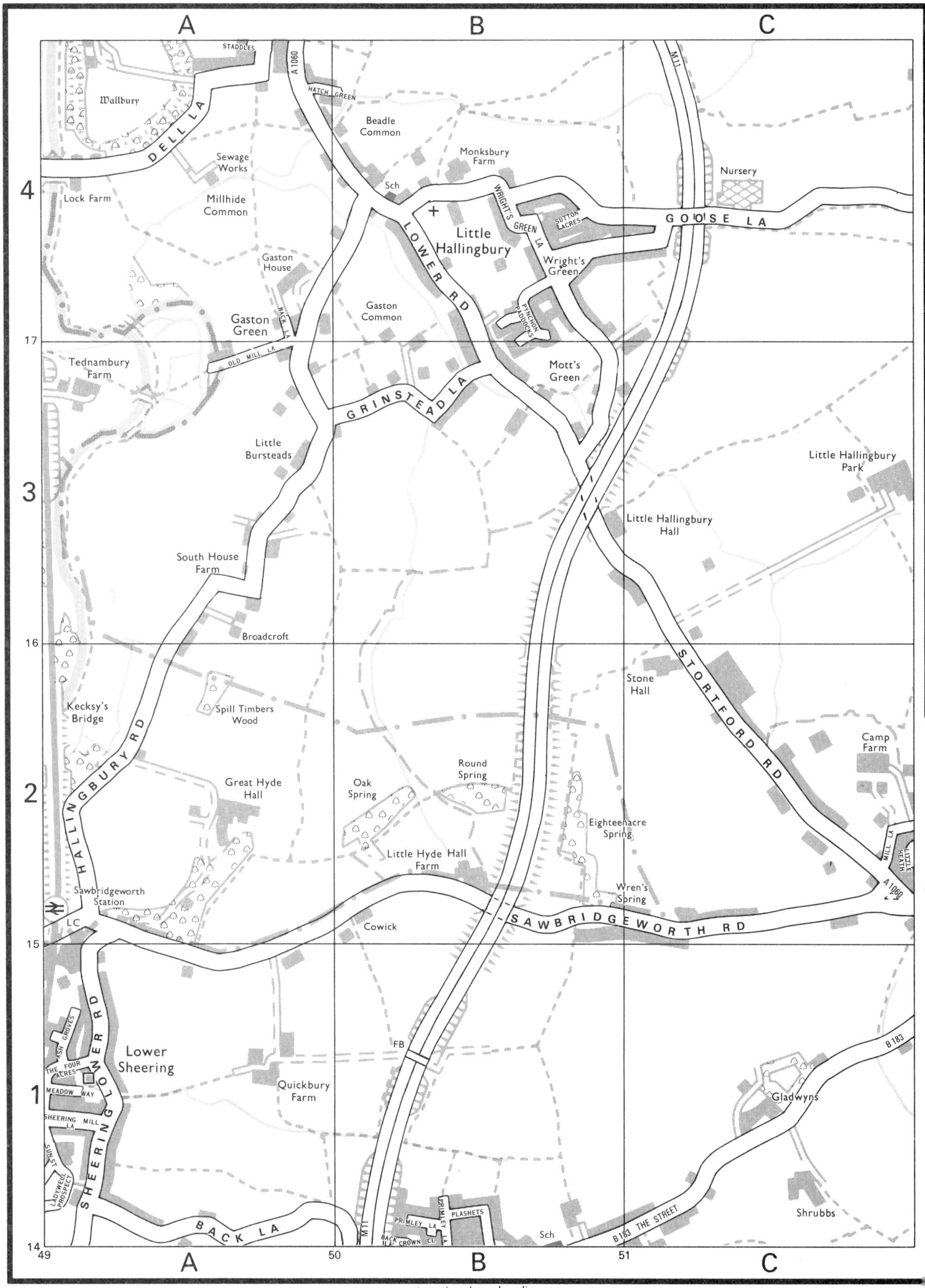
A
B
C
4
3
2
1
17
16
15
14
49
50
51
STADDLES
A 1060
HATCH GREEN
Wallbury
DELL LA
Beadle Common
Sewage Works
Monksbury Farm
Nursery
Lock Farm
Millhide Common
Sch
WRIGHT'S GREEN LA
SUTTON ACRES
GOOSE LA
Little Hallingbury
LOWER RD
Wright's Green
Gaston House
M11
Gaston Common
PYNCHON PADDOCKS
Gaston Green
BACK LA
OLD MILL LA
Tednambury Farm
Mott's Green
GRINSTEAD LA
Little Bursteads
Little Hallingbury Park
Little Hallingbury Hall
South House Farm
Broadcroft
STORTFORD RD
Stone Hall
Kecksy's Bridge
Spill Timbers Wood
Camp Farm
Round Spring
HALLINGBURY RD
Great Hyde Hall
Oak Spring
Eighteenacre Spring
MILL LA
LITTLE HEATH
Little Hyde Hall Farm
Sawbridgeworth Station
Wren's Spring
A 1060
LC
Cowick
SAWBRIDGEWORTH RD
LOWER RD
ASH GROVES
Lower Sheering
FB
B 183
THE FOUR ACRES
MEADOW WAY
Quickbury Farm
Gladwyns
SHEERING MILL LA
SHEERING LOWER RD
SUNSET
LADYWELL PROSPECT
PLASHETS
PRIMLEY LA
PRIMLEY LA
BACK LA
CROWN CL
Shrubbs
Sch
B 183 THE STREET
BACK LA

79

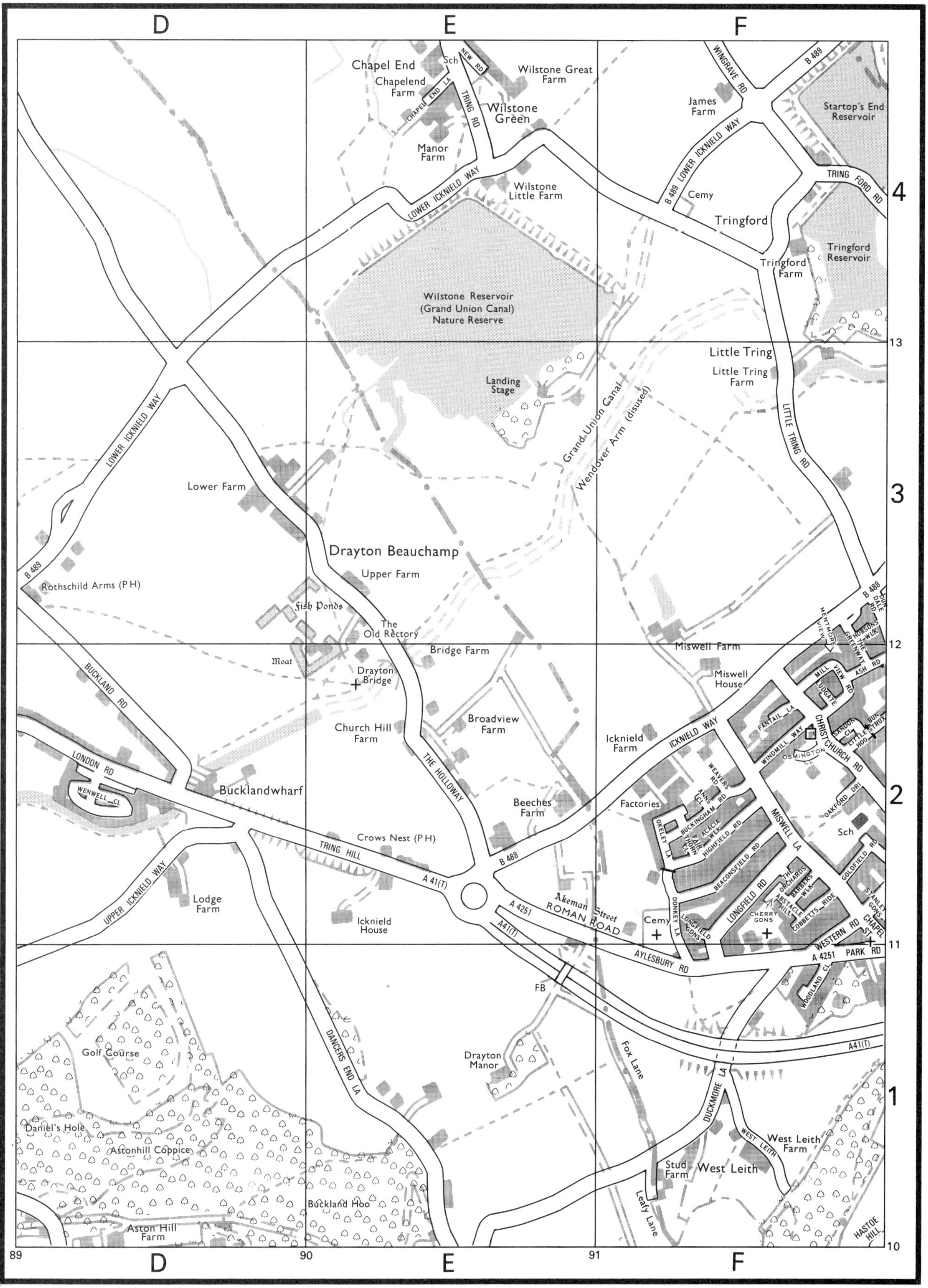
D
E
F
Chapel End
Chapelend Farm
Sch
NEW RD
CHAPEL END LA
TRING RD
Wilstone Great Farm
Wilstone Green
Manor Farm
WINGRAVE RD
B 489
James Farm
Startop's End Reservoir
LOWER ICKNIELD WAY
TRING FORD RD
Wilstone Little Farm
Cemy
Tringford
Tringford Farm
Tringford Reservoir
Wilstone Reservoir (Grand Union Canal) Nature Reserve
Little Tring
Little Tring Farm
Landing Stage
Grand Union Canal Wendover Arm (disused)
LITTLE TRING RD
Lower Farm
Drayton Beauchamp
Upper Farm
Rothschild Arms (PH)
Fish Ponds
The Old Rectory
Bridge Farm
Miswell Farm
Miswell House
Moat
Drayton Bridge
BUCKLAND RD
Broadview Farm
Church Hill Farm
Icknield Farm
ICKNIELD WAY
THE HOLLOWAY
LONDON RD
WENWELL CL
Bucklandwharf
Beeches Farm
Factories
Crows Nest (PH)
TRING HILL
A 41(T)
B 488
Lodge Farm
UPPER ICKNIELD WAY
Icknield House
A 4251
Akeman Street
ROMAN ROAD
Cemy
AYLESBURY RD
FB
Golf Course
DANCERS END LA
Drayton Manor
Fox Lane
DUCKMORE LA
Daniel's Hole
Astonhill Coppice
West Leith Farm
WEST LEITH
Stud Farm
West Leith
Leafy Lane
Buckland Hoo
Aston Hill Farm
HASTOE HILL
MENTMORE VIEW
THE GREENWAY
HOBSONS WLK
DUNSDALE RD
ASH RD
MILL VIEW RD
LUDGATE
FANTAIL LA
CHRISTCHURCH RD
WINDMILL WAY
OSMINGTON CL
SANDON CL
LITTLE HOO
BUNSTRUX
WEAVERS RD
ANNE CL
BUCKINGHAM RD
FAIRTHORN CL
ACACIA WLK
HIGHFIELD RD
OKELEY LA
MISWELL LA
OAKFORD DRI
Sch
GOLDFIELD RD
BEACONSFIELD RD
LONGFIELD RD
THE ORCHARDS
BARBERS WLK
ABSTACLE HILL
CHERRY GDNS
COBBETTS RIDE
STANLEY GDNS
CHAPEL ST
DONKEY LA
LONGFIELD GDNS
WESTERN RD
PARK RD
WOODLAND CL
1
2
3
4
10
11
12
13
89
90
91

100

119

80

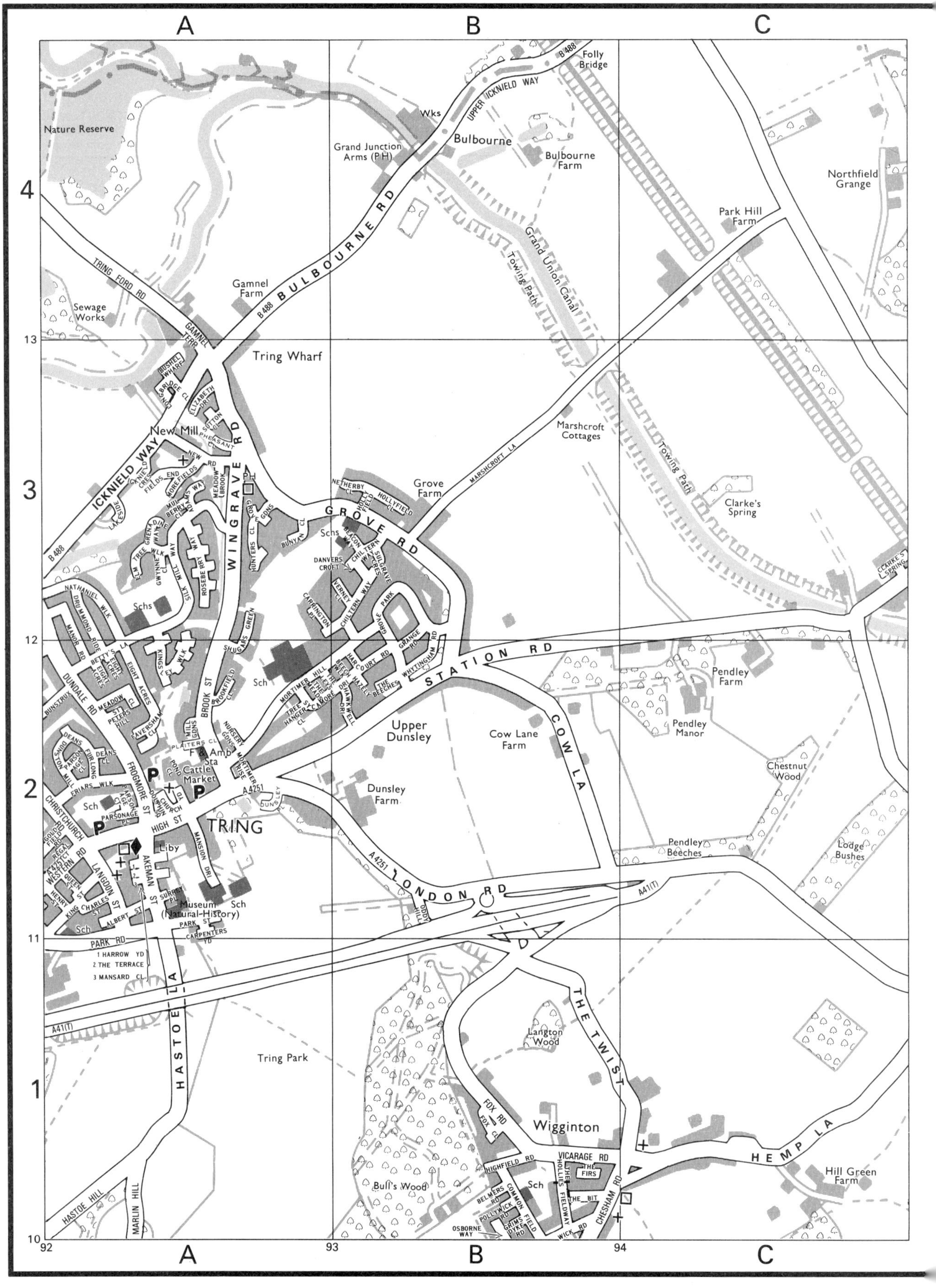
A
B
C
4
3
2
1
13
12
11
10
92
93
94
Nature Reserve
Grand Junction Arms (P.H)
Wks
Bulbourne
Bulbourne Farm
Folly Bridge
B 488
UPPER ICKNIELD WAY
Northfield Grange
Park Hill Farm
Grand Union Canal
Towing Path
BULBOURNE RD
Gamnel Farm
TRING FORD RD
Sewage Works
GAMNEL TERR
Tring Wharf
BUSHEL WHARF
ELIZABETH DRI
SUTTON
PHEASANT
New Mill
ICKNIELD WAY
WINGRAVE RD
Marshcroft Cottages
MARSHCROFT LA
Grove Farm
Clarke's Spring
CLARKE'S SPRING
GROVE RD
NETHERBY CL
HOLLYFIELD
HUNTERS CL
GROVE GDNS
BUNYAN CL
Schs
BEACON WAY
CHILTERN WAY
DANVERS CROFT
SULGRAVE CRES
VERNEY CL
CARRINGTON PL
GROVE PARK
LAKESIDE
MORE FIELDS
MEADOW BROOK
MULBERRY WAY
GRENADINE WAY
ELM TREE WLK
GWYNNE CL
SILK MILL WAY
ROSEBERY WAY
NATHANIEL WLK
DRUMMOND RIDE
MANOR RD
Schs
SHUGARS GREEN
BETTY'S LA
EIGHT ACRES
KINGSLEY WLK
DUNDALE RD
MEADOW CL
ST PETERS HILL
FAVERSHAM CL
BROOK ST
BROOKFIELD CL
Sch
MORTIMER HILL
TREE HANGER CL
HAWKWELL DRI
HAZELY
THE BEECHES
HARCOURT RD
GRANGE RD
WHYTINGHAM RD
STATION RD
Pendley Farm
Pendley Manor
Upper Dunsley
Cow Lane Farm
COW LA
Chestnut Wood
BUNSTRUX
DEANS FURLONG
DEANS CL
PLAITERS CL
F & Amb Sta
Cattle Market
NURSERY GDNS
MORTIMER RISE
A 4251
DUNSLEY PL
Dunsley Farm
Pendley Beeches
Lodge Bushes
FROGMORE ST
FRIARS WLK
CHRISTCHURCH RD
PARSONAGE PL
Sch
CHURCH YD
HIGH ST
TRING
MANSION DRI
Liby
AKEMAN ST
LANGDON ST
WESTERN RD
QUEEN ST
HENRY ST
KING ST
CHARLES ST
ALBERT ST
SURREY PL
Museum (Natural History)
Sch
PARK ST
CARPENTERS YD
LONDON RD
DUNDALE HILL
A41(T)
PARK RD
1 HARROW YD
2 THE TERRACE
3 MANSARD CL
HASTOE LA
Tring Park
Langton Wood
THE TWIST
FOX RD
FOX CL
Wigginton
VICARAGE RD
HIGHFIELD RD
THE FIRS
Sch
HOLLIES
FIELDWAY
THE BIT
CHESHAM RD
BELMERS RD
POLLYWICK RD
COMMON FIELD
GRIMS DYKE RD
OSBORNE WAY
WICK RD
Bull's Wood
HEMP LA
Hill Green Farm
HASTOE HILL
MARLIN HILL

99

120

not continued, see key diagram

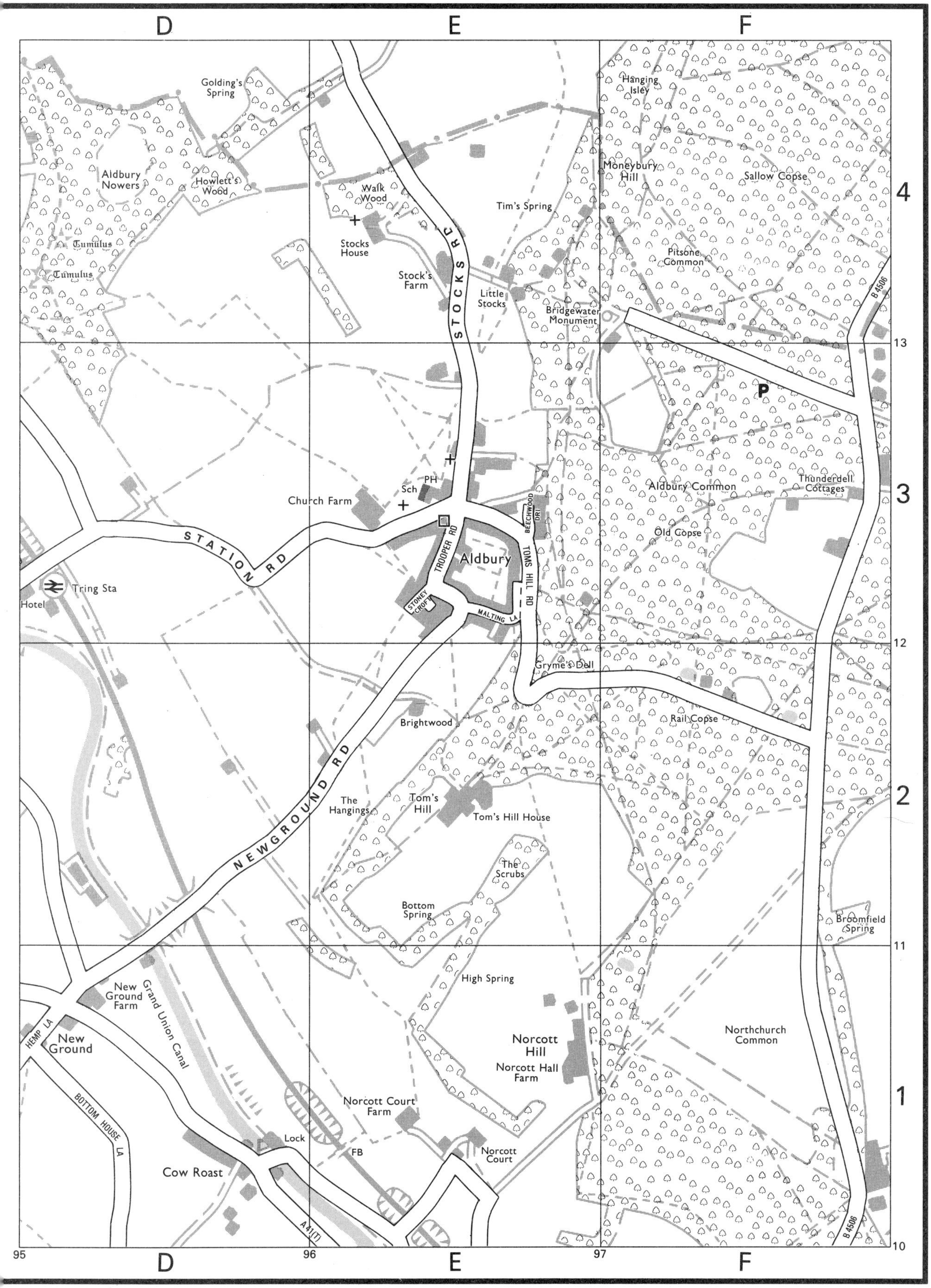

102

121

81

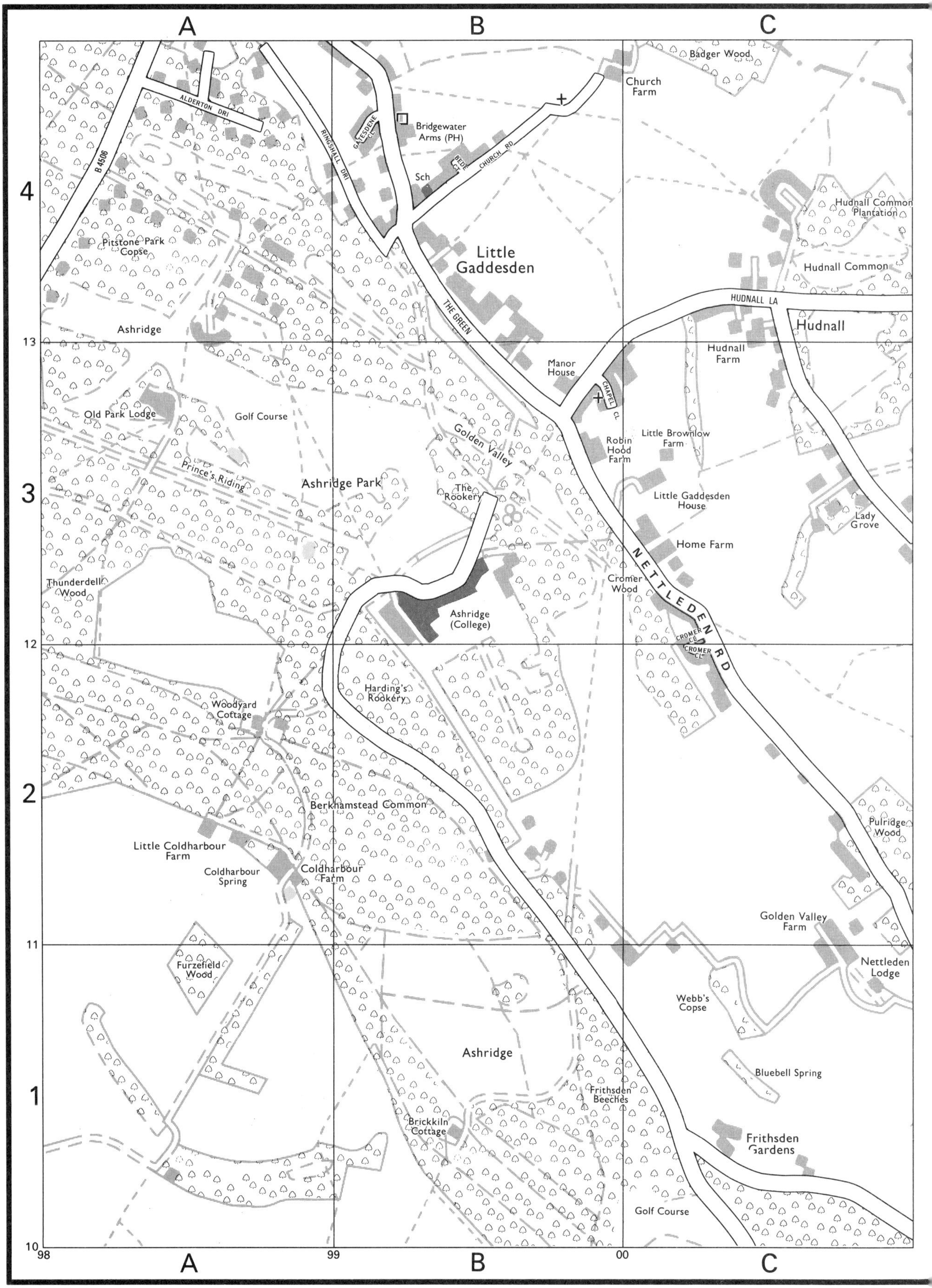

A
B
C
4
3
2
1
13
12
11
10
98
99
00
B 4506
ALDERTON DRI
RINGSHALL DRI
GATESDENE CL
Bridgewater Arms (PH)
Sch
BEDE CL
CHURCH RD
Church Farm
Badger Wood
Hudnall Common Plantation
Hudnall Common
HUDNALL LA
Hudnall
Hudnall Farm
Pitstone Park Copse
Little Gaddesden
THE GREEN
Ashridge
Manor House
CHAPEL CL
Old Park Lodge
Golf Course
Golden Valley
Robin Hood Farm
Little Brownlow Farm
Prince's Riding
Ashridge Park
The Rookery
Little Gaddesden House
Lady Grove
Home Farm
NETTLEDEN RD
Thunderdell Wood
Cromer Wood
Ashridge (College)
CROMER CL
CROMER CL
Harding's Rookery
Woodyard Cottage
Berkhamstead Common
Pulridge Wood
Little Coldharbour Farm
Coldharbour Spring
Coldharbour Farm
Golden Valley Farm
Furzefield Wood
Nettleden Lodge
Webb's Copse
Ashridge
Bluebell Spring
Frithsden Beeches
Brickkiln Cottage
Frithsden Gardens
Golf Course

101

122

82

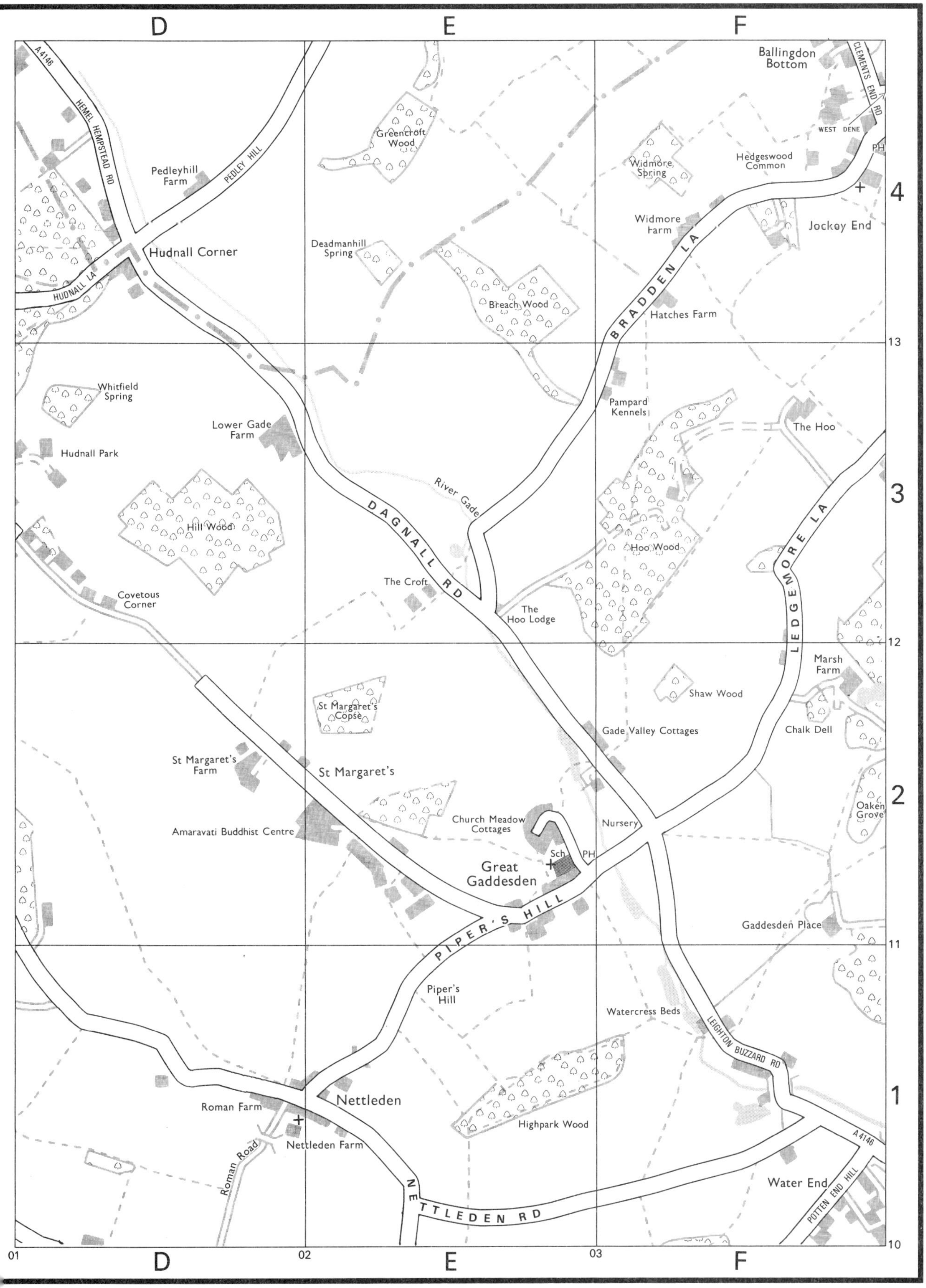
D
E
F
Ballingdon Bottom
CLEMENTS END RD
WEST DENE
PH
A4146
HEMEL HEMPSTEAD RD
PEDLEY HILL
Pedleyhill Farm
Greencroft Wood
Widmore Spring
Hedgeswood Common
4
Widmore Farm
Jockey End
Hudnall Corner
Deadmanhill Spring
HUDNALL LA
BRADDEN LA
Breach Wood
Hatches Farm
13
Whitfield Spring
Pampard Kennels
Lower Gade Farm
The Hoo
Hudnall Park
River Gade
3
DAGNALL RD
LEDGEMORE LA
Hill Wood
Hoo Wood
The Croft
Covetous Corner
The Hoo Lodge
12
Marsh Farm
Shaw Wood
St Margaret's Copse
Gade Valley Cottages
Chalk Dell
St Margaret's Farm
St Margaret's
2
Oaken Grove
Church Meadow Cottages
Nursery
Amaravati Buddhist Centre
Sch
PH
Great Gaddesden
PIPER'S HILL
Gaddesden Place
11
Piper's Hill
Watercress Beds
LEIGHTON BUZZARD RD
1
Roman Farm
Nettleden
Highpark Wood
A4146
Nettleden Farm
Roman Road
Water End
POTTEN END HILL
NETTLEDEN RD
10
01
02
03
D
E
F

104

123

83

103

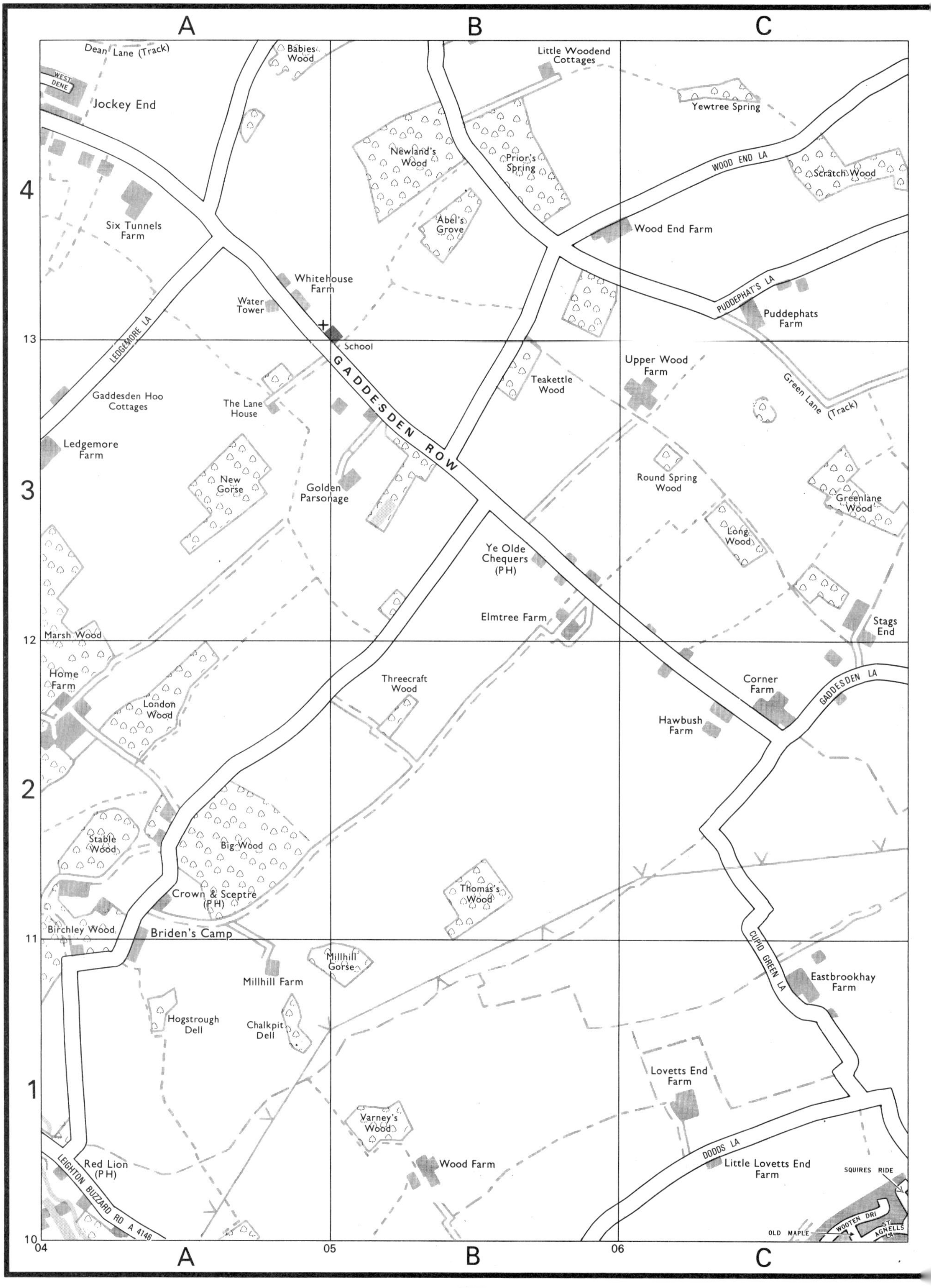
A
B
C
Dean Lane (Track)
WEST DENE
Jockey End
Babies Wood
Little Woodend Cottages
Yewtree Spring
Newland's Wood
Prior's Spring
WOOD END LA
Scratch Wood
4
Six Tunnels Farm
Abel's Grove
Wood End Farm
Whitehouse Farm
Water Tower
PUDDEPHAT'S LA
Puddephats Farm
LEDGEMORE LA
13
School
GADDESDEN ROW
Upper Wood Farm
Teakettle Wood
Green Lane (Track)
Gaddesden Hoo Cottages
The Lane House
Ledgemore Farm
Round Spring Wood
3
New Gorse
Golden Parsonage
Greenlane Wood
Long Wood
Ye Olde Chequers (PH)
Elmtree Farm
Stags End
Marsh Wood
12
Home Farm
Threecraft Wood
Corner Farm
GADDESDEN LA
London Wood
Hawbush Farm
2
Stable Wood
Big Wood
Thomas's Wood
Crown & Sceptre (PH)
Birchley Wood
Briden's Camp
11
CUPID GREEN LA
Millhill Gorse
Millhill Farm
Eastbrookhay Farm
Hogstrough Dell
Chalkpit Dell
Lovetts End Farm
1
Varney's Wood
DODDS LA
Red Lion (PH)
Wood Farm
Little Lovetts End Farm
LEIGHTON BUZZARD RD A 4146
SQUIRES RIDE
OLD MAPLE
WOOTEN DRI
ST AGNELLS LA
10
04
05
06
A
B
C

124

84

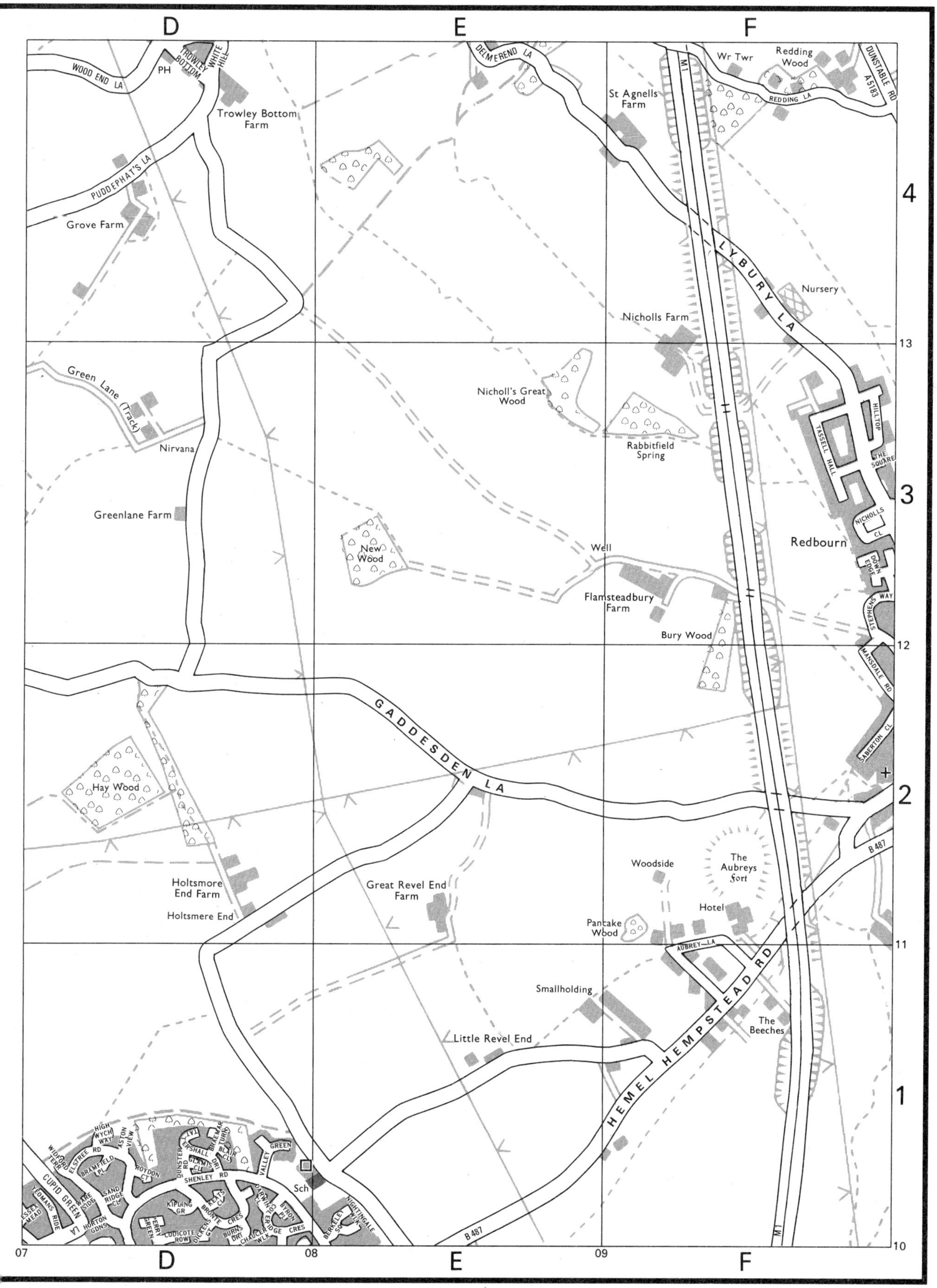

D
E
F
WOOD END LA
PH
TROWLEY BOTTOM
WHITE HILL
Trowley Bottom Farm
PUDDEPHAT'S LA
Grove Farm
DELMEREND LA
St Agnells Farm
M1
Wr Twr
Redding Wood
REDDING LA
DUNSTABLE RD
A5183
4
LYBURY LA
Nursery
Nicholls Farm
13
Green Lane (Track)
Nirvana
Nicholl's Great Wood
Rabbitfield Spring
TASSELL HALL
HILLTOP
THE SQUARE
3
NICHOLLS CL
Redbourn
Greenlane Farm
New Wood
Well
DOWN EDGE
WAY
Flamsteadbury Farm
ST STEPHENS
Bury Wood
12
MANSDALE RD
GADDESDEN LA
SABERTON CL
Hay Wood
2
B 487
Woodside
The Aubreys Fort
Holtsmore End Farm
Great Revel End Farm
Holtsmere End
Hotel
Pancake Wood
11
AUBREY LA
HEMEL HEMPSTEAD RD
Smallholding
The Beeches
Little Revel End
1
HIGH WYCH WAY
ASTON VIEW
ELSTREE RD
WIDFORD TERR
BRAMFIELD PL
ROYDON CT
DUNSTER RD
ERSHALL CL
BRAEMAR TURN
BLAIR CL
GLAMIS CL
GREEN
VALLEY
SHENLEY RD
Sch
CUPID GREEN LA
WARE SIDE
SAND RIDGE CL
KIPLING GR
BRONTE CL
KEATS CL
DARWIN CL
COLERIDGE
BYRON PL
NIGHTINGALE WLK
ESSEX MEAD
YEOMANS RIDE
HORTON GDNS
PERRY GREEN
CUDICOTE ROW
DICKENS CT
BURNS DRI
CRES
CHAUCER WLK
RIDGE CRES
BERKELEY SQ
B 487
M1
07
08
09
10

106

125

85

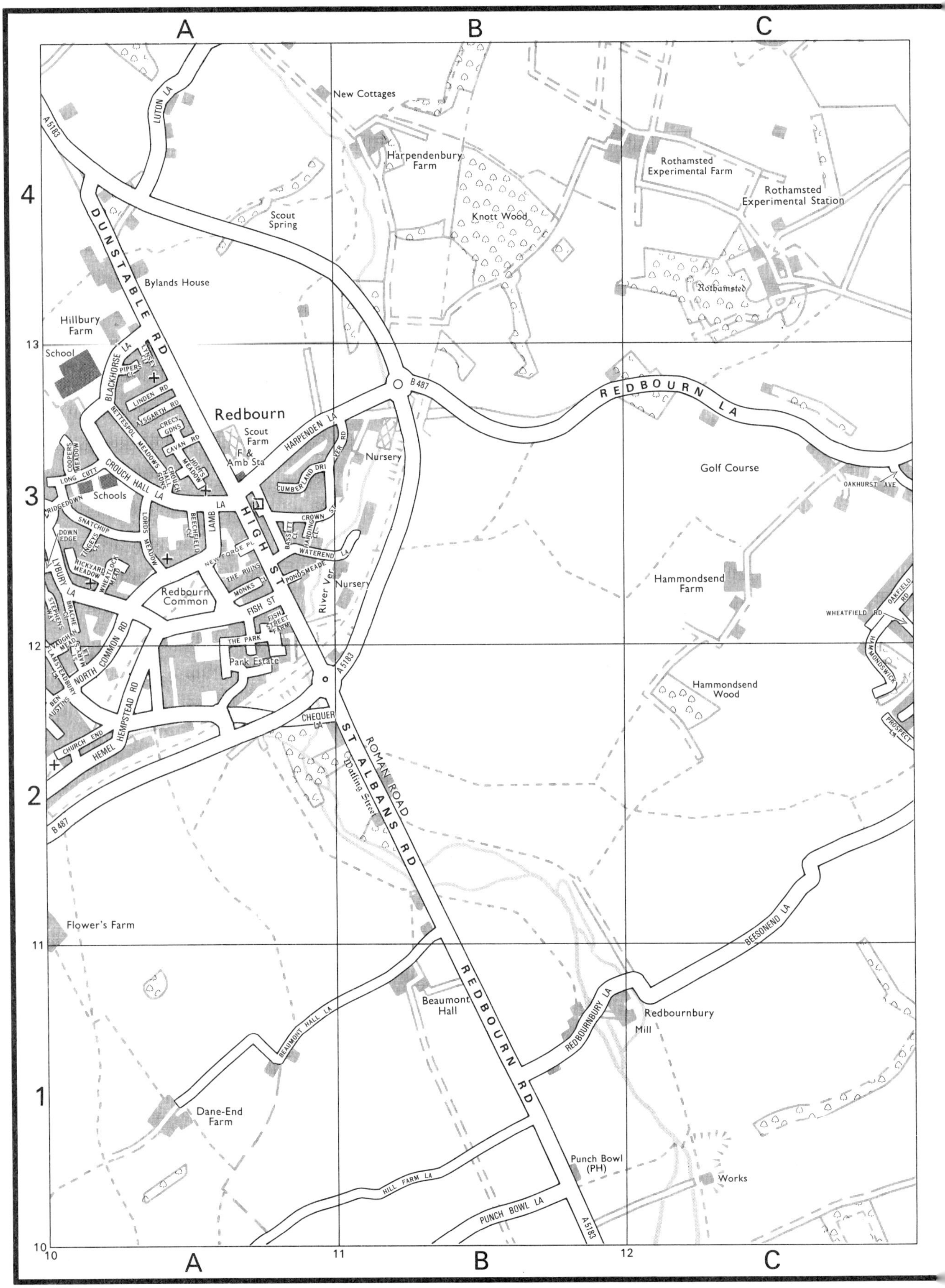
A
B
C
4
13
3
12
2
11
1
10
10
11
12
New Cottages
Harpendenbury Farm
Rothamsted Experimental Farm
Rothamsted Experimental Station
Knott Wood
Rothamsted
Scout Spring
Bylands House
Hillbury Farm
School
Redbourn
Scout Farm
F & Amb Sta
Nursery
Golf Course
OAKHURST AVE
Schools
Hammondsend Farm
Redbourn Common
Park Estate
WHEATFIELD RD
OAKFIELD RD
HAMMONDSWICK
Hammondsend Wood
PROSPECT
Flower's Farm
Beaumont Hall
Redbournbury Mill
Dane-End Farm
Punch Bowl (PH)
Works
LUTON LA
A5183
DUNSTABLE RD
B487
REDBOURN LA
HARPENDEN LA
BLACKHORSE LA
PIPERS CL
LINDEN RD
AYSGARTH RD
CRECY GDNS
CAVAN RD
BETTESPOL MEADOWS
CROUCH HALL GDNS
HOLTS MEADOW
COOPERS MEADOW
LONG CUTT
CROUCH HALL LA
RIDGEDOWN
SNATCHUP
DOWN EDGE
TINGEYS CL
LORDS MEADOW
BEECHFIELD CL
LAMB LA
HIGH ST
CUMBERLAND DRI
CROWN ST
BASSETT CL
HARDING CL
WATEREND LA
NEW FORGE PL
THE RUINS
PONDSMEADE
MONKS CL
FISH ST
FISH STREET FARM
River Ver
RICKYARD MEADOW
WHEATLOCK MEAD
LYBURY LA
BRACHE CL
STEPHENS WAY
VAUGHAN MEAD
LAMSTEADBURY
NORTH COMMON RD
THE PARK
BEN AUSTINS
CHURCH END
HEMEL HEMPSTEAD RD
CHEQUER LA
ST ALBANS RD
ROMAN ROAD
Watling Street
BEESONEND LA
REDBOURN RD
REDBOURNBURY LA
BEAUMONT HALL LA
HILL FARM LA
PUNCH BOWL LA

105

126

86

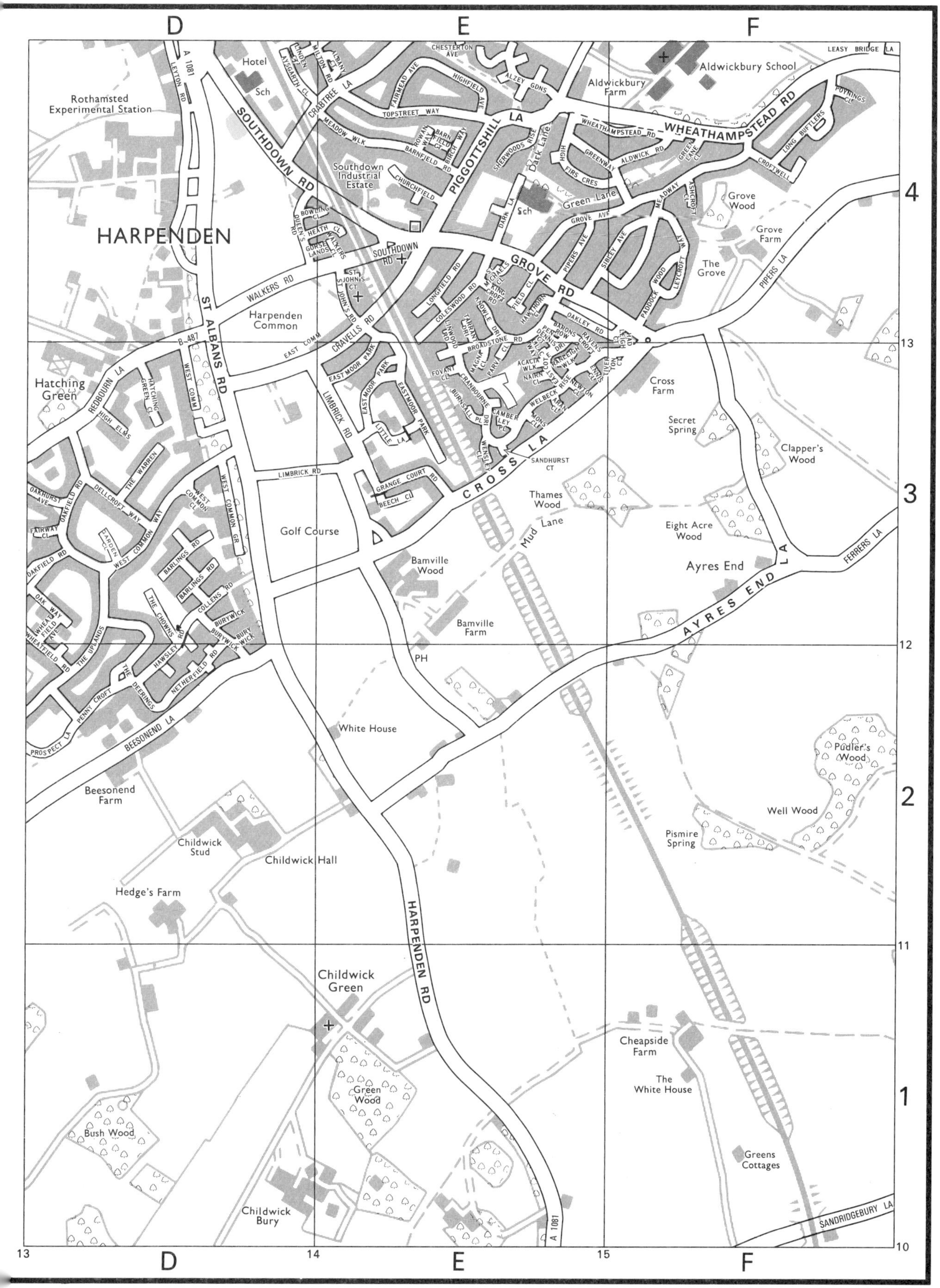

D
E
F
HARPENDEN
Rothamsted Experimental Station
Hotel
Sch
A 1081
LEYTON RD
SOUTHDOWN RD
CRABTREE LA
TOPSTREET WAY
MEADOW WLK
BARNFIELD RD
PIGGOTTSHILL LA
CHESTERTON AVE
HIGHFIELD AVE
ALZEY GDNS
FAIRMEAD AVE
Southdown Industrial Estate
CHURCHFIELD
Aldwickbury School
Aldwickbury Farm
LEASY BRIDGE LA
WHEATHAMPSTEAD RD
ALDWICK RD
GREENWAY
FIRS CRES
Green Lane
Dark Lane
SHERWOODS RISE
GREEN LANE CL
POYNINGS CL
LONG BUFTLERS
CROFTWELL
Grove Wood
Grove Farm
The Grove
MEADWAY
ASHCROFT
GROVE AVE
GROVE RD
PIPERS AVE
SIBLEY AVE
PADDOCK WOOD
LEYCROFT
PIPERS LA
WALKERS RD
SOUTHDOWN RD
ST JOHNS CT
ST JOHN'S RD
Harpenden Common
EAST COMM
CRAVELLS RD
LONGFIELD RD
COLESWOOD RD
KNOWLE DRI
OAKLEY RD
BROADSTONE RD
ST ALBANS RD
B 487
WEST COMM
Hatching Green
REDBOURN LA
HIGH ELMS
THE WARREN
EASTMOOR PARK
LIMBRICK RD
LITTLE LA
GRANGE COURT RD
BEECH CL
CROSS LA
SANDHURST CT
Cross Farm
Secret Spring
Clapper's Wood
Thames Wood
Mud Lane
Eight Acre Wood
Golf Course
Bamville Wood
Ayres End
AYRES END LA
FERRERS LA
Bamville Farm
PH
DELLCROFT WAY
WEST COMMON WAY
WEST COMMON GR
BARLINGS RD
COLLENS RD
BURYWICK
THE CHOWNS
HAWSLEY RD
NETHERFIELD RD
THE DEERINGS
THE UPLANDS
PENNY CROFT
PROSPECT LA
BEESONEND LA
White House
Beesonend Farm
Childwick Stud
Childwick Hall
Hedge's Farm
Pudler's Wood
Well Wood
Pismire Spring
HARPENDEN RD
Childwick Green
Cheapside Farm
The White House
Green Wood
Bush Wood
Greens Cottages
Childwick Bury
SANDRIDGEBURY LA
A 1081
4
3
2
1
13
12
11
10
14
15

108

127

87

107

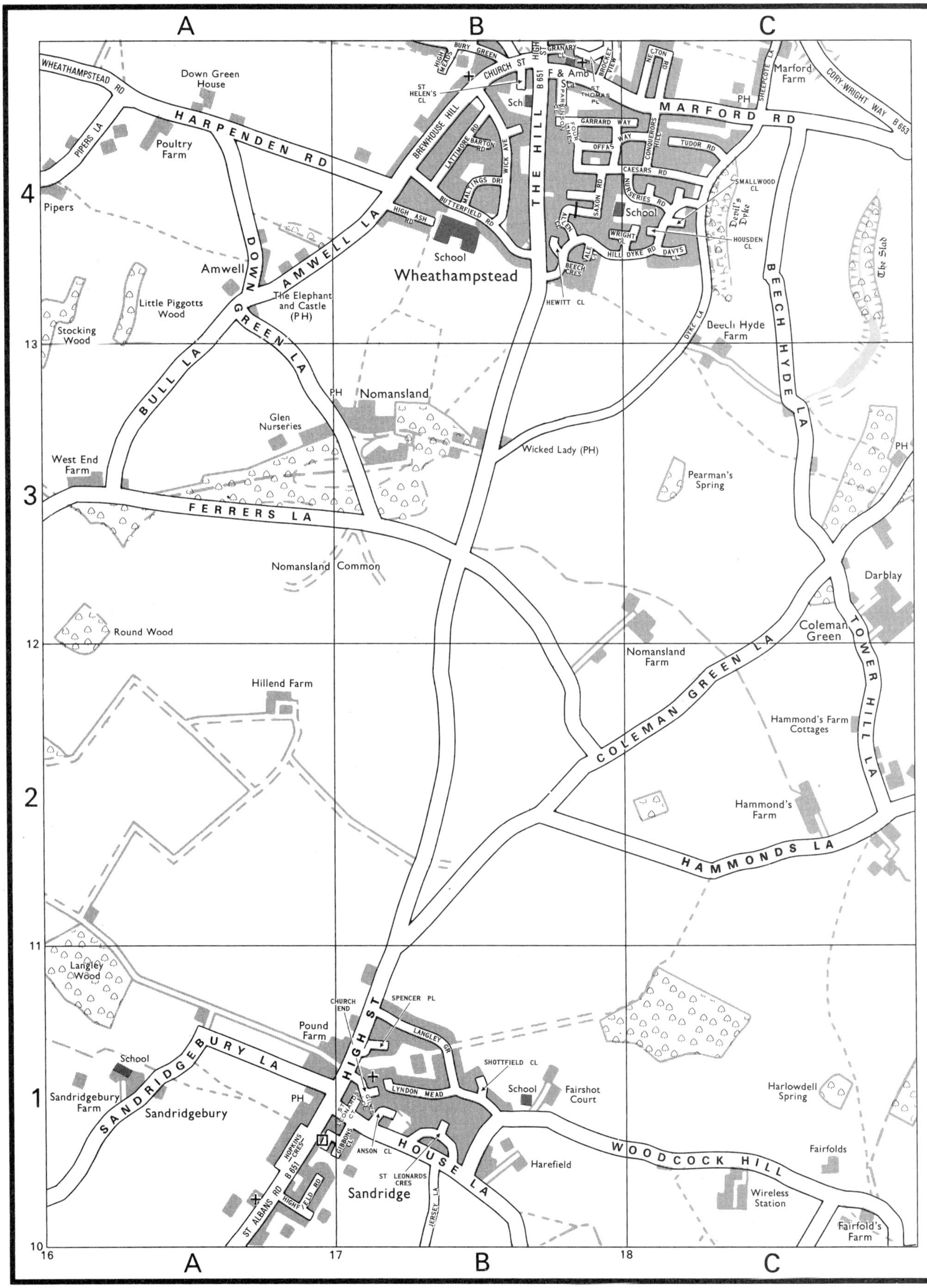

A
B
C
4
3
2
1
13
12
11
10
16
17
18
WHEATHAMPSTEAD RD
Down Green House
HARPENDEN RD
PIPERS LA
Poultry Farm
Pipers
HIGH MEADS
BURY GREEN
CHURCH ST
HIGH ST
GRANARY CL
BROCKET VIEW
NECTON RD
SHEEPCOTE LA
Marford Farm
CORY-WRIGHT WAY
B 653
ST HELEN'S CL
B 651
F & Amb Sta
ST THOMAS PL
Sch
PARKINSON CL
FOUR ACRES
GARRARD WAY
MARFORD RD
PH
BREWHOUSE HILL
LATTIMORE RD
BARTON RD
WICK AVE
OFFAS WAY
CONQUERORS HILL
TUDOR RD
CAESARS RD
MALTINGS DRI
THE HILL
SAXON RD
NURSERIES RD
SMALLWOOD CL
Devil's Dyke
BUTTERFIELD RD
HIGH ASH RD
School
ALLEN CL
WRIGHT CL
HOUSDEN CL
VALE CL
HILL DYKE RD
DAVYS CL
The Slad
BEECH CRES
School
Wheathampstead
HEWITT CL
DOWN GREEN LA
AMWELL LA
Amwell
Little Piggotts Wood
The Elephant and Castle (PH)
Stocking Wood
DYKE LA
Beech Hyde Farm
BEECH HYDE LA
BULL LA
PH
Nomansland
Glen Nurseries
Wicked Lady (PH)
PH
West End Farm
Pearman's Spring
FERRERS LA
Nomansland Common
Darblay
Round Wood
Coleman Green
Nomansland Farm
COLEMAN GREEN LA
TOWER HILL LA
Hillend Farm
Hammond's Farm Cottages
Hammond's Farm
HAMMONDS LA
Langley Wood
CHURCH END
SPENCER PL
LANGLEY GR
Pound Farm
SHOTTFIELD CL
School
SANDRIDGEBURY LA
HIGH ST
LYNDON MEAD
School
Fairshot Court
Harlowdell Spring
Sandridgebury Farm
PH
Sandridgebury
ST LEONARDS CT
GILES CL
GIBBONS CL
ANSON CL
HOUSE LA
WOODCOCK HILL
HOPKINS CRES
Harefield
Fairfolds
B 651
HIGHFIELD RD
ST LEONARDS CRES
Sandridge
JERSEY LA
Wireless Station
ST ALBANS RD
Fairfold's Farm

128

88

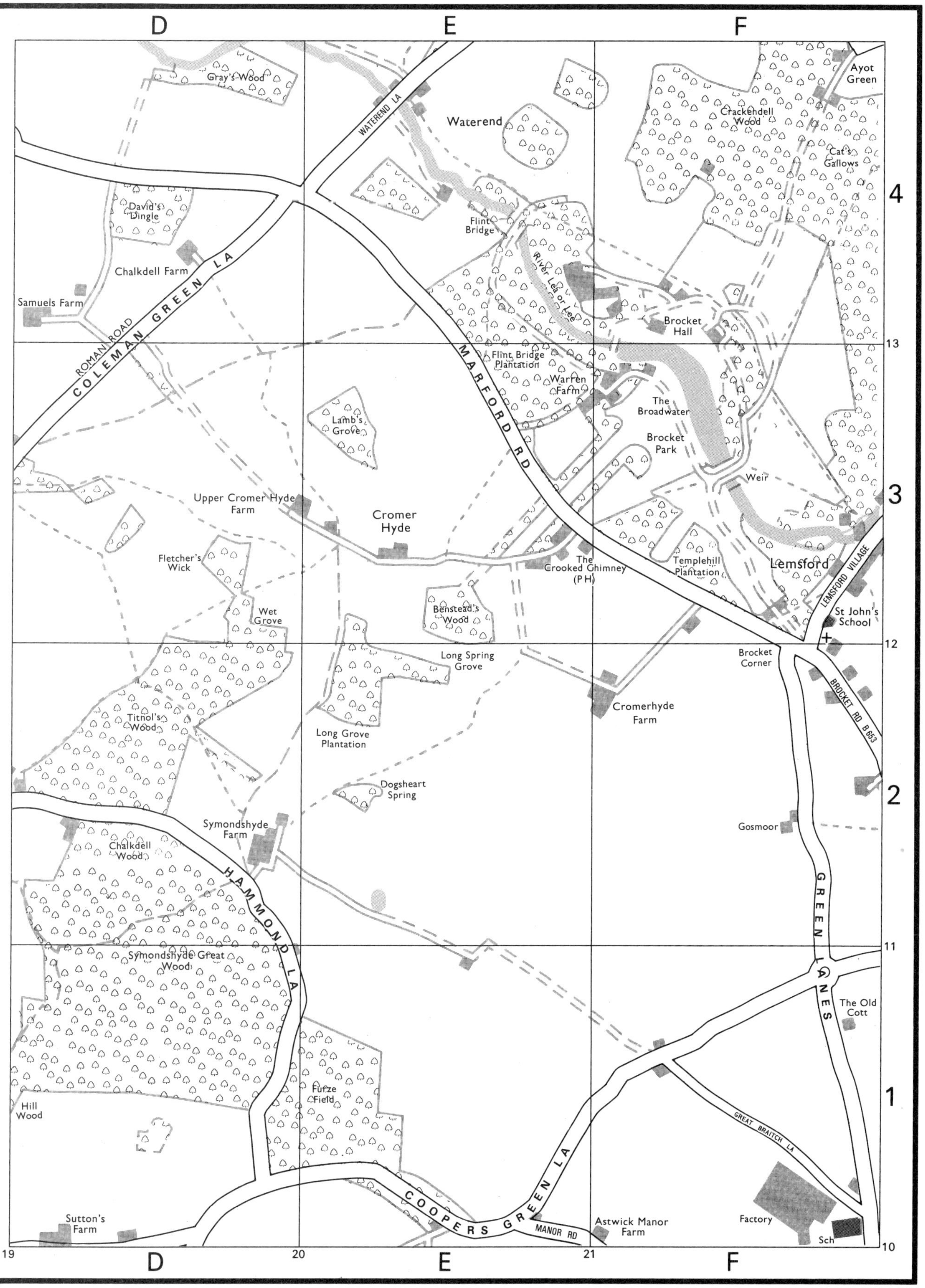
D
E
F
Gray's Wood
Waterend
WATEREND LA
Ayot Green
Crackendell Wood
Cat's Gallows
David's Dingle
Flint Bridge
River Lea or Lee
Chalkdell Farm
Samuels Farm
ROMAN ROAD
COLEMAN GREEN LA
Brocket Hall
Flint Bridge Plantation
Warren Farm
MARFORD RD
The Broadwater
Lamb's Grove
Brocket Park
Weir
Upper Cromer Hyde Farm
Cromer Hyde
Fletcher's Wick
The Crooked Chimney (PH)
Templehill Plantation
Lemsford
LEMSFORD VILLAGE
Wet Grove
Benstead's Wood
St John's School
Long Spring Grove
Brocket Corner
BROCKET RD B 653
Titnol's Wood
Cromerhyde Farm
Long Grove Plantation
Dogsheart Spring
Symondshyde Farm
Gosmoor
Chalkdell Wood
HAMMOND LA
GREEN LANES
Symondshyde Great Wood
The Old Cott
Furze Field
Hill Wood
GREAT BRAITCH LA
COOPERS GREEN LA
Sutton's Farm
MANOR RD
Astwick Manor Farm
Factory
Sch
4
3
2
1
13
12
11
10
19
20
21
D
E
F

110

129

89

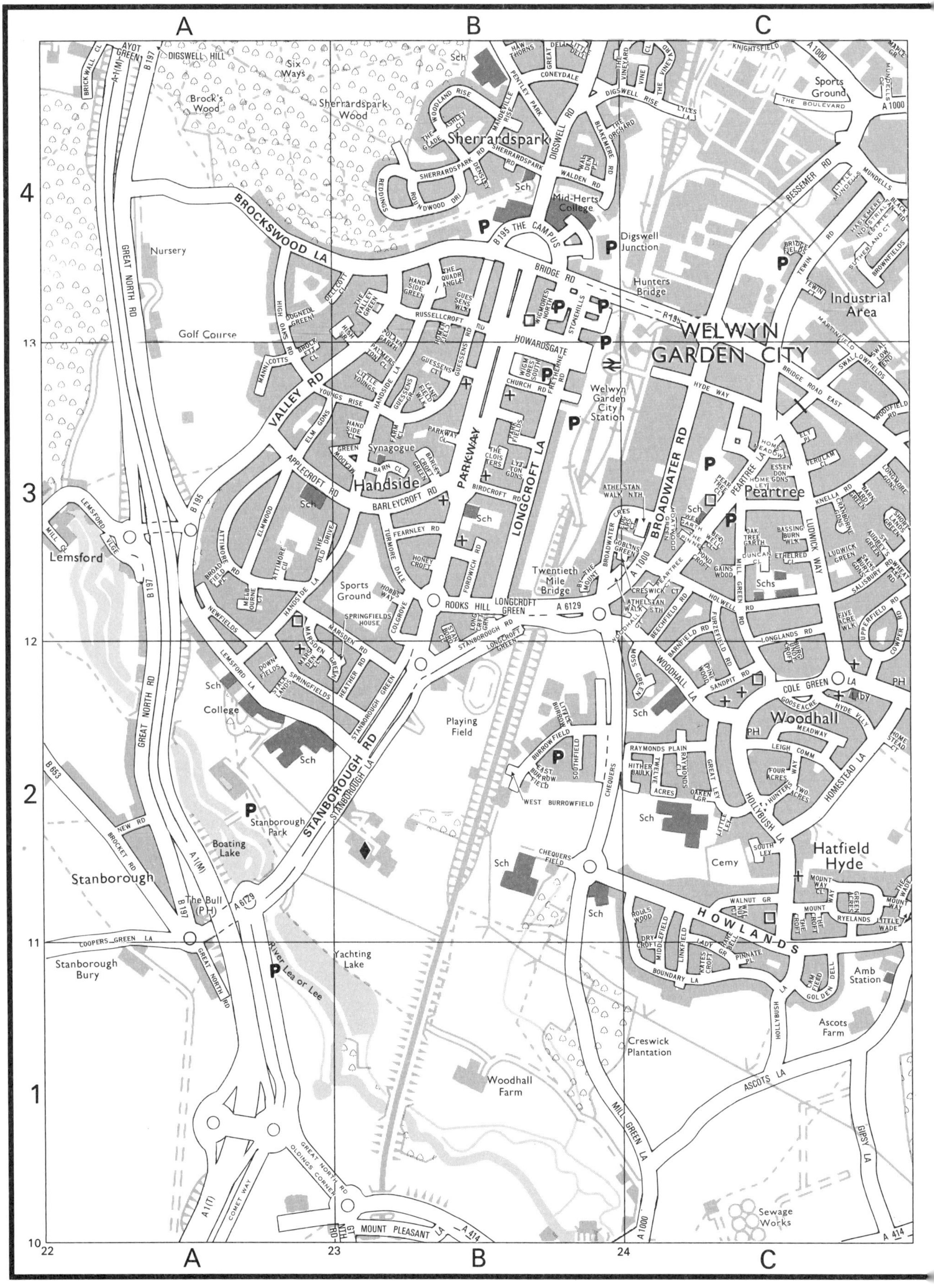

A
B
C
4
3
2
1
13
12
11
10
22
23
24
Six Ways
Brock's Wood
Sherrardspark Wood
Sherrardspark
Sch
Mid-Herts College
Digswell Junction
Hunters Bridge
Sports Ground
THE BOULEVARD
A 1000
KNIGHTSFIELD
DIGSWELL HILL
AYOT GREEN
BRICKWALL CL
A1(M)
B 197
GREAT NORTH RD
Nursery
Golf Course
BROCKSWOOD LA
B 195 THE CAMPUS
BRIDGE RD
HOWARDSGATE
CONEYDALE
DIGSWELL RD
DIGSWELL RISE
PENTLEY PARK
SHERRARDSPARK RD
ROUNDWOOD DRI
REDDINGS
WALDEN RD
BLAKEMERE RD
THE ORCHARD
BESSEMER RD
MUNDELLS
Industrial Area
WELWYN GARDEN CITY
Welwyn Garden City Station
HYDE WAY
BRIDGE ROAD EAST
SWALLOWFIELDS
TEWIN RD
WOODFIELD RD
VALLEY RD
HIGH OAKS
MANNICOTTS
RUSSELLCROFT RD
GUESSENS RD
HANDSIDE LA
PARKWAY
CHURCH RD
LONGCROFT LA
Synagogue
Handside
APPLECROFT RD
BARLEYCROFT RD
BIRDCROFT RD
FEARNLEY RD
TURMORE DALE
Sch
Lemsford
LEMSFORD VLGE
MILL CL
ATTIMORE RD
ELMWOOD
THE OLD DRIVE
Sports Ground
SPRINGFIELDS HOUSE
ROOKS HILL
LONGCROFT GREEN
A 6129
Twentieth Mile Bridge
FORDWICH RD
STANBOROUGH RD
HOBBS WAY
COLGROVE
NEWFIELDS
LEMSFORD LA
SPRINGFIELDS
HEATHER RD
MARSDEN RD
STANBOROUGH GREEN
College
Sch
Playing Field
BROADWATER RD
Peartree
PEARTREE LA
KNELLA RD
LUDWICK WAY
HOLWELL RD
LONGLANDS RD
COLE GREEN LA
Woodhall
MEADWAY
LEIGH COMM
HOMESTEAD LA
HYDE VLLY
WOODHALL LA
BARNFIELD RD
FURZEFIELD RD
SANDPIT RD
CRESWICK CT
MOSS GREEN
BURROWFIELD
SOUTHFIELD
WEST BURROWFIELD
CHEQUERS
CHEQUERS FIELD
RAYMONDS PLAIN
HITHER BAULK
TWELVE ACRES
OAKEN GR
GREAT LEY
HOLLYBUSH LA
FOUR ACRES
TWO ACRES
Sch
Cemy
SOUTH LEY
Hatfield Hyde
HOWLANDS
RYELANDS
LITTLE WADE
MOUNT WAY
BOUNDARY LA
PINNATE PL
LINKFIELD
MIDDLEFIELD
Amb Station
GOLDEN DELL
Ascots Farm
ASCOTS LA
HOLLYBUSH LA
GIPSY LA
B 653
NEW RD
BROCKET RD
Stanborough
Stanborough Park
Boating Lake
STANBOROUGH LA
The Bull (PH)
COOPERS GREEN LA
Stanborough Bury
GREAT NORTH RD
Yachting Lake
River Lea or Lee
Creswick Plantation
Woodhall Farm
MILL GREEN LA
A 1000
Sewage Works
A1(T)
COMET WAY
GREAT NORTH RD
OLDINGS CORNER
MOUNT PLEASANT LA
A 414
GT NTH RD

109

130

90

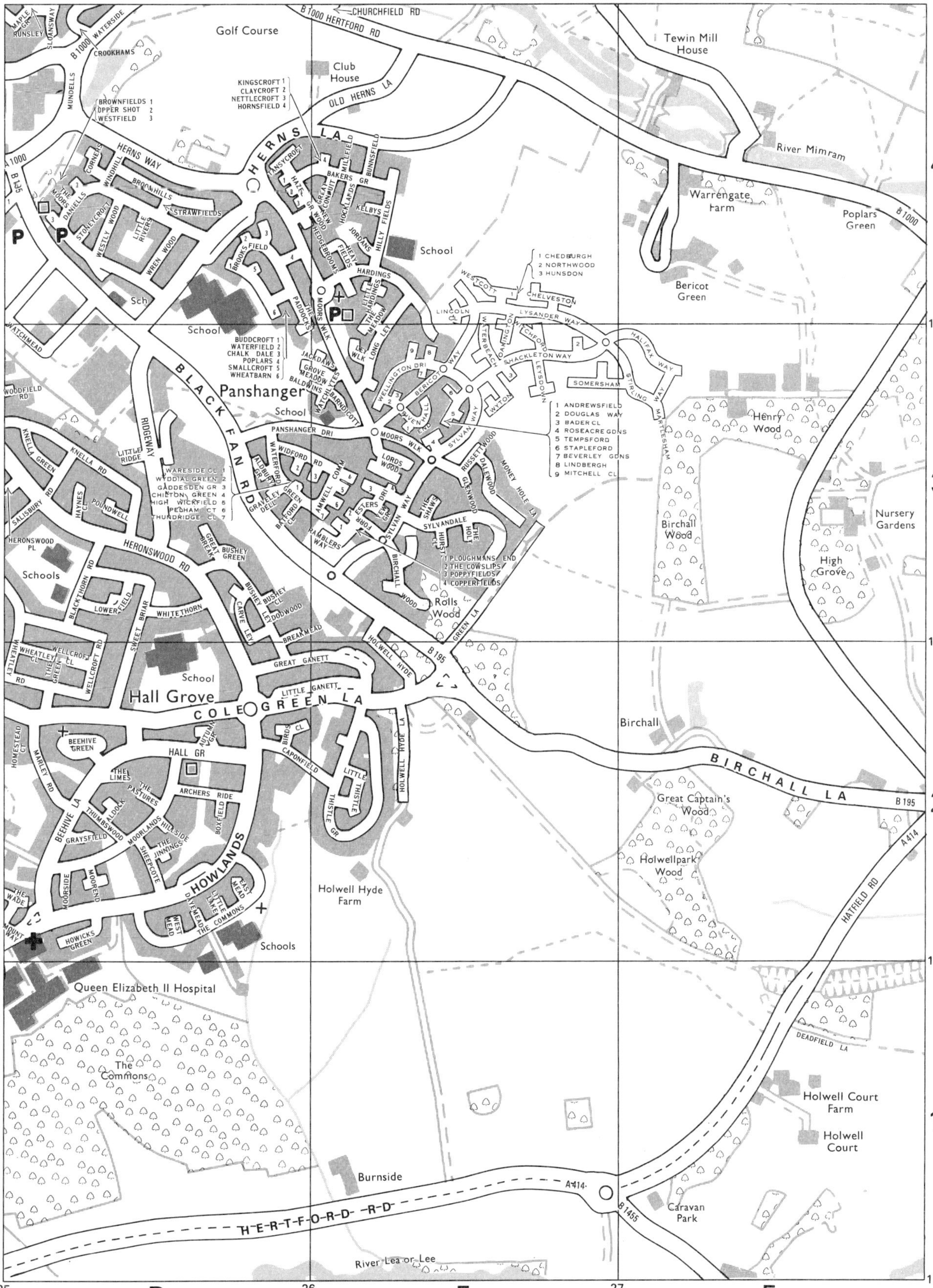
D
E
F
Golf Course
Club House
B1000 HERTFORD RD
CHURCHFIELD RD
Tewin Mill House
River Mimram
Warrengate Farm
Poplars Green
B1000
Bericot Green
School
OLD HERNS LA
HERNS LA
HERNS WAY
KINGSCROFT 1
CLAYCROFT 2
NETTLECROFT 3
HORNSFIELD 4
BROWNFIELDS 1
UPPER SHOT 2
WESTFIELD 3
MUNDELLS
CROOKHAMS
B1000 WATERSIDE
RUNSLEY
SLOANSWAY
MAPLE
A1000
B195
STRAWFIELDS
BROOMHILLS
WINDHILL
CORNERS
DANIELLS
THE MOORS
STONEYCROFT
WESTLY WOOD
LITTLE RIVERS
WREN WOOD
TANSYCROFT
BAKERS GR
MILLFIELD
BUNNSFIELD
KELBYS
HILLY FIELDS
JORDANS
HOCKLANDS
HEDGEBROWS
BROOKS FIELD
HARDINGS
LITTLE HARDINGS
THE MEADOW
PADDOCKS
MOORS WLK
LONG LEY
LEY WLK
Sch
School
WATCHMEAD
BUDDCROFT 1
WATERFIELD 2
CHALK DALE 3
POPLARS 4
SMALLCROFT 5
WHEATBARN 6
1 CHEDBURGH
2 NORTHWOOD
3 HUNSDON
WESTCOTT
CHELVESTON
LINCOLN
LYSANDER WAY
HALIFAX WAY
WATERBEACH
SHACKLETON WAY
LEYSDOWN
SOMERSHAM
STIRLING WAY
MARTLESHAM
WELLINGTON DR
BERICOT WAY
WYTON
SYLVAN WAY
1 ANDREWSFIELD
2 DOUGLAS WAY
3 BADER CL
4 ROSEACRE GDNS
5 TEMPSFORD
6 STAPLEFORD
7 BEVERLEY GDNS
8 LINDBERGH
9 MITCHELL CL
Panshanger
School
BLACK FAN RD
JACKDAWS
GROVE MEADOW
BALDWINS
WATCHLYTES
BARNDCOTT
PANSHANGER DRI
MOORS WLK
WOODFIELD RD
KNELLA GREEN
KNELLA RD
RIDGEWAY
LITTLE RIDGE
WARESIDE CL 1
WYDDIAL GREEN 2
GADDESDEN GR 3
CHILTON GREEN 4
HIGH WICKFIELD 5
PELHAM CT 6
THUNDRIDGE CL 7
SALISBURY RD
HAYNES CL
POUNDWELL
WIDFORD RD
WATERFORD GREEN
ALDBURY GR
GRAVELEY DELL
BATFORD CL
AMWELL COMM
LORDS WOOD
FESTERS DRI
FORD
SYLVAN WAY
RAMBLERS WAY
RUSSETTWOOD
GLENWOOD
DALEWOOD
MONEY HOLE LA
THE SHAWS
SYLVANDALE
HURST
THE HOLT
1 PLOUGHMANS END
2 THE COWSLIPS
3 POPPYFIELDS
4 COPPERFIELDS
BIRCHALL WOOD
Rolls Wood
GREEN LA
Henry Wood
Nursery Gardens
Birchall Wood
High Grove
HERONSWOOD PL
Schools
HERONSWOOD RD
GREAT BRAMBLE
BUSHEY GREEN
BUSHEY CL
BUSHEY LY
CARVE LEY
DODWOOD
BLACKTHORN RD
LOWERFIELD
SWEET BRIAR
WHITETHORN
BREAKMEAD
HOLWELL HYDE
B195
WHEATLEY CL
WELLCROFT CL
THE GREEN
WELLCROFT RD
WHEATLEY RD
GREAT GANETT
LITTLE GANETT
School
Hall Grove
COLE GREEN LA
Birchall
BIRCHALL LA
B195
BEEHIVE GREEN
HOMESTEAD CT
MARLEY RD
AUTUMN GR
HALL GR
BIRDS CL
CAPONFIELD
LITTLE THISTLE
THISTLE GR
HOLWELL HYDE LA
THE LIMES
THE PASTURES
ARCHERS RIDE
BOXFIELD
BEEHIVE LA
THUMBSWOOD
ALDOCK
MOORLANDS
HILLSIDE
GRAYSFIELD
THE JINNINGS
SHEEPCOTE
HOWLANDS
Great Captain's Wood
Holwellpark Wood
A414
HATFIELD RD
THE WADE
MOORSIDE
MOOREND
EAST MEAD
LITTLE LAKE
DAYEMEAD
WEST MEAD
THE COMMONS
Holwell Hyde Farm
MOUNT WAY
HOWICKS GREEN
Schools
Queen Elizabeth II Hospital
DEADFIELD LA
The Commons
Holwell Court Farm
Holwell Court
Burnside
A414
HERTFORD RD
B1455
Caravan Park
River Lea or Lee
13
12
11
10
25
26
27
4
3
2
1
D
E
F

112

131

91

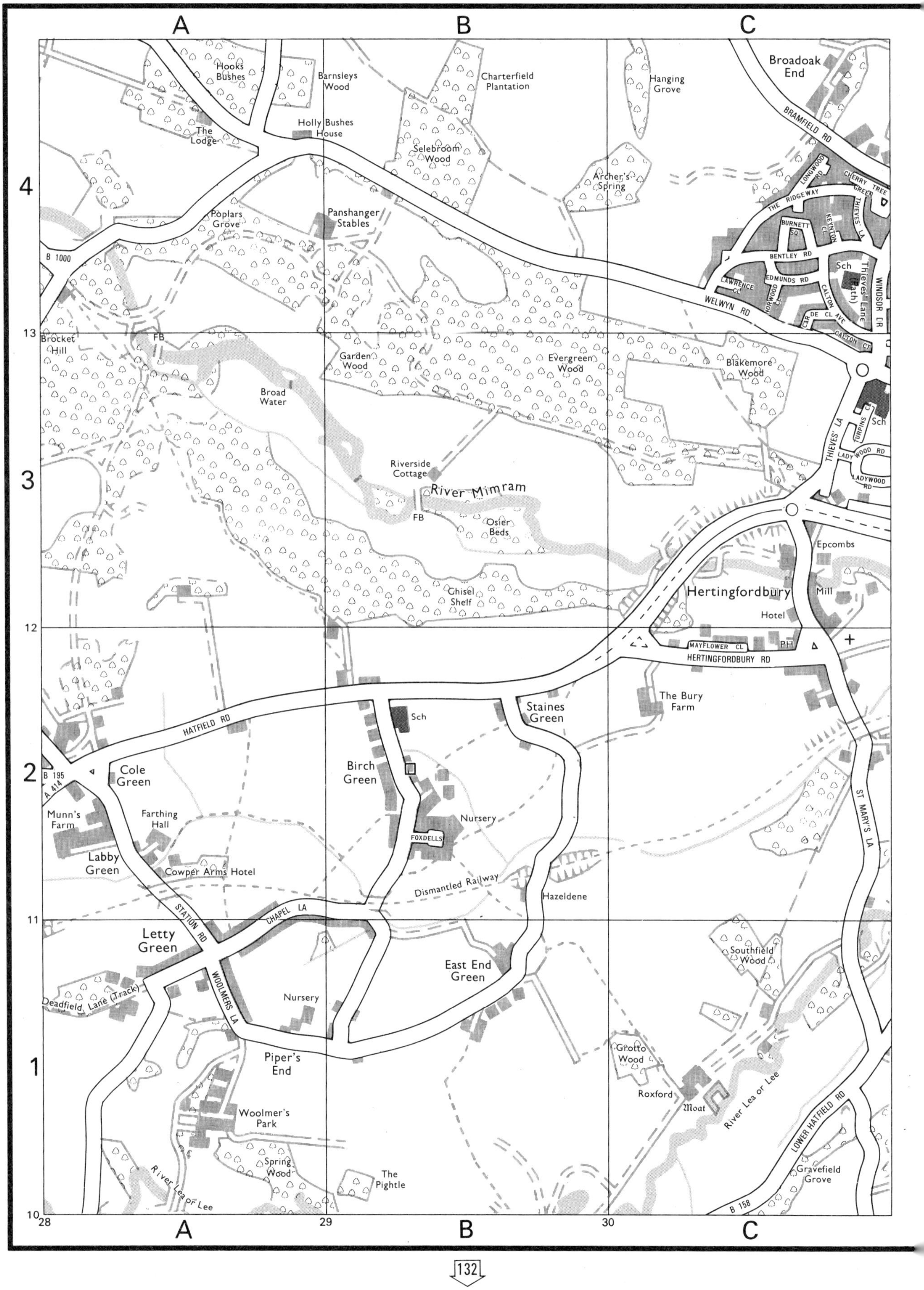
A
B
C
4
3
2
1
13
12
11
10
28
29
30
Hooks Bushes
Barnsleys Wood
Charterfield Plantation
Hanging Grove
Broadoak End
The Lodge
Holly Bushes House
Selebroom Wood
Archer's Spring
BRAMFIELD RD
LONGWOOD RD
CHERRY TREE GREEN
THE RIDGEWAY
THIEVES LA
Poplars Grove
Panshanger Stables
BURNETT SQ
KEYNTON CL
BENTLEY RD
Sch
Thieves' Lane (Path)
WINDSOR CR
B 1000
LAWRENCE CL
EDMUNDS RD
NORWOOD CL
CALTON AVE
CAR DE CL
CALTON CT
WELWYN RD
Brocket Hill
FB
Garden Wood
Evergreen Wood
Blakemore Wood
Broad Water
TURPINS CL
THIEVES' LA
LADY WOOD RD
LADYWOOD RD
Riverside Cottage
River Mimram
Osier Beds
Epcombs
Chisel Shelf
Hertingfordbury
Mill
Hotel
MAYFLOWER CL
PH
HERTINGFORDBURY RD
HATFIELD RD
Staines Green
The Bury Farm
B 195
A 414
Cole Green
Birch Green
Munn's Farm
Farthing Hall
Nursery
FOXDELLS
ST MARY'S LA
Labby Green
Cowper Arms Hotel
Dismantled Railway
Hazeldene
STATION RD
CHAPEL LA
Letty Green
Southfield Wood
East End Green
WOOLMERS LA
Deadfield Lane (Track)
Piper's End
Grotto Wood
Roxford
Moat
River Lea or Lee
LOWER HATFIELD RD
Woolmer's Park
Spring Wood
The Pightle
Gravefield Grove
B 158

111

132

92

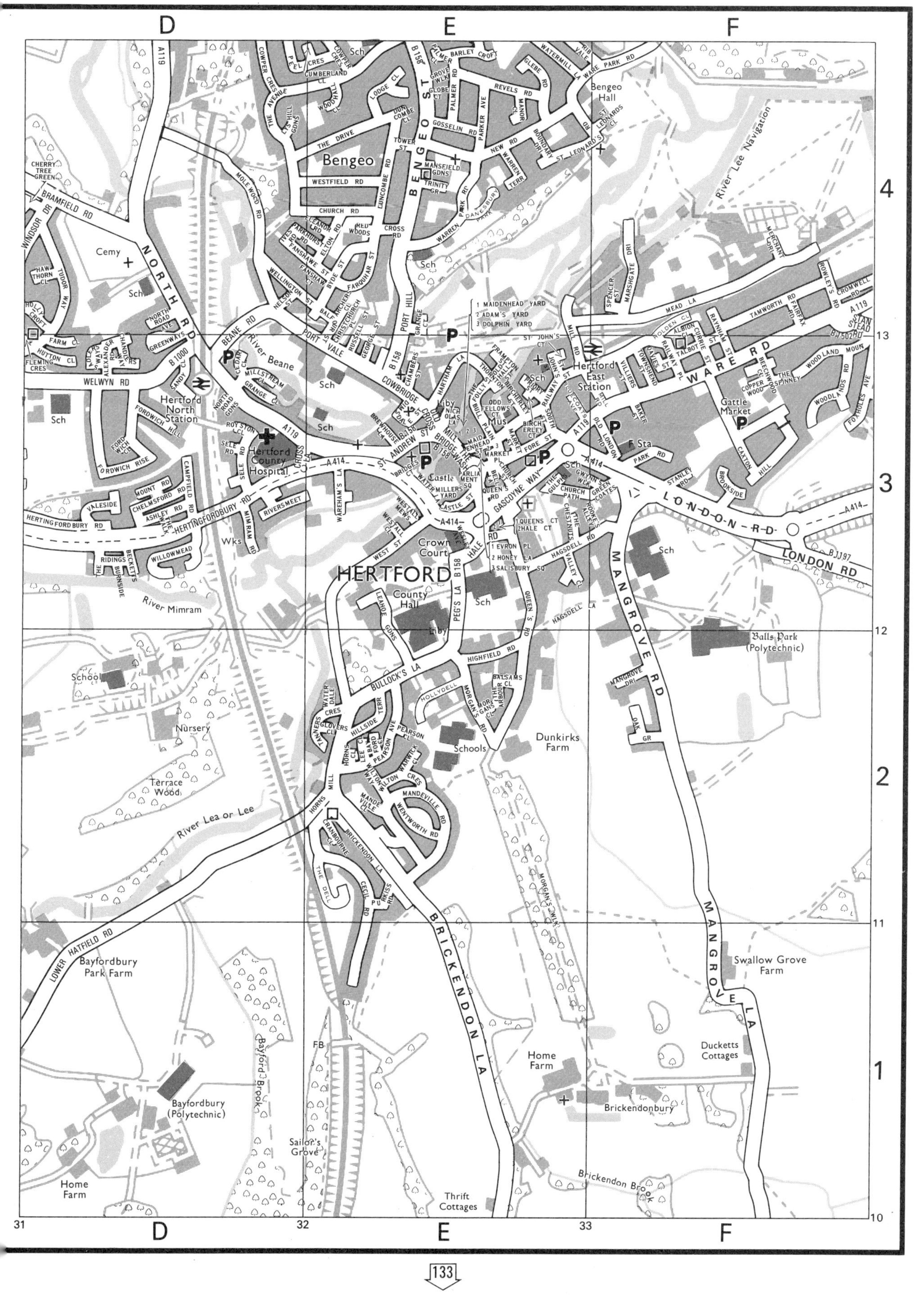
D
E
F
4
3
2
1
13
12
11
10
31
32
33
Bengeo
Bengeo Hall
HERTFORD
Hertford North Station
Hertford East Station
Hertford County Hospital
Crown Court
County Hall
Castle
Mus
Liby
Cemy
Sch
Schools
School
Nursery
Terrace Wood
Wks
Cattle Market
F Sta
Balls Park (Polytechnic)
Dunkirks Farm
Swallow Grove Farm
Ducketts Cottages
Home Farm
Brickendonbury
Bayfordbury Park Farm
Bayfordbury (Polytechnic)
Sailor's Grove
Thrift Cottages
FB
River Beane
River Mimram
River Lea or Lee
River Lee Navigation
Bayford Brook
Brickendon Brook
NORTH RD
WELWYN RD
BRAMFIELD RD
HERTINGFORDBURY RD
LOWER HATFIELD RD
BRICKENDON LA
MANGROVE RD
MANGROVE LA
LONDON RD
WARE RD
BENGEO ST
PORT HILL
PORT VALE
COWBRIDGE
GASCOYNE WAY
QUEEN'S RD
BULLOCK'S LA
PEG'S LA
HAGSDELL RD
HIGHFIELD RD
MEAD LA
WARE PARK RD
WATERMILL LA
A119
A414
B158
B1000
B1197
B1502
1 MAIDENHEAD YARD
2 ADAM'S YARD
3 DOLPHIN YARD
1 QUEENS CT
2 HALE CT
1 EVRON PL
2 HONEY LA
3 SALISBURY SQ

114

133

93

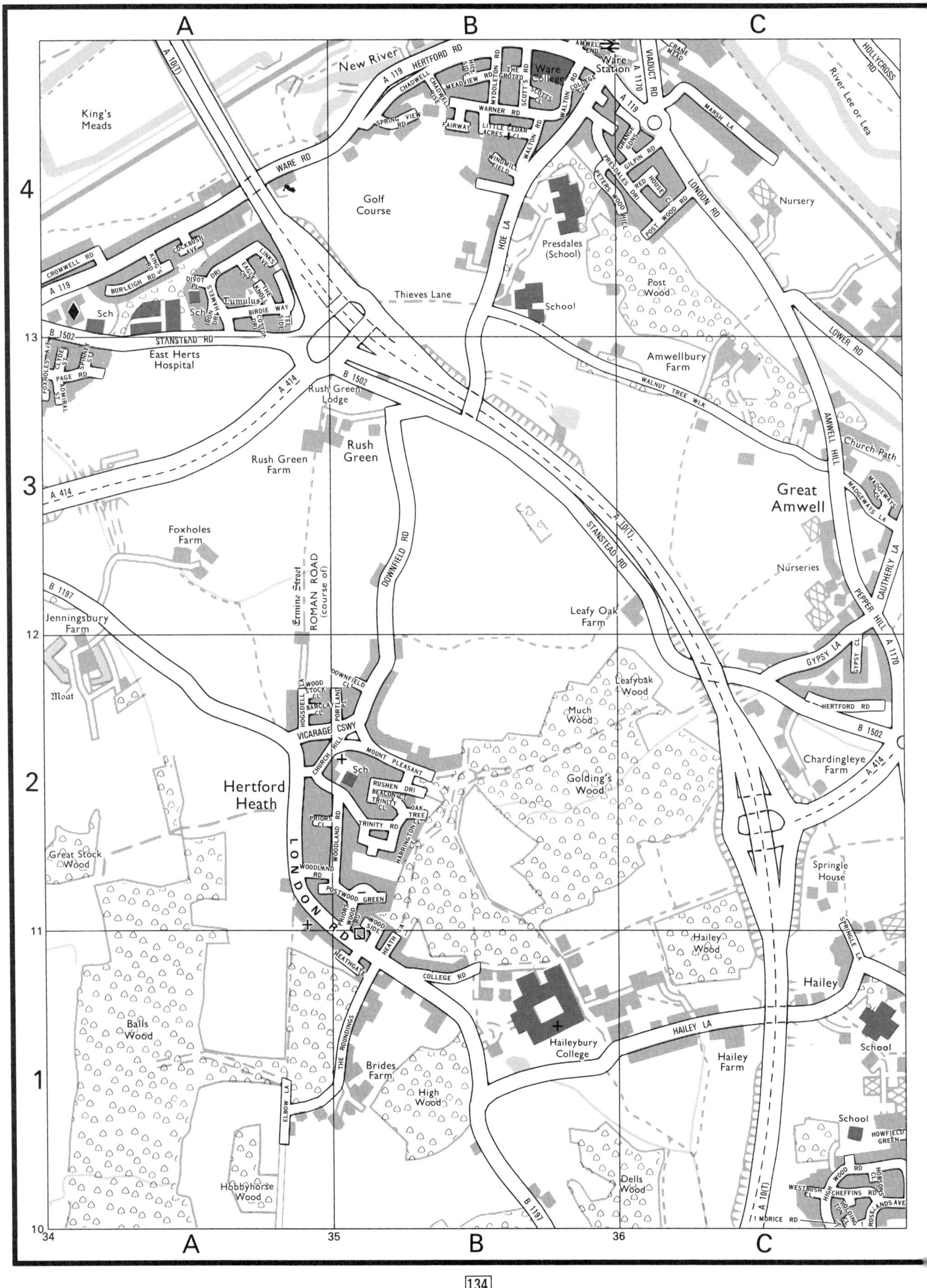

A
B
C
4
3
2
1
13
12
11
10
34
35
36
King's Meads
New River
A 119 HERTFORD RD
WARE RD
A 10(T)
Golf Course
Ware College
Ware Station
AMWELL END
VIADUCT RD
A 1170
CRANE MEAD
HOLLYCROSS RD
River Lee or Lea
MARSH LA
CHADWELL
CHADWELL RISE
SPRING VIEW RD
MEADVIEW RD
HILLSIDE
MYDDLETON RD
THE GROTTO
SCOTT'S RD
SCOTTS CL
WARNER RD
FAIRWAY
LITTLE ACRES
CEDAR CL
WALTON RD
COLLEGE CL
WINDMILL FIELD
GRANGE GDNS
GILPIN RD
RED HOUSE CL
PRESDALES DRI
PETERS WOOD HILL
POST WOOD RD
LONDON RD
Nursery
HOE LA
Presdales (School)
Post Wood
School
CROMWELL RD
A 119
BURLEIGH RD
KING'S RD
COCKBUSH AVE
DIVOT PL
DRI
LINKS AVE
EAGLE
THE KNOLL
Tumulus
BIRDIE WAY
TEE SIDE
COTTON DRI
HAMELS DRI
IRON DRI
Sch
Sch
Thieves Lane
B 1502
STANSTEAD RD
East Herts Hospital
FOXHOLES AVE
CLYDE ST
SPINNEY ST
PAGE RD
ADMIRAL ST
A 414
Rush Green Lodge
B 1502
Amwellbury Farm
WALNUT TREE WLK
LOWER RD
Rush Green
Rush Green Farm
AMWELL HILL
Church Path
Great Amwell
MADGEWAYS CL
MADGEWAYS LA
A 414
Foxholes Farm
A 10(T)
STANSTEAD RD
DOWNFIELD RD
CAUTHERLY LA
Nurseries
PEPPER HILL
A 1170
B 1197
Jenningsbury Farm
Ermine Street
ROMAN ROAD (course of)
Leafy Oak Farm
Moat
GYPSY LA
GYPSY CL
HERTFORD RD
B 1502
A 414
Leafyoak Wood
Much Wood
WOODSTOCK CL
DOWNFIELD CL
HOGSDELL LA
BARCLAY CL
PORTLAND PL
VICARAGE CSWY
CHURCH HILL
MOUNT PLEASANT
Sch
Hertford Heath
RUSHEN DRI
BEADLON CL
TRINITY CL
OAK TREE CL
TRINITY RD
PRIORS CL
WOODLAND RD
HARRINGTON CL
Golding's Wood
Chardingleye Farm
Great Stock Wood
Springle House
WOODLAND RD
POSTWOOD GREEN
PRIORS WOOD RD
WOOD SIDE
HEATH LA
LONDON RD
HEATHGATE
COLLEGE RD
Hailey Wood
SPRINGLE LA
Hailey
Balls Wood
THE ROUNDINGS
Haileybury College
HAILEY LA
School
Hailey Farm
Brides Farm
High Wood
ELBOW LA
School
HOWFIELD GREEN
Hobbyhorse Wood
Dells Wood
B 1197
A 10(T)
WESTBUSH CL
HIGH WOOD RD
CHEFFINS RD
HOBSONS CL
GOLDINGTON CL
ROSELANDS AVE
1 MORICE RD

113

134

94

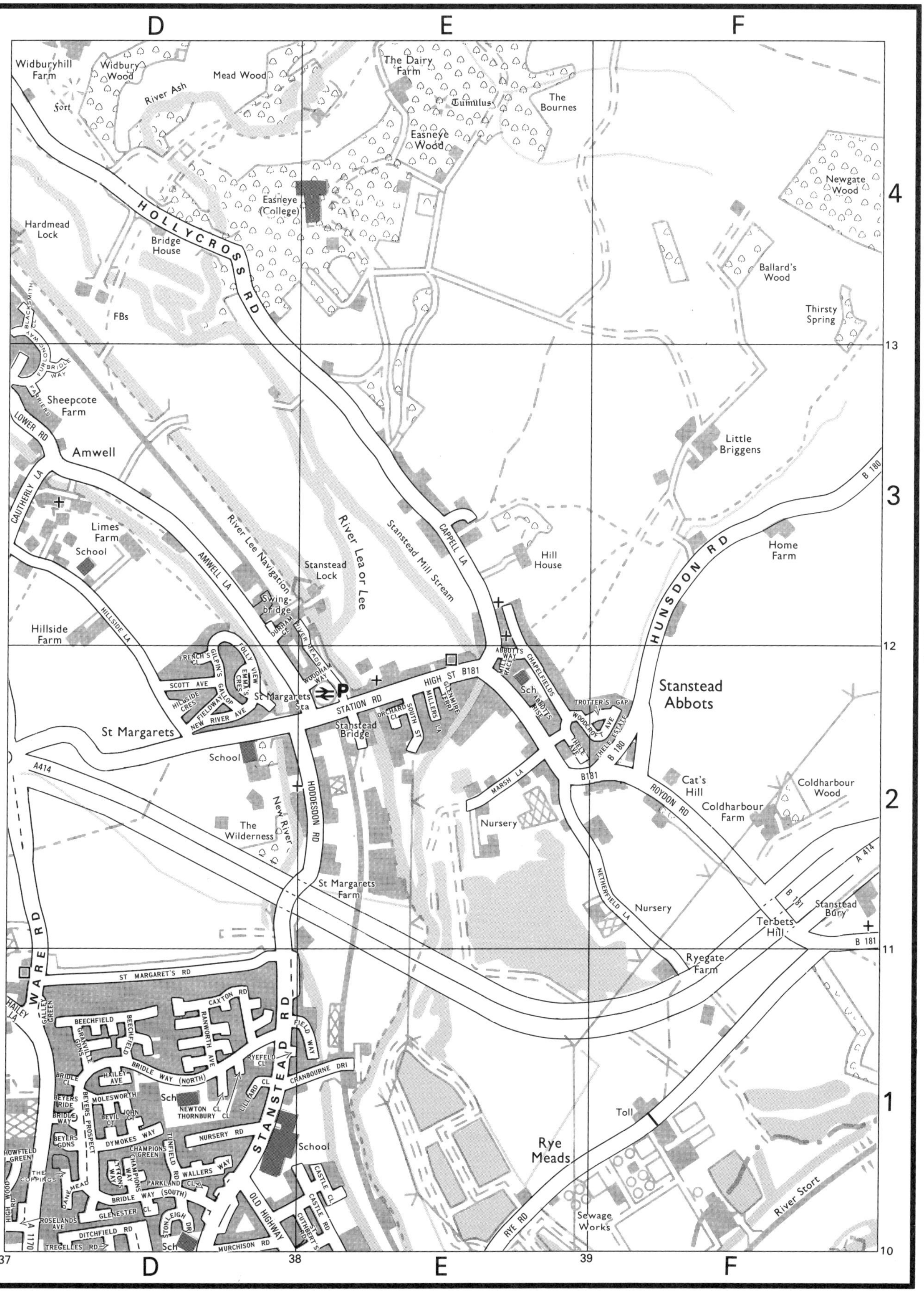
D
E
F
Widburyhill Farm
Widbury Wood
Mead Wood
River Ash
Fort
The Dairy Farm
Tumulus
The Bournes
Easneye Wood
Newgate Wood
Easneye (College)
Hardmead Lock
Bridge House
HOLLYCROSS RD
Ballard's Wood
Thirsty Spring
FBs
BLACKSMITH WAY
LONDON RD
FURLONG WAY
BRIDLE WAY
FARRIERS
Sheepcote Farm
LOWER RD
Amwell
Little Briggens
CAUTHERLY LA
Limes Farm
School
AMWELL LA
River Lee Navigation
River Lea or Lee
Stanstead Mill Stream
CAPPELL LA
Hill House
HUNSDON RD
Home Farm
B 180
Stanstead Lock
Swing-bridge
Hillside Farm
HILLSIDE LA
DURHAM CL
RIVER MEADS
WOODHAM WAY
ABBOTTS WAY
MILL RACE
CHAPELFIELDS
FRENCH'S CL
GILPIN'S GALLOP
FOLLY VIEW
EMMA'S CRES
SCOTT AVE
HILLSIDE CRES
FIELDWAY
NEW RIVER AVE
St Margarets Sta
STATION RD
HIGH ST B181
GLENMIRE TERR
ORCHARD CL
SOUTH ST
MILLERS LA
Sch
ABBOTS RISE
TROTTER'S GAP
WOODCROFT AVE
THELE AVE
THELE ESTATE
Stanstead Abbots
St Margarets
Stanstead Bridge
School
A414
B181
MARSH LA
Cat's Hill
Coldharbour Wood
Coldharbour Farm
ROYDON RD
HODDESDON RD
New River
The Wilderness
Nursery
St Margarets Farm
NETHERFIELD LA
Nursery
A 414
B 181
Stanstead Bury
Terbets Hill
WARE RD
Ryegate Farm
ST MARGARET'S RD
CAXTON RD
HAILEY LA
GALLEY GREEN
BEECHFIELD
GRANVILLE GDNS
RANWORTH AVE
FIELD WAY
RYEFELD CL
BRIDLE WAY (NORTH)
CRANBOURNE DRI
BRIDLE CL
HAILEY AVE
MOLESWORTH
BEYERS RIDE
BEYERS PROSPECT
JOHN CT
BEVIL CT
NEWTON CL
THORNBURY CL
LILLIARD CL
STANSTEAD RD
Toll
BRIDLE WAY
BEYERS GDNS
DYMOKES WAY
CHAMPIONS GREEN
NURSERY RD
School
HOWFIELD GREEN
LYTTONS WAY
CHAMPIONS WAY
TUNFIELD RD
WALLERS WAY
Rye Meads
THE COPPINGS
DANEMEAD
PARKLAND CL
CASTLE CL
BRIDLE WAY (SOUTH)
HIGH WOOD RD
GLENESTER CL
OLD HIGHWAY
CASTLE RD
River Stort
ROSELANDS AVE
STONLEIGH DR
CUTHBERT'S
RYE RD
Sewage Works
A 1170
DITCHFIELD RD
TREGELLES RD
Sch
MURCHISON RD
4
3
2
1
13
12
11
10
37
38
39

116

135

95

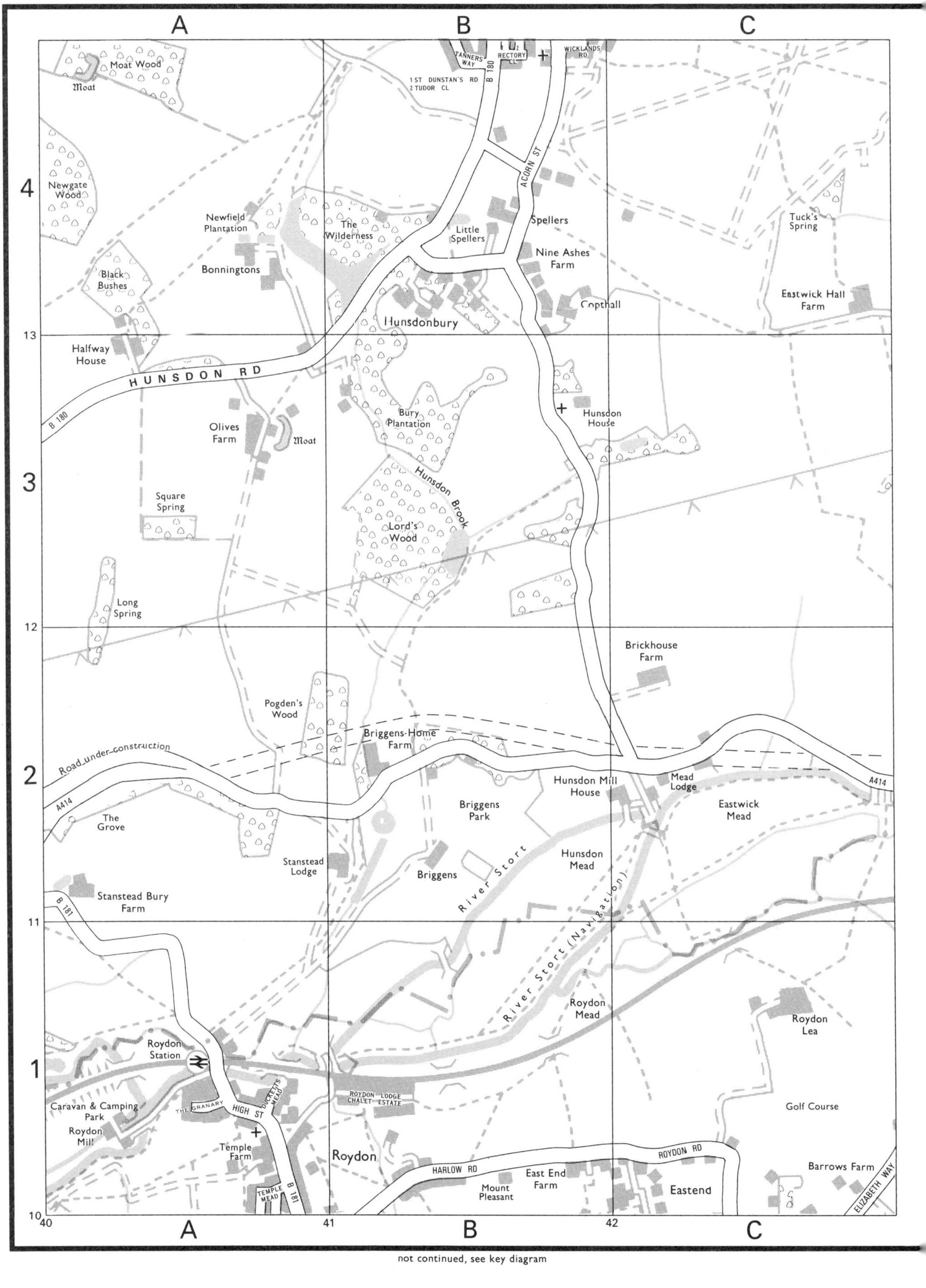

115

not continued, see key diagram

96

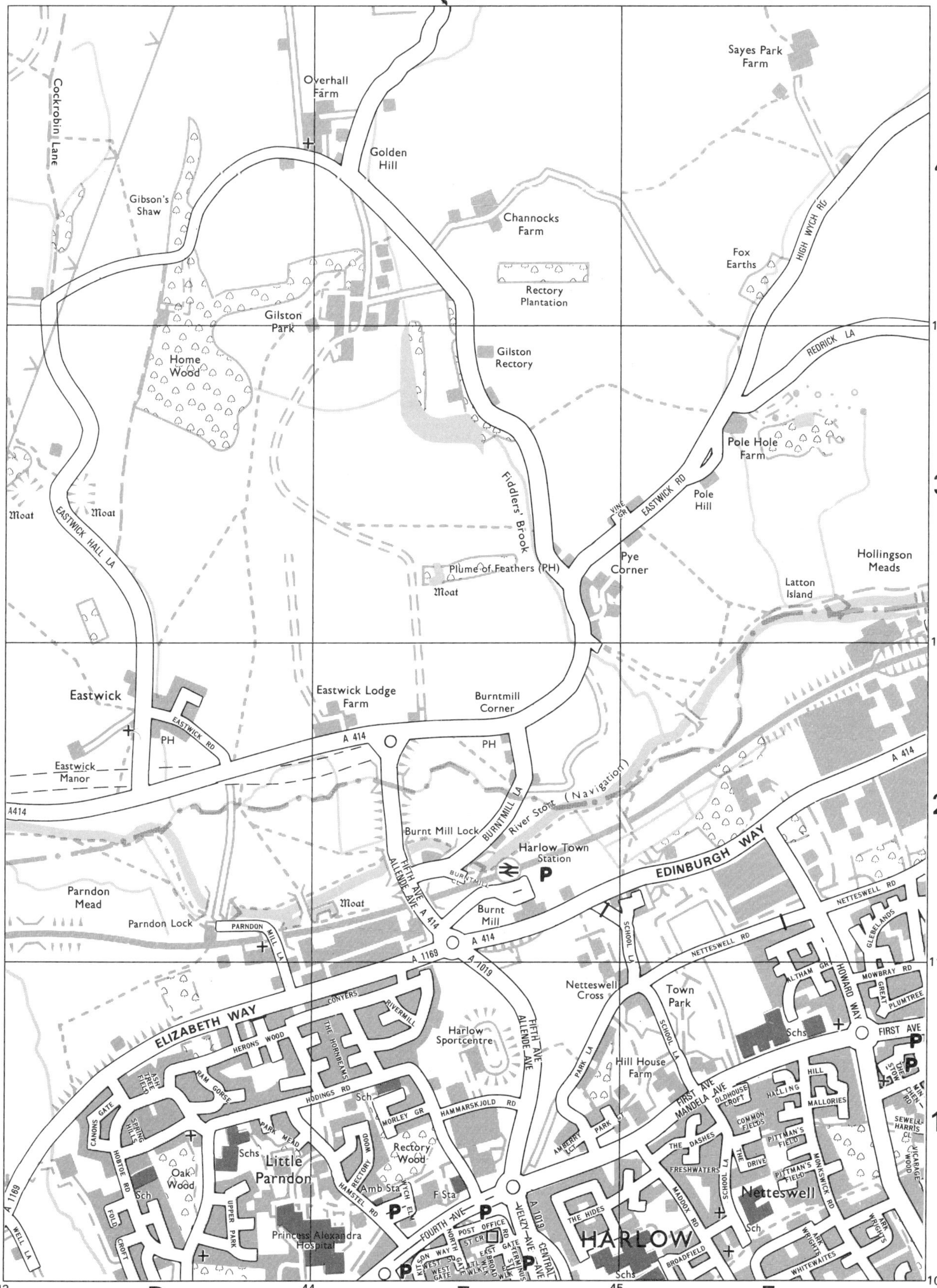

not continued, see key diagram

97

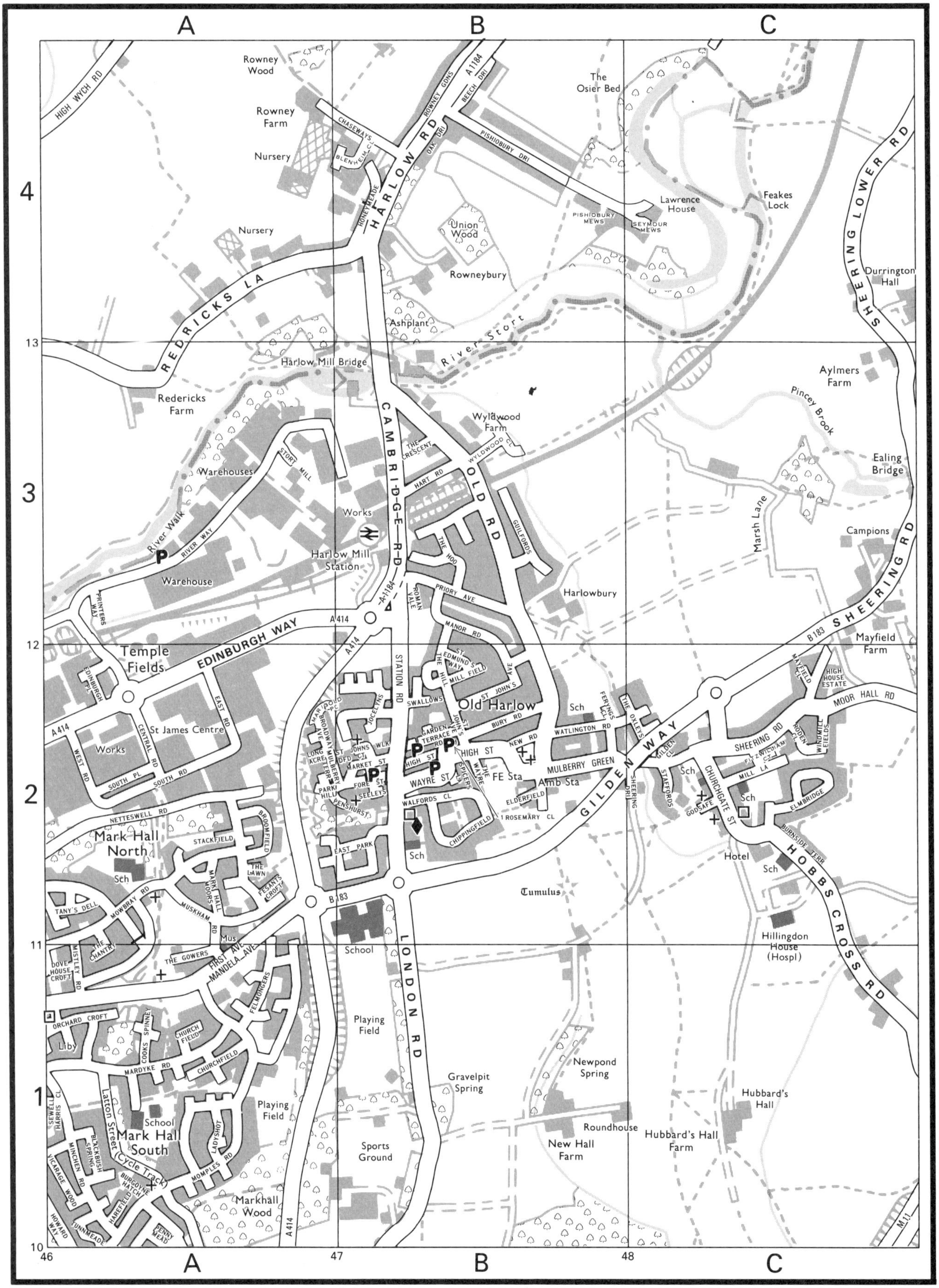
A
B
C
4
3
2
1
13
12
11
10
46
47
48
Rowney Wood
Rowney Farm
Nursery
Nursery
HIGH WYCH RD
REDRICKS LA
HARLOW RD
A1184
ROWNEY GDNS
BEECH DRI
OAK DRI
PISHIOBURY DRI
CHASEWAYS
BLENHEIM CL
HONEYMEADE
The Osier Bed
Lawrence House
Feakes Lock
PISHIOBURY MEWS
SEYMOUR MEWS
Union Wood
Rowneybury
Ashplant
River Stort
Harlow Mill Bridge
Redericks Farm
Durrington Hall
SHEERING LOWER RD
Aylmers Farm
Pincey Brook
Wyldwood Farm
WYLDWOOD CL
THE CRESCENT
CAMBRIDGE RD
OLD RD
HART RD
Warehouses
STORT MILL
Works
River Walk
RIVER WAY
Harlow Mill Station
Warehouse
PRINTERS WAY
GUILFORDS
THE HOO
ROMAN VALE
PRIORY AVE
Harlowbury
Marsh Lane
Ealing Bridge
Campions
SHEERING RD
B183
Mayfield Farm
A414
EDINBURGH WAY
Temple Fields
EDINBURGH PL
EAST RD
MANOR RD
ST EDMUND'S WAY
THE HILL
MILL FIELD
ST JOHN'S AVE
STATION RD
SWALLOWS
Old Harlow
Sch
FERINGS CL
THE OXLEYS
MAYFIELD CL
HIGH HOUSE ESTATE
MOOR HALL RD
St James Centre
CENTRAL RD
WEST RD
Works
SOUTH PL
SOUTH RD
JOCELYNS
MARROWBONE CL
BROADWAY AVE
MULBERRY TERR
LONG ACRE
JOHNS WLK
MARKET ST
FORE ST
PARK HILL
SEELEYS
PENSHURST
GARDEN TERRACE RD
ST JOHN'S AVE
BURY RD
NEW RD
WATLINGTON RD
GILDEN WAY
HIGH ST
WAYRE ST
EPICERS
THE WAYRE
FE Sta
Amb Sta
MULBERRY GREEN
ELDERFIELD
ROSEMARY CL
WALFORDS CL
CHIPPINGFIELD
SHEERING DRI
GILDEN CL
STAFFORDS
Sch
CHURCHGATE ST
GOOSAFE
FITZWILLIAM CT
MILL LA
RODEN
WINDMILL FIELDS
ELMBRIDGE
Sch
BURNSIDE TERR
Hotel
Sch
HOBBS CROSS RD
NETTESWELL RD
BROOMFIELD
STACKFIELD
Mark Hall North
THE LAWN
FESANTS CROFT
MARK HALL MOORS
EAST PARK
Sch
Sch
TANY'S DELL
MOWBRAY RD
MUSKHAM RD
B183
Tumulus
School
Hillingdon House (Hospl)
THE CHANTRY
MISTLEY RD
DOVE HOUSE CROFT
Mus
FIRST AVE
MANDELA AVE
THE GOWERS
FELMONGERS
LONDON RD
ORCHARD CROFT
SPINNEY
COOKS
CHURCH FIELD
Liby
Playing Field
MARDYKE RD
CHURCHFIELD
Newpond Spring
Gravelpit Spring
Hubbard's Hall
Playing Field
SEWELL HARRIS CL
Latton Street (Cycle Track)
School
Mark Hall South
BLACKBUSH SPRING
LADYSHOT
Roundhouse
Hubbard's Hall Farm
New Hall Farm
Sports Ground
MINCHEN RD
VICARAGE WOOD
BURGOYNE HATCH
HAREFIELD
MOMPLES RD
Markhall Wood
HOWARD WAY
TUNNMEADE
PENNY MEAD
A414
M11

117

99

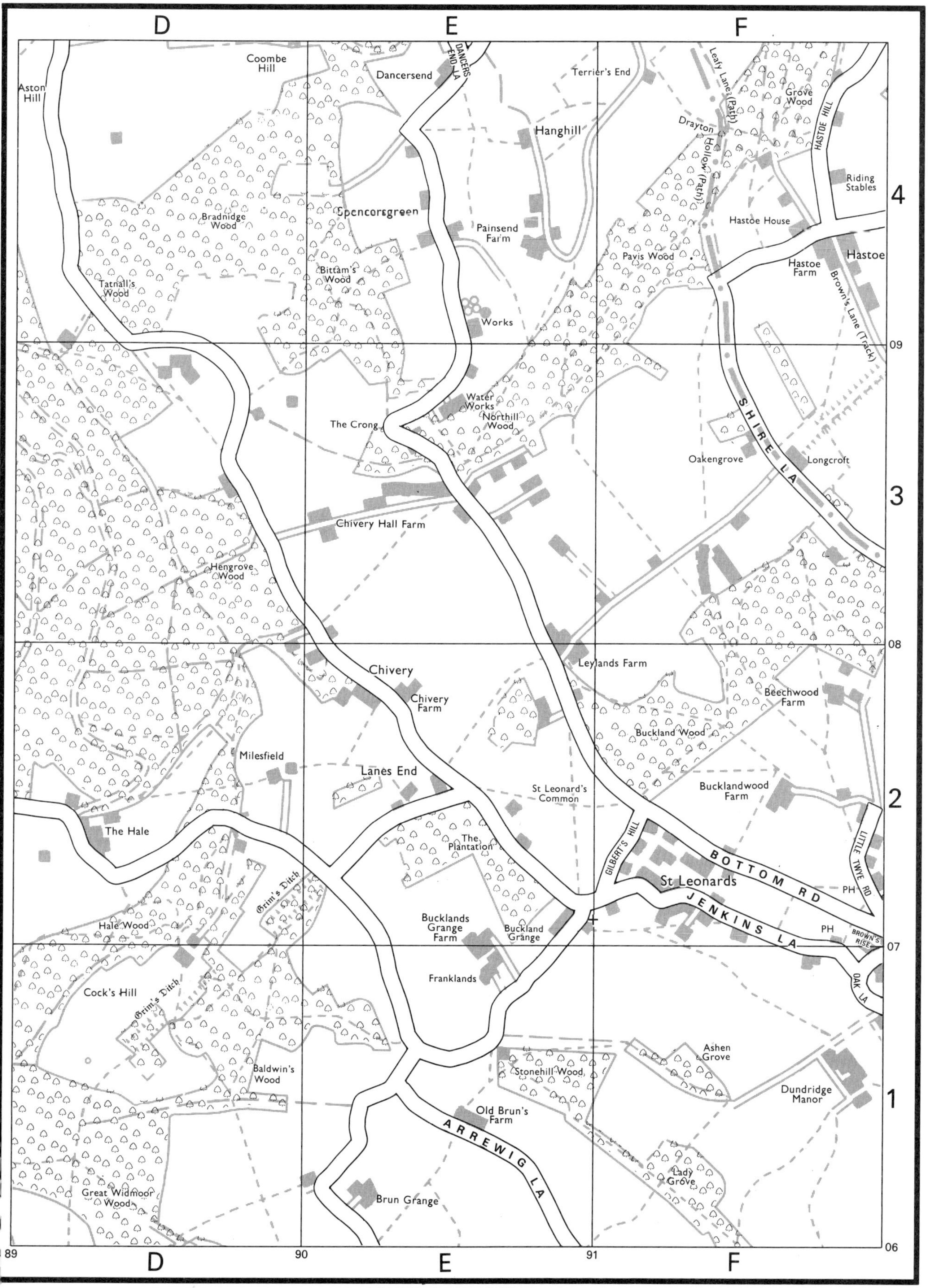

120

not continued, see key diagram

100

119

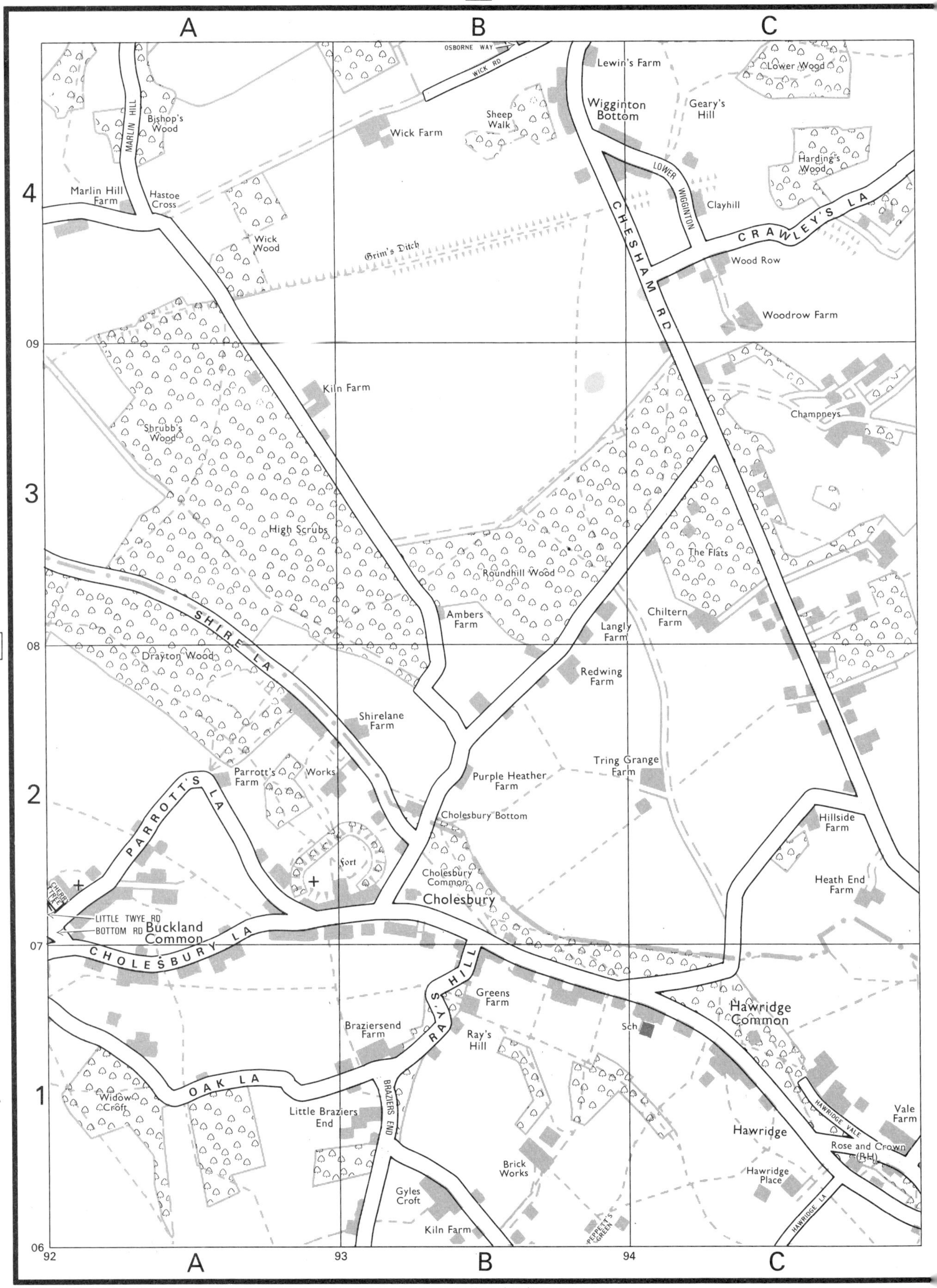
A
B
C
OSBORNE WAY
WICK RD
Lewin's Farm
Lower Wood
Wigginton Bottom
Geary's Hill
MARLIN HILL
Bishop's Wood
Sheep Walk
Wick Farm
Harding's Wood
LOWER WIGGINTON
Clayhill
Marlin Hill Farm
Hastoe Cross
CHESHAM RD
CRAWLEY'S LA
Wick Wood
Grim's Ditch
Wood Row
Woodrow Farm
09
Kiln Farm
Champneys
Shrubb's Wood
3
High Scrubs
The Flats
Roundhill Wood
SHIRE LA
Ambers Farm
Chiltern Farm
Langly Farm
08
Drayton Wood
Redwing Farm
Shirelane Farm
Tring Grange Farm
Purple Heather Farm
Parrott's Farm
Works
2
PARROTT'S LA
Cholesbury Bottom
Hillside Farm
Fort
Cholesbury Common
Cholesbury
Heath End Farm
LITTLE TWYE RD
BOTTOM RD
Buckland Common
07
CHOLESBURY LA
RAY'S HILL
Greens Farm
Hawridge Common
Braziersend Farm
Ray's Hill
Sch
1
OAK LA
BRAZIERS END
Widow Croft
Little Braziers End
Vale Farm
HAWRIDGE VALE
Hawridge
Rose and Crown (PH)
Brick Works
Hawridge Place
Gyles Croft
HAWRIDGE LA
Kiln Farm
PEPPETT'S GREEN
06
92
93
94

101

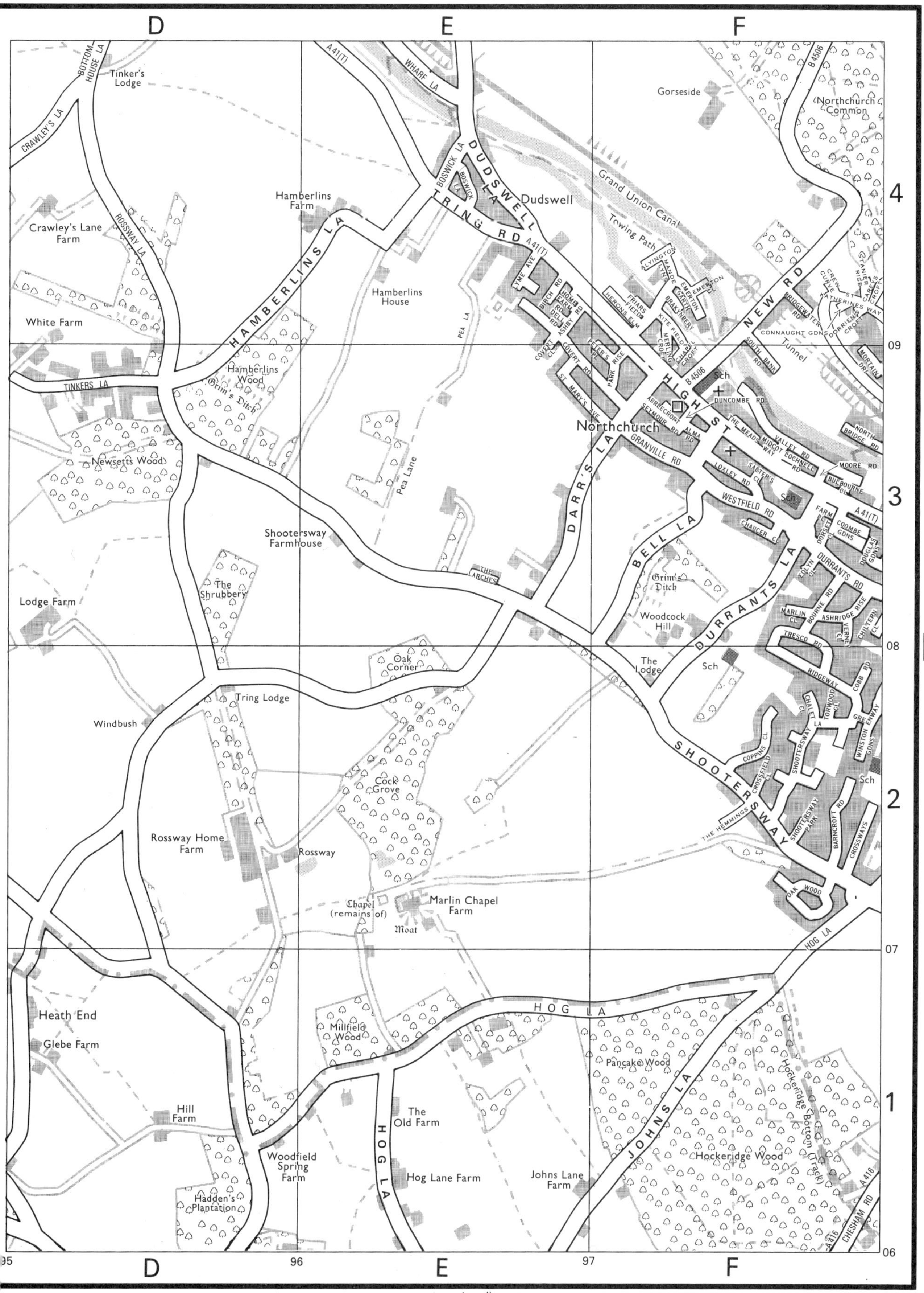

122

not continued, see key diagram

102

121

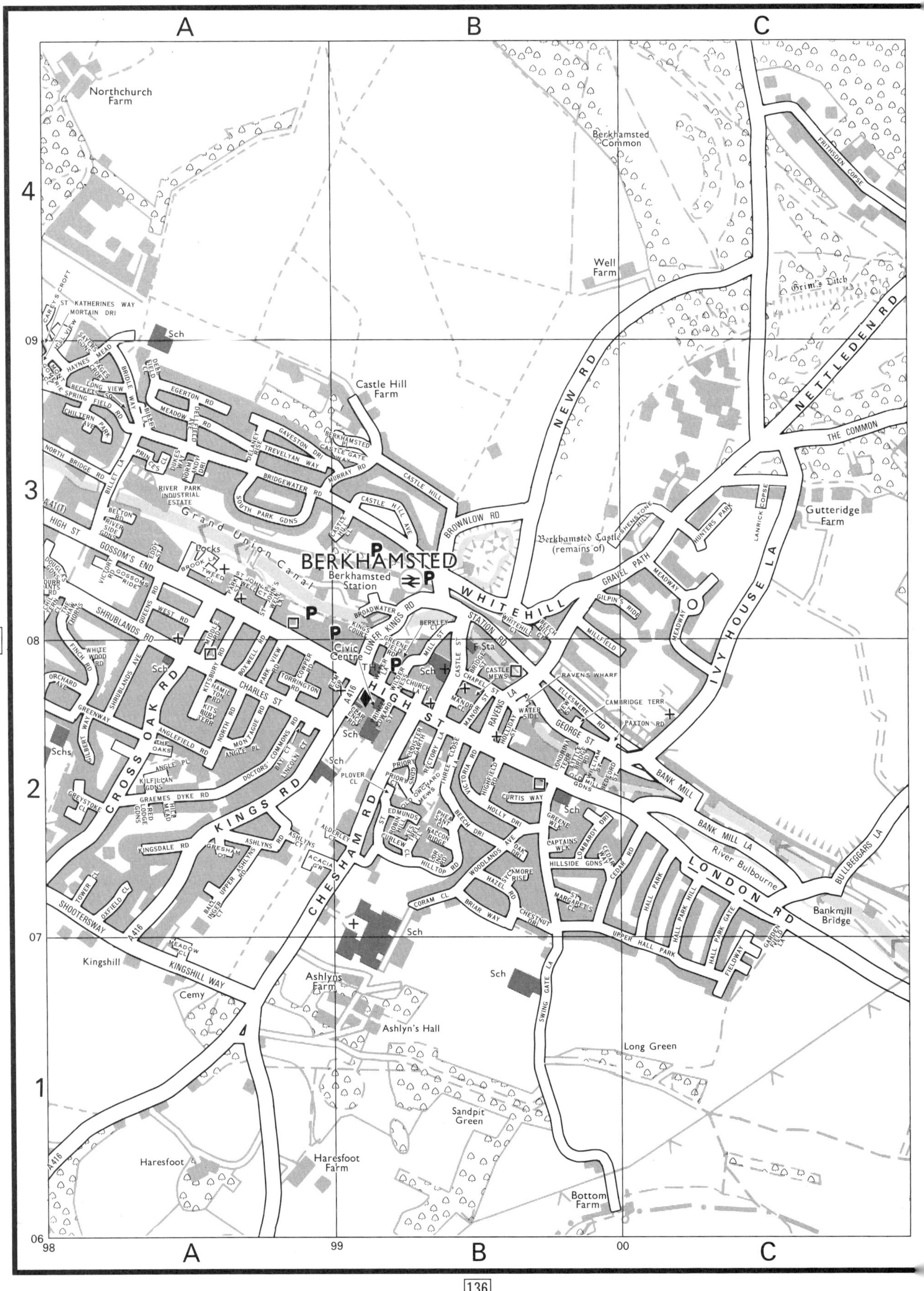
A
B
C
4
3
2
1
09
08
07
06
98
99
00
Northchurch Farm
Berkhamsted Common
Well Farm
Grim's Ditch
NETTLEDEN RD
THE COMMON
FRITHSDEN COPSE
Castle Hill Farm
NEW RD
Sch
Schs
CAREY'S CROFT
ST KATHERINES WAY
MORTAIN DRI
HAYNES MEAD
LONG VIEW
BECKETS SQ
SPRING FIELD RD
CHILTERN PARK AVE
BRIDLE WAY
EGERTON RD
MEADOW RD
GAVESTON DRI
TREVELYAN WAY
BRIDGEWATER RD
MURRAY RD
CASTLE HILL
CASTLE HILL AVE
BROWNLOW RD
NORTH BRIDGE RD
BILLET LA
PRINCES CL
RIVER PARK INDUSTRIAL ESTATE
SOUTH PARK GDNS
A41(T)
HIGH ST
BELTON RD
RIVERSIDE GDNS
Grand Union Canal
Locks
GOSSOM'S END
GOSSOMS RIDE
VICTORY RD
BROOK ST
TWEED CL
BERKHAMSTED
Berkhamsted Station
Berkhamsted Castle (remains of)
SHENSTONE HILL
HUNTERS PARK
LANRICK COPSE
Gutteridge Farm
GRAVEL PATH
MEADWAY
IVY HOUSE LA
WHITEHILL
GILPIN'S RIDE
MILLFIELD
SHRUBLANDS RD
QUEENS RD
WEST RD
BROADWATER
LOWER KINGS RD
BERKLEY CT
STATION RD
F Sta
CASTLE MEWS
Civic Centre
MIDDLE RD
BOXWELL RD
PARK VIEW
COWPER RD
TORRINGTON RD
CHARLES ST
KITSBURY RD
KITSBURY TERR
FINCH RD
WHITE WOOD RD
ORCHARD AVE
SHRUBLANDS AVE
GREENWAY
GILBERT WAY
CROSS OAK RD
ANGLEFIELD RD
ANGLE PL
NORTH RD
MONTAGUE RD
DOCTORS COMMONS RD
LINCOLN CT
HIGH ST
A416
CASTLE ST
CHAPEL ST
MANOR ST
RAVENS LA
HOLLIDAY ST
RAVENS WHARF
ELLESMERE RD
CAMBRIDGE TERR
PAXTON RD
GEORGE ST
BANK MILL
PLOVER CL
PRIORY GDNS
RECTORY LA
THREE CLOSE LA
ORCHARD MEWS
VICTORIA RD
HIGHFIELD RD
CURTIS WAY
HOLLY DRI
BEECH DRI
GREENE WLK
CAPTAINS WLK
LOMBARDY DRI
HILLSIDE GDNS
CEDAR RD
CEDAR WAY
BANK MILL LA
River Bulbourne
LONDON RD
BULLBEGGARS LA
Bankmill Bridge
KILFILLAN GDNS
GRAEMES DYKE RD
GREYSTOKE CL
KINGS RD
KINGSDALE RD
GRESHAM CT
ASHLYNS CT
ASHLYNS RD
UPPER ASHLYNS RD
BALLINGER CT
ALDERLEY CT
ACACIA GR
CHESHAM RD
ST EDMUNDS
CURLEW CL
HILLTOP RD
WOODLANDS AVE
HAZEL RD
SYCAMORE RISE
ST MARGARET'S CL
CHESTNUT DRI
BRIAR WAY
CORAM CL
HALL PARK
HALL PARK HILL
HALL PARK GATE
UPPER HALL PARK
FIELDWAY
GARDEN FIELD LA
TOWER CL
OXFIELD CL
SHOOTERSWAY
MEADOW CL
KINGSHILL WAY
Kingshill
Cemy
Ashlyns Farm
Ashlyn's Hall
SWING GATE LA
Long Green
Sandpit Green
Haresfoot
Haresfoot Farm
Bottom Farm

136

103

D
E
F
Holly Bush Farm
Frithsden Vines (Vineyard)
Frithsden
Little Frithsden Copse
Crossways Farm
Heizdin's Wood
Strathgade Farm
Bingham's Park Farm
Bingham's Park
NETTLEDEN RD
POTTEN END HILL
Brown's Spring
Rumblers Farm
Hollybush Wood
HOLLYBUSH CL
Brown's Spring
Catstail Wood
4
FRITHSDEN CPS
THE HAMLET
BROWNS SPR
OLIVER'S CL
WATER END RD
Woodcroft Farm
VICARAGE RD
VICARAGE GDNS
HOME FIELD
PLOUGH LA
THE BACK
Pottenend Farm
HEDGESIDE
BRIAR CL
THE FRONT
RAMBLING WAY
09
COMMON GREEN
CHURCH RD
Sch
SCHOOL GDNS
CHESTNUT CL
THE LAURELS
THE COMMON
HEMPSTEAD LA
Boxted Farm
Potten End
Amersfort
BERKHAMSTED RD
FENNYCROFT RD
HOWARDS DR
CHASDEN RD
3
School
CHERRY ORCH
POLEHANGER LA
Little Heath
Little Heath Farm
Boxted House
School
Gutteridge Wood
ELM GREEN
MAPLE GREEN
WHITE BROOM RD
DAGGS DELL RD
LYNE WAY
SOMERIES RD
GALLEY HILL
SPRING LA
SACOMBE RD
MARK RD
WARREN RD
ROBE END
FIELDS END LA
THE AVENUE
BOXTED RD
08
BULLBEGGARS LA
Littleheath Great Farm
Fields End
THE COPSE
THE LAWNS
PULLEYS LA
BIRCH GREEN
Sch
HITCHENS CL
Fields End Farm
Lower Little Heath Farm
THE GLADES
THE SHRUBBERY
HOLLYBUSH LA
Sch
MARTINDALE RD
HAREPARK CL
HARDINS CL
MICKLEM DRI
GOOSECROFT
ROSEWOOD CT
Warners End
PULLEYS CL
PULLEYS CL
FRIMLEY RD
HAWTHORN LA
PULLEYS LA
LITTLE HEATH LA
POUCHEN END LA
ROSEHEATH
RIPLEY WAY
EAST FLINT
RAVENS DELL
YOUNGFIELD RD
Bullbeggars Wood
MYRTLE GREEN
MERROW DRI
2
NEWLANDS RD
JUNIPER GREEN
VARNEY CL
GREAT STURGESS RD
PARKWOOD DRI
GREEN END LA
SMALL ACRE
VARNEY RD
SIDFORD CL
STONEY CROFT
PADDOCK WAY
VALLEYSIDE
LEGGFIELD TERR
MOUNT CL
GREEN END LA
LONG CHAULDEN
ST NICHOLAS MOUNT
WESTRIDGE CL
Shrub Hill Common
RIDGE LEA
MIDDLEHILL
LUCKS HILL
JOCKETTS HILL
07
ROWCROFT
BROOM RISE
TUDORS RD
SCHOOL ROW
JOCKETTS RD
SHRUB HILL RD
WHITE HILL
Pouchen End Hall
Pouchen End Farm
MUSK HILL
HONEYCROSS RD
Sch
DAMASK GREEN
COTESMORE RD
SHEPHERDS GREEN
CUTTSFIELD TERR
CHAULDEN TERR
NORTHRIDGE WAY
UPPER SALES
Pix Farm
Pouchen End
FURZE RD
LINDLINGS
LONDON RD
OLDFIELD RD
HUNTS MILL
HAZELDELL RD
Broadway Farm
PIX FARM LA
Chaulden
RAMSON RISE
FOXGLOVES
HAZELDELL LINK
Sch
PIXIES HILL RD
PIXIES HILL CRES
LOWER SALES
THISTLE CL
BENCHLEYS RD
Grand Union Canal
THE COLTSFOOT
CHAULDEN HOUSE GDNS
1
SHARPES LA
CHAULDEN LA
Cress Farm
Winkwell
WINKWELL
MOORLAND RD
River Bulbourne
Broadway Orchard
Motel
LONDON RD
SUGAR LA
Bourne End Farm
Bourne End
BOURNE END LA
OLD FISHERY LA
A41(T)
Saw Mill
Moorend Farm
06
1
02
03
D
E
F

124

137

104

123

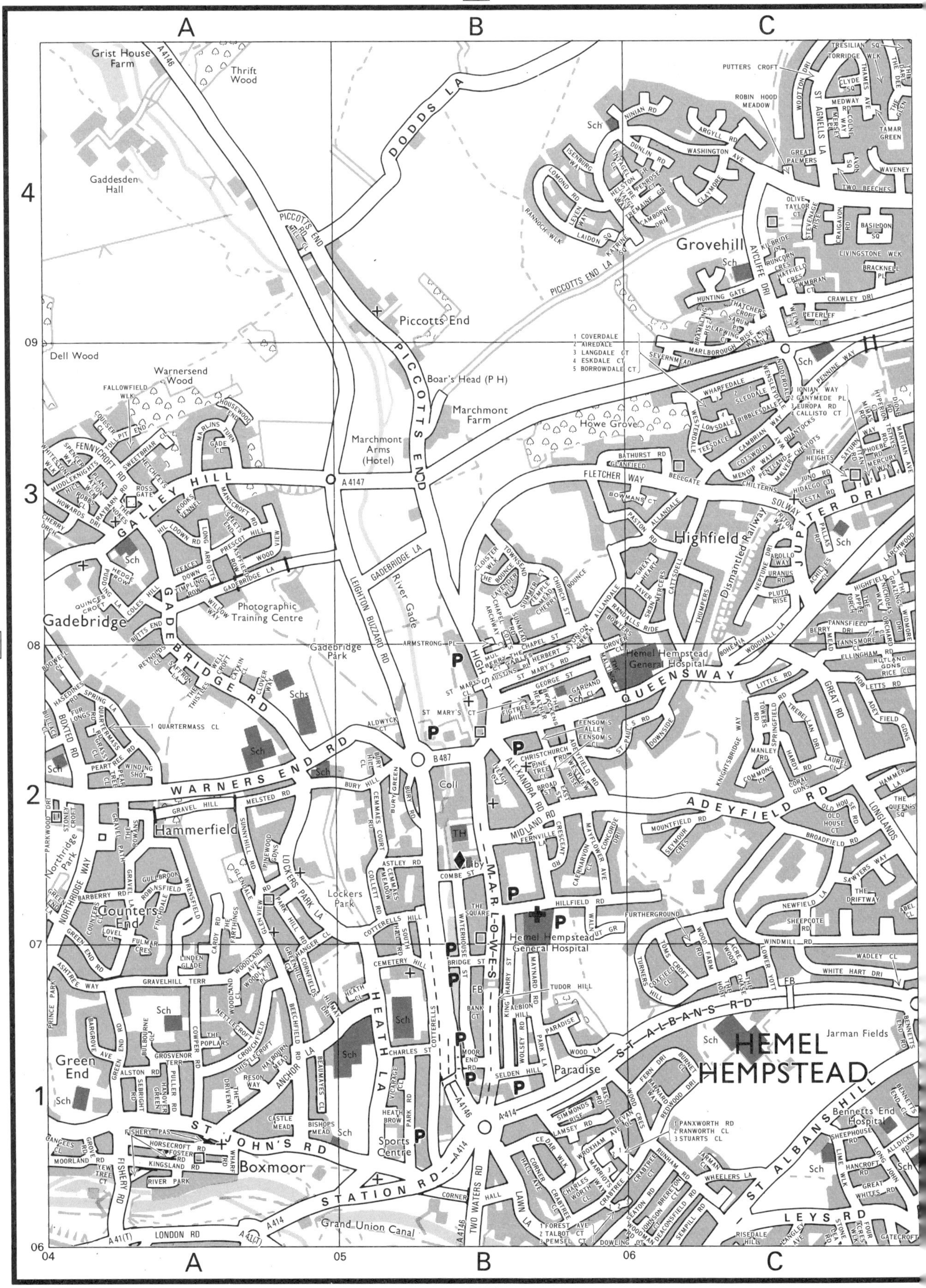
A
B
C
A
B
C
4
3
2
1
09
08
07
06
04
05
06
Grist House Farm
Thrift Wood
Gaddesden Hall
DODDS LA
PICCOTTS END
Piccotts End
PICCOTTS END LA
Dell Wood
Warnersend Wood
Boar's Head (P H)
Marchmont Farm
Marchmont Arms (Hotel)
Howe Grove
Grovehill
Sch
NINIAN RD
ARGYLL RD
WASHINGTON AVE
DUNLIN RD
ISENBURG WAY
LOMOND RD
RANNOCH WLK
LEVEN WAY
LAIDON SQ
CLAYMORE
AYCLIFFE DRI
HUNTING GATE
MARLBOROUGH RISE
SEVERNMEAD
PUTTERS CROFT
ROBIN HOOD MEADOW
GREAT PALMERS
ST AGNELLS LA
TWO BEECHES
WAVENEY
OLIVE TAYLOR CT
CRAIGAVON RD
BASILDON SQ
LIVINGSTONE WLK
BRACKNELL PL
CRAWLEY DRI
PETERLEE CT
TAMAR GREEN
TRESILIAN SQ
TORRIDGE WLK
THAMES AVE
MEDWAY RD
1 COVERDALE
2 AIREDALE
3 LANGDALE CT
4 ESKDALE CT
5 BORROWDALE CT
WHARFEDALE
WESTERDALE
LONSDALE
TEESDALE
RIBBLESDALE
PENNINE WAY
1 IONIAN WAY
2 GANYMEDE PL
3 EUROPA RD
4 CALLISTO CT
QUANTOCKS
CHEVIOTS
COTSWOLD
MENDIP WAY
PENTLAND
MALVERN WAY
CHILTERNS
SOLWAY
BATHURST RD
GLANFIELD
FLETCHER WAY
BELLGATE
BOWMANS CT
ALLANDALE
PASTON RD
Highfield
Dismantled Railway
JUPITER DRI
APOLLO WAY
URANUS RD
NEPTUNE DRI
PLUTO RISE
ACHILLES CL
PALLAS RD
JUNO RD
HIDALGO CT
VESTA RD
THE HEIGHTS
SATURN WAY
PHOEBE RD
MERCURY WLK
MARTIAN AVE
LARCHWOOD RD
HIGHFIELD LA
ORCHARD
TANNSFIELD DRI
TANNSMORE CL
ELLINGHAM RD
RUTLAND GDNS
HOBLETTS RD
LITTLE RD
BOHEMIA
WOODHALL LA
QUEENSWAY
Hemel Hempstead General Hospital
CATTSDELL
THUMPERS
MERCERS
RANDALLS RIDE
CLOISTER WLK
TOWNSEND
THE BOUNCE
LAVENDER WLK
CHURCH ST
CHAPEL ST
ST MARY'S RD
GEORGE ST
GARLAND CL
HIGH ST
ARMSTRONG PL
ST MARY'S CL
ST MARY'S CT
FIGTREE HILL
FENSOM'S ALLEY
FENSOM'S CL
ST PAUL'S RD
DOWNSIDE
CHRISTCHURCH RD
PINE TREE CL
ALEXANDRA RD
BROAD ST
EAST ST
WESTVIEW RISE
ADEYFIELD RD
KNIGHTSBRIDGE WAY
TOWERS RD
SPRINGFIELD RD
TREBELLAN DRI
GREAT RD
ADEY FIELD GDNS
MANLEY RD
COMMONS LA
HARDY RD
LAUREL CL
CORAL GDNS
OLD HOUSE CT
OLD HOUSE RD
LONGLANDS
HAMMER LA
THE QUEEN'S SQ
MOUNTFIELD RD
SEYMOUR CRES
BROADFIELD RD
SAWYERS WAY
THE DRIFTWAY
NEWFIELD LA
SHEEPCOTE RD
WINDMILL RD
WADLEY CL
WHITE HART DRI
FURTHERGROUND
WOOD FARM RD
ACRE WOOD
TOMS CROFT
TURNERS HILL
OXFIELD CL
THE HOLT
THE CHASE
LOWER YOTT
FB
ST ALBANS RD
Sch
HEMEL HEMPSTEAD
Jarman Fields
BENNETTS END RD
Bennetts End Hospital
ST ALBANS HILL
SHEEPHOUSE RD
LIME WLK
HANCROFT RD
GREAT WHITES RD
ALLDICKS RD
LEYS RD
RISEDALE HILL
STONE CL
FOUR TREES
GATECROFT
FERN DRI
BARNARD WAY
REDWOOD DRI
WOOD CRES
1 PANXWORTH RD
2 RANWORTH CL
3 STUARTS CL
JARMAN CL
WHEELERS LA
RUNHAM RD
CRABTREE LA
WROXHAM AVE
BEVAN CL
SIMMONDS RISE
LAMSEY RD
BASSIL RD
CEDAR WLK
CORNER HALL AVE
CHARLES WORTH CL
MARRIOTS WAY
SEATON RD
BRERETON RD
DEACONSFIELD RD
SEMPILL RD
DOWLING CT
1 FOREST AVE
2 TALBOT CT
3 PEMSEL CT
LAWN LA
TWO WATERS RD
CORNER HALL
A414
A4146
Paradise
WOOD LA
PARADISE
TUDOR HILL
SELDEN HILL
PARK LA
WOLSEY RD
ALBION HILL
KING HARRY ST
MAYNARD RD
Hemel Hempstead General Hospital
HILLFIELD RD
WALNUT GR
MIDLAND RD
FERNVILLE LA
CRESCENT RD
CAERNARVON CL
MAYFLOWER AVE
CONCORDE DRI
MARLOWES
COMBE ST
Liby
TH
Coll
B487
THE SQUARE
WATERHOUSE ST
BRIDGE ST
FB
BANK CT
MOOR END RD
COTTERELLS
COTTERELLS HILL
CHARLES ST
VICARAGE CL
HEATH BROW
PARK RD
Sports Centre
BISHOPS MEAD
BEAUMAYES CL
HEATH LA
CEMETERY HILL
SOUTH HILL RD
HEATH CL
ASTLEY RD
CEMMAES MEADOW
COLLETT RD
CEMMAES COURT
BURY HILL
BURY RD
BURY GREEN
BURY HILL CL
ALDWYCK CT
Lockers Park
LOCKERS PARK LA
PARK HILL RD
HANGER CL
CORNFIELDS
GREENHILL
HILLWAY DRI
BEECHFIELD RD
ANCHOR LA
CASTLE MEAD
Schs
Sch
LEIGHTON BUZZARD RD
GADEBRIDGE LA
River Gade
Gadebridge Park
Photographic Training Centre
Gadebridge
GADEBRIDGE RD
GADEBRIDGE LA
GALLEY HILL
A4147
A4146
FALLOWFIELD WLK
FENNYCROFT RD
SWEETBRIAR CL
MARLINS TURN
GADE CL
HOUSEWOOD END
MIDDLEKNIGHTS HILL
HOWARDS DRI
CHERRY ORCH
ROSS GATE
RAYBARN RD
COOKS VENNEL
MANSCROFT RD
HILLDOWN RD
LONG ARROTTS
PRESCOT HILL
WOOD VIEW
EFFACEY DOWN
PUDDING LA
HEDGE ROW
QUINCES CROFT
COLES HILL
BUTTS END
REYNOLDS CRES
SAFFRON CL
THISTLES
WELL CROFT
CATKIN CL
CLOVER WAY
1 QUARTERMASS CL
BODWELL CL
HASEDINES RD
SPRING LA
FURLONGS
BULLACE CL
BOXTED RD
PEARTREE CL
WINDING SHOT
WARNERS END RD
MELSTED RD
GRAVEL HILL
Hammerfield
PARKWOOD DRI
STONEY CROFT
Northridge Park
NORTHRIDGE WAY
GRAVEL PATH
GULL BROOK
ROBINSFIELD
WRENSFIELD
FINCHDALE
BARBERRY RD
Counters End
LOVEL CL
FULMAR CRES
LINDEN GLADE
CARDY RD
THE FARTHINGS
GLENVIEW RD
SUNNYHILL RD
PINEWOOD DRI
GLENDALE
ASHTREE WAY
GRAVELHILL TERR
WOODLAND AVE
WOODLAND RISE
PRINCE PARK
BARGROVE AVE
GREEN END RD
BURNS CL
Sch
THE POPLARS
COWPER RD
GROSVENOR TERR
NETTLECROFT
CROUCHFIELD
THISTLECROFT
HAYBOURN MEAD
RESON WAY
THE DRIVEWAY
Green End
ALSTON RD
SEBRIGHT RD
HANOVER GREEN
PULLER RD
ST JOHN'S RD
FISHERY PAS
HORSECROFT RD
FOSTER RD
KINGSLAND RD
WHARF RD
Boxmoor
RIVER PARK
GANGELS CL
GROVE RD
MOORLAND RD
YEW TREE CT
FISHERY RD
STATION RD
Grand Union Canal
A414
LONDON RD
A41(T)

138

105

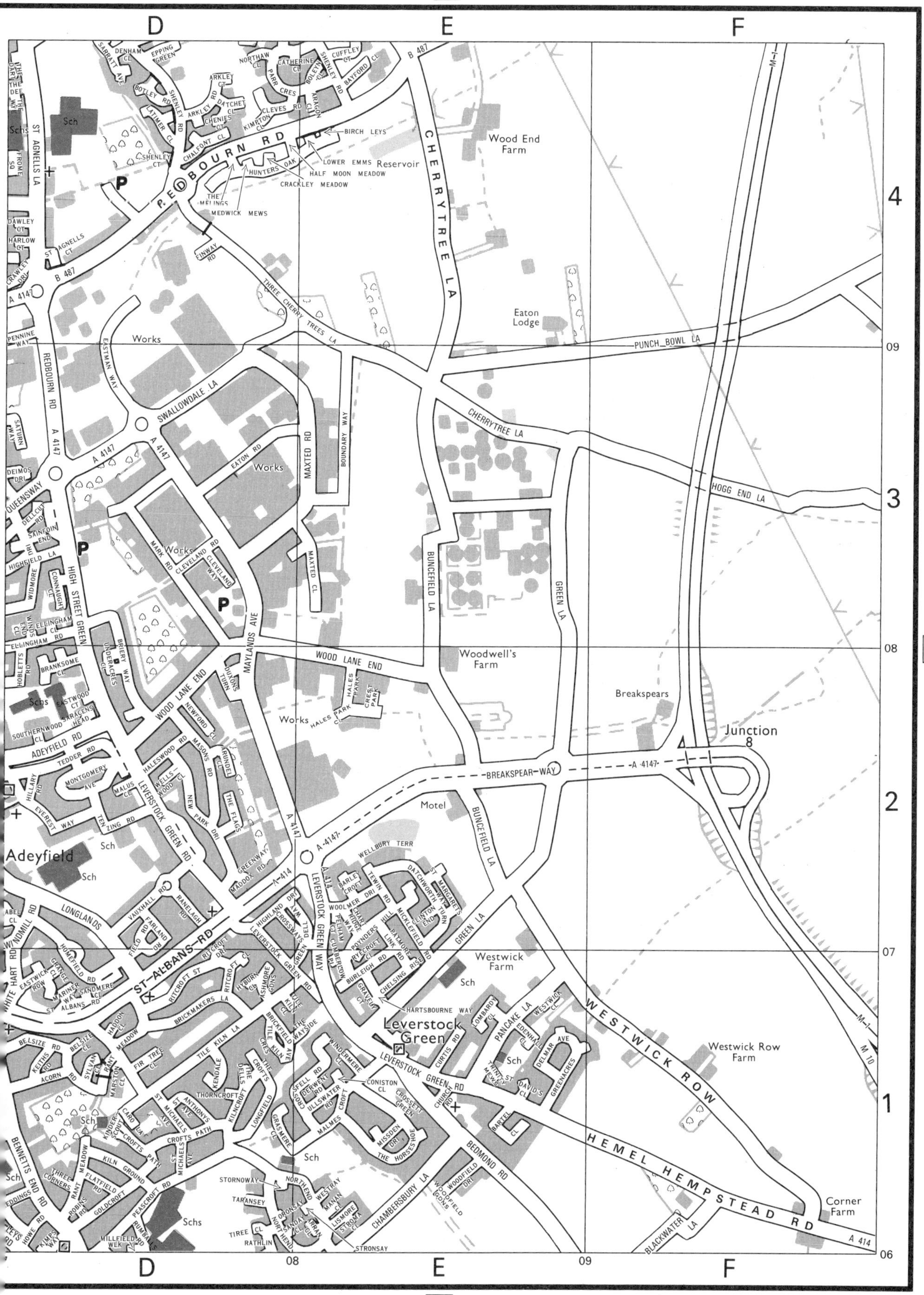
D
E
F
4
3
2
1
09
08
07
06
09
08
REDBOURN RD
CHERRYTREE LA
Wood End Farm
Reservoir
BIRCH LEYS
LOWER EMMS
HALF MOON MEADOW
CRACKLEY MEADOW
HUNTERS OAK
THE MELINGS
MEDWICK MEWS
ST AGNELLS LA
ST AGNELLS CT
DAWLEY CT
HARLOW CT
CRAWLEY DRI
B 487
A 4147
PENNINE WAY
Works
EASTMAN WAY
THREE CHERRY TREES LA
Eaton Lodge
PUNCH BOWL LA
M-1
SWALLOWDALE LA
MAXTED RD
BOUNDARY WAY
HOGG END LA
EATON RD
QUEENSWAY
HIGH STREET GREEN
MAYLANDS AVE
MARK RD
CLEVELAND RD
BUNCEFIELD LA
GREEN LA
MAXTED CL
WOOD LANE END
Woodwell's Farm
Breakspears
Junction 8
BREAKSPEAR WAY
Motel
HALES PARK
CREST PARK
ADEYFIELD RD
Adeyfield
Sch
Schs
LEVERSTOCK GREEN RD
LEVERSTOCK GREEN WAY
WELLBURY TERR
LONGLANDS
ST ALBANS RD
WINDMILL RD
WHITE HART RD
Westwick Farm
WESTWICK ROW
Westwick Row Farm
Leverstock Green
PANCAKE LA
HARTSBOURNE WAY
M 10
HEMEL HEMPSTEAD RD
A 414
BEDMOND RD
CHAMBERSBURY LA
BLACKWATER LA
Corner Farm
BENNETTS END RD
BRICKMAKERS LA
TILE KILN LA
CROFTS PATH
STORNOWAY
TARANSEY
TIREE
RATHLIN
STRONSAY

126

139

106

125

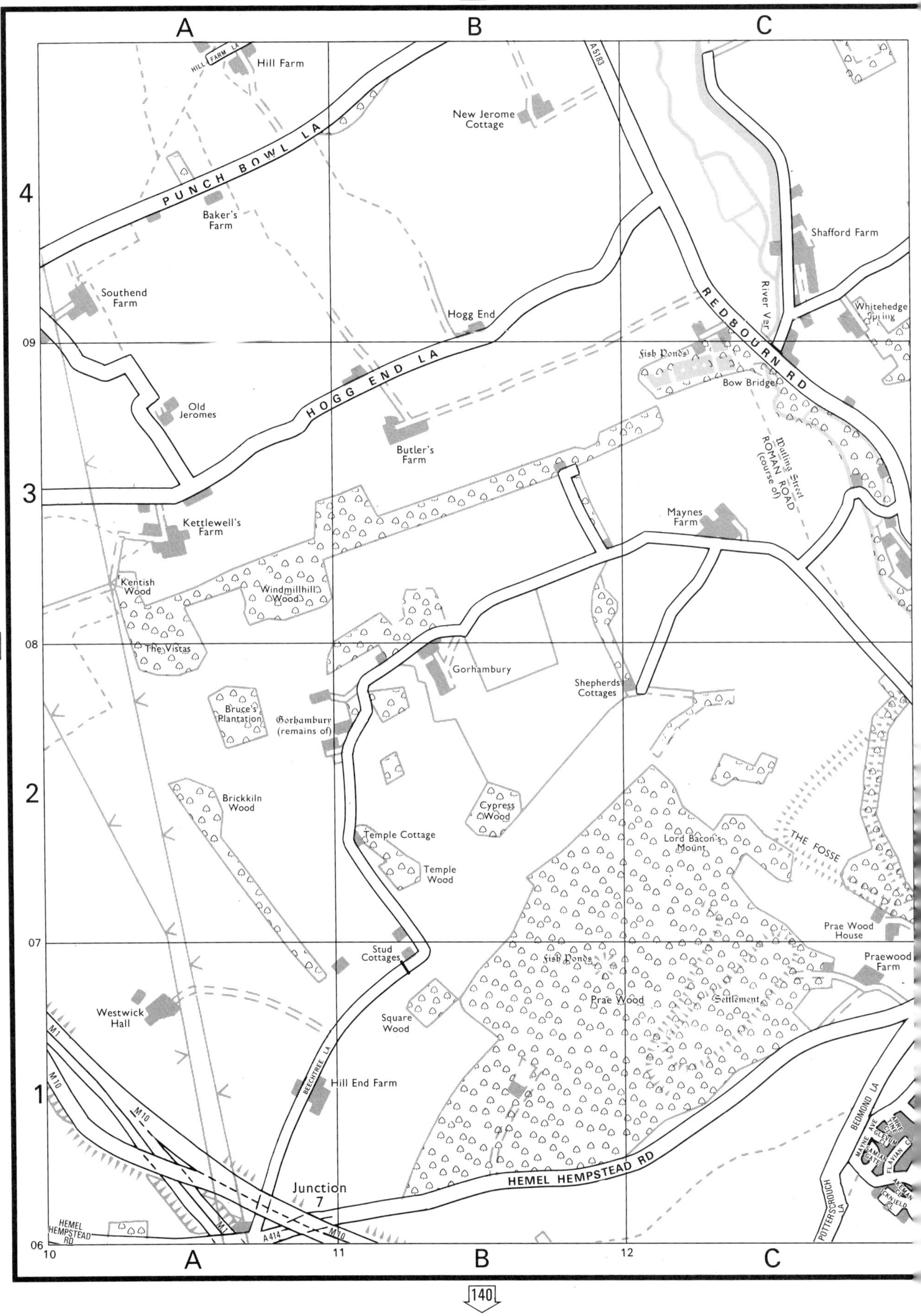
A
B
C
A
B
C
4
3
2
1
09
08
07
06
10
11
12
HILL FARM LA
Hill Farm
A5183
New Jerome
Cottage
PUNCH BOWL LA
Baker's
Farm
Shafford Farm
Southend
Farm
Hogg End
River Ver
Whitehedge
Spring
REDBOURN RD
Fish Ponds
Bow Bridge
Old
Jeromes
HOGG END LA
Butler's
Farm
Watling Street
ROMAN ROAD
(course of)
Kettlewell's
Farm
Maynes
Farm
Kentish
Wood
Windmillhill
Wood
The Vistas
Gorhambury
Shepherds
Cottages
Bruce's
Plantation
Gorhambury
(remains of)
Brickkiln
Wood
Cypress
Wood
Temple Cottage
Lord Bacon's
Mount
THE FOSSE
Temple
Wood
Prae Wood
House
Stud
Cottages
Fish Ponds
Praewood
Farm
Westwick
Hall
Prae Wood
Settlement
Square
Wood
M1
M10
BEECHTREE LA
Hill End Farm
BEDMOND LA
MAYNE AVE
GLEVUM CL
SAMIAN GATE
FLAVIAN CL
AKEMAN CL
ICKNIELD CL
POTTERSCROUCH LA
HEMEL HEMPSTEAD RD
Junction
7
HEMEL
HEMPSTEAD
RD
A414
M10
M1

140

107

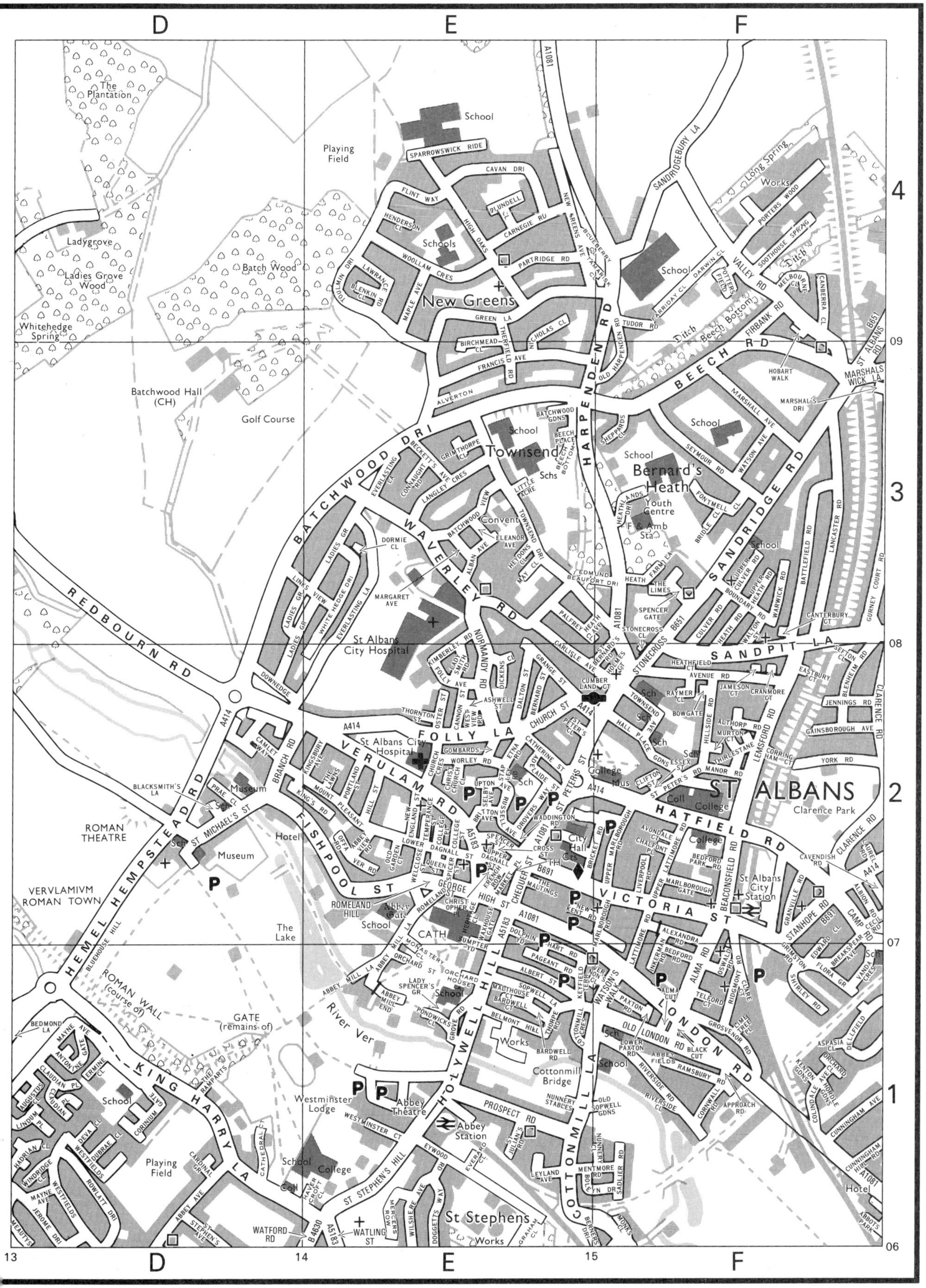
D
E
F
The Plantation
School
Playing Field
SPARROWSWICK RIDE
CAVAN DRI
FLINT WAY
HENDERSON CL
Schools
HIGH OAKS
CARNEGIE RU
Ladygrove
Batch Wood
Ladies Grove Wood
WOOLLAM CRES
PARTRIDGE RD
New Greens
MAPLE AVE
BLENKIN CL
LAWRANCE RD
TOULMIN DRI
Whitehedge Spring
GREEN LA
BIRCHMEAD CL
THERFIELD RD
NICHOLAS CL
FRANCIS AVE
ALVERTON
A1081
NEW GREENS AVE
BLUEBERRY CL
SANDRIDGEBURY LA
School
Long Spring
Works
PORTERS WOOD
SOOTHOUSE SPRING
DARWIN CL
Ditch
VALLEY RD
MELBOURNE CL
CANBERRA CL
TUDOR RD
FARRIDAY CL
POTTERS FIELD
Beech Bottom
FIRBANK RD
B651
ST ALBANS RD
HARPENDEN RD
OLD HARPENDEN RD
BEECH RD
HOBART WALK
MARSHALS WICK LA
MARSHALS DRI
4
09
Batchwood Hall (CH)
Golf Course
School
Townsend
BATCHWOOD GDNS
BEECH PLACE
BEECH BOTTOM
SHEPPARDS CL
School
MARSHALL AVE
SEYMOUR RD
WATSON AVE
School
Bernard's Heath
Youth Centre
F & Amb Sta
FONTMELL CL
BRIDLE CL
SANDRIDGE RD
BATCHWOOD DRI
EVERLASTING LA
BECKETT'S AVE
CONNAUGHT RD
GRIMTHORPE CL
LANGLEY CRES
LITTLE ACRE
Schs
WAVERLEY RD
Convent
BATCHWOOD VIEW
ELEANOR AVE
ALBAN AVE
TOWNSEND DRI
HEYDONS CL
MAY CL
EDMUND BEAUFORT DRI
HEATHLANDS DRI
HEATH FARM LA
THE LIMES
School
UPPER CULVER RD
UPPER HEATH RD
BOUNDARY RD
BATTLEFIELD RD
LANCASTER RD
GURNEY COURT RD
3
DORMIE CL
LADIES GR
LINKS VIEW
WHITE HEDGE DRI
MARGARET AVE
REDBOURN RD
St Albans City Hospital
SPENCER GATE
STONECROSS CL
PALFREY HEATH CL
CULVER RD
HEATH RD
WARWICK RD
WALTON ST
CANTERBURY CT
SANDPIT LA
SEFTON CL
08
KIMBERLEY RD
NORMANDY RD
DICKENS CL
GRANGE ST
CARLISLE AVE
BERNARD'S CL
HOLMES CT
STONECROSS
HEATHFIELD CT
AVENUE RD
EASTBURY CT
BLENHEIM RD
CLARENCE RD
DOWNEDGE
FOLLY AVE
LADY SMITH WAY
DALTON ST
BERNARD ST
CUMBERLAND CT
JAMESON CT
CRANMORE CT
RAYMER CL
TOWNSEND AVE
BOWGATE
JENNINGS RD
THORNTON ST
OSTER ST
CANNON ST
WEST VIEW RD
ASHWELL ST
CHURCH ST
A414
ST PETER'S CL
HALL PLACE GDNS
HILLSIDE RD
ALTHORP RD
MURTON CT
LEMSFORD RD
GAINSBOROUGH AVE
CAMLET WAY
BRANCH RD
KINGSBURY AVE
THE LAWNS
FOLLY LA
St Albans City Hospital
GOMBARDS
WORLEY RD
ETNA RD
CATHERINE ST
College
Sch
ESSEX RD
THIRLESTANE
CORRINGHAM CT
YORK RD
BLACKSMITH'S LA
Museum
PRAE CL
VERULAM RD
PORTLAND ST
MOUNT PLEASANT
HILL ST
KING'S RD
CHRIST CHURCH CL
UPTON AVE
SELBY AVE
RUSSELL AVE
DROVERS WAY
ST PETERS ST
Mus
CLIFTON ST
ST PETER'S RD
MANOR RD
Coll
College
ST ALBANS
Clarence Park
2
ROMAN THEATRE
Sch
ST MICHAEL'S ST
Museum
Hotel
FISHPOOL ST
OFFA RD
ABBEY VIEW RD
VER RD
LOWER DAGNALL ST
NEW ENGLAND ST
TEMPERANCE ST
COLLEGE PL
A5183
SPENCER ST
UPPER DAGNALL ST
CROSS ST
WADDINGTON RD
City Hall
Cts
BRICKET RD
UPPER MARLBOROUGH RD
AVONDALE RD
CHALFONT PL
LATTIMORE RD
College
HATFIELD RD
BEDFORD PARK RD
CAVENDISH RD
VERULAMIVM ROMAN TOWN
WELLCLOSE ST
QUEEN ST
GEORGE ST
CHRISTOPHER PL
FRENCH ROW
MARKET PL
CHEQUER ST
THE MALTINGS
B691
NEW KENT RD
LIVERPOOL RD
UPPER LATTIMORE RD
MARLBOROUGH GATE
St Albans City Station
VICTORIA ST
BEACONSFIELD RD
GRANVILLE RD
STANHOPE RD
CAMP RD
ALBION RD
CECIL RD
ROMELAND HILL
Abbey Gate
School
HIGH ST
WAXHOUSE GATE
The Lake
CATH
A1081
DOLPHIN YD
SUMPTER YD
ALEXANDRA RD
BEDFORD RD
ALMA RD
OSWALD RD
RIDGMONT RD
EDWARD CL
BREAKSPEAR AVE
07
BLUEHOUSE HILL
HEMEL HEMPSTEAD RD
ROMAN WALL (course of)
ABBEY MILL LA
MONASTERY CL
ORCHARD ST
HART RD
PAGEANT RD
ALBERT ST
KEYFIELD TERR
WATSON'S WALK
LATTIMORE RD
INKERMAN RD
CLARE RD
GRIMSTON RD
FLORA GR
SHIRLEY RD
VANDA CRES
LADY SPENCER'S GR
ABBEY MILL END
ORCHARD HOUSE
School
MALTHOUSE CT
SOPWELL LA
BARDWELL CT
PAXTON RD
ALMA CUT
TELFORD CT
LIME TREE PL
BEDMOND LA
MAYNE AVE
ANTONINE GATE
ERMINE CL
GATE (remains of)
River Ver
PONDWICKS CL
GROVE RD
HOLYWELL HILL
BELMONT HILL
THORPE RD
Works
COTTONMILL CRES
OLD LONDON RD
LONDON RD
GROSVENOR RD
ASPASIA CL
DELLFIELD
ORCHARD CL
CLAUDIAN PL
AUGUSTUS CL
School
CORINIUM GATE
THE RAMPARTS
KING HARRY LA
BARDWELL RD
Sch
Cottonmill Bridge
LOWER PAXTON RD
ABBEY FIELDS
BLACK CUT
RAMSBURY RD
RIVERSIDE RD
KENTON GDNS
COLINDALE AVE
NORBROKE GDNS
1
LINDUM PL
DEVA CL
WESTFIELDS
DUBRAE CL
PP
Westminster Lodge
Abbey Theatre
NUNNERY STABLES
OLD SOPWELL GDNS
RIVERSIDE CL
CORNWALL RD
APPROACH RD
CUNNINGHAM AVE
HADRIAN CL
WINDRIDGE CL
ROWLATT DRI
Playing Field
CARDINAL GR
CATHEDRAL CT
WESTMINSTER CT
PROSPECT RD
Abbey Station
ST JULIAN'S RD
NUNNERY CL
School
College
EYWOOD RD
EVERARD CL
LEYLAND AVE
MENTMORE RD
SADLIER RD
BOLEYN DR
CUNNINGHAM HILL RD
A1081
Hotel
MAYNE AVE
JEROME DRI
MEAUTYS
ABBEY AVE
ST STEPHEN'S AVE
WATFORD RD
B4630
Coll
HAVERCROFT CL
A5183
ST STEPHEN'S HILL
WILSHERE AVE
MERCERS ROW
DOGGETTS WAY
St Stephens
WATLING ST
Works
GRAHAM CL
COTTONMILL LA
BERNERS DRI
ABBOTS PARK
06
13
14
15
D
E
F

128

141

108

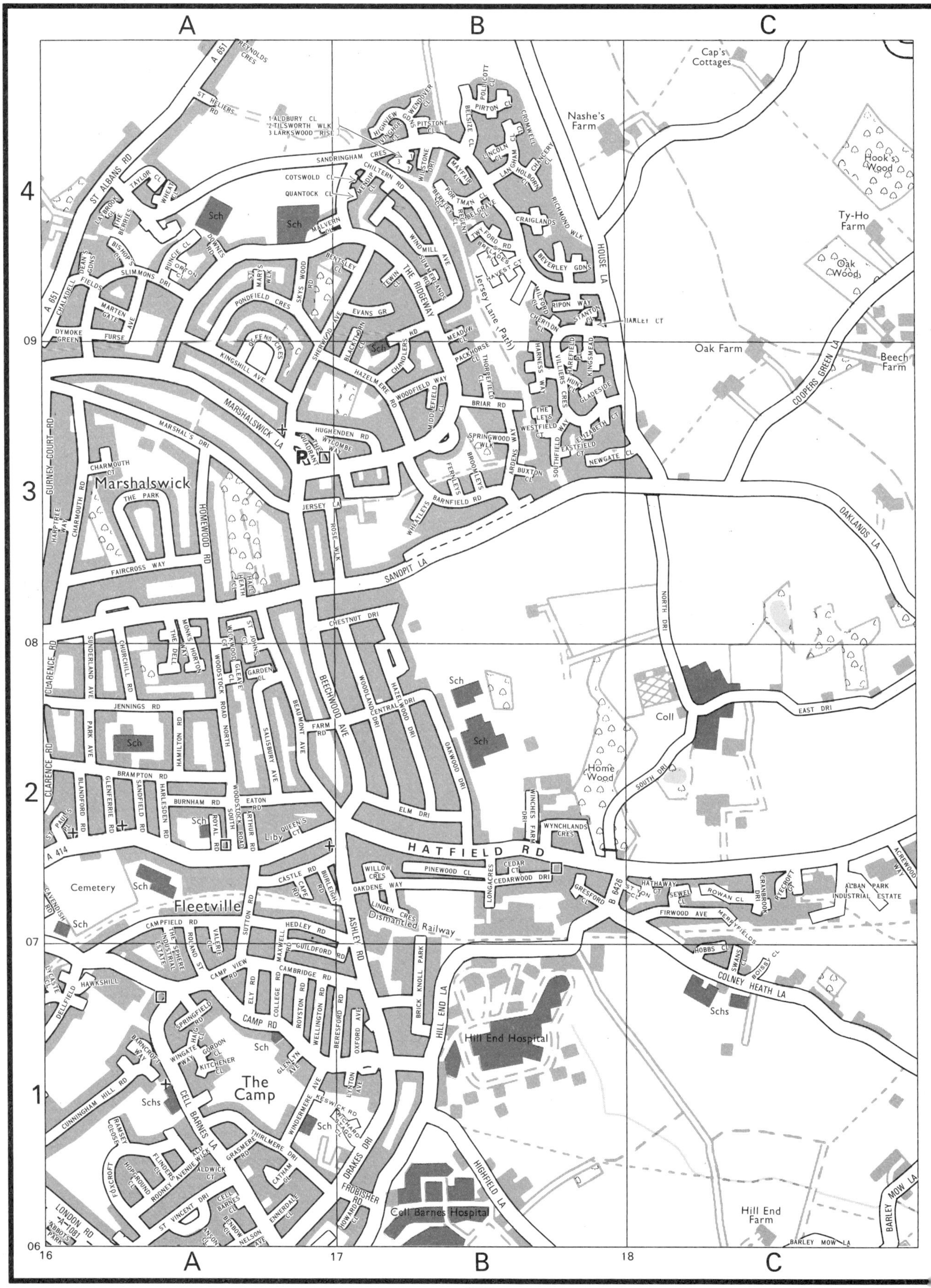

A
B
C
4
3
2
1
09
08
07
06
16
17
18
Cap's Cottages
Nashe's Farm
Hook's Wood
Ty-Ho Farm
Oak Wood
Oak Farm
Beech Farm
COOPERS GREEN LA
OAKLANDS LA
NORTH DRI
EAST DRI
SOUTH DRI
Coll
Home Wood
HOUSE LA
RICHMOND WLK
Jersey Lane (Path)
THE RIDGEWAY
SANDPIT LA
MARSHALSWICK LA
Marshalswick
HOMEWOOD RD
GURNEY COURT RD
ST ALBANS RD
A 651
REYNOLDS CRES
ST HELIERS RD
SANDRINGHAM CRES
1 ALDBURY CL
2 TILSWORTH WLK
3 LARKSWOOD RISE
COTSWOLD CL
QUANTOCK CL
CHILTERN RD
MENDIP
MALVERN
SLIMMONS DRI
FURSE AVE
DYMOKE GREEN
KINGSHILL AVE
POND FIELD CRES
EVANS GR
HAZELMERE RD
WOODFIELD WAY
BRIAR RD
NEWGATE CL
BARNFIELD RD
JERSEY LA
ROSE WLK
FAIRCROSS WAY
CHESTNUT DRI
JENNINGS RD
BRAMPTON RD
BURNHAM RD
EATON RD
BEECHWOOD AVE
ELM DRI
OAKWOOD DRI
HATFIELD RD
A 414
B 6426
PINEWOOD CL
CEDARWOOD DRI
WYNCHLANDS CRES
Cemetery
Fleetville
Dismantled Railway
ASHLEY RD
CAMPFIELD RD
HAWKSHILL
CAMP RD
HILL END LA
BRICK KNOLL PARK
Hill End Hospital
COLNEY HEATH LA
FIRWOOD AVE
ALBAN PARK INDUSTRIAL ESTATE
Schs
The Camp
CELL BARNES LA
CUNNINGHAM HILL RD
Cell Barnes Hospital
HIGHFIELD LA
DRAKES DRI
FROBISHER
LONDON RD
A 1081
Hill End Farm
BARLEY MOW LA
Sch
Liby

127

142

109

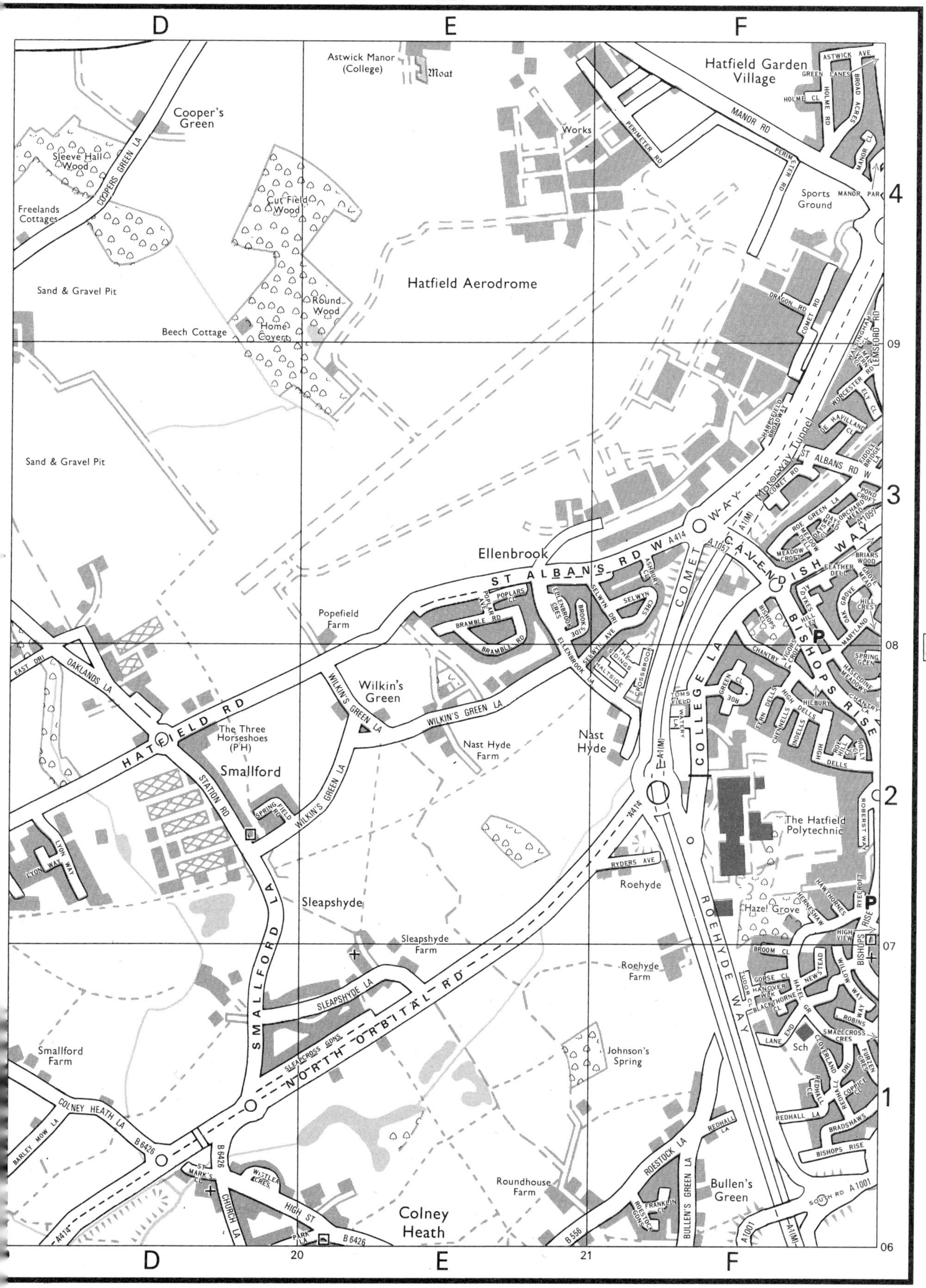
D
E
F
Astwick Manor
(College)
Moat
Hatfield Garden
Village
ASTWICK AVE
GREEN LANES
HOLME CL
HOLME RD
BROAD ACRES
MANOR CL
MANOR PAR
MANOR RD
Cooper's
Green
COOPERS GREEN LA
Sleeve Hall
Wood
Freelands
Cottages
Works
PERIMETER RD
Sports
Ground
4
Cut Field
Wood
Sand & Gravel Pit
Hatfield Aerodrome
Round
Wood
Beech Cottage
Home
Covert
DRAGON RD
COMET RD
LEMSFORD RD
09
WORCESTER RD
ELY CL
DE HAVILLAND CL
HARPSFIELD BROADWAY
Motorway Tunnel
ST ALBANS RD W
Sand & Gravel Pit
3
COMET RD
POND CROFT
ROE GREEN LA
ORCHARD MEAD
A1057
A1(M)
CAVENDISH WAY
Ellenbrook
ST ALBAN'S RD W
A414
A1057
MEADOW CROFT
BRIARS WOOD
FEATHER DELL
ASHBURY CL
SELWYN CRES
SELWYN DRI
COMET WAY
POPLARS CL
POPLAR AVE
ELLENBROOK CRES
BROOKSIDE
BRAMBLE RD
Popefield
Farm
BISHOPS RISE
MARYLAND
HILL CREST
OAK GROVE
08
130
EAST DRI
OAKLANDS LA
SELWYN AVE
ELLENBROOK LA
THE SIDINGS
CROSSBROOK
HALTSIDE
CHANTRY LA
VIGORS CROFT
SPRING GLEN
HASEDINE MEADOWS
CHANTRY LA
Wilkin's
Green
WILKIN'S GREEN LA
WILKIN'S GREEN LA
TOMS FIELD
WATERY LA
COLLEGE LA
ROE GREEN CL
FERN DELLS
HIGH DELLS
CHENNELLS
INDELLS
HILBURY
ROE HILL CL
HOLLY
HIGH DELLS
HATFIELD RD
The Three
Horseshoes
(P.H)
Smallford
Nast Hyde
Farm
Nast
Hyde
A1(M)
2
STATION RD
SPRINGFIELD RD
WILKIN'S GREEN LA
A414
The Hatfield
Polytechnic
ROBERTS WAY
LYON WAY
LYON WAY
RYDERS AVE
Roehyde
RYECROFT
HAWTHORNES
HERNESHAW
Sleapshyde
Hazel Grove
BISHOPS RISE
HIGH VIEW
P
Sleapshyde
Farm
ROEHYDE WAY
BROOM CL
07
Roehyde
Farm
NEWSTEAD
WILLOW WAY
GORSE CL
HANOVER WLK
TUDOR CL
BLACKTHORNE CL
HAZEL GR
ROBINS WAY
SLEAPSHYDE LA
NORTH ORBITAL RD
SMALLFORD LA
LANE END
Sch
SMALLCROSS CRES
Smallford
Farm
SLEAPCROSS GDNS
Johnson's
Spring
CLOVERLAND
FURZEN CRES
COPPICE CL
REDHALL CL
1
COLNEY HEATH LA
B6426
REDHALL LA
REDHALL LA
BRADSHAWS
BARLEY MOW LA
B6426
ROESTOCK LA
BULLEN'S GREEN LA
BISHOPS RISE
ST MARK'S CL
WISTLEA CRES
Roundhouse
Farm
Bullen's
Green
SOUTH RD
A1001
HIGH ST
CHURCH LA
FRANKLIN CL
ROESTOCK GDNS
A414
PARK LA
B6426
Colney
Heath
B556
A1001
A1(M)
06
D
20
E
21
F

143

110

129

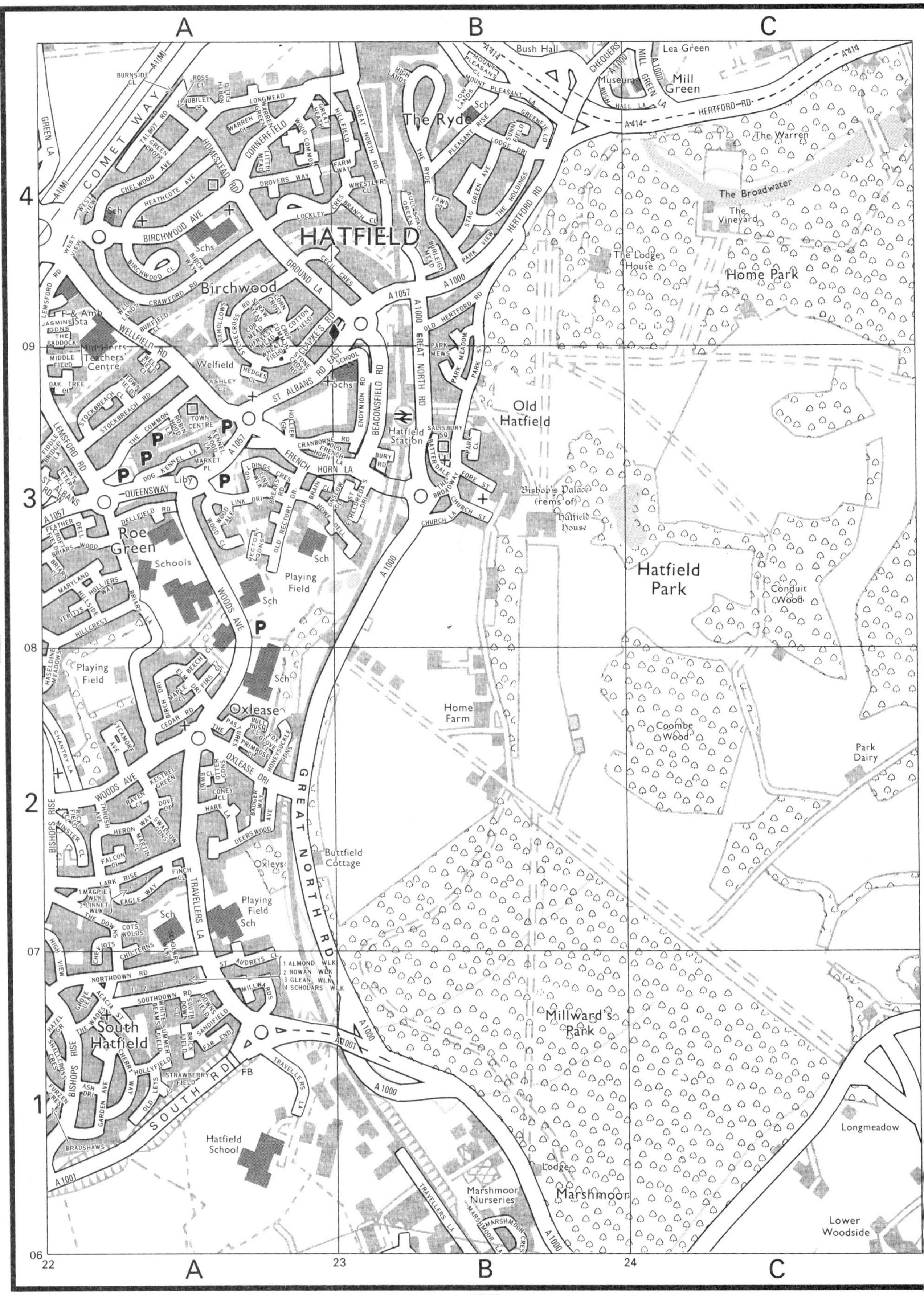
A
B
C
4
3
2
1
09
08
07
06
22
23
24
Bush Hall
Lea Green
Mill Green
Museum
CHEQUERS
MILL GREEN LA
BUSH HALL LA
A414
HERTFORD RD
The Warren
The Broadwater
The Vineyard
The Lodge House
Home Park
The Ryde
HATFIELD
Birchwood
Welfield
GREEN LA
COMET WAY
A1(M)
BURNSIDE CL
ROSS CL
JUBILEE CT
NORTH FIELD
TALBOT RD
GREEN CROFT
CHELWOOD AVE
HEATHCOTE AVE
HOMESTEAD RD
LONGMEAD
WARREN CL
CORNERFIELD
DROVERS WAY
FARM WAY
WRESTLERS CL
HILLFIELD
GREAT NORTH RD
HIGH LANDS
MOUNT PLEASANT
MOUNT PLEASANT LA
LOW LANDS
PLEASANT RISE
LODGE DRI
GREENFIELD
STAG GREEN AVE
THE HOLDINGS
PARK VIEW
HERTFORD RD
THE RYDE
BULLS LAND
BURLEIGH MEAD
LOCKLEY CRES
BRANCH CL
BIRCHWOOD AVE
BIRCHWOOD CL
BIRCH WAY
WEST VIEW
GROUND LA
CECIL CRES
CRAWFORD RD
A1057
A1000
OLD HERTFORD RD
PARK MEWS
PARK MEADOW
PARK ST
LEMSFORD RD
WELLFIELD RD
F & Amb Sta
JASMINE GDNS
THE PADDOCK
Mid-Herts Teachers' Centre
MIDDLE FIELD
OAK TREE CL
STOCKBREACH CL
STOCKBREACH RD
TOWN CENTRE
THE COMMON
ROBIN HOOD
KENNEL LA
DOG KENNEL LA
MARKET PL
ST ALBANS RD EAST
ASHLEY CT
HEDGES CL
SCHOOL LA
ENDYMION RD
BEACONSFIELD RD
Hatfield Station
SALISBURY SQ
BATTERDALE
FORE ST
PARK CL
BURY RD
THE BROADWAY
CHURCH ST
CHURCH LA
Old Hatfield
Bishop's Palace (rems of) Hatfield House
Hatfield Park
Conduit Wood
QUEENSWAY
Liby
CRANBORNE RD
FRENCH HORN LA
LINK DRI
OLD RECTORY DRI
RECTORY GDNS
WOOD CL
HOWE DELL
BRAIN CL
ETHELREDA'S DRI
DELLFIELD RD
Roe Green
Schools
FEATHER DELL
BRIARS WOOD
BRIARS LA
MARYLAND
HILLSIDE
HOLLIERS WAY
VERITYS
HILLCREST
WOODS AVE
Playing Field
Sch
Schs
HASELDINE MEADOWS
ELM DRI
BEECH DRI
MAPLE CL
BIRCH DRI
CEDAR RD
Oxlease
BULL RUSH CL
PASTURES
PRIMROSE CL
FOXGLOVE
HONEYSUCKLE GDNS
OXLEASE DRI
OTTER GDNS
CONEY CL
HARE LA
BADGER WAY
DEERSWOOD AVE
SYCAMORE AVE
CHANTRY LA
Home Farm
Coombe Wood
Park Dairy
BISHOPS RISE
MINSTER CL
THRUSH LA
RAVEN CT
KESTREL GREEN
DOVE CT
HERON WAY
MARTIN CL
SWALLOW GDNS
FALCON CL
LARK RISE
FINCH CL
MAGPIE WLK
LINNET WLK
EAGLE WAY
THE DOWNS
COTSWOLDS
CHILTERNS
CHEVIOTS
HIGH VIEW
TRAVELLERS LA
SCHOLARS WLK
ST AUDREYS CL
1 ALMOND WLK
2 ROWAN WLK
3 GLEAN WLK
4 SCHOLARS WLK
MILLWARDS
Buttfield Cottage
Oxleys
GREAT NORTH RD
NORTHDOWN RD
SOUTHDOWN RD
ACACIA ST
GROVE LEA
WHITE BEAMS
SOUTH DOWN
DOWNS CT
SANDIFIELD
South Hatfield
THE WADES
CHERRY WAY
HOLLYFIELD
BRICK FIELD
FAR END
HAZEL GR
SHALLCROSS CRES
FURZEN CRES
BISHOPS RISE
ASH DRI
GARDEN AVE
OLD LEYS
STRAWBERRY FIELD
SOUTH RD
FB
BRADSHAWS
A1001
TRAVELLERS LA
Hatfield School
Millward's Park
Lodge
Marshmoor
Marshmoor Nurseries
MARSHMOOR LA
MARSHMOOR CRES
Longmeadow
Lower Woodside

144

111

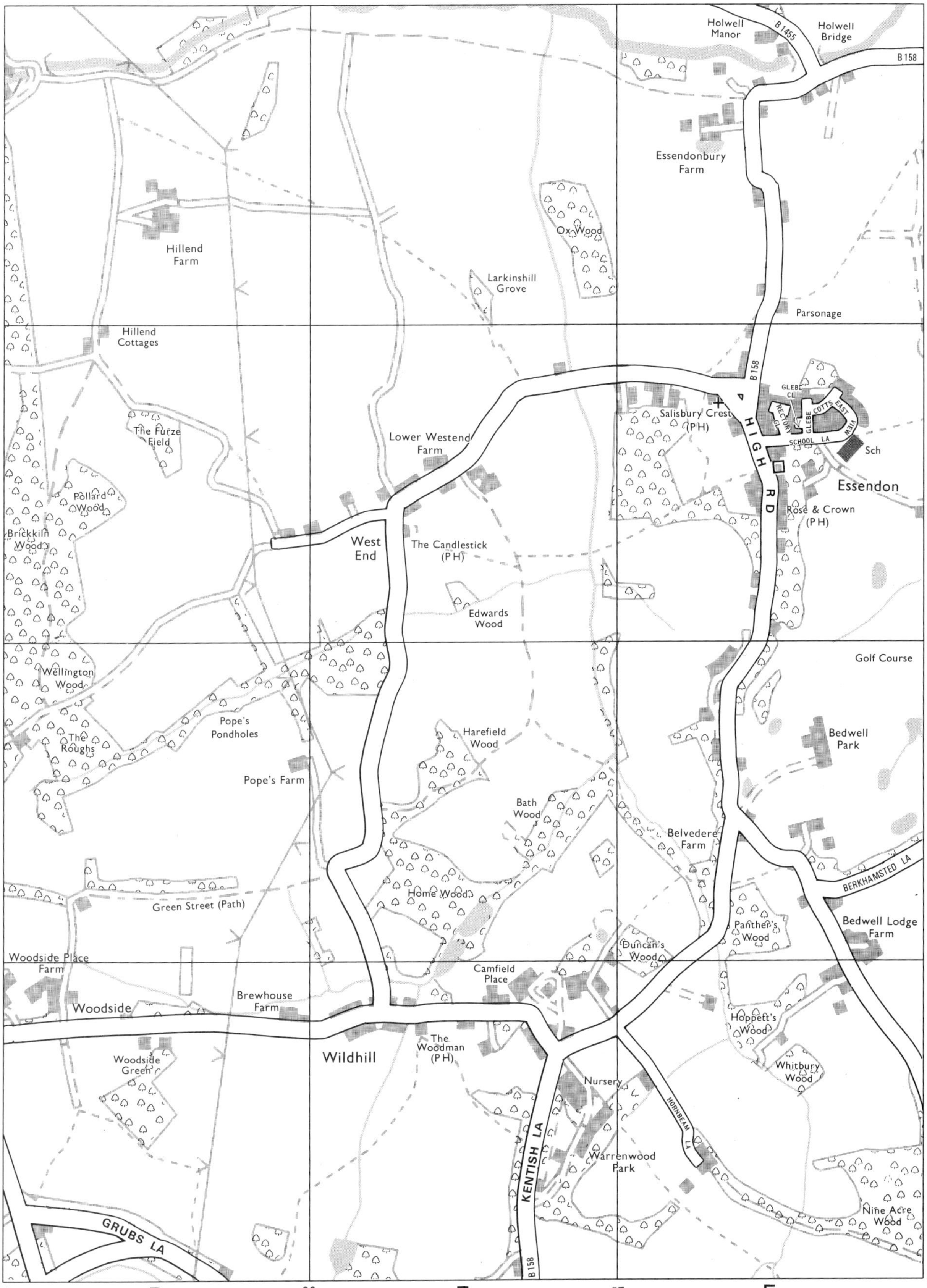
D
E
F
Holwell Manor
B 1455
Holwell Bridge
B 158
Essendonbury Farm
Hillend Farm
Ox Wood
Larkinshill Grove
Parsonage
Hillend Cottages
B 158
GLEBE CL
RECTORY CL
GLEBE COTTS
EAST VIEW
SCHOOL LA
Salisbury Crest (PH)
Sch
The Furze Field
Lower Westend Farm
HIGH RD
Essendon
Pollard Wood
Rose & Crown (PH)
Brickkiln Wood
West End
The Candlestick (PH)
Edwards Wood
Golf Course
Wellington Wood
Pope's Pondholes
Harefield Wood
Bedwell Park
The Roughs
Pope's Farm
Bath Wood
Belvedere Farm
BERKHAMSTED LA
Home Wood
Green Street (Path)
Panther's Wood
Bedwell Lodge Farm
Woodside Place Farm
Duncan's Wood
Camfield Place
Woodside
Brewhouse Farm
Hoppett's Wood
The Woodman (PH)
Wildhill
Woodside Green
Whitbury Wood
Nursery
HORNBEAM LA
KENTISH LA
Warrenwood Park
Nine Acre Wood
GRUBS LA
B 158
4
09
3
08
2
07
1
06
25
26
27
D
E
F

132

145

112

131

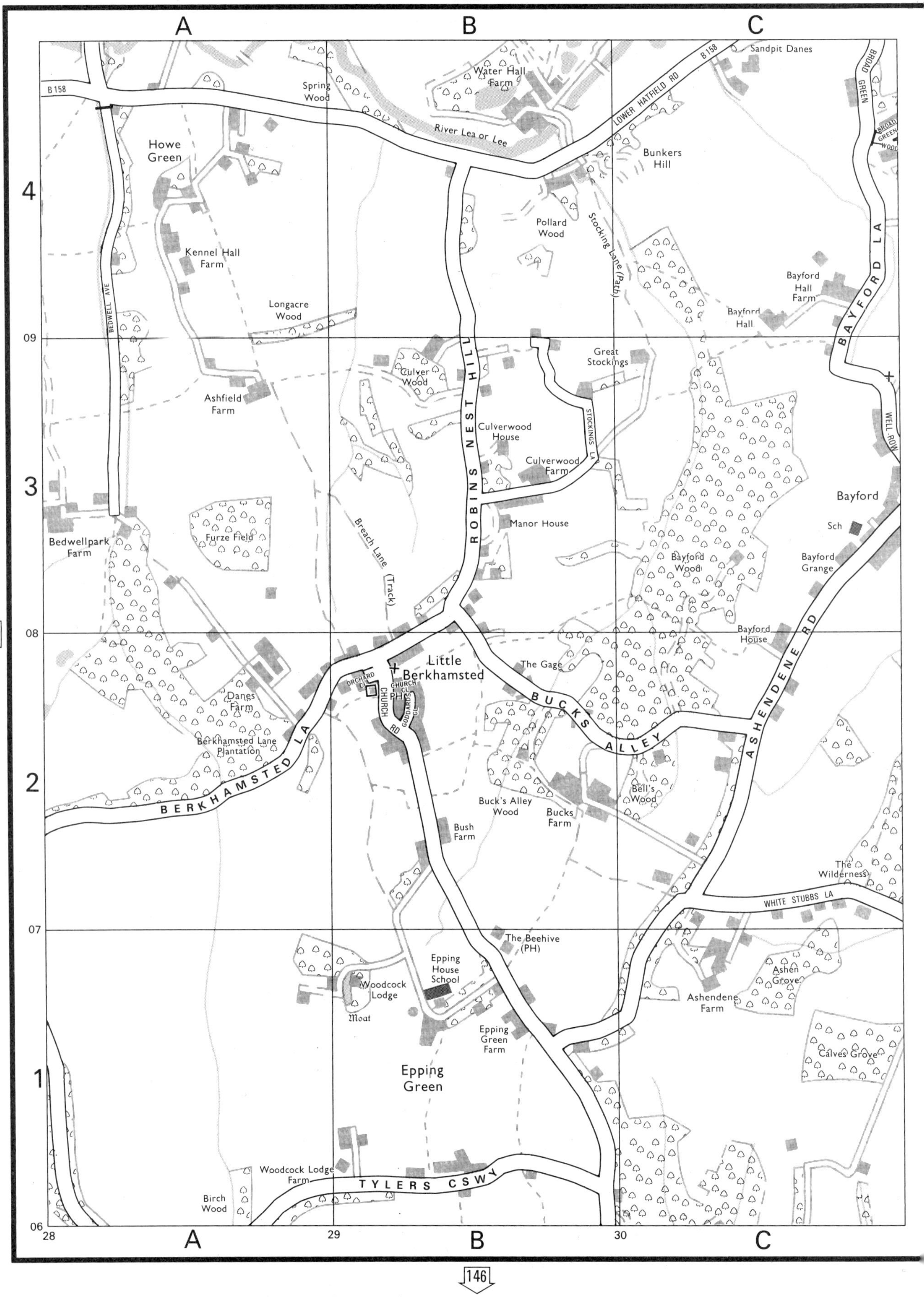
A
B
C
4
3
2
1
09
08
07
06
28
29
30
B 158
Spring Wood
Water Hall Farm
Sandpit Danes
LOWER HATFIELD RD
BROAD GREEN
BROAD GREEN WOOD
River Lea or Lee
Howe Green
Bunkers Hill
Pollard Wood
Stocking Lane (Path)
Kennel Hall Farm
BEDWELL AVE
Longacre Wood
Bayford Hall Farm
Bayford Hall
BAYFORD LA
Great Stockings
Culver Wood
Ashfield Farm
ROBINS NEST HILL
STOCKINGS LA
WELL ROW
Culverwood House
Culverwood Farm
Bayford
Furze Field
Breach Lane (Track)
Manor House
Sch
Bedwellpark Farm
Bayford Wood
Bayford Grange
Bayford House
ASHENDENE RD
Little Berkhamsted
The Gage
ORCHARD CL
CHURCH CL
CHURCH RD
GODDARDS CL
PH
Danes Farm
BUCKS ALLEY
Berkhamsted Lane Plantation
BERKHAMSTED LA
Bell's Wood
Buck's Alley Wood
Bucks Farm
Bush Farm
The Wilderness
WHITE STUBBS LA
The Beehive (PH)
Epping House School
Woodcock Lodge
Moat
Ashen Grove
Ashendene Farm
Epping Green Farm
Calves Grove
Epping Green
Woodcock Lodge Farm
TYLERS CSWY
Birch Wood

146

113

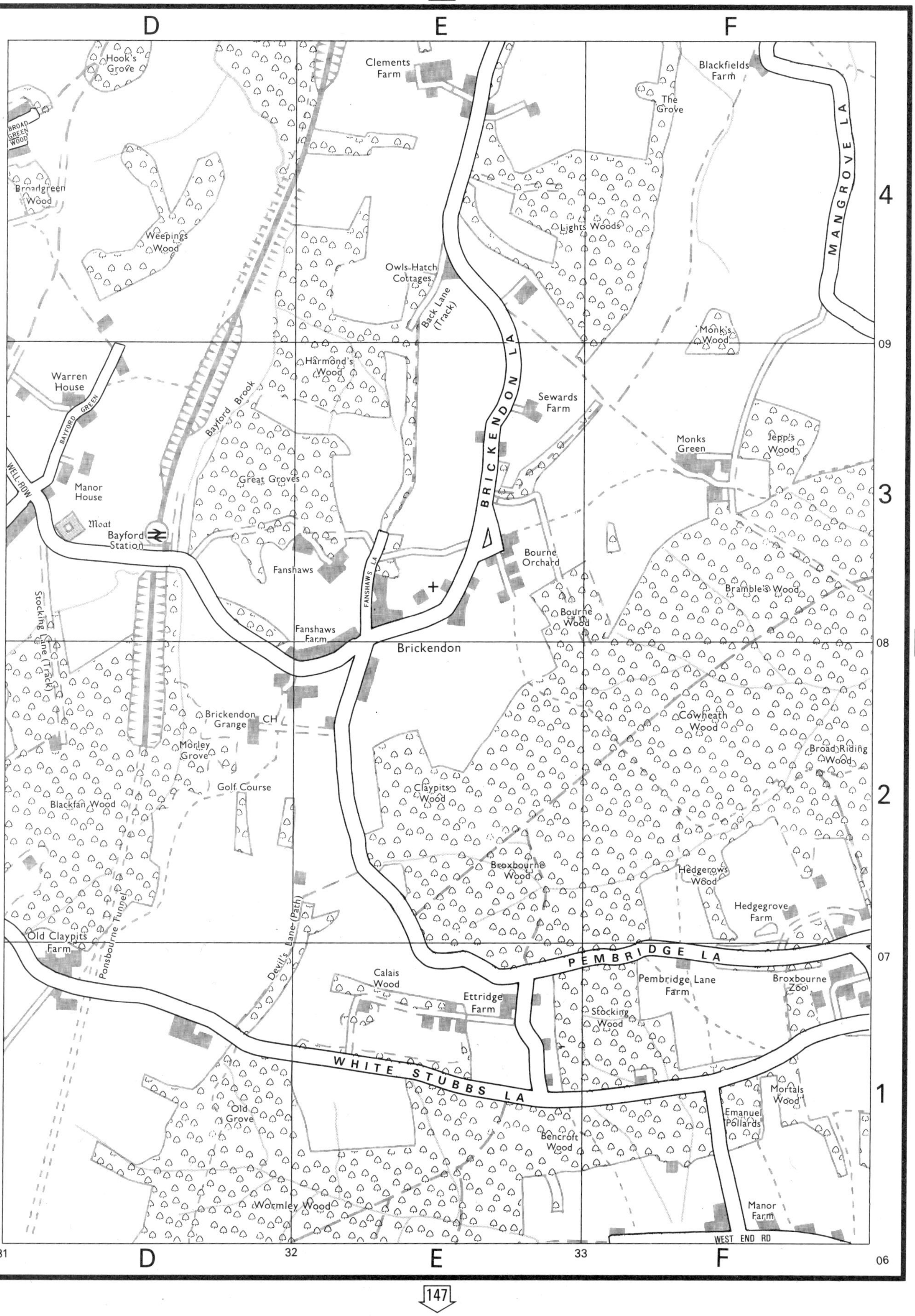
D
E
F
Hook's Grove
Clements Farm
Blackfields Farm
BROAD GREEN WOOD
The Grove
MANGROVE LA
Broadgreen Wood
4
Lights Woods
Weepings Wood
Owls Hatch Cottages
Back Lane (Track)
Monk's Wood
09
Harmond's Wood
Warren House
BRICKENDON LA
Sewards Farm
BAYFORD GREEN
Bayford Brook
Monks Green
Jepp's Wood
WELL-ROW
Manor House
Great Groves
3
Moat
Bayford Station
Bourne Orchard
Fanshaws
FANSHAWS LA
Bramble's Wood
Stocking Lane (Track)
Bourne Wood
Fanshaws Farm
Brickendon
08
Brickendon Grange
CH
Cowheath Wood
Morley Grove
Broad Riding Wood
Golf Course
Claypits Wood
2
Blackfan Wood
Broxbourne Wood
Hedgerows Wood
Hedgegrove Farm
Old Claypits Farm
Ponsbourne Tunnel
Devil's Lane (Path)
PEMBRIDGE LA
07
Calais Wood
Pembridge Lane Farm
Broxbourne Zoo
Ettridge Farm
Stocking Wood
WHITE STUBBS LA
1
Mortals Wood
Old Grove
Emanuel Pollards
Bencroft Wood
Wormley Wood
Manor Farm
WEST END RD
31
32
33
06
D
E
F

134

147

114

133

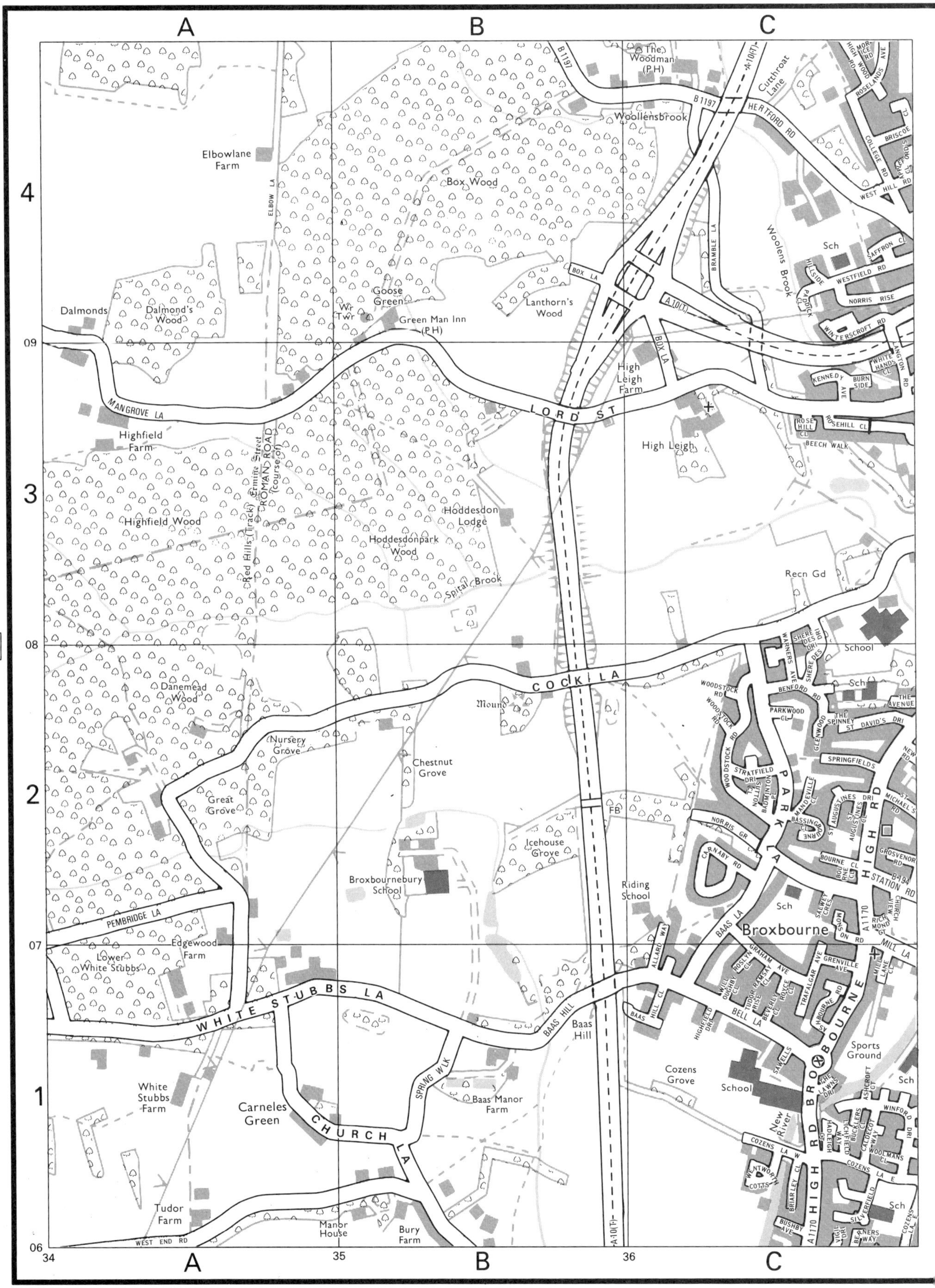
A
B
C
4
3
2
1
09
08
07
06
34
35
36
The Woodman (PH)
B1197
A10(T)
Cutthroat Lane
Woollensbrook
HERTFORD RD
Elbowlane Farm
ELBOW LA
Box Wood
BRAMBLE LA
Woolens Brook
Sch
HILLSIDE
PADDOCK CL
WESTFIELD RD
SAFFRON CL
NORRIS RISE
WINTERSCROFT RD
COLLEGE RD
BRISCOE CL
WEST HILL RD
ROSELANDS AVE
BOX LA
Lanthorn's Wood
Goose Green
Wr Twr
Green Man Inn (PH)
Dalmonds
Dalmond's Wood
High Leigh Farm
KENNEDY AVE
BURNSIDE
WHITE HANDS CL
LANGTON RD
MANGROVE LA
LORD ST
ROSE HILL CL
ROSEHILL CL
BEECH WALK
Highfield Farm
High Leigh
Red Hills (Track) Ermine Street
ROMAN ROAD (course of)
Highfield Wood
Hoddesdon Lodge
Hoddesdonpark Wood
Spital Brook
Recn Gd
School
Sch
Danemead Wood
COCK LA
Mound
WARNERS AVE
SHERE DES DRI
BENFORD RD
WOODSTOCK RD
PARKWOOD CL
THE SPINNEY
ST DAVID'S DRI
THE AVENUE
GLENWOOD
SPRINGFIELDS
Nursery Grove
Chestnut Grove
STRATFIELD DRI
NOLLIS CL
BADMINTON
PARK LA
MANDEVILLE CL
ST AUGUSTINES DRI
ST MICHAEL'S RD
Great Grove
FB
NORRIS GR
BASSINGBOURNE CL
Icehouse Grove
CARNABY RD
BOURNE CL
GROSVENOR RD
HIGH RD
B194
STATION RD
Broxbournebury School
Riding School
Sch
SALWEY CRES
CHURCH VIEW
RICHMOND CT
Broxbourne
A1170
PEMBRIDGE LA
ALLARD WAY
BAAS LA
GRAHAM AVE
ROSLYN CL
MONSON RD
MILL LA
Edgewood Farm
Lower White Stubbs
WILLOUGHBY CL
TUDOR RISE
RAMSAY CL
BEVERLEY CL
ROYCE CL
TRAFALGAR AVE
GRENVILLE AVE
MILL LANE CL
WHITE STUBBS LA
BAAS HILL
Baas Hill
BAAS HILL CL
HIGHFIELD DRI
BELL LA
SEYBOURNE RD
BROXBOURNE
Sports Ground
White Stubbs Farm
SPRING WLK
Cozens Grove
SAWELLS
School
THE LAWNS DRI
ASHCROFT CT
Sch
Carneles Green
Baas Manor Farm
New River
HADLEIGH WAY
BUCKLERS CL
LICHFIELD WAY
CALDICOT WAY
WINFORD DRI
CHURCH LA
COZENS LA W
WOOLMANS CL
COZENS LA E
WENTWORTH COTTS
BRIARLEY CL
Tudor Farm
Manor House
Bury Farm
BUSHBY AVE
SILVERFIELD
Sch
WEST END RD
A10(T)
A1170
VIGIL DRI
BERNERS WAY
COZENS LA E

148

115

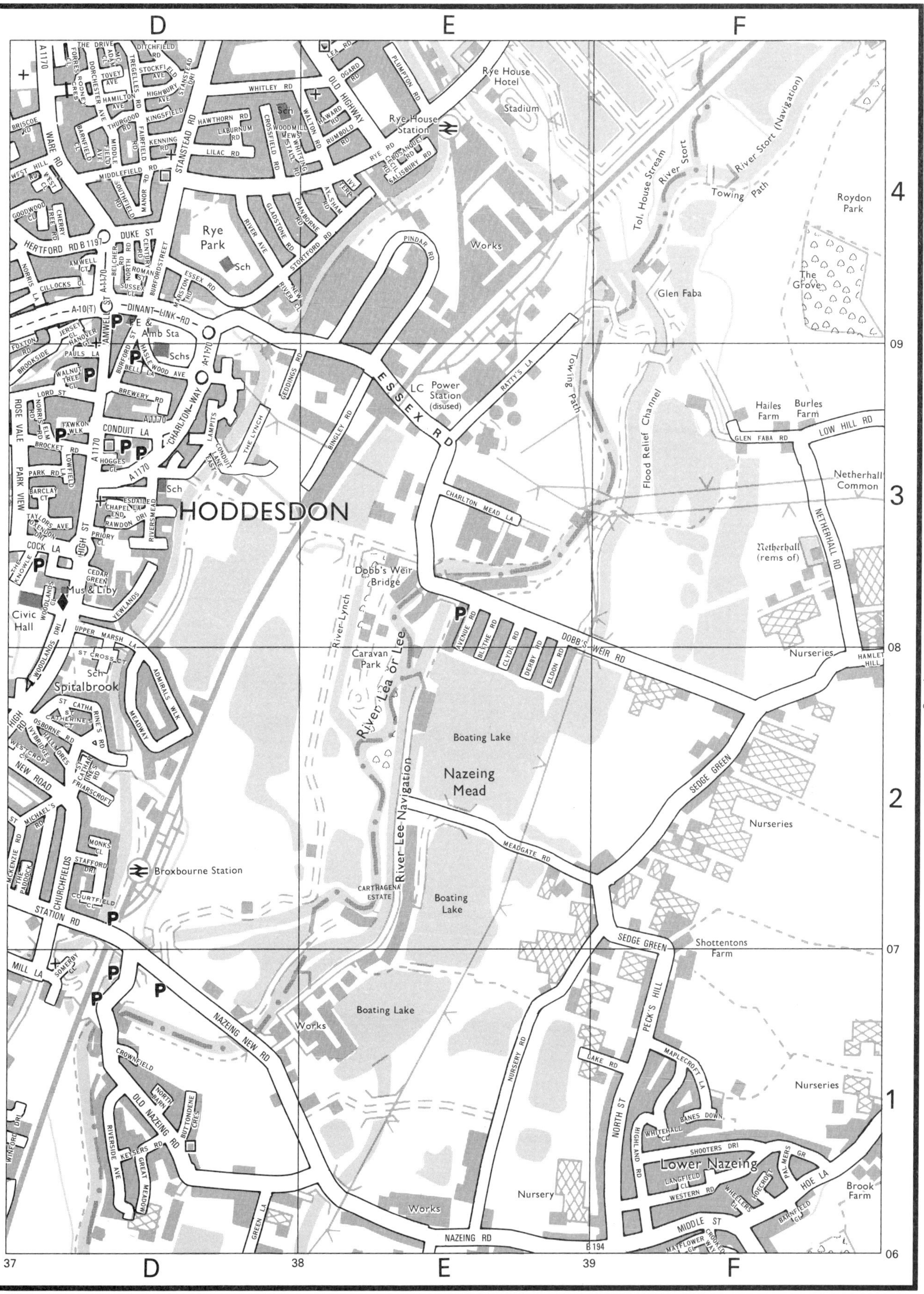

not continued, see key diagram

149

122

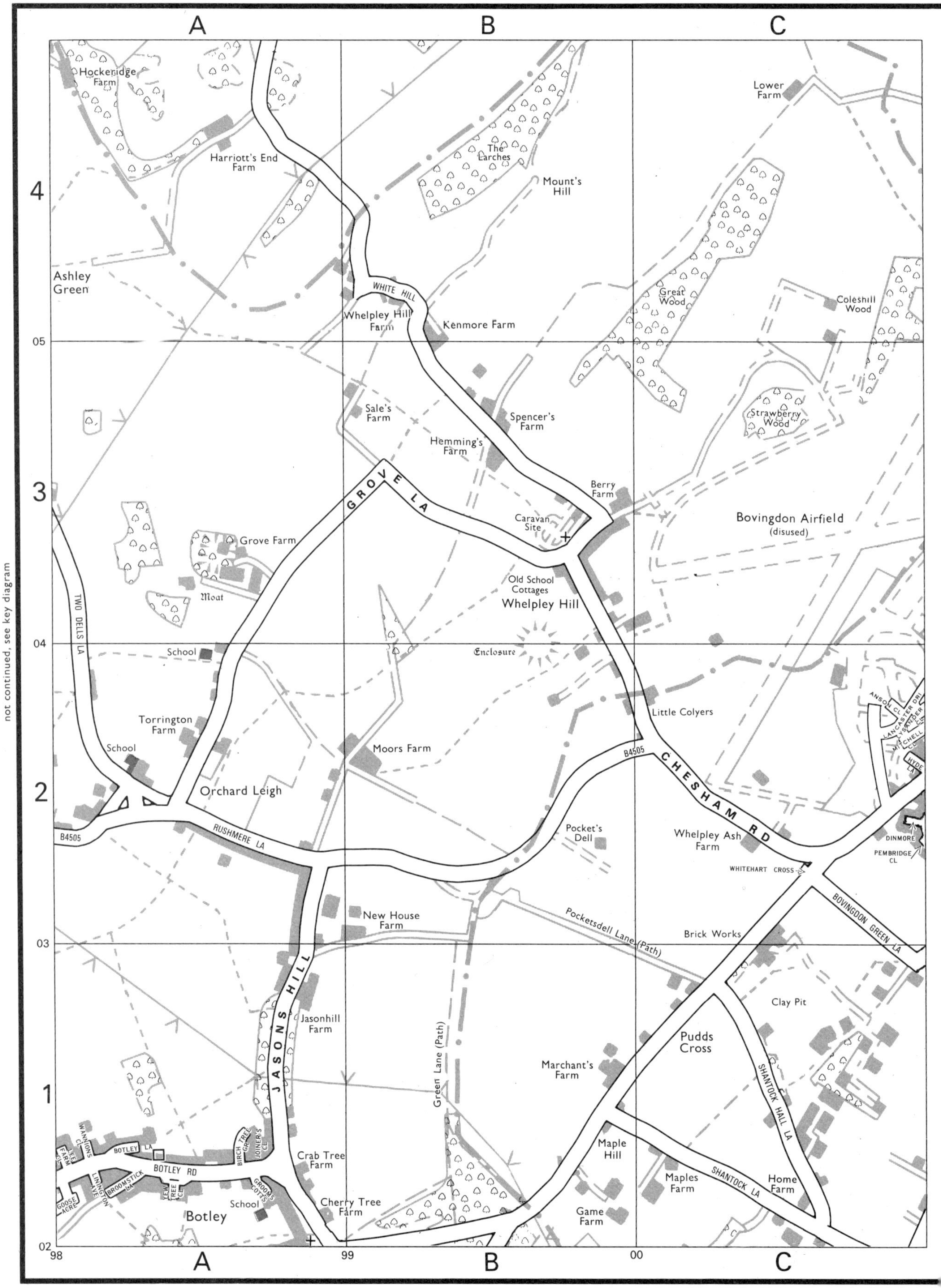

not continued, see key diagram

150

123

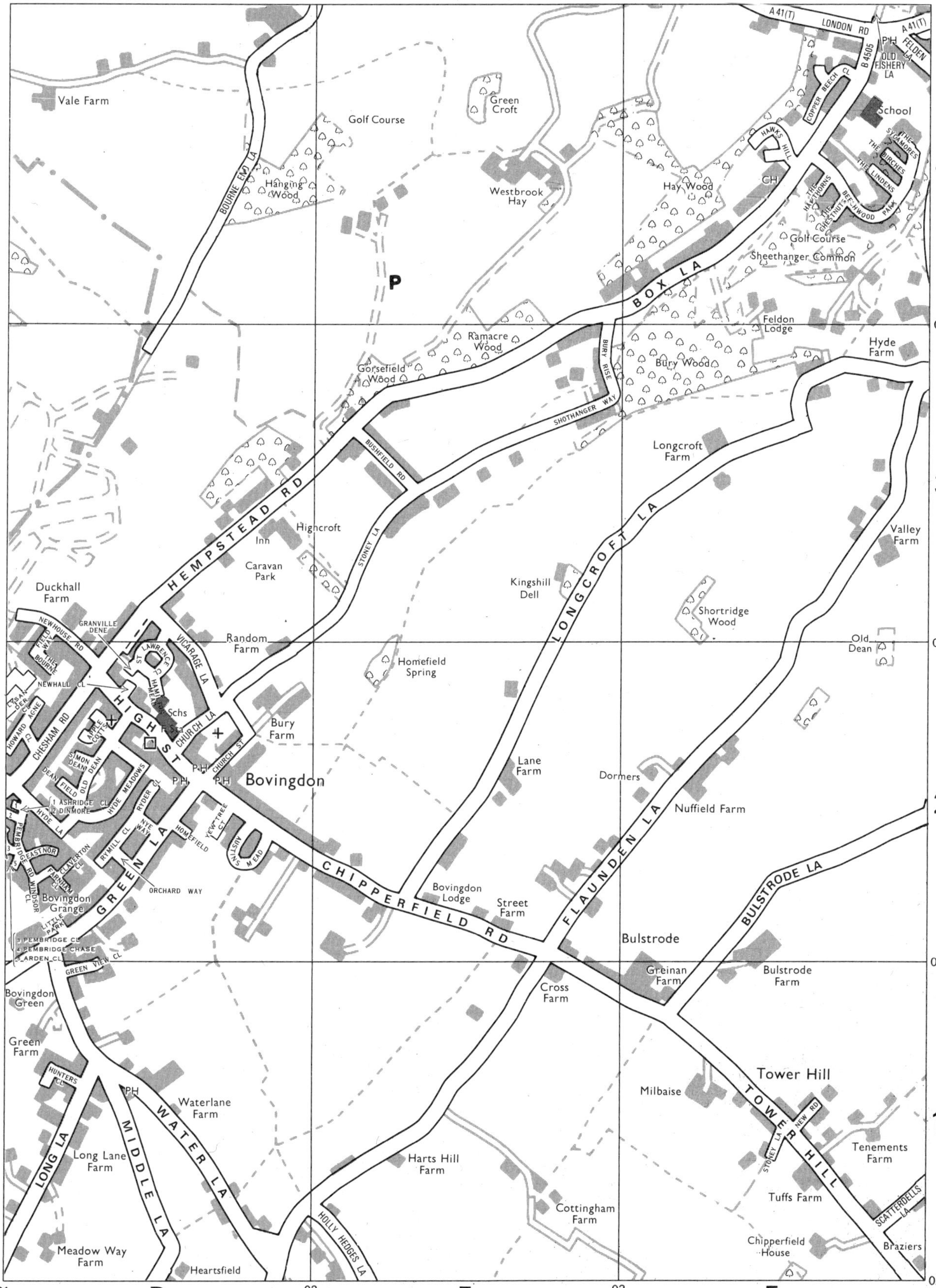
D
E
F
A 41(T) LONDON RD
A 41(T)
FELDEN LA
PH
OLD FISHERY LA
B 4505
COPPER BEECH CL
School
THE SYCAMORES
THE BIRCHES
THE LINDENS
HAWKS HILL
Vale Farm
Golf Course
Green Croft
Hanging Wood
BOURNE END LA
Westbrook Hay
Hay Wood
CH
THE HAWTHORNS
THE CHESTNUTS
BEECHWOOD PARK
Golf Course
Sheethanger Common
P
BOX LA
Feldon Lodge
Ramacre Wood
BURY RISE
Bury Wood
Hyde Farm
Gorsefield Wood
SHOTHANGER WAY
Longcroft Farm
BUSHFIELD RD
HEMPSTEAD RD
Highcroft
Inn
Caravan Park
STONEY LA
LONGCROFT LA
Valley Farm
Kingshill Dell
Shortridge Wood
Duckhall Farm
GRANVILLE DENE
NEWHOUSE RD
FIELD WAY
THE BOURNE
NEWHALL CL
ST LAWRENCE CL
VICARAGE LA
Random Farm
Old Dean
Homefield Spring
HIGH ST
CHESHAM RD
HOWARD AGNE
APPLE COTTS
Schs
F Sta
CHURCH LA
CHURCH ST
Bury Farm
SIMON DEAN
DEAN FIELD
OLD DEAN
HYDE MEADOWS
RYDER CL
PH
PH
PH
Bovingdon
Lane Farm
Dormers
Nuffield Farm
1 ASHRIDGE CL
2 DINMORE
HYDE LA
PEMBRIDGE RD
EASTNOR
CLAVERTON CL
FARNHAM CL
WINDSOR CL
RYMILL CL
NYE WAY
GREEN LA
HOMEFIELD
YEW TREE CT
AUSTINS MEAD
FLAUNDEN LA
ORCHARD WAY
CHIPPERFIELD RD
Bovingdon Lodge
Street Farm
BULSTRODE LA
Bovingdon Grange
LITTLE PARK
1 PEMBRIDGE CL
4 PEMBRIDGE CHASE
5 ARDEN CL
Bulstrode
GREEN VIEW CL
Greinan Farm
Bulstrode Farm
Bovingdon Green
Cross Farm
Green Farm
Tower Hill
HUNTERS CL
PH
Milbaise
Waterlane Farm
TOWER HILL
NEW RD
STONEY LA
Tenements Farm
LONG LA
MIDDLE LA
WATER LA
Long Lane Farm
Harts Hill Farm
Tuffs Farm
Cottingham Farm
SCATTERDELLS LA
HOLLY HEDGES LA
Chipperfield House
Meadow Way Farm
Braziers
Heartsfield
4
05
3
04
2
03
1
02
01
02
03

138

151

124

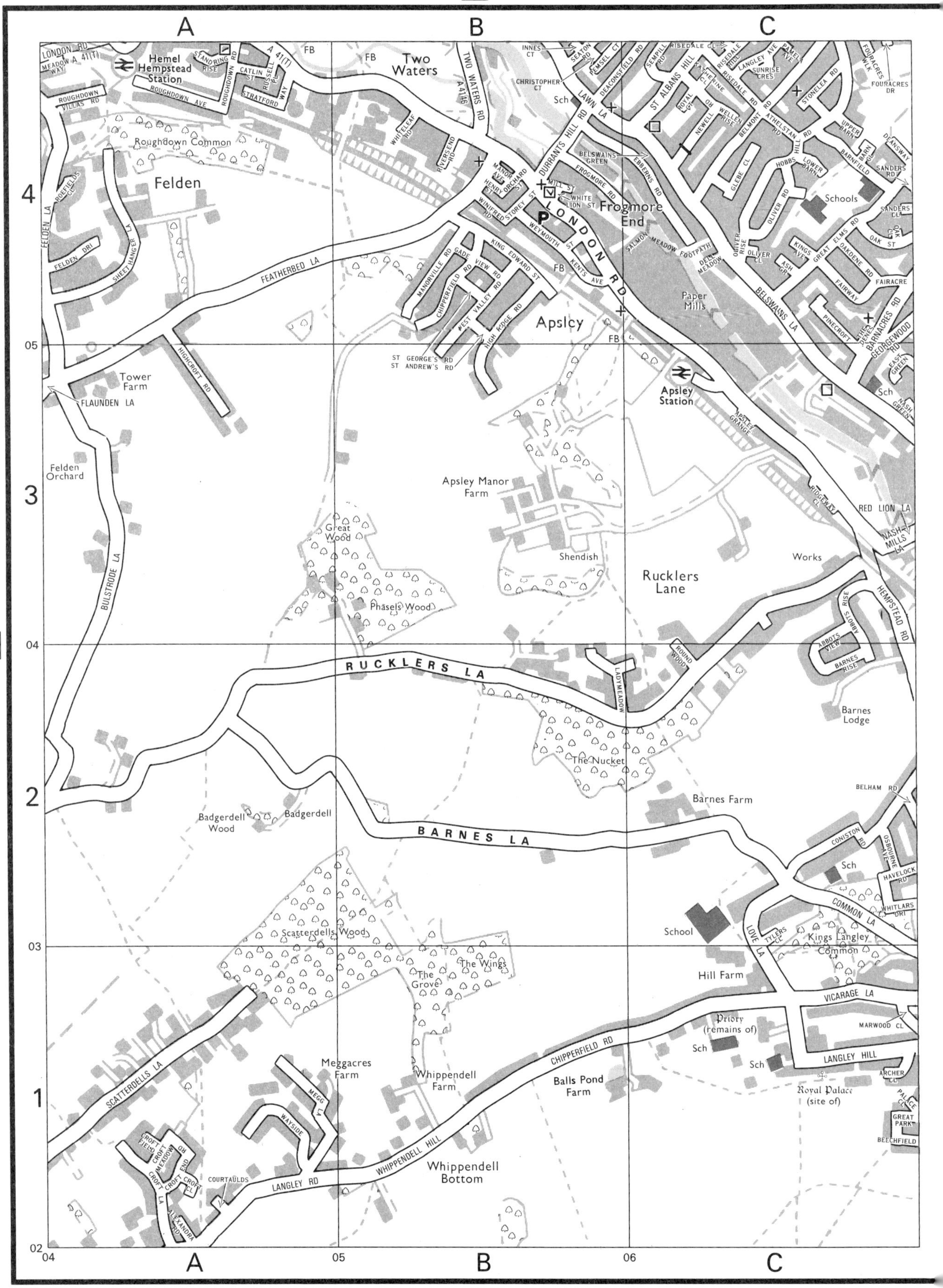
A
B
C
4
3
2
1
05
04
03
02
06
Hemel Hempstead Station
Two Waters
Roughdown Common
Felden
Frogmore End
Apsley
Apsley Station
Paper Mills
Schools
Tower Farm
Felden Orchard
Apsley Manor Farm
Great Wood
Shendish
Rucklers Lane
Works
Phasels Wood
RUCKLERS LA
The Nucket
Barnes Lodge
Barnes Farm
Badgerdell Wood
Badgerdell
BARNES LA
School
Scatterdells Wood
The Wings
The Grove
Kings Langley Common
Hill Farm
Priory (remains of)
Meggacres Farm
Whippendell Farm
Balls Pond Farm
Royal Palace (site of)
Whippendell Bottom
FEATHERBED LA
LONDON RD
BULSTRODE LA
FLAUNDEN LA
HIGHCROFT RD
SCATTERDELLS LA
LANGLEY RD
WHIPPENDELL HILL
CHIPPERFIELD RD
COMMON LA
VICARAGE LA
LANGLEY HILL
LOVE LA
HEMPSTEAD RD
BELSWAINS LA
RED LION LA
LADYMEADOW
ROUND WOOD
TWO WATERS RD
A 4146
A 41(T)
ROUGHDOWN AVE
STRATFORD WAY
ST ALBANS HILL
DURRANTS HILL RD
LAWN LA
KING EDWARD ST
HIGH RIDGE RD
WEST VALLEY RD
GADE VIEW RD
CHIPPERFIELD RD
MANORVILLE RD
ST GEORGE'S RD
ST ANDREW'S RD
KENTS AVE
WEYMOUTH ST
STOREY ST
WINIFRED RD
FROGMORE RD
BELSWAINS GREEN
EBBERNS RD
SALMON MEADOW FOOTPATH
DELL MEADOW
APSLEY GRANGE
RIDGEWAY CL
FELDEN LA
FELDEN DRI
SHEETHANGER LA
ROUGHDOWN VILLAS RD
MEGG LA
WAYSIDE
COURTAULDS
ALEXANDRA RD
CROFT MEADOW
CROFT FIELD
TYLERS CL
CONISTON RD
BELHAM RD
MARWOOD CL
ARCHER CL
BEECHFIELD
GREAT PARK
ABBOTS RISE
ABBOTS VIEW
BARNES RISE
NASH MILLS LA
FB
Sch

137

152

125

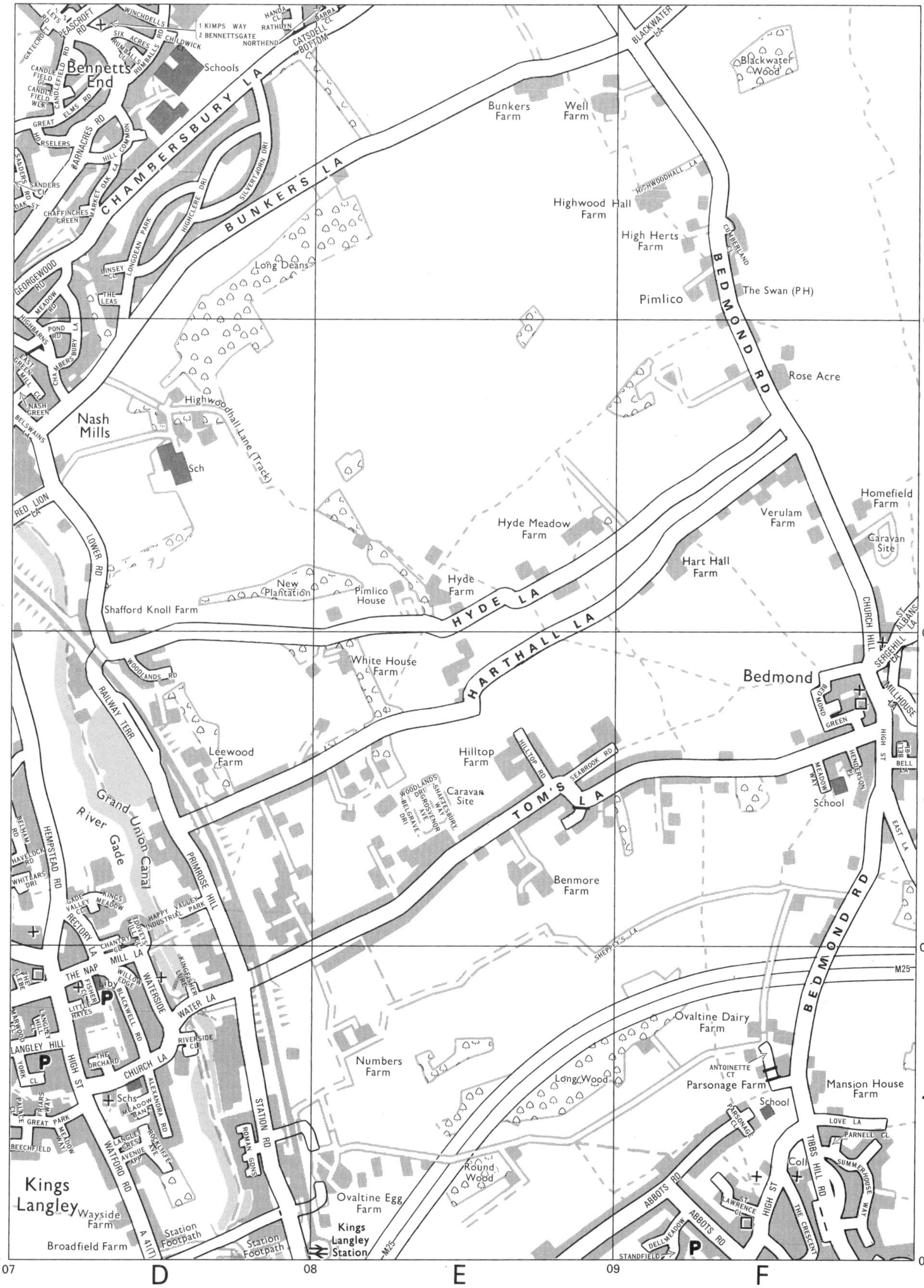
D
E
F
4
3
2
1
05
04
03
02
07
08
09
Bennetts End
Schools
Chambersbury La
Bunkers La
Bunkers Farm
Well Farm
Blackwater Wood
Highwood Hall Farm
High Herts Farm
Pimlico
The Swan (PH)
Bedmond Rd
Rose Acre
Long Deans
Nash Mills
Highwoodhall Lane (Track)
Sch
Homefield Farm
Verulam Farm
Caravan Site
Hyde Meadow Farm
Hart Hall Farm
Hyde Farm
New Plantation
Pimlico House
Shafford Knoll Farm
Hyde La
Harthall La
White House Farm
Bedmond
Leewood Farm
Hilltop Farm
Tom's La
School
Grand Union Canal
River Gade
Benmore Farm
M25
Ovaltine Dairy Farm
Numbers Farm
Long Wood
Parsonage Farm
Mansion House Farm
Round Wood
Ovaltine Egg Farm
Kings Langley Station
Kings Langley
Wayside Farm
Broadfield Farm
Station Footpath
Lower Rd
Railway Terr
Primrose Hill
Station Rd
High St
Watford Rd
A 41(T)
Church La
Abbots Rd
Tibbs Hill Rd
Love La
Church Hill
Sergehill La
St Albans La
Millhouse La
Bell La
East La
Coll
Liby

140

153

126

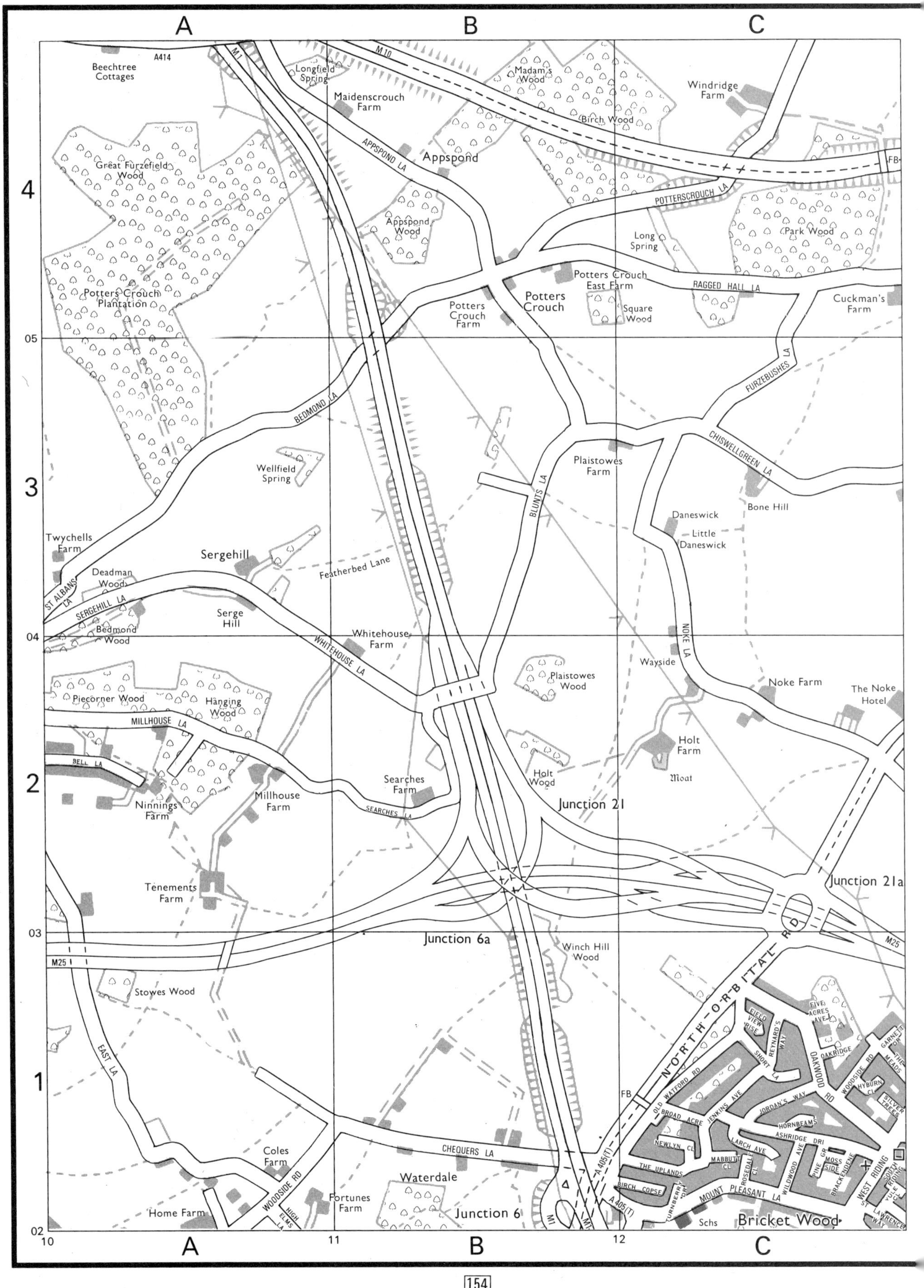

A
B
C
4
3
2
1
05
04
03
02
10
11
12
A414
M1
M10
Beechtree Cottages
Longfield Spring
Maidenscrouch Farm
Madam's Wood
Birch Wood
Windridge Farm
FB
Great Furzefield Wood
APPSPOND LA
Appspond
Appspond Wood
POTTERSCROUCH LA
Long Spring
Park Wood
Potters Crouch Plantation
Potters Crouch Farm
Potters Crouch
Potters Crouch East Farm
Square Wood
RAGGED HALL LA
Cuckman's Farm
FURZEBUSHES LA
BEDMOND LA
CHISWELLGREEN LA
Plaistowes Farm
Wellfield Spring
BLUNTS LA
Bone Hill
Daneswick
Little Daneswick
Twychells Farm
Sergehill
Featherbed Lane
Deadman Wood
ST ALBANS LA
SERGEHILL LA
Serge Hill
Bedmond Wood
WHITEHOUSE LA
Whitehouse Farm
NOKE LA
Wayside
Plaistowes Wood
Noke Farm
The Noke Hotel
Piecorner Wood
Hanging Wood
MILLHOUSE LA
BELL LA
Holt Farm
Holt Wood
Moat
Searches Farm
Millhouse Farm
Ninnings Farm
SEARCHES LA
Junction 21
Tenements Farm
Junction 21a
Junction 6a
Winch Hill Wood
M25
NORTH ORBITAL RD
Stowes Wood
FIVE ACRES AVE
EIFIELD VIEW RISE
REYNARD'S WAY
SHORT LA
OAKWOOD RD
OAKRIDGE
WOODSIDE RD
GARNETT DR
THE MEADS
HYBURN CL
SILVER TREES
EAST LA
OLD WATFORD RD
BROAD ACRE
JENKINS AVE
JORDAN'S WAY
HORNBEAMS
ASHRIDGE DRI
FB
CHEQUERS LA
NEWLYN CL
LARCH AVE
MABBUTT CL
ROSEDALE CL
WILDWOOD AVE
PINE GR
MOSS SIDE
BRACKENDENE
WEST RIDING
SOUTH RIDING
Coles Farm
Waterdale
A 405(T)
THE UPLANDS
BIRCH COPSE
MOUNT PLEASANT LA
WOODSIDE RD
Fortunes Farm
Junction 6
Home Farm
HIGH ELMS LA
TURNBERRY DR
Schs
Bricket Wood
ST LAWRENCE WAY

139

154

127

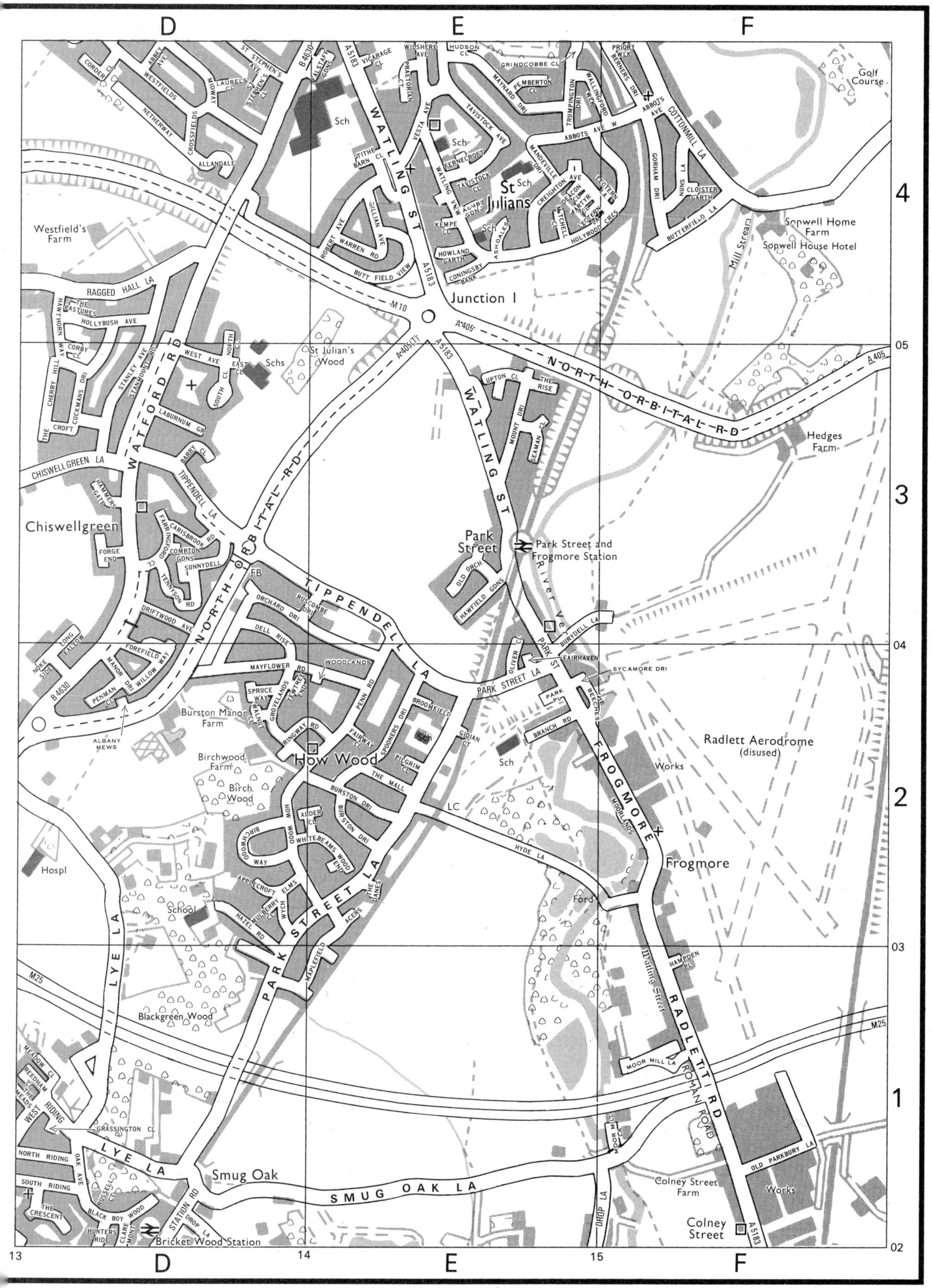
D
E
F
4
3
2
1
05
04
03
02
13
14
15
St Julians
Junction 1
Westfield's Farm
RAGGED HALL LA
HOLLYBUSH AVE
Chiswellgreen
CHISWELL GREEN LA
WATFORD RD
WEST AVE
Schs
St Julian's Wood
NORTH ORBITAL RD
A405
M10
A5183
WATLING ST
TIPPENDELL LA
Park Street
Park Street and Frogmore Station
River Ver
Sopwell Home Farm
Sopwell House Hotel
Golf Course
Mill Stream
Hedges Farm
Radlett Aerodrome (disused)
Works
FROGMORE
Frogmore
Ford
HYDE LA
Burston Manor Farm
Birchwood Farm
Birch Wood
How Wood
PARK STREET LA
PARK STREET
Hospl
School
Blackgreen Wood
LYE LA
M25
Watling Street
RADLETT RD
ROMAN ROAD
MOOR MILL LA
Smug Oak
SMUG OAK LA
DROP LA
Colney Street Farm
Colney Street
OLD PARKBURY LA
Bricket Wood Station
STATION RD
NORTH RIDING
SOUTH RIDING
WEST RIDING
THE CRESCENT
Sch
FB
LC

142

155

128

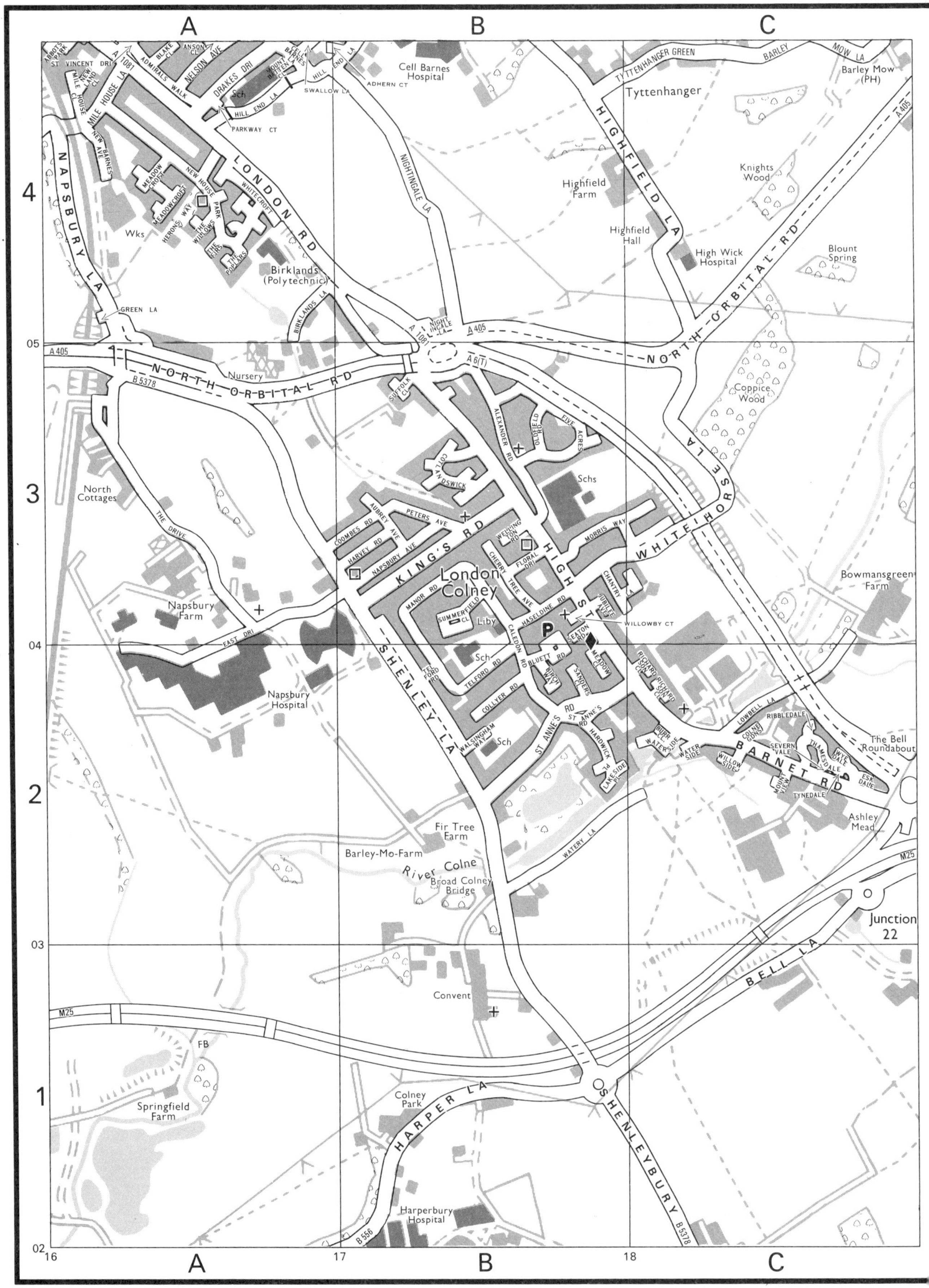
A
B
C
4
3
2
1
05
04
03
02
16
17
18
Cell Barnes Hospital
Tyttenhanger
TYTTENHANGER GREEN
BARLEY MOW LA
Barley Mow (PH)
A 405
ST VINCENT DRI
ABBOTS PARK
A 1081
BLAKE CL
ANSON CL
NELSON AVE
ADMIRALS WALK
DRAKES DRI
MOUNT BATTEN CL
CELL BARNES LA
HILL END LA
ADHERN CT
SWALLOW LA
PARKWAY CT
Sch
MILE HOUSE LA
MILE HOUSE CL
NEW LAND CL
NEW BARNES AVE
NAPSBURY LA
MEADOW CROFT
MEADOWCROFT
HERONS WAY
THE WILLOWS
THE FIRS
THE POPLARS
NEW HOUSE PARK
WHITECROFT
LONDON RD
NIGHTINGALE LA
HIGHFIELD LA
Highfield Farm
Highfield Hall
High Wick Hospital
Knights Wood
Blount Spring
NORTH ORBITAL RD
Wks
Birklands (Polytechnic)
BIRKLANDS LA
GREEN LA
NIGHTINGALE LA
A 405
A 1081
A 6(T)
Nursery
B 5378
SUFFOLK CL
Coppice Wood
ALEXANDER RD
OLDFIELD RD
FIVE ACRES
Schs
COTLANDSWICK
WHITEHORSE LA
North Cottages
THE DRIVE
AUBREY AVE
PETERS AVE
COOMBES RD
HARVEY RD
NAPSBURY AVE
KING'S RD
WEDDINGTON RD
FLORAL DRI
HIGH ST
MORRIS WAY
CHERRY TREE AVE
London Colney
MANOR RD
SUMMERFIELD CL
Liby
HASELDINE RD
JUBILEE AVE
CHANTRY LA
WILLOWBY CT
Bowmansgreen Farm
Napsbury Farm
EAST DRI
CALEDON RD
SEATON RD
P
Sch
TELFORD RD
TELFORD RD
BLUETT RD
BIRCH WAY
SANDERS RD
MEADOW CL
RICHARD CL
RICHARD SQ
Napsbury Hospital
SHENLEY LA
COLLYER RD
ST ANNE'S RD
HARDWICK PL
WALSINGHAM WAY
Sch
BURR CL
WATERSIDE
LOWBELL LA
RIBBLEDALE
COLNE GDNS
SEVERN VALE
THAMESDALE
WYE DALE
ESK DALE
WILLOW SIDE
BARNET RD
MOUNT VIEW
TYNEDALE
The Bell Roundabout
LAKESIDE PL
Ashley Mead
Fir Tree Farm
Barley-Mo-Farm
WATERY LA
River Colne
Broad Colney Bridge
M25
Junction 22
BELL LA
Convent
M25
FB
Springfield Farm
Colney Park
HARPER LA
SHENLEYBURY
B 5378
Harperbury Hospital
B 556

141

156

129

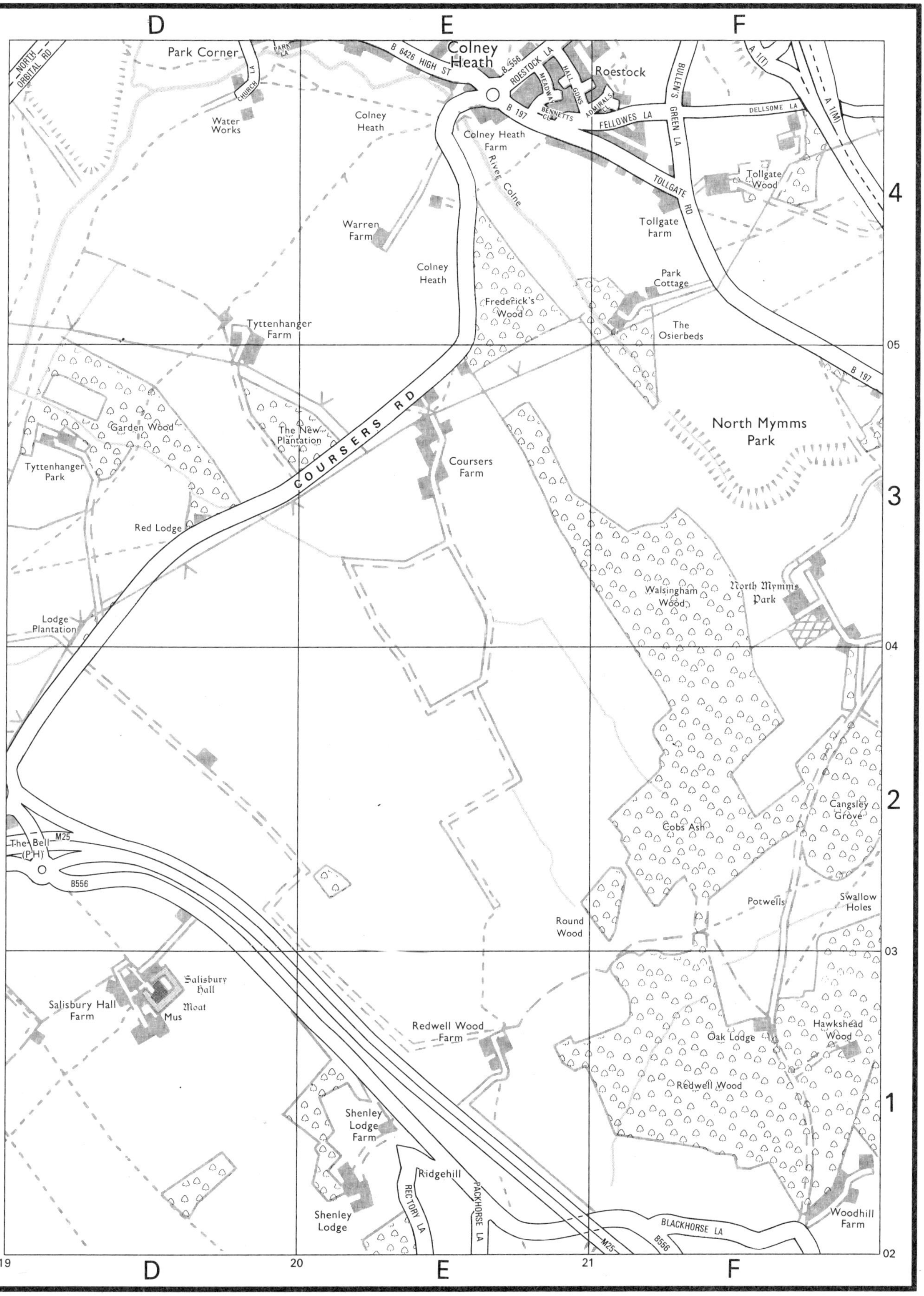
D
E
F
Park Corner
PARK LA
CHURCH LA
NORTH ORBITAL RD
Water Works
B 6426 HIGH ST
Colney Heath
B 556
ROESTOCK LA
MEADWAY
HALL GDNS
BENNETTS CL
ADMIRALS CL
Roestock
B 197
FELLOWES LA
BULLEN'S GREEN LA
DELLSOME LA
A 1(T)
A 1(M)
Colney Heath
Colney Heath Farm
River Colne
Tollgate Wood
TOLLGATE RD
Tollgate Farm
Warren Farm
Colney Heath
Park Cottage
Frederick's Wood
The Osierbeds
Tyttenhanger Farm
B 197
North Mymms Park
Garden Wood
The New Plantation
COURSERS RD
Coursers Farm
Tyttenhanger Park
Red Lodge
Walsingham Wood
North Mymms Park
Lodge Plantation
Cangsley Grove
Cobs Ash
The Bell (PH)
M25
B556
Potwells
Swallow Holes
Round Wood
Salisbury Hall
Moat
Mus
Salisbury Hall Farm
Redwell Wood Farm
Oak Lodge
Hawkshead Wood
Redwell Wood
Shenley Lodge Farm
Ridgehill
RECTORY LA
PACKHORSE LA
Shenley Lodge
BLACKHORSE LA
M25
B556
Woodhill Farm
4
3
2
1
05
04
03
02
19
20
21
D
E
F

144

157

130

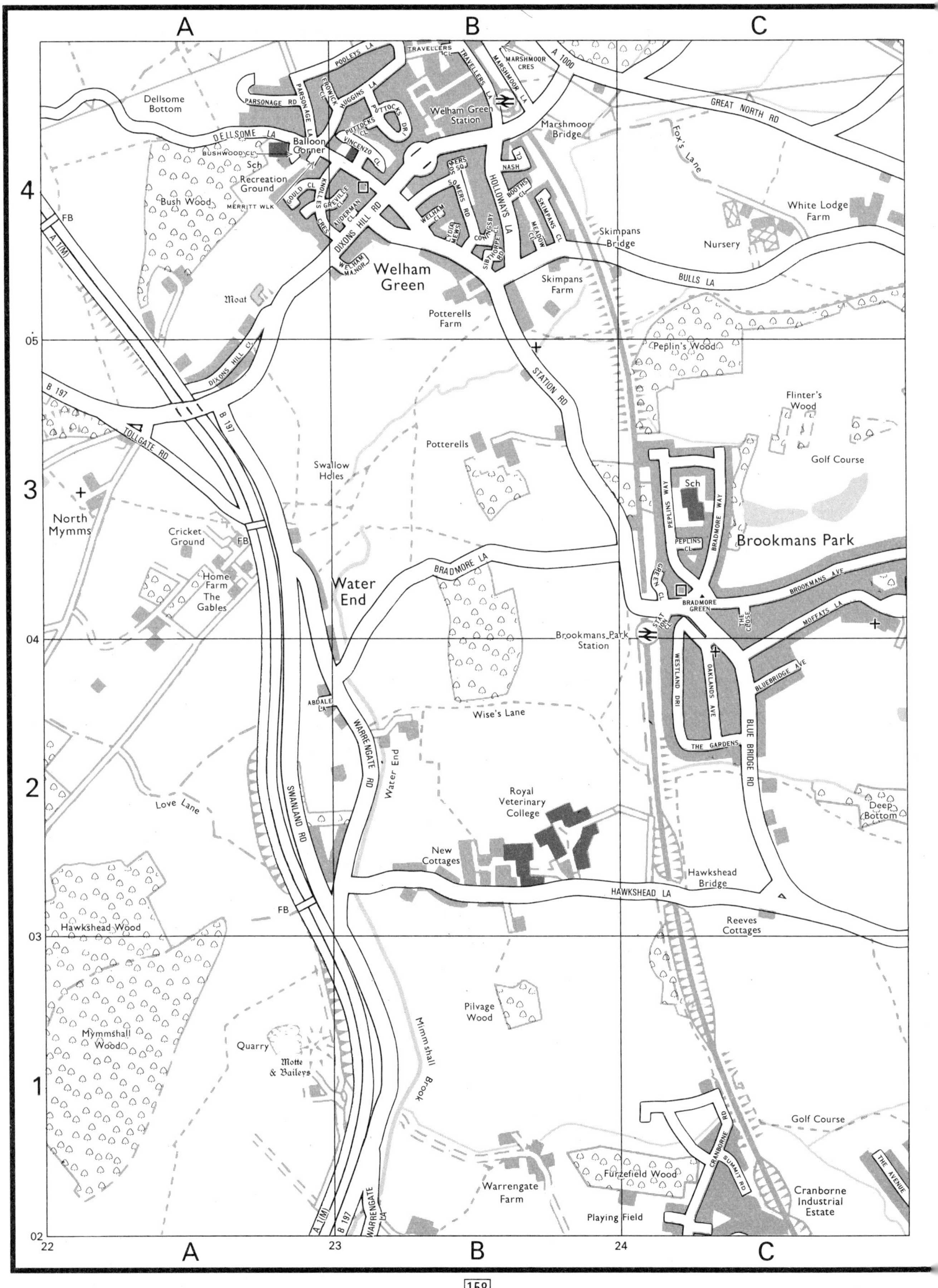

A
B
C
Dellsome Bottom
DELLSOME LA
PARSONAGE RD
PARSONAGE LA
POOLEYS LA
TRAVELLERS CL
TRAVELLERS LA
MARSHMOOR CRES
MARSHMOOR LA
A 1000
GREAT NORTH RD
HUGGINS LA
PUTTOCKS CL
PUTTOCKS DR
Welham Green Station
Marshmoor Bridge
Fox's Lane
Balloon Corner
BUSHWOOD CL
VINCENZO CL
Sch
Recreation Ground
Bush Wood
MERRITT WLK
GOULD CL
KNOLLES CRES
GREVILLE CL
DIXONS HILL RD
NASH
HOLLOWAYS LA
BOOTHS CL
SKIMPANS CL
MEADOW CL
SOMERS RD
WELHAM CL
LYDIA MEWS
SIBTHORPE RD
Skimpans Bridge
White Lodge Farm
Nursery
WELHAM MANOR
Welham Green
Skimpans Farm
BULLS LA
FB
A 1(M)
Moat
Potterells Farm
05
Peplin's Wood
DIXONS HILL CL
STATION RD
B 197
Flinter's Wood
TOLLGATE RD
Potterells
Golf Course
Swallow Holes
Sch
3
North Mymms
PEPLINS WAY
BRADMORE WAY
Cricket Ground
Brookmans Park
PEPLINS CL
BRADMORE LA
Home Farm
The Gables
Water End
GREEN CL
BROOKMANS AVE
BRADMORE GREEN
THE CLOSE
MOFFATS LA
143
04
Brookmans Park Station
WESTLAND DRI
OAKLANDS AVE
BLUEBRIDGE AVE
ABDALE LA
Wise's Lane
WARRENGATE RD
Water End
SWANLAND RD
THE GARDENS
BLUE BRIDGE RD
2
Love Lane
Royal Veterinary College
Deep Bottom
New Cottages
Hawkshead Bridge
HAWKSHEAD LA
FB
Reeves Cottages
Hawkshead Wood
03
Pilvage Wood
Mimmshall Brook
Mymmshall Wood
Quarry
Motte & Baileys
1
Golf Course
CRANBORNE RD
SUMMIT RD
Furzefield Wood
Warrengate Farm
Cranborne Industrial Estate
THE AVENUE
Playing Field
A 1(M)
B 197
WARRENGATE LA
02
22
23
24

158

131

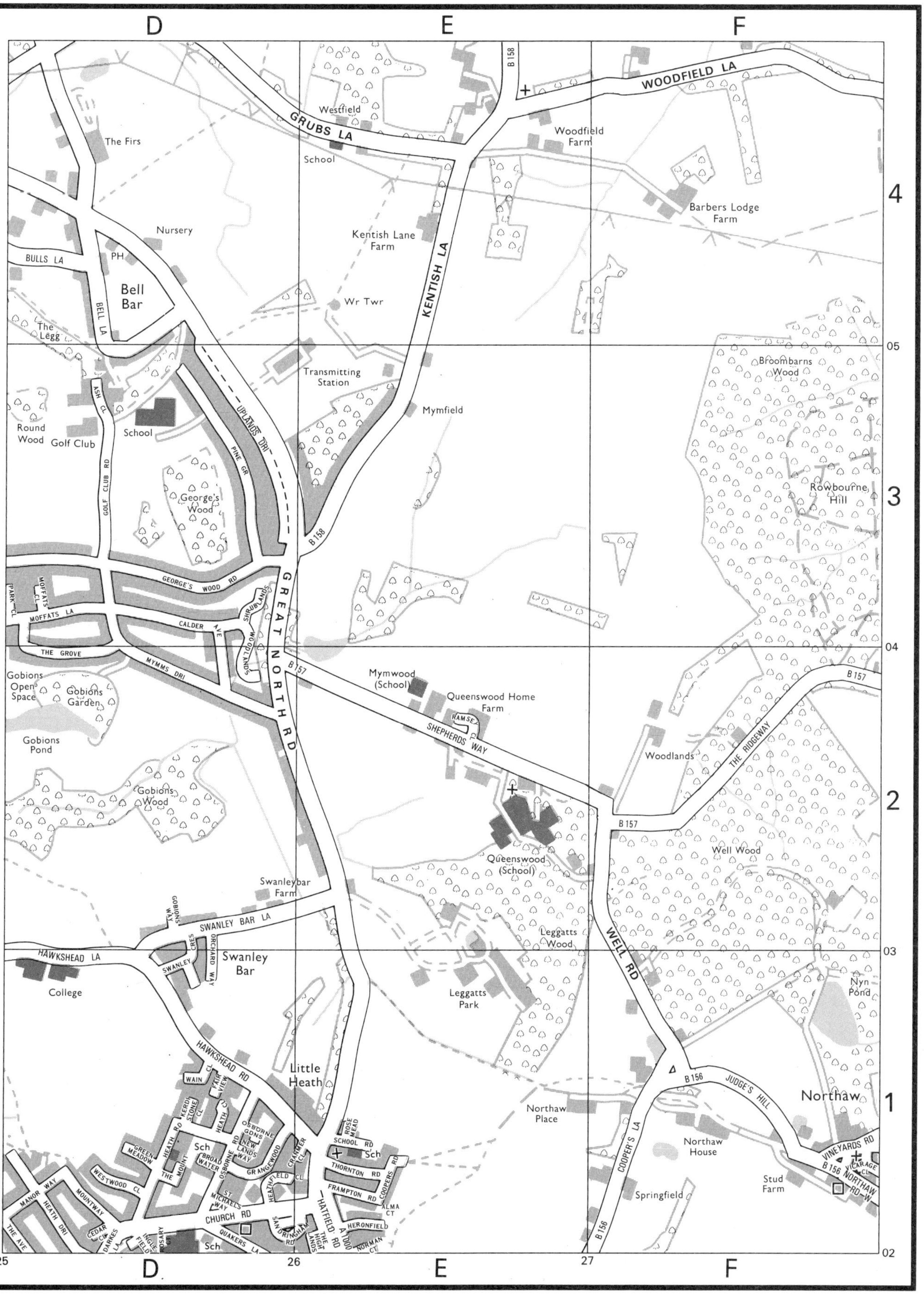
D
E
F
4
3
2
1
05
04
03
02
25
26
27
WOODFIELD LA
GRUBS LA
B 158
Westfield
School
The Firs
Woodfield Farm
Barbers Lodge Farm
Nursery
Kentish Lane Farm
KENTISH LA
BULLS LA
PH
Bell Bar
BELL LA
Wr Twr
The Legg
Transmitting Station
Broombarns Wood
ASH CL
Mymfield
Round Wood
Golf Club
School
UPLANDS DRI
PINE GR
GOLF CLUB RD
George's Wood
Rowbourne Hill
B 158
GEORGE'S WOOD RD
MOFFATS CL
PARK CL
MOFFATS LA
CALDER AVE
SHRUBLANDS
WOODLANDS
GREAT NORTH RD
THE GROVE
MYMMS DRI
B 157
Mymwood (School)
Queenswood Home Farm
RAMSEY
SHEPHERDS WAY
B 157
Gobions Open Space
Gobions Garden
Gobions Pond
Woodlands
THE RIDGEWAY
Gobions Wood
B 157
Well Wood
Queenswood (School)
Swanleybar Farm
GOBIONS WAY
SWANLEY BAR LA
Leggatts Wood
WELL RD
HAWKSHEAD LA
SWANLEY CRES
ORCHARD WAY
Swanley Bar
Nyn Pond
College
Leggatts Park
HAWKSHEAD RD
Little Heath
B 156
JUDGE'S HILL
Northaw
WAIN CL
FAIR VIEW
Northaw Place
KERDISTONE CL
HEATH CL
HEATH RD
OSBORNE GDNS
NEW LANDS WAY
ROSE MEAD
SCHOOL RD
COOPER'S LA
Northaw House
VINEYARDS RD
GREEN MEADOW
Sch
BROADWATER
OSBORNE WAY
GRANGEWOOD
CRANMER CL
Sch
THORNTON RD
COOPERS RD
VICARAGE CL
B 156 NORTHAW RD W
THE MOUNT
WESTWOOD CL
HEATHFIELD CL
FRAMPTON RD
ALMA CT
Stud Farm
MANOR WAY
MOUNTWAY
ST MICHAELS WAY
CHURCH RD
HATFIELD RD
A 1000
Springfield
HEATH DRI
CEDAR CL
DARKES LA
INGLEFIELD
ROSARY
SANDRINGHAM RD
THE HIGHLANDS
HERONFIELD
QUAKERS LA
Sch
NORMAN CT
B 156
THE AVE

146

159

132

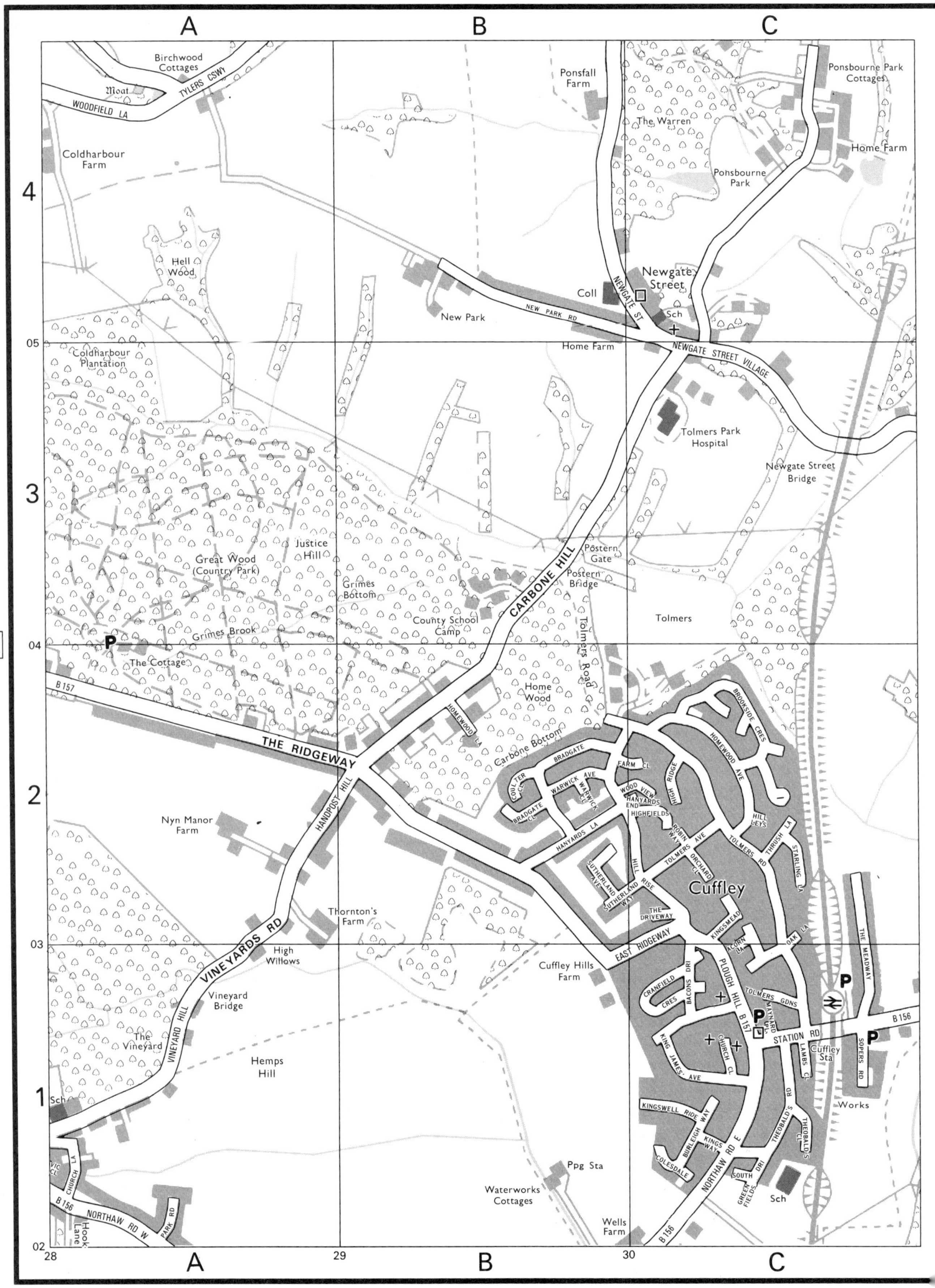
A
B
C
Birchwood Cottages
Moat
TYLERS CSWY
WOODFIELD LA
Ponsfall Farm
The Warren
Ponsbourne Park Cottages
Home Farm
Ponsbourne Park
Coldharbour Farm
4
Hell Wood
Newgate Street
Coll
NEWGATE ST
Sch
NEW PARK RD
New Park
Home Farm
NEWGATE STREET VILLAGE
05
Coldharbour Plantation
Tolmers Park Hospital
Newgate Street Bridge
3
Justice Hill
Great Wood (Country Park)
Postern Gate
Postern Bridge
CARBONE HILL
Grimes Bottom
Tolmers
County School Camp
Grimes Brook
Tolmers Road
P
04
The Cottage
B 157
Home Wood
HOMEWOOD LA
BROOKSIDE CRES
THE RIDGEWAY
Carbone Bottom
BRADGATE
FARM CL
HOMEWOOD AVE
COULTER CL
WARWICK AVE
WARWICK CL
WOOD VIEW
HIGH RIDGE
HANYARDS END
HIGHFIELDS
HANDPOST HILL
2
BRADGATE CL
HANYARDS LA
ROBIN WAY
HILL LEYS
THRUSH LA
Nyn Manor Farm
TOLMERS AVE
TOLMERS RD
STARLING LA
ORCHARD CL
SUTHERLAND AVE
HILL RISE
SUTHERLAND WAY
Cuffley
THE DRIVEWAY
KINGSMEAD
Thornton's Farm
VINEYARDS RD
EAST RIDGEWAY
ACORN LA
OAK LA
THE MEADWAY
03
High Willows
Cuffley Hills Farm
BACONS DRI
PLOUGH HILL
P
CRANFIELD CRES
TOLMERS GDNS
Vineyard Bridge
B 157
MAYNARD PL
B 156
STATION RD
P
KING JAMES' AVE
CHURCH CL
LAMBS CL
Cuffley Sta
SOPERS RD
The Vineyard
VINEYARD HILL
Hemps Hill
1
Sch
KINGSWELL RIDE
THEOBALD'S RD
Works
BURLEIGH WAY
KINGS WAY
THEOBALD'S CL
CHURCH LA
VIC CL
NORTHAW RD E
COLESDALE
SOUTH DRI
GREEN FIELDS
Ppg Sta
Sch
Waterworks Cottages
B 156
NORTHAW RD W
PARK RD
Hook Lane
Wells Farm
B 156
02
28
A
29
B
30
C

145

160

133

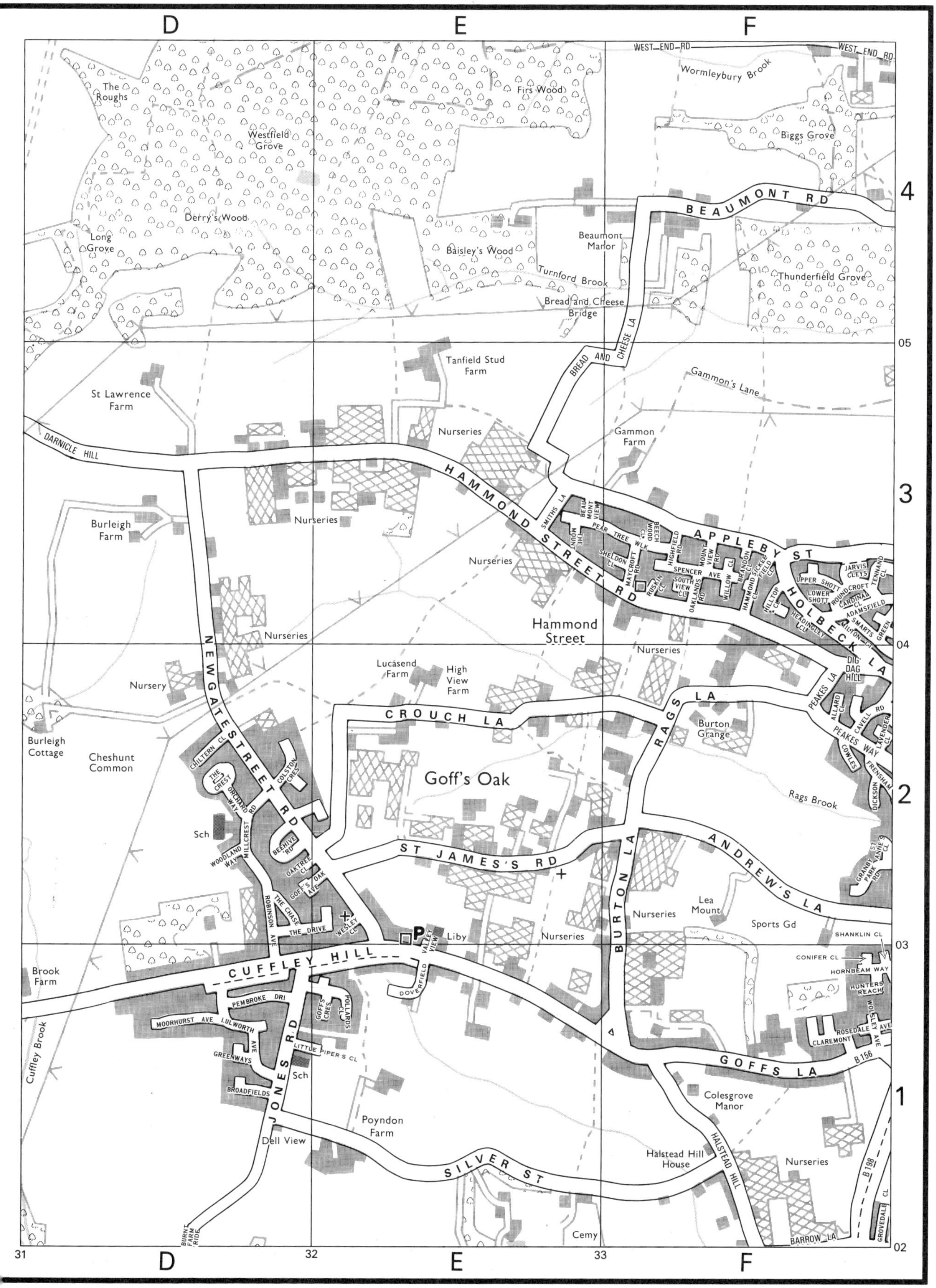

D
E
F
4
3
2
1
05
04
03
02
31
32
33
The Roughs
Westfield Grove
Firs Wood
WEST END RD
Wormleybury Brook
Biggs Grove
BEAUMONT RD
Derry's Wood
Long Grove
Baisley's Wood
Beaumont Manor
Turnford Brook
Thunderfield Grove
Bread and Cheese Bridge
BREAD AND CHEESE LA
Tanfield Stud Farm
St Lawrence Farm
Gammon's Lane
DARNICLE HILL
Nurseries
Gammon Farm
HAMMOND STREET RD
SMITHS LA
BEAUMONT VIEW
THE MOUNT
PEAR TREE WLK
SHELDON CL
MAYCROFT RD
BEECH WOOD CL
HIGHFIELD RD
RUSKIN CL
SOUTH VIEW CL
SPENCER AVE
MOUNT VIEW RD
OAKLANDS RD
WILLOW CL
BRANDON CL
HAMMOND CL
SICKLEFIELD CL
HILLTOP CL
APPLEBY ST
UPPER SHOTT
LOWER SHOTT
ROUNDCROFT
CARDINAL CL
JARVIS CLEYS
TENNAND CL
ADAMSFIELD
SMARTS GREEN
MILSON CL
HEADINGLEY CL
HOLBECK LA
Burleigh Farm
Nursery
Hammond Street
DIG DAG HILL
PEAKES LA
ALLARD CL
CAVELL RD
LAVENDER CL
PEAKES WAY
COWLES
FRENSHAM
DICKSON
Lucasend Farm
High View Farm
CROUCH LA
RAGS LA
Burton Grange
Burleigh Cottage
Cheshunt Common
NEWGATESTREET RD
CHILTERN CL
THE CREST
ORCHARD WAY
COLSTON CRES
Goff's Oak
Rags Brook
Sch
MILLCREST RD
WOODLAND WAY
BEEHIVE RD
OAKTREE CL
GOFF'S OAK AVE
ST JAMES'S RD
ST ANDREW'S LA
BURTON LA
GRANBY PARK RD
ST ANNE'S CL
ROBINSON AVE
THE CHASE
THE DRIVE
WESLEY CL
P
VALLEY VIEW
Liby
Lea Mount
Sports Gd
SHANKLIN CL
CONIFER CL
HORNBEAM WAY
HUNTERS REACH
Brook Farm
CUFFLEY HILL
DOVERFIELD
PEMBROKE DRI
GOFFS CRES
POLLARDS CL
MOORHURST AVE
LULWORTH AVE
GREENWAYS
LITTLE PIPERS CL
JONES RD
ROSEDALE
CLAREMONT
WOLSEY AVE
GOFFS LA
B156
Cuffley Brook
BROADFIELDS
Colesgrove Manor
Poyndon Farm
Dell View
Halstead Hill House
HALSTEAD HILL
SILVER ST
B198
GROVEDALE CL
BARROW LA
BURNT FARM RIDE
Cemy

148

161

134

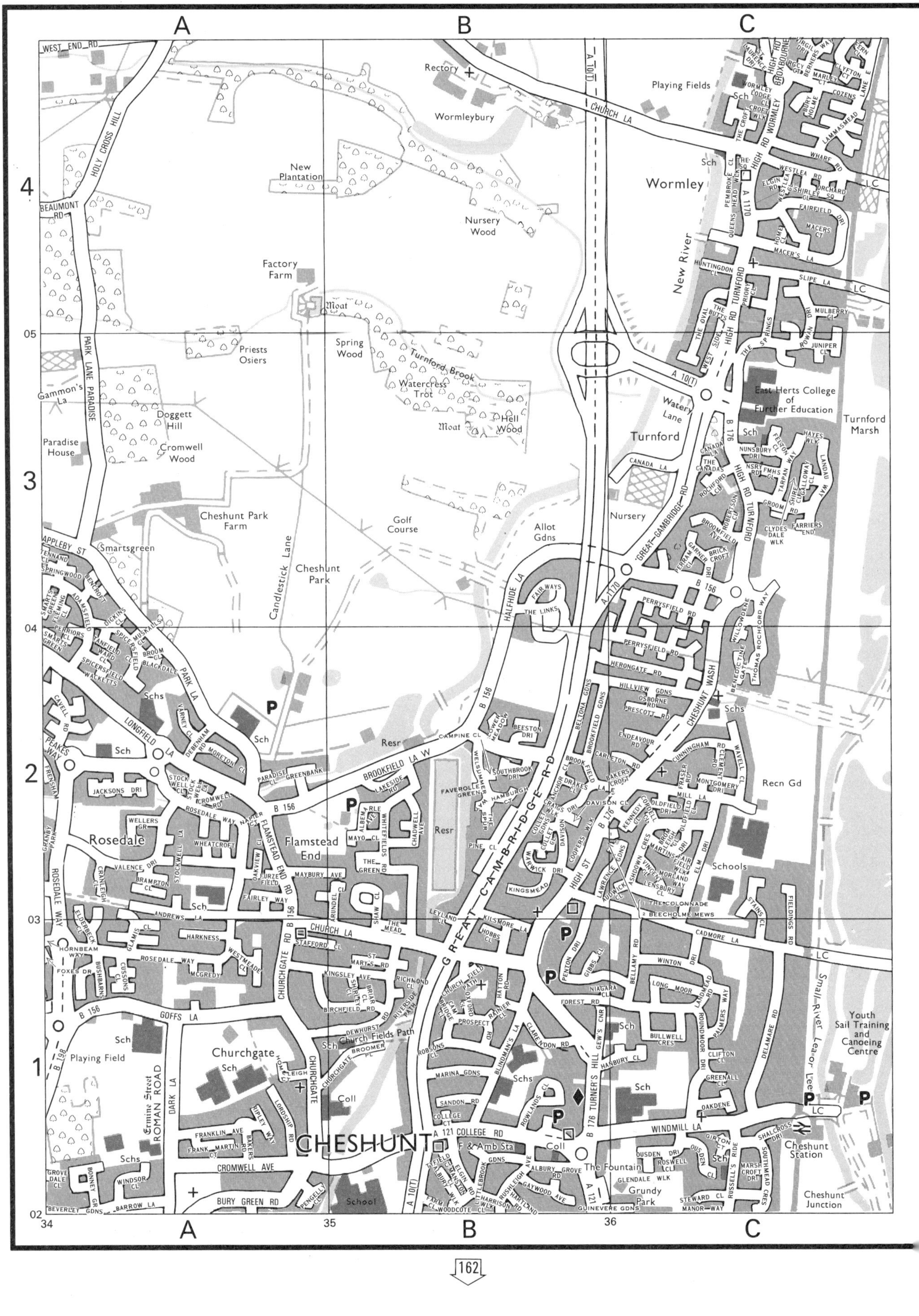
A
B
C
Rectory
Wormleybury
Playing Fields
Wormley
New Plantation
Nursery Wood
Factory Farm
Moat
Priests Osiers
Spring Wood
Turnford Brook
Watercress Trot
Hell Wood
Doggett Hill
Cromwell Wood
Paradise House
Gammon's La
Cheshunt Park Farm
Golf Course
Allot Gdns
Nursery
Turnford
East Herts College of Further Education
Turnford Marsh
New River
Smartsgreen
Cheshunt Park
Candlestick Lane
Schs
Sch
Resr
Rosedale
Flamstead End
Recn Gd
Schools
Churchgate
Playing Field
Coll
CHESHUNT
F & Amb Sta
The Fountain
Grundy Park
Cheshunt Station
Cheshunt Junction
Youth Sail Training and Canoeing Centre
Small River Lea or Lee
School
Ermine Street
ROMAN ROAD
GREAT CAMBRIDGE RD
HIGH RD TURNFORD
CHURCH LA
HOLY CROSS HILL
PARK LANE PARADISE
BROOKFIELD LA W
GOFFS LA
WINDMILL LA
COLLEGE RD
CHESHUNT WASH
HIGH ST
TURNER'S HILL
CHURCHGATE
DARK LA
CROMWELL AVE
BURY GREEN RD
LONGFIELD LA
APPLEBY ST
34
35
36
02
03
04
05
1
2
3
4

147

162

135

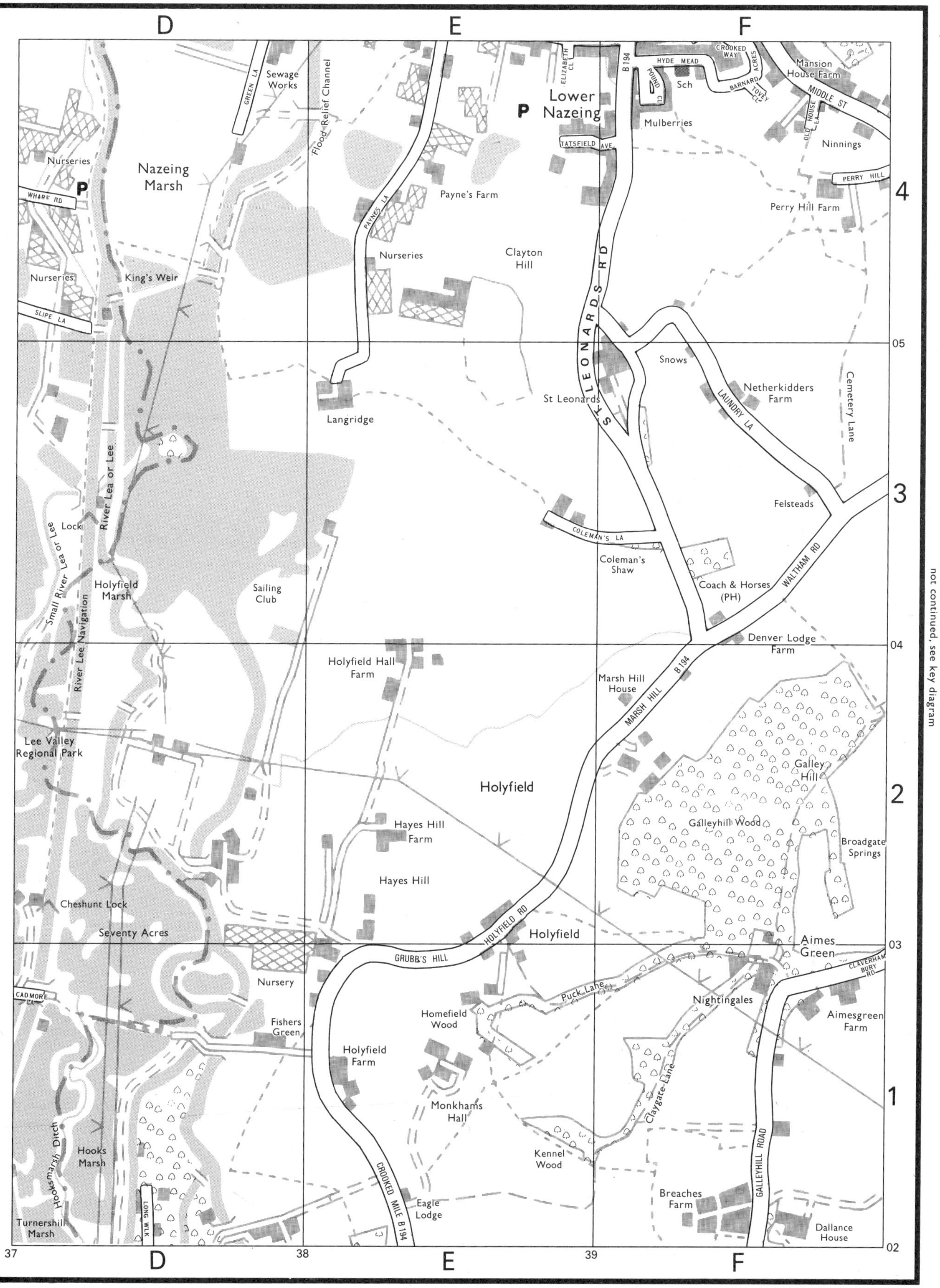

not continued, see key diagram

163

136

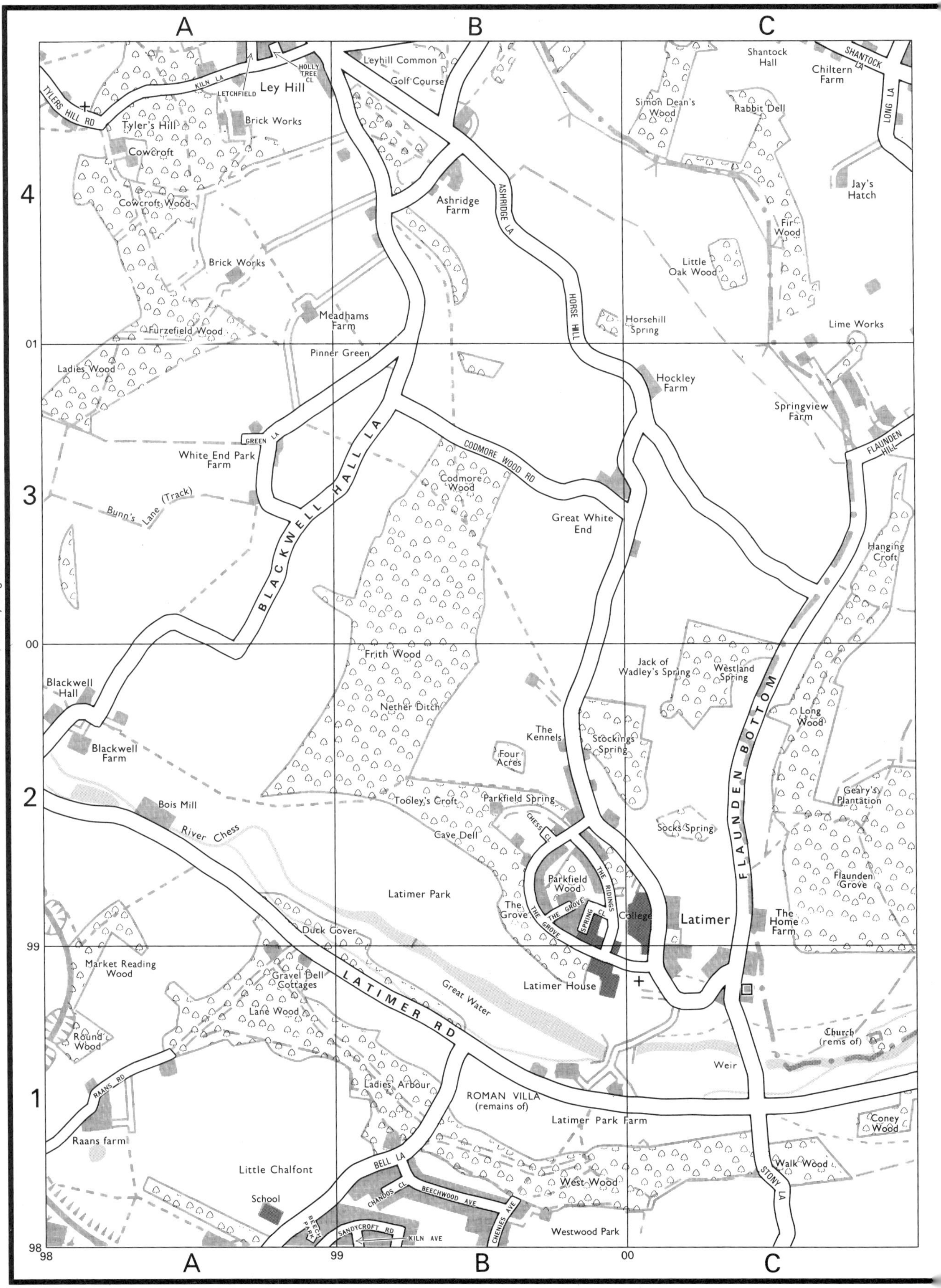

not continued, see key diagram

not continued, see key diagram

137

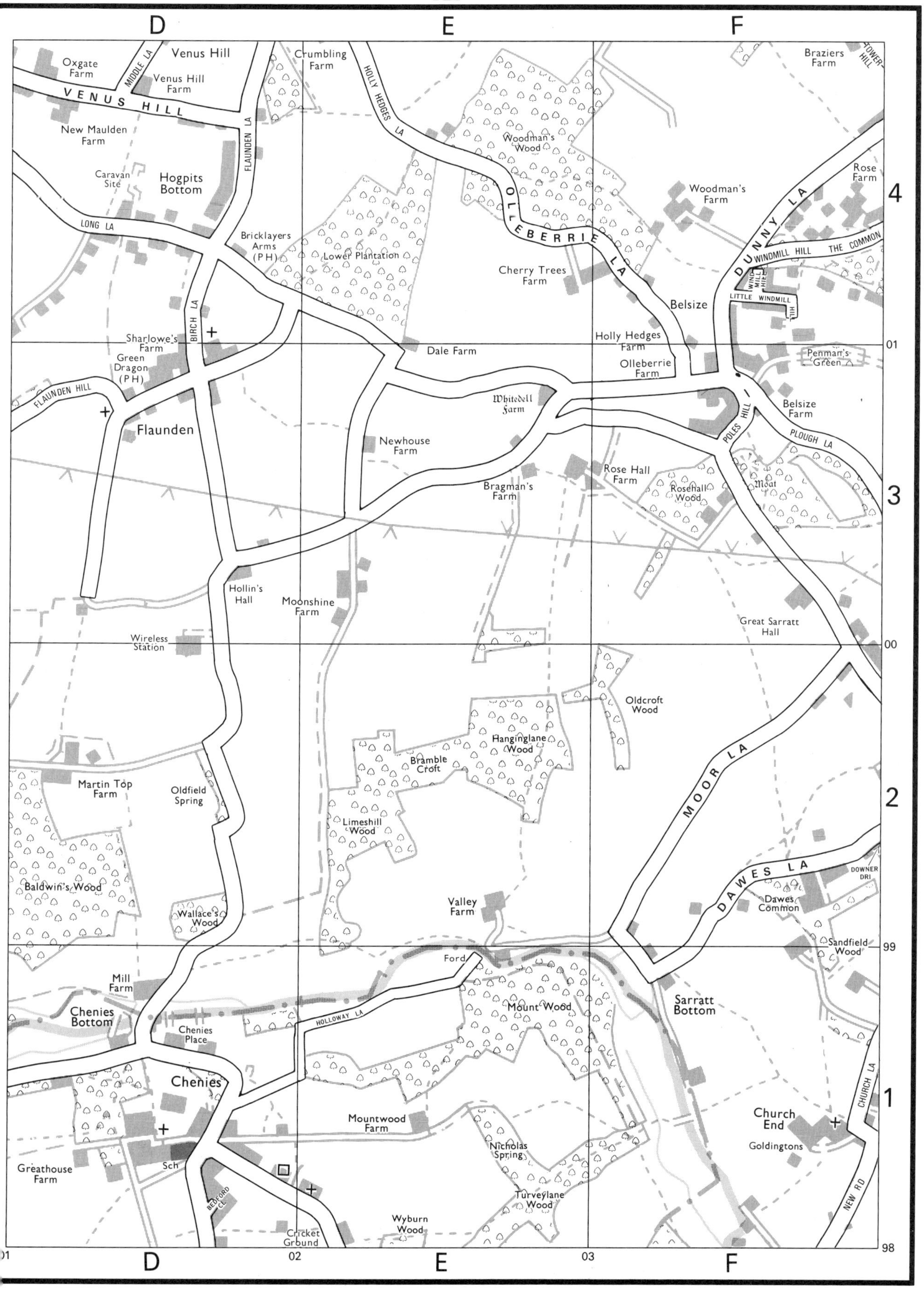
D
E
F
Oxgate Farm
Venus Hill
Venus Hill Farm
MIDDLE LA
VENUS HILL
Crumbling Farm
HOLLY HEDGES LA
Braziers Farm
TOWER HILL
New Maulden Farm
FLAUNDEN LA
Woodman's Wood
Caravan Site
Hogpits Bottom
OLLEBERRIE LA
Woodman's Farm
Rose Farm
4
DUNNY LA
LONG LA
Bricklayers Arms (PH)
Lower Plantation
Cherry Trees Farm
WINDMILL HILL
THE COMMON
LITTLE WINDMILL HILL
Belsize
BIRCH LA
Sharlowe's Farm
Green Dragon (PH)
Dale Farm
Holly Hedges Farm
Olleberrie Farm
01
Penman's Green
FLAUNDEN HILL
Whitedell Farm
Belsize Farm
Flaunden
POLES HILL
Newhouse Farm
PLOUGH LA
Rose Hall Farm
Rosehall Wood
Moat
Bragman's Farm
3
Hollin's Hall
Moonshine Farm
Great Sarratt Hall
Wireless Station
00
Oldcroft Wood
Hanginglane Wood
Bramble Croft
MOOR LA
Martin Top Farm
Oldfield Spring
2
Limeshill Wood
DAWES LA
DOWNER DRI
Baldwin's Wood
Valley Farm
Dawes Common
Wallace's Wood
Sandfield Wood
99
Ford
Mill Farm
Mount Wood
Sarratt Bottom
Chenies Bottom
Chenies Place
HOLLOWAY LA
CHURCH LA
Chenies
1
Church End
Mountwood Farm
Goldingtons
Nicholas Spring
Greathouse Farm
Sch
BEDFORD CL
Turveylane Wood
NEW RD
Wyburn Wood
Cricket Ground
98
01
02
03
D
E
F

152

164

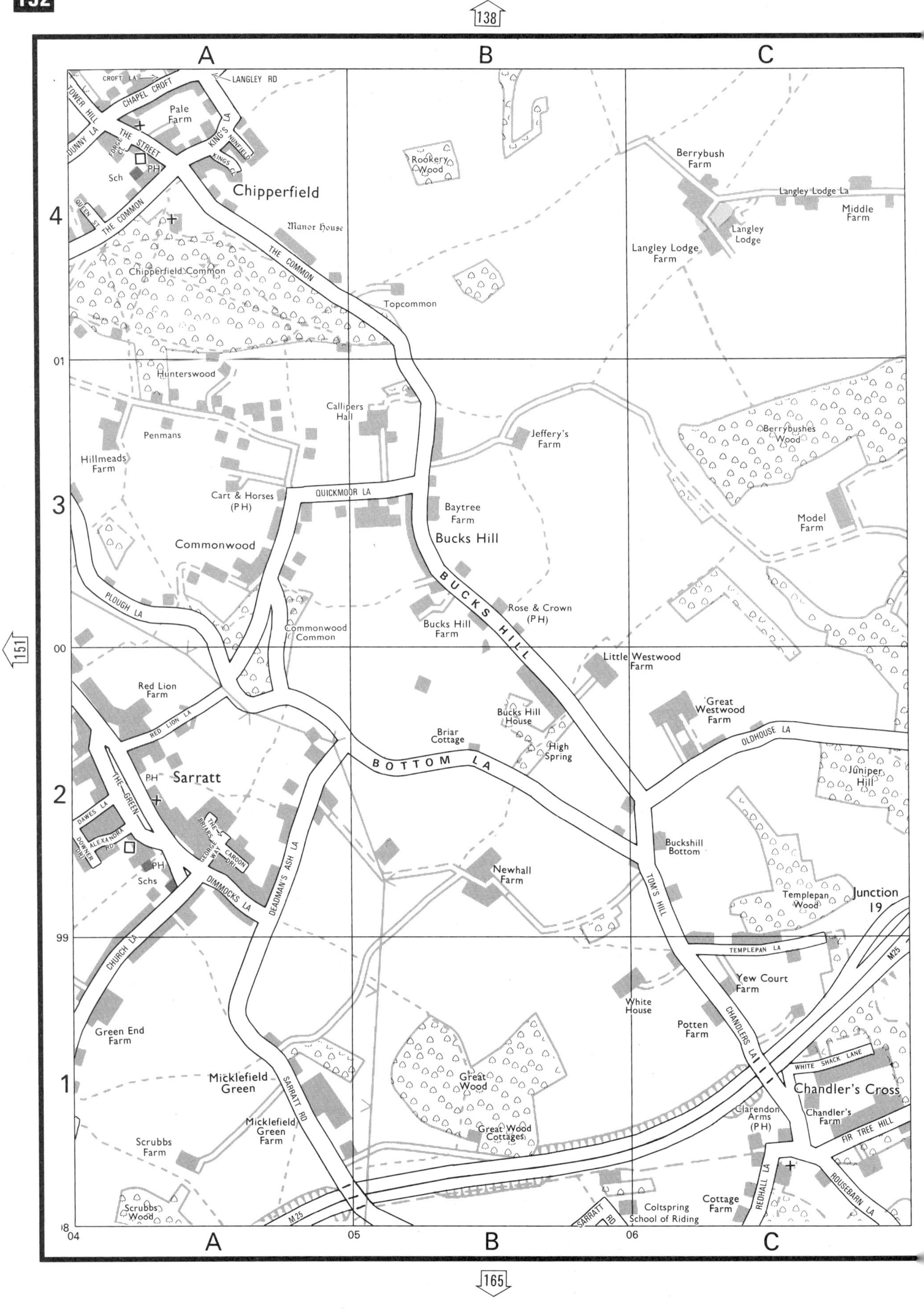

138
A
B
C
4
3
2
1
01
00
99
04
05
06
151
165
Chipperfield
Pale Farm
Sch
PH
Manor House
Chipperfield Common
Topcommon
Rookery Wood
Berrybush Farm
Langley Lodge La
Middle Farm
Langley Lodge
Langley Lodge Farm
Hunterswood
Callipers Hall
Penmans
Hillmeads Farm
Jeffery's Farm
Berrybushes Wood
Cart & Horses (PH)
Baytree Farm
Bucks Hill
Model Farm
Commonwood
Rose & Crown (PH)
Bucks Hill Farm
Commonwood Common
Little Westwood Farm
Red Lion Farm
Great Westwood Farm
Bucks Hill House
Briar Cottage
High Spring
Juniper Hill
Sarratt
Buckshill Bottom
Newhall Farm
Templepan Wood
Junction 19
Schs
Yew Court Farm
White House
Potten Farm
Green End Farm
Micklefield Green
Great Wood
Chandler's Cross
Clarendon Arms (PH)
Chandler's Farm
Micklefield Green Farm
Great Wood Cottages
Scrubbs Farm
Scrubbs Wood
Coltspring School of Riding
Cottage Farm
CROFT LA
LANGLEY RD
TOWER HILL
CHAPEL CROFT
DUNNY LA
FORGE CL
THE STREET
KING'S LA
NUNFIELD
KINGS CL
QUEEN ST
THE COMMON
QUICKMOOR LA
BUCKS HILL
PLOUGH LA
RED LION LA
OLDHOUSE LA
BOTTOM LA
THE GREEN
DAWES LA
ALEXANDRA RD
DOWNER DRI
THE BRIARS
GEORGE WAY
CAROON DRI
DIMMOCKS LA
DEADMAN'S ASH LA
TOM'S HILL
TEMPLEPAN LA
M25
CHURCH LA
CHANDLERS LA
WHITE SHACK LANE
FIR TREE HILL
SARRATT RD
ROUSEBARN LA
REDHALL LA

139

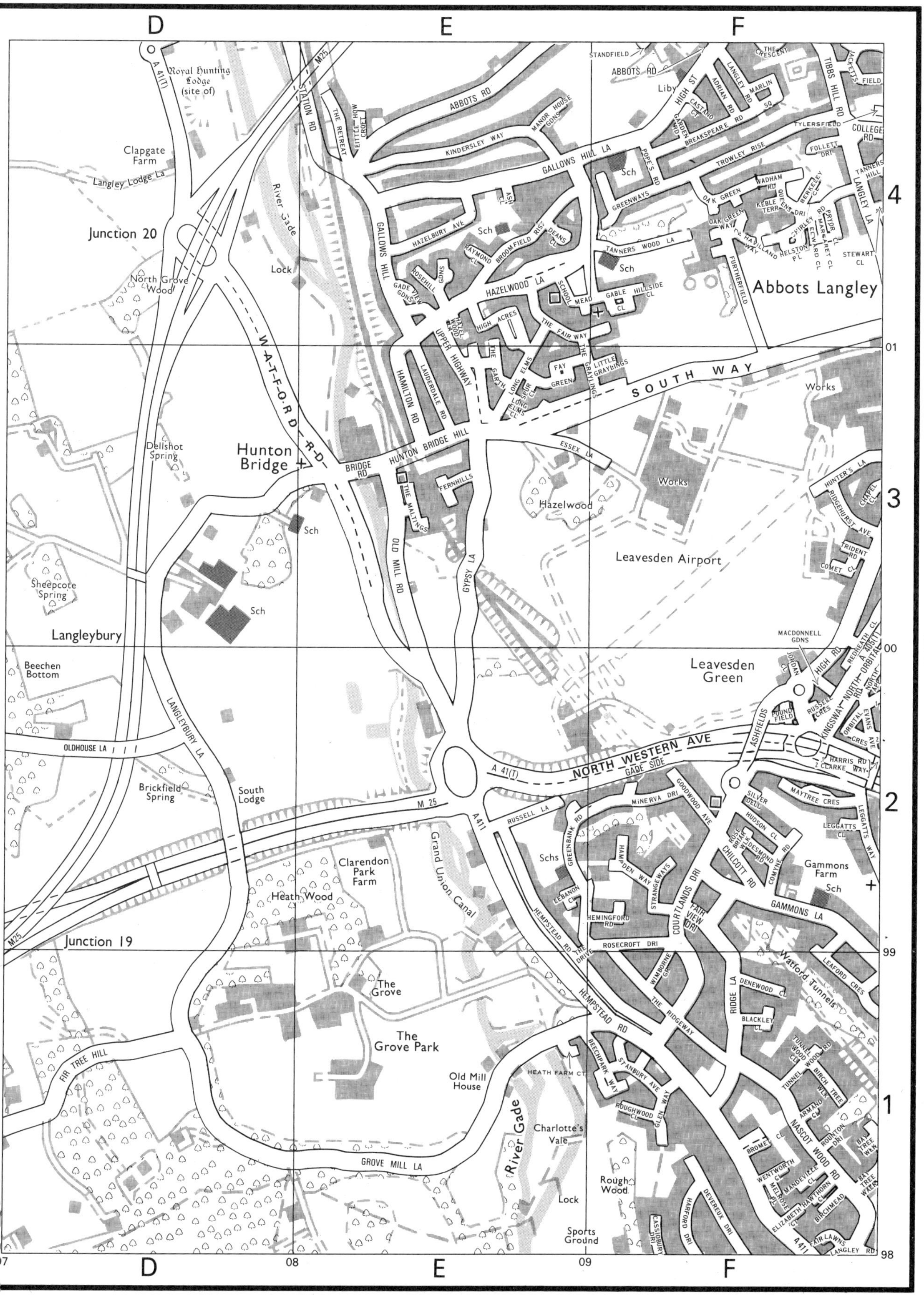
D
E
F
Royal Hunting Lodge (site of)
A 41(T)
M25
STATION RD
THE RETREAT
LITTLE HOW CROFT
ABBOTS RD
MANOR HOUSE GDNS
KINDERSLEY WAY
GALLOWS HILL LA
STANDFIELD
ABBOTS RD
Liby
HIGH ST
CASTANO CT
GARDEN RD
ADRIAN RD
LANGLEY RD
MARLIN SQ
THE CRESCENT
BREAKSPEARE RD
TIBBS HILL RD
JACKETTS FIELD
TYLERSFIELD
COLLEGE RD
FOLLETT DRI
TANNERS HILL
LANGLEY LA
TROWLEY RISE
POPE'S RD
Sch
WADHAM RD
QUEENS DRI
BERKELEY CL
OAK GREEN
OAK GREEN WAY
KEBLE TERR
HAVILLAND WAY
HELSTON PL
PRYOR CL
MARGARET CL
EDWARD CL
PIRLEY
STEWART CL
GREENWAYS
TANNERS WOOD LA
Clapgate Farm
Langley Lodge La
River Gade
Junction 20
North Grove Wood
Lock
GALLOWS HILL
HAZELBURY AVE
ASH CL
Sch
BROOMFIELD RISE
DEANS CL
RAYMOND CL
ROSEHILL GDNS
GADE VIEW GDNS
HAZELWOOD LA
SCHOOL MEAD
GABLE CL
HILLSIDE CL
Sch
FURTHERFIELD
Abbots Langley
HAZEL WOOD
HIGH ACRES
THE FAIR WAY
W-A-T-F-O-R-D R-D
UPPER HIGHWAY
HAMILTON RD
LAUDERDALE RD
THE GARTH
LONG ELMS
LONG SPUR CL
LONG ELMS CL
FAY GREEN
THE GRAYLINGS
LITTLE GRAYLINGS
SOUTH WAY
01
Works
Hunton Bridge
Dellshot Spring
BRIDGE RD
HUNTON BRIDGE HILL
FERNHILLS
THE MALTINGS
ESSEX LA
Sch
Hazelwood
Works
HUNTER'S LA
RIDGEHURST AVE
CHAPEL CL
3
TRIDENT RD
COMET CL
Leavesden Airport
OLD MILL RD
GYPSY LA
Sheepcote Spring
Sch
Langleybury
MACDONNELL GDNS
REDHEATH CL
JORDAN
HIGH RD
A 405(T)
NORTH ORBITAL RD
00
Beechen Bottom
Leavesden Green
ASHFIELDS
POUND FIELD
RUSSELL CRES
KINGSWAY
EVANS AVE
CRES
HARRIS RD
CLARKE WAY
OLDHOUSE LA
LANGLEYBURY LA
A 41(T)
NORTH WESTERN AVE
GADE SIDE
GOODWOOD AVE
MINERVA DRI
SILVER DELL
MAYTREE CRES
2
Brickfield Spring
South Lodge
M 25
A 411
RUSSELL LA
GREENBANK RD
HUDSON CL
LEGGATTS CL
LEGGATTS WAY
ROSE BRIAR WLK
DESMOND RD
COMYNE RD
CHILCOTT RD
Gammons Farm
Sch
Clarendon Park Farm
Grand Union Canal
Schs
HAMPDEN WAY
STRANGEWAYS
COURTLANDS DRI
FAIR VIEW DRI
GAMMONS LA
Heath Wood
LEBANON CL
HEMINGFORD RD
M25
Junction 19
HEMPSTEAD RD
THE DRIVE
ROSECROFT DRI
99
Watford Tunnels
LEAFORD CRES
WIMBORNE GR
RIDGE LA
DENEWOOD CL
The Grove
THE RIDGEWAY
BLACKLEY CL
HEMPSTEAD RD
TUNNEL WOOD CL
TUNNEL WOOD RD
BIRCH TREE WLK
The Grove Park
FIR TREE HILL
Old Mill House
HEATH FARM CT
BEECHPARK WAY
STANBURY AVE
GLEN WAY
ARMAND CL
1
Charlotte's Vale
River Gade
ROUGHWOOD CL
BROMET CL
NASCOT WOOD RD
ROUNTON DRI
BAY TREE WLK
GROVE MILL LA
Rough Wood
WENTWORTH CL
MELROSE PL
MANDEVILLE CL
HAWTHORN CL
BIRCHMEAD
Lock
HARFORD DRI
DEVEREUX DRI
ELIZABETH CT
Sports Ground
CASSIOBURY DRI
A 411
FAIR LAWNS
LANGLEY RD
98
07
08
09
D
E
F

154

166

140

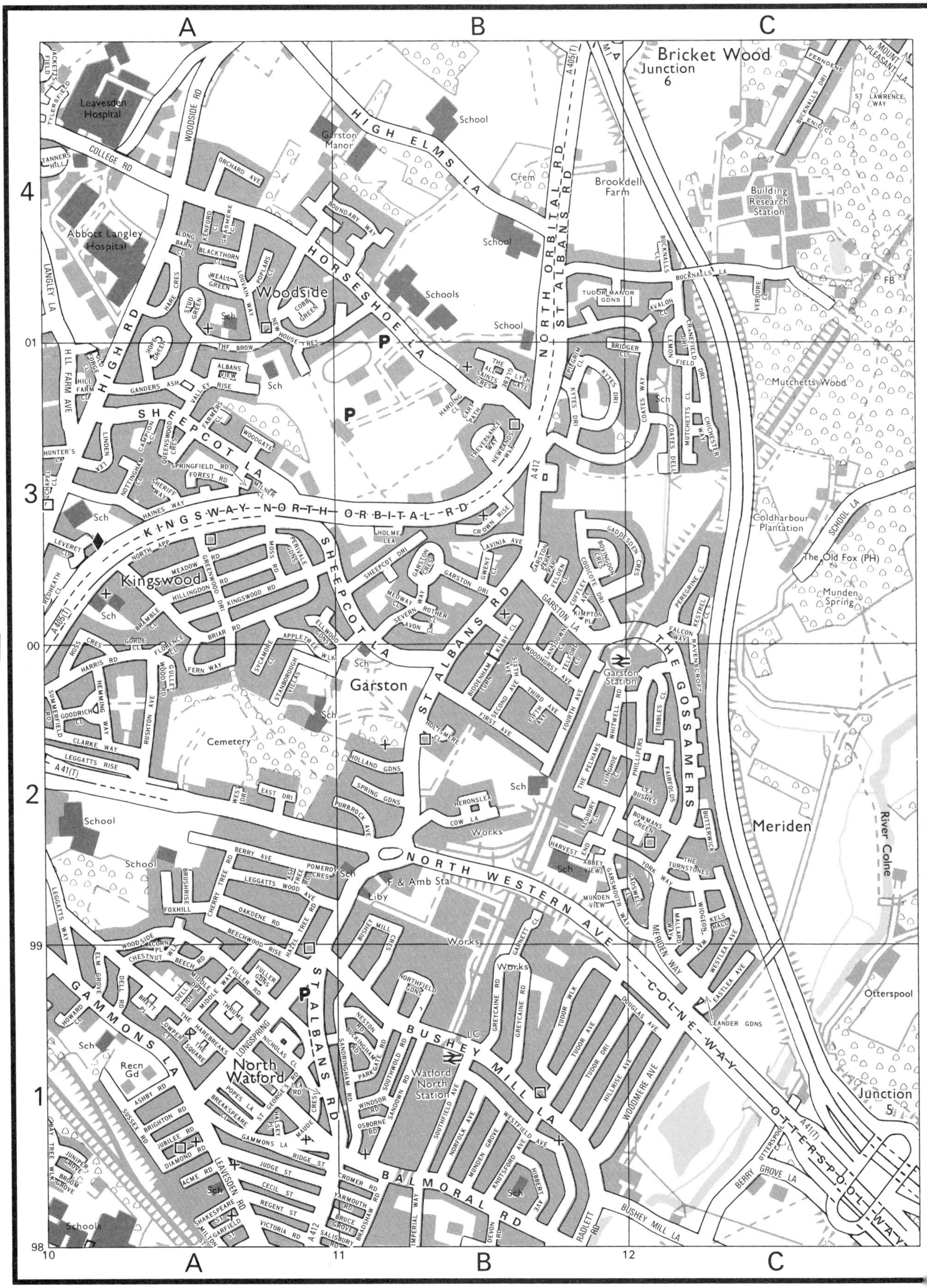
A
B
C
1
2
3
4
Bricket Wood
Junction 6
Leavesden Hospital
Abbots Langley Hospital
Garston Manor
School
HIGH ELMS LA
Crem
Brookdell Farm
Building Research Station
COLLEGE RD
WOODSIDE RD
ORCHARD AVE
HORSESHOE LA
Woodside
Schools
NORTH ORBITAL RD
ST ALBANS RD
BUCKNALLS LA
TUDOR MANOR GDNS
Mutchetts Wood
HIGH RD
SHEEPCOT LA
KINGSWAY NORTH ORBITAL RD
Kingswood
Coldharbour Plantation
SCHOOL LA
The Old Fox (PH)
Munden Spring
Garston
Garston Station
THE GOSSAMERS
Cemetery
A41(T)
A405(T)
A412
LEGGATTS RISE
NORTH WESTERN AVE
Meriden
River Colne
F & Amb Sta
Liby
Works
COLNE WAY
Otterspool
GAMMONS LA
North Watford
Recn Gd
BUSHEY MILL LA
Watford North Station
BALMORAL RD
OTTERSPOOL WAY
Junction 5
BERRY GROVE LA
BUSHEY MILL LA
Schools
10
11
12
98
99
00
01

153

167

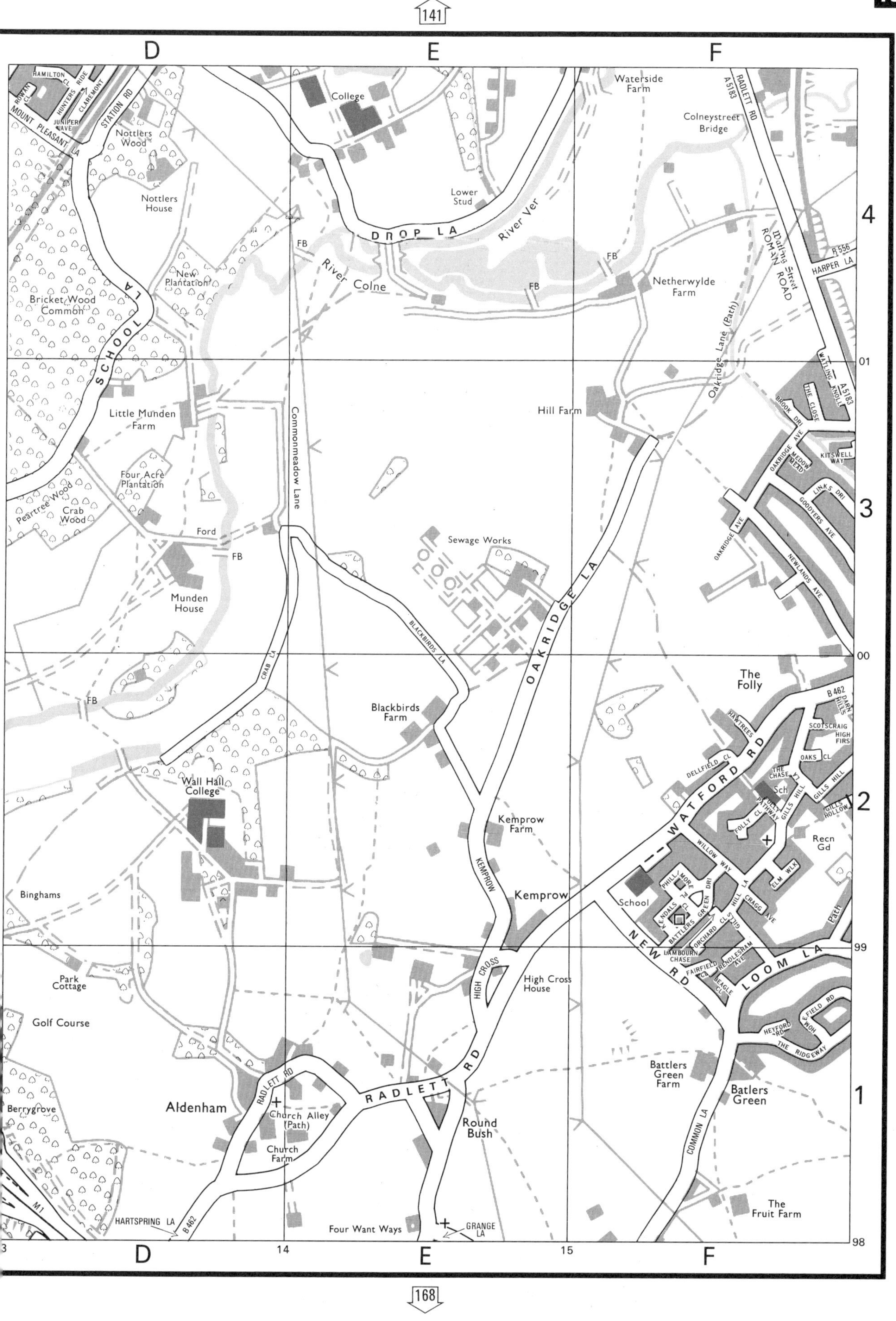
141
D
E
F
College
Waterside Farm
A5183
RADLETT RD
Colneystreet Bridge
Nottlers Wood
Nottlers House
Lower Stud
DROP LA
River Ver
River Colne
Watling Street
ROMAN ROAD
Netherwylde Farm
New Plantation
Bricket Wood Common
SCHOOL LA
STATION RD
MOUNT PLEASANT LA
HAMILTON CL
HUNTERS RIDE
CLAREMONT
ROWAN CL
JUNIPER AVE
B556
HARPER LA
Oakridge Lane (Path)
FB
4
01
Little Munden Farm
Hill Farm
Commonmeadow Lane
Four Acre Plantation
Peartree Wood
Crab Wood
Ford
Munden House
Sewage Works
OAKRIDGE LA
BLACKBIRDS LA
CRAB LA
OAKRIDGE AVE
WATLING KNOLL
THE CLOSE
BROOK DRI
MEDOW MEAD
KITSWELL WAY
LINKS DRI
GOODYERS AVE
NEWLANDS AVE
3
00
156
The Folly
B462
DARN HILLS
SCOTSCRAIG
HIGH FIRS
HAWTREES
DELLFIELD CL
OAKS CL
THE CHASE
Sch
GILLS HILL
GILLS HOLLOW
GILLS HILL LA
FOLLY PATHWAY
FOLLY CL
WATFORD RD
WILLOW WAY
Recn Gd
ELM WLK
CRAGG AVE
Path
Blackbirds Farm
Wall Hall College
Kemprow Farm
KEMPROW
Kemprow
School
PHILLIMORE PL
BATTLERS GREEN DRI
KENDALS CL
BATTLERS CL
GILL'S CL
ORCHARD CL
LAMBOURN CHASE
TRENDLESHAM AVE
FAIRFIELD CL
BEAGLE CL
NEW RD
LOOM LA
2
99
Binghams
Park Cottage
Golf Course
HIGH CROSS
High Cross House
HEYFORD RD
THE RIDGEWAY
FIELD RD
Battlers Green Farm
Batlers Green
Aldenham
RADLETT RD
Church Alley (Path)
Church Farm
Round Bush
Berrygrove
COMMON LA
1
M1
HARTSPRING LA
B462
Four Want Ways
GRANGE LA
The Fruit Farm
13
14
15
98
168

142

155

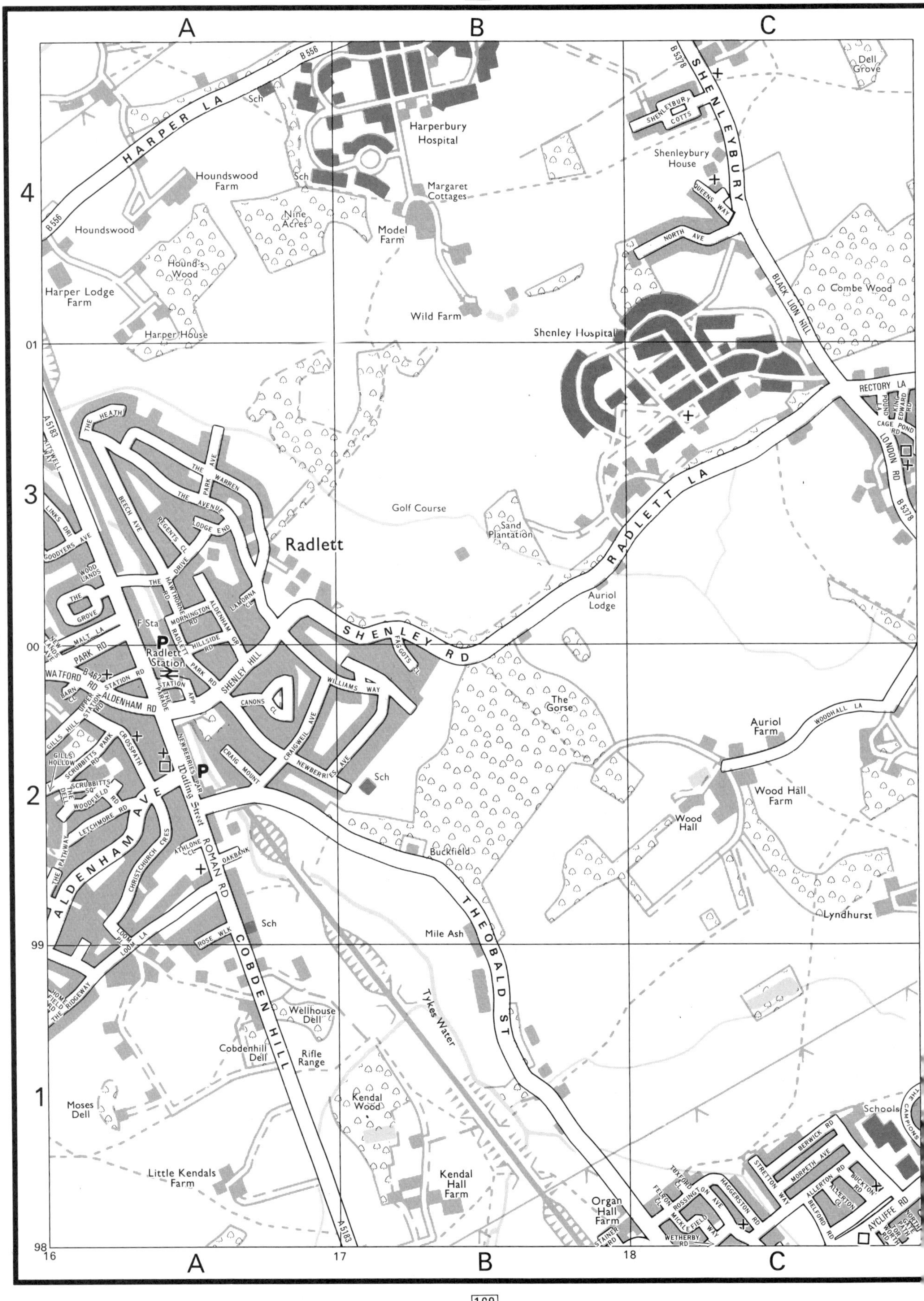

A
B
C
4
3
2
1
01
00
99
98
16
17
18
B556
HARPER LA
Sch
Harperbury
Hospital
Houndswood
Farm
Houndswood
Nine
Acres
Margaret
Cottages
Model
Farm
Hound's
Wood
Harper Lodge
Farm
Harper House
Wild Farm
B5378
SHENLEYBURY
SHENLEYBURY COTTS
Shenleybury
House
QUEENS WAY
NORTH AVE
BLACK LION HILL
Dell
Grove
Combe Wood
Shenley Hospital
RECTORY LA
POUND LA
KING EDWARD RD
CAGE POND RD
LONDON RD
A5183
KITSWELL WAY
LINKS DRI
THE HEATH
THE AVE
PARK WARREN
THE AVENUE
BEECH AVE
REGENTS CL
LODGE END
THE DRIVE
GOODYERS AVE
WOOD LANDS
THE GROVE
HAWTHORNE RD
MORNINGTON RD
ALDENHAM GR
LAMORNA CL
HILLSIDE RD
Golf Course
Sand
Plantation
Radlett
RADLETT LA
Auriol
Lodge
F Sta
NEW LANDS
MALT LA
PARK RD
Radlett
Station
RADLETT PARK RD
SHENLEY HILL
SHENLEY RD
FAGGOTS CL
WATFORD RD
B462
STATION RD
STATION APP
THE PARADE
BARN CL
UPPER STATION RD
ALDENHAM RD
CANONS CL
WILLIAMS WAY
The
Gorse
Auriol
Farm
WOODHALL LA
GILLS HILL
CROSSPATH
SCRUBBITTS PARK RD
GILLS HOLLOW
SCRUBBITTS SQ
THE DELL
WOODFIELD RD
NEWBERRIES PAR
CRAIG MOUNT
CRAIGWEIL AVE
NEWBERRIES AVE
Sch
Watling Street
Wood Hall
Farm
Wood
Hall
LETCHMORE RD
ALDENHAM AVE
THE PATHWAY
CHRISTCHURCH CRES
ATHLONE CL
OAKBANK
ROMAN RD
Buckfield
THEOBALD ST
Lyndhurst
LOOM PL
LOOM LA
ROSE WLK
COBDEN HILL
Sch
Mile Ash
HOMEFIELD RD
THE RIDGEWAY
Wellhouse
Dell
Tykes Water
Cobdenhill
Dell
Rifle
Range
Moses
Dell
Kendal
Wood
Schools
THE CAMPIONS
Little Kendals
Farm
Kendal
Hall
Farm
Organ
Hall
Farm
BERWICK RD
STRETTON WAY
MORPETH AVE
TUXFORD CL
FELTON CL
ROSSINGTON AVE
HAGGERSTON RD
MICKLEFIELD WAY
ALLERTON RD
BUCKTON RD
ALLERTON CL
BELFORD RD
AYCLIFFE RD
NORTHGATE PATH
STAINER RD
WETHERBY RD

169

143

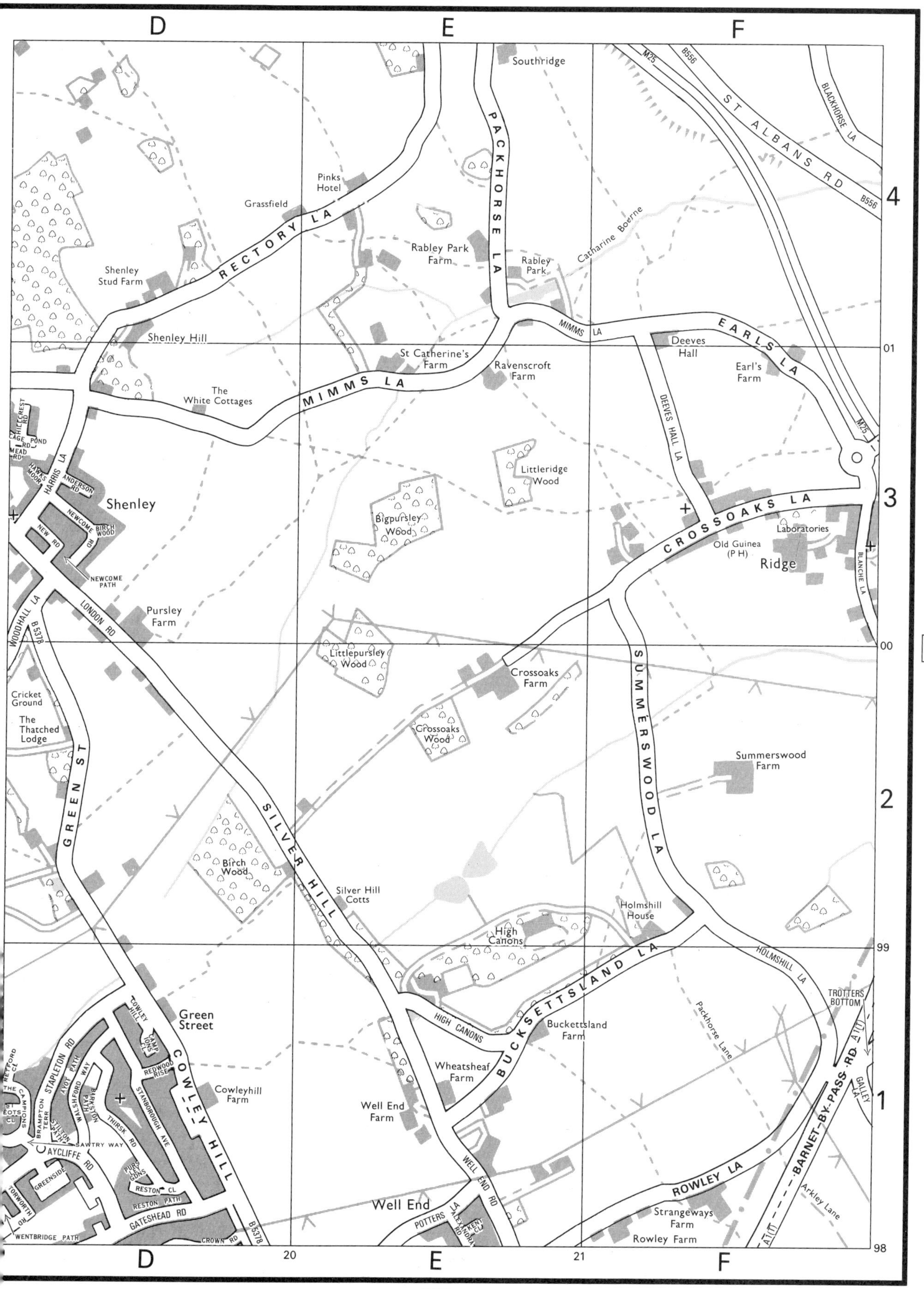
D
E
F
4
3
2
1
01
00
99
98
20
21
Southridge
M25
B556
ST ALBANS RD
B556
BLACKHORSE LA
PACKHORSE LA
Pinks Hotel
Grassfield
RECTORY LA
Rabley Park Farm
Rabley Park
Catharine Bourne
Shenley Stud Farm
Shenley Hill
MIMMS LA
EARLS LA
Deeves Hall
Earl's Farm
St Catherine's Farm
Ravenscroft Farm
The White Cottages
MIMMS LA
DEEVES HALL LA
M25
HILLCREST RD
CAGE POND RD
MEAD RD
HAWKS MOOR
HARRIS LA
ANDERSON RD
Shenley
NEWCOME RD
BIRCH WOOD
NEW RD
NEWCOME PATH
Littleridge Wood
Bigpursley Wood
CROSSOAKS LA
Laboratories
Old Guinea (P H)
Ridge
BLANCHE LA
WOODHALL LA
B5378
LONDON RD
Pursley Farm
Littlepursley Wood
Crossoaks Farm
SUMMERSWOOD LA
Cricket Ground
The Thatched Lodge
Crossoaks Wood
Summerswood Farm
GREEN ST
SILVER HILL
Birch Wood
Silver Hill Cotts
Holmshill House
High Canons
HOLMSHILL LA
TROTTERS BOTTOM
BUCKSETTSLAND LA
HIGH CANONS
Buckettsland Farm
Packhorse Lane
Green Street
COWLEY HILL
CAMP CL
REDWOOD RISE
Wheatsheaf Farm
Cowleyhill Farm
A1(T)
BARNET-BY-PASS RD
GALLEY LA
RETFORD CL
THE CAMPIONS
STAPLETON RD
BRAMPTON TERR
ELTOTS CL
STILTON PATH
AYLOT PATH
WALSHFORD WAY
BARKSTON PATH
THIRSK RD
STANBOROUGH AVE
SAWTRY WAY
AYCLIFFE RD
Well End Farm
WELL END RD
GREENSIDE
PURSLEY GONS
RESTON CL
RESTON PATH
GATESHEAD RD
TORWORTH RD
WENTBRIDGE PATH
CROWN RD
B5378
Well End
POTTERS LA
ALEXANDRA RD
KENT CL
ROWLEY LA
Strangeways Farm
Rowley Farm
Arkley Lane
A1(T)

158

170

144

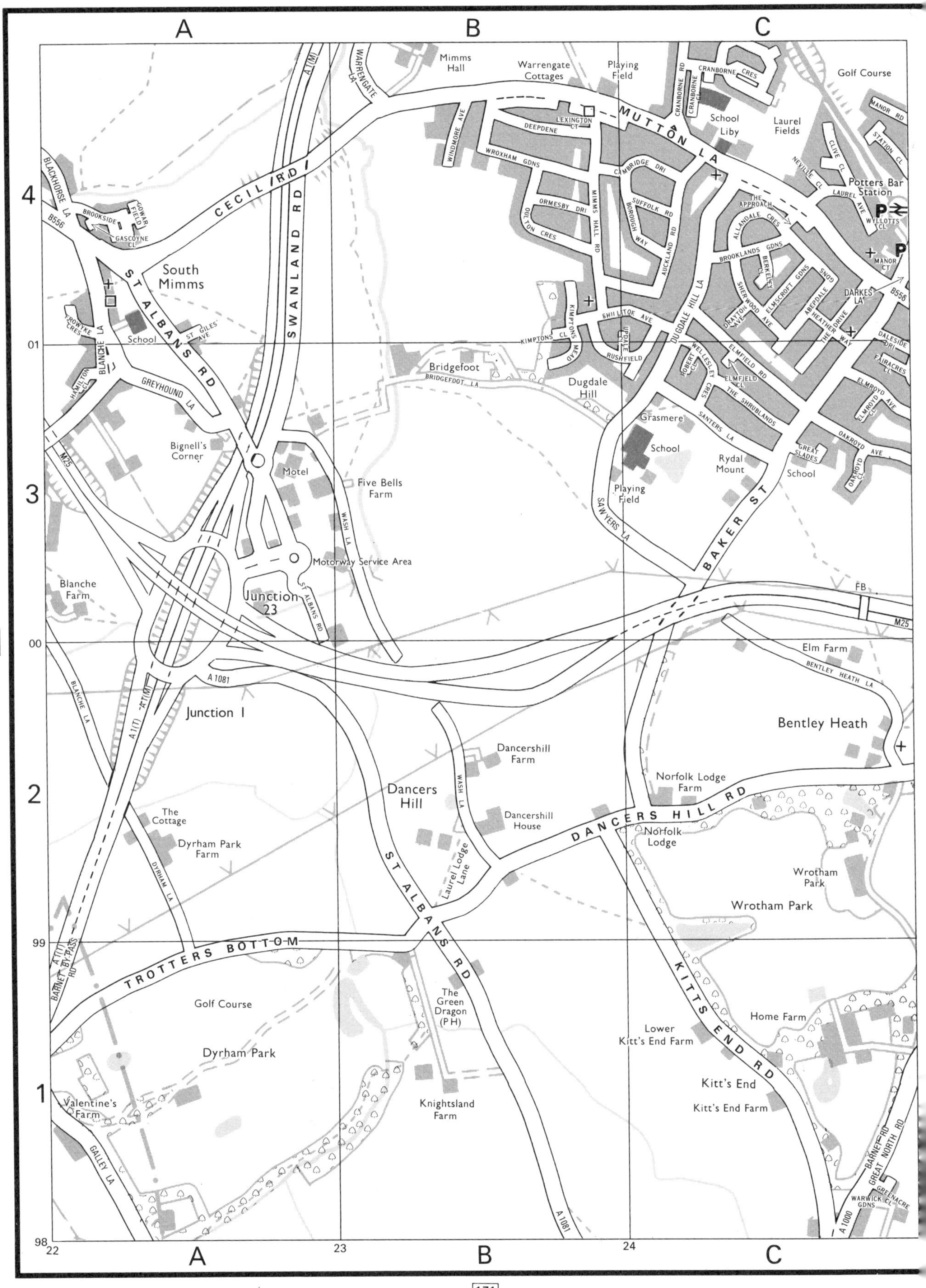
A
B
C
4
3
2
1
01
00
99
98
22
23
24
Mimms Hall
Warrengate Cottages
Playing Field
Golf Course
School
Liby
Laurel Fields
MUTTON LA
CECIL RD
SWANLAND RD
ST ALBANS RD
South Mimms
School
Potters Bar Station
Bridgefoot
Dugdale Hill
Grasmere
School
Rydal Mount
School
Playing Field
Bignell's Corner
Motel
Five Bells Farm
Motorway Service Area
Junction 23
Blanche Farm
Junction 1
M25
A 1081
Elm Farm
Bentley Heath
Dancershill Farm
Dancers Hill
Norfolk Lodge Farm
Dancershill House
DANCERS HILL RD
Norfolk Lodge
The Cottage
Dyrham Park Farm
Wrotham Park
Wrotham Park
TROTTERS BOTTOM
KITTS END RD
Golf Course
The Green Dragon (PH)
Home Farm
Lower Kitt's End Farm
Dyrham Park
Kitt's End
Kitt's End Farm
Valentine's Farm
Knightsland Farm
GALLEY LA
A1000
BAKER ST
SAWYERS LA
DUGDALE HILL LA
WASH LA
BLANCHE LA
DYRHAM LA
GREYHOUND LA
BLACKHORSE LA
BENTLEY HEATH LA
GREAT NORTH RD
BARNET RD
Laurel Lodge Lane
WARRENGATE LA
A1(M)
A1(T)
BARNET BY-PASS RD
B556
FB

157

171

145

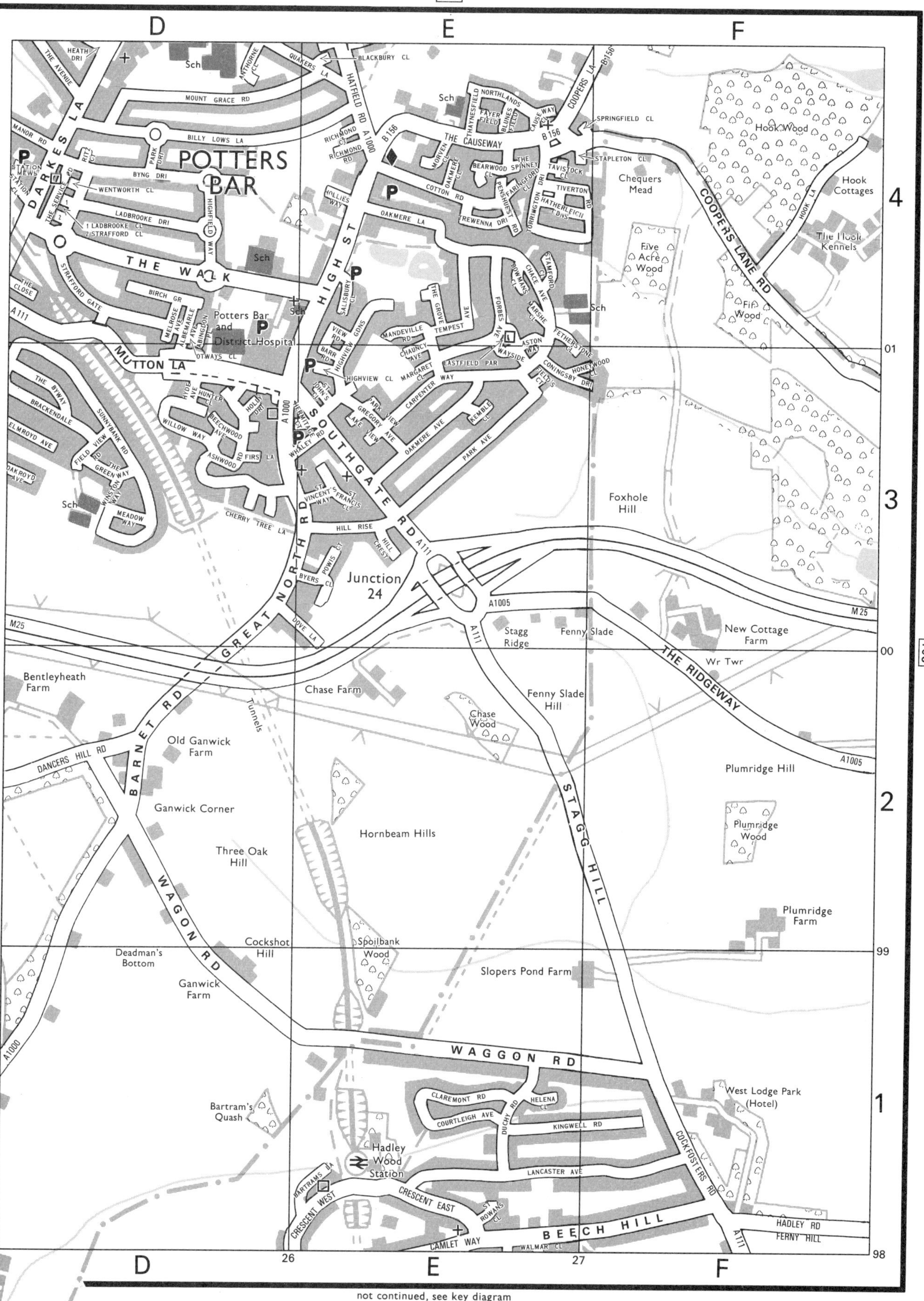

160

not continued, see key diagram

146

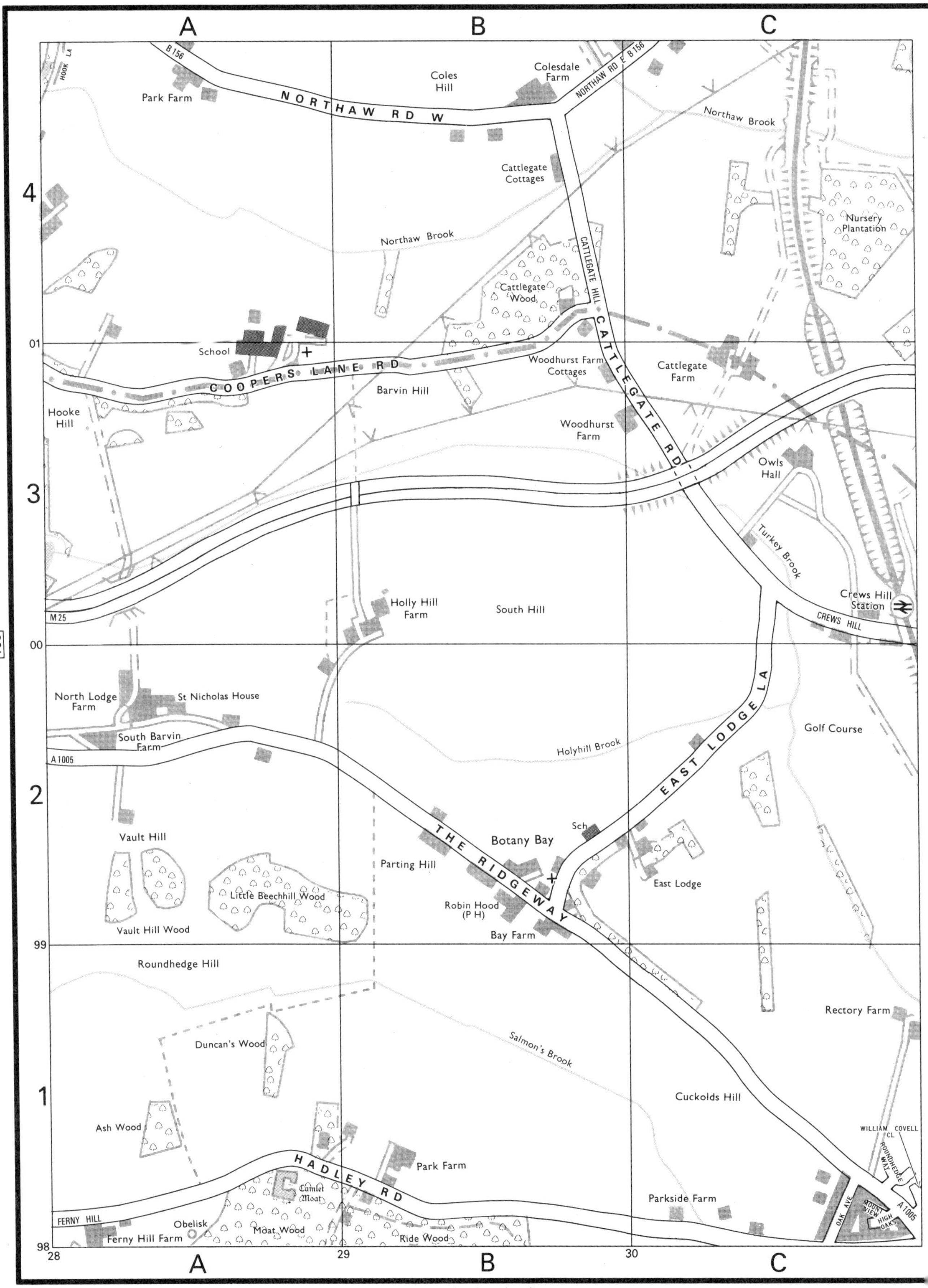

159

not continued, see key diagram

147

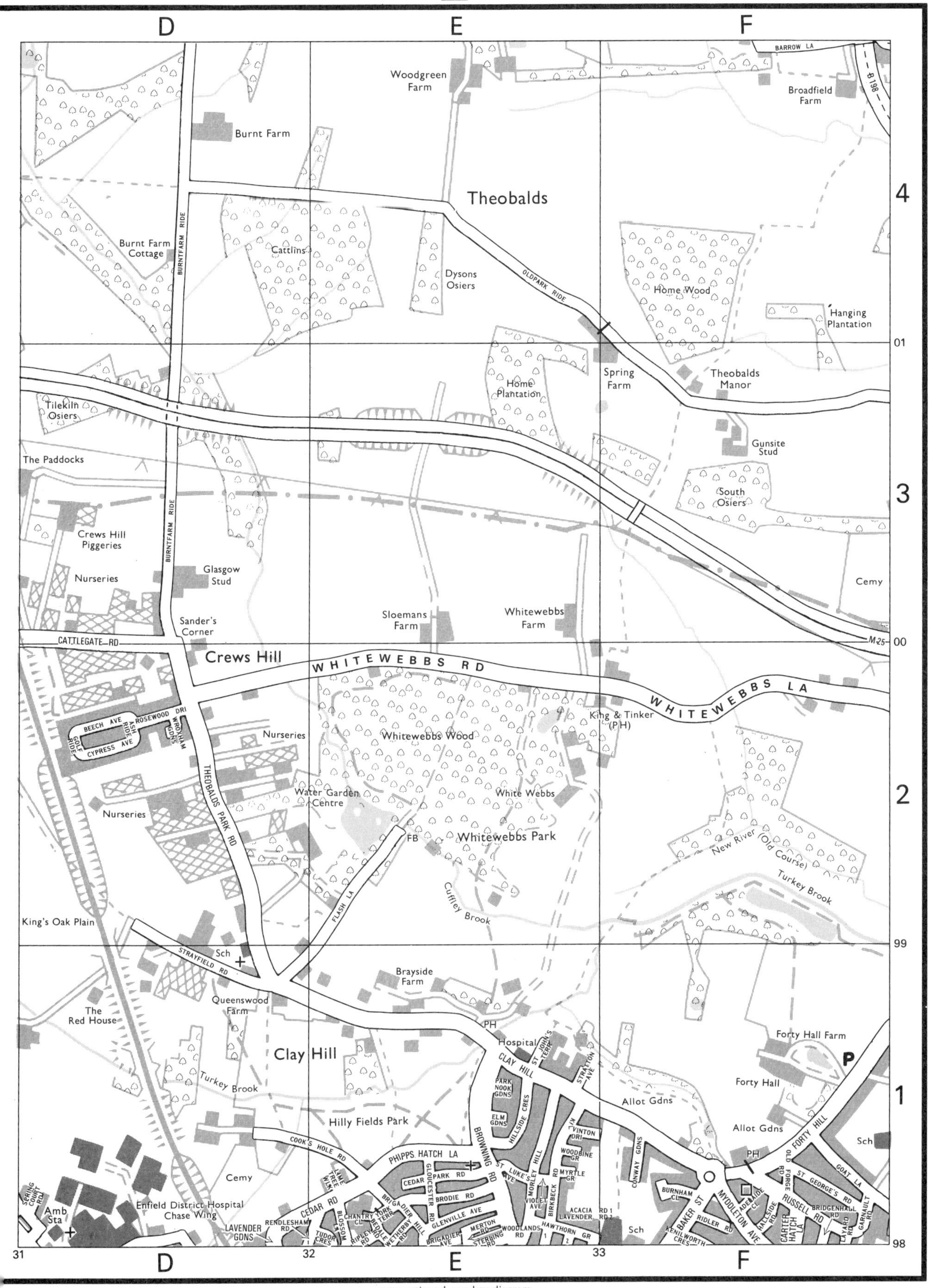
D
E
F
Woodgreen Farm
Burnt Farm
BARROW LA
Broadfield Farm
B 198
Theobalds
4
Burnt Farm Cottage
BURNTFARM RIDE
Cattlins
Dysons Osiers
OLDPARK RIDE
Home Wood
Hanging Plantation
01
Home Plantation
Spring Farm
Theobalds Manor
Tilekiln Osiers
The Paddocks
Gunsite Stud
South Osiers
3
Crews Hill Piggeries
Nurseries
Glasgow Stud
Cemy
Sloemans Farm
Whitewebbs Farm
Sander's Corner
CATTLEGATE RD
M25
00
Crews Hill
WHITEWEBBS RD
WHITEWEBBS LA
BEECH AVE
ROSEWOOD DRI
ASH RIDE
WROXHAM GDNS
GOLF RIDE
CYPRESS AVE
King & Tinker (PH)
Nurseries
Whitewebbs Wood
THEOBALDS PARK RD
Water Garden Centre
White Webbs
2
Nurseries
FB
Whitewebbs Park
New River (Old Course)
Turkey Brook
Cuffley Brook
FLASH LA
King's Oak Plain
99
Sch
STRAYFIELD RD
Brayside Farm
Queenswood Farm
The Red House
PH
Hospital
Clay Hill
ST JOHN'S TERR
CLAY HILL
STRATTON AVE
Forty Hall Farm
P
Turkey Brook
PARK NOOK GDNS
HILLSIDE CRES
Forty Hall
1
ELM GDNS
Allot Gdns
Hilly Fields Park
VINTON DRI
Allot Gdns
Sch
COOK'S HOLE RD
PHIPPS HATCH LA
BROWNING RD
WOODBINE GR
CONWAY GDNS
PH
FORTY HILL
OLD FORGE RD
ST GEORGE'S RD
GOAT LA
LIME TREE WLK
CEDAR RD
GLOUCESTER RD
PARK RD
ST LUKE'S AVE
MORLEY HILL
MYRTLE GR
BURNHAM CL
MYDDLETON AVE
ADELAIDE CL
HALSIDE
RUSSELL RD
Cemy
BRODIE RD
VIOLET AVE
BIRKBECK RD
SPRING COURT RD
CEDAR RD
BRIGADIER HILL
GLENVILLE AVE
ACACIA RD 1
LAVENDER RD 2
BAKER ST
BRIDGENHALL RD
GARNAULT RD
Amb Sta
Enfield District Hospital Chase Wing
CHANTRY CL
YORK TERR
WOODLANDS RD
HAWTHORN GR
Sch
RIDLER RD
CARTER HATCH LA
LYNDHURST RD
LAVENDER GDNS
RENDLESHAM RD
TUDOR CRES
BLOSSOM LA
RIPLEY RD
BEDALE RD
WETHERBY RD
MERTON RD
BRIGADIER AVE
STERLING RD
KENILWORTH CRES
98
31
32
33
D
E
F

162

148

161

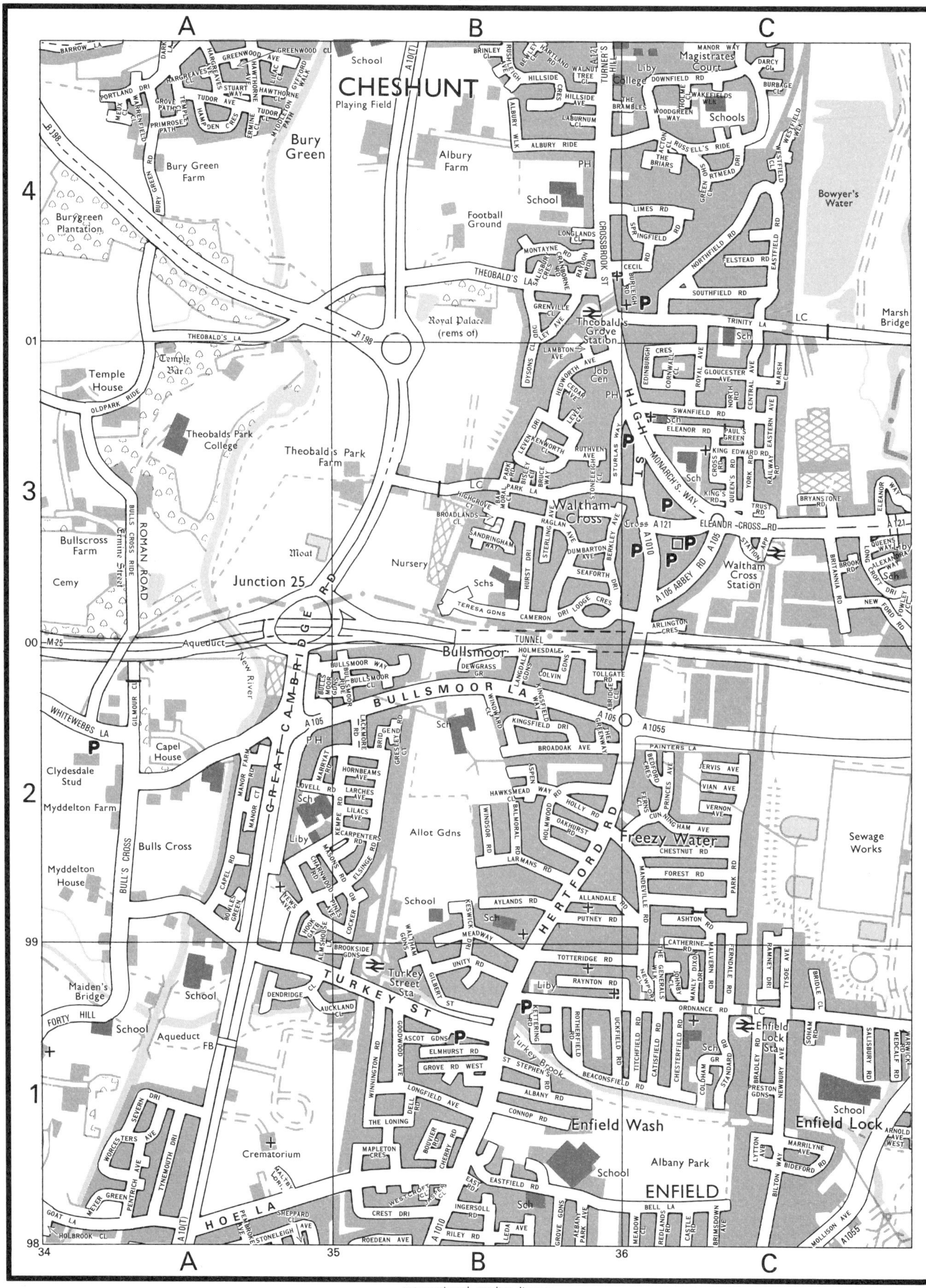
A
B
C
4
3
2
1
01
00
99
98
34
35
36
CHESHUNT
Playing Field
School
Bury Green
Bury Green Farm
Burygreen Plantation
Albury Farm
Football Ground
Magistrates Court
College
Schools
Bowyer's Water
Marsh Bridge
Royal Palace (rems of)
Theobalds Grove Station
Temple Bar
Temple House
Theobalds Park College
Theobalds Park Farm
Waltham Cross
Waltham Cross Station
Bullscross Farm
Cemy
Moat
Nursery
Junction 25
Aqueduct
TUNNEL
Bullsmoor
New River
BULLSMOOR LA
GREAT CAMBRIDGE RD
Capel House
Clydesdale Stud
Myddelton Farm
Bulls Cross
Myddelton House
Allot Gdns
Freezy Water
Sewage Works
Maiden's Bridge
Turkey Street Sta
TURKEY ST
Enfield Lock Sta
Crematorium
Enfield Wash
Albany Park
ENFIELD
Enfield Lock
HOE LA
M 25
A10(T)
A105
A1055
A121
A1010
B198

149

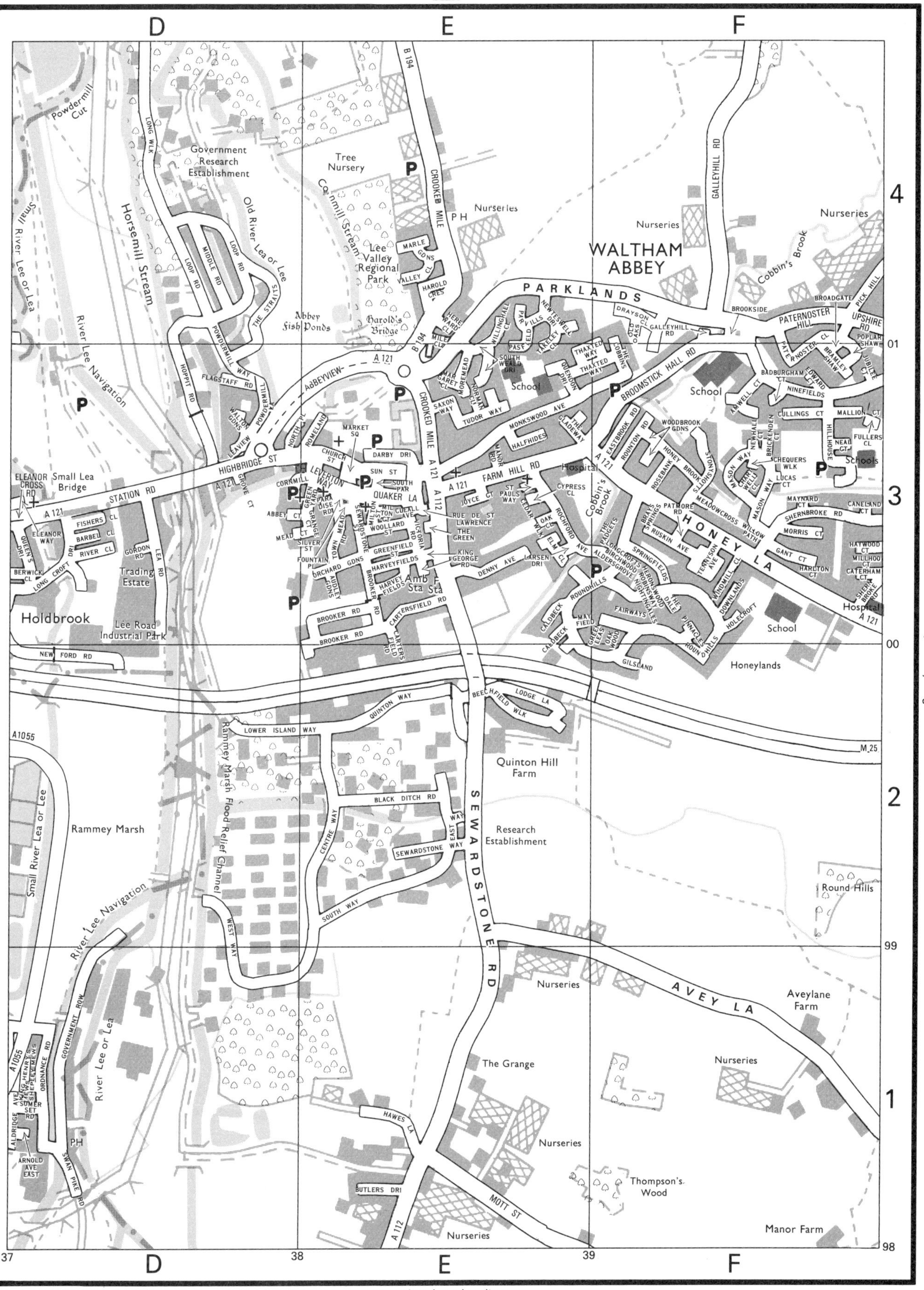

not continued, see key diagram

not continued, see key diagram

151

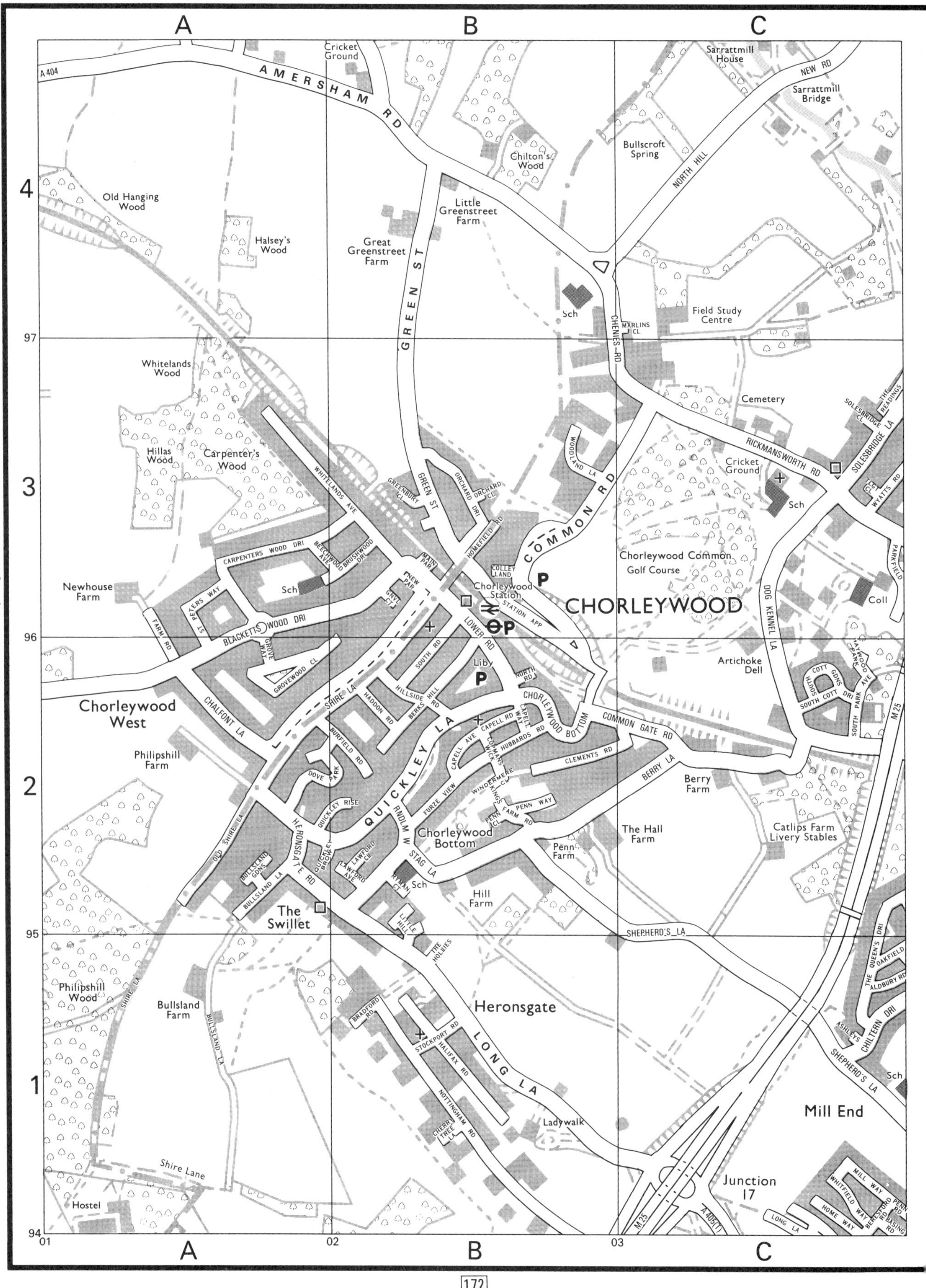

not continued, see key diagram

172

152

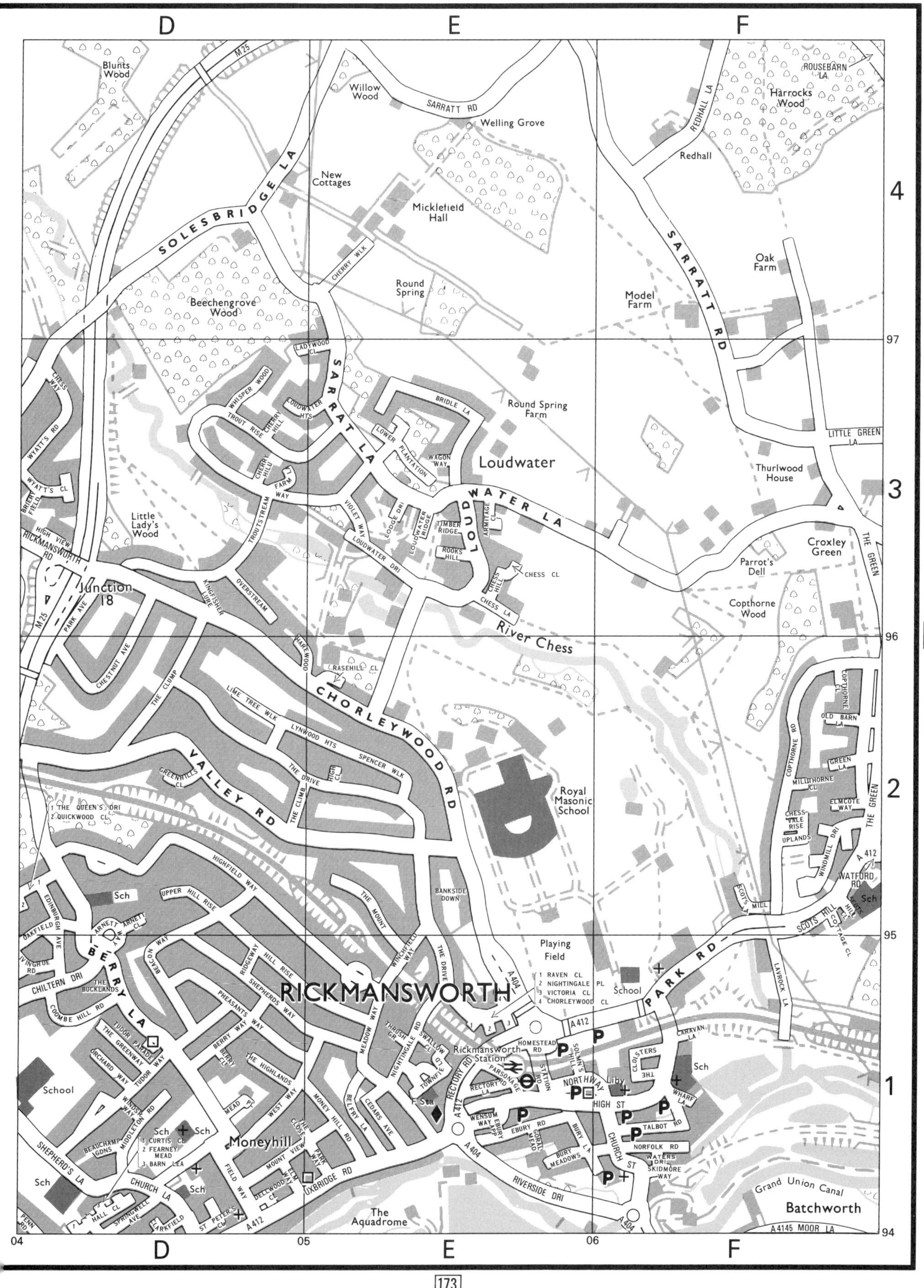
D
E
F
Blunts Wood
Willow Wood
SARRATT RD
Welling Grove
M25
REDHALL LA
Harrocks Wood
ROUSEBARN LA
Redhall
New Cottages
Mickletield Hall
SOLESBRIDGE LA
SARRATT RD
Oak Farm
CHERRY WLK
Round Spring
Beechengrove Wood
Model Farm
LADYWOOD CL
SARRAT LA
BRIDLE LA
Round Spring Farm
CHESS WAY
WHISPER WOOD
LOUDWATER HTS
TROUT RISE
CHERRY HILL
LOWER PLANTATION
WAGON WAY
Loudwater
LITTLE GREEN LA
WYATT'S RD
Thurlwood House
WYATT'S CL
CHERRY HILL
FARM WAY
TROUTSTREAM
LOUDWATER LA
ARMITAGE CL
VIOLET WAY
LODGE DRI
LOUDWATER RIDGE
TIMBER RIDGE
ROOKS HILL
Little Lady's Wood
Croxley Green
THE GREEN
Parrot's Dell
HIGH VIEW
RICKMANSWORTH RD
LOUDWATER DRI
CHESS CL
CHESS HILL
CHESS LA
Copthorne Wood
Junction 18
KINGFISHER LURE
OVERSTREAM
PARK AVE
M25
River Chess
HAREWOOD
RASEHILL CL
CHESTNUT AVE
CHORLEYWOOD RD
COPTHORNE CL
THE CLUMP
LIME TREE WLK
LYNWOOD HTS
OLD BARN LA
COPTHORNE RD
SPENCER WLK
GREENHILLS CL
VALLEY RD
THE DRIVE
HIGH CL
GREEN LA
MILLTHORNE CL
Royal Masonic School
ELMCOTE WAY
1 THE QUEEN'S DRI
2 QUICKWOOD CL
THE CLIMB
CHESS VALE RISE
UPLANDS
WINDMILL DRI
THE GREEN
A 412
HIGHFIELD WAY
WATFORD RD
Sch
UPPER HILL RISE
BANKSIDE DOWN
THE MOUNT
SCOTS MILL
SCOTS HILL
Sch
EDINBURGH AVE
ARNETT WAY
ARNETT HILLS
COTTAGE CL
OAKFIELD
Playing Field
PARK RD
LAVROCK LA
BERRY LA
BEACON WAY
RIDGEWAY
HILL RISE
WINCHFIELD WAY
THE DRIVE
A 404
1 RAVEN CL
2 NIGHTINGALE PL
3 VICTORIA CL
4 CHORLEYWOOD CL
School
CHILTERN DRI
THE BUCKLANDS
SHEPHERDS WAY
RICKMANSWORTH
COOMBE HILL RD
PHEASANTS WAY
A 412
THE GREENWAY
TUDOR PARADE
BERRY WAY
MEADOW WAY
THRUSH GR
NIGHTINGALE RD
SWALLOW CL
HOMESTEAD RD
SOLOMON'S HILL
THE CLOISTERS
CARAVAN LA
ORCHARD WAY
TUDOR WAY
BERRY CL
THE HIGHLANDS
Rickmansworth Station
STATION RD
Sch
School
PARSONAGE RD
RECTORY LA
NORTHWAY
Liby
WINDSOR WAY
WEST WAY
MONEY HILL RD
BELFRY LA
CEDARS AVE
TOWNFIELD
RECTORY RD
F Sta
HIGH ST
WHARF LA
MEAD PL
WENSUM WAY
EBURY APP
EBURY RD
CORAL MEAD
BURY LA
CHURCH ST
TALBOT RD
BEAUCHAMP GDNS
MIDDLETON RD
Sch
Sch
1 CURTIS CL
2 FEARNEY MEAD
3 BARN LEA
Moneyhill
THE CLOSE
PARK WAY
A 412
A 404
BURY MEADOWS
NORFOLK RD
WATERS DRI
SKIDMORE WAY
SHEPHERD'S LA
Sch
MOUNT VIEW
ELM WAY
DELLWOOD CL
FIELD WAY
UXBRIDGE RD
RIVERSIDE DRI
Grand Union Canal
CHURCH LA
Sch
HALL CL
SPRINGWELL AVE
LARKFIELD
ST PETER'S CL
The Aquadrome
A 404
Batchworth
PENN RD
A4145 MOOR LA
97
96
95
94
4
3
2
1
04
05
06
D
E
F

166

173

153

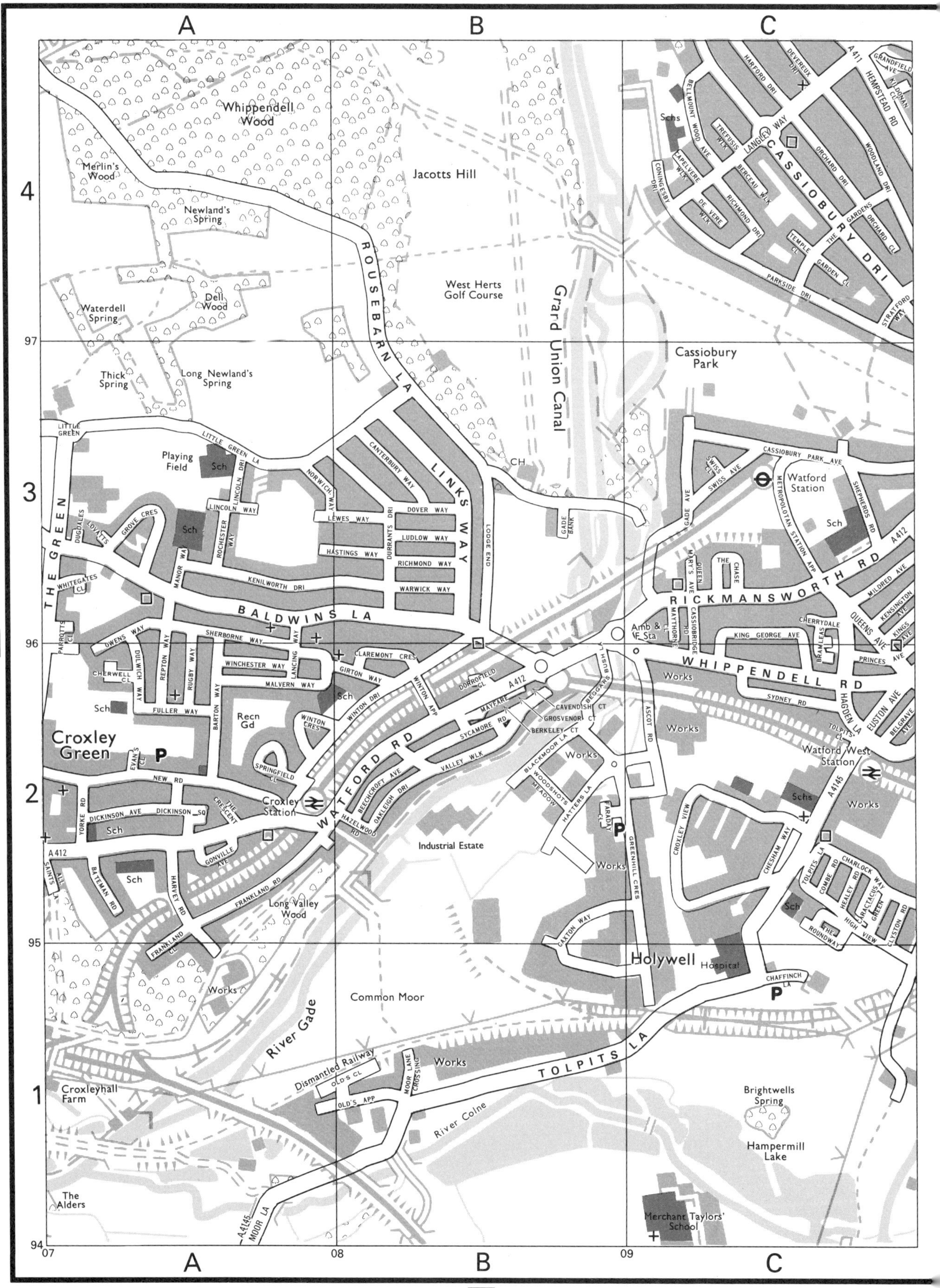
A
B
C
4
3
2
1
97
96
95
94
07
08
09
Whippendell Wood
Merlin's Wood
Newland's Spring
Jacotts Hill
Dell Wood
Waterdell Spring
West Herts Golf Course
Grand Union Canal
Thick Spring
Long Newland's Spring
Cassiobury Park
ROUSEBARN LA
LINKS WAY
LITTLE GREEN LA
LITTLE GREEN
Playing Field
Sch
Schs
CASSIOBURY DRI
CASSIOBURY PARK AVE
Watford Station
RICKMANSWORTH RD
WHIPPENDELL RD
BALDWINS LA
THE GREEN
KENILWORTH DRI
Amb & F Sta
Works
Croxley Green
Croxley Station
WATFORD RD
Recn Gd
Industrial Estate
Watford West Station
Holywell
Hospital
Long Valley Wood
Common Moor
River Gade
Dismantled Railway
TOLPITS LA
River Colne
Croxleyhall Farm
Brightwells Spring
Hampermill Lake
The Alders
Merchant Taylors' School
MOOR LA
A412
A4145
A411

165

174

154

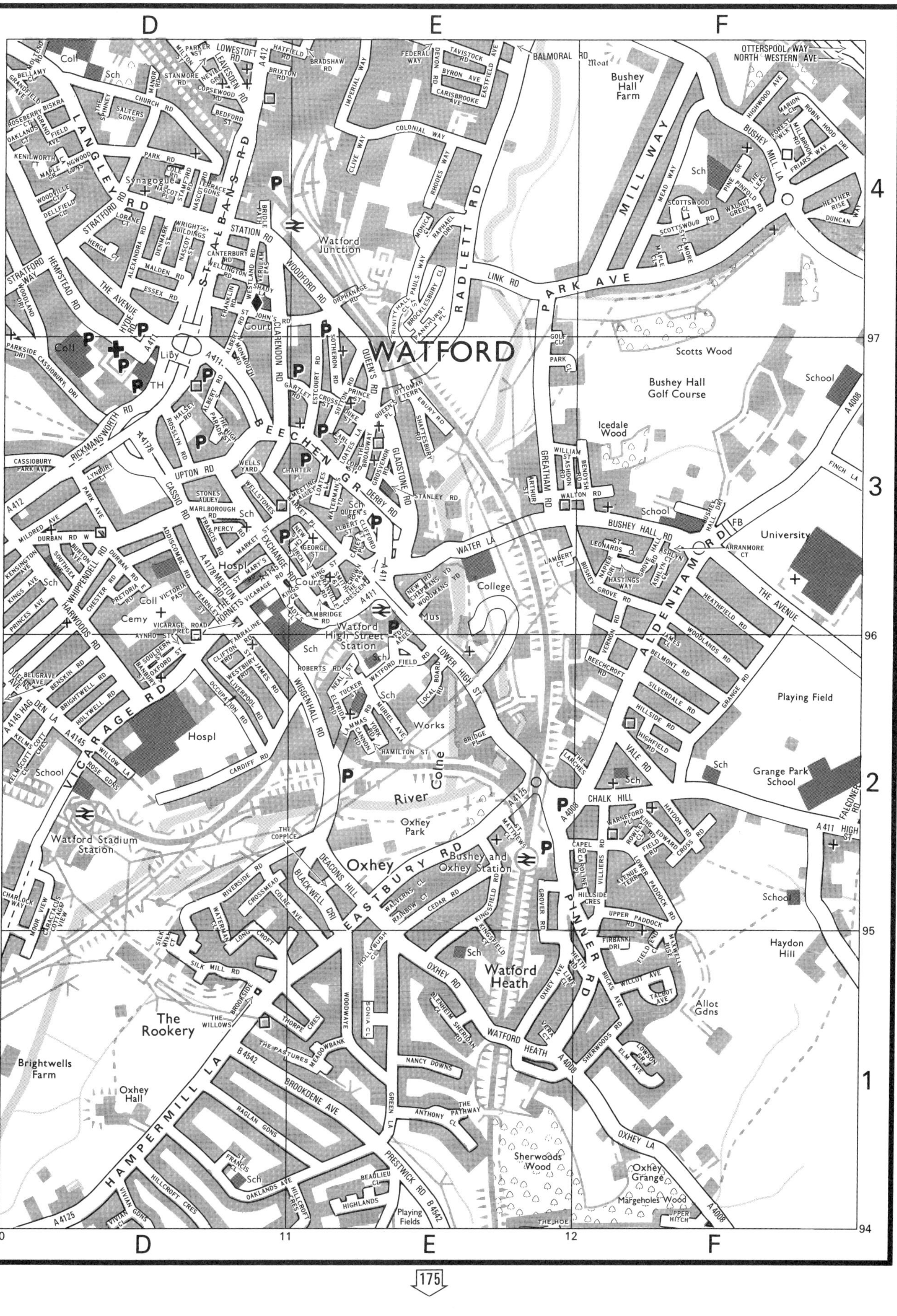
D
E
F
4
3
2
1
97
96
95
94
10
11
12
WATFORD
Watford Junction
Watford High Street Station
Watford Stadium Station
Bushey and Oxhey Station
Bushey Hall Farm
Moat
Scotts Wood
Bushey Hall Golf Course
Icedale Wood
University
Playing Field
Grange Park School
School
Sch
Coll
College
Hospl
Cemy
Mus
Works
Synagogue
LiBy
TH
Court
River Colne
Oxhey Park
Oxhey
Watford Heath
The Rookery
Brightwells Farm
Oxhey Hall
Sherwoods Wood
Oxhey Grange
Margeholes Wood
Haydon Hill
Allot Gdns
Playing Fields
ST ALBANS RD
LANGLEY RD
STATION RD
PARK AVE
RADLETT RD
MILL WAY
WOODFORD RD
ORPHANAGE RD
CLARENDON RD
BEECHEN GR
QUEEN'S RD
DERBY RD
GLADSTONE RD
WATER LA
LOWER HIGH ST
ALDENHAM RD
BUSHEY HALL RD
BUSHEY MILL LA
RICKMANSWORTH RD
HEMPSTEAD RD
THE AVENUE
UPTON RD
CASSIO RD
VICARAGE RD
WHIPPENDELL RD
HARWOODS RD
WIGGENHALL RD
EASTBURY RD
PINNER RD
CHALK HILL
OXHEY RD
WATFORD HEATH
HAMPERMILL LA
BROOKDENE AVE
PRESTWICK RD
OXHEY LA
DEACONS HILL
BLACKWELL DRI
SILK MILL RD
BALMORAL RD
OTTERSPOOL WAY
NORTH WESTERN AVE
A 411
A 412
A 4008
A 4125
A 4145
A 4178
B 4542

168

175

155

167

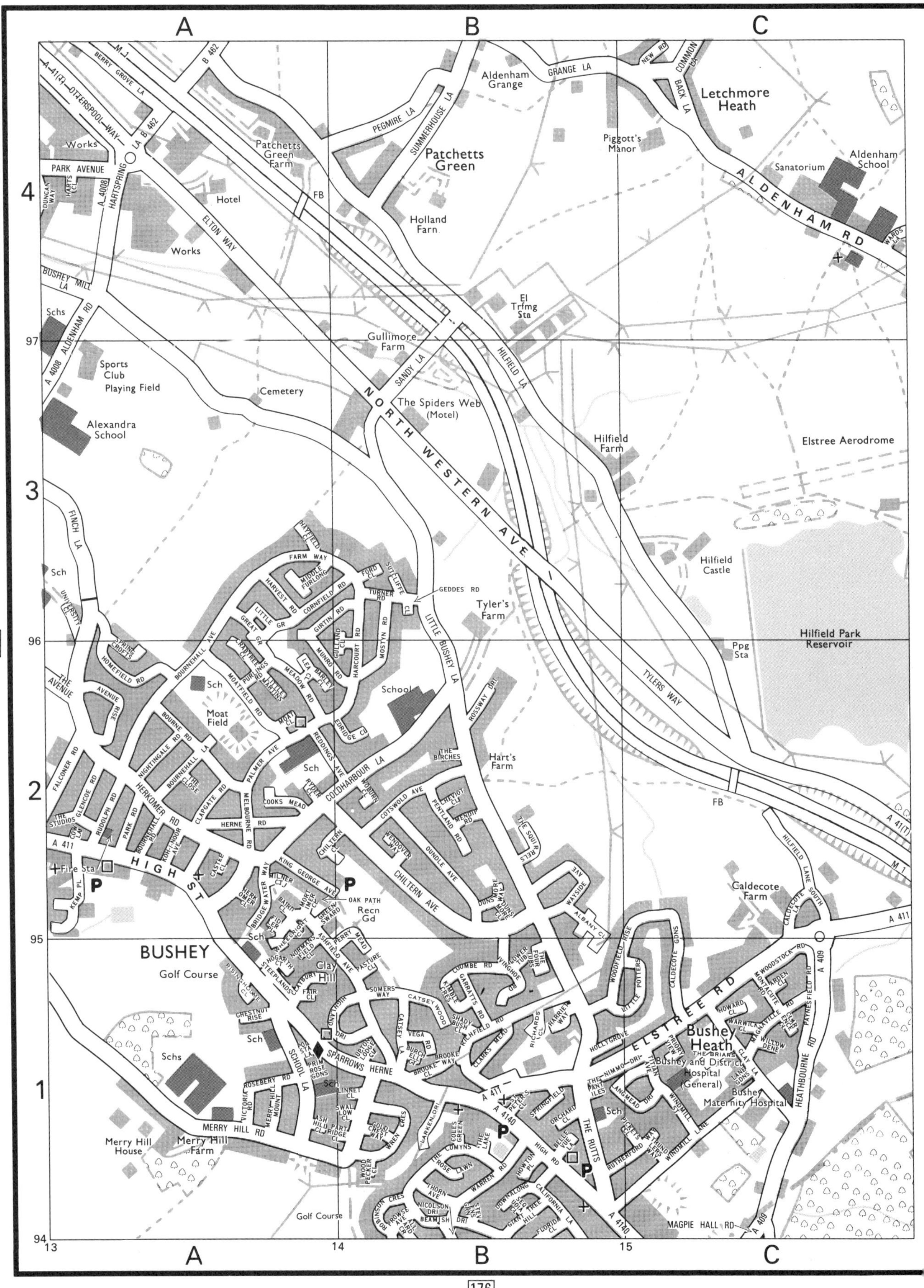
A
B
C
4
3
2
1
97
96
95
94
13
14
15
M 1
A 41(T)
BERRY GROVE LA
OTTERSPOOL WAY
B 462
LA B 462
Works
PARK AVENUE
HARTS CL
DUNCAN WAY
A 4008
HARTSPRING
Hotel
ELTON WAY
Works
BUSHEY MILL LA
Schs
ALDENHAM RD
A 4008
Sports Club
Playing Field
Alexandra School
Cemetery
Patchetts Green Farm
FB
PEGMIRE LA
SUMMERHOUSE LA
Patchetts Green
Holland Farm
Aldenham Grange
GRANGE LA
NEW RD
COMMON LA
BACK LA
Letchmore Heath
Piggott's Manor
Sanatorium
Aldenham School
ALDENHAM RD
WARDS LA
El Trfmg Sta
Gullimore Farm
SANDY LA
HILFIELD LA
NORTH WESTERN AVE
The Spiders Web (Motel)
Hilfield Farm
Elstree Aerodrome
Hilfield Castle
Tyler's Farm
Hilfield Park Reservoir
Ppg Sta
TYLERS WAY
FINCH LA
Sch
UNIVERSITY CL
SPRING CROFTS
HOMEFIELD RD
THE AVENUE
AVENUE RISE
BOURNEHALL AVE
HAYFIELD CL
FARM WAY
MIDDLE FURLONG
HARVEST RD
FORD CL
SUTCLIFFE CL
GEDDES RD
TURNER RD
CORNFIELD RD
LITTLE GR
GREAT GR
GIRTIN RD
MOSTYN RD
MUNRO RD
HARCOURT RD
LITTLE BUSHEY LA
Sch
Moat Field
MOATFIELD RD
MEADOW RD
School
ROSSWAY DRI
EDRIDGE CL
REDDINGS AVE
Sch
PALMER AVE
COLDHARBOUR LA
THE BIRCHES
Hart's Farm
FALCONER RD
NIGHTINGALE RD
BOURNEHALL LA
BOURNE RD
THE CLOSE
CLAPGATE RD
MELBOURNE RD
COOKS MEAD
RYDER CL
WOBURN CL
COTSWOLD AVE
CHEVIOT CL
PENTLAND RD
MENDIP RD
THE SQUIRRELS
GLENCOE RD
RUDOLPH RD
HERKOMER RD
PARK RD
BOURNEHALL RD
KOH-I-NOOR AVE
HERNE RD
THE STUDIOS
CONWAY LA
A 411
Fire Sta
HIGH ST
KEMP PL
P
CASTLE CL
KING GEORGE AVE
CHILTERN CL
WENDOVER WAY
OUNDLE AVE
CHILTERN AVE
DUNSMORE WAY
WAYSIDE AVE
ALBANY CL
MILNER CT
BRIDGE WATER WAY
OAK PATH
Recn Gd
GREEN SWARD
PERRY MEAD
Caldecote Farm
CALDECOTE LA
HILFIELD LANE SOUTH
A 411
BUSHEY
Golf Course
Sch
HOGARTH CT
STEEPLANDS
ASHFIELD AVE
PASTURE CL
Clay Hill
FAIR CL
COUMBE RD
IVINGHOE RD
LOWER TUBBS
THE FOUR TUBBS
WOODFIELD RISE
LITTLE POTTERS
CALDECOTE GDNS
WOODSTOCK RD
ELSTREE RD
A 409
CHESTNUT RISE
SOMERS WAY
CATSEY WOOD
GARRATTS RD
KESTREL CRES
SHADY BUSH CL
RICHFIELD RD
RICHARDS CL
HARRIET WAY
HOLLYGROVE
HOWARD CL
MONTAGUE RD
WARWICK CL
Bushey Heath
PRIORY VIEW
THE BRIARS
Bushey and District Hospital (General)
Schs
Sch
SCHOOL LA
SPARROWS HERNE
CATSEY LA
VEGA RD
BURCH CL
BROOKE WAY
CLARKS MEAD
THE NIMMO DRI
THE PANTILES
CLAY LA
LANE GDNS
WILLOW DENE
PAYNESFIELD RD
HEATHBOURNE RD
Bushey Maternity Hospital
ROSEBERY RD
VICTORIA RD
MERRY HILL MOUNT
LINNET CL
SWALLOW CL
A 411
A 4140
SPRINGFIELD
ORCHARD CL
THE RUTTS
LANGMEAD DRI
WINDMILL LA
Sch
MERRY HILL RD
Merry Hill House
Merry Hill Farm
GOLDCREST WAY
WREN CRES
LARKEN DRI
COLES GREEN
THE LAKE
COMYNS
THE ROSE LAWN
WARREN RD
HIGH RD
RUTHERFORD WAY
WOODPECKER CL
THORN AVE
NICOLSON DRI
BEAMISH DRI
DOWN ALONG
CALIFORNIA LA
FLORIDA CL
A 4140
ROBINSON CRES
Golf Course
MAGPIE HALL RD
A 409

176

156

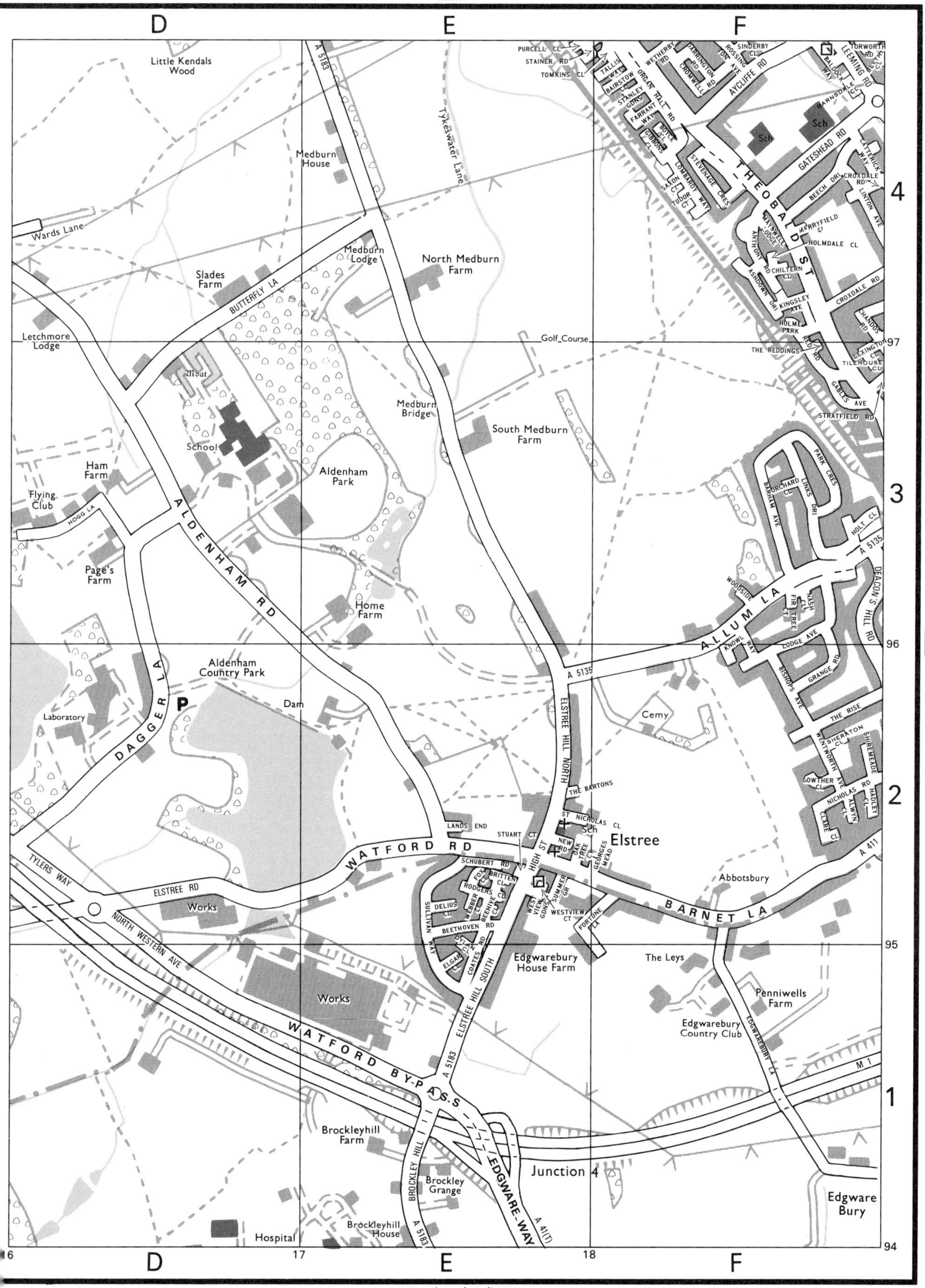

170

not continued, see key diagram

157

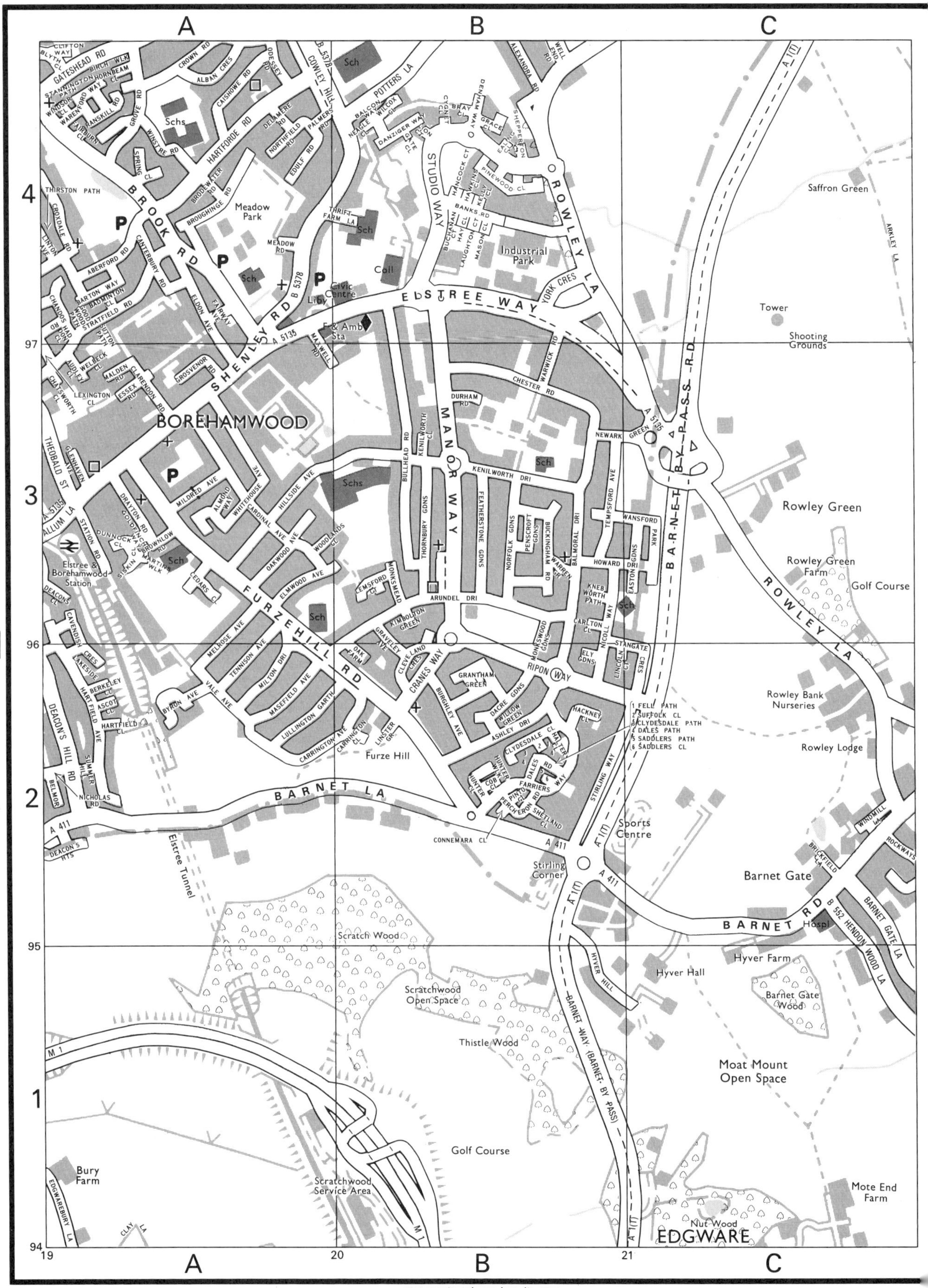

169

not continued, see key diagram

158

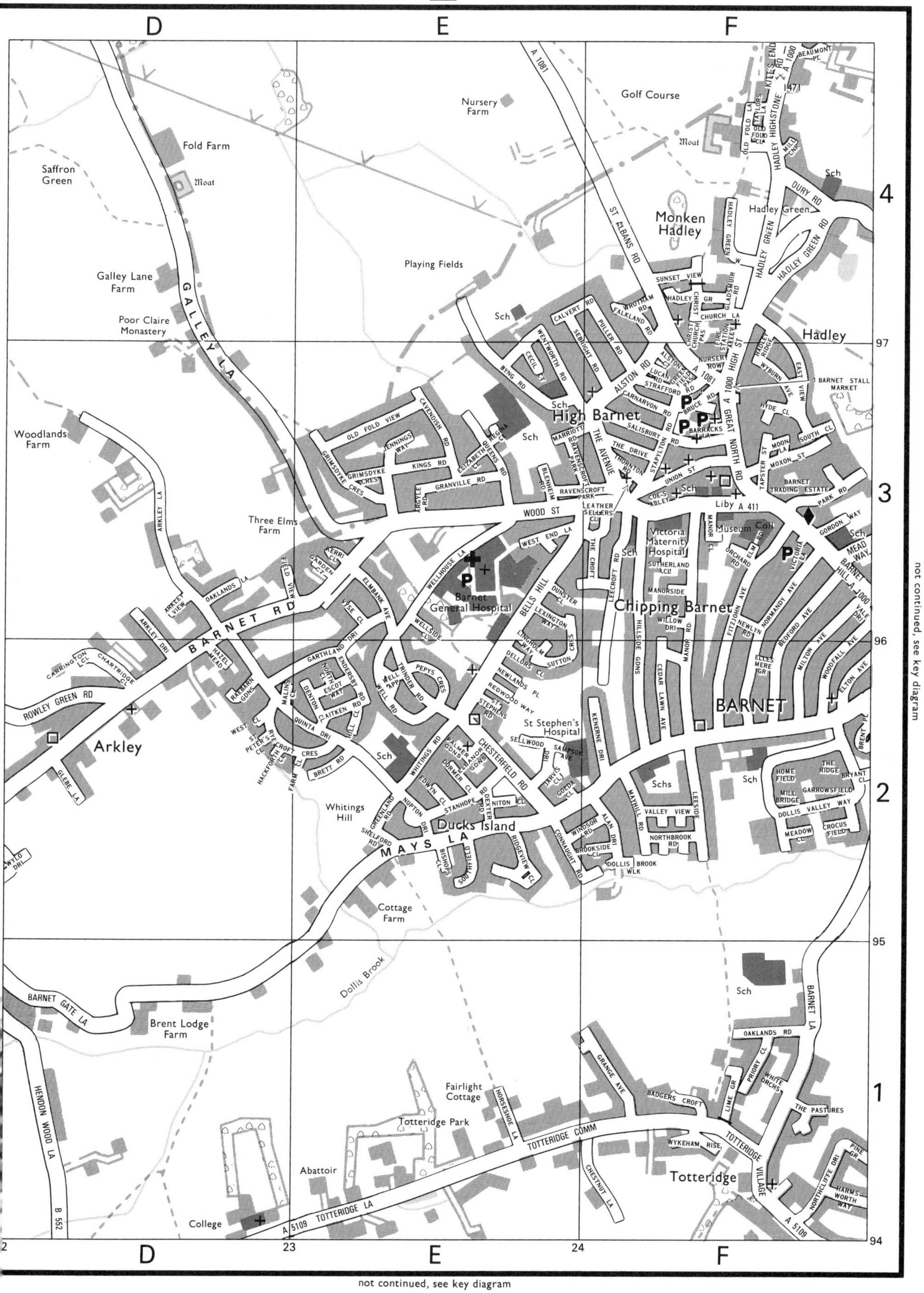

not continued, see key diagram

not continued, see key diagram

164

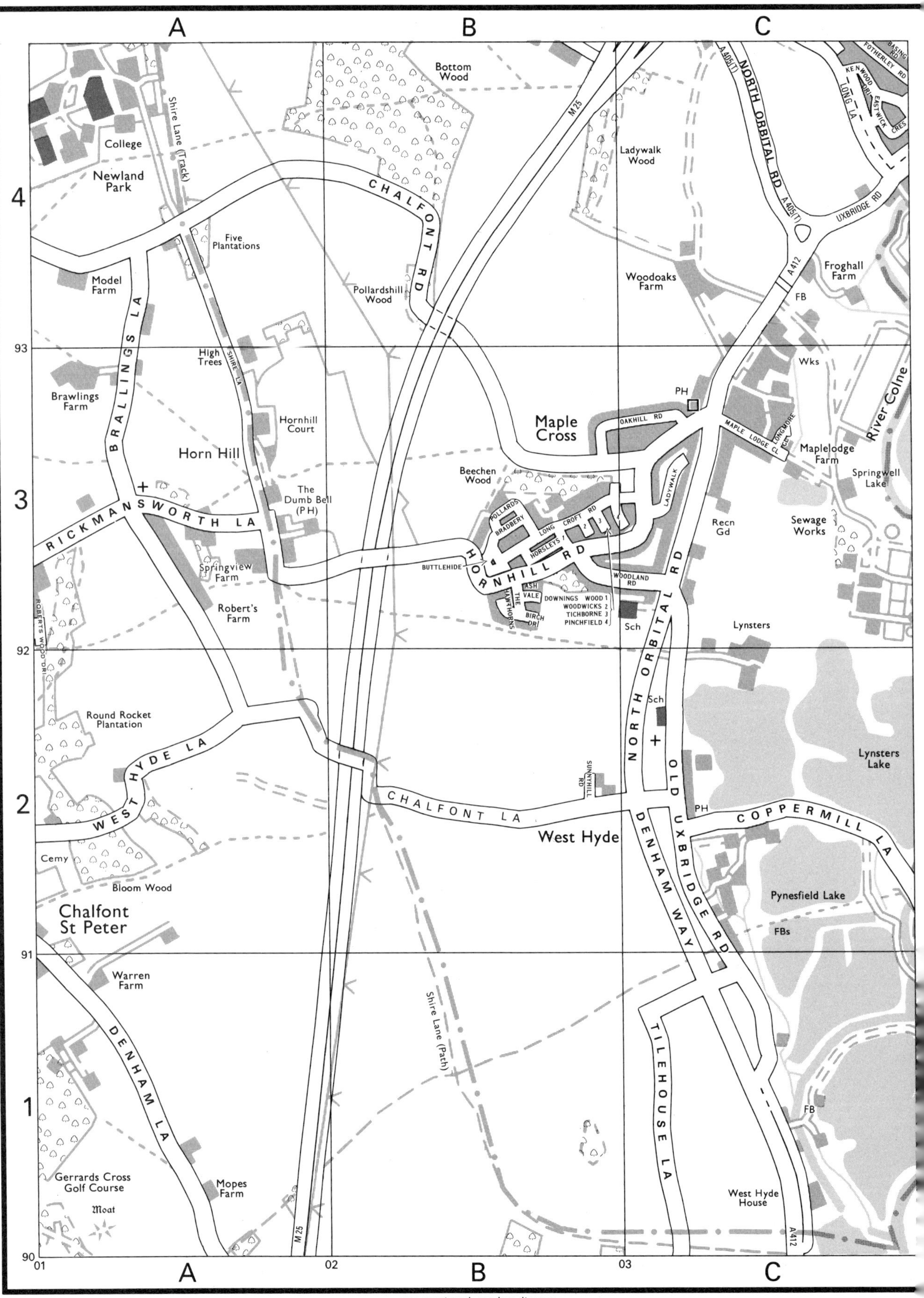

not continued, see key diagram

not continued, see key diagram

165

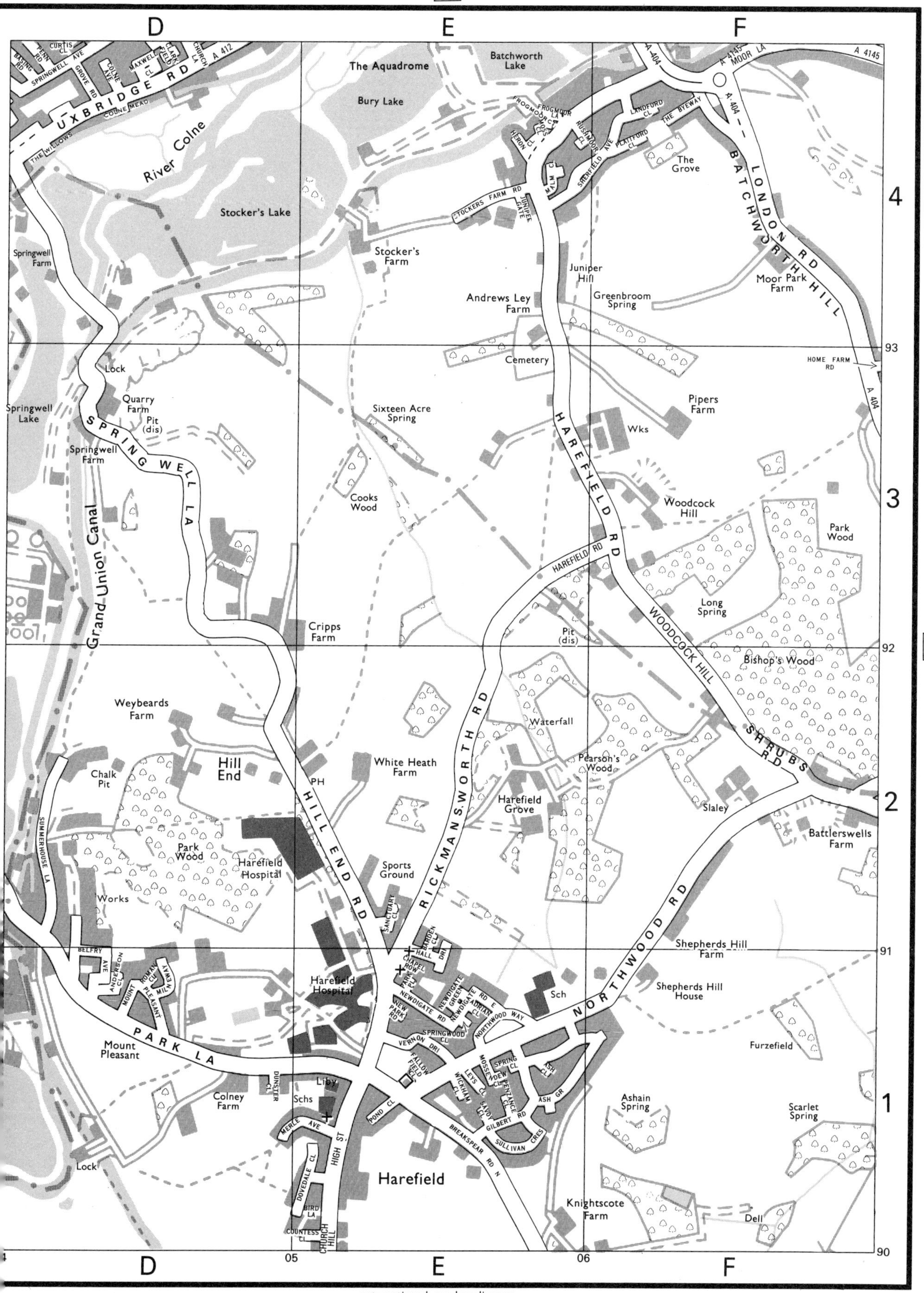

174

not continued, see key diagram

166

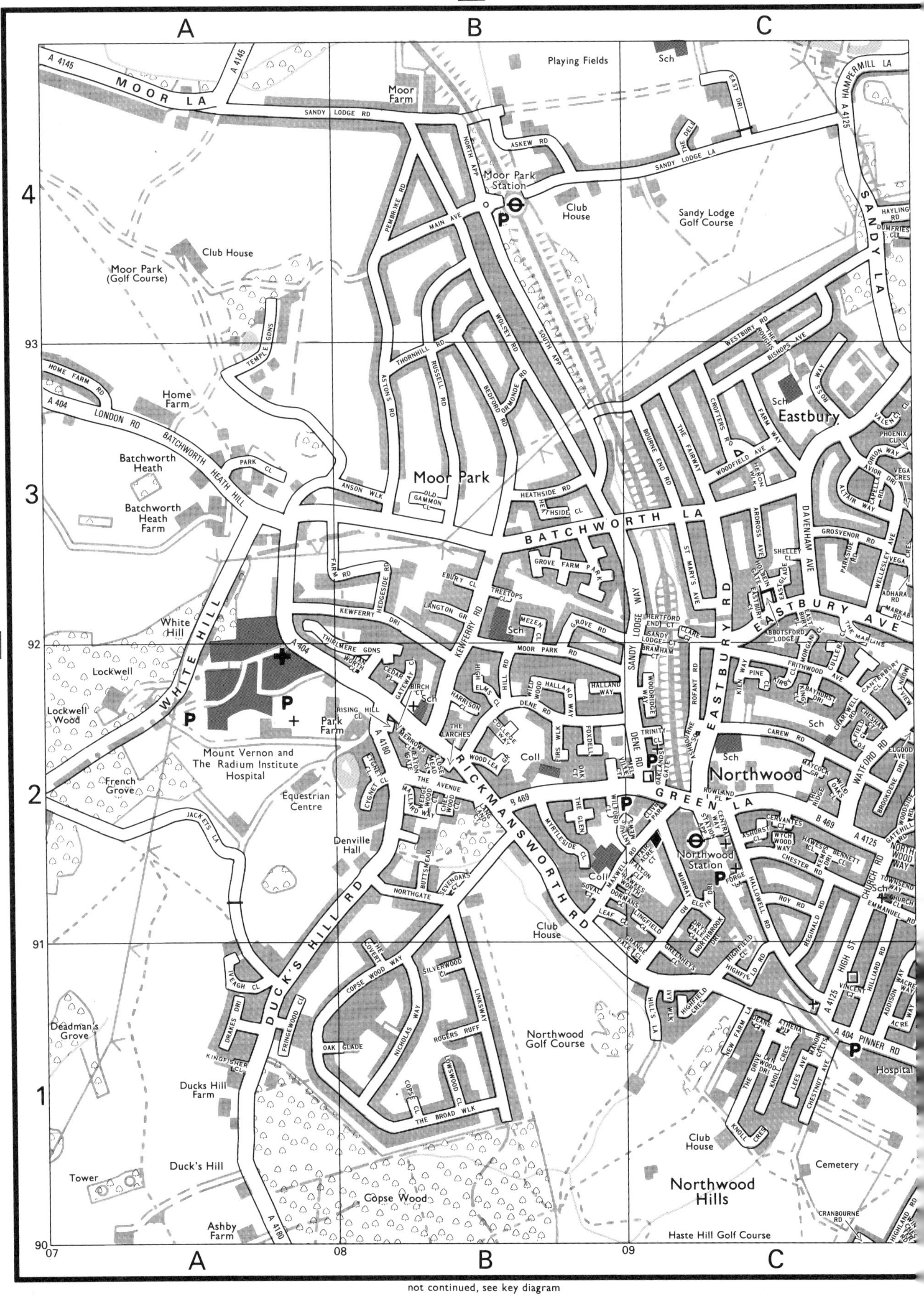

173

not continued, see key diagram

167

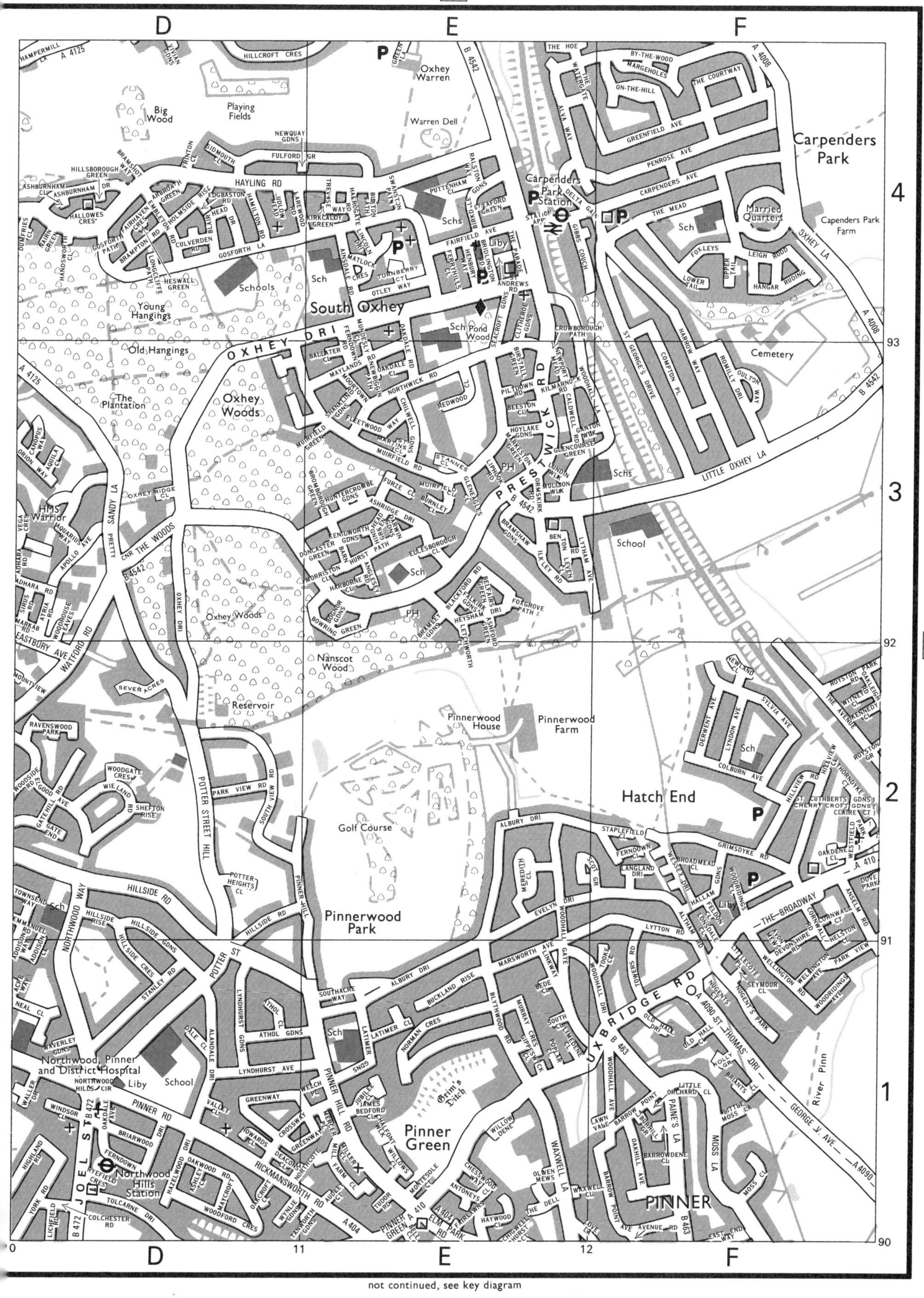
D
E
F
4
3
2
1
93
92
91
90
0
11
12
Carpenders Park
Carpenders Park Station
Oxhey Warren
Warren Dell
Big Wood
Playing Fields
South Oxhey
Young Hangings
Old Hangings
The Plantation
Oxhey Woods
Pond Wood
Nanscot Wood
Reservoir
HMS Warrior
Pinnerwood House
Pinnerwood Farm
Golf Course
Pinnerwood Park
Hatch End
Cemetery
Married Quarters
Capenders Park Farm
Northwood, Pinner and District Hospital
Northwood Hills Station
Pinner Green
Grim's Ditch
PINNER
River Pinn
Schools
School
Sch
Schs
Liby
PH
HAYLING RD
GOSFORTH LA
OXHEY DRI
PRESTWICK RD
LITTLE OXHEY LA
OXHEY LA
SANDY LA
WATFORD RD
POTTER STREET HILL
HILLSIDE RD
NORTHWOOD WAY
PINNER RD
PINNER HILL RD
UXBRIDGE RD
RICKMANSWORTH RD
GEORGE V AVE
ST GEORGE'S DRIVE
HARROW WAY
COMPTON PL
GRIMSDYKE RD
THE BROADWAY
ALBURY DRI
EVELYN DRI
WOODHALL DRI
WAXWELL LA
MOSS LA
PAINE'S LA
JOEL ST
A 4125
B 4542
A 4008
A 410
A 4090
A 404
B 463
B 472

176

168

175

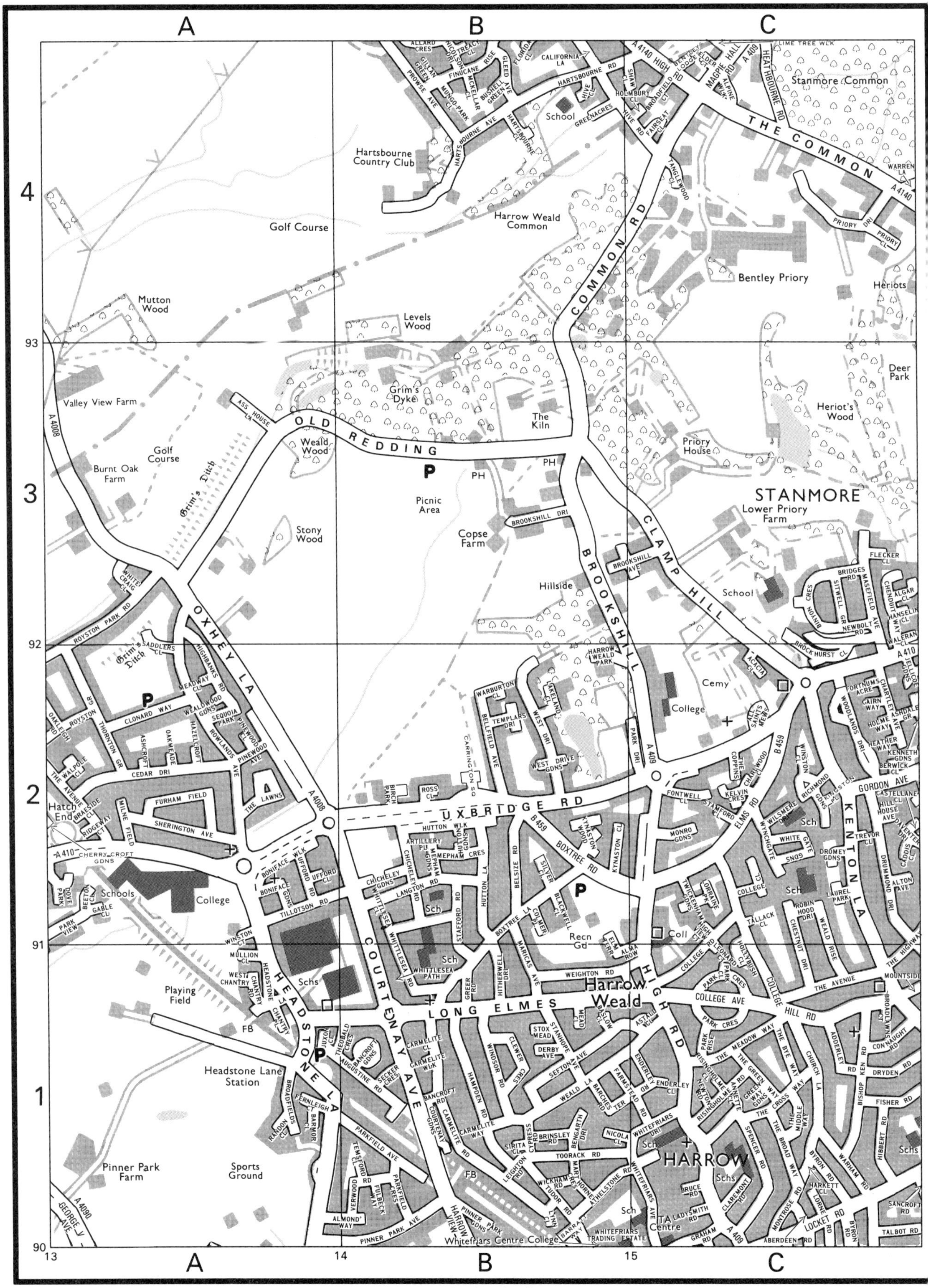

not continued, see key diagram

USER'S NOTES

EXPLANATION OF THE STREET INDEX REFERENCE SYSTEM

Street names are listed alphabetically and show the locality, the map page number and a reference to the square in which the name falls on the map page.

Example:	Ordnance Rd. Enf..*162* C1
Ordnance Rd	This is the full street name, which may have been abbreviated on the map.
Enf	This is the abbreviation for the town, village or locality in which the street falls. Postal codes have been used for street names in the London Postal District.
162	This is the page number of the map on which the street name appears.
C1	The letter and figure indicate the square on the map in which the centre of the street falls. The square can be found at the junction of the vertical column carrying the appropriate letter and the horizontal row carrying the appropriate figure.

ABBREVIATIONS USED IN THE INDEX

Road Names

Approach	App	North	N
Avenue	Ave	Orchard	Orch
Broadway	Bwy	Parade	Par
By-Pass	By-Ps	Passage	Pas
Causeway	Cswy	Place	Pl
Common	Comm	Pleasant	Plea
Corner	Cnr	Precinct	Prec
Cottages	Cotts	Promenade	Prom
Court	Ct	Road	Rd
Crescent	Cres	South	S
Drive	Dri	Square	Sq
Drove	Dro	Street, Saint	St
East	E	Terrace	Terr
Gardens	Gdns	Walk	Wlk
Grove	Gr	West	W
Heights	Hts	Yard	Yd
Lane	La		

Towns, Villages and Rural Localities

Abbots Langley	Abb L	153	F4
Albury	Alb	57	D3
Aldbury	Ald	101	E3
Aldenham	Aldhm	155	D1
Anstey	Ans	29	D3
Apsley End	Aps En	19	F4
Ardeley	Ard	38	C2
Arlesey	Arl	11	D3
Ashley Green	Ash Gr	136	A4
Ashwell	Ashw	4	B2
Aspenden	Asp	40	B3
Aston	Ast	51	F1
Aston End	Ast En	51	F3
Ayot St Lawrence	A St L	88	A3
Ayot St Peter	A St P	88	C2
Baldock	Bal	23	F4
Barkway	Bark	17	E2
Barley	Bar	8	C1
Barnet	Barn	171	F2
Bayford	Bay	132	C3
Bedmond	Bed	139	F2
Benington	Benn	52	C2
Berkhamsted	Berk	122	B3
Birchanger	Birhr	59	F1
Birch Green	Bir Gr	112	B2
Bird Green	Brd Gr	30	C4
Bishop's Stortford	Bis St	76	C4
Blackmore End	Bla En	87	E3
Borehamwood	Bor	170	A3
Botley	Bot	136	A1
Bourne End	Bor En	123	D1
Bovingdon	Bov	137	D2
Bramfield	Bram	91	E2
Braughing	Brag	55	F3
Breachwood Green	Bre Gr	47	F1
Brent Pelham	Bre P	30	A1
Brickendon	Bric	133	E2
Bricket Wood	Bri Wd	140	C1
Brookmans Park	Bro Pk	144	C3
Buckland	Buck	27	E4
Buckland Common	Buc Co	120	A2
Bull's Green	Bul Gr	90	C4
Buntingford	Bun	40	C4
Burnham Green	Brn Gr	90	B3
Bury Green	Bry Gr	75	F4
Bushey	Bus	170	A1
Bygrave	Byg	13	E3
Caddington	Cad	62	C2
Caldecote	Cal	3	E1
Chalfont St Peter	C St P	172	A2
Chandler's Cross	Cha Cr	152	C1
Chapmore End	Cha En	92	B3
Cheddington	Ched	80	A4
Chenies	Chen	151	D1
Cheshunt	Ches	148	B1
Chipperfield	Chipf	152	A4
Chipping	Chipp	27	E3
Chiswellgreen	Chis	141	D3
Cholesbury	Chol	120	B2
Chorleywood	Chor	164	B3
Church End	Ch En	11	D4
Clapgate	Clap	57	E3
Clothall	Clo	24	C2
Cockernhoe Green	Cok Gr	46	C2
Codicote	Cod	67	F1
Colliers End	Col En	73	D3
Colney Heath	Coln H	143	E4
Colney Street	Col St	141	F1
Cottered	Cotrd	39	E4
Crafton	Cra	60	C2
Cromer	Cro	38	B3
Croxley Green	Cro Gr	166	A2
Cuffley	Cuf	146	C2
Dagnall	Dagn	81	E3
Dane End	Dan En	71	F4
Datchworth	Dat	69	F1
Digswell	Digs	89	F2
Drayton Beauchamp	Dra B	99	E3
Dunstable	Dun	44	A1
Eastwick	East	117	D2
Edgware	Edg	170	C1
Edworth	Edw	3	D3
Elstree	Elst	169	F2
Enfield	Enf	162	C1
Epping Green	Ep Gr	132	B1
Essendon	Ess	131	F3
Farnham	Far	58	B3
Felden	Fel	138	A4
Flamstead	Fla	84	A1
Flaunden	Flau	151	D3
Ford End	Fo En	30	C2
Frogmore	Fro	141	F2
Furneux Pelham	Fur P	43	D3
Goff's Oak	Gofs O	147	E2
Gosmore	Gos	34	C2
Graveley	Gra	36	B2
Gravesend	Gravnd	57	D4
Great Amwell	Gt Am	114	C3
Great Chiswell	Gt Ch	9	F1
Great Gaddesden	Gt Ga	103	E2
Great Hallingbury	Gt Ha	77	F2
Great Hormead	Gt Ho	42	A4
Great Munden	Gt Mu	54	B3
Great Offley	Gt Of	33	E1
Great Wymondley	Gt Wy	35	F3
Green End	Gr En	26	B4
Green End, (Braughing)	Gr En	75	E1
Green Tye	Gr Ty	75	E1
Guilden Morden	Gu M	1	C3
Hadham Cross	Had Cr	74	C1
Hall's Green	Hal Gr	37	F3
Hammond Street	Ham St	147	E3
Harefield	Hare	173	E1
Hare Street, (Ardeley)	H St A	38	C3
Hare Street, (Hormead)	H St H	41	F4
Harlow	Harl	117	F1
Harmer Green	Har Gr	90	A3
Harpenden	Harp	86	A1
Harrow	Har	176	C1
Harrow Weald	Har W	176	B1
Hastoe	Has	119	F4
Hatfield	Hat	130	B4
Haultwick	Hault	53	F2
Hay Street	Hay St	41	F1
Hebing End	Heb En	52	C1
Hemel Hempstead	Heml H	124	C1
Henlow	Henlw	10	B4
Heronsgate	Heron	164	B1
Hertford	Hert	114	A2
Hertingfordbury	Hertng	112	C3
Hexton	Hex	19	D1
High Cross	H Cr	72	C1
Higham Gobion	H Gobn	19	D3
High Wych	H Wy	97	D1
Hinxworth	Hin	3	E3
Hitchin	Hit	34	C4
Hoddesdon	Hod	135	D3
Holwell	Hol	21	D4
Horn Hill	Hrn H	172	A3
Hunsdon	Hun	95	E1
Ickleford	Ick	21	F2
Ivinghoe	Ivin	80	C4
Kelsall	Kel	15	E3
Kensworth Common	Ken Co	82	C4
Kimpton	Kim	66	B1
Kings Langley	Kin L	139	D1
Kings Walden	Kin Wd	48	A2
Kinsbourne Green	Kin Gr	85	D3
Knebworth	Kneb	69	D3
Kneesworth	Knee	2	A3
Langley	Lan	49	F1
Latimer	Lat	150	C2
Lemsford	Lem	110	A3
Letchmore Heath	Let H	168	C4
Letchworth	Letw	22	C4
Letty Green	Let Gr	112	A1
Levens Green	Lev Gr	54	B1
Lilley	Lily	32	B1
Little Almshoe	L Alm	49	D1
Little Berkhamsted	L Berk	132	B2
Little Chalfont	L Chal	150	A1
Little Chishill	L Chis	18	C4
Little Gaddesden	L Gad	102	B4
Little Hadham	L Had	57	E1
Little Hallingbury	L Hal	98	B4
Little Hormead	L Hor	42	A3
Little Wymondley	L Wym	35	F2
London Colney	Lon C	142	B3
Long Marston	Lon M	79	D2
Lower Nazeing	Lo Naz	149	E4
Luffenhall	Luf	38	B4
Luton	Luton	45	E2
Mangrove Green	Man Gr	46	C2
Maple Cross	Map Cr	172	B3
Markyate	Mark	83	F3
Marsworth	Mars	80	A1
Meesden	Mee	29	F3
Mentmore	Men	61	E2
Mill End	Mil En	26	C3
Much Hadham	Muc H	74	C2
Nettleden	Net	103	E1
Newgate Street	New St	146	C4
Newmill End	Nwml E	85	F4
Newnham	Newn	12	C4
Newsells	News	17	E4
Northaw	Nort	145	F1
Northchurch	Nthch	121	F3
North Mymms	N Mym	144	A3
Northwood	Norwd	174	C2
Norton	Nor	12	A1
Nuthampstead	Nut	18	A1
Odsey	Odsey	5	E1
Oldhall Green	Odh Gr	54	C1
Old Knebworth	Old K	68	B3
Park Street	Pk St	141	E3
Patchetts Green	Pat Gr	168	B4
Pegsdon	Pegs	19	E1
Peter's Green	Pet Gr	65	E2
Piccotts End	Pic En	124	B4
Pirton	Pirt	20	B2
Pitstone	Pit	80	B2
Pinner	Pnr	175	F1
Potten End	Pot En	123	D3
Potters Bar	Pot B	159	D4
Preston	Pres	48	B3
Puckeridge	Puc	55	E2
Puttenham	Put	78	C1
Radlett	Radl	156	A3
Radwell	Radw	12	B2
Redbourn	Red	106	A3
Reed	Reed	16	C3
Rickmansworth	Ric	165	E1
Ridge	Ridge	157	F3
Ringshall	Rin	81	D1
Roast Green	Rst Gr	30	C3
Roe Green	Ro Gr	26	A4
Roydon	Roy	116	B1
Royston	Royst	7	E3
Rushden	Rus	25	F2
St Albans	St Alb	127	F2
St Ippolitts	St Ipp	35	D2
St Leonards	St Le	119	F2
St Pauls Walden	St P W	49	D1
Sacombe	Sac	71	F2
Sacombe Green	Sac Gr	72	A2
Sandon	San	15	D1
Sandridge	Sand	108	B1
Sarratt	Sar	152	A2
Sawbridgeworth	Saw	97	F1
Shenley	Shen	157	D3
Smallford	Sal	129	D2
Southern Green	Stn Gr	26	A2
South Oxhey	Sth Ox	175	E4
Spellbrook	Spel	97	F4
Stanborough	Stanb	110	A2
Standon	Stand	55	F1
Stanmore	Stan	176	C3
Stanstead Abbotts	Sta Ab	115	F2
Stanstead Mountfitchet	Sta M	59	E4
Stapleford	Stap	92	A4
Starlings Green	Sta Gr	30	C2
Steeple Morden	Ste Mo	5	D4
Stevenage	Stev	50	B4
Stocking Pelham	Sto P	43	F4
Stotford	Stot	11	F4
Streatley	Str	31	D3
Studham	Stu	82	B2
Tea Green	T Gr	47	D2
Tewin	Tewin	90	C1
Therfield	Ther	15	F4
Thorley	Thor	76	B1
Throcking	Tho	26	C1
Thundridge	Thun	93	F4
Tonwell	Tonw	92	C4
Tring	Tri	100	A2
Tyttenhanger	Tyt	142	C4
Wadesmill	Wad	93	E4
Wallington	Wal	25	E4
Walkern	Wal	38	A1
Waltham Abbey	Wa Aby	163	E3
Waltham Cross	Wa Cr	162	B3
Ware	Ware	93	F1
Wareside	Wars	94	C2
Warren's Green	Wa Gr	37	E3
Water End	Wa En	144	B3
Waterford	Wat	92	A1
Watford	Watf	167	E3
Watton at Stone	Wat St	70	C2
Welham Green	Wel Gr	144	B4
Wellpond Green	Wep Gr	56	B1
Welwyn	Welw	89	D2
Welwyn Garden City	WelGC	110	C3
Westland Green	Wes Gr	56	C1
Westmill	West	40	C2
Weston	Wes	24	B1
Wheathampstead	Whea	108	B4
Whitwell	Whit	66	C3
Widford	Widf	95	F2
Wigginton	Wigg	100	B1
Wildhill	Wild	131	E1
Willian	Will	23	D1
Wilstone	Wils	79	E1
Wingrave	Wing	60	B2
Wood End	Wd En	53	E4
Woolmer Green	Wl Gr	69	D1
Wyddial	Wyd	28	A2

Abbey Ave. St Alb 127 D1
Abbey Ct. Wa Aby 163 D3
Abbey Dri. Luton 46 A1
Abbey Mill End. St Alb 127 E1
Abbey Mill La. St Alb 127 E1
Abbey Rd. Ches 162 C3
Abbey View. Watf 154 B2
Abbey View Rd. St Alb 127 E2
Abbeyfields. St Alb 127 F1
Abbeyview. Wa Aby 163 E3
Abbis Orch. Ick 21 F3
Abbots Ave. St Alb 141 F4
Abbots Ave W. St Alb 141 E4
Abbots Cl. Dat 69 E1
Abbots Gr. Stev 50 C3
Abbots Park. St Alb 128 A1
Abbots Rd. Abb L 153 E4
Abbots Rise. Kin L 138 C3
Abbots View. Kin L 138 C2
Abbots Wood Rd. Luton 46 A1
Abbotsford Lodge. Norwd 174 C3
Abbotts La. Widf 95 E2
Abbotts Rd. Letw 22 B3
Abbotts Rise. Sta Ab 115 E2
Abbotts Way. Bis St 76 C2
Abbotts Way. Sta Ab 115 E2
Abbotts Way. Wing 60 A2
Abdale La. Wa En 144 A2
Abel Cl. Heml H 125 D2
Aberdale Gdns. Pot B 158 C4
Aberdeen Rd. Har 176 C1
Aberford Rd. Bor 170 A4
Abigail Cl. Luton 45 E2
Abingdon Pl. Pot B 159 D4
Abingdon Rd. Luton 44 B2
Abridge Cl. Enf 162 B2
Abstacle Hill. Tri 99 F2
Acacia Cl. Stan 176 B2
Acacia Gr. Berk 122 A2
Acacia Rd. Enf 161 E1
Acacia St. Hat 130 A1
Acacia Wlk. Harp 107 E3
Acacia Wlk. Tri 99 F2
Acers. Chis 141 E2
Achilles Cl. Heml H 124 C3
Ackroyd Rd. Roystn 7 F4
Acme Rd. Watf 154 A1
Acorn La. Cuf 146 C1
Acorn Pl. Watf 154 A1
Acorn Rd. Heml H 125 D1
Acorn St. Hun 116 B4
Acre Way. Norwd 174 C1
Acre Wood. Heml H 124 C1
Acremore St. Bry Gr 75 E4
Acrewood Way. St Alb 128 C2
Acton Cl. Ches 162 C4
Acworth Cres. Luton 44 B3
Adams Way. Tri 100 A3
Adam's Yard. Hert 113 E3
Adamsfield. Ham St 148 A3
Adderley Rd. Bis St 76 C4
Adderley Rd. Har 176 C1
Addiscombe Rd. Watf 167 D3
Addison Cl. Norwd 175 D1
Addison Way. Norwd 174 C1
Adelaide Cl. Enf 161 F1
Adelaide St. Luton 63 E4
Adelaide St. St Alb 127 E2
Adele Ave. Har Gr 89 F2
Adeyfield Gdns. Heml H 124 C2
Adeyfield Rd. Heml H 124 C2
Adhara Rd. Norwd 175 D3
Adhern Ct. St Alb 142 B4
Adinger Cl. Stev 50 C2
Admiral St. Hert 114 A3
Admirals Cl. Coln H 143 F4
Admirals Wlk. Hod 135 D2
Admirals Wlk. St Alb 142 A4
Adrian Cl. Hare 173 E1
Adrian Rd. Abb L 153 F4
Adstone Rd. Cad 62 C2
Ailsworth Rd. Luton 45 D4
Ainsdale Rd. Sth Ox 175 E4
Aintree Rd. Roystn 7 F3
Airedale. Heml H 124 C3
Airport Approach Rd. Luton 64 B4
Airport Way. Luton 64 A4
Airport Way. Nwml E 64 A3
Aitken Rd. Barn 171 E2
Akeman St. Tri 100 A2
Alan Dri. Barn 171 F2
Alandale Dri. Pnr 175 D1
Alban Ave. St Alb 127 E3
Alban Cres. Bor 170 A4
Alban Park Industrial Estate. St 128 C2
Alban Rd. Letw 23 E2
Albans View. Watf 154 A3
Albany Cl. Bus 168 B2
Albany Ct. Harp 107 E4
Albany Mews. Chis 141 D2
Albany Park Ave. Enf 162 B1
Albany Rd. Enf 162 B1
Albemarle Ave. Ches 148 B2
Albemarle Ave. Pot B 159 D4
Albert Rd. Arl 11 D2
Albert Rd. Luton 63 F3
Albert Rd N. Watf 167 D3
Albert Rd S. Watf 167 D3
Albert St. Mark 83 F3
Albert St. St Alb 127 E1
Albert St. Stev 50 B4
Albert St. Tri 100 A2
Albert St. Watf 167 E3
Albion Cl. Hert 113 F4
Albion Hill. Heml H 124 B1
Albion Rd. Luton 63 F4
Albion Rd. Pit 80 B3
Albion Rd. St Alb 127 F2
Albury Cl. Luton 31 D1
Albury Dri. Pnr 175 E2
Albury Grove Rd. Ches 148 B1
Albury Rd. L Had 57 E1
Albury Ride. Ches 162 B4
Albury Wlk. Ches 162 B4
Alconbury. Bis St 59 D1
Aldbury Cl. St Alb 128 B4
Aldbury Cl. Watf 154 B2
Aldbury Gr. Wel GC 111 D3
Aldbury Rd. Ric 164 C1
Aldeburgh Cl. Stev 36 A1
Aldenham Gr. Radl 156 A3
Aldenham Rd. Bus 167 F3
Aldenham Rd. Elst 169 D3
Aldenham Rd. Radl 156 A2
Alder Cl. Bal 23 F4
Alder Cl. Bis St 76 B2
Alder Cl. Chis 141 E2
Alder Cres. Luton 45 D2
Alder Ct. Luton 45 D2
Alderbury Rd. Sta Mo 59 F4
Alderley Ct. Berk 122 B2
Alderman Cl. Wel Gr 144 B4
Alders End La. Harp 85 F1
Aldersgrove. Wa Aby 163 F3
Alderton Cl. Luton 46 B1
Alderton Dri. Rin 102 A4
Aldhouse Cl. Luton 45 D3
Aldock. Wel GC 111 D2
Aldock Rd. Stev 50 C4
Aldridge Ave. Enf 163 D1
Aldwick. St Alb 128 A1
Aldwick Ct. St Alb 128 A1
Aldwick Rd. Harp 107 F4
Aldwickbury Cres. Harp 86 B1
Aldwyck Ct. Heml H 124 B2
Aldwyke Rise. Ware 93 E2
Aldykes. Hat 129 F3
Alesia Rd. Luton 44 C3
Alexander Rd. Hertng 113 D3
Alexander Rd. Lon C 142 B3
Alexander Rd. Stot 11 F3
Alexandra Ave. Luton 45 E1
Alexandra Rd. Bor 170 B4
Alexandra Rd. Chipf 138 A1
Alexandra Rd. Heml H 124 B2
Alexandra Rd. Hit 21 F1
Alexandra Rd. Kin L 139 D1
Alexandra Rd. St Alb 127 F2
Alexandra Rd. Watf 167 D4
Alexandra Way. Ches 162 C3
Aleyn Way. Clo 13 D1
Alfriston Cl. Luton 46 B2
Algar Cl. Stan 176 C3
Alington La. Letw 22 C2
All Saints Cl. Bis St 77 D4
All Saints Cres. Watf 154 B3
All Saints La. Cro Gr 166 A2
All Saints Mews. Har 176 B2
Allandale. Heml H 124 C3
Allandale. St Alb 141 D4
Allandale Cres. Pot B 158 C4
Allandale Rd. Enf 162 B2
Allard Cl. Ham St 147 F2
Allard Cres. Bus 176 B4
Allard Way. Hod 134 C1
Alldicks Rd. Heml H 124 C1
Allen Cl. Whea 108 B4
Allenby Ave. Dun 44 A1
Allendale. Luton 31 D1
Allende Ave. Harl 117 E1
Allerton Cl. Bor 156 C1
Allerton Rd. Bor 156 C1
Alleyns Rd. Stev 50 B4
Allison. Letw 23 E3
Allton Rd. Henlw 10 A2
Allum La. Elst 169 F3
Alma Ct. Pot B 145 E1
Alma Cut. St Alb 127 F1
Alma Link. Luton 63 E4
Alma Rd. Nthch 121 F3
Alma Rd. St Alb 127 F1
Alma Row. Har 176 B1
Alma St. Luton 63 E4
Almond Cl. Luton 45 D2
Almond Way. Bor 170 A3
Almond Way. Har 176 B1
Almond Wlk. Hat 130 A1
Almonds La. Stev 50 C4
Alms La. Ashw 4 B2
Almshouse La. Enf 162 A1
Alnwick Dri. Lon M 78 C4
Alpha Pl. Bis St 76 C4
Alpine Cl. Hit 35 D3
Alpine Way. Luton 44 B4
Alpine Wlk. Bus 176 C4
Alston Ct. Barn 171 F3
Alston Rd. Barn 171 F3
Alston Rd. Heml H 124 A1
Altair Way. Norwd 174 C3
Altham Gr. Harl 117 F1
Altham Rd. Pnr 175 F2
Althorp Rd. Luton 45 E1
Althorp Rd. St Alb 127 F2
Alton Ave. Stan 176 C2
Alton Rd. Luton 63 F3
Altwood. Harp 86 B1
Alva Way. Watf 175 E4
Alverton. St Alb 127 E3
Alwyn Cl. Elst 169 F2
Alwyn Cl. Luton 45 F1
Alyington. Nthch 121 F4
Alzey Gdns. Harp 107 E4
Amberley Cl. Harp 86 A1
Amberley Cl. Luton 46 B2
Amberley Green. Ware 93 E2
Amberry Ct. Harl 117 E1
Ambleside. Harp 86 B1
Ambleside. Luton 44 C3
Ambrose La. Harp 85 F2
Amenbury La. Harp 86 A1
Amersham Rd. Chen 164 A4
Ames Cl. Luton 44 C4
Amwell Comm. Wel GC 111 E3
Amwell Ct. Hod 135 D4
Amwell Ct. Wa Aby 163 F3
Amwell End. Ware 93 E1
Amwell Hill. Hert H 114 C3
Amwell La. Sta Ab 115 D3
Amwell La. Whea 108 A4
Amwell St. Hod 135 D4
Anchor Cl. Ches 148 B2
Anchor La. Heml H 124 A1
Anchor La. Wad 93 E4
Anchor Rd. Bal 23 F4
Anchor St. Bis St 77 D3
Anderson Cl. Hare 173 D1
Anderson Rd. Shen 157 D3
Anderson Rd. Stev 51 E3
Anderson's La. Gt Ho 29 D1
Andover Cl. Luton 44 B3
Andrews La. Ches 148 A2
Andrew's La. Ham St 147 F2
Andrewsfield. Wel GC 111 E3
Anershall. Wing 60 A2
Angel Pavement. Royston 7 E3
Angell's Meadow. Ashw 4 B2
Angle Pl. Berk 122 A2
Angle Ways. Stev 51 D1
Anglefield Rd. Berk 122 A2
Anglesey Rd. Sth Ox 175 E3
Angotts Mead. Stev 50 A3
Angus Cl. Luton 44 A2
Anmer Gdns. Luton 44 A2
Annables La. Kin Gr 85 D2
Annette Cl. Har 176 C1
Anns Cl. Tri 99 F2
Anselm Rd. Pnr 175 F2
Anson Cl. Bov 136 C2
Anson Cl. Sand 108 B1
Anson Cl. St Alb 142 A4
Anson Wlk. Norwd 174 B3
Anstee Rd. Luton 44 A3
Anthony Cl. Watf 167 E1
Anthony Gdns. Luton 63 E3
Anthony Rd. Bor 169 F4
Anthorne Cl. Pot B 159 D4
Anthus Mews. Norwd 174 C2
Antoinette Ct. Abb L 139 F1
Antoneys Cl. Pnr 175 E1
Antonine Gate. St Alb 127 D1
Aplins Cl. Harp 86 A1
Apollo Ave. Norwd 175 D3
Apollo Way. Heml H 124 C3
Apple Cotts. Bov 137 D2
Apple Orch The. Heml H 124 C3
Appleby St. Ham St 147 F3
Applecroft. Chis 141 D2
Applecroft. Nthch 121 F3
Applecroft Rd. Luton 46 B2
Applecroft Rd. Wel GC 110 A3
Appleford's Cl. Hod 134 C4
Appleton Fields. Bis St 76 C2
Appletree Wlk. Watf 154 A2
Applewood Cl. Harp 85 F2
Approach Rd. St Alb 127 F1
Approach The. Pot B 158 C4
Appspond La. Chis 140 B4
April Pl. Saw 97 F2
Apsley Cl. Bis St 76 C2
Apsley End Rd. Aps En 19 F3
Apsley Grange. Heml H 138 C3
Apton Ct. Bis St 76 C4
Apton Fields. Bis St 76 C3
Apton Rd. Bis St 76 C4
Aquarius Way. Norwd 175 D3
Aquila Cl. Norwd 175 D3
Aragon Cl. Heml H 125 E4
Aran Cl. Harp 107 E3
Arbour Cl. Luton 31 D1
Arbour The. Hert 113 E2
Arbroath Green. Sth Ox 175 D4
Arcade The. Letw 22 C3
Arcade Wlk. Hit 34 C4
Arch Rd. Gt Wy 35 F3
Archer Cl. Kin L 138 C1
Archer Rd. Stev 51 D3
Archers. Bun 40 C4
Archers Cl. Hert 113 E4
Archers Ride. Wel GC 111 D2
Archers Way. Letw 22 B3
Archfield. Wel GC 89 F1
Archway Ct. Heml H 124 B3
Archway Rd. Luton 44 C2
Arden Cl. Bov 137 D2
Arden Cl. Bus 168 C1
Arden Gr. Harp 86 A1
Arden Pl. Luton 45 F1
Ardens Way. St Alb 128 B3
Ardleigh Green. Luton 46 C1
Ardross Ave. Norwd 174 C3
Arena Par. Letw 22 C3
Argyle Rd. Barn 171 E3
Argyle Way. Stev 50 B3
Argyll Ave. Luton 45 E1
Argyll Rd. Heml H 124 C4
Arkley Ct. Heml H 125 D4
Arkley Dri. Barn 171 D2
Arkley La. Barn 171 D3
Arkley Rd. Heml H 125 D4
Arkley View. Barn 171 D3
Arkwrights. Harl 117 F1
Arlesey Rd. Henlw 10 C4
Arlesey Rd. Hit 21 F3
Arlesey Rd. Ick 21 F2
Arlesey Rd. Stot 11 F3
Arlington Cres. Ches 162 C3
Armand Cl. Watf 153 F1
Armitage Cl. Chor 165 E3
Armitage Gdns. Luton 44 B1
Armour Rise. Hit 22 A1
Armstrong Pl. Heml H 124 B2
Arncliffe Cres. Luton 45 F1
Arnett Cl. Chor 165 D2
Arnett Way. Chor 165 D2
Arnold Ave East. Enf 163 D1
Arnold Ave West. Enf 162 C1
Arnold Cl. Luton 46 A2
Arnold Cl. Stev 36 B1
Arnolds La. Hin 3 E3
Arran Cl. Heml H 125 E1
Arranmore Ct. Bus 167 F3
Arretine Cl. St Alb 126 C1
Arrewig La. St Le 119 E1
Arrow Cl. Luton 44 C3
Arthur Rd. St Alb 128 A2
Arthur St. Bus 167 E3
Arthur St. Luton 63 F3
Artillery Pl. Har 176 B2
Arundel Cl. Ches 148 B2
Arundel Cl. Heml H 125 D2
Arundel Cl. Stev 51 F2
Arundel Dri. Bor 170 B3
Arundel Rd. Luton 44 C1
Ascot Cl. Bis St 77 F4
Ascot Cl. Elst 170 A2
Ascot Cres. Stev 37 D1
Ascot Gdns. Enf 162 B1
Ascot Rd. Luton 45 D1
Ascot Rd. Roystn 7 F3
Ascot Rd. Watf 166 C2
Ascots La. Wel GC 110 C1
Ash Cl. Abb L 153 E4
Ash Cl. Bro Pk 145 D3
Ash Cl. Hare 173 E1
Ash Dri. Hat 130 A1
Ash Gr. Hare 173 E1
Ash Gr. Heml H 138 C4
Ash Gr. Whea 87 E1
Ash Groves. Saw 98 A1
Ash Hill. Bark 17 E2
Ash Hill Cl. Bus 168 A1
Ash Meadow. Muc H 74 C1
Ash Rd. Luton 63 D4
Ash Rd. Tri 99 F2
Ash Rd. Ware 94 A2
Ash Ride. Enf 161 D2
Ash Tree Field. Harl 117 D1
Ash Tree Rd. Watf 154 A2
Ash Vale. Map Cr 172 B3
Ash Way. Roystn 7 F3
Ashanger La. Clo 24 B2
Ashbourne Cl. Letw 23 D2
Ashbourne Rd. Hod 134 C1
Ashbourne Sq. Norwd 174 C2
Ashbrook La. St Ipp 35 D2
Ashburnam Wlk. Stev 50 C1
Ashburnham Cl. Sth Ox 175 D4
Ashburnham Dr. Sth Ox 175 D4
Ashburnham Rd. Luton 63 E4
Ashbury Cl. Hat 129 F3
Ashby Gdns. St Alb 141 E4
Ashby Rd. Nthch 121 E4
Ashby Rd. Watf 154 A1
Ashby Rise. Bis St 59 D1
Ashcombe. Wel GC 89 F1
Ashcroft. Pnr 176 A2
Ashcroft Cl. Harp 107 F4
Ashcroft Ct. Hod 134 C1
Ashcroft Rd. Luton 46 A1
Ashdale. Bis St 76 B2
Ashdale Gdns. Luton 31 D1
Ashdale Gr. Stan 176 C2
Ashdales. St Alb 141 E4
Ashdon Rd. Bus 167 E3
Ashdown. Letw 11 F1
Ashdown Cres. Ches 148 C2
Ashdown Dri. Bor 169 F4
Ashdown Rd. Stev 69 D4
Ashendene. Bay 133 D3
Ashendene Rd. Bay 132 C2
Ashfield Ave. Bus 168 B1
Ashfield Way. Luton 45 D3
Ashfields. Watf 153 F2
Ashford Green. Sth Ox 175 E3
Ashfords. Bun 40 C4
Ashleigh. Stev 51 D2
Ashley Cl. Pnr 175 D1
Ashley Cl. Wel GC 110 B4
Ashley Ct. Hat 130 A3
Ashley Dri. Bor 170 B2
Ashley Gdns. Harp 85 E2
Ashley Rd. Hertng 113 D3
Ashley Rd. St Alb 128 B1
Ashleys. Ric 164 C1
Ashlyn Cl. Bus 167 F3
Ashlyn Ct. Bus 167 F3
Ashlyns Ct. Berk 122 A2
Ashlyns Rd. Berk 122 A2
Ashmore Gdns. Heml H 125 D1
Ashridge Cl. Bov 137 D2
Ashridge Dri. Bri Wd 140 C1
Ashridge Dri. Sth Ox 175 E3
Ashridge La. Bot 150 B4
Ashridge Rise. Berk 121 F3
Ashton Rd. Enf 162 C2
Ashton Rd. Luton 63 F3
Ashton's La. Bal 23 F3
Ashtree Way. Heml H 124 A1
Ashurst Cl. Norwd 174 C2
Ashville Way. Bal 13 D1
Ashwell Ave. Luton 44 B4
Ashwell Cl. Gra 36 A2
Ashwell Common. Gra 36 A2
Ashwell Park. Harp 86 B1
Ashwell Rd. Byg 13 E2
Ashwell Rd. Gu M 1 C1
Ashwell Rd. Hin 3 F3
Ashwell Rd. Newn 12 C4
Ashwell Rd. Ste Mo 5 D4
Ashwell St. Ashw 4 B2
Ashwell St. Knee 2 A2
Ashwell St. St Alb 127 E2
Ashwood Rd. Pot B 159 D3
Askew Rd. Norwd 174 B4
Aspasia Cl. St Alb 127 F1
Aspen Cl. Stev 69 D4
Aspen Way. Enf 162 B2
Aspenden Rd. Bun 40 C3
Aspens The. Hit 35 D3
Aspfield Row. Heml H 124 A3
Ass House La. Har 176 A3
Astall Cl. Har 176 B1
Astley Green. Luton 46 B1
Astley Rd. Heml H 124 B2
Aston End Rd. Ast 51 F2
Aston La. Ast 69 F4
Aston Rd. Stand 55 E1
Aston Rise. Hit 35 D3
Aston View. Heml H 105 D1
Aston Way. Pot B 159 E4
Astons Rd. Norwd 174 B3
Astra Ct. Luton 45 F1
Astrope La. Lon M 79 D2
Astwick Ave. Hat 129 F4
Astwick Rd. Stot 3 D1
Astwick Rd. Stot 11 F4
Athelstan Rd. Heml H 138 C4
Athelstan Wlk N. Wel GC 110 C3
Athelstan Wlk S. Wel GC 110 B3
Athelstone Rd. Har 176 B1
Athena Pl. Norwd 174 C1
Atherstone Rd. Luton 44 B1
Atherton End. Saw 97 F2
Athlone Cl. Radl 156 A2
Athol Cl. Pnr 175 D1
Athol Gdns. Pnr 175 D1
Atholl Cl. Luton 44 B4
Atria Rd. Norwd 175 D3
Attimore Cl. Wel GC 110 A3
Attimore Rd. Wel GC 110 A3
Aubrey La. Red 105 F1
Aubrey Rd. Lon C 142 B3
Aubreys. Letw 23 D1
Aubreys Rd. Heml H 123 F2
Aubries. Wal 38 A1
Auckland Cl. Enf 162 B1
Auckland Rd. Pot B 158 C4
Audley Cl. Bor 170 A3
Audley Ct. Pnr 175 E1
Audley Gdns. Wa Aby 163 E3
Audrey Gdns. Bis St 76 C2
Audwick Cl. Ches 148 C2
Augustine Rd. Har 176 B1
Augustus Cl. St Alb 127 D1
Austen Paths. Stev 51 E3
Austin Rd. Luton 45 E2
Austins Mead. Bov 137 D2
Austins Pl. Heml H 124 B2
Autumn Gr. Wel GC 111 D2
Avalon Cl. Watf 154 C4
Ave Grimaldi. Luton 45 D2
Ave The. Luton 44 B3
Avebury Ave. Luton 45 E2
Avenue App. Kin L 139 D1
Avenue One. Letw 23 E3
Avenue Rd. Bis St 77 D3
Avenue Rd. Pnr 175 F1
Avenue Rd. Roy 135 E3
Avenue Rd. St Alb 127 F2
Avenue Rise. Bus 168 A2
Avenue St Nicholas. Harp 86 A1
Avenue Terr. Watf 167 F2
Avenue The. Barn 171 F3
Avenue The. Bus 167 F3
Avenue The. Har 176 C1
Avenue The. Heml H 123 F3
Avenue The. Hert 113 D4
Avenue The. Hit 35 D4
Avenue The. Norwd 174 B2
Avenue The. Pnr 175 F2
Avenue The. Pot B 159 D4
Avenue The. Radl 156 A3
Avenue The. Stev 50 B4
Avenue The. Stot 11 F3
Avenue The. Watf 167 D4
Avenue The. Wl Gr 89 E4
Avey La. Wa Aby 163 F1
Avior Dri. Norwd 174 C3
Avocet. Letw 11 F1
Avon Cl. Watf 154 B3
Avon Mews. Pnr 175 F2
Avon Rd. Henlw 10 B2
Avon Sq. Heml H 124 C4
Avondale Ct. St Alb 127 F2
Avondale Rd. Luton 63 E4
Axe Cl. Luton 44 C3
Aycliffe Dri. Heml H 124 C4
Aycliffe Rd. Bor 156 C1
Aydon Rd. Luton 45 D3
Aylands Rd. Enf 162 B2
Aylesbury Rd. Tri 99 F1
Aylsham Rd. Hod 135 E4
Aynho St. Watf 167 D2
Aynsworth Ave. Bis St 59 D1
Ayot Green. A St P 89 D1
Ayot Little Green La. A St P 88 C1
Ayot Path. Bor 157 D1
Ayot St Peter Rd. A St P 88 C2
Ayres End La. Harp 107 F3
Aysgarth Cl. Harp 107 D4
Aysgarth Rd. Red 106 A3

Baas Hill. Hod 134 B1
Baas Hill Cl. Hod 134 C1

Baas La. Hod 134 C2
Babbage Rd. Stev 50 A3
Back La. Aldhm 168 C4
Back La. Buck 27 E4
Back La. Hal 98 A4
Back La. Letw 23 E4
Back La. Pres 48 B3
Back La. Saw 98 A1
Back La. Tewin 90 C1
Back St. Ashw 4 B2
Back St. Luton 63 F4
Back The. Pot En 123 D4
Bacons Dri. Cuf 146 C1
Bacon's Yd. Ashw 4 B2
Dadburgham Ct. Wa Aby 163 F3
Baddeley Cl. Stev 51 D1
Bader Cl. Stev 36 C1
Bader Cl. Wel GC 111 E3
Badger Cl. Kneb 69 D3
Badger Way. Hat 130 A2
Badgers. Bis St 76 C3
Badgers Cl. Bor 169 F4
Badgers Cl. Stev 50 C2
Badgers Croft. N20 171 F1
Badminton Cl. Bor 170 A4
Badminton Cl. Stev 69 D4
Badminton Pl. Hod 134 C2
Bagwicks Cl. Luton 44 C4
Bailey St. Luton 63 F3
Baines La. Dat 69 E2
Baird Cl. Bus 168 A2
Bairstow Cl. Bor 169 F4
Baker St. Enf 161 F1
Baker St. Hert 113 F3
Baker St. Luton 63 F3
Baker St. Pot B 158 C3
Baker St. Stev 50 B4
Bakers Ct. Bis St 77 D4
Bakers Gr. Wel GC 111 E4
Baker's La. Bar 8 C1
Baker's La. Cod 67 F1
Bakers La. Ken Co 82 C4
Bakers Rd. Ches 148 A1
Bakerscroft. Ches 148 C2
Bakewell Cl. Luton 44 B1
Balcombe Cl. Luton 46 B2
Balcon Way. Bor 170 B4
Baldock La. Letw 23 E2
Baldock La. Will 23 D1
Baldock Rd. Bun 40 B4
Baldock Rd. Letw 23 E3
Baldock Rd. Roystn 7 D3
Baldock Rd. Ste Mo 6 B2
Baldock Rd. Stot 12 A3
Baldock St. Roystn 7 E3
Baldock St. Ware 93 E1
Baldock Way. Bor 169 F4
Baldways Cl. Wing 60 B2
Baldwins. Wel GC 111 E3
Baldwins La. Cro Gr 166 A3
Balfour St. Hert 113 E4
Baliol Rd. Hit 34 C4
Ballater Cl. Sth Ox 175 E3
Ballinger Ct. Berk 122 A2
Ballslough Hill. Kim 66 C1
Balmoral Cl. Ches 162 B3
Balmoral Cl. Stev 69 E4
Balmoral Dri. Bor 170 B3
Balmoral Rd. Enf 162 B2
Balmoral Rd. Hit 21 F1
Balmoral Rd. Watf 154 B1
Balsams Cl. Hert 113 E2
Bampton Rd. Luton 44 A1
Banbury Cl. Luton 44 C2
Banbury St. Watf 167 D2
Bancroft. Hit 34 C4
Bancroft Ct. Hit 34 C4
Bancroft Gdns. Har 176 B1
Bancroft Rd. Har 176 B1
Bancroft Rd. Luton 45 D3
Bandley Rise. Stev 51 E2
Banes Down. Lo Naz 135 F1
Bank Cl. Luton 44 B2
Bank Ct. Heml H 124 B1
Bank Mill. Berk 122 C2
Bank Mill La. Berk 122 C2
Bank Mill La. Pot En 122 C2
Banks Rd. Bor 170 B4
Bankside Down. Ric 165 E2
Baracroft Way. St Alb 128 A1
Barbel Cl. Ches 163 D3
Barberry Rd. Heml H 124 A2
Barbers Wlk. Tri 99 F2
Barchester Rd. Har 176 B1
Barclay Cl. Hert H 114 A2
Barclay Cres. Stev 50 C4
Barclay Ct. Hod 135 D3
Barden Cl. Hare 173 E2
Bardwell Ct. St Alb 127 E1
Bardwell Rd. St Alb 127 E1
Barford Rise. Luton 46 B1
Bargrove Ave. Heml H 124 A1
Barham Ave. Elst 169 F3
Barkham Cl. Ched 79 F4
Barking Cl. Luton 44 A3
Barkston Path. Bor 157 D1
Barkway Hill. Bark 17 F3
Barkway Rd. Roystn 7 F3
Barkway St. Roystn 7 E3
Barley Cl. Bus 168 A2
Barley Croft. Heml H 125 E2
Barley Croft. Hert 113 E4
Barley Hills. Bis St 76 C2
Barley La. Luton 44 B3
Barley Mow La. Tyt 128 C1
Barley Ponds Cl. Ware 93 F1
Barley Ponds Rd. Ware 93 F1
Barley Rd. Gt Ch 9 D4
Barley Rd. Gt Ch 9 E1
Barley Rise. Bal 24 A4
Barleycroft. Stev 51 E2
Barleycroft. Tonw 92 C4
Barleycroft. Wat 92 A2
Barleycroft Green. Wel GC 110 B3
Barleycroft Rd. Wel GC 110 B3
Barleyvale. Luton 45 D4
Barlings Rd. Harp 107 D3
Barmor Cl. Har 176 A1
Barn Cl. Heml H 138 C4
Barn Cl. Radl 156 A2
Barn Cl. Wel GC 110 B3
Barn Lea. Ric 165 D1
Barnacres Rd. Heml H 139 D4
Barnard Acres. Lo Naz 149 F4
Barnard Green. Wel GC 110 C3
Barnard Rd. Luton 63 D4
Barnard Rd. Saw 97 F2
Barnard Way. Heml H 124 C1
Barncroft. Gravnd 57 E4
Barncroft Rd. Berk 121 F2
Barndell Cl. Stot 11 F3
Barndicott. Wel GC 111 E3
Barnes La. Chipf 138 B2
Barnes Rise. Kin L 138 C2
Barnet By-Ps Rd. Barn 170 C3
Barnet Gate La. Barn 170 C2
Barnet Hill. Barn 171 F3
Barnet La. Bor 170 B2
Barnet La. Elst 169 F2
Barnet La. N20 171 F1
Barnet Rd. Barn 171 D2
Barnet Rd. Lon C 142 C2
Barnet Rd. Pot B 159 D2
Barnet Stall Market. Barn 171 F3
Barnet Trading Estate. Barn 171 F3
Barnet Way. NW7 170 B1
Barnfield. Heml H 138 C4
Barnfield Ave. Luton 45 E3
Barnfield Cl. Hod 135 D4
Barnfield Cl. Lo Naz 135 F1
Barnfield Ct. Harp 107 E4
Barnfield Rd. Harp 107 E4
Barnfield Rd. St Alb 128 B3
Barnfield Rd. Wel GC 110 C2
Barnhurst Path. Sth Ox 175 E3
Barns Dene. Harp 85 F1
Barnsdale Cl. Bor 169 F4
Barnside Ct. Wel GC 110 B3
Barnston Cl. Luton 46 B1
Barnwell. Stev 51 D1
Baron Ct. Stev 36 A1
Barons Row. Harp 107 E4
Barons The. Bis St 76 B3
Barr Rd. Pot B 159 E3
Barra Cl. Heml H 139 E4
Barracks La. Barn 171 F3
Barratt Way. Har 176 B1
Barrells Down Rd. Bis St 58 C1
Barrett La. Bis St 76 C4
Barrington Rd. Letw 22 C2
Barrow La. Ches 147 F1
Barrow Point Ave. Pnr 175 F1
Barrow Point La. Pnr 175 F1
Barrowby Cl. Luton 46 B1
Barrowdene Cl. Pnr 175 F1
Barry Cl. Chis 141 D3
Bartel Cl. Heml H 125 E1
Bartholomew Rd. Bis St 76 C3
Bartletts Mead. Hert 92 B1
Barton Cl. Harp 86 B2
Barton Rd. Hex 19 D1
Barton Rd. Luton 45 E4
Barton Rd. Whea 108 B4
Barton Way. Bor 170 A4
Barton Way. Cro Gr 166 A2
Bartons The. Elst 169 E2
Bartrams La. Barn 159 E1
Basbow La. Bis St 76 C4
Basildon Sq. Heml H 124 C4
Basils Rd. Stev 50 B4
Basing Rd. Ric 173 D4
Baslow Cl. Har 176 B1
Bassett Cl. Red 106 A3
Bassil Rd. Heml H 124 B1
Bassingbourne Cl. Hod 134 C2
Bassingburn Wlk. Wel GC 110 C3
Batchelors. Stand 55 F1
Batchwood Dri. St Alb 127 E3
Batchwood Gdns. St Alb 127 E3
Batchwood View. St Alb 127 E3
Batchworth Heath Hill. Ric 174 A3
Batchworth Hill. Ric 173 F4
Batchworth La. Norwd 174 B3
Bateman Rd. Cro Gr 166 A2
Batford Cl. Wel GC 111 D3
Batford Rd. Harp 86 B2
Bath Rd. Luton 45 E1
Bathurst Rd. Heml H 124 C3
Batterdale. Hat 130 B3
Battlefield Rd. St Alb 127 F3
Battlers Green Dri. Radl 155 F2
Baulk The. Ched 79 F4
Baulk The. Ivin 80 C3
Baulk The. Lily 32 B1
Bawdsey Cl. Stev 50 A4
Bay Ct. Berk 122 A2
Bay Tree Wlk. Watf 154 A1
Bayford Cl. Heml H 125 E4
Bayford Cl. Hert 113 E2
Bayford Green. Bay 133 D3
Bayford La. Bay 132 C4
Bayhurst Dri. Norwd 174 C2
Bayworth. Letw 23 D3
Beacon Ct. Hert H 114 B2
Beacon Rd. Rin 81 D1
Beacon Rd. Ware 94 A1
Beacon Way. Ric 165 D1
Beacon Way. Tri 100 B3
Beaconsfield. Luton 64 A4
Beaconsfield Rd. Enf 162 C1
Beaconsfield Rd. Hat 130 B3
Beaconsfield Rd. St Alb 127 F2
Beaconsfield Rd. Tri 99 F2
Beadlow Rd. Luton 44 A2
Beagle Cl. Radl 155 F1
Beale Cl. Stev 51 E3
Beamish Dri. Bus 168 B1
Beane Ave. Stev 51 E3
Beane Rd. Hert 113 D4
Beane Rd. Wat St 70 B2
Beane Wlk. Stev 51 E3
Beanfield Rd. H Wy 97 D2
Beanley Cl. Luton 46 C1
Bear La. Ashw 4 B2
Bearton Ave. Hit 34 C4
Bearton Green. Hit 21 F1
Bearton Rd. Hit 21 F1
Bearwood Cl. Pot B 159 E4
Beauchamp Gdns. Ric 165 D1
Beaulieu Cl. Watf 167 E1
Beaumayes Cl. Heml H 124 A1
Beaumont Ave. St Alb 128 A2
Beaumont Cl. Hit 34 B4
Beaumont Hall La. Red 106 A1
Beaumont Pl. Barn 171 F4
Beaumont Rd. Ham St 147 F4
Beaumont Rd. Luton 45 D1
Beaumont View. Ham St 147 E3
Becket Gdns. Welw 89 E2
Beckets Sq. Berk 122 A3
Becketts. Hertng 113 D3
Beckett's Ave. St Alb 127 E3
Beckfield La. Gr En 26 B4
Beckham Cl. Luton 45 E4
Becks Cl. Mark 83 E3
Bedale Rd. Enf 161 E1
Bede Cl. Pnr 175 E1
Bede Ct. L Gad 102 B4
Bedford Ave. Barn 171 F3
Bedford Cl. Chen 151 D1
Bedford Cres. Enf 162 C2
Bedford Park Rd. St Alb 127 F2
Bedford Rd. Henlw 10 A2
Bedford Rd. Hit 21 E1
Bedford Rd. Hol 21 E4
Bedford Rd. Ick 21 E2
Bedford Rd. Letw 22 B4
Bedford Rd. Norwd 174 B3
Bedford Rd. St Alb 127 F1
Bedford St. Berk 122 B2
Bedford St. Hit 34 B4
Bedford St. Watf 167 D4
Bedmond Green. Bed 139 F2
Bedmond La. Abb L 139 F1
Bedmond La. Bed 140 A3
Bedmond La. Chis 140 B4
Bedmond La. St Alb 126 C1
Bedmond Rd. Bed 139 F3
Bedwell Ave. L Berk 132 A4
Bedwell Cl. Wel GC 110 C3
Bedwell Cres. Stev 50 C3
Bedwell La. Stev 50 C3
Bedwell Rise. Stev 50 C3
Beech Ave. Enf 161 D2
Beech Ave. Radl 156 A3
Beech Bottom. St Alb 127 E3
Beech Cl. Harp 107 E3
Beech Cl. Hat 130 A2
Beech Dri. Berk 122 B2
Beech Dri. Bor 169 F4
Beech Dri. Saw 118 B4
Beech Dri. Stev 51 D2
Beech Hill. Barn 159 F1
Beech Hill. Letw 22 B4
Beech Hill. Lily 46 B4
Beech Hill Ct. Berk 122 B3
Beech Hyde La. Sand 108 C3
Beech Hyde La. Whea 108 C4
Beech Park. L Chal 150 A1
Beech Pl. St Alb 127 E3
Beech Rd. Luton 63 E4
Beech Rd. St Alb 127 F3
Beech Rd. Watf 154 A1
Beech Way. Bla En 87 D3
Beech Wlk. Hod 134 C3
Beech Wlk. Tri 100 B2
Beechcroft Ave. Cro Gr 166 B2
Beechcroft Rd. Bus 167 F2
Beechen Gr. Watf 167 E3
Beeches The. Hit 35 D3
Beeches The. Pk St 141 E2
Beeches The. Tri 100 B2
Beeches The. Welw 89 E2
Beechfield. Hod 115 D1
Beechfield. Kin L 139 D1
Beechfield. Saw 97 F1
Beechfield Cl. Red 106 A3
Beechfield Rd. Heml H 124 A1
Beechfield Rd. Ware 93 F1
Beechfield Rd. Wel GC 110 C3
Beechfield Wlk. Wa Aby 163 E2
Beeching Cl. Harp 86 A2
Beechlands. Bis St 76 C3
Beecholme Mews. Ches 148 C2
Beechpark Way. Watf 153 F1
Beechtree La. St Alb 126 A1
Beechwood Ave. Chor 164 A3
Beechwood Ave. L Chal 150 B1
Beechwood Ave. Po B 159 D3
Beechwood Ave. St Alb 128 A2
Beechwood Cl. Bal 23 F3
Beechwood Cl. Ham St 147 F3
Beechwood Cl. Hert 113 F3
Beechwood Dri. Ald 101 E3
Beechwood Park. Fel 137 F4
Beechwood Rd. Luton 44 C2
Beechwood Rise. Watf 154 A1
Beecroft La. Wal 38 B1
Beehive Cl. Elst 169 E2
Beehive Green. Wel GC 111 D2
Beehive La. Wel GC 111 D2
Beehive Rd. Gofs O 147 D2
Beesonend La. Harp 106 C2
Beeston Cl. Sth Ox 175 E3
Beeston Dri. Ches 148 B2
Beethoven Rd. Elst 169 E2
Beeton Cl. Pnr 176 A2
Beggarman's La. Lev Gr 72 B4
Beggars Bush La. Watf 166 B2
Belcher Rd. Hod 135 D4
Beldam Ave. Roystn 7 E3
Beldams La. Bis St 77 D3
Belfairs Green. Sth Ox 175 E3
Belford Rd. Bor 156 C1
Belfry Ave. Hare 173 D2
Belfry La. Ric 165 E1
Belgrave Ave. Watf 166 C2
Belgrave Cl. St Alb 128 B4
Belgrave Dri. Bed 139 E2
Belgrave Rd. Luton 44 B3
Belham Rd. Bed 139 D2
Bell Acre. Letw 23 D2
Bell Acre Gdns. Letw 23 D2
Bell Cl. Bed 139 F2
Bell Cl. Hit 35 D3
Bell Cl. Kneb 69 D3
Bell Cl. Pnr 175 E1
Bell La. Bed 140 A2
Bell La. Bro Pk 144 C4
Bell La. Enf 162 C1
Bell La. Hert 113 E3
Bell La. Hod 134 C1
Bell La. Hod 135 D3
Bell La. L Chal 150 B1
Bell La. Lon C 142 C1
Bell La. Nthch 121 F3
Bell La. Stev 50 B4
Bell La. Widf 95 E2
Bell Leys. Wing 60 A2
Bell Mead. Saw 97 F1
Bell St. Saw 97 F1
Bellamy Cl. Watf 167 D4
Bellamy Rd. Ches 148 C1
Belle Vue La. Bus 168 B1
Belle Vue Rd. Ware 93 F1
Bellerby Rise. Luton 44 A3
Bellfield Ave. Har 176 B2
Bellgate. Heml H 124 C3
Bellmount Wood Ave. Watf 166 C4
Bells Hill. Barn 171 E3
Bells Hill. Bis St 76 C4
Belmers Rd. Wigg 100 B2
Belmont Hill. St Alb 127 E1
Belmont Rd. Bus 167 F2
Belmont Rd. Heml H 138 C4
Belmont Rd. Luton 63 E4
Belmor. Elst 170 A2
Belper Rd. Luton 44 B1
Belsham Pl. Luton 46 C1
Belsize Cl. Heml H 125 D1
Belsize Cl. St Alb 128 B4
Belsize Rd. Har 176 B2
Belsize Rd. Heml H 125 D1
Belswains Green. Heml H 138 C4
Belswains La. Heml H 138 C4
Belton Rd. Berk 122 A3
Beltona Gdns. Ches 148 B2
Belvedere Rd. Luton 45 D3
Bembridge Gdns. Luton 44 C4
Ben Austins. Red 106 A2
Benbow Cl. St Alb 128 A1
Benchley Hill. Hit 35 E4
Benchleys Rd. Heml H 123 F1
Bencroft. Ham St 148 A3
Bendish La. Whit 66 B4
Bendysh Rd. Bus 167 F3
Benedictine Gate. Ches 148 C2
Benford Rd. Hod 134 C2
Bengarth Dri. Har 176 B1
Bengeo St. Hert 113 E4
Benhooks Ave. Bis St 76 C3
Benington Cl. Luton 45 F3
Benington Rd. Ast 51 F1
Benington Rd. Wal 52 A3
Bennett Cl. Norwd 174 C2
Bennett Ct. Letw 23 D3
Bennetts Cl. Coln H 143 E4
Bennetts End Cl. Heml H 124 C1
Bennetts End Rd. Heml H 125 D1
Bennettsgate. Heml H 139 D4
Benningfield Cl. Widf 95 E3
Benningfield Rd. Widf 95 E2
Benskin Rd. Watf 167 D2
Benslow La. Hit 35 D4
Benslow Rise. Hit 35 D4
Benson Cl. Luton 44 C4
Benstede. Stev 69 E4
Bentfield End Cswy. Sta Mo 59 E4
Bentfield Gdns. Sta Mo 59 E4
Bentfield Rd. Sta Mo 59 E4
Bentick Way. Cod 67 F1
Bentley Heath La. Pot B 158 C2
Bentley Lodge. Bus 176 C4
Bentley Rd. Hertng 112 C4
Benton Rd. Sth Ox 175 E3
Bentsley Cl. St Alb 128 B4
Berceau Wlk. Watf 166 C4
Beresford Rd. Luton 45 D1
Beresford Rd. Ric 164 C1
Beresford Rd. St Alb 128 B1
Bericot Way. Wel GC 111 E3
Berkeley. Letw 23 D2
Berkeley Cl. Abb L 153 F4
Berkeley Cl. Elst 170 A2
Berkeley Cl. Hit 34 B4
Berkeley Cl. Pot B 158 C4
Berkeley Cl. Stev 69 D4
Berkeley Cl. Ware 93 E1
Berkeley Ct. Cro Gr 166 B2
Berkeley Ct. Harp 86 A1
Berkeley Sq. Red 105 E1
Berkhamsted La. L Berk 132 A2
Berkhamsted Pl. Berk 122 A3
Berkhamsted Rd. Heml H 123 E3
Berkley Ave. Ches 162 B3
Berkley Cl. St Alb 128 B4
Berkley Ct. Berk 122 B2
Berks Hill. Chor 164 B2
Bernard St. St Alb 127 E2
Berners Dri. St Alm 141 F4
Berners Way. Hod 148 C4
Bernhardt Cres. Stev 51 E3
Berries The. St Alb 128 A4
Berrow Cl. Luton 46 C1
Berry Ave. Watf 154 A2
Berry Cl. Ric 165 D1
Berry Grove La. Bus 168 A4
Berry Grove La. Bus 154 C1
Berry La. Chor 164 C2
Berry La. Ric 165 D1
Berry Leys. Luton 44 C4
Berry Way. Ric 165 D1
Berryfield. Ched 79 F4
Berrymead. Heml H 124 C3
Berwick Cl. Ches 163 D3
Berwick Cl. Stan 176 C2
Berwick Rd. Bor 156 C1
Bessemer Dri. Stev 50 A2
Bessemer Rd. Wel GC 89 F1
Bethune Cl. Luton 63 D3
Betony Vale. Roystn 7 F3
Bettespol Meadows. Red 106 A3
Betty's La. Tri 100 A2
Bevan Cl. Heml H 124 C1
Beverley Gdns. Ches 148 A1
Beverley Gdns. St Alb 128 B4
Beverley Gdns. Wel GC 111 E3
Beverley Rd. Luton 44 C1
Beverley Rd. Stev 37 D1
Beverly Cl. Hod 134 C1
Bevil Ct. Hod 115 D1
Bewley Cl. Ches 162 B4
Bexhill Rd. Luton 46 B1
Beyers Gdns. Hod 115 D1
Beyers Prospect. Hod 115 D1
Beyers Ride. Hod 115 D1
Bibbs Hall La. A St L 87 F3
Biddenham Turn. Watf 154 B2
Bideford Gdns. Luton 45 E2
Bideford Rd. Enf 162 C1
Bidwell Cl. Letw 23 D3
Biggin Hill. Ans 28 B4
Biggin La. Hit 34 C4
Billet La. Berk 122 A3
Billy Lows La. Pot B 159 D4
Bilton Rd. Hit 21 F1
Bilton Way. Enf 162 C1
Bilton Way. Luton 62 C4
Bingen Rd. Hit 21 E1
Bingley Rd. Hod 135 E3
Binham Cl. Luton 45 E4
Binyon Cres. Stan 176 C3
Birch Copse. Bri Wd 140 C1
Birch Ct. Norwd 174 B2
Birch Dri. Hat 130 A2
Birch Dri. Map Cr 172 B3
Birch Gr. Luton 45 F2
Birch Gr. Pot B 159 D4
Birch Gr. Wl Gr 89 F4
Birch Green. Heml H 123 F3
Birch La. Flau 151 D4
Birch Leys. Heml H 125 E4
Birch Link. Luton 45 E1
Birch Park. Har 176 B2
Birch Rd. Nthch 121 E4
Birch Rd. Wl Gr 69 D1
Birch Tree Gr. Bot 136 A1
Birch Tree Wlk. Watf 153 F1
Birch Way. Harp 107 E4
Birch Way. Lon C 142 B2
Birch Wlk. Bor 170 A4
Birchall La. Wel GC 111 F2
Birchall Wood. Wel GC 111 E3
Birchanger La. Birhr 59 F1
Bircherley Ct. Hert 113 E3
Bircherley St. Hert 113 E3
Birches The. Bus 168 B2
Birches The. Fel 137 F4
Birches The. Letw 22 C4
Birchfield Rd. Ches 148 B1
Birchmead. Watf 153 F1
Birchmead Cl. St Alb 127 E3
Birchway. Hat 130 A4
Birchwood. Birhr 59 E1
Birchwood. Shen 157 D3
Birchwood. Wa Aby 163 F3
Birchwood Ave. Hat 130 A4
Birchwood Cl. Hat 130 A4
Birchwood Way. Chis 141 D2
Bird La. Hare 173 E1
Birdcroft Rd. Wel GC 110 B3
Birdie Way. Hert 114 A4
Birds Cl. Wel GC 111 D2
Birds Hill. Letw 23 D3
Birdsfoot La. Luton 45 D3
Birkbeck Rd. Enf 161 E1
Birkdale Gdns. Sth Ox 175 E4
Birklands La. St Alb 142 A4
Birling Dri. Luton 46 B2
Birstall Green. Sth Ox 175 E3
Birtley Croft. Luton 46 C1
Biscot Rd. Luton 45 E1
Bishop Ken Rd. Har 176 C1
Bishop's Ave. Bis St 76 C2
Bishops Ave. Elst 169 F2

Bishops Ave. Norwd 174 C4
Bishops Cl. Barn 171 E2
Bishops Cl. Hat 129 F3
Bishop's Cl. St Alb 128 A4
Bishops Mead. Heml H 124 A1
Bishops Park Way. Bis St 76 A4
Bishops Rd. Tewin 90 B3
Bishops Rise. Hat 129 F2
Bishopscote Rd. Luton 45 D2
Biskra. Watf 167 D4
Bisley Cl. Ches 162 B3
Bit The. Wigg 100 B1
Bittern Cl. Stev 51 E1
Bittern Way. Letw 11 F1
Black Boy Wood. Bri Wd 141 D1
Black Cut. St Alb 127 F1
Black Ditch Rd. Wa Aby 163 E2
Black Fan Rd. Wel GC 110 C4
Black Fan Rd. Wel GC 111 D3
Black Lion Hill. Shen 156 C4
Black Swan La. Luton 45 D3
Blackberry Mead. Stev 51 E2
Blackbirds La. Aldhm 155 E3
Blackbury Cl. P Bar 159 E4
Blackbush Spring. Harl 118 A1
Blackbushe. Bis St 59 E1
Blackdale. Ham St 148 A2
Blackendale Gr. Luton 45 D3
Blacketts Wood Dri. Chor 164 A3
Blackford Rd. Sth Ox 175 E3
Blackhorn Dri. Luton 46 D2
Blackhorse Cl. Hit 35 D3
Blackhorse La. Hit 35 D3
Blackhorse La. Pot B 157 F4
Blackhorse La. Red 106 A3
Blackhorse La. Ridge 143 F1
Blackhorse Rd. Letw 23 E4
Blackley Cl. Watf 153 F1
Blackmoor La. Watf 166 B2
Blackmore. Letw 23 D2
Blackmore Way. Bla En 87 D3
Blacksmith Cl. Gt Am 115 D4
Blacksmiths Hill. Benn 52 C2
Blacksmith's La. Reed 16 B3
Blacksmith's St. St Alb 127 D2
Blackthorn Cl. St Alb 128 B3
Blackthorn Cl. Watf 154 A4
Blackthorn Rd. Wel GC 111 D3
Blackthorne Cl. Hat 129 F1
Blackwater La. Heml H 125 F1
Blackwell Cl. Har 176 B2
Blackwell Dri. Watf 167 E2
Blackwell Hall La. Lat 150 B3
Blackwell Rd. Kin L 139 D1
Bladon Cl. L Wym 35 F2
Blair Cl. Heml H 105 D1
Blairhead Dr. Sth Ox 175 D4
Blake Cl. St Alb 142 A4
Blakemere Rd. Wel GC 110 B4
Blakeney Dri. Luton 45 E4
Blakeney Rd. Stev 50 A4
Blakes Way. Welw 89 E3
Blanche La. Pot B 158 A3
Blandford Ave. Luton 45 E3
Blandford Rd. St Alb 128 A2
Blanes The. Ware 93 E2
Blaydon Rd. Luton 64 A4
Blenheim Cl. Saw 118 B4
Blenheim Cl. Watf 167 E1
Blenheim Cres. Luton 45 E1
Blenheim Rd. Barn 171 E3
Blenheim Rd. St Alb 127 F2
Blenheim Way. Stev 69 E4
Blenkin Cl. St Alb 127 E4
Blind La. h st A 38 C3
Blindman's La. Ches 148 B1
Bloomfield Ave. Luton 46 A1
Bloomfield Rd. Harp 85 F2
Blossom La. Enf 161 E1
Blue Bridge Rd. Bro Pk 144 C2
Bluebell Wood Cl. Luton 62 C4
Bluebells. Wl Gr 89 F4
Blueberry Cl. St Alb 127 E4
Bluebridge Ave. Bro Pk 144 C2
Bluecoat Yard. Ware 93 E1
Bluecoats Ave. Hert 113 E3
Bluecoats Ct. Hert 113 E3
Bluehouse Hill. St Alb 127 D2
Bluett Rd. Lon C 142 B2
Blundell Cl. St Alb 127 E4
Blundell Rd. Luton 45 D2
Blunesfield. P Bar 159 E4
Blunts La. Chis 140 B3
Blyth Cl. Bor 170 A4
Blyth Cl. Stev 50 A4
Blythe Rd. Roy 135 E3
Blythway. Wel GC 89 F1
Blythwood Gdns. Sta Mo 59 E3
Blythwood Rd. Pnr 175 E1
Bockings. Wal 38 B1
Bodmin Rd. Luton 44 C2
Bodwell Cl. Heml H 124 A2
Boech Cres. Whea 108 B4
Bogmoor Rd. Bar 18 A4
Bognor Gdns. Sth Ox 175 E3
Bohemia. Heml H 124 C2
Boissy Cl. St Alb 128 C1
Boleyn Cl. Heml H 125 E4
Bollingbroke Rd. Luton 63 D3
Bolney Green. Luton 46 B2
Bolton Rd. Luton 63 F4
Boniface Gdns. Har 176 A2
Boniface Wlk. Har 176 A2
Bonks Hill. Saw 97 E1
Bonney Gr. Ches 148 A1
Bonnick Cl. Luton 63 E3
Booths Cl. Wel Gr 144 B4
Borough Way. Pot B 158 C4
Borrowdale Ct. Heml H 124 C3
Borton Ave. Henlw 10 A2
Bosanquet Rd. Hod 135 E4
Boscombe Ct. Letw 23 D3
Bosmore Rd. Luton 44 C3
Boswell Dri. Ick 21 F2
Boswell Gdns. Stev 36 B1
Boswick La. Nthch 121 E4
Botley La. Bot 136 A1
Botley Rd. Bot 136 A1
Botley Rd. Heml H 125 D4
Bottom House La. Wigg 101 D1
Bottom La. Sar 152 B2
Bottom Rd. St Le 119 F2
Boulevard The. Wel GC 110 C4
Boulton Rd. Stev 37 E1
Bounce The. Heml H 124 B3
Boundary Dri. Hert 113 E4
Boundary La. Wel GC 110 C1
Boundary Rd. Bis St 77 D3
Boundary Rd. St Alb 127 F3
Boundary Way. Heml H 125 E3
Boundary Way. Watf 154 B4
Bourne Cl. Hod 134 C2
Bourne Cl. Ware 93 E1
Bourne End La. Heml H 137 D4
Bourne End Rd. Norwd 174 C3
Bourne Honour. Tonw 92 C4
Bourne Rd. Berk 121 F3
Bourne Rd. Bus 168 A2
Bourne The. Bov 137 D2
Bourne The. Ware 93 E1
Bournehall Ave. Bus 168 A2
Bournehall La. Bus 168 A2
Bournehall Rd. Bus 168 A2
Bournemouth Rd. Stev 50 A4
Bouvier Rd. Enf 162 B1
Bovingdon Cres. Watf 154 B3
Bovingdon Green La. Bov 136 C2
Bowbrook Vale. Luton 46 C1
Bowcock Wlk. Stev 50 C2
Bower Heath La. Harp 86 B3
Bowers Way. Harp 86 A1
Bowershott. Letw 23 D2
Bowgate. St Alb 127 F2
Bowlers Mead. Bun 40 B4
Bowles Green. Enf 162 A2
Bowling Cl. Harp 107 E4
Bowling Green. Stev 50 B4
Bowling Green La. Bun 40 B4
Bowling Green La. Luton 45 F1
Bowling Rd. Ware 93 F1
Bowman Trading Estate. Stev 50 A3
Bowmans Ave. Hit 35 D4
Bowmans Cl. Pot B 159 E4
Bowmans Cl. Welw 89 E3
Bowmans Ct. Heml H 124 C3
Bowmans Green. Watf 154 C2
Bowring Green. Sth Ox 175 E3
Bowyers. Heml H 124 B3
Bowyer's Cl. Hit 21 E1
Box La. Fel 137 F4
Box La. Hod 134 C3
Boxberry Cl. Stev 50 C3
Boxfield. Wel GC 111 D2
Boxfield Green. Stev 51 E4
Boxgrove Cl. Luton 46 B3
Boxted Cl. Luton 44 B3
Boxted Rd. Heml H 123 F3
Boxtree La. Har 176 B2
Boxtree Rd. Har 176 B2
Boxwell Rd. Berk 122 A2
Boyce Cl. Bor 169 F4
Boyd Cl. Bis St 77 D4
Boyle Cl. Luton 63 F4
Braceby Cl. Luton 44 C3
Brache Cl. Red 106 A3
Bracken La. Wl Gr 89 F4
Brackendale. Pot B 159 D3
Brackendale Gr. Harp 85 E2
Brackendene. Bri Wd 140 C1
Brackens The. Heml H 124 B2
Bracklesham Gdns. Luton 46 B2
Bracknell Pl. Heml H 124 C4
Bradbery. Map Cr 172 B3
Bradden La. Gt Ga 103 F4
Bradford Rd. Heron 164 B1
Bradgate. Cuf 146 B2
Bradgate Cl. Cuf 146 B2
Bradgers Hill Rd. Luton 45 F2
Bradley Common. Birhr 59 E2
Bradley Rd. Enf 162 C1
Bradley Rd. Luton 44 B1
Bradleys Cnr. Hit 35 E4
Bradman Way. Stev 37 D1
Bradmore Green. Bro Pk 144 C3
Bradmore La. Wa En 144 B3
Bradmore Way. Bro Pk 144 C3
Bradshaw Rd. Watf 154 B1
Bradshaws. Hat 129 F1
Bradway. Whit 66 C3
Braemar Cl. Stev 69 D4
Braemar Turn. Heml H 105 D1
Braeside Cl. Pnr 176 A2
Bragbury Cl. Stev 69 E4
Bragbury La. Dat 69 E3
Brain Cl. Hat 130 A3
Brakynbery. Nthch 121 F4
Brallings La. C St P 172 A3
Bramble Cl. Harp 85 F2
Bramble Cl. Luton 44 B2
Bramble Cl. Watf 154 A3
Bramble La. Hod 134 C4
Bramble Rd. Hat 129 E3
Bramble Rd. Luton 44 B2
Brambles The. Ches 162 C4
Brambles The. Roystn 7 F3
Brambles The. Stev 36 B1
Brambles The. Ware 93 E2
Brambles The. Wl Gr 89 F4
Brambling Rise. Heml H 124 C4
Bramfield. Hit 35 D3
Bramfield La. Wat 91 F2
Bramfield Pl. Heml H 105 D1
Bramfield Rd. Dat 90 C4
Bramfield Rd. Hertng 112 C4
Bramham Ct. Norwd 174 C2
Bramhanger Acre. Luton 44 B4
Bramingham Business Park. Luton 45 D4
Bramingham Rd. Luton 44 C3
Bramleas. Watf 166 C3
Bramley Cl. Bal 12 C1
Bramley Gdns. Sth Ox 175 E3
Bramley Shaw. Wa Aby 163 F3
Brampton Cl. Ches 148 A2
Brampton Cl. Harp 86 B1
Brampton Park Rd. Hit 21 F1
Brampton Rd. Roystn 7 F3
Brampton Rd. St Alb 128 A2
Brampton Rd. Sth Ox 175 D4
Brampton Terr. Bor 157 D1
Bramshaw Gdns. Sth Ox 175 E3
Bramshot Way. Sth Ox 175 D4
Bramshott Cl. Hit 34 C3
Branch Cl. Hat 130 B4
Branch Rd. Fro 141 E2
Branch Rd. St Alb 127 D2
Brand St. Hit 34 C4
Brandles Rd. Letw 23 D2
Branksome Cl. Heml H 125 D2
Branton Cl. Luton 46 C1
Brantwood Rd. Luton 63 E4
Braunds Alley. Hit 34 C4
Bray Cl. Bor 170 B4
Brayes Manor. Stot 11 F3
Brays Rd. Luton 46 A2
Brays Springs. Wa Aby 163 F3
Braziers End. Chol 120 B1
Bread and Cheese La. Ham St 147 F4
Breadcroft La. Harp 86 A1
Breakmead. Wel GC 111 D3
Breaks Rd. Hat 130 A3
Breakspear. Stev 51 E2
Breakspear Ave. St Alb 127 F1
Breakspear Rd N. Hare 173 E1
Breakspear Way. Heml H 125 E2
Breakspear Way. St Alb 125 F2
Breakspeare Cl. Watf 154 A1
Breakspeare Rd. Abb L 153 F4
Brecon Cl. Luton 63 E3
Breeze Terr. Ches 148 B2
Brendon Ave. Luton 46 B1
Brent Ct. Stev 50 C3
Brent Pl. Barn 171 F2
Brereton Ct. Heml H 124 C1
Brett Pl. Watf 154 A1
Brett Rd. Barn 171 E2
Bretts Mead. Luton 63 E3
Brewery La. Bal 12 C1
Brewery La. Sta Mo 59 F4
Brewery Rd. Hod 135 D3
Brewhouse Hill. Whea 108 B4
Brewhouse La. Hert 113 E3
Briants Cl. Pnr 175 F1
Briar Cl. Ches 148 B1
Briar Cl. Luton 46 B2
Briar Cl. Pot En 123 D4
Briar Patch La. Letw 22 B2
Briar Rd. St Alb 128 B3
Briar Rd. Watf 154 A3
Briar Way. Berk 122 B2
Briardale. Stev 50 C2
Briardale. Ware 93 E2
Briarley Cl. Hod 134 C1
Briars Cl. Hat 130 A3
Briars La. Hat 130 A3
Briars The. Bus 168 C1
Briars The. Ches 162 C4
Briars Wood. Hat 129 F3
Briarwood Dri. Norwd 175 D1
Briary La. Roystn 7 E3
Briary Wood End. Wl Gr 89 F4
Briary Wood La. Wl Gr 89 F4
Brick Kiln La. Hit 34 C2
Brick Knoll Park. St Alb 128 B1
Brickcroft. Ches 148 C3
Brickenden Ct. Wa Aby 163 F3
Brickendon La. Bric 133 E4
Brickendon La. Hert 113 E2
Bricket Rd. St Alb 127 F2
Brickfield. Hat 130 A1
Brickfield Ave. Heml H 125 D1
Brickfield La. Barn 170 C2
Brickfields The. Ware 93 D1
Brickkiln Rd. Stev 50 B3
Brickly Rd. Luton 44 B3
Brickmakers La. Heml H 125 D1
Brickwall Cl. A St P 110 A4
Brickyard La. Reed 16 C3
Bride Hall La. A St L 88 A3
Bridewell Cl. Bun 40 C4
Bridge End. Bun 40 C4
Bridge Foot. Ware 93 E1
Bridge Pl. Watf 167 E2
Bridge Rd. Abb L 153 E3
Bridge Rd. Letw 22 C3
Bridge Rd. Stev 50 A4
Bridge Rd. Wel GC 110 B4
Bridge Rd. Wl Gr 69 D1
Bridge Rd E. Wel GC 110 C3
Bridge St. Berk 122 B2
Bridge St. Bis St 76 C4
Bridge St. Heml H 124 B1
Bridge St. Hit 34 C3
Bridge St. Knee 2 A4
Bridge St. Luton 63 F4
Bridgefields. Wel GC 110 C4
Bridgefoot. Bun 40 C4
Bridgefoot La. Pot B 158 B3
Bridgend Rd. Enf 162 B2
Bridgenhall Rd. Enf 161 F1
Bridger Cl. Watf 154 B3
Bridges Ct. Hert 113 E3
Bridges Rd. Stan 176 C3
Bridgewater Rd. Berk 122 A3
Bridgewater Rd. Nthch 121 F4
Bridgewater Way. Bus 168 A2
Bridle Cl. Enf 162 C1
Bridle Cl. Hod 115 D1
Bridle Cl. St Alb 127 F3
Bridle La. Chor 165 E3
Bridle Path. Watf 167 D4
Bridle Way. Berk 122 A3
Bridle Way. Gt Am 115 D3
Bridle Way. Hod 115 D1
Bridle Way (N). Hod 115 D1
Bridle Way (S). Hod 115 D1
Bridlington Rd. Sth Ox 175 E4
Brierley Cl. Luton 46 B1
Briery Field. Chor 165 D3
Briery Way. Heml H 125 D2
Brigadier Ave. Enf 161 E1
Brigadier Hill. Enf 161 E1
Brighton Rd. Watf 154 A1
Brighton Way. Stev 50 A4
Brightwell Rd. Watf 167 D2
Brill Cl. Luton 46 B1
Brimfield Cl. Luton 46 C1
Brimsdown Ave. Enf 162 C1
Brinley Cl. Ches 162 B4
Brinsley Rd. Har 176 B1
Briscoe Cl. Hod 134 C4
Briscoe Rd. Hod 134 C4
Bristol Rd. Luton 45 D2
Britannia. Stand 55 F1
Britannia Ave. Luton 45 D2
Britannia Rd. Ches 162 C3
Britten Cl. Elst 169 E2
Britton Ave. St Alb 127 E2
Brixham Cl. Stev 50 A4
Brixton Rd. Watf 167 D4
Broad Acre. Bri Wd 140 C1
Broad Acres. Hat 129 F4
Broad Green. Bay 132 C4
Broad Green Wood. Bay 132 C4
Broad Mead. Luton 45 D2
Broad Oak Way. Stev 50 C1
Broad St. Heml H 124 B2
Broad Way The. Har 176 C1
Broad Wlk. Harl 117 E1
Broad Wlk The. Norwd 174 B1
Broadcroft. Letw 22 C4
Broadfield. Bis St 58 C1
Broadfield. Harl 117 F1
Broadfield Cl. Had Cr 74 C1
Broadfield Ct. Har 176 C4
Broadfield Pl. Wel GC 110 A3
Broadfield Rd. Heml H 124 C2
Broadfield Rd. Wl Gr 69 D1
Broadfield Way. Had Cr 74 C1
Broadfields. Gofs O 147 D1
Broadfields. H Wy 97 D1
Broadfields. Har 176 A1
Broadfields. Harp 85 F1
Broadgate. Wa Aby 163 F3
Broadhall Way. Stev 51 D1
Broadlands Cl. Ches 162 B3
Broadlawns Ct. Har 176 C1
Broadleaf Ave. Bis St 76 B2
Broadmead. Hit 35 D3
Broadmead Cl. Pnr 175 F2
Broadmeads. Ware 93 E1
Broadoak Ave. Enf 162 B2
Broadstone Rd. Harp 107 E4
Broadview. Stev 50 C3
Broadwater. Berk 122 B3
Broadwater. Pot B 145 D1
Broadwater Ave. Letw 22 C3
Broadwater Cres. Stev 69 D4
Broadwater Cres. Wel GC 110 B3
Broadwater Dale. Letw 22 C3
Broadwater La. Stev 51 E1
Broadwater Rd. Wel GC 110 C3
Broadway. Letw 22 C3
Broadway Ave. Harl 118 A2
Broadway The. Bla En 87 D3
Broadway The. Hat 130 B3
Broadway The. Pnr 175 F2
Broadway The. Watf 167 E3
Brocket Rd. Hod 135 D3
Brocket Rd. Stanb 110 A2
Brocket View. Whea 108 B4
Brockett Cl. Wel GC 110 A3
Brockhurst Cl. Stan 176 C2
Brockley Hill. Stan 169 E1
Brockswood La. Wel GC 110 A4
Brockwell Shott. Wal 38 A1
Brodewater Rd. Bor 170 A4
Brodie Rd. Enf 161 E1
Bromborough Green. Sth Ox 175 E3
Bromet Cl. Watf 153 F1
Bromleigh Cl. Ches 148 C2
Bromley. Lon M 79 D2
Brompton Cl. Luton 44 C4
Bronte Cres. Heml H 105 D1
Bronte Paths. Stev 51 E3
Brook Dri. Radl 155 F3
Brook Dri. Stev 69 D4
Brook End. Saw 97 E1
Brook Field. Ast 51 F1
Brook La. Berk 122 A3
Brook La. Saw 97 E1
Brook Rd. Bor 170 A4
Brook Rd. Ches 162 C3
Brook Rd. Saw 97 F1
Brook Rd. Sta Mo 59 F3
Brook St. Luton 63 E4
Brook St. Stot 11 F3
Brook St. Tri 100 A2
Brook View. Hit 35 E3
Brookbridge La. Dat 69 E1
Brookdene Ave. Watf 167 E1
Brookdene Dri. Norwd 174 C2
Brooke Cl. Bus 168 B1
Brooke Rd. Roystn 7 E4
Brooke Way. Bus 168 B1
Brooker Rd. Wa Aby 163 E3
Brookfield Cl. Tri 100 A2
Brookfield Gdns. Ches 148 B2
Brookfield La. Ast 51 F2
Brookfield La E. Ches 148 B2
Brookfield La W. Ches 148 B2
Brookfields. Saw 97 E1
Brookhill. Stev 68 C4
Brooklands Cl. Luton 44 B3
Brooklands Gdns. Pot B 158 C4
Brookmans Ave. Bro Pk 144 C3
Brooksfield. Wel GC 111 D4
Brookshill. Har 176 B3
Brookshill Ave. Har 176 C3
Brookshill Dri. Har 176 B3
Brookside. Hat 129 E3
Brookside. Hert 113 F3
Brookside. Hod 135 D3
Brookside. Letw 22 C3
Brookside. Pot B 158 A4
Brookside. Wa Aby 163 F4
Brookside. Watf 167 D1
Brookside Cl. Barn 171 F2
Brookside Cres. Cuf 146 C2
Brookside Gdns. Enf 162 B1
Broom Cl. Ham St 148 A2
Broom Cl. Hat 129 F1
Broom Gr. Kneb 68 C3
Broom Gr. Watf 154 A1
Broom Hill. Heml H 123 F1
Broom Hill. Wl Gr 90 A4
Broom Wlk. Stev 50 C3
Broomer Pl. Ches 148 B1
Broomfield. Chis 141 E2
Broomfield. Harl 118 A2
Broomfield Ave. Ches 148 C3
Broomfield Cl. Welw 89 E2
Broomfield Rd. Welw 89 E2
Broomfield Rise. Abb L 153 E4
Broomhills. Wel GC 111 D4
Broomleys. St Alb 128 B3
Brooms Cl. Wel GC 89 E1
Brooms Rd. Luton 64 A4
Broomstick Hall Rd. Wa Aby 163 F3
Broomstick La. Bot 136 A1
Broughinge Rd. Bor 170 A4
Broughton Ave. Luton 45 E3
Broughton Hill. Letw 23 D3
Brow The. Watf 154 A3
Brownfield Way. Bla En 87 D3
Brownfields. Wel GC 110 C4
Browning Dri. Hit 35 D4
Browning Rd. Enf 161 E1
Browning Rd. Harp 86 B1
Browning Rd. Luton 44 A1
Brownlow La. Ched 80 A4
Brownlow Rd. Berk 122 B3
Brownlow Rd. Bor 170 A3
Brown's Cl. Luton 44 B3
Brown's Rise. Buc Co 119 F2
Browns Spr. Heml H 123 E4
Brox Dell. Stev 50 C3
Broxley Mead. Luton 44 B3
Bruce Grove. Watf 154 B1
Bruce Rd. Barn 171 F3
Bruce Rd. Har 176 C1
Bruce Way. Ches 162 B3
Brunel Rd. Stev 51 D4
Brunswick St. Luton 63 F4
Brushrise. Watf 154 A2
Brushwood Dri. Chor 164 B3
Brussels Way. Luton 44 B4
Bryan Rd. Bis St 76 C4
Bryanstone Rd. Ches 162 C3
Bryant Cl. Barn 171 F2
Bryant Ct. Harp 86 A2
Bryce Cl. Ware 93 E2
Buchanan Ct. Bor 170 B4
Buchanan Dri. Luton 64 A4
Buckettsland. Shen 157 E1
Buckettsland La. Ridge 157 F1
Buckingham Dri. Luton 46 B1
Buckingham Rd. Bor 170 B3
Buckingham Rd. Tri 99 F2
Buckingham Rd. Watf 154 B1
Buckland Rd. Dra B 99 D2
Buckland Rise. Pnr 175 E1
Bucklands The. Ric 165 D1
Buckle Cl. Luton 44 C4
Bucklers Cl. Hod 134 C1
Bucklersbury. Hit 34 C3
Bucknalls Cl. Watf 154 C4
Bucknalls Dri. Bri Wd 154 C4
Bucknalls La. Watf 154 C4
Bucks Alley. L Berk 132 B2
Bucks Ave. Watf 167 F1
Bucks Hill. Sar 152 B3
Buckthorn Ave. Stev 50 C2
Buckton Rd. Bor 156 C1
Buckwood La. Stu 82 B4
Buckwood Rd. Mark 83 E3
Buddcroft. Wel GC 111 D4
Bude Cres. Stev 50 A4
Bulbourne Cl. Berk 121 F3
Bulbourne Cl. Heml H 124 A1
Bulbourne Rd. Tri 100 B4
Bull La. Buck 27 E4
Bull La. Whea 108 A3
Bull Plain. Hert 113 E3
Bull Stag Green. Hat 130 B4

Bullace Cl. Heml H 124 A2
Bullbeggars La. Pot En 123 D2
Bullen's Green La. Coln H 143 F4
Bullfields. Saw 97 F2
Bullhead Rd. Bor 170 B3
Bullock's Hill. St P W 49 D1
Bullock's La. Hert 113 E2
Bullrush Cl. Hat 130 A2
Bull's Cross. Enf 162 A2
Bulls Cross Ride. Ches 162 C4
Bulls La. Wel Gr 144 C4
Bullsland Gdns. Chor 164 A2
Bullsland La. Chor 164 A2
Bullsmoor Cl. Enf 162 B2
Bullsmoor Gdns. Enf 162 A2
Bullsmoor La. Enf 162 B2
Bullsmoor Ride. Enf 162 B2
Bullsmoor Way. Enf 162 B2
Bullwell Cres. Ches 148 C1
Bulstrode La. Chipf 138 A3
Bulwer Link. Stev 50 C2
Buncefield La. Heml H 125 E3
Bungalows The. Harp 86 B2
Bunkers La. Heml H 139 D4
Bunnsfield. Wel GC 111 E4
Bunstrux. Tri 100 A2
Bunting Rd. Luton 44 A2
Buntingford Rd. Puc 55 E2
Bunyan Cl. Pirt 20 B2
Bunyan Cl. Tri 100 A3
Bunyan Rd. Hit 34 C4
Bunyans Cl. Luton 45 D3
Burbage Cl. Ches 162 C4
Burchell Ct. Bus 168 B1
Burfield Cl. Hat 130 A4
Burfield Rd. Chor 164 B2
Burford Cl. Luton 31 D1
Burford St. Hod 135 D3
Burford Way. Hit 21 E1
Burfordstreet. Hod 135 D4
Burge End La. Pirt 20 B3
Burghley Ave. Bor 170 B2
Burghley Cl. Stev 69 D4
Burgoyne Hatch. Harl 118 A1
Burgundy Croft. Wel GC 110 C2
Burhill Gr. Pnr 175 F1
Burleigh Mead. Hat 130 B4
Burleigh Rd. Ches 162 C4
Burleigh Rd. Heml H 125 E1
Burleigh Rd. Hert 114 A4
Burleigh Rd. St Alb 128 A2
Burleigh Way. Cuf 146 C1
Burley. Letw 11 F1
Burley Rd. Bis St 77 D2
Burnell Rise. Letw 22 C3
Burnell Wlk. Letw 22 C3
Burnells Way. Sta Mo 59 F4
Burnet Cl. Heml H 124 C1
Burnett Ave. Henlw 10 A2
Burnett Sq. Hertng 112 C4
Burnham Cl. Enf 161 F1
Burnham Green Rd. Brn Gr 90 B3
Burnham Rd. Luton 46 A1
Burnham Rd. St Alb 128 A2
Burnley Cl. Sth Ox 175 E3
Burns Cl. Hit 35 D4
Burns Cl. Stev 51 E4
Burns Dri. Heml H 105 D1
Burns Rd. Roystn 7 E4
Burnsall Pl. Harp 107 E3
Burnside. Hertng 113 D3
Burnside. Hod 134 C3
Burnside. Saw 97 E1
Burnside Cl. Hat 130 A4
Burnside Terr. Harl 118 C2
Burnt Cl. Luton 44 C4
Burntfarm Ride. Ches 161 D4
Burntfarm Ride. Enf 161 D3
Burntmill Cl. Harl 117 E2
Burntmill La. H Wy 117 E2
Burr Cl. Lon C 142 C2
Burr St. Luton 63 F4
Burrowfield. Wel GC 110 B2
Burrs La. Bark 17 E2
Burr's Pl. Luton 63 F4
Bursland. Letw 22 B3
Burston Dri. Chis 141 E2
Burton Ave. Watf 167 D3
Burton Cl. Bla En 87 E3
Burton La. Gofs O 147 F2
Burtons Mill. Saw 97 F2
Burwell Rd. Stev 51 E2
Bury End. Pirt 20 B2
Bury Green. Heml H 124 B2
Bury Green. Whea 108 B4
Bury Green Rd. Ches 148 A1
Bury Hill. Heml H 124 B2
Bury Hill Cl. Heml H 124 B2
Bury Holme. Hod 148 C4
Bury La. Bram 91 D2
Bury La. Cod 67 F1
Bury La. Dat 69 E2
Bury La. Ric 165 E1
Bury La. Str 31 D3
Bury Mead. Ch En 11 D4
Bury Mead Rd. Hit 21 F1
Bury Meadows. Ric 165 E1
Bury Park Rd. Luton 63 E4
Bury Plntn. Roystn 7 F3
Bury Rd. Harl 118 B2
Bury Rd. Hat 130 B3
Bury Rd. Heml H 124 B2
Bury Rise. Fel 137 E3
Burycroft. Wel GC 89 F1
Burydale. Stev 69 D4
Burydell La. Pk St 141 E3
Burymead. Stev 36 B1
Burywick. Harp 107 D3
Bush Hall La. Hat 130 B4
Bush Spring. Bal 13 D1
Bushbarns. Ches 148 A1
Bushby Ave. Hod 134 C1
Bushel Wharf. Tri 100 A3
Bushell Green. Bus 176 B4
Bushey Cl. Wel GC 111 D3
Bushey Green. Wel GC 111 D3
Bushey Grove Rd. Bus 167 F3
Bushey Hall Dri. Bus 167 F3
Bushey Hall Rd. Bus 167 F3
Bushey Ley. Wel GC 111 D3
Bushey Mill Cres. Watf 154 B1
Bushey Mill La. Bus 167 F4
Bushey Mill La. Watf 154 B1
Bushfield Rd. Bov 137 E3
Bushmead Rd. Luton 45 F3
Bushwood Cl. Wel Gr 144 A4
Butcher's La. Hit 34 C3
Butcher's La. Pres 48 B3
Bute St. Luton 63 F4
Butely Rd. Luton 44 A3
Butlers Dri. Wa Aby 163 E1
Butlin Rd. Luton 63 D4
Butt Field View. St Alb 141 E4
Butterfield Green Rd. Luton 46 A3
Butterfield La. St Alb 141 F4
Butterfield Rd. Whea 108 B4
Butterfly La. Elst 169 D4
Buttersweet Rise. Saw 97 F1
Butterwick. Watf 154 C2
Buttlehide. Map Cr 172 B3
Buttondene Cres. Lo Naz 135 D1
Butts End. Heml H 124 A3
Butts The. Hod 148 C4
Buttsmead. Norwd 174 B2
Buxton Cl. St Alb 128 B3
Buxton La. Gu M 1 C2
Buxton Path. Sth Ox 175 E4
Buxton Rd. Luton 63 E4
Buzzard Rd. Luton 44 A2
By The Mount. Wel GC 110 B3
Byde St. Hert 113 E4
Bye Way The. Har 176 C1
Byers Cl. Pot B 159 E3
Byeway The. Ric 173 F4
Byfield. Wel GC 89 F1
Byfield Cl. Luton 44 A1
Bygrave Rd. Bal 12 C1
Bylands Cl. Bis St 76 B3
Byng Dri. Pot B 159 D4
Byng Rd. Barn 171 E3
Byrd Wlk. Bal 24 A4
Byron Ave. Bor 170 A2
Byron Ave. Watf 167 E4
Byron Cl. Hit 35 D4
Byron Cl. Stev 51 E4
Byron Pl. Heml H 105 D1
Byron Rd. Har 176 C1
Byron Rd. Harp 86 A1
Byron Rd. Luton 44 A1
Byron Rd. Roystn 7 F4
Byslips Rd. Stu 82 C3
By-The-Wood. Watf 175 F4
Byway The. Pot B 159 D3

Caddington Comm. Cad 83 F4
Caddis Cl. Stan 176 C2
Cade Cl. Letw 12 B1
Cades Cl. Luton 63 D3
Cades La. Luton 63 D3
Cadmore La. Ches 148 C1
Cadwell La. Hit 21 F1
Caernarvon Cl. Heml H 124 B2
Caernarvon Cl. Stev 69 D4
Caesars Rd. Whea 108 C4
Cage Pond Rd. Shen 156 C3
Cairn Way. Stan 176 C2
Caishowe Rd. Bor 170 A4
Caistor Cl. Stev 36 A1
Caldbeck. Wa Aby 163 E3
Caldecot Way. Hod 134 C1
Caldecote Gdns. Bus 168 C1
Caldecote La. Bus 168 C2
Caldecote Rd. Newn 12 C4
Calder Ave. Bro Pk 145 D3
Caldercote Rd. Cal 3 E1
Caldwell Rd. Sth Ox 175 E3
Caleb Cl. Luton 44 C1
Caledon Rd. Lon C 142 B3
California. Bal 12 C1
California La. Bus 168 B1
Callisto Ct. Heml H 124 C3
Calnwood Rd. Luton 44 A1
Calton Ave. Hertng 112 C4
Calton Ct. Hertng 112 C3
Calverley Cl. Bis St 76 C2
Calvert Rd. Barn 171 F4
Calverton Rd. Luton 45 D3
Camberley Pl. Harp 107 E3
Camborne Dri. Heml H 124 C4
Cambrian Way. Heml H 124 C3
Cambridge Cl. Ches 148 B1
Cambridge Cres. Knee 2 A4
Cambridge Dri. Pot B 158 C4
Cambridge Rd. Bar 17 F4
Cambridge Rd. Bark 17 F3
Cambridge Rd. Harl 118 B3
Cambridge Rd. Hit 22 B1
Cambridge Rd. Puc 55 E1
Cambridge Rd. Saw 97 F2
Cambridge Rd. St Alb 128 A1
Cambridge Rd. Sta Mo 59 F4
Cambridge Rd. Watf 167 E3
Cambridge St. Luton 63 F3
Cambridge Terr. Berk 122 B2
Cameron Dri. Ches 162 B3
Camfield. Wel GC 110 C1
Camford Way. Luton 44 A4
Camlet Way. Barn 159 E1
Camlet Way. St Alb 127 D2
Camp Rd. St Alb 128 A1
Camp View Rd. St Alb 128 A1
Campania Gr. Luton 45 D4
Campbell Cl. Hit 35 D4
Campers Ave. Letw 22 C3
Campers Rd. Letw 22 C3
Campers Wlk. Letw 22 C3
Campfield Rd. Hertng 113 D3
Campfield Rd. St Alb 128 A2
Campfield Way. Letw 22 B3
Campine Cl. Ches 148 B2
Campion Cl. Watf 154 A3
Campion Ct. Stev 50 B4
Campion Way. Roystn 7 F3
Campions Cl. Bor 157 D1
Campions The. Bor 157 D1
Campions The. Sta Mo 59 F4
Campkin Mead. Stev 51 E2
Campus The. Wel GC 110 B4
Canada La. Ches 148 C3
Canadas The. Ches 148 C3
Canberra Cl. Knee 2 A3
Canberra Cl. St Alb 127 F4
Canberra Gdns. Luton 45 D3
Candlefield Cl. Heml H 139 D4
Candlefield Rd. Heml H 139 D4
Candlefield Wlk. Heml H 139 D4
Caneland Ct. Wa Aby 163 F3
Canfield. Bis St 76 C4
Cangels Cl. Heml H 124 A1
Canham Cl. Kim 66 B1
Cannix Cl. Stev 51 D1
Cannon La. Luton 46 A3
Cannon Rd. Watf 167 E2
Cannon St. St Alb 127 E2
Cannons Cl. Bis St 59 D1
Cannon's Cl. Gu M 1 C3
Cannons Mead. Sta Mo 59 E4
Cannons Meadow. Tewin 90 C1
Cannons Mill La. Bis St 59 D1
Canons Cl. Radl 156 A2
Canons Field. Whea 87 E1
Canons Field. Wl Gr 89 F4
Canons Gate. Harl 117 D1
Canons Rd. Ware 93 E1
Canonsfield Rd. Wl Gr 89 F4
Canopus Way. Norwd 175 D3
Canterbury Cl. Luton 44 C2
Canterbury Cl. Norwd 174 C2
Canterbury Ct. St Alb 127 F2
Canterbury Rd. Bor 170 A4
Canterbury Rd. Watf 167 D4
Canterbury Way. Cro Gr 166 B3
Canterbury Way. Stev 36 C1
Cape Rd. St Alb 128 A2
Capel Rd. Enf 162 A2
Capel Rd. Watf 167 F2
Capell Ave. Chor 164 B2
Capell Rd. Chor 164 B2
Capell Way. Chor 164 B2
Capella Rd. Norwd 174 C3
Capelvere Wlk. Watf 166 C4
Caponfield. Wel GC 111 D2
Cappell La. Sta Ab 115 E3
Capron Rd. Luton 44 C2
Captains Wlk. Berk 122 B2
Caractacus Cottage View. Watf 167 D2
Caractacus Green. Watf 166 C2
Caravan La. Ric 165 F1
Carbone Hill. Cuf 146 B3
Carde Cl. Hertng 112 C4
Cardiff Gr. Luton 63 E4
Cardiff Pl. Knee 2 A4
Cardiff Rd. Luton 63 E4
Cardiff Rd. Watf 167 D2
Cardigan St. Luton 63 E4
Cardinal Ave. Bor 170 A3
Cardinal Cl. Ham St 147 F3
Cardinal Gr. St Alb 127 D1
Cardy Rd. Heml H 124 A2
Carew Rd. Norwd 174 C2
Carey Pl. Watf 167 E3
Careys Croft. Nthch 121 F4
Carisbrook. Chis 141 D3
Carisbrook Rd. Luton 44 C1
Carisbrooke Ave. Watf 167 E4
Carisbrooke Rd. Harp 86 B1
Carleton Rd. Ches 148 C2
Carleton Rise. Welw 89 E3
Carlisle Ave. St Alb 127 E2
Carlton Cl. Bor 170 B3
Carlton Cl. Luton 45 E1
Carlton Cres. Luton 45 E2
Carlton Rd. Harp 86 A1
Carmelite Cl. Har 176 B1
Carmelite Rd. Har 176 B1
Carmelite Rd. Luton 44 A2
Carmelite Way. Har 176 B1
Carmelite Wlk. Har 176 B1
Carnaby Rd. Hod 134 C2
Carnarvon Rd. Barn 171 F3
Carnecie Rd. St Alb 127 E4
Carnegie Gdns. Luton 45 D4
Caro La. Heml H 125 D1
Carol Cl. Luton 45 D2
Caroline Pl. Watf 167 F2
Carpenders Ave. Watf 175 F4
Carpenders Cl. Harp 85 E2
Carpenter Way. Pot B 159 E3
Carpenters Rd. Enf 162 B2
Carpenters Wood Dri. Chor 164 A3
Carpenters Yd. Tri 100 A2
Carrigans. Bis St 76 C4
Carrington Ave. Bor 170 A2
Carrington Cl. Barn 171 D2
Carrington Cl. Bor 170 B2
Carrington Pl. Tri 100 A3
Carrington Sq. Har 176 B2
Carsdale Cl. Luton 45 D3
Cart Path. Watf 154 B3
Carteret Rd. Luton 46 B1
Carterhatch La. Enf 161 F1
Carters Cl. Ch En 11 D4
Carters Cl. Stev 51 E2
Carters Leys. Bis St 76 B4
Carters Way. Ch En 11 D4
Carters Wlk. Ch En 11 D4
Cartersfield Rd. Wa Aby 163 E3
Carthagena Estate. Lo Naz 135 E2
Cartwright Rd. Roystn 7 E3
Cartwright Rd. Stev 37 E1
Carve Ley. Wel GC 111 D3
Cashio La. Letw 23 D4
Caslon Way. Letw 11 F1
Cassio Rd. Watf 167 D3
Cassiobridge Rd. Watf 166 C3
Cassiobury Dri. Watf 166 C4
Cassiobury Park Ave. Watf 180 C3
Castano Ct. Abb L 153 F4
Castellane Cl. Stan 176 C2
Castle Cl. Bus 168 A2
Castle Cl. Hod 115 E1
Castle Croft Rd. Luton 63 D3
Castle Gate Way. Berk 122 B3
Castle Hill. Berk 122 B3
Castle Hill Ave. Berk 122 B3
Castle Mead. Heml H 124 A1
Castle Mens. Berk 122 B2
Castle Rd. Enf 162 C1
Castle Rd. Hod 115 E1
Castle Rd. St Alb 128 A2
Castle Rise. Bla En 86 C1
Castle St. Berk 122 B2
Castle St. Bis St 76 C3
Castle St. Hert 113 E3
Castle St. Luton 63 F3
Castle St. Wing 60 A2
Castles' Cl. Stot 11 F4
Caterham Ct. Wa Aby 163 F3
Catesby Green. Luton 31 D1
Catham Cl. St Alb 128 A1
Cathedral Ct. St Alb 127 D1
Catherall Rd. Luton 45 D3
Catherine Cl. Heml H 125 D4
Catherine Rd. Enf 162 C2
Catherine St. St Alb 127 E2
Catisfield Rd. Enf 162 C1
Catkin Cl. Heml H 124 A2
Catlin St. Heml H 138 A4
Catsbrook Rd. Luton 45 D3
Catsdell Bottom. Heml H 139 E4
Catsey La. Bus 168 B1
Catsey Wood. Bus 168 B1
Catterick Way. Bor 169 F4
Cattlegate Hill. Nort 160 B4
Cattlegate Rd. Enf 160 B3
Cattsdell. Heml H 124 C3
Causeway Cl. Pot B 159 E4
Causeway The. Bis St 76 C4
Causeway The. Bre P 30 A1
Causeway The. Bun 40 C4
Causeway The. Fur P 43 D2
Causeway The. Knee 2 A3
Causeway The. P Bar 159 E4
Causeway The. Ther 15 F4
Cautherly La. Gt Am 115 D3
Cavan Dri. St Alb 127 E4
Cavan Rd. Red 106 A3
Cavell Rd. Ham St 148 A2
Cavell Wlk. Stev 51 E3
Cavendish Cres. Bor 170 A3
Cavendish Ct. Cro Gr 166 B2
Cavendish Rd. Barn 171 E3
Cavendish Rd. Luton 45 D1
Cavendish Rd. Mark 83 E3
Cavendish Rd. St Alb 127 F2
Cavendish Rd. Stev 50 A3
Cavendish Way. Hat 129 F3
Cawkell Cl. Sta Mo 59 E4
Caxton Hill. Hert 113 F3
Caxton Rd. Hod 115 D1
Caxton Way. Stev 50 A2
Caxton Way. Watf 166 B2
Cecil Cl. Bis St 77 E4
Cecil Cres. Hat 130 A4
Cecil Ct. Barn 171 E3
Cecil Rd. Ches 162 C4
Cecil Rd. Hert 113 E2
Cecil Rd. Hod 135 E4
Cecil Rd. Pot B 158 A4
Cecil Rd. St Alb 127 F2
Cecil St. Watf 154 A1
Cedar Ave. Ches 162 B3
Cedar Ave. Ick 21 F2
Cedar Cl. Gt Am 114 B4
Cedar Cl. Hert 113 D3
Cedar Cl. Pot B 145 D1
Cedar Cl. Saw 97 F1
Cedar Cres. Roystn 7 D3
Cedar Ct. St Alb 128 B2
Cedar Dri. Pnr 176 A2
Cedar Green. Hod 135 D3
Cedar Lawn Ave. Barn 171 F2
Cedar Park. Bis St 76 B2
Cedar Park Rd. Enf 161 E1
Cedar Pl. Norwd 174 B2
Cedar Rd. Berk 122 C2
Cedar Rd. Enf 161 E1
Cedar Rd. Hat 130 A2
Cedar Rd. Watf 167 E2
Cedar Way. Berk 122 B2
Cedar Wlk. Heml H 124 B1
Cedar Wlk. Wa Aby 163 E3
Cedars Ave. Ric 165 E1
Cedars Cl. Bor 170 A3
Cedars The. Harp 86 A1
Cedarwood Dri. St Alb 128 B2
Celandine Dri. Luton 45 D4
Cell Barnes Cl. St Alb 128 A1
Cell Barnes La. St Alb 128 A1
Cemetery Hill. Heml H 124 B1
Cemetery Rd. Bis St 76 C3
Cemmaes Court Rd. Heml H 124 B2
Cemmaes Meadow. Heml H 124 B2
Central App. Letw 22 C3
Central Ave. Ches 162 C3
Central Ave. Harl 117 E1
Central Ave. Henlw 10 A2
Central Dri. St Alb 128 B2
Central Rd. Harl 118 A2
Central Way. Norwd 174 C2
Centre Way. Wa Aby 163 E2
Century Rd. Hod 135 D4
Century Rd. Ware 93 E1
Cervantes Ct. Norwd 174 C2
Chace Ave. Pot B 159 E4
Chace The. Stev 50 C1
Chad La. Fla 84 B2
Chadwell. Gt Am 114 A4
Chadwell Ave. Ches 148 B2
Chadwell Cl. Luton 45 F1
Chadwell Rd. Stev 50 A2
Chadwell Rise. Gt Am 114 A4
Chaffinch La. Watf 166 C1
Chaffinches Green. Heml H 139 D4
Chagney Cl. Letw 22 C3
Chalet Cl. Berk 121 F2
Chalfont Cl. Heml H 125 D4
Chalfont La. Chor 164 A2
Chalfont La. Map Cr 172 B2
Chalfont Pl. St Alb 127 F2
Chalfont Rd. Map Cr 172 B4
Chalfont Way. Luton 46 B1
Chalfont Wlk. Pnr 175 E1
Chalk Dale. Wel GC 111 D4
Chalk Hill. Cok Gr 47 D3
Chalk Hill. Watf 167 F2
Chalk Hills. Bal 23 F3
Chalkdell Fields. St Alb 128 A4
Chalkdell Path. Hit 34 B4
Chalkdown. Stev 51 E4
Chalkfield. Letw 23 E2
Chalks Ave. Saw 97 E2
Challney Cl. Luton 44 B1
Chalton Rd. Luton 44 B3
Chamberlaines. Kin Gr 85 D2
Chambers La. Ick 21 F2
Chambers' St. Hert 113 E3
Chambersbury La. Heml H 139 D4
Champions Green. Hod 115 D1
Champions Way. Hod 115 D1
Chancellors Rd. Stev 36 B1
Chancery Cl. St Alb 128 B4
Chandlers La. Cha Cr 152 C1
Chandlers Rd. St Alb 128 B3
Chandlers Way. Hertng 113 D3
Chandos Cl. L Chal 150 B1
Chandos Rd. Bor 170 A4
Chandos Rd. Luton 44 C1
Chantry Cl. Bis St 76 C4
Chantry Cl. Enf 161 E1
Chantry Cl. Kin L 139 D1
Chantry La. Hat 130 A2
Chantry La. Hat 129 F2
Chantry La. Lon C 142 B3
Chantry Pl. Har 176 A1
Chantry Rd. Bis St 76 C4
Chantry Rd. Har 176 A1
Chantry The. Harl 118 A1
Chaomans. Letw 22 C2
Chapel Cl. L Gad 102 B3
Chapel Cl. Luton 45 E4
Chapel Cl. Watf 153 F3
Chapel Cotts. Heml H 124 B3
Chapel Croft. Chipf 152 A4
Chapel Croft. Nthch 121 F3
Chapel End. Bun 40 C4
Chapel End. Hod 135 D3
Chapel End La. Wils 99 E4
Chapel Hill. Sta Mo 59 F3
Chapel La. L Had 75 D4
Chapel La. Let Gr 112 A2
Chapel La. Lon M 79 D2
Chapel Pl. Stot 11 F3
Chapel Rd. Bre Gr 65 F4
Chapel Rd. Fla 84 A1
Chapel Row. Bis St 76 C3
Chapel Row. Hare 173 E1
Chapel St. Berk 122 B2
Chapel St. Heml H 124 B2
Chapel St. Hin 3 E3
Chapel St. Luton 63 F3
Chapel St. Tri 99 F2
Chapel Viaduct. Luton 63 F4
Chapelfields. Sta Ab 115 E2
Chapman Rd. Stev 36 A1
Chapmans End. Puc 55 E2
Chapmans Yd. Watf 167 E3
Chapter House Rd. Luton 44 A2
Chard Dri. Luton 31 D1
Chardins Cl. Heml H 123 F2
Charles St. Berk 122 A2
Charles St. Heml H 124 B1
Charles St. Luton 63 F4
Charles St. Tri 100 A2
Charlesworth Cl. Heml H 124 B1
Charlock Way. Watf 166 C2
Charlton Mead La. Hod 135 E3
Charlton Rd. Hit 34 B3
Charlton Way. Hod 135 D3
Charlwood Cl. Har 176 B2
Charlwood Rd. Luton 44 A1
Charmouth Ct. St Alb 128 A3
Charmouth Rd. St Alb 128 A3
Charnwood Rd. Enf 162 A2
Chartley Ave. Stan 176 C2

Chartridge Cl. Barn 171 D2
Chartridge Way. Heml H 125 E2
Chartwell Cl. Wa Aby 163 F3
Chartwell Dri. Luton 45 F2
Chartwell Rd. Norwd 174 C2
Chasden Rd. Heml H 123 F3
Chase Cl. Ch En 11 D4
Chase Hill Rd. Ch En 11 D4
Chase St. Luton 63 F3
Chase The. Bis St 76 C3
Chase The. Gofs O 147 D2
Chase The. Heml H 124 C1
Chase The. Radl 155 F2
Chase The. Watf 166 C3
Chase The. Wl Gr 89 F4
Chaseside Cl. Ched 80 A4
Chaseways. Saw 118 B4
Chatsworth Cl. Bor 170 A3
Chatsworth Ct. Stev 51 D1
Chatsworth Rd. Luton 45 D1
Chatteris Cl. Luton 44 B2
Chatterton. Letw 23 D3
Chatton Cl. Luton 46 C1
Chaucer Cl. Berk 121 F3
Chaucer Rd. Luton 45 E1
Chaucer Rd. Roystn 7 E4
Chaucer Way. Hit 35 E4
Chaucer Wlk. Heml H 105 D1
Chaul End La. Luton 44 C1
Chaul End Rd. Cad 44 A1
Chaul End Rd. Cad 62 B3
Chaulden House Gdns. Heml H 123 F1
Chaulden La. Heml H 123 F1
Chaulden Terr. Heml H 123 F1
Chauncy Ave. Pot B 159 E3
Chauncy Cl. Ware 93 E2
Chauncy Gdns. Clo 13 D1
Chauncy Rd. Stev 50 C3
Chaworth Green. Luton 44 B3
Cheapside. Luton 63 F4
Chedburgh. Wel GC 111 E4
Cheddington La. Lon M 79 E3
Cheddington Rd. Pit 80 B2
Cheffins Rd. Hod 114 C1
Chells La. Stev 51 E4
Chells Way. Stev 51 E3
Chelmsford Rd. Hertng 113 D3
Chelsing Rise. Heml H 125 E1
Chelsworth Cl. Luton 46 B1
Chelveston. Wel GC 111 E4
Chelwood Ave. Hat 130 A4
Chelwood Cl. Norwd 174 B2
Chenduit Way. Stan 176 C3
Cheney Rd. Luton 44 B3
Chenies Ave. L Chal 150 B1
Chenies Ct. Heml H 125 D4
Chenies Green. Bis St 76 B3
Chenies Rd. Chor 164 B4
Chennells. Hat 129 F2
Chequer La. Red 106 A2
Chequer St. Luton 63 F3
Chequer St. St Alb 127 E2
Chequers. Bis St 76 B4
Chequers. Hat 130 B4
Chequers. Wel GC 110 B2
Chequers Bridge Rd. Stev 50 B3
Chequers Cl. Bun 40 B4
Chequers Cl. Pit 80 B2
Chequers Cl. Stot 12 A3
Chequers Field. Wel GC 110 B2
Chequers Hill. Fla 84 B1
Chequers La. Abb L 140 B1
Chequers La. Pit 80 B3
Chequers La. Pres 48 B4
Chequers Wlk. Wa Aby 163 F3
Cheriton Cl. St Alb 128 B4
Cherry Bounce. Heml H 124 B3
Cherry Cl. Kneb 68 C2
Cherry Croft. Wel GC 89 E1
Cherry Croft Gdns. Pnr 175 F2
Cherry Dri. Roystn 7 F4
Cherry Gdns. Bis St 77 D4
Cherry Gdns. Saw 97 F2
Cherry Gdns. Tri 99 F2
Cherry Hill. Chis 141 D3
Cherry Hill. Chor 165 D3
Cherry Orch. Heml H 124 A3
Cherry Rd. Enf 162 B1
Cherry Tree Ave. Lon C 142 B3
Cherry Tree Cl. Arl 11 D2
Cherry Tree Cl. Luton 46 A1
Cherry Tree Green. Hertng 112 C4
Cherry Tree La. Buc Co 120 A2
Cherry Tree La. Harp 87 D1
Cherry Tree La. Heron 164 B1
Cherry Tree La. Pot B 159 D3
Cherry Tree Rd. Hod 135 D4
Cherry Tree Rd. Watf 154 A2
Cherry Tree Rise. Wal 38 A1
Cherry Trees. Henlw 10 A2
Cherry Way. Hat 130 A1
Cherry Wlk. Chor 165 E4
Cherrydale. Watf 166 C3
Cherrytree La. Heml H 125 E4
Chertsey Cl. Luton 64 B4
Chertsey Rise. Stev 51 E2
Cherwell Cl. Cro Gr 166 A2
Chesfield Cl. Bis St 76 C3
Chesford Rd. Luton 46 B2
Chesham Ct. Norwd 174 C2
Chesham Rd. Ash Gr 121 F1
Chesham Rd. Berk 122 A1
Chesham Rd. Bov 136 C2
Chesham Rd. Wigg 120 C4
Chesham Way. Watf 166 C2
Chess Cl. Chor 165 E3
Chess Cl. Lat 150 B2
Chess Hill. Chor 165 E3
Chess La. Chor 165 E3
Chess Vale Rise. Cro Gr 165 F2
Chess Way. Chor 165 D3
Chesswood Way. Pnr 175 E1
Chester Ave. Luton 44 C2
Chester Cl. Luton 44 C1
Chester Rd. Bor 170 B3
Chester Rd. Norwd 174 C2
Chester Rd. Stev 37 D1
Chester Rd. Watf 167 D3
Chesterfield Rd. Barn 171 E2
Chesterfield Rd. Enf 162 C1
Chesterton Ave. Harp 86 B1
Chestnut Ave. Chor 165 D2
Chestnut Ave. Henlw 10 B2
Chestnut Ave. Luton 44 B4
Chestnut Ave. Norwd 174 C1
Chestnut Ave. Ware 93 F2
Chestnut Cl. Bis St 76 C3
Chestnut Cl. Dagn 81 E3
Chestnut Cl. Pot En 123 D3
Chestnut Dri. Berk 122 B2
Chestnut Dri. Har 176 C1
Chestnut Dri. St Alb 128 B3
Chestnut La. Knee 2 A3
Chestnut La. N20 171 F1
Chestnut Rd. Enf 162 C2
Chestnut Rise. Bus 168 A1
Chestnut Wash. Ches 148 C2
Chestnut Wlk. Roystn 7 F3
Chestnut Wlk. Stev 36 B1
Chestnut Wlk. Watf 154 A1
Chestnut Wlk. Wl Gr 89 F4
Chestnuts The. Cod 67 F1
Chestnuts The. Fel 137 F4
Chestnuts The. Hert 113 E3
Cheverells Cl. Mark 83 E2
Cheverells Green. Mark 83 E2
Cheviot Cl. Bus 168 B2
Cheviot Cl. Luton 44 B4
Cheviot Rd. Luton 44 B4
Cheviots. Hat 130 A2
Cheviots. Heml H 124 C3
Cheyne Cl. Pit 80 B2
Cheyne Cl. Ware 93 E2
Chicheley Gdns. Har 176 B2
Chicheley Rd. Har 176 B2
Chichester Way. Watf 154 C3
Chigwell Hurst Ct. Pnr 175 E1
Chilcott Rd. Watf 153 F2
Chilcourt. Roystn 7 E3
Childwick Ct. Heml H 139 D4
Chiltern Ave. Bus 168 B2
Chiltern Cl. Berk 122 A3
Chiltern Cl. Bor 169 F4
Chiltern Cl. Bus 168 A2
Chiltern Cl. Gofs O 147 D2
Chiltern Cl. Ware 93 E2
Chiltern Ct. Harp 86 A1
Chiltern Dri. Ric 165 D1
Chiltern Gdns. Luton 44 C2
Chiltern Park Ave. Berk 122 A3
Chiltern Rd. Bal 23 F3
Chiltern Rd. Hit 35 D4
Chiltern Rd. St Alb 128 B4
Chiltern Rd. Wing 60 A2
Chiltern Rise. Luton 63 E3
Chiltern View. Letw 22 B3
Chiltern Way. Tri 100 B3
Chilterns. Hat 130 A1
Chilterns. Heml H 124 C3
Chilterns The. Hit 35 D3
Chilterns The. Ken Co 82 C4
Chilton Green. Wel GC 111 E3
Chilvers Bank. Bal 23 F4
Chilwell Gdns. Sth Ox 175 E3
Chinnery Hill. Bis St 76 C3
Chipperfield Rd. Bov 137 E2
Chipperfield Rd. Fel 138 B4
Chipperfield Rd. Kin L 138 B1
Chippingfield. Harl 118 B2
Chishill Rd. Bar 9 D1
Chiswellgreen La. Chis 140 C3
Chobham St. Luton 63 F3
Chobham Wlk. Luton 63 F3
Cholesbury La. Buc Co 120 A1
Cholwell Rd. Stev 51 E2
Chorleywood Bottom. Chor 164 B2
Chorleywood Cl. Ric 165 E1
Chorleywood Rd. Chor 165 D3
Chorleywood Rd. Ric 165 E2
Chouler Gdns. Stev 36 B1
Christ Church La. Barn 171 F4
Christ Church Pas. Barn 171 F4
Christchurch Cl. St Alb 127 E2
Christchurch Cres. Radl 156 A2
Christchurch Pl. Hert 113 E3
Christchurch Rd. Heml H 124 B2
Christchurch Rd. Tri 99 F2
Christie Rd. Stev 51 E3
Christopher Ct. Heml H 138 B4
Christopher Pl. St Alb 127 E2
Church Cl. Cod 67 F1
Church Cl. Cuf 146 C1
Church Cl. L Berk 132 A2
Church Cl. Norwd 174 C2
Church Cl. Stu 82 A2
Church Cres. Saw 97 F1
Church Cres. St Alb 127 E2
Church End. Bar 9 D1
Church End. Ch En 11 D4
Church End. Fla 84 B1
Church End. Mark 83 E3
Church End. Red 106 A2
Church End. Sand 108 B1
Church End. Wal 38 B1
Church Field. Ware 93 D2
Church Field Path. Ches 148 B1
Church Green. Benn 52 B2
Church Green. Harp 86 A1
Church Hill. Bed 139 F3
Church Hill. Ched 79 F4
Church Hill. Hare 173 E1
Church Hill. Hert H 114 A2
Church La. Ashw 4 B2
Church La. Bark 17 E2
Church La. Berk 122 B2
Church La. Bov 137 D2
Church La. Ch En 11 D4
Church La. Ched 80 A4
Church La. Ches 148 B1
Church La. Coln H 129 D1
Church La. Dan En 71 F4
Church La. Gra 36 B2
Church La. Gu M 1 C3
Church La. Har 176 C1
Church La. Hat 130 B3
Church La. Hod 148 B4
Church La. Kim 66 B1
Church La. Kin L 139 D1
Church La. Letw 12 B1
Church La. Mars 79 F1
Church La. Muc H 74 C2
Church La. Nort 146 A1
Church La. Reed 16 C3
Church La. Ric 165 D1
Church La. Roystn 7 E3
Church La. Sar 152 A2
Church La. Stap 92 A3
Church La. Stev 50 B4
Church La. Ther 15 F4
Church La. Thor 76 B2
Church Manor. Bis St 77 D4
Church Mead. Stu 82 A2
Church Path. Gt Am 115 D3
Church Path. Hert 113 E3
Church Path. Ick 21 F2
Church Path. L Wym 35 F2
Church Rd. Cad 63 E1
Church Rd. Fla 84 A1
Church Rd. Gt Ha 77 F2
Church Rd. Heml H 125 E1
Church Rd. Hert 113 E4
Church Rd. Ivin 80 C3
Church Rd. Kin Wd 47 F2
Church Rd. L Berk 132 B2
Church Rd. L Gad 102 B4
Church Rd. L Hal 77 D1
Church Rd. Norwd 174 C2
Church Rd. Pit 80 C2
Church Rd. Pot B 145 D1
Church Rd. Pot En 123 D3
Church Rd. Sta Mo 59 F3
Church Rd. Stot 11 F3
Church Rd. Str 31 D3
Church Rd. Stu 82 A2
Church Rd. Watf 167 D4
Church Rd. Wel GC 110 B3
Church Row Mews. Ware 93 E1
Church St. Bal 12 C1
Church St. Bis St 76 C4
Church St. Bov 137 D2
Church St. Bun 40 C4
Church St. Gu M 1 C3
Church St. Hat 130 B3
Church St. Heml H 124 B3
Church St. Hert 113 E3
Church St. Luton 63 F4
Church St. Ric 165 F1
Church St. Saw 97 F1
Church St. St Alb 127 E2
Church St. Wa Aby 163 E3
Church St. Ware 93 E1
Church St. Watf 167 E3
Church St. Welw 89 E3
Church St. Whea 108 B4
Church St. Wing 60 A1
Church View. Hod 134 C2
Church View. Lon M 79 D2
Church Wlk. Saw 97 F1
Church Yd. Tri 100 A2
Churchfield. Bar 9 D1
Churchfield. Harl 118 A1
Churchfield. Harp 107 E4
Churchfield Rd. Tewin 90 B1
Churchfields. Hod 135 D2
Churchfields. Stand 55 F1
Churchgate. Ches 148 A1
Churchgate. Hit 34 C4
Churchgate Rd. Ches 148 A1
Churchgate St. Harl 118 C2
Churchill Rd. Luton 45 D1
Churchill Rd. St Alb 128 A2
Churchyard. Hit 34 C4
Churchyard Wlk. Hit 34 C4
Cicero Dri. Luton 45 D4
Cillocks Cl. Hod 135 D4
Claggy Rd. Kim 66 A1
Claire Ct. Pnr 175 F2
Clamp Hill. Stan 176 C3
Clapgate Rd. Bus 168 A2
Clare Cl. Elst 169 F2
Clare Cres. Bal 23 F3
Clare Ct. Norwd 174 C3
Clare Ct. St Alb 127 F1
Claremont. Bric 155 D4
Claremont. Ches 147 F1
Claremont Cres. Cro Gr 166 B2
Claremont Rd. Barn 159 E1
Claremont Rd. Har 176 C1
Claremont Rd. Luton 45 D1
Clarence Cl. Bus 168 C1
Clarence Rd. Berk 122 B2
Clarence Rd. Harp 86 A2
Clarence Rd. St Alb 128 A2
Clarence Rd. Sta Mo 59 F4
Clarendon Ct. Harp 86 A2
Clarendon Rd. Bor 170 A3
Clarendon Rd. Ches 148 B1
Clarendon Rd. Harp 86 A2
Clarendon Rd. Luton 45 F1
Clarendon Rd. Watf 167 D3
Clarion Cl. Gt Of 33 E1
Clark Rd. Roystn 7 E4
Clarke Way. Watf 154 A2
Clarke's Rd. Hat 130 A4
Clarke's Spring. Tri 100 C3
Clarkfield. Ric 173 D4
Clarks Cl. Ware 93 E2
Clarks Mead. Bus 168 B1
Claudian Pl. St Alb 127 D1
Claverhambury Rd. Wa Aby 149 F1
Claverley Green. Luton 46 C1
Claverton Cl. Bov 137 D2
Clay Hall Rd. Ken Co 82 C4
Clay Hill. Enf 161 E1
Clay La. Bus 168 C1
Clay La. Edg 170 A1
Claybury. Bus 168 A1
Claybush Rd. Ashw 4 B2
Claycroft. Wel GC 111 D4
Claydown Way. Cad 63 D1
Claygate Ave. Harp 85 F1
Claymore. Heml H 124 C4
Claymore Dri. Ick 21 F3
Claymores. Stev 50 C3
Clayponds. Bis St 77 D4
Cleall Ave. Wa Aby 163 E3
Cleave The. Harp 86 B1
Clement Pl. Tri 100 A2
Clement Rd. Ches 148 C2
Clements End Rd. Gt Ga 103 F4
Clements End Rd. Stu 82 C1
Clements Rd. Chor 164 B2
Clements St. Ware 93 F1
Clevedon Rd. Luton 46 A1
Cleveland Cres. Bor 170 B2
Cleveland Rd. Heml H 125 D3
Cleveland Rd. Mark 83 F3
Cleveland Way. Heml H 125 D3
Cleves Rd. Heml H 125 D4
Cleviscroft. Stev 50 C2
Clewer Cres. Har 176 B1
Clifford Cres. Luton 44 B3
Clifford St. Watf 167 E3
Clifton Cl. Ches 148 C1
Clifton Rd. Luton 63 D4
Clifton Rd. Watf 167 D2
Clifton St. St Alb 127 F2
Clifton Way. Bor 170 A4
Clifton Way. Ware 93 E2
Climb The. Chor 165 D2
Clinton Ave. Luton 45 F2
Clinton End. Heml H 125 E2
Clitheroe Gdns. Sth Ox 175 E4
Clive Cl. Pot B 158 C4
Clive Par. Norwd 174 C2
Clive Way. Watf 167 E4
Cloister Garth. Berk 122 B2
Cloister Garth. St Alb 141 F4
Cloister Wlk. Heml H 124 B3
Cloisterlawns. Letw 22 C2
Cloisters Rd. Letw 23 D2
Cloisters Rd. Luton 44 A2
Cloisters The. Ric 165 F1
Cloisters The. Wel GC 110 B3
Clonard Way. Pnr 176 A2
Close The. Bal 23 F4
Close The. Bro Pk 144 C3
Close The. Bus 168 A2
Close The. Cod 67 F1
Close The. Harp 85 E2
Close The. Hin 3 E3
Close The. Luton 45 D3
Close The. Mark 83 F3
Close The. Pot B 159 D4
Close The. Radl 155 F3
Close The. Ric 165 E1
Close The. Roystn 7 F4
Close The. Wall 25 F3
Close The. Ware 93 F1
Closemead Cl. Norwd 174 B2
Clothall Rd. Bal 23 F4
Clothall Rd. Clo 24 B3
Clovelly Way. Stev 50 A4
Clover Cl. Luton 44 A2
Clover Way. Heml H 124 A2
Cloverfield. Wel GC 89 F1
Cloverland. Hat 129 F1
Clowns The. Harp 107 D3
Clump The. Chor 165 D2
Clusterbolts. Stap 92 A4
Clyde Rd. Roy 135 E2
Clyde Sq. Heml H 124 C4
Clyde St. Hert 114 A3
Clydesdale Cl. Bor 170 B2
Clydesdale Path. Bor 170 B2
Clydesdale Rd. Luton 44 A2
Clydesdale Rd. Roystn 7 F3
Clydesdale Wlk. Ches 148 C3
Clyfton Cl. Hod 148 C4
Clyston Rd. Watf 166 C2
Coach Dri. Hit 34 C3
Coachman's La. Bal 23 E4
Coates Dell. Watf 154 C3
Coates Rd. Elst 169 E1
Coates Way. Watf 154 C3
Cob Cl. Bor 170 B2
Cobb Green. Watf 154 A4
Cobb Rd. Berk 121 F2
Cobbetts Ride. Tri 99 F2
Cobbins The. Wa Aby 163 F3
Cobblers Wick. Wing 60 A2
Cobden St. Luton 45 F1
Cobham Rd. Ware 93 F1
Cobmead. Hat 130 A4
Cock La. Hod 134 B2
Cock La. Sta Gr 30 C2
Cockbush Ave. Hert 114 A4
Cocker Rd. Enf 162 B2
Cockfosters Rd. Barn 159 F1
Codicote Dri. Watf 154 B3
Codicote Heights. Cod 68 A1
Codicote Rd. A St L 88 B2
Codicote Rd. Welw 89 D3
Codicote Rd. Whea 87 F1
Codicote Rd. Whit 66 C3
Codicote Row. Heml H 105 D1
Codmore Wood Rd. Lat 150 B3
Coe's Alley. Barn 171 F3
Colburn Ave. Pnr 175 F2
Colchester Rd. Norwd 175 D1
Cold Christmas La. Thun 93 F3
Coldham Gr. Enf 162 C1
Coldharbour La. Bus 168 B2
Coldharbour La. Harp 86 B2
Cole Green La. Wel GC 111 D2
Cole Rd. Watf 167 D4
Colebrook Ave. Luton 44 B4
Coleman Green La. Sand 108 C2
Coleman Green La. Whea 109 D4
Coleman's La. Lo Naz 149 F3
Colemans Rd. Bre Wd 47 E1
Coleridge Cl. Hit 35 D4
Coleridge Cres. Heml H 105 D1
Coles Green. Bus 168 B1
Coles Hill. Heml H 124 A3
Colesdale. Cuf 146 C1
Colestrete. Stev 50 C3
Colestrete Cl. Stev 50 C3
Coleswood Rd. Harp 107 E4
Colgrove. Wel GC 110 B3
Colin Rd. Luton 45 F1
Colindale Ave. St Alb 127 F1
College Ave. Har 176 C1
College Cl. Fla 84 A1
College Cl. Gt Am 114 B4
College Cl. Har 176 C2
College Ct. Ches 148 B1
College Hill Rd. Har 176 C1
College La. Hat 129 F2
College Pl. St Alb 127 E2
College Rd. Abb L 154 A4
College Rd. Ast C 78 B1
College Rd. Ches 148 B1
College Rd. Har 176 B1
College Rd. Hert H 114 B1
College Rd. Hod 134 C4
College Rd. St Alb 128 A1
College St. St Alb 127 E2
College Way. Norwd 174 B2
Collens Rd. Harp 107 D3
Collenswood Rd. Stev 51 D2
Collet Cl. Ches 148 B2
Collet Gdns. Ches 148 B2
Collett Rd. Heml H 124 B2
Collett Rd. Ware 93 E1
Colley Land. Chor 164 B3
Collingdon St. Luton 63 E4
Collings Wells Cl. Cad 62 C2
Collingtree. Luton 46 A2
Collins Cross. Bis St 59 D1
Collison Cl. Hit 22 B1
Collyer Rd. Lon C 142 B2
Colmer Pl. Har 176 B2
Colne Ave. Ric 173 D4
Colne Ave. Watf 167 E2
Colne Gdns. Lon C 142 C2
Colne Mead. Ric 173 D4
Colne Way. Heml H 124 C4
Colne Way. Watf 154 C1
Colney Heath La. St Alb 128 C1
Colonial Way. Watf 167 E4
Colonnade The. Ches 148 C2
Colston Cres. Gofs O 147 D2
Colts Cnr. Stev 51 D2
Colts Croft. Gt Ch 9 F1
Colts The. Bis St 76 C2
Coltsfield. Sta Mo 59 F4
Coltsfoot Dri. Roystn 7 F3
Coltsfoot Green. Luton 44 A3
Coltsfoot La. Dat 90 B4
Coltsfoot Rd. Ware 93 F2
Coltsfoot The. Heml H 123 F1
Colvin Gdns. Enf 162 B2
Colwell Rise. Luton 46 C1
Colyer Cl. Har Gr 89 F2
Combe Rd. Watf 166 C2
Combe St. Heml H 124 B2
Comet Cl. Watf 153 F3
Comet Rd. Hat 129 F3
Comet Rd. Hat 129 F4
Comet Way. Hat 129 F3
Comet Way. Stanb 110 A1
Commerce Way. Letw 22 C3
Common Field. Wigg 100 B2
Common Gate Rd. Chor 164 C2
Common Green. Pot En 123 D3
Common La. Ashw 4 A3
Common La. Kim 66 A1
Common La. Kim 86 B3
Common La. Kin L 138 C2
Common La. Radl 155 F1
Common Rd. Chor 164 C4
Common Rd. Ken Co 82 C4
Common Rd. Stan 176 B4
Common Rd. Stot 11 F4
Common Rd. Stu 82 A2
Common Rise. Hit 22 A1
Common The. Chipf 151 F4
Common The. Hat 130 A3
Common The. Kin Gr 85 E2
Common The. Pot En 123 D3
Common The. Stan 176 C4
Common View. Letw 23 D4
Common View Sq. Letw 23 D4
Commonfields. Harl 117 F1

Commons La. Heml H 124 C2
Commons The. Wel GC 111 D2
Compton Ave. Luton 44 C2
Compton Gdns. Chis 141 D3
Compton Pl. Watf 175 F3
Comyne Rd. Watf 153 F2
Comyns The. Bus 168 B1
Concorde Dri. Heml H 124 B2
Concorde St. Luton 63 F4
Conduit La. Gt Ho 29 D1
Conduit La. Hod 135 D3
Conduit La E. Hod 135 D3
Coney Cl. Hat 130 A2
Coney Green. Saw 97 E2
Coneydale. Wel GC 110 B4
Conifer Cl. Ches 147 F1
Conifer Wlk. Stev 51 E4
Coningsby Dri. Watf 166 C4
Coningsby Bank. St Alb 141 E4
Coningsby Cl. Wel Gr 144 B4
Coningsby Dri. Pot B 159 E3
Coniston Cl. Heml H 125 E1
Coniston Rd. Kin L 138 C2
Coniston Rd. Luton 44 C3
Connaught Cl. Heml H 125 D3
Connaught Gdns. Nthch 121 F4
Connaught Rd. Barn 171 E2
Connaught Rd. Har 176 C1
Connaught Rd. Harp 86 A1
Connaught Rd. Luton 44 C1
Connaught Rd. St Alb 127 E3
Connemara Cl. Bor 170 B2
Connop Rd. Enf 162 B1
Conquerors Hill. Whea 108 C4
Conquest Cl. Hit 34 C3
Constantine Cl. Stev 36 C1
Constantine Pl. Bal 13 D1
Convent Cl. Hit 34 C4
Conway Gdns. Enf 161 F1
Conway Rd. Luton 45 D1
Conyers. Harl 117 E1
Cook Rd. Stev 51 D4
Cook's Hole Rd. Enf 161 E1
Cooks Mead. Bus 168 A2
Cooks Spinney. Harl 118 A1
Cooks Vennel. Heml H 124 A3
Cooks Way. Hit 22 A1
Coombe Gdns. Berk 121 F3
Coombe Hill Rd. Ric 165 D1
Coombe Rd. Bus 168 B1
Coombe Rd. Kel 6 A1
Coombelands Rd. Roystn 2 C1
Coombes Rd. Lon C 142 B3
Coopers Alley. Hit 34 C4
Cooper's Cl. Kim 66 A1
Coopers Cl. Stev 51 E2
Coopers Green La. St Alb 128 C3
Coopers Green La. Stanb 109 E1
Cooper's Hill. Kim 87 D4
Cooper's La. Nort 145 F1
Coopers Lane Rd. Nort 160 A3
Coopers Meadow. Red 106 A3
Coopers Rd. Pot B 145 E1
Coopers Wlk. Ches 148 B2
Cooters End La. Harp 85 F3
Copenhagen Cl. Luton 44 B4
Copmans Wick. Chor 164 B2
Coppens The. Stot 12 A3
Copper Beech Cl. Fel 137 F4
Copper Ct. Saw 97 F1
Copperfields. Roystn 7 E3
Copperfields. Wel GC 111 E3
Coppermill La. Map Cr 172 C2
Copperwood. Hert 113 F3
Coppice Cl. Hat 129 F1
Coppice Mead. Stot 11 F3
Coppice The. Watf 167 E2
Coppings The. Hod 115 D1
Coppins Cl. Berk 121 F2
Coppins The. Har 176 B2
Coppins The. Mark 83 E3
Copse Cl. Norwd 174 B1
Copse Hill. Wl Gr 90 A4
Copse The. Bis St 77 E4
Copse The. Heml H 123 F3
Copse Way. Luton 44 B4
Copse Wood Way. Norwd 174 B1
Copsewood Rd. Watf 167 D4
Copthorne. Luton 46 B2
Copthorne Cl. Cro Gr 165 F2
Copthorne Rd. Cro Gr 165 F2
Coral Gdns. Heml H 124 C2
Corbridge Dri. Luton 46 C1
Corby Cl. Chis 141 D3
Cordell Cl. Ches 148 C2
Corder Cl. St Alb 141 D4
Coreys Mill La. Stev 36 B1
Corinium Gate. St Alb 127 D1
Corinium Gdns. Luton 45 D4
Corn Mead. Wel GC 89 E1
Corncastle Rd. Luton 63 E3
Corncrake Cl. Luton 46 B3
Corncroft. Hat 130 A4
Cornel Cl. Luton 63 D4
Corner Hall. Heml H 124 B1
Corner Hall Ave. Heml H 124 B1
Corner Wood. Mark 83 E3
Cornerfield. Hat 130 A4
Corners. Wel GC 111 D4
Cornfield Rd. Bus 168 A3
Cornfields. Heml H 124 A1
Cornmill. Wa Aby 163 D3
Cornwall Cl. Ches 162 C3
Cornwall Ct. Pnr 175 F2
Cornwall Rd. Harp 86 A1
Cornwall Rd. Pnr 175 F2
Cornwall Rd. St Alb 127 F1
Coronation Ave. Roystn 7 E3
Coronation Rd. Bis St 76 C3
Coronation Rd. Ware 93 E1
Corringham Ct. St Alb 127 F2
Corton Cl. Stev 50 A4
Cory-Wright Way. Whea 87 F1
Cosgrove Way. Luton 62 C4
Cotefield. Luton 44 B2
Cotesmore Rd. Heml H 123 F1
Cotlandswick. Lon C 142 B3
Cotney Croft. Stev 51 E2
Cotswold. Heml H 124 C3
Cotswold Ave. Bus 168 B2
Cotswold Cl. St Alb 128 B4
Cotswold Gdns. Luton 44 B4
Cotswolds. Hat 130 A2
Cottage Cl. Cro Gr 165 F2
Cottered Rd. Thro 26 C1
Cotterells. Heml H 124 B1
Cotterells Hill. Heml H 124 B2
Cotton Dri. Hert 114 A4
Cotton Field. Hat 130 A4
Cotton Rd. Pot B 159 E4
Cottonmill Cres. St Alb 127 E1
Cottonmill La. St Alb 127 E1
Coulser Cl. Heml H 124 A3
Coulter Cl. Cuf 146 B2
Council Rd. Bis St 77 D4
Counters Cl. Heml H 124 A2
Countess Cl. Hare 173 E1
Coursers Rd. Coln H 143 E4
Coursers Rd. Lon C 143 D3
Courtaulds. Chipf 138 A1
Courtenay Ave. Har 176 B1
Courtenay Gdns. Har 176 B1
Courtfield Cl. Hod 135 D2
Courtfields. Harp 86 B1
Courtlands Dri. Watf 153 F2
Courtleigh Ave. Barn 159 E1
Courtway The. Watf 175 F4
Covent Garden Cl. Luton 44 C2
Coventry Cl. Stev 37 D1
Coverdale. Heml H 124 C3
Coverdale. Luton 44 A3
Covert Cl. Nthch 121 E3
Covert Rd. Nthch 121 E3
Covert The. Norwd 174 B1
Cow La. Bus 168 A2
Cow La. Tri 100 B2
Cow La. Watf 154 B2
Cowards La. Cod 88 C4
Cowbridge. Hert 113 E3
Cowdray Cl. Luton 46 B2
Cowles. Ham St 147 F2
Cowley Hill. Bor 157 D1
Cowper Cres. Hert 92 A1
Cowper Ct. Watf 154 A1
Cowper Rd. Berk 122 A2
Cowper Rd. Harp 86 B1
Cowper Rd. Heml H 124 A1
Cowper Rd. Mark 83 E3
Cowper Rd. Wel GC 110 C3
Cowper Rise. Mark 83 E3
Cowper St. Luton 63 F3
Cowpers Way. Tewin 90 B3
Cowridge Cres. Luton 46 A1
Cowslip Cl. Roystn 7 F3
Cowslip Hill. Letw 22 C4
Cowslips The. Wel GC 111 E3
Coxfield Cl. Heml H 124 C1
Cox's Way. Arl 11 D3
Coyney Green. Luton 45 E1
Cozens La E. Hod 134 C1
Cozens La W. Hod 134 C1
Cozens Rd. Ware 94 A1
Crab La. Aldhm 155 D3
Crab Tree La. Pirt 20 B2
Crab Tree Rd. Kneb 68 C2
Crabb's La. Sto P 43 F3
Crabtree Cl. Bus 168 A2
Crabtree Cl. Heml H 124 B1
Crabtree Ct. Heml H 124 C1
Crabtree Dell. Letw 23 E2
Crabtree La. Bal 23 F4
Crabtree La. Harp 107 E4
Crabtree La. Heml H 124 B1
Crackley Meadow. Heml H 125 D4
Cradock Rd. Luton 44 A1
Cragg Ave. Radl 155 F2
Cragside. Kneb 69 E4
Craig Mount. Radl 156 A2
Craigavon Rd. Heml H 124 C4
Craiglands. St Alb 128 B4
Craigs Wlk. Ches 148 B2
Craigweil Ave. Radl 156 A2
Cranborne Ave. Hit 34 B3
Cranborne Cl. Hert 113 E2
Cranborne Cl. Pot B 158 C4
Cranborne Cres. Pot B 158 C4
Cranborne Gdns. Wel GC 110 C3
Cranborne Rd. Ches 162 B4
Cranborne Rd. Hat 130 A3
Cranborne Rd. Hod 135 E4
Cranbourne Dri. Harp 107 E3
Cranbourne Dri. Hod 115 E1
Cranbourne Rd. Norwd 174 C1
Cranbrook Cl. Ware 93 E2
Cranbrook Dri. Luton 44 B4
Cranbrook Dri. St Alb 128 C2
Crane Mead. Ware 114 C4
Cranefield Dri. Watf 154 C3
Cranes Way. Bor 170 B2
Cranfield Cres. Cuf 146 C1
Cranleigh Cl. Ches 148 A2
Cranleigh Gdns. Luton 45 E2
Cranmer Cl. Pot B 145 E1
Cranmore Ct. St Alb 127 F2
Cranwell Gdns. Bis St 59 E1
Cravells Rd. Harp 107 E4
Crawford Rd. Hat 130 A4
Crawley Cl. Cad 63 E1
Crawley Dri. Heml H 124 C4
Crawley Green Rd. Luton 64 A4
Crawley Rd. Luton 63 E4
Crawley's La. Wigg 120 C4
Crecy Gdns. Red 106 A3
Creighton Ave. St Alb 141 E4
Crescent E. Barn 159 E1
Crescent Rd. Bis St 77 D3
Crescent Rd. Heml H 124 B2
Crescent Rd. Luton 63 F4
Crescent Rise. Luton 63 F4
Crescent The. Abb L 139 F1
Crescent The. Bri Wd 141 D1
Crescent The. Cad 62 C2
Crescent The. Cotrd 39 E4
Crescent The. Cro Gr 166 A2
Crescent The. Gos 35 D2
Crescent The. Harl 118 B3
Crescent The. Henlw 10 B2
Crescent The. Hit 21 E1
Crescent The. Letw 23 D3
Crescent The. Mars 80 A1
Crescent The. Pit 80 B2
Crescent The. Watf 167 E3
Crescent The. Welw 89 D2
Crescent W. Barn 159 E1
Cresswick. Whit 66 C4
Crest Dri. Enf 162 B1
Crest Park. Heml H 125 E2
Crest The. Gofs O 147 D2
Crest The. Luton 45 D4
Crest The. Saw 97 E1
Crest The. Ware 93 E2
Crest The. Wl Gr 89 E4
Cresta Cl. Dun 44 A1
Creswick Ct. Wel GC 110 B3
Crew Curve. Nthch 121 F4
Crews Hill. Nort 160 C3
Crib St. Ware 93 E1
Cricketer's Rd. Arl 11 D2
Cricketfield La. Bis St 76 C4
Crispin Field. Pit 80 B2
Croasdaile Rd. Sta Mo 59 F4
Croasdale Cl. Sta Mo 59 F4
Crocus Field. Barn 171 F2
Croft Cl. Chipf 138 A1
Croft End Rd. Chipf 138 A1
Croft Field. Chipf 138 A1
Croft Field. Hat 130 A3
Croft La. Chipf 138 A1
Croft La. Letw 12 A1
Croft Meadow. Chipf 138 A1
Croft Rd. Luton 46 A2
Croft Rd. Ware 93 E1
Croft The. Barn 171 F3
Croft The. Chis 141 D3
Croft The. Hod 148 C4
Croft The. Luton 44 B4
Croft The. Wel GC 110 C2
Croft Wlk. Hod 148 C4
Crofters. Saw 97 F2
Crofters End. Saw 97 F2
Crofters Rd. Norwd 174 C3
Crofts Path. Heml H 125 D1
Crofts The. Heml H 125 D1
Crofts The. Stot 11 F3
Croftwell. Harp 107 F4
Cromer Cl. L Gad 102 C2
Cromer Rd. Watf 154 B1
Cromer Way. Luton 45 E4
Crompton Rd. Stev 50 A3
Cromwell Ave. Ches 148 A1
Cromwell Cl. St Alb 128 B4
Crmwell Green. Letw 23 D4
Cromwell Hill. Luton 45 E1
Cromwell Rd. Bor 169 F4
Cromwell Rd. Ches 148 A2
Cromwell Rd. Hert 114 A4
Cromwell Rd. Letw 23 D4
Cromwell Rd. Luton 45 E1
Cromwell Rd. Stev 51 E3
Cromwell Rd. Ware 93 F1
Cromwell Way. Pirt 20 B2
Crooked Mile. Wa Aby 163 E4
Crooked Way. Lo Naz 135 F1
Crookhams. Wel GC 90 A1
Crop Common. Hat 130 A4
Crosby Cl. Luton 45 D1
Cross La. Harp 107 E3
Cross La. Hert 113 D3
Cross Oak Rd. Berk 122 A2
Cross Rd. Ches 162 C3
Cross Rd. Hert 113 E4
Cross Rd. Watf 167 F2
Cross St. Letw 22 C4
Cross St. Luton 63 F4
Cross St. St Alb 127 E2
Cross St. Ware 93 F1
Cross St. Watf 167 E3
Cross Way. Harp 86 B2
Cross Way The. Har 176 C1
Cross Way The. Luton 63 E3
Crossbrook. Hat 129 F2
Crossbrook St. Ches 162 B4
Crossett Green. Heml H 125 E1
Crossfell Rd. Heml H 125 E1
Crossfield Cl. Berk 121 F2
Crossfield Rd. Hod 135 D4
Crossfields. St Alb 141 D4
Crossgates. Stev 50 C3
Crosslands. Cad 62 C2
Crossleys. Letw 11 F1
Crossmead. Watf 167 D2
Crossoaks La. Pot B 157 F3
Crossoaks La. Ridge 157 F3
Crosspath. Radl 156 A2
Crosspaths. Harp 85 E2
Crossway. Pnr 175 D1
Crossway. Wel GC 89 E1
Crossways. Berk 121 F2
Crossways. Heml H 125 E2
Crouch Hall Gdns. Red 106 A3
Crouch Hall La. Red 106 A3
Crouch La. Gofs O 147 E2
Crouchfield. Heml H 124 A1
Crouchfield. Hert 92 B1
Crow Furlong. Hit 34 B4
Crow La. Reed 16 C3
Crowborough Path. Sth Ox 175 E3
Crowland Rd. Luton 46 B3
Crown Cl. Saw 98 B1
Crown Pas. Watf 167 E3
Crown Rd. Bor 170 A4
Crown Rise. Watf 154 B3
Crown St. Red 106 A3
Crown Terr. Bis St 77 D4
Crownfield. Hod 135 D1
Croxdale Rd. Bor 170 A4
Croxley View. Watf 166 C2
Croxton Cl. Luton 45 D4
Crunell's Green. Pres 48 C3
Cubbington Cl. Luton 45 D4
Cubitts Cl. Har Gr 89 F2
Cuckmans Dri. Chis 141 D3
Cuckoo's Nest. Luton 64 A4
Cuffley Ave. Watf 154 B3
Cuffley Cl. Luton 44 C2
Cuffley Ct. Heml H 125 E4
Cuffley Hill. Gofs O 147 D1
Cullera Cl. Norwd 174 C2
Cullings Ct. Wa Aby 163 F3
Culver Rd. St Alb 127 F3
Culverden Rd. Sth Ox 175 D4
Culverhouse Rd. Luton 45 E2
Culworth Cl. Cad 62 C2
Cumberland Cl. Bed 139 F4
Cumberland Cl. Hert 113 E4
Cumberland Ct. St Alb 127 F2
Cumberland Dri. Red 106 A3
Cumberland St. Luton 63 F3
Cumberlow Pl. Heml H 125 E1
Cundalls Rd. Ware 93 F1
Cunningham Ave. Enf 162 C2
Cunningham Ave. St Alb 127 F1
Cunningham Hill Rd. St Alb 128 A1
Cunningham Rd. Ches 148 C2
Cupid Green La. Gt Ga 104 C2
Cupid Green La. Heml H 105 D1
Cupthall Cl. Gt Ha 77 F2
Curam Cl. Berk 122 B2
Curlew Cl. Berk 122 B2
Curlew Cl. Letw 11 F1
Curlew Rd. Luton 46 B3
Currie St. Hert 113 F3
Curtis Cl. Ric 165 D1
Curtis Rd. Heml H 125 E1
Curtis Way. Berk 122 B2
Curzon Rd. Luton 45 E1
Cussons Cl. Ches 148 A1
Cutenhoe Rd. Luton 63 F3
Cutforth Rd. Saw 97 F2
Cuttsfield Terr. Heml H 123 F1
Cuttys La. Stev 50 C3
Cwmbran Ct. Heml H 124 C4
Cygnet Cl. Bor 170 B4
Cygnet Cl. Norwd 174 B2
Cylers Thicket. Welw 89 E3
Cypress Ave. Enf 161 D2
Cypress Cl. Wa Aby 163 E3
Cypress Rd. Har 176 B1

Dacre Cres. Kim 66 B1
Dacre Gdns. Bor 170 B2
Dacre Green. Roystn 7 F3
Dacre Rd. Hit 35 D4
Dagger La. Elst 169 D2
Daggs Dell Rd. Heml H 123 F3
Dagnall Rd. Gt Ga 103 E3
Dagnalls. Letw 22 C1
Dalby Cl. Luton 44 A2
Dale Ave. Bla En 87 D3
Dale Cl. Hit 34 C2
Dale Cl. Pnr 175 D1
Dale Ct. Saw 97 E1
Dale Rd. Luton 63 E4
Dale The. Letw 22 C3
Dale The. Wa Aby 163 F3
Dales Path. Bor 170 B2
Dales Rd. Bor 170 B2
Daleside Dri. Pot B 158 C3
Dalewood. Harp 86 B1
Dalewood. Wel GC 111 E3
Dalkeith Rd. Harp 86 B1
Dallow Rd. Luton 63 D4
Dalroad Industrial Estate. Luton 63 D4
Dalton Gdns. Bis St 76 C2
Dalton St. St Alb 127 E2
Dalton Way. Whit 66 C4
Daltry Cl. Stev 36 B1
Daltry Rd. Stev 36 B1
Damask Cl. Wes 37 D4
Damask Green. Heml H 123 F1
Damask Green Rd. Wes 37 D4
Dammersey Cl. Mark 83 F2
Dancers End La. Dra B 99 E1
Dancers Hill Rd. Pot B 158 C2
Dancote. Kneb 68 C3
Dane Acres. Bis St 76 B4
Dane Bridge La. Gr Ty 75 D1
Dane Cl. Harp 86 B2
Dane Cl. Stot 11 F4
Dane End La. Hal Gr 37 F3
Dane End Rd. H Cr 72 C2
Dane O'Coys Rd. Bis St 58 C1
Dane Park. Bis St 76 B4
Dane Rd. Luton 45 E1
Dane St. Bis St 77 D4
Danebridge Rd. Gr Ty 75 D1
Danefield Rd. Pirt 20 B2
Danemead. Hod 115 D1
Danes The. Chis 141 E2
Danesbury La. Wl Gr 89 E4
Danesbury Park. Hert 113 E4
Danesbury Park Rd. Wl Gr 89 E4
Danescroft. Letw 12 A1
Danesgate. Stev 50 B3
Danestrete. Stev 50 B3
Daniells. Wel GC 111 D4
Danvers Croft. Tri 100 B3
Danziger Way. Bor 170 B4
Darby Dri. Wa Aby 163 E3
Darby Dri. Wl Gr 68 C2
Darcy Cl. Ches 162 C4
Dark La. Ches 148 A1
Dark La. Harp 107 E4
Dark La. San 15 D1
Dark La. Ware 93 F2
Dark La. Wing 60 B1
Darkes La. Pot B 159 D4
Darley Rd. Bre Gr 47 E1
Darnicle Hill. Ham St 147 D3
Darrington Rd. Bor 169 F4
Darr's La. Nthch 121 E3
Dart The. Heml H 125 D4
Darwin Cl. Heml H 105 D1
Darwin Cl. St Alb 127 F4
Darwin Gdns. Sth Ox 175 E3
Darwin Rd. Stev 51 D3
Dashes The. Harl 117 F1
Datchet Cl. Heml H 125 D4
Datchworth Turn. Heml H 125 E2
Davenham Ave. Norwd 174 C3
Daventer Dri. Stan 176 C2
Davies St. Hert 113 F3
Davis Cres. Pirt 20 B3
Davis' Row. Arl 11 D2
Davison Cl. Ches 148 B2
Davison Dri. Ches 148 B2
Davys Cl. Whea 108 C4
Dawes La. Sar 151 F2
Dawley. Wel GC 89 F1
Dawley. Wel GC 89 F1
Dawley Ct. Heml H 125 D4
Dawlish Cl. Stev 69 E4
Dawlish Rd. Luton 44 C2
Dawson Cl. Henlw 10 B3
Dayemead. Wel GC 111 D2
Days Cl. Hat 129 F3
Day's Cl. Roystn 7 E3
Days Mead. Hat 129 F3
De Havilland Cl. Hat 129 F3
De Havilland Way. Abb L 153 F4
De Vere Wlk. Watf 166 C4
Deacon Cl. St Alb 141 E4
Deacons Cl. Bor 170 A3
Deacons Cl. Pnr 175 D1
Deacons Hill. Watf 167 E2
Deacon's Hill Rd. Elst 170 A2
Deacon's Hts. Elst 170 A2
Deacons Way. Hit 21 E1
Deaconsfield Rd. Heml H 138 B4
Dead Woman's La. Pres 48 B3
Deadman's Ash La. Sar 152 A2
Dean Field. Bov 137 D2
Dean The. Wing 60 A2
Deane Ct. Norwd 174 C1
Deans Cl. Abb L 153 E4
Deans Cl. Tri 100 A2
Deans Furlong. Tri 100 A2
Dean's Gdns. St Alb 128 A4
Deans Meadow. Dagn 81 E3
Deanscroft. Kneb 68 C3
Deansway. Heml H 138 C4
Deard's End La. Kneb 68 C3
Deards Wood. Kneb 68 C3
Debenham Rd. Ches 148 A2
Dee The. Heml H 124 C4
Deep Denes. Luton 46 A1
Deepdene. Pot B 158 B4
Deeping Cl. Kneb 68 C2
Deerfield Cl. Ware 93 E1
Deerings The. Harp 107 D2
Deerswood Ave. Hat 130 A2
Deeves Hall La. Shen 157 F3
Deimos Dri. Heml H 125 D3
Delahay Rise. Berk 122 A3
Delamare Rd. Ches 148 C1
Delamere Rd. Bor 170 A4
Delfcroft. Ware 93 E1
Delfield Cl. Cad 62 C2
Delius Cl. Elst 169 E2
Dell Cl. Harp 86 A2
Dell La. Bis St 77 D4
Dell La. L Hal 98 A4
Dell Meadow. Heml H 138 C4
Dell Rd. Enf 162 B1
Dell Rd. Nthch 121 E4
Dell Rd. Watf 154 A1
Dell Rise. Chis 141 D3
Dell Side. Watf 154 A1
Dell The. Bal 23 F3
Dell The. Cad 62 C2
Dell The. Hert 113 E2
Dell The. Luton 46 C1
Dell The. Norwd 174 C4
Dell The. Pnr 175 E1
Dell The. Radl 156 A2
Dell The. Roystn 7 E3
Dell The. St Alb 128 A2
Dell The. Stev 50 C3
Dellcot Cl. Luton 46 A2
Dellcott Cl. Wel GC 110 B4
Dellcroft Way. Harp 107 D3
Dellcut Rd. Heml H 125 D3
Dellfield. St Alb 128 A1
Dellfield. Wad 93 E4
Dellfield Ave. Berk 122 A3

Dellfield Cl. Berk 122 A3
Dellfield Cl. Radl 155 F2
Dellfield Cl. Watf 167 D4
Dellfield Ct. Harl 118 B2
Dellfield Rd. Hat 130 A3
Dellmeadow. Abb L 139 F1
Dellors Cl. Barn 171 E2
Dells The. Bis St 76 C4
Dells The. Heml H 125 D1
Dellsome La. Coln H 143 F4
Dellsome La. Wel Gr 144 A4
Dellsprings. Bun 40 C4
Dellwood Cl. Ric 165 D1
Delmar Ave. Heml H 125 E1
Delmerend La. Fla 84 B1
Delphine Cl. Luton 63 D3
Delta Gain. Watf 175 E4
Demontfort Rise. Ware 93 E2
Denbigh Rd. Luton 45 D1
Denby. Letw 23 D3
Dendridge Cl. Enf 162 A1
Dene La. Ast 51 F1
Dene Rd. Norwd 174 B2
Denes The. Heml H 138 C3
Denewood Cl. Watf 153 F1
Denham Cl. Heml H 125 D4
Denham Cl. Luton 44 C4
Denham La. C St P 172 A1
Denham Way. Bor 170 B4
Denham Way. Map Cr 172 C2
Denmark Cl. Luton 44 C4
Denmark St. Watf 167 D4
Denny Ave. Wa Aby 163 E3
Denny Ct. Bis St 59 D1
Densley Cl. Wel GC 110 B4
Denton Cl. Barn 171 E2
Denton Cl. Luton 44 A2
Denton Rd. Stev 50 C2
Dents Cl. Letw 23 E2
Derby Ave. Har 176 B1
Derby Rd. Luton 44 B1
Derby Rd. Roy 135 E2
Derby Rd. Watf 167 E3
Derby Way. Stev 51 D4
Derwent Ave. Luton 45 D4
Derwent Ave. Pnr 175 F2
Derwent Rd. Harp 85 E2
Derwent Rd. Heml H 125 E1
Derwent Rd. Henlw 10 A2
Derwent Rd. Luton 64 A4
Desborough Cl. Hert 92 B1
Desborough Dri. Tewin 90 B3
Desborough Rd. Hit 35 E4
Desmond Rd. Watf 153 F2
Deva Cl. St Alb 127 D1
Devereux Dri. Watf 153 F1
Devoils La. Bis St 76 C4
Devon Rd. Luton 64 A4
Devon Rd. Watf 167 E4
Devonshire Cl. Stev 69 D4
Devonshire Rd. Harp 86 A1
Devonshire Rd. Pnr 175 F1
Dewars Cl. Welw 89 E3
Dewes Green Rd. Sta Gr 30 C1
Dewgrass Gr. Enf 162 B2
Dewhurst Rd. Ches 148 B1
Dewpond Cl. Stev 50 B4
Dewsbury Rd. Luton 45 E3
Dexter Cl. Luton 31 D1
Dexter Rd. Barn 171 E2
Diamond Rd. Watf 154 A1
Dickens Cl. St Alb 127 E2
Dickens Ct. Heml H 105 D1
Dicket Mead. Welw 89 E3
Dickins Cl. Ham St 148 A3
Dickinson Ave. Cro Gr 166 A2
Dickinson Sq. Cro Gr 166 A2
Dickson. Ham St 147 F2
Dig Dag Hill. Ham St 147 F2
Digswell Hill. Welw 89 D1
Digswell La. Wel GC 89 F1
Digswell Park Rd. Wel GC 89 E2
Digswell Park Rd. Wel GC 89 F2
Digswell Rd. Wel GC 110 B4
Digswell Rise. Wel GC 110 C4
Dimmocks La. Sar 152 A2
Dimsdale Cres. Bis St 77 D3
Dimsdale St. Hert 113 E3
Dinant Link Rd. Hod 135 D4
Dinmore. Bov 137 D2
Dione Rd. Heml H 124 C3
Ditchfield Rd. Hod 115 D1
Ditchling Cl. Luton 46 B2
Ditchmore La. Stev 50 B3
Divot Pl. Hert 114 A4
Dixies Cl. Ashw 4 B2
Dixon Pl. Bun 40 C4
Dixons Hill Cl. Wel Gr 144 A3
Dixons Hill Rd. Wel Gr 144 B4
Dobb's Weir Rd. Roy 135 E2
Docklands. Pirt 20 B2
Doctors' Commons Rd. Berk 122 A2
Dodds La. Heml H 104 C1
Dodds La. Pic En 124 B4
Dodwood. Wel GC 111 D3
Dog Kennel La. Chor 164 C3
Dog Kennel La. Hat 130 A3
Dog Kennel La. Roy 7 E3
Doggetts Way. St Alb 127 E1
Dognell Green. Wel GC 110 A4
Dolesbury Dri. Wl Gr 89 F4
Dollis Brook Wlk. Barn 171 F2
Dollis Valley Way. Barn 171 F2
Dolphin Sq. Tri 100 A2
Dolphin Way. Bis St 77 D4
Dolphin Yd. Hert 113 E3
Dolphin Yd. St Alb 127 E2
Doncaster Green. Sth Ox 175 E3
Donkey La. Tri 99 F2
Donne Cl. Roystn 7 E4
Dorchester Ave. Hod 135 D4
Dordans Rd. Luton 44 C2
Dorel Cl. Luton 45 F1
Dormans Cl. Norwd 174 B2
Dormer Cl. Barn 171 E2
Dormie Cl. St Alb 127 E3
Dorrien's Croft. Berk 121 F4
Dorrington Cl. Luton 45 E1
Dorrofield Cl. Cro Gr 166 B2
Dorset Cl. Berk 121 F3
Douglas Ave. Watf 154 C1
Douglas Dri. Stev 51 D4
Douglas Gdns. Berk 122 A3
Douglas House. Ches 148 B2
Douglas Rd. Harp 85 F1
Douglas Rd. Luton 45 D1
Douglas Way. Wel GC 111 E3
Dove Cl. Bis St 76 C2
Dove Cl. Sta Mo 59 F4
Dove Ct. Hat 130 A2
Dove House La. Ken Co 82 B4
Dove La. Pot B 159 E3
Dove Park. Chor 164 B2
Dove Park. Pnr 176 A2
Dovedale. Stev 51 D2
Dovedale. Ware 93 E2
Dovedale Cl. Hare 173 E1
Dovehouse Croft. Harl 118 A1
Dovehouse Hill. Luton 46 A1
Dover Cl. Luton 45 D2
Dover Way. Cro Gr 166 B3
Doverfield. Gofs O 147 E1
Dowling Ct. Heml H 124 B1
Down Edge. Red 105 F3
Down Green La. Whea 108 A4
Downalong. Bus 168 B1
Downedge. St Alb 127 D2
Downes Rd. St Alb 128 A4
Downfield Cl. Hert H 114 B2
Downfield Rd. Ches 162 B4
Downfield Rd. Hert H 114 B3
Downfields. Wel GC 110 A2
Downhall Ley. Bun 40 C4
Downings Wood. Map Cr 172 B3
Downlands. Luton 44 B4
Downlands. Roystn 7 E3
Downlands. Stev 51 E4
Downlands. Wa Aby 163 F3
Downs Rd. Luton 63 E4
Downs The. Hat 130 A2
Downsfield. Hat 130 A1
Downside. Heml H 124 C2
Dragon Rd. Hat 129 F4
Drakes Cl. Ches 148 B2
Drakes Dri. Norwd 174 A1
Drakes Dri. St Alb 128 B1
Drakes Dri. Stev 51 D4
Drapers Way. Stev 50 B4
Drayson Cl. Wa Aby 163 F4
Drayton Ave. Pot B 158 C4
Drayton Rd. Bor 170 A3
Drayton Rd. Luton 44 A2
Driftway The. Heml H 124 C2
Driftwood Ave. Chis 141 D3
Drive The. Barn 171 F3
Drive The. Bla En 87 D4
Drive The. Chor 165 E2
Drive The. Gofs O 147 E2
Drive The. Harl 117 F1
Drive The. Harp 86 A1
Drive The. Hert 113 E4
Drive The. Hod 135 D4
Drive The. Lon C 142 A3
Drive The. Norwd 174 C1
Drive The. Pot B 158 C4
Drive The. Radl 156 A3
Drive The. Saw 97 E1
Drive The. Watf 153 E1
Drive The. Wl Gr 69 D1
Driver's End La. Cod 67 F2
Driveway The. Cuf 146 C2
Driveway The. Heml H 124 A1
Dromey Gdns. Har 176 C2
Drop La. Bric 155 E4
Drovers Way. Hat 130 A4
Drovers Way. St Alb 127 E2
Drummond Dri. Stan 176 C2
Drummond Ride. Tri 100 A3
Drury La. Hun 95 E1
Drycroft. Wel GC 110 C1
Dryden Cres. Stev 51 E4
Dryden Rd. Har 176 C1
Drysdale Cl. Norwd 174 C2
Dubbs Knoll Rd. Gu M 1 C3
Dubrae Cl. St Alb 127 D1
Duchy Rd. Barn 159 E1
Duck La. Benn 52 C2
Ducketts La. Gr Ty 75 E1
Ducketts Mead. Roy 116 A1
Ducketts Wood. Thun 93 E4
Duckling La. Saw 97 F2
Duckmore La. Tri 99 F1
Duck's Hill Rd. Norwd 174 A1
Dudley Ave. Ches 162 B4
Dudley Hill Cl. Wl Gr 89 F4
Dudley St. Luton 63 F4
Dudswell La. Nthch 121 E4
Dugdale Ct. Hit 21 E1
Dugdale Hill La. Pot B 158 C4
Dugdales. Cro Gr 166 A3
Duke St. Hod 135 D4
Duke St. Luton 63 F4
Duke St. Watf 167 E3
Duke's La. Hit 34 C4
Dukes Ride. Bis St 76 B4
Dukes Way. Berk 122 A3
Dulwich Way. Cro Gr 166 A2
Dumbarton Ave. Ches 162 B3
Dumfries Cl. Sth Ox 175 D4
Dumfries St. Luton 63 E3
Duncan Cl. Wel GC 110 C3
Duncan Way. Bus 167 F4
Duncombe Cl. Hert 113 E4
Duncombe Cl. Luton 45 E3
Duncombe Rd. Hert 113 E4
Duncombe Rd. Nthch 121 F3
Dundale Rd. Tri 100 A2
Dunham's La. Letw 23 E3
Dunlin. Letw 11 F1
Dunlin Rd. Heml H 124 C4
Dunmow Ct. Luton 45 E1
Dunmow Rd. Birhr 77 F4
Dunmow Rd. Bis St 77 E4
Dunn Cl. Stev 50 C2
Dunnock Cl. Bor 170 A3
Dunny La. Chipf 151 F4
Dunny La. Sar 151 F3
Dunsby Rd. Luton 45 D3
Dunsley Pl. Tri 100 A2
Dunsmore Cl. Bus 168 B2
Dunsmore Rd. Luton 63 E3
Dunsmore Way. Bus 168 B2
Dunstable Cl. Luton 45 D1
Dunstable Pl. Luton 63 E4
Dunstable Rd. Cad 62 B2
Dunstable Rd. Dagn 81 E4
Dunstable Rd. Luton 44 B1
Dunstable Rd. Rod 106 A4
Dunstable Rd. Stu 82 A3
Dunster Cl. Barn 171 E3
Dunster Cl. Hare 173 D1
Dunster Rd. Heml H 105 D1
Dunston Hill. Tri 100 A2
Durban Rd E. Watf 167 D3
Durban Rd W. Watf 167 D3
Durbar Rd. Luton 45 D1
Durham Cl. Saw 97 E1
Durham Cl. Sta Ab 115 D3
Durham Rd. Bor 170 B3
Durham Rd. Luton 64 A4
Durham Rd. Stev 37 D1
Durler Gdns. Luton 63 E3
Durrants Dri. Cro Gr 166 B3
Durrants Hill Rd. Heml H 138 B4
Durrants La. Nthch 121 F3
Durrants Rd. Berk 121 F3
Dury Rd. Barn 171 F4
Duxford Cl. Luton 45 D4
Duxons Turn. Heml H 125 D2
Dyes La. Lan 49 F2
Dyes La. Stev 50 A2
Dyke La. Whea 108 C4
Dylan Cl. Elst 169 E1
Dymoke Green. St Alb 128 A4
Dymokes Way. Hod 115 D1
Dyrham La. Pot B 158 A2
Dysons Cl. Ches 162 B3
E Circular Rd. Luton 64 B4
Eagle Cl. Luton 44 A2
Eagle Ct. Hert 114 A4
Eagle Way. Hat 130 A2
Ealing Cl. Bor 170 B4
Earl St. Watf 167 E3
Earls Cl. Bis St 76 B3
Earls Hill Gdns. Roystn 7 E3
Earls La. Pot B 157 F3
Earls La. Ridge 157 F4
Earlsmead. Letw 22 C2
Easington Rd. Dan En 71 F4
Easingwood Gdns. Luton 62 C4
East Burrowfield. Wel GC 110 B2
East Cl. Chis 141 D3
East Cl. Hit 22 A1
East Cl. Stev 50 C3
East Comm. Harp 107 E4
East Dri. Lon C 142 A3
East Dri. Norwd 174 C4
East Dri. Saw 97 F1
East Dri. St Alb 128 C2
East Dri. Watf 154 A2
East End Way. Pnr 175 F1
East Flint. Heml H 123 F2
East Gate. Harl 117 E1
East Green. Heml H 139 D3
East Hill. Luton 45 D3
East La. Abb L 140 A1
East La. Bed 139 F2
East La. Whea 87 E1
East Lodge La. Enf 160 C2
East Mead. Wel GC 111 D2
East Mount. Whea 87 E1
East Park. Harl 118 B2
East Park. Saw 97 F1
East Rd. Bis St 77 D4
East Rd. Enf 162 B1
East Rd. Harl 118 A2
East Reach. Stev 51 D1
East Ridgeway. Cuf 146 C2
East Riding. Tewin 90 B3
East St. Heml H 124 B2
East St. Lily 32 B1
East St. Ware 93 E1
East View. Barn 171 F3
East View. Ess 131 F3
East View. St Ipp 35 E1
East Way. Wa Aby 163 E2
East Wlk. Harl 117 E1
Eastbourne Ave. Stev 50 A3
Eastbrook Rd. Wa Aby 163 F3
Eastbury Ave. Norwd 174 C3
Eastbury Cl. Norwd 174 C3
Eastbury Ct. St Alb 127 F2
Eastbury Pl. Norwd 174 C3
Eastbury Rd. Norwd 174 C2
Eastbury Rd. Watf 167 E2
Eastcheap. Letw 22 C3
Eastcote Dri. Harp 107 E3
Eastcott Cl. Luton 46 B1
Eastern Ave. Ches 162 C3
Eastern Ave. Henlw 10 B2
Eastern Way. Letw 12 A1
Eastfield Ave. Watf 167 E4
Eastfield Cl. Luton 46 B2
Eastfield Ct. St Alb 128 B3
Eastfield Par. Pot B 159 E4
Eastfield Rd. Ches 162 C4
Eastfield Rd. Enf 162 B1
Eastfield Rd. Roystn 7 F3
Eastgate. Stev 50 C3
Eastglade. Norwd 174 C3
Eastholm. Letw 23 D4
Eastholm Green. Letw 23 D4
Eastlea Ave. Watf 154 C1
Eastman Way. Heml H 125 D3
Eastmoor Park. Harp 107 E3
Eastnor. Bov 137 D2
Easton Gdns. Bor 170 C3
Eastor. Wel GC 90 A1
Eastwick Cres. Ric 172 C4
Eastwick Hall La. East 117 D3
Eastwick Rd. East 117 D2
Eastwick Rd. H Wy 117 F3
Eastwick Row. Heml H 125 D1
Eastwood Ct. Heml H 125 D2
Eaton Gate. Norwd 174 D2
Eaton Green Rd. Luton 46 C1
Eaton Rd. Heml H 125 D3
Eaton Rd. St Alb 128 A2
Eaton Valley Rd. Luton 46 A1
Ebberns Rd. Heml H 138 C4
Ebenezer St. Luton 63 E3
Ebury App. Ric 165 E1
Ebury Cl. Norwd 174 B3
Ebury Rd. Ric 165 E1
Ebury Rd. Watf 167 E3
Echo Hill. Roystn 7 E3
Eddy St. Berk 122 A3
Edenhall Cl. Heml H 125 E1
Edens Cl. Bis St 77 D4
Edens Mount. Saw 97 F2
Edgars Ct. Wel GC 110 C3
Edgbaston Rd. Sth Ox 175 D4
Edgcott Cl. Luton 31 D1
Edgecote Cl. Cad 62 C2
Edgehill Gdns. Luton 44 B4
Edgewood Dri. Luton 46 B3
Edgeworth Cl. Stev 51 E1
Edgware Way (Watford By-Ps) 169 E1
Edgwarebury La. Elst 169 F1
Edinburgh Ave. Chor 165 D2
Edinburgh Cres. Ches 162 C3
Edinburgh Pl. Harl 118 A2
Edinburgh Sq. Knee 2 A3
Edinburgh Way. Harl 117 F2
Edison Rd. Stev 51 D3
Edlyn Cl. Berk 121 F3
Edmonds Dri. Stev 51 E2
Edmund Beaufort Dri. St Alb 127 F3
Edmunds Rd. Hertng 112 C4
Edridge Cl. Bus 168 B2
Edulf Rd. Bor 170 A4
Edward Cl. Abb L 153 F4
Edward Cl. St Alb 127 F1
Edward Ct. Wa Aby 163 F3
Edward St. Luton 45 F1
Edwyn Cl. Barn 171 E2
Egdon Dri. Luton 45 E3
Egerton Rd. Berk 122 A3
Eight Acres. Tri 100 A2
Eighth Ave. Luton 44 B4
Eisenberg Cl. Bal 13 D1
Elaine Gdns. Cad 63 D1
Elbow La. Hert H 114 A1
Elbow La. Stev 69 D4
Eldefield. Letw 22 B4
Elder Ct. Bus 176 C4
Elder Rd. Ware 93 F2
Elder Way. Stev 50 B2
Elderbeck Cl. Ches 148 A1
Elderberry Cl. Luton 46 A2
Elderfield. Harl 118 B2
Eldon Ave. Bor 170 A4
Eldon Rd. Luton 44 B1
Eldon Rd. Roy 135 E2
Eleanor Ave. St Alb 127 E3
Eleanor Cross Rd. Ches 162 C3
Eleanor Gdns. Barn 171 E2
Eleanor Rd. Ches 162 C3
Eleanor Rd. Hert 113 E4
Eleanor Way. Ches 162 C3
Eleanor Way. Wa Aby 163 D3
Elfrida Rd. Watf 167 E2
Elgar Cl. Elst 169 E1
Elgin Dri. Norwd 174 C2
Elgin Rd. Ches 148 B1
Elgin Rd. Hod 148 C4
Elgood Ave. Norwd 175 D2
Eliot Rd. Roystn 7 E4
Eliot Rd. Stev 51 E3
Elizabeth Cl. Barn 171 E3
Elizabeth Cl. Lo Naz 149 E4
Elizabeth Ct. St Alb 128 B3
Elizabeth Ct. Watf 153 F1
Elizabeth Dri. Tri 100 A3
Elizabeth Rd. Bis St 76 C3
Elizabeth St. Luton 63 E3
Elizabeth Way. Harl 117 D1
Ellenborough Cl. Bis St 76 B3
Ellenbrook Cres. Hat 129 E3
Ellenbrook La. Hat 129 E2
Ellenhall Cl. Luton 45 E1
Ellerdine Cl. Luton 45 D2
Ellesborough Cl. Sth Ox 175 E3
Ellesfield. Welw 89 D3
Ellesmere Gr. Barn 171 F2
Ellesmere Rd. Berk 122 B2
Ellice. Letw 23 D2
Ellingham Cl. Heml H 125 D3
Ellingham Rd. Heml H 124 C2
Ellis Ave. Stev 50 C4
Elliswick Rd. Harp 86 A1
Ellwood Gdns. Watf 154 A3
Elm Ave. Cad 62 C2
Elm Ave. Watf 167 F1
Elm Cl. Wa Aby 163 E3
Elm Dri. Ches 148 C2
Elm Dri. Hat 130 A2
Elm Dri. St Alb 128 B2
Elm Gdns. Enf 161 E1
Elm Gdns. Wel GC 110 A3
Elm Gr. Berk 122 B2
Elm Green. Heml H 123 F3
Elm Grove. Bis St 77 D4
Elm Grove. Watf 154 A1
Elm Park. Bal 23 F4
Elm Park Rd. Pnr 175 E1
Elm Rd. Barn 171 F3
Elm Rd. Bis St 76 C4
Elm Rd. Hod 135 D3
Elm Rd. Ware 94 A1
Elm Terr. Har 176 B1
Elm Tree Wlk. Tri 100 A3
Elm Way. Ric 165 D1
Elm Wlk. Radl 155 F2
Elm Wlk. Roystn 7 F4
Elm Wlk. Stev 51 D2
Elmbank Ave. Barn 171 E3
Elmbridge. Harl 118 C2
Elmbrook Cl. Bis St 76 C2
Elmcote Way. Cro Gr 165 F2
Elmfield Cl. Pot B 158 C3
Elmfield Rd. Pot B 158 C3
Elmhurst Cl. Bis St 76 C4
Elmhurst Rd. Enf 162 B1
Elmoor Ave. Welw 89 D3
Elmoor Cl. Welw 89 D2
Elmore Rd. Luton 46 A1
Elmroyd Ave. Pot B 158 C3
Elmroyd Cl. Pot B 158 C3
Elms Rd. Har 176 C2
Elms The. Cod 67 F1
Elmscroft Gdns. Pot B 158 C4
Elmside. Ken Co 82 C4
Elmside Wlk. Hit 34 C4
Elmtree Ave. Cok Gr 46 C2
Elmwood. Saw 97 F1
Elmwood. Wel GC 110 A3
Elmwood Ave. Bal 23 F4
Elmwood Ave. Bor 170 A3
Elmwood Cres. Luton 45 F2
Elsinge Rd. Enf 162 B2
Elstree Hill N. Elst 169 E2
Elstree Hill S. Elst 169 E1
Elstree Rd. Bus 168 C1
Elstree Rd. Heml H 105 D1
Elstree Way. Bor 170 B4
Elton Ave. Barn 171 F2
Elton Rd. Hert 113 E4
Elton Way. Bus 168 A4
Ely Cl. Hat 129 F3
Ely Cl. Stev 37 D1
Ely Gdns. Bor 170 B2
Ely Pl. Wel GC 110 C3
Ely Rd. St Alb 128 A1
Ely Way. Luton 44 B2
Embleton Rd. Sth Ox 175 D4
Emerald Rd. Luton 44 A2
Emerton Cl. Nthch 121 F4
Emerton Garth. Nthch 121 F4
Emmanuel Rd. Norwd 174 C2
Emma's Cres. Sta Ab 115 D2
Empress Rd. Luton 44 C2
Endeavour Rd. Ches 148 C2
Enderby Rd. Luton 45 E3
Enderley Cl. Har 176 B1
Enderley Rd. Har 176 B1
Endersby Rd. Barn 171 E2
Endymion Rd. Hat 130 B3
Englefield. Luton 45 F2
Englehurst. Harp 86 B1
Enid Cl. Bri Wd 154 C4
Ennerdale Cl. St Alb 128 A1
Ennis Cl. Harp 107 E3
Ennismore Cl. Letw 23 E2
Enslow Cl. Cad 62 C2
Enterprise Centre The. Stev 50 A4
Enterprise Way. Luton 45 D4
Epping Green. Heml H 125 D4
Epping Way. Luton 44 B4
Ereswell Rd. Luton 45 D4
Erin Cl. Luton 45 D1
Ermine Cl. Ches 162 A4
Ermine Cl. Roystn 7 E4
Ermine Cl. St Alb 127 D1
Ermine Ct. Bun 40 C4
Ermine St. Thun 93 E4
Escot Way. Barn 171 E2
Esdaile La. Hod 135 D3
Eskdale. Lon C 142 C2
Eskdale Ct. Heml H 124 C3
Essendon Gdns. Wel GC 110 C3
Essex Cl. Luton 63 F3
Essex La. Abb L 153 E3
Essex Mead. Heml H 105 D1
Essex Rd. Bor 170 A3
Essex Rd. Hod 135 F3
Essex Rd. Stev 50 B4
Essex Rd. Watf 167 D4
Essex St. St Alb 127 F2
Estcourt Rd. Watf 167 E3
Ethelred Cl. Wel GC 110 C3
Etna Rd. St Alb 127 E2
Europa Rd. Heml H 124 C3
Euston Ave. Watf 166 C2

Evans Ave. Watf 153 F2
Evan's Cl. Cro Gr 166 A2
Evans Gr. St Alb 128 B4
Evedon Cl. Luton 44 C3
Evelyn Dri. Pnr 175 E2
Evelyn Rd. Dun 44 A1
Everard Cl. St Alb 127 E1
Everest Cl. Arl 11 D3
Everest Way. Heml H 125 D2
Evergreen Cl. Wl Gr 69 D1
Evergreen Rd. Ware 93 F2
Evergreen Way. Luton 45 D4
Everlasting La. St Alb 127 E3
Evron Pl. Hert 113 E3
Exchange Rd. Stev 50 C3
Exchange Rd. Watf 167 D3
Exchange Yard. Hit 34 C4
Exeter Cl. Stev 37 D1
Exton Ave. Luton 46 A1
Eynsford Ct. Hit 34 C3
Eywood Rd. St Alb 127 E1

Faggots Cl. Radl 156 B2
Fair Cl. Bus 168 A1
Fair Oak Dri. Luton 45 F2
Fair View. Pot B 145 D1
Fairacre. Heml H 138 C4
Fairacre Ct. Norwd 174 C2
Fairacres Cl. Pot B 158 C3
Fairburn Cl. Bor 170 A4
Faircross Way. St Alb 128 A3
Fairfax Ave. Luton 44 B4
Fairfax Rd. Hert 113 F4
Fairfield. Bun 40 C3
Fairfield Ave. Sth Ox 175 E4
Fairfield Cl. Harp 86 B1
Fairfield Cl. Radl 155 F1
Fairfield Dri. Hod 148 C4
Fairfield Rd. Hod 135 D4
Fairfield Way. Hit 35 E4
Fairfield Wlk. Ches 148 C2
Fairfolds. Watf 154 C2
Fairford Ave. Luton 45 F2
Fairgreen Rd. Cad 62 C2
Fairhaven. Pk St 141 E2
Fairhaven Cres. Sth Ox 175 D4
Fairlands Way. Stev 50 B3
Fairlawns. Pnr 175 E1
Fairlawns. Watf 153 F1
Fairley Way. Ches 148 A2
Fairmead Ave. Harp 107 E4
Fairseat Cl. Har 176 C4
Fairthorn Cl. Tri 99 F2
Fairview Dri. Watf 153 F2
Fairview Rd. Stev 50 A3
Fairway. Bis St 77 E3
Fairway. Gt Am 114 B4
Fairway. Heml H 138 C4
Fairway. Saw 97 F1
Fairway Ave. Bor 170 A4
Fairway Cl. Chis 141 E2
Fairway Cl. Harp 107 D3
Fairway The. Abb L 153 E4
Fairway The. Norwd 174 C3
Fairways. Ches 148 B3
Fairways. Wa Aby 163 F3
Falcon Cl. Hat 130 A2
Falcon Cl. Norwd 174 C2
Falcon Cl. Saw 97 E1
Falcon Cl. Stev 51 E1
Falcon Ridge. Berk 122 B2
Falcon Way. Watf 154 C3
Falconer Rd. Bus 168 A2
Falconers Field. Harp 85 F2
Falconers Park. Saw 97 E1
Falconers Rd. Luton 46 A1
Falkirk Gdns. Sth Ox 175 E3
Falkland Rd. Barn 171 F4
Fallowfield. Luton 45 E2
Fallowfield. Stev 51 E2
Fallowfield. Wel GC 89 F1
Fallowfield Cl. Hare 173 E1
Fallowfield Wlk. Heml H 124 A3
Fallows Green. Harp 86 A2
Falstaff Gdns. St Alb 141 F4
Falstone Green. Luton 46 C1
Fanhams Hall Rd. Ware 93 F2
Fanhams Rd. Ware 93 F1
Fanshaw Ct. Hert 113 E4
Fanshawe Cres. Ware 93 E1
Fanshawe St. Hert 113 D4
Fanshaws La. Bric 133 E3
Fantail La. Tri 99 F2
Far End. Hat 130 A1
Faraday Cl. Watf 166 B2
Faraday Rd. Stev 51 D3
Faringdon Rd. Luton 44 B2
Faringford Cl. Pot B 159 E4
Farland Rd. Heml H 125 D2
Farley Farm Rd. Luton 63 D3
Farley Hill. Luton 63 E3
Farm Ave. Harp 85 E2
Farm Cl. Barn 171 E2
Farm Cl. Ches 148 B1
Farm Cl. Cuf 146 C2
Farm Cl. Hertng 113 D3
Farm Cl. Letw 12 A1
Farm Cl. Stev 50 C2
Farm Cl. Wel GC 110 B3
Farm Green. Luton 63 E3
Farm Hill Rd. Wa Aby 163 E3
Farm La. Chor 165 E3
Farm La. Stand 73 D4
Farm Pl. Berk 121 F3
Farm Rd. Chor 164 A2
Farm Rd. Norwd 174 B3
Farm Rd. Nwml E 85 D4
Farm Rd. St Alb 128 A2
Farm Way. Bus 168 A3
Farm Way. Hat 130 B4
Farm Way. Norwd 174 C3
Farmers Cl. Watf 154 A3
Farmhouse Cl. Ches 148 C3
Farmstead Rd. Har 176 B1
Farnham Cl. Bov 137 D2
Farnham Cl. Saw 97 E1
Farquhar St. Hert 113 E4
Farraline Rd. Watf 167 D3
Farrant Way. Bor 169 F4
Farrer Top. Mark 83 F3
Farriday Cl. St Alb 127 F4
Farriers. Gt Am 115 D3
Farriers Cl. Bal 12 C1
Farriers Cl. Cod 67 F1
Farriers End. Ches 148 C3
Farriers Way. Bor 170 B2
Farringford Cl. Chis 141 D3
Farr's La. Nwml E 65 D1
Farthing Dri. Letw 23 E2
Farthings The. Heml H 124 A2
Faverolle Green. Ches 148 B2
Faversham Cl. Tri 100 A2
Fawcett Rd. Stev 51 D4
Fawkon Wlk. Hod 135 D3
Fawn Ct. Hat 130 B4
Fay Green. Abb L 153 E3
Fayerfield. P Bar 159 E4
Feacey Down. Heml H 124 A3
Fearney Mead. Ric 165 D1
Fearnley Rd. Wel GC 110 B3
Fearnley St. Watf 167 D3
Fears Green. San 15 E2
Feather Dell. Hat 130 A3
Featherbed La. Fel 138 A4
Featherbed La. Heml H 138 B4
Featherston Rd. Stev 51 E2
Featherstone Gdns. Bor 170 B3
Federal Way. Watf 167 E4
Felden Cl. Watf 154 B3
Felden Cl. Kin L 139 D1
Felden Dri. Fel 138 A4
Felden La. Fel 138 A4
Feldon Cl. Pnr 175 F2
Felix Ave. Luton 46 A1
Fell Path. Bor 170 B2
Fellowes La. Coln H 143 F4
Fellowes Way. Stev 51 D1
Fells Cl. Hit 34 C4
Felmersham Ct. Luton 63 D4
Felmersham Rd. Luton 63 D4
Felmongers. Harl 118 A1
Felstead Cl. Luton 45 F2
Felstead Rd. Ches 162 C4
Felstead Way. Luton 45 F2
Felton Cl. Bor 156 C1
Felton Cl. Ches 148 C3
Felton Cl. Luton 46 B1
Fen End. Stot 11 F4
Fennycroft Rd. Heml H 124 C4
Fensom's Alley. Heml H 124 B2
Fensom's Cl. Heml H 124 B2
Fenwick Cl. Luton 45 D3
Fermor Cres. Luton 46 B1
Fern Cl. Hod 148 C4
Fern Dells. Hat 129 F2
Fern Dri. Heml H 124 C1
Fern Gr. Wel GC 89 E1
Fern Way. Watf 154 A2
Ferndale Rd. Enf 162 C1
Ferndale Rd. Luton 63 D4
Ferndene. Bri Wd 154 C4
Ferndown. Norwd 175 D1
Ferndown Cl. Pnr 175 F2
Ferndown Rd. Sth Ox 175 E3
Fernecroft. St Alb 141 E4
Fernheath. Luton 31 D1
Fernhills. Abb L 153 E3
Fernleigh Ct. Har 176 A1
Fernleys. St Alb 128 B3
Ferns Cl. Enf 162 C2
Fernville La. Heml H 124 B2
Ferny Hill. Barn 159 F1
Ferrars Cl. Luton 44 A1
Ferrers La. Whea 108 A3
Ferrier Rd. Stev 51 E3
Ferryhills Cl. Sth Ox 175 E4
Feryngs Cl. Harl 118 B2
Fesants Croft. Harl 118 A2
Fetherstone Cl. Pot B 159 E4
Fiddle Bridge La. Hat 129 F3
Fidler Pl. Bus 168 A2
Field Cl. Harp 107 E4
Field Cres. Roystn 7 F4
Field End Cl. Luton 46 B2
Field End Cl. Watf 167 F1
Field Fare Green. Luton 44 A3
Field House Ct. Harp 86 A1
Field La. Letw 22 C2
Field Rd. Heml H 125 D2
Field Rd. Watf 167 F2
Field View. Barn 171 D3
Field View Rd. Pot B 159 D3
Field View Rise. Bri Wd 140 C1
Field Way. Bov 137 D2
Field Way. Hod 115 E1
Field Way. Ric 165 D1
Fieldfare. Letw 11 F1
Fieldgate Rd. Luton 44 B1
Fieldings Rd. Ches 148 C1
Field's Ct. Pot B 159 E3
Fields End. Tri 100 A2
Fields End La. Heml H 123 F3
Fieldway. Berk 122 C1
Fieldway. Sta Ab 115 D2
Fieldway. Wigg 100 B1
Fifth Ave. Harl 117 E1
Fifth Ave. Letw 23 E3
Fifth Ave. Watf 154 B2
Figtree Mill. Heml H 124 B2
Filey Cl. Stev 50 A4
Filmer Rd. Luton 44 C2
Finch Cl. Hat 130 A2
Finch Cl. Luton 44 A2
Finch La. Bus 168 A3
Finch Rd. Berk 122 A2
Finchdale. Heml H 124 A2
Finches The. Hit 35 D4
Finley Rd. Harp 86 B2
Finsbury Rd. Luton 44 B3
Finucane Rise. Bus 176 B4
Finway. Luton 62 C4
Finway Rd. Heml H 125 D4
Fir Cl. Stev 50 C1
Fir Station Alley. Barn 171 F4
Fir Tree Cl. Heml H 125 D1
Fir Tree Ct. Elst 169 F3
Fir Tree Hill. Cha Cr 153 D1
Firbank Dri. Watf 167 F1
Firbank Rd. St Alb 127 F4
Firecrest. Letw 11 F1
Firlands. Bis St 76 C3
Firs Cl. Hat 130 A2
Firs Cl. Hit 34 B4
Firs Dri. Bla En 87 E3
Firs La. Pot B 159 D3
Firs The. St Alb 142 A4
Firs The. Wel GC 89 E1
Firs The. Wigg 100 B2
Firs Wlk. Norwd 174 B2
Firs Wlk. Tewin 90 C3
First Ave. Harl 117 F1
First Ave. Watf 154 B2
Firway. Wl Gr 89 F4
Firway Cl. Wl Gr 89 F4
Firwood Ave. St Alb 128 C2
Fish Hill. Roystn 7 E3
Fish St. Red 106 A3
Fish Street Farm. Red 106 A3
Fisher Cl. Kin L 139 D1
Fisher Rd. Har 176 C1
Fishers Cl. Ches 163 D3
Fishers Cl. Puc 55 E2
Fishers Green. Stev 36 A1
Fisher's Green Rd. Stev 50 A4
Fishers Mead. Puc 55 E2
Fishery Pas. Heml H 124 A1
Fishery Rd. Heml H 124 A1
Fishponds Rd. Hit 34 C4
Fishpool St. St Alb 127 E2
Fitzjohn Ave. Barn 171 F3
Fitzroy Ave. Luton 45 D2
Fitzwarin Cl. Luton 44 C4
Fitzwilliam Ct. Harl 118 C2
Five Acre Wlk. Wel GC 110 C3
Five Acres. Lon C 142 B3
Five Acres. Sta M 59 F4
Five Acres Ave. Bri Wd 140 C1
Five Oaks. Cad 62 C2
Five Springs. Luton 44 C3
Flags The. Heml H 125 D2
Flagstaff Rd. Wa Aby 163 D3
Flamstead End Rd. Ches 148 A2
Flamsteadbury La. Red 106 A2
Flash La. Enf 161 E2
Flatfield Rd. Heml H 125 D1
Flaunden Bottom. Lat 150 C2
Flaunden Hill. Flau 151 D3
Flaunden La. Bov 137 F2
Flaunden La. Fel 138 A3
Flaunden La. Flau 151 D4
Flavian Cl. St Alb 126 C1
Flax Mews. Mark 83 F3
Flecker Cl. Stan 176 C3
Fleet The. Roystn 7 E3
Fleetwood. Letw 23 D2
Fleetwood Way. Sth Ox 175 E3
Fleming Cl. Ham St 148 A3
Fleming Cres. Hertng 113 D3
Fletcher Way. Heml H 124 B3
Flexley Wood. Wel GC 90 A1
Flinders Cl. St Alb 128 A1
Flinders Cl. Stev 51 E3
Flint Cl. Luton 44 C4
Flint Rd. Letw 23 E4
Flint Way. St Alb 127 E4
Flora Gr. St Alb 127 F1
Floral Dri. Lon C 142 B3
Florence Ave. Luton 44 B3
Florence Cl. Watf 154 A2
Florence St. Hit 34 C4
Florida Cl. Bus 168 B1
Flowers Industrial Estate. Luton 63 F3
Fold Croft. Harl 117 D1
Foldingshott. Dat 69 E2
Follett Dri. Abb L 153 F4
Folly Ave. St Alb 127 E2
Folly Cl. Hit 35 D3
Folly Cl. Radl 155 F2
Folly Fields. Whea 87 D1
Folly La. Cad 62 C2
Folly La. St Alb 127 E2
Folly Pathway. Radl 155 F2
Folly The. Bun 40 B4
Folly The. Hert 113 E3
Folly View. Sta Ab 115 D2
Fontmell Cl. St Alb 127 F3
Fontwell Cl. Har 176 B2
Football Cl. Bal 12 C1
Forbes Ave. Pot B 159 E4
Ford Cl. Bus 168 B3
Ford Hill. L Had 75 D4
Ford St. Brag 55 F3
Fordham Cl. Ashw 4 B3
Fordham Rd. Roystn 7 F3
Fordwich Cl. Hertng 113 D3
Fordwich Mill. Hertng 113 D3
Fordwich Rd. Wel GC 110 B3
Fordwich Rise. Hertng 113 D3
Fore St. Harl 118 B2
Fore St. Hat 130 B3
Fore St. Hert 113 E3
Fore St. Wes 24 A1
Forebury Ave. Saw 97 F1
Forebury Cres. Saw 97 F1
Forebury The. Saw 97 F1
Forefield. Chis 141 D2
Forelands Pl. Saw 97 F2
Forest Ave. Heml H 124 B1
Forest Rd. Ches 148 B1
Forest Rd. Enf 162 C2
Forest Rd. Watf 154 A3
Forest Row. Stev 50 C1
Forest Wlk. Bus 167 F4
Foresthall Rd. Birhr 59 F2
Forge Cl. Chipf 152 A4
Forge Cl. Hit 34 C4
Forge End. Chis 141 D3
Forge La. Norwd 174 C2
Forge La. Welw 89 E3
Forres Cl. Hod 135 D4
Forrest Cres. Luton 46 A2
Forresters Dri. Wel GC 111 E3
Fortnums Acre. Stan 176 C2
Fortune La. Elst 169 E2
Forty Hill. Enf 161 F1
Forum The. Stev 50 B3
Fosman Cl. Hit 34 B4
Foster Cl. Stev 36 B1
Foster Dri. Hit 35 D3
Foster Rd. Heml H 124 A1
Foston Cl. Luton 44 C3
Fotherley Rd. Ric 172 C4
Founceley Ave. Dan En 71 F4
Fountain Pl. Wa Aby 163 E3
Fountain's Rd. Luton 45 E2
Four Acres. Stev 50 C4
Four Acres. Wel GC 110 C2
Four Acres The. Saw 98 A1
Four Limes. Whea 108 B4
Four Tubs The. Bus 168 B1
Fouracres. Letw 23 D2
Fouracres Wlk. Heml H 138 C4
Fourth Ave. Harl 117 E1
Fourth Ave. Letw 23 E4
Fourth Ave. Luton 44 B4
Fourth Ave. Watf 154 B2
Fovant Cl. Harp 107 E3
Fowley Cl. Ches 162 C3
Fowlmere Rd. Gt Ch 9 F4
Fox Alley. Watf 167 E2
Fox Cl. Elst 169 E2
Fox Cl. Wigg 100 B2
Fox Cnr. Gu M 1 C3
Fox HILL. Gu M 1 C3
Fox HILL RD. Gu M 1 C3
Fox La. Ther 15 F4
Fox Rd. Stev 50 C2
Fox Rd. Wigg 100 B1
Foxbury Cl. Luton 45 E3
Foxcroft. St Alb 128 A1
Foxdell. Norwd 174 B2
Foxdells. Bir Gr 112 B2
Foxdells La. Bis St 58 C1
Foxes Dr. Ches 148 A1
Foxfield. Stev 51 E2
Foxfield Cl. Norwd 174 C2
Foxglove Bank. Roystn 7 F3
Foxglove Cl. Hat 130 A2
Foxglove Way. Wl Gr 89 F4
Foxgloves The. Heml H 123 F1
Foxgrove Path. Sth Ox 175 E3
Foxhill. Luton 45 F3
Foxhill. Watf 154 A2
Foxholes Ave. Hert 113 F3
Foxhollows. Hat 130 A4
Foxley Dri. Bis St 77 D4
Foxley Gr. Har Gr 89 F2
Foxleys. Watf 175 F4
Foxton Rd. Hod 135 D3
Frampton Rd. Pot B 145 E1
Frampton St. Hert 113 E3
Francis Ave. St Alb 127 E3
Francis Cl. Hit 35 D3
Francis Rd. Hin 3 E3
Francis Rd. Ware 93 E1
Francis Rd. Watf 167 D3
Francis St. Luton 63 E4
Frank Martin Ct. Ches 148 A1
Frankland Cl. Watf 166 A1
Frankland Rd. Cro Gr 166 A2
Franklin Ave. Ches 148 A1
Franklin Cl. Coln H 129 F1
Franklin Cl. Pirt 20 B2
Franklin Gdns. Hit 22 A1
Franklin Rd. Watf 167 D4
Franklin's Rd. Stev 50 B4
Franks Cl. Henlw 10 A2
Fraser Rd. Ches 148 C2
Frederick St. Luton 45 F1
Freeman Ave. Luton 45 D4
Freemans Cl. Hit 21 E1
Freewaters Cl. Ick 21 F2
Freman Dri. Bun 40 B4
French Horn La. Hat 130 A3
French Row. St Alb 127 E2
French's Cl. Sta Ab 115 D2
Frensham. Ham St 148 A2
Frensham Dri. Hit 22 B1
Freshwater Cl. Luton 44 C4
Freshwaters. Harl 117 F1
Fretherne Rd. Wel GC 110 B3
Friars Cl. Luton 63 D3
Friars Field. Nthch 121 F4
Friars Rd. Brag 56 A4
Friars Rd. Wes 24 A1
Friars Way. Bus 167 F4
Friars Way. Kin L 139 D1
Friars Way. Luton 63 D3
Friars Wlk. Tri 100 A2
Friars Wood. Bis St 77 E4
Friarscroft. Hod 135 D2
Friday Furlong. Hit 34 B4
Friedburg Ave. Bis St 76 B2
Friendless La. Fla 83 F2
Friesian Cl. Luton 44 A2
Frimley Rd. Heml H 123 F2
Fringewood Cl. Norwd 174 A1
Frinton Cl. Sth Ox 175 D4
Friston Green. Luton 46 B1
Frithsden Copse. Pop En 122 C4
Frithwood Ave. Norwd 174 C2
Frobisher Dri. Stev 51 D4
Frobisher Rd. St Alb 128 B1
Froghall La. Wal 38 A1
Frogmoor Ct. Ric 173 E4
Frogmoor La. Ric 173 E4
Frogmore. Fro 141 F2
Frogmore Hill. Ast 70 A4
Frogmore Rd. Heml H 138 B4
Frogmore St. Tri 100 A2
Frogs Hall La. Hault 53 F2
Frome Cl. Luton 44 C2
Frome Sq. Heml H 125 D4
Front St. Cad 63 E1
Front The. Pot En 123 D4
Frowick Cl. Wel Gr 144 A4
Frowyke Cres. Pot B 158 A4
Fry Rd. Stev 51 E3
Fulbeck Way. Har 176 B1
Fulford Gr. Sth Ox 175 D4
Fuller Ct. Bis St 77 D4
Fuller Gdns. Watf 154 A1
Fuller Rd. Watf 154 A1
Fuller Way. Cro Gr 166 A2
Fullers Cl. Wa Aby 163 F3
Fulling Mill La. Welw 89 D3
Fullmore Cl. Harp 86 B2
Fulmar Cres. Heml H 124 A2
Fulton Cl. Stev 50 B3
Fulton Cres. Bis St 77 E4
Furham Field. Pnr 176 A2
Furlong Way. Gt Am 115 D3
Furlongs. Heml H 124 A2
Furrows The. Luton 45 D4
Furse Ave. St Alb 128 A4
Furtherfield. Abb L 153 F4
Furtherground. Heml H 124 C2
Furze Cl. Sth Ox 175 E3
Furze Gr. Roystn 7 F3
Furze Rd. Heml H 123 F1
Furze View. Chor 164 B2
Furzebushes La. Chis 140 C3
Furzedown. Stev 51 D2
Furzedown Ct. Harp 86 A1
Furzefield. Ches 148 A2
Furzefield Rd. Wel GC 110 C2
Furzehill Rd. Bor 170 A2
Furzen Cres. Hat 130 A1

Gable Cl. Abb L 153 F4
Gable Cl. Pnr 176 A2
Gables Ave. Bor 169 F3
Gables The. Heml H 124 B2
Gaddesden Cres. Watf 154 C3
Gaddesden Gr. Wel GC 111 E3
Gaddesden La. Red 105 E2
Gaddesden Row. Gt Ga 104 B3
Gade Ave. Watf 166 C3
Gade Bank. Cro Gr 166 B3
Gade Cl. Heml H 124 A3
Gade Side. Watf 153 F2
Gade Valley Cl. Bed 139 D2
Gade View Gdns. Abb L 153 E4
Gade View Rd. Fel 138 B4
Gadebridge La. Heml H 124 A3
Gadebridge La. Pic En 124 B3
Gadebridge Rd. Heml H 124 A2
Gadswell Cl. Watf 154 C2
Gage Cl. Roystn 7 E4
Gainsborough Ave. St Alb 127 F2
Gainsford Cres. Hit 22 B1
Gainswood. Wel GC 110 C3
Gall End La. Sta Mo 59 F4
Galley Green. Hod 115 D1
Galley Hill. Heml H 124 A3
Galley La. Barn 171 D3
Galleyhill Rd. Wa Aby 163 F4
Galloway Cl. Bis St 76 C4
Galloway Cl. Ches 148 C3
Galloway Rd. Bis St 58 C1
Gallows Hill. Abb L 153 E4
Gallows Hill La. Abb L 153 E4
Galston Rd. Luton 44 B4
Gammons La. Watf 154 A1
Gamnel Terr. Tri 100 A3
Ganders Ash. Watf 154 A3
Gangies Hill. H Wy 97 D2
Gant Ct. Wa Aby 163 F3
Ganton Wlk. Sth Ox 175 F3
Ganymede Pl. Heml H 124 C3
Gaping La. Hit 34 B4
Garden Ave. Hat 130 A1
Garden Cl. Harp 107 E3
Garden Cl. Roystn 7 F4
Garden Cl. St Alb 128 A2
Garden Cl. Watf 166 C4
Garden Cl. Wl Gr 69 D1
Garden Ct. Barn 171 E3
Garden Ct. Whea 87 E1
Garden Field. Ast 51 F1
Garden Field La. Berk 122 C1
Garden La. Roystn 7 E3
Garden Rd. Abb L 153 F4
Garden Rd. Bun 40 C4
Garden Rd. Wl Gr 69 D1
Garden Row. Hit 34 C4

Garden Terrace Rd. Harl 118 B2
Garden Wlk. Roystn 7 F4
Garden Wlk. Stev 50 C3
Gardenia Ave. Luton 45 D2
Gardens The. Bro Pk 144 C2
Gardens The. Henlw 10 B4
Gardens The. Stot 11 F3
Gardens The. Watf 166 C4
Gardiners La. Ashw 4 B2
Garfield St. Watf 154 A1
Garland Cl. Heml H 124 B2
Garland Rd. Ware 93 F1
Garnault Rd. Enf 161 F1
Garner Dri. Ches 148 C3
Garnett Cl. Watf 154 B2
Garnett Dr. Bri Wd 140 C1
Garrard Way. Whea 108 B4
Garratts Rd. Bus 168 B1
Garretts Mead. Luton 46 A2
Garrowsfield. Barn 171 F2
Garsmouth Way. Watf 154 B2
Garston Cres. Watf 154 B3
Garston Dri. Watf 154 B3
Garston La. Watf 154 B3
Garston Park Par. Watf 154 B3
Garth Rd. Letw 22 C2
Garth The. Abb L 153 E3
Garthland Dri. Barn 171 E2
Gartlet Rd. Watf 167 E3
Gas La. Bark 17 E2
Gascoyne Cl. Pot B 150 A4
Gascoyne Way. Hert 113 E3
Gate Cl. Bor 170 B4
Gate End. Norwd 175 D2
Gatecroft. Heml H 124 C1
Gatehill Rd. Norwd 175 D2
Gatehouse Mews. Bun 40 C4
Gates Way. Stev 50 B3
Gatesdene Cl. L Gad 102 B4
Gateshead Rd. Bor 170 A4
Gateway Cl. Norwd 174 B2
Gatwick Cl. Bis St 59 D1
Gauldie Way. Stand 55 E1
Gaunts Way. Letw 12 A1
Gaveston Dri. Berk 122 A3
Gayland Ave. Luton 64 A4
Gayton Cl. Luton 45 D2
Gaywood Ave. Ches 148 B1
Gdns The. Bal 23 F4
Gean Wlk. Hat 130 A1
Geddes Rd. Bus 168 B3
Geddings Rd. Hod 135 D3
General Wlk The. Enf 162 C1
George La. Roystn 7 E3
George St. Berk 122 B2
George St. Heml H 124 B2
George St. Hert 113 E3
George St. Luton 63 F4
George St. Mark 83 F3
George St. Watf 167 E3
George St W. Luton 63 F4
George V Ave. Pnr 175 F1
George V Way. Sar 152 A2
Georges Mead. Elst 169 E2
George's Wood Rd. Bro Pk 145 D3
Georgewood Rd. Heml H 139 D4
Gerard Ave. Bis St 76 C2
German Wlk. Letw 22 C3
Gernon Rd. Letw 22 C3
Gew's Car. Ches 148 B1
Giant Tree Hill. Bus 168 B1
Gibbons Cl. Bor 169 F4
Gibbons Cl. Sand 108 B1
Gibbons Way. Kneb 68 C3
Gibbs Cl. Ches 148 B1
Gibbs Couch. Watf 175 E4
Gibbs Field. Bis St 76 B3
Gidian Ct. Chis 141 E2
Gifford's La. Hault 54 A1
Gilbert Rd. Hare 173 E1
Gilbert St. Enf 162 B1
Gilbert Way. Berk 122 A2
Gilbert's Hill. St Le 119 F2
Gilbey Ave. Bis St 77 D3
Gilbey Cres. Sta Mo 59 F4
Gilden Cl. Harl 118 C2
Gilden Way. Harl 118 C2
Gilder Cl. Luton 45 D4
Gilderdale. Luton 44 A3
Gilders. Saw 97 E1
Giles Cl. Sand 108 B1
Gillan Green. Bus 176 B4
Gilliam St. Luton 63 F4
Gillian Ave. St Alb 141 E4
Gills Hill La. Radl 155 F2
Gills Hollow. Radl 155 F2
Gills Mill. Radl 156 A2
Gilmour Cl. Enf 162 A2
Gilpin Green. Harp 86 B1
Gilpin Rd. Gt Am 114 C4
Gilpin's Gallop. Sta Ab 115 D2
Gilpin's Ride. Berk 122 C3
Gilsland. Wa Aby 163 F2
Ginns Rd. Sto P 43 E3
Gippeswyck Cl. Pnr 175 E1
Gipsy La. Hat 110 C1
Gipsy La. Kneb 68 C2
Gipsy La. Luton 64 A3
Gipsy La. Sta Mo 59 E2
Girdle Rd. Hit 22 A1
Girons Cl. Hit 35 D4
Girtin Rd. Bus 168 B3
Girton Ct. Ches 148 C1
Girton Way. Cro Gr 166 B2
Glade The. Bal 23 F4
Glade The. Letw 22 C2
Glade The. Wel GC 110 B4
Glades The. Heml H 123 F2
Gladeside. St Alb 128 B3
Gladeway The. Wa Aby 163 E3
Gladsmuir Rd. Barn 171 F4
Gladstone Ave. Luton 63 E4
Gladstone Rd. Dan En 71 F4
Gladstone Rd. Hod 135 D4
Gladstone Rd. Ware 93 E1
Gladstone Rd. Watf 167 E3
Glamis Cl. Ches 148 A1
Glamis Cl. Heml H 105 D1
Glanfield. Heml H 124 C3
Gleave Cl. St Alb 128 A2
Glebe Ave. Ch En 11 D4
Glebe Cl. Ess 131 F3
Glebe Cl. Heml H 138 C4
Glebe Cl. Pit 80 B3
Glebe Cl. Wat St 70 B2
Glebe Cotts. Ess 131 F3
Glebe Ct. Bis St 77 D4
Glebe La. Barn 171 D2
Glebe Rd. Hert 113 E4
Glebe Rd. Letw 23 D4
Glebe Rd. Welw 89 D3
Glebe The. Kin L 139 D1
Glebe The. Watf 154 B3
Glebelands. Harl 117 F2
Gleed Ave. Bus 176 B4
Glemsford Cl. Luton 44 A3
Glemsford Dri. Harp 86 B1
Glen Faba Rd. Roy 135 F3
Glen The. Heml H 124 C4
Glen The. Norwd 174 B2
Glen Way. Watf 153 F1
Glencoe Rd. Bus 168 A2
Glencourse Green. Sth Ox 175 E3
Glendale. Heml H 124 A2
Glendale Wlk. Ches 148 C1
Gleneagles Cl. Sth Ox 175 E3
Glenester Cl. Hod 115 D1
Glenferrie Rd. St Alb 128 A2
Glenfield Rd. Luton 45 E3
Glenhaven Ave. Bor 170 A3
Glenlyn Ave. St Alb 128 A1
Glenmire Terr. Sta Ab 115 E2
Glenview Rd. Heml H 124 A2
Glenville Ave. Enf 161 E1
Glenwood. Hod 134 C2
Glenwood. Wel GC 111 E3
Glenwood Cl. Stev 51 E1
Glevum Cl. St Alb 126 C1
Globe Cres. Far 58 B3
Globe Ct. Hert 113 E4
Globe Ct. Hod 148 C4
Gloucester Ave. Ches 162 C3
Gloucester Rd. Enf 161 E1
Gloucester Rd. Luton 63 F3
Glovers Cl. Hert 113 E2
Glynde The. Stev 69 D4
Goat La. Enf 161 F1
Gobions Way. Pot B 145 D2
Goblins Green. Wel GC 110 B3
Goddard End. Ast 51 E1
Goddard End. Stev 69 E4
Goddards Cl. L Berk 132 B2
Goddfreys Cl. Luton 63 D3
Godfrey Cl. Stev 51 D2
Godfries Cl. Tewin 90 C2
Godsafe. Harl 118 C2
Goffs Cres. Gofs O 147 E1
Goffs La. Ches 147 F1
Goffs La. Gofs O 147 F1
Goff's Oak Ave. Gofs O 147 E2
Gold Crest Cl. Luton 44 A3
Golda Cl. Barn 171 E2
Goldcrest Way. Bus 168 B1
Goldcroft. Heml H 125 D1
Golden Dell. Wel GC 110 C1
Goldfield Rd. Tri 99 F2
Goldfinch Way. Bor 170 A3
Goldings. Bis St 77 D4
Goldings Cres. Hat 130 A3
Goldings La. Wat 92 A1
Goldington Cl. Hod 114 C1
Goldon. Letw 23 E2
Goldstone Cl. Ware 93 E1
Golf Cl. Bus 167 E3
Golf Club Rd. Bro Pk 145 D3
Golf Ride. Enf 161 D2
Gombards. St Alb 127 E2
Gombard's Alley. St Alb 127 E2
Gomer Cl. Cod 67 F1
Gonville Ave. Cro Gr 166 A2
Gonville Cres. Stev 51 E1
Goodey Meade. Heb En 52 C1
Goodrich Cl. Watf 154 A2
Goodwin Stile. Bis St 76 B3
Goodwins Mead. Ched 80 A4
Goodwood Ave. Enf 162 B1
Goodwood Ave. Watf 153 F2
Goodwood Cl. Hod 135 D4
Goodwood Path. Bor 170 A4
Goodwood Rd. Roystn 7 F3
Goodyers Ave. Radl 155 F3
Goose Acre. Bot 136 A1
Goose Acre. Ched 80 A4
Goose La. Gt Ha 98 C4
Gooseacre. Wel GC 110 C2
Gooseberry Hill. Luton 45 D4
Gooseberry Hill S. Luton 45 D4
Goosecroft. Heml H 123 F2
Goral Mead. Ric 165 E1
Gordon Ave. Stan 176 C2
Gordon Cl. St Alb 128 A1
Gordon Rd. Wa Aby 163 D3
Gordon St. Luton 63 E4
Gordon Way. Barn 171 F3
Gore La. Stand 73 E2
Gorham Dri. St Alb 141 F4
Gorle Cl. Watf 154 A2
Gorleston Cl. Stev 36 A1
Gorse Cl. Hat 129 F1
Gorselands. Harp 107 E4
Gorst Cl. Letw 22 C3
Gosforth La. Sth Ox 175 D4
Gosforth Path. Sth Ox 175 D4
Goshawk Cl. Luton 44 A2
Gosling Ave. Gt Of 33 E1
Gosmore Rd. Hit 34 C3
Gossamers The. Watf 154 C2
Gosselin Rd. Hert 113 E4
Gossom's End. Berk 122 A3
Gossoms Ride. Berk 122 A3
Gothic Way. Arl 11 D3
Gould Cl. Wel Gr 144 A4
Government Row. Enf 163 D1
Gowar Field. Pot B 158 A4
Gower Rd. Roystn 7 E4
Gowers The. Harl 118 A1
Grace Cl. Bor 170 B4
Grace Gdns. Bis St 76 C2
Grace Way. Stev 50 C4
Graces Maltings. Tri 100 A2
Graemes Dyke Rd. Berk 122 A2
Graham Ave. Hod 134 C1
Graham Cl. St Alb 127 E1
Graham Gdns. Luton 45 E2
Graham Rd. Har 176 C1
Grailands. Bis St 76 B4
Grammar School Wlk. Hit 34 C4
Grampian Way. Luton 44 B4
Granary Cl. Whea 108 B4
Granary La. Harp 86 B1
Granary The. Roy 116 A1
Granby Ave. Harp 86 B1
Granby Park Rd. Ham St 147 F2
Granby Rd. Luton 44 C1
Granby Rd. Stev 36 B1
Grandfield Ave. Watf 167 D4
Grange Ave. Luton 44 B3
Grange Ave. N20 171 F1
Grange Bottom. Roystn 7 F3
Grange Cl. Heml H 125 D1
Grange Cl. Hert 113 D3
Grange Cl. Hit 35 D2
Grange Cl. Mark 83 E3
Grange Court Rd. Harp 107 E3
Grange Ct. Hert 113 E4
Grange Ct. Wa Aby 163 E3
Grange Dri. Stot 11 F3
Grange Gdns. Gt Am 114 C4
Grange Hill. Welw 89 E3
Grange La. Aldhm 168 B4
Grange Park. Bis St 58 C1
Grange Rd. Bis St 77 D4
Grange Rd. Bus 167 F2
Grange Rd. Elst 169 F2
Grange Rd. Letw 22 C4
Grange Rd. Pit 80 B3
Grange Rd. Tri 100 B2
Grange Rd. Wils 79 E1
Grange Rise. Cod 67 F1
Grange St. St Alb 127 E2
Grange Wlk. Bis St 77 D4
Grangedale Cl. Norwd 174 C1
Grangeside. Bis St 59 D1
Grangewood. Pot B 145 D1
Gransden Cl. Luton 45 D4
Grant Gdns. Harp 86 A1
Grantham Cl. Roystn 7 D4
Grantham Gdns. Ware 93 F1
Grantham Green. Bor 170 B2
Grantham Rd. Luton 45 D1
Granville Dene. Bov 137 D2
Granville Gdns. Hod 115 D1
Granville Rd. Barn 171 E3
Granville Rd. Hit 22 B1
Granville Rd. Luton 63 D4
Granville Rd. Nthch 121 F3
Granville Rd. St Alb 127 F2
Granville Rd. Watf 167 E3
Grasmere Ave. Harp 86 B1
Grasmere Ave. Luton 45 D4
Grasmere Cl. Heml H 125 D1
Grasmere Cl. Watf 154 A4
Grasmere Rd. Luton 45 E4
Grasmere Rd. St Alb 128 A1
Grasmere Rd. Ware 93 F2
Grass Meadows. Stev 51 E4
Grass Warren. Tewin 90 C1
Grassington Cl. Bri Wd 141 D1
Grassy Cl. Heml H 124 A2
Gravel Hill. Heml H 124 A2
Gravel La. Heml H 124 A2
Gravel Path. Berk 122 A3
Gravel Path. Heml H 124 A2
Graveley Ave. Bor 170 B2
Graveley Dell. Wel GC 111 D3
Graveley La. Gt Wy 36 A3
Gravelhill Terr. Heml H 124 A1
Gravely Ct. Heml H 125 E1
Graylings The. Abb L 153 E3
Grays Cl. Roystn 7 E4
Grays Ct. Bis St 76 C4
Gray's La. Hit 34 B4
Graysfield. Wel GC 111 D2
Grazings The. Heml H 124 C3
Great Braitch La. Hat 109 F1
Great Break. Wel GC 111 D3
Great Cambridge Rd. Ches 148 B2
Great Cambridge Rd. Enf 162 A2
Great Conduit. Wel GC 111 E4
Great Dell. Wel GC 89 E1
Great Elms Rd. Heml H 138 C4
Great Ganett. Wel GC 111 E2
Great Gr. Bus 168 A2
Great Hadham Rd. Bis St 76 B3
Great Heart. Heml H 124 C3
Great Heath. Hat 130 A4
Great Innings N. Wat St 70 B2
Great Innings S. Wat St 70 B2
Great Lawne. Dat 69 E1
Great Ley. Wel GC 110 C2
Great Meadow. Lo Naz 135 D1
Great Molewood. Hert 92 A1
Great North Rd. A St P 110 A4
Great North Rd. Barn 171 F3
Great North Rd. Bro Pk 145 D2
Great North Rd. Hat 130 A2
Great North Rd. Lem 110 A3
Great North Rd. Pot B 159 E3
Great North Rd. Rad 12 B2
Great North Rd. Stanb 110 A2
Great North Rd. Stot 12 B3
Great North Rd. Wel Gr 144 C4
Great North Rd. Wl Gr 89 F4
Great Palmers. Heml H 124 C4
Great Park. Kin L 139 D1
Great Plumtree. Harl 117 F1
Great Rd. Heml H 124 C2
Great Slades. Pot B 158 C3
Great Sturgess Rd. Heml H 123 F2
Great Whifes Rd. Heml H 124 C1
Greatfield Cl. Harp 85 E2
Greatham Rd. Watf 167 E3
Green Acres. Lily 32 B1
Green Acres. Stev 51 E1
Green Acres Wel GC 110 C2
Green Cl. Bro Pk 144 C3
Green Cl. Ches 162 C4
Green Cl. Luton 44 B3
Green Cl. Stev 51 D1
Green Croft. Hat 130 A4
Green Dell Way. Heml H 125 E2
Green Drift. Roystn 7 D4
Green End La. Heml H 123 F2
Green End Rd. Heml H 124 A1
Green Hill Cl. Brag 55 F4
Green La. Ashw 4 C3
Green La. Bov 137 D2
Green La. Brag 55 F4
Green La. Cro Gr 165 F2
Green La. Harp 107 E4
Green La. Hat 109 F1
Green La. Heml H 125 E2
Green La. Hit 22 A1
Green La. Ivin 80 C3
Green La. Ken Co 82 C4
Green La. Lat 150 A3
Green La. Letw 23 E4
Green La. Lo Naz 149 D4
Green La. Luton 46 B2
Green La. Norwd 174 C2
Green La. St Alb 142 A4
Green La. St Alb 127 E4
Green La. Stanb 109 F2
Green La. Watf 167 E1
Green La. Wel GC 111 E3
Green Lane Cl. Harp 107 F4
Green Meadow. Pot B 145 D1
Green Oaks. Luton 45 F2
Green St. Bor 157 D1
Green St. Chen 164 B4
Green St. Chor 164 B3
Green St. Roystn 7 E4
Green St. Shen 157 D2
Green St. Stev 50 B4
Green The. Bis St 76 C2
Green The. Ched 80 A4
Green The. Ches 148 B2
Green The. Cod 67 F1
Green The. Cro Gr 165 F2
Green The. Ivin 80 B2
Green The. L Gad 102 B4
Green The. Luton 44 B3
Green The. Newn 12 C4
Green The. Old K 68 B3
Green The. Pet Gr 65 E2
Green The. Roystn 7 E3
Green The. Sar 152 A2
Green The. Stot 11 F4
Green The. Wa Aby 163 E3
Green The. Ware 93 E2
Green The. Wel GC 111 D2
Green The. Welw 89 D3
Green View Cl. Bov 137 D1
Green Way Gdns. Har 176 C1
Green Way The. Har 176 C1
Green Wlk. Roystn 7 E3
Greenacre Cl. Pot B 158 C1
Greenacres. Bus 176 B4
Greenacres. Heml H 125 E1
Greenacres. Pit 80 B2
Greenall Cl. Ches 148 C1
Greenbank. Ches 148 A2
Greenbank Rd. Watf 153 E2
Greenbury Cl. Chor 164 B3
Greencoates. Hert 113 F3
Greene Field Rd. Berk 122 B2
Greene Wlk. Berk 122 B2
Greenfield. Hat 130 B4
Greenfield. Roystn 7 D4
Greenfield. Wel GC 89 E1
Greenfield Ave. Ick 21 E2
Greenfield Ave. Watf 175 F4
Greenfield La. Ick 21 F2
Greenfield Pas. Barn 171 F3
Greenfield Rd. Stev 50 C4
Greenfield St. Wa Aby 163 E3
Greenfields. Cuf 146 C1
Greenfields. Sta Mo 59 F4
Greengate. Luton 44 B4
Greenheys Cl. Norwd 174 C1
Greenhill Ave. Luton 45 F2
Greenhill Cres. Watf 166 C2
Greenhill Ct. Heml H 124 A1
Greenhill Park. Bis St 76 B3
Greenhills. Ware 93 E2
Greenhills Cl. Chor 165 D2
Greenland Rd. Barn 171 E2
Greenlane Industrial Estate. Letw 23 E4
Greenleas. Wa Aby 163 F3
Greenside. Bor 157 D1
Greenside Dri. Hit 34 B4
Greenstead. Saw 97 F1
Greensward. Bus 168 A2
Greenway. Berk 122 A2
Greenway. Bis St 77 E3
Greenway. Harp 107 F4
Greenway. Heml H 125 D2
Greenway. Letw 23 D1
Greenway. Pnr 175 D1
Greenway. Wal 52 A4
Greenway The. Enf 162 B2
Greenway The. Pot B 159 D3
Greenway The. Ric 165 D1
Greenway The. Tri 99 F3
Greenways. Abb L 153 F4
Greenways. Bun 40 B4
Greenways. Gofs O 147 D1
Greenways. Hertng 113 D3
Greenways. Luton 46 A3
Greenways. Stev 50 C3
Greenwood Ave. Ches 162 A4
Greenwood Cl. Ches 162 A4
Greenwood Dri. Watf 154 A3
Greenyard. Wa Aby 163 E3
Greer Rd. Har 176 B1
Gregories Cl. Luton 45 E1
Gregory Ave. Pot B 159 E3
Grenadine Way. Tri 100 A3
Grenville Ave. Hod 134 C1
Grenville Cl. Ches 162 B4
Grenville Ct. Chor 164 B3
Gresford Cl. St Alb 128 A2
Gresham Cl. Luton 64 B4
Gresham Ct. Berk 122 A2
Gresley Ct. Enf 162 B2
Gresley Way. Stev 51 E2
Gresley Way. Stev 51 E4
Greville Cl. Wel Gr 144 B4
Greycaine Rd. Watf 154 B1
Greydells Rd. Stev 50 C4
Greyfriars. Ware 93 D2
Greyhound La. Pot B 158 A3
Greystoke Cl. Berk 122 A2
Grimsdyke Cres. Barn 171 E3
Grimsdyke Rd. Pnr 175 F2
Grimsdyke Rd. Wigg 100 B1
Grimston Rd. St Alb 127 F1
Grimstone Rd. L Wym 35 F2
Grimthorpe Cl. St Alb 127 E3
Grindcobbe Cl. St Alb 141 E4
Grinstead La. L Hal 98 B3
Groom Rd. Ches 148 C3
Grooms Cotts. Bot 136 A1
Groomsby Dri. Ivin 80 C3
Grosvenor Ave. Bed 139 E2
Grosvenor Ct. Cro Gr 166 B2
Grosvenor Rd. Bal 12 C1
Grosvenor Rd. Bor 170 A3
Grosvenor Rd. Hod 134 C2
Grosvenor Rd. Luton 45 D3
Grosvenor Rd. Norwd 174 C3
Grosvenor Rd. St Alb 127 F1
Grosvenor Rd. Watf 167 E3
Grosvenor Rd W. Bal 12 C1
Grosvenor Terr. Heml H 124 A1
Grotto The. Gt Am 114 A4
Ground La. Hat 130 A4
Grove Ave. Harp 107 E4
Grove Cres. Cro Gr 166 A3
Grove Ct. Wa Aby 163 D3
Grove Farm Park. Norwd 174 B3
Grove Gdns. Enf 162 B1
Grove Gdns. Tri 100 A3
Grove Hall Rd. Bus 167 F3
Grove Hill. Sta Mo 59 F4
Grove La. Ash Gr 136 B3
Grove Lea. Hat 130 A1
Grove Mead. Hat 129 F3
Grove Meadow. Wel GC 111 E3
Grove Mill La. Watf 153 E1
Grove Park. Tri 100 B3
Grove Park Rd. Cad 63 D1
Grove Path. Ches 162 A4
Grove Pl. Bis St 76 C4
Grove Rd. Bor 170 A4
Grove Rd. Cad 63 D1
Grove Rd. Harp 107 E4
Grove Rd. Heml H 124 A1
Grove Rd. Hit 21 F1
Grove Rd. Luton 63 E4
Grove Rd. Norwd 174 B3
Grove Rd. Ric 173 D4
Grove Rd. Stev 50 B4
Grove Rd. Tri 100 A2
Grove Rd. Ware 93 F1
Grove Rd West. Enf 162 B1
Grove The. Bro Pk 145 D2
Grove The. Bry Gr 75 F4
Grove The. Gt Ha 77 F2
Grove The. Lat 150 B2
Grove The. Luton 63 D3
Grove The. Pot B 159 E4
Grove The. Radl 156 A3
Grove Way. Chor 164 A2
Grove Wlk. Hert 113 E4
Grovedale Cl. Ches 147 F1
Groveland Way. Stot 12 A3
Grovelands. Chis 141 D2
Grovelands Ave. Hit 22 B1
Grover Cl. Heml H 124 B2
Grover Rd. Watf 167 E2
Grovesnor Cl. Bis St 76 B2
Grovewood Cl. Chor 164 A2
Grubb's Hill. Wa Aby 149 E1
Grubs La. Wild 145 E4

Guernsey Cl. Luton 44 A2
Guessens Ct. Wel GC 110 B3
Guessens Gr. Wel GC 110 B3
Guessens Rd. Wel GC 110 B3
Guessens Wlk. Wel GC 110 B4
Guildford Rd. St Alb 128 A1
Guildford St. Luton 63 F4
Guilfords. Harl 118 B3
Guinevere Gdns. Ches 148 C1
Gulland Cl. Bus 168 B2
Gullbrook. Heml H 124 A2
Gullet Wood Rd. Watf 154 A2
Gulphs The. Hert 113 E3
Gun La. Kneb 68 C2
Gun Meadow Ave. Kneb 69 D2
Gun Rd. Kneb 69 D2
Gun Road Gdns. Kneb 68 C2
Gunnels Wood Industrial Estate 50 B2
Gunnels Wood Rd. Stev 50 A3
Gurney Court Rd. St Alb 128 A3
Gurney's La. Hol 21 D4
Gwent Cl. Watf 154 B3
Gwynfa Cl. Wl Gr 89 E4
Gwynne Cl. Tri 100 A3
Gwynn's Wlk. Hert 113 F3
Gyford Walk. Ches 162 A4
Gypsy Cl. Gt Am 114 C2
Gypsy La. Abb L 153 E3
Gypsy La. Gt Am 114 C2

Hackforth Cl. Barn 171 D2
Hackney Cl. Bor 170 B2
Haddon Cl. Bor 170 A3
Haddon Cl. Heml H 125 D1
Haddon Cl. Stev 69 E4
Haddon Ct. Harp 86 A1
Haddon Rd. Chor 164 B2
Haddon Rd. Luton 63 F4
Hadham Rd. Bis St 76 B4
Hadham Rd. Stand 55 F1
Hadleigh Ct. Harp 107 F3
Hadleigh Ct. Hod 134 C1
Hadley Cl. Elst 169 F2
Hadley Gr. Barn 171 F4
Hadley Green. Barn 171 F4
Hadley Green Rd. Barn 171 F4
Hadley Green W. Barn 171 F4
Hadley Highstone. Barn 171 F4
Hadley Rd. Enf 160 A1
Hadley Ridge. Barn 171 F3
Hadlow Down Cl. Luton 45 D3
Hadrian Cl. St Alb 127 D1
Hadrian Way. Letw 23 E4
Hadrians Way. Bal 23 E4
Hadwell Cl. Stev 51 D2
Haelfoot. Letw 22 C3
Hagdell Rd. Luton 63 E3
Hagden La. Watf 166 C2
Haggerston Rd. Bor 156 C1
Hagsdell La. Hert 113 E3
Hagsdell Rd. Hert 113 E3
Haig Cl. St Alb 128 A1
Hailey Ave. Hod 115 D1
Hailey La. Hert H 114 C1
Hailey La. Hod 114 C1
Haines Way. Watf 154 A3
Haldens. Wel GC 89 F1
Hale Ct. Hert 113 E3
Hale Rd. Hert 113 E3
Hales Park. Heml H 125 E2
Hales Park Cl. Heml H 125 E2
Haleswood Rd. Heml H 125 D2
Half Acres. Bis St 76 C4
Half Moon La. Cad 63 E1
Half Moon La. Mark 84 A4
Half Moon Meadow. Heml H 125 D4
Halfacre La. Gt Ho 29 D1
Halfhide La. Ches 148 B3
Halfhides. Wa Aby 163 E3
Halfway Ave. Luton 44 B1
Halifax Rd. Heron 164 B1
Halifax Way. Wel Gc 111 F3
Hall Cl. Ric 165 D1
Hall Dri. Hare 173 E1
Hall Gdns. Coln H 143 E4
Hall Gr. Wel GC 111 D2
Hall Heath Cl. St Alb 128 A3
Hall La. Gt Ch 9 F1
Hall La. Gt Ho 29 D1
Hall La. Kim 66 B1
Hall Mead. Letw 22 B3
Hall Park. Berk 122 C2
Hall Park Gate. Berk 122 C2
Hall Park Hill. Berk 122 C2
Hall Place Gdns. St Alb 127 F2
Hallam Gdns. Pnr 175 F2
Halland Way. Norwd 174 B2
Halling Hill. Harl 117 F1
Hallingbury Cl. L Hal 77 D1
Hallingbury Rd. Bis St 77 D2
Hallingbury Rd. Saw 98 A2
Hallmores. Hod 135 D2
Hallowell Rd. Norwd 174 C2
Hallowes Cres. Sth Ox 175 D4
Hallside Rd. Enf 161 F1
Hallwicks Rd. Luton 46 A2
Hallworth Dri. Stot 11 F3
Halsey Dri. Hit 35 D4
Halsey Pl. Watf 154 A1
Halsey Rd. Watf 167 D3
Halstead Hill. Ches 147 F1
Halter Cl. Bor 170 B2
Haltside. Hat 129 F2
Halyard Cl. Luton 45 D3
Hamberlins La. Nthch 121 D4
Hambro Cl. Nwml E 85 F4
Hamburgh Ct. Ches 148 B2
Hamels Dri. Hert 114 A4
Hamilton Ave. Hod 135 D4
Hamilton Cl. Bric 155 D4
Hamilton Cl. Pot B 158 A3
Hamilton Mead. Bov 137 D2
Hamilton Rd. Abb L 153 E3
Hamilton Rd. Berk 122 A2
Hamilton Rd. St Alb 128 A2
Hamilton Rd. Sth Ox 175 D4
Hamilton St. Watf 167 E2
Hamlet Hill. Roy 135 F2
Hamlet The. Pot En 123 D4
Hammarskjold Rd. Harl 117 E1
Hammer La. Heml H 124 C2
Hammers Gate. Chis 141 D3
Hammond Cl. Ham St 147 F3
Hammond Cl. Stev 50 B3
Hammond La. Stanb 109 D2
Hammond Street Rd. Ham St 147 E3
Hammonds La. Sand 108 C2
Hammondswick. Harp 106 C2
Hamonte. Letw 23 E2
Hampden. Kim 66 B1
Hampden Cl. Letw 23 D4
Hampden Cres. Ches 162 A4
Hampden Hill. Ware 93 F1
Hampden Hill Cl. Ware 93 F1
Hampden Pl. Fro 141 F1
Hampden Rd. Har 176 B1
Hampden Rd. Hit 22 B1
Hampden Rd. Letw 23 D4
Hampden Rise. Roy 7 F2
Hampden Way. Watf 153 F2
Hampermill La. Watf 167 D1
Hampton Cl. Stev 69 E4
Hampton Rd. Luton 63 D4
Hamstel Rd. Harl 117 E1
Hanbury Cl. Ches 148 C1
Hanbury Cl. Ware 93 F1
Hancock Ct. Bor 170 B4
Hancroft Rd. Heml H 124 C1
Hand La. Saw 97 E1
Handa Cl. Heml H 139 D4
Handcross Rd. Luton 46 B1
Handpost Hill. Cuf 146 A2
Handside Cl. Wel GC 110 B3
Handside Green. Wel GC 110 B4
Handside La. Wel GC 110 B3
Handsworth Cl. Sth Ox 175 D4
Hangar Ruding. Watf 175 F4
Hanger Cl. Heml H 124 A1
Hangmans La. Wl Gr 89 F4
Hanover Cl. Stev 50 C1
Hanover Ct. Hod 135 D4
Hanover Green. Heml H 124 A1
Hanover Wlk. Hat 129 F1
Hanscombe End Rd. Aps En 19 E4
Hanselin Cl. Stan 176 C3
Hanswick Cl. Luton 46 A1
Hanworth Cl. Luton 45 E4
Hanyards End. Cuf 146 C2
Hanyards La. Cuf 146 B2
Happy Valley Industrial Park. Bed 139 D2
Harborne Cl. Sth Ox 175 E3
Harbury Dell. Luton 45 D4
Harcourt Rd. Bus 168 B2
Harcourt Rd. Tri 100 B2
Harcourt St. Luton 63 F3
Harding Cl. Luton 44 C4
Harding Cl. Red 106 A3
Harding Cl. Watf 154 B3
Hardings. Wel GC 111 E4
Hardwick Cl. Stev 69 E4
Hardwick Green. Luton 45 D4
Hardwick Pl. Lon C 142 B2
Hardy Cl. Hit 35 E4
Hardy Rd. Heml H 124 C2
Hare Cres. Watf 154 A4
Hare La. Hat 130 A2
Hare Street Rd. Bun 41 D4
Hare Street Rd. H St H 41 E4
Harebell. Wel GC 110 C2
Harebreaks The. Watf 154 A1
Harefield. Harl 118 A1
Harefield. Stev 51 E2
Harefield Pl. St Alb 128 B3
Harefield Rd. Luton 62 C4
Harefield Rd. Ric 173 F3
Harepark Cl. Heml H 123 F2
Harewood. Chor 165 E2
Harewood Rd. Sth Ox 175 D4
Hargrave Cl. Sta Mo 59 F4
Hargreaves Ave. Ches 162 A4
Hargreaves Cl. Ches 162 A4
Hargreaves Rd. Roystn 7 E3
Harkett Cl. Har 176 C1
Harkness. Ches 148 A1
Harkness Way. Hit 22 B1
Harlesden Rd. St Alb 128 A2
Harlestone Cl. Luton 31 D1
Harley Ct. St Alb 128 B4
Harlow Ct. Heml H 125 D4
Harlow Rd. Roy 116 B1
Harlow Rd. Saw 118 B4
Harlton Ct. Wa Aby 163 F3
Harmer Green La. Har Gr 90 A3
Harmsworth Way. N20 171 F1
Harness Way. St Alb 128 B3
Harold Cres. Wa Aby 163 E4
Harpenden Rd. St Alb 107 E1
Harpenden Rd. Whea 108 A4
Harpenden Rise. Harp 85 F2
Harpendon La. Red 106 A3
Harper La. Lon C 156 A4
Harps Hill. Mark 83 F3
Harpsfield Bwy. Hat 129 F3
Harptree Way. St Alb 128 A3
Harriet Way. Bus 168 B1
Harrington Ct. Hert H 114 B2
Harris La. Gt Of 33 E1
Harris La. Luton 46 A2
Harris La. Shen 157 D3
Harris Rd. Watf 154 A2
Harrison Cl. Norwd 174 B2
Harrison Wlk. Ches 148 B1
Harrisons. Birhr 59 E1
Harris's La. Ware 93 E1
Harrogate Rd. Sth Ox 175 E4
Harrow Ct. Stev 50 C3
Harrow View. Har 176 B1
Harrow Way. Watf 175 F3
Harrow Weald Park. Har 176 B2
Harrow Yd. Tri 100 A2
Harrowden Rd. Luton 64 B4
Harrowdene. Stev 51 E2
Hart Hill Dri. Luton 63 F4
Hart Hill La. Luton 64 A4
Hart La. Luton 46 A1
Hart Rd. Harl 118 B3
Hart Rd. St Alb 127 E1
Hart Wlk. Luton 46 A1
Hartfield Ave. Elst 170 A2
Hartfield Cl. Elst 170 A2
Hartfield Ct. Ware 93 E1
Hartford Dri. Watf 166 C4
Hartforde Rd. Bor 170 A4
Harthall La. Bed 139 E2
Hartham La. Hert 113 E3
Hartland Ct. Hit 34 B4
Hartland Rd. Ches 148 B1
Hartley Rd. Luton 63 F4
Harts Cl. Bus 168 A4
Hartsbourne Ave. Bus 176 B4
Hartsbourne Cl. Bus 176 B4
Hartsbourne Rd. Bus 176 B4
Hartsbourne Way. Heml H 125 E1
Hartsfield Rd. Luton 46 A1
Hartspring La. Bus 168 A4
Hartwell Gdns. Harp 85 F1
Harvest Cl. Luton 44 A2
Harvest Ct. Wl Gr 89 F4
Harvest End. Watf 154 B2
Harvest Mead. Hat 130 A4
Harvest Rd. Bus 168 A3
Harvey Rd. Cro Gr 166 A2
Harvey Rd. Lon C 142 B3
Harvey Rd. Stev 51 D3
Harveyfields. Wa Aby 163 E3
Harveys Hill. Luton 45 F3
Harwood Cl. Tewin 90 C1
Harwood Cl. Wel GC 89 F1
Harwood Hill. Wel GC 89 F1
Hasedines Rd. Heml H 124 A2
Haseldine Meadows. Hat 129 F2
Haseldine Rd. Lon C 142 B3
Hasketon Dri. Luton 44 A3
Haslewood Ave. Hod 135 D3
Haslingden Cl. Harp 85 E2
Hastings Cl. Stev 50 A4
Hastings St. Luton 63 E3
Hastings Way. Bus 167 F3
Hastings Way. Cro Gr 166 B3
Hastoe Hill. Has 119 F4
Hastoe La. Tri 100 A1
Hatch Green. L Hal 98 A4
Hatch La. Wes 24 A2
Hatching Green Cl. Harp 107 D3
Hatfield Cres. Heml H 124 C4
Hatfield Rd. Bir Gr 112 A2
Hatfield Rd. Hat 111 F2
Hatfield Rd. P Bar 159 E4
Hatfield Rd. St Alb 128 B2
Hatfield Rd. Watf 167 D4
Hathaway Cl. Luton 44 A1
Hathaway Ct. St Alb 128 C2
Hatherleigh Gdns. Pot B 159 E4
Hatters La. Watf 166 B2
Hatton Rd. Ches 148 B1
Havelock Rd. Kin L 138 C2
Havelock Rd. Luton 45 F1
Havelock Rise. Luton 45 F1
Haven Cl. Hat 129 F3
Havercroft Cl. St Alb 127 E1
Havers La. Bis St 76 C3
Havest Ct. St Alb 128 B4
Haward Rd. Hod 135 E4
Hawbush Rise. Welw 89 D3
Hawes Cl. Norwd 174 C2
Hawes La. Wa Aby 163 E1
Hawfield Gdns. Pk St 141 E3
Hawkbush Cl. Welw 89 D2
Hawkesworth Cl. Norwd 174 C2
Hawkfield. Letw 22 C4
Hawkfields. Luton 45 F3
Hawkins Cl. Bor 170 B4
Hawkins Hall La. Dat 69 F1
Hawks Dri. Fel 137 F4
Hawkshead La. Bro Pk 144 C2
Hawkshead Rd. Pot B 145 D1
Hawkshill. St Alb 128 A1
Hawksmead Cl. Enf 162 B2
Hawksmoor. Shen 157 D3
Hawkwell Dri. Tri 100 B2
Hawridge La. Chol 120 C1
Hawridge Vale. Chol 120 C1
Hawsley Rd. Harp 107 D2
Hawthorn Ave. Luton 46 A2
Hawthorn Cl. Harp 107 E4
Hawthorn Cl. Hertng 113 D4
Hawthorn Cl. Hit 34 C3
Hawthorn Cl. Roystn 7 F4
Hawthorn Cl. Watf 153 F1
Hawthorn Cres. Cad 62 C2
Hawthorn Gr. Enf 161 E1
Hawthorn Hill. Letw 22 C4
Hawthorn La. Heml H 123 F2
Hawthorn Rd. Hod 135 D4
Hawthorn Rise. Thor 76 C2
Hawthorn Way. Chis 141 D4
Hawthorn Way. Roystn 7 F4
Hawthorne Ave. Ches 162 A4
Hawthorne Cl. Ches 162 A4
Hawthorne Rd. Radl 156 A3
Hawthornes. Hat 129 F2
Hawthorns. Wel GC 110 B4
Hawthorns The. Berk 122 A3
Hawthorns The. Fel 137 F4
Hawthorns The. Map Cr 172 B3
Hawthorns The. Stev 51 D2
Hay Cl. Bor 170 B4
Hay La. Harp 86 A1
Haybourn Mead. Heml H 124 A1
Haycroft. Bis St 77 E4
Haycroft Rd. Stev 50 B4
Haydock Rd. Roystn 7 F3
Haydon Rd. Watf 167 F2
Hayes Cl. Luton 46 B3
Hayes Wlk. Ches 148 C3
Hayfield Cl. Bus 168 A3
Haygarth. Kneb 69 D2
Hayhurst Rd. Luton 44 A1
Hayley Bell Gdns. Bis St 76 C2
Hayley Comm. Stev 51 E2
Hayling Dri. Luton 46 B2
Hayling Rd. Sth Ox 175 D4
Haymeads. Wel GC 89 F1
Haymeads La. Bis St 77 E3
Haymoor. Letw 22 C4
Haynes Cl. Wel GC 111 D3
Haynes Mead. Berk 122 A3
Haysman Cl. Letw 23 D4
Haywood Cl. Pnr 175 E1
Haywood Ct. Wa Aby 163 F3
Haywood La. Ther 16 A3
Haywood Park. Chor 164 C2
Haywoods La. Roystn 7 F4
Hazel Cl. Har Gr 89 F2
Hazel Gdns. Saw 97 F2
Hazel Gr. Hat 129 F1
Hazel Gr. Stot 11 F3
Hazel Gr. Wel GC 111 D4
Hazel Mead. Barn 171 D2
Hazel Rd. Berk 122 B2
Hazel Rd. Chis 141 D2
Hazel Tree Rd. Watf 154 A2
Hazelbury Ave. Abb L 153 E4
Hazelbury Cres. Luton 63 E4
Hazelcroft. Pnr 176 A2
Hazeldell. Wat St 70 B2
Hazeldell Link. Heml H 123 F1
Hazeldell Rd. Heml H 123 F1
Hazelend Rd. Sta Mo 59 D2
Hazelmere Rd. St Alb 128 B3
Hazelmere Rd. Stev 69 D4
Hazels The. Tewin 90 C1
Hazelwood Cl. Hit 34 C4
Hazelwood Cl. Luton 46 A2
Hazelwood Dri. Pnr 175 D1
Hazelwood Dri. St Alb 128 B2
Hazelwood La. Abb L 153 E4
Hazelwood Rd. Cro Gr 166 B2
Hazely. Tri 100 B2
Heacham Cl. Luton 44 A2
Headingley Cl. Ham St 147 F3
Headingley Cl. Stev 50 C4
Headstone La. Har 176 A1
Healey Rd. Watf 166 C2
Heath Ave. Roystn 7 E3
Heath Ave. St Alb 127 E3
Heath Brow. Heml H 124 B1
Heath Cl. Harp 107 E4
Heath Cl. Heml H 124 B1
Heath Cl. Luton 63 D3
Heath Cl. Pot B 145 D1
Heath Dri. Pot B 145 D1
Heath Dri. Ware 93 E2
Heath Farm La. St Alb 127 F3
Heath Hill. Cod 67 E1
Heath La. Cod 67 E1
Heath La. Heml H 124 B1
Heath La. Hert H 114 B1
Heath Rd. Bre Wd 47 E1
Heath Rd. Pot B 145 D1
Heath Rd. St Alb 127 F3
Heath Rd. Watf 167 F1
Heath Rd. Wl Gr 68 C1
Heath Row. Bis St 59 D1
Heath The. Bre Wd 47 E1
Heathbourne Rd. Bus 168 C1
Heathbrow Rd. Wl Gr 89 F4
Heathcote Ave. Hat 130 A4
Heather Rd. Wel GC 110 B2
Heather Rise. Bus 167 F4
Heather Way. Heml H 124 B2
Heather Way. Pot B 158 C4
Heather Way. Stan 176 C2
Heathermere. Letw 11 F1
Heathfield. Roystn 7 D3
Heathfield Cl. Cad 62 C2
Heathfield Cl. Pot B 145 D1
Heathfield Ct. St Alb 127 F2
Heathfield Rd. Bus 167 F3
Heathfield Rd. Hit 21 F1
Heathfield Rd. Luton 45 E2
Heathgate. Hert H 114 B1
Heathlands. Wl Gr 68 C1
Heathlands Dri. St Alb 127 F3
Heathside Cl. Norwd 174 B3
Heathside Rd. Norwd 174 B3
Heaton Dell. Luton 46 C1
Heay Fields. Wel GC 111 E4
Hebden Cl. Luton 44 A2
Hedge Row. Heml H 124 A3
Hedgebrooms. Wel GC 111 E4
Hedgerows. Saw 97 F1
Hedgerows The. Stev 51 E4
Hedges Cl. Hat 130 A3
Hedgeside. Pot En 123 D4
Hedgeside Rd. Norwd 174 B3
Hedley Rd. St Alb 128 A2
Hedley Rise. Luton 46 C1
Heights The. Heml H 124 C3
Helena Cl. Barn 159 E1
Hellards Rd. Stev 50 B4
Helmsley Cl. Luton 44 B3
Helston Cl. Pnr 175 F2
Helston Gr. Heml H 124 B4
Helston Pl. Abb L 153 F4
Hemel Hempstead Rd. Dagn 81 F1
Hemel Hempstead Rd. Heml H 125 F1
Hemel Hempstead Rd. L Gad 103 D4
Hemel Hempstead Rd. Red 105 F1
Hemel Hempstead Rd. St Alb 126 B1
Hemingford Dri. Luton 45 E3
Hemingford Rd. Watf 153 F2
Hemming Way. Watf 154 A2
Hemmings The. Berk 121 F2
Hemp La. Wigg 100 C1
Hempstead La. Pot En 123 E3
Hempstead Rd. Bov 137 D3
Hempstead Rd. Kin L 139 D2
Hempstead Rd. Watf 153 F1
Henbury Way. Sth Ox 175 E4
Henderson Cl. St Alb 127 E4
Henderson Pl. Bed 139 F2
Hendon Wood La. NW7 171 D1
Henge Way. Luton 44 C4
Henry St. Heml H 138 B4
Henry St. Tri 100 A2
Hensley Cl. Hit 35 D3
Hensley Cl. Welw 89 E3
Hensteau Pl. Luton 46 B1
Henth The. Radl 156 A3
Herald Cl. Bis St 76 B3
Herbert St. Heml H 124 B2
Hereford Rd. Luton 44 A2
Hereward Cl. Wa Aby 163 E4
Herga Ct. Watf 167 D4
Heritage Cl. St Alb 127 E2
Herkomer Cl. Bus 168 A2
Herkomer Rd. Bus 168 A2
Hermitage Ct. Pot B 159 E3
Hermitage Rd. Hit 34 C4
Herne Rd. Bus 168 A2
Herne Rd. Stev 36 A1
Herneshaw. Hat 129 F2
Herns La. Wel GC 111 D4
Herns Way. Wel GC 111 D4
Heron Cl. Ric 173 E4
Heron Cl. Saw 97 E1
Heron Ct. Bis St 77 D4
Heron Dri. Luton 45 F3
Heron Trading Estate. Luton 44 B4
Heron Way. Hat 130 A2
Heron Wlk. Norwd 174 C3
Heronfield. Pot B 145 E1
Herongate Rd. Ches 148 C2
Herons Elm. Nthch 121 F4
Herons Way. St Alb 142 A4
Herons Wood. Harl 117 D1
Heronsgate Rd. Chor 164 A2
Heronslea. Watf 154 B2
Heronswood. Wa Aby 163 F3
Heronswood Pl. Wel GC 111 D3
Heronswood Rd. Wel GC 111 D3
Hertford End Ct. Norwd 174 C3
Hertford Rd. Enf 162 B2
Hertford Rd. Gt Am 114 C2
Hertford Rd. Hat 130 B4
Hertford Rd. Hod 134 C4
Hertford Rd. Stev 69 D4
Hertford Rd. Tewin 90 C1
Hertford Rd. Ware 93 E1
Hertford Rd. Wel GC 90 A1
Hertford Rd. Welw 89 E2
Hertingfordbury Rd. Hert 113 D3
Hertingfordbury Rd. Hertng 113 D3
Heswall Green. Sth Ox 175 D4
Hetchleys. Heml H 124 A3
Hewitt Cl. Whea 108 B4
Hewlett Rd. Luton 44 C3
Hexton Rd. Gt Of 33 F4
Hexton Rd. Lily 32 A2
Heydon Rd. Gt Ch 9 F2
Heydons Cl. St Alb 127 E3
Heyford Rd. Radl 155 F1
Heysham Dri. Sth Ox 175 E3
Heywood Dri. Luton 45 F1
Hibbert Ave. Watf 154 B1
Hibbert Rd. Har 176 C1
Hibbert St. Luton 63 F3
Hickling Cl. Luton 46 B1
Hickling Way. Harp 86 B2
Hicks Rd. Mark 83 F3
Hidalgo Ct. Heml H 124 C3
Hides The. Harl 117 E1
High Acres. Abb L 153 E4
High Ash Rd. Whea 108 B4
High Ave. Letw 22 C2
High Beech Rd. Luton 44 B4
High Canons. Shen 157 E1
High Cl. Chor 165 E2
High Cross. Aldhm 155 E1
High Dane. Hit 22 A1
High Dells. Hat 129 F2
High Elms. Harp 107 D3
High Elms Cl. Norwd 174 B2
High Elms La. Abb L 154 B4
High Elms La. Heb En 70 C4
High Firs Cres. Harp 107 E4
High Gr. Wel GC 110 B4
High House Estate. Harl 118 C2
High La. Sta Mo 59 F4
High Mead. Luton 45 D2
High Meads. Whea 108 B4
High Oak Rd. Ware 93 E2
High Oaks. Enf 160 C1
High Oaks. St Alb 127 E4

High Oaks Rd. Wel GC 110 A4
High Plash. Stev 50 C3
High Rd. Aps En 19 F4
High Rd. Bus 168 B1
High Rd. Ess 131 F3
High Rd. Har 176 C1
High Rd. Hod 134 C2
High Rd. Stap 91 F3
High Rd. Wat 92 A2
High Rd. Watf 154 A3
High Rd Broxbourne. Hod 134 C1
High Rd Turnford. Ches 148 C3
High Rd Wormley. Hod 148 C4
High Ridge. Cuf 146 C2
High Ridge. Harp 85 F2
High Ridge. Luton 46 B1
High Ridge Rd. Fel 138 B4
High St. Abb L 139 F1
High St. Arl 11 D3
High St. Ashw 4 B2
High St. Bal 23 F4
High St. Bar 8 C1
High St. Bark 17 E2
High St. Barn 171 F3
High St. Bed 139 F2
High St. Berk 122 B2
High St. Bis St 76 C4
High St. Bov 137 D2
High St. Bun 40 C4
High St. Bus 168 A2
High St. Ch En 11 D4
High St. Ched 80 A4
High St. Ches 148 B2
High St. Cod 67 F1
High St. Coln H 129 D1
High St. Wa. Cr 162 C3
High St. Elst 169 E2
High St. Fla 84 A1
High St. Gos 34 C2
High St. Gra 36 B2
High St. Gt Of 33 E2
High St. Gu M 1 C2
High St. Har 176 C1
High St. Hare 173 E1
High St. Harl 118 B2
High St. Harp 86 A1
High St. Heml H 124 B2
High St. Hin 3 E3
High St. Hit 34 C4
High St. Hod 135 D3
High St. Hun 95 E1
High St. Kim 66 B1
High St. Kin L 139 D1
High St. Luton 44 B2
High St. Mark 83 F3
High St. Muc H 74 C2
High St. Norwd 174 C1
High St. Nthch 121 F3
High St. Pirt 20 B2
High St. Pot B 159 E4
High St. Puc 55 E2
High St. Red 106 A3
High St. Reed 16 C3
High St. Ric 165 F1
High St. Roy 116 A1
High St. Roystn 7 E3
High St. Sand 108 B1
High St. St Alb 127 E2
High St. Sta Ab 115 E2
High St. Stand 55 F1
High St. Stev 50 B4
High St. Stot 11 F3
High St. Tri 100 A2
High St. Wal 38 A1
High St. Ware 93 E1
High St. Wat St 70 B2
High St. Welw 89 E3
High St. Whea 87 E1
High St. Whit 66 C4
High St. Widf 95 F2
High Street Green. Heml H 125 D3
High Town Rd. Luton 45 F1
High View. Birhr 59 E2
High View. Chor 165 D3
High View. Hat 130 A1
High View. Hit 34 B4
High View. Mark 83 F2
High View. Watf 166 C2
High View Ct. Har 176 C2
High Wickfield. Wel GC 111 E3
High Wood Cl. Luton 62 C4
High Wood Rd. Hod 114 C1
High Wych La. Saw 97 D1
High Wych Rd. H Wy 117 F4
High Wych Rd. Saw 97 E1
High Wych Way. Heml H 105 D1
Higham Dri. Luton 46 B1
Highbanks Rd. Pnr 176 A2
Highbarns. Heml H 139 D3
Highbury Ave. Hod 135 D4
Highbury Rd. Hit 35 D4
Highbury Rd. Luton 45 E1
Highbush Rd. Stot 11 F3
Highclere Dri. Heml H 139 D4
Highcroft Rd. Fel 138 A3
Highfield. Heml H 124 C3
Highfield. Letw 22 C2
Highfield Ave. Bis St 77 E3
Highfield Ave. Harp 107 E4
Highfield Cl. Norwd 174 C1
Highfield Cres. Norwd 174 C1
Highfield Dri. Hod 134 C1
Highfield La. Heml H 124 C3
Highfield La. St Alb 128 B1
Highfield La. Tyt 142 C4
Highfield Rd. Berk 122 B2
Highfield Rd. Bus 167 F2
Highfield Rd. Ham St 147 F3
Highfield Rd. Hert 113 E2
Highfield Rd. Luton 45 D1
Highfield Rd. Norwd 174 C1
Highfield Rd. Sand 108 A1
Highfield Rd. Tri 99 F2
Highfield Rd. Wigg 100 B2
Highfield Way. Pot B 159 D4
Highfield Way. Ric 165 D2
Highfields. Cuf 146 C2
Highgrove Ct. Ches 162 B3
Highland Dri. Bus 168 A1
Highland Dri. Heml H 125 D2
Highland Rd. Lo Naz 135 F1
Highland Rd. Norwd 174 C1
Highland Rd. Thor 76 C2
Highlands. Hat 130 B4
Highlands. Roystn 7 F3
Highlands. Watf 167 E1
Highlands The. Pot B 145 E1
Highlands The. Ric 165 D1
Highmead. Sta Mo 59 F4
Highmoor. Harp 86 A2
Highover Cl. Luton 46 A1
Highover Rd. Letw 22 B3
Highover Way. Hit 22 A1
Highview Cl. Pot B 159 E3
Highview Gdns. Pot B 159 E3
Highview Gdns. St Alb 128 B4
Highway The. Stan 176 C1
Highwood Ave. Bus 167 F4
Highwoodhall La. Heml H 139 E4
Hilbury. Hat 129 F2
Hilfield La. Bus 168 B4
Hilfield La S. Bus 168 C2
Hill Cl. Barn 171 E2
Hill Cl. Harp 86 B2
Hill Cl. Luton 45 E4
Hill Cl. Pic En 124 A4
Hill Common. Heml H 139 D4
Hill Crest. Pot B 159 E3
Hill Crest. Stev 50 C3
Hill Crest. Whit 66 C3
Hill Croft Cl. Luton 44 B3
Hill Dyke Rd. Whea 108 B4
Hill End La. St Alb 128 B1
Hill End Rd. Hare 173 E2
Hill Farm Ave. Watf 154 A3
Hill Farm Cl. Watf 154 A3
Hill Farm La. A St L 88 A3
Hill Farm La. Red 106 B1
Hill House Ave. Stan 176 C2
Hill Ley. Hat 129 F3
Hill Leys. Cuf 146 C2
Hill Rd. Cod 67 F1
Hill Rd. Norwd 174 B2
Hill Rise. Cuf 146 C2
Hill Rise. Luton 44 B4
Hill Rise. Pot B 159 E3
Hill Rise. Ric 165 D1
Hill Side. Ched 79 F4
Hill St. St Alb 127 E2
Hill The. Harl 118 B2
Hill The. Whea 108 B4
Hill Top. Bal 23 F4
Hill View. Buck 27 E4
Hill View. Nthch 122 A4
Hill View. Whit 66 C3
Hillary Cl. Luton 44 B4
Hillary Cres. Luton 63 E3
Hillary Rd. Heml H 125 D2
Hillary Rise. Arl 11 D3
Hillborough Rd. Luton 63 E3
Hillbrow. Letw 22 B2
Hillcrest. Bal 23 F4
Hillcrest. Hat 130 A3
Hillcrest Ave. Luton 45 E4
Hillcrest Rd. Shen 157 D3
Hillcroft Cres. Watf 175 D4
Hilldown Rd. Heml H 124 A3
Hillfield. Hat 130 B4
Hillfield Ave. Hit 22 A1
Hillfield Rd. Heml H 124 B2
Hillgate. Hit 22 A2
Hillhouse. Wa Aby 163 F3
Hilliard Rd. Norwd 174 C1
Hillingdon Rd. Watf 154 A3
Hillmead. Berk 122 A2
Hillmead. Stev 51 D3
Hillrise Ave. Watf 154 B1
Hill's La. Norwd 174 C1
Hillsborough Green. Sth Ox 175 D4
Hillshott. Letw 23 D3
Hillside. Cod 67 F1
Hillside. Gt Am 114 A4
Hillside. Hat 130 A3
Hillside. Hod 134 C4
Hillside. Roystn 7 E3
Hillside. Stev 50 C3
Hillside. Wel GC 111 D2
Hillside Ave. Bis St 77 D4
Hillside Ave. Bor 170 A3
Hillside Ave. Ches 162 B4
Hillside Cl. Abb L 153 F4
Hillside Cres. Ches 162 B4
Hillside Cres. Enf 161 E1
Hillside Cres. Norwd 175 D1
Hillside Cres. Sta Ab 115 D2
Hillside Cres. Watf 167 F2
Hillside Gdns. Barn 171 F3
Hillside Gdns. Berk 122 B2
Hillside Gdns. Norwd 175 D2
Hillside La. Sta Ab 115 D2
Hillside Rd. Bus 167 F2
Hillside Rd. Chor 164 B2
Hillside Rd. Harp 85 F2
Hillside Rd. Luton 63 E4
Hillside Rd. Norwd 175 D2
Hillside Rd. Pnr 175 D2
Hillside Rd. Radl 156 A2
Hillside Rd. St Alb 127 F2
Hillside Rise. Norwd 175 D2
Hillside Terr. Hert 113 E2
Hillside Way. Wl Gr 90 A4
Hilltop. Red 105 F3
Hilltop Cl. Ham St 147 F3
Hilltop Ct. Luton 63 E4
Hilltop Rd. Bed 139 E2
Hilltop Rd. Berk 122 B2
Hillview Cl. Pnr 175 F2
Hillview Cres. Luton 45 E4
Hillview Gdns. Ches 148 C2
Hillview Rd. Pnr 175 F2
Hilly Fields. Wel GC 111 E4
Hilmay Dri. Heml H 124 A1
Hindhead Green. Sth Ox 175 E3
Hine Way. Hit 21 E1
Hinxworth Rd. Ashw 4 A2
Hinxworth Rd. Hin 3 E2
Hipkins. Bis St 76 C2
Hishbridge St. Wa Aby 163 F4
Hitchens Cl. Heml H 123 F2
Hitchin Hill. Hit 34 C3
Hitchin Hill Path. Hit 34 C3
Hitchin Rd. Arl 11 D1
Hitchin Rd. Gos 34 C2
Hitchin Rd. Gt Wy 35 F3
Hitchin Rd. Henlw 10 A3
Hitchin Rd. Hit 33 F4
Hitchin Rd. Kim 66 B1
Hitchin Rd. Letw 22 C2
Hitchin Rd. Luton 46 A2
Hitchin Rd. Pegs 19 E1
Hitchin Rd. Pirt 20 C1
Hitchin Rd. Stev 36 A1
Hitchin Rd. Stot 11 E2
Hitchin Rd. Wes 24 A1
Hitchin St. Bal 23 F4
Hither Field. Ware 93 F2
Hitherbaulk. Wel GC 110 C2
Hitherway. Wel GC 89 E1
Hitherwell Dri. Har 176 B1
Hive Cl. Bus 176 B4
Hive Rd. Bus 176 B4
Hive Rd. Har 176 C4
Hobart Walk. St Alb 127 F4
Hobbs Cl. Ches 148 B1
Hobbs Cl. St Alb 128 C1
Hobbs Cross Rd. Harl 118 C2
Hobbs Hill. Welw 89 E2
Hobbs Hill Rd. Heml H 138 C4
Hobbs Way. Wel GC 110 B3
Hobletts Rd. Heml H 124 C2
Hobsons Cl. Hod 114 C1
Hobsons Wlk. Tri 99 F3
Hobtoe Rd. Harl 117 D1
Hockerill. Wat St 70 C2
Hockerill St. Bis St 77 D4
Hocklands. Wel GC 111 E4
Hockwell Ring. Luton 44 B2
Hoddesdon Rd. Sta Ab 115 E2
Hodings Rd. Harl 117 E1
Hodwell. Ashw 4 B2
Hoe La. Enf 162 A1
Hoe La. Gt Am 114 B4
Hoe La. Lo Naz 135 F1
Hoe The. Watf 175 E4
Hoecroft. Lo Naz 135 F1
Hoestock Rd. Saw 97 E1
Hog Hall La. Dagn 81 D3
Hog La. Ash Gr 121 E1
Hogarth Ct. Bus 168 A1
Hogg End La. Heml H 125 F3
Hogg End La. Red 126 A3
Hogg La. Elst 169 D3
Hogges Cl. Hod 135 D3
Hogsdell La. Hert H 114 A2
Holbeck La. Ham St 147 F3
Holbein Gate. Norwd 174 C3
Holborn Cl. St Alb 128 B4
Holbrook Cl. Enf 162 A1
Holcroft Rd. Harp 86 B2
Holdbrook. Hit 35 D4
Holden Cl. Hert 113 F4
Holders La. Stev 51 F3
Holdings The. Hat 130 B4
Holecroft. Wa Aby 163 F3
Holford Way. Luton 31 D1
Holgate Dri. Luton 44 A2
Holkham Cl. Luton 44 A2
Holland Gdns. Watf 154 B2
Holland Rd. Luton 45 D1
Holland's Croft. Hun 95 E1
Holliday St. Berk 122 B2
Hollier Ct. Hat 130 A3
Holliers Way. Hat 130 A3
Hollies Cl. Roystn 7 F3
Hollies The. Heron 164 B1
Hollies The. Wigg 100 B2
Hollies Way. P Bar 159 E4
Hollow La. Hit 34 C4
Holloway La. Chen 151 E1
Holloway The. Dra B 99 E2
Holloways La. Wel Gr 144 B4
Holly Cl. Hat 129 F2
Holly Copse. Stev 50 C2
Holly Croft. Hertng 113 D4
Holly Dri. Berk 122 B2
Holly Dri. Pot B 159 D3
Holly Farm Cl. Cad 62 C2
Holly Gr. Pnr 175 F1
Holly Grove Rd. Bram 91 E2
Holly Hedges La. Bov 151 E4
Holly La. Kim 86 C3
Holly Leys. Stev 69 E4
Holly Rd. Enf 162 B2
Holly Rd. Wl Gr 69 D1
Holly Shaws. Stev 51 D1
Holly St. Luton 63 F3
Holly Tree Cl. Bot 150 A4
Holly Wlk. Harp 86 B1
Holly Wlk. Wel GC 89 E1
Hollybush Ave. Chis 141 D4
Hollybush Cl. Har 176 B1
Hollybush Cl. Heml H 123 E4
Hollybush Cl. Watf 167 E1
Hollybush Cl. Wl Gr 89 F4
Hollybush Hill. Lily 32 C1
Hollybush La. Dat 69 E2
Hollybush La. Fla 84 A2
Hollybush La. Harp 86 A2
Hollybush La. Heml H 123 F2
Hollybush La. Wel GC 110 C1
Hollybush La. Wel GC 110 C2
Hollybush La. Whit 66 A4
Hollybush Rd. Luton 46 B1
Hollycross Rd. Ware 115 D4
Hollydell. Hert 113 E2
Hollyfield. Hat 130 A1
Hollyfield. Tri 100 B3
Hollyfield Cl. Tri 100 B3
Hollygrove. Bus 168 B1
Holmbrook Ave. Luton 45 E3
Holmbury Cl. Har 176 C4
Holmdale. Letw 23 D3
Holmdale Cl. Bor 169 F4
Holme Cl. Ches 162 B4
Holme Cl. Hat 129 F4
Holme Lea. Watf 154 B3
Holme Park. Bor 169 F4
Holme Rd. Hat 129 F4
Holme Way. Stan 176 C2
Holmes Ct. St Alb 127 F2
Holmesdale. Enf 162 B2
Holmfield Cl. Luton 63 E3
Holmscroft Rd. Luton 44 C3
Holmshill La. Ridge 157 F1
Holmside Rise. Sth Ox 175 D4
Holmwood Rd. Enf 162 B2
Holroyd Cres. Bal 23 F4
Holt Cl. Elst 169 F3
Holt The. Heml H 124 C1
Holt The. Wel GC 111 E3
Holts Mdw. Red 106 A3
Holtsmere Cl. Luton 46 B1
Holtsmere Cl. Watf 154 B2
Holwell Hyde. Wel GC 111 E2
Holwell Hyde La. Wel GC 111 E2
Holwell Rd. Hol 21 D4
Holwell Rd. Pirt 20 C3
Holwell Rd. Wel GC 110 C3
Holy Cross Hill. Ham St 148 A4
Holyfield Rd. Wa Aby 149 E2
Holyrood Cres. St Alb 141 E4
Holywell Cl. Stu 82 B3
Holywell Ct. Luton 45 D2
Holywell Hill. St Alb 127 E1
Holywell Rd. Stu 82 A4
Holywell Rd. Watf 167 D2
Home Cl. Hod 148 C4
Home Cl. Luton 44 B2
Home Cl. Stot 11 F4
Home Farm Rd. Nthch 121 E4
Home Farm Rd. Ric 174 A3
Home Field. Barn 171 F2
Home Field. Pot En 123 D4
Home Ley. Wel GC 110 C3
Home Meadow. Wel GC 110 C3
Home Way. Ric 164 C1
Homedale Dri. Luton 44 B1
Homefield. Bov 137 D2
Homefield La. Lan 49 F1
Homefield Rd. Bus 168 A2
Homefield Rd. Chor 164 B3
Homefield Rd. Heml H 125 D1
Homefield Rd. Radl 155 F1
Homefield Rd. Ware 93 F1
Homeleigh Ct. Ches 148 A1
Homerfield. Wel GC 110 B4
Homerswood La. Welw 89 D1
Homerton Rd. Luton 45 D3
Homestead Ct. Wel GC 110 C2
Homestead La. Wel GC 110 C2
Homestead Moat. Stev 50 C3
Homestead Rd. Hat 130 A4
Homestead Rd. Ric 165 E1
Homestead Way. Luton 63 E3
Homewood Ave. Cuf 146 C2
Homewood La. Cuf 146 B2
Homewood Rd. St Alb 128 A3
Honey Bourne. Bis St 76 C3
Honey Brook. Wa Aby 163 F3
Honey La. Bun 40 C4
Honey La. Hert 113 E3
Honey La. Sta Gr 30 C2
Honey La. Wa Aby 163 F3
Honeycroft. Wel GC 110 B3
Honeycross Rd. Heml H 123 F1
Honeygate. Luton 45 F2
Honeymeade. Saw 118 B4
Honeysuckle Gdns. Hat 130 A2
Honeyway. Roystn 7 F3
Honeywood Cl. Pot B 159 E3
Hoo St. Luton 63 F3
Hoo The. Harl 118 B3
Hook Gate. Enf 162 A2
Hook La. Nort 159 F4
Hookers Way. Luton 44 B3
Hoops La. Ther 15 F3
Hope Green. Watf 154 A3
Hopewell Rd. Bal 23 E4
Hopground Cl. St Alb 128 A1
Hopkins Cres. Sand 108 A1
Hoppit Rd. Wa Aby 163 D3
Hopton Rd. Stev 50 A4
Horace Brightman Cl. Luton 45 D4
Hordle Gdns. St Alb 127 F1
Horn Hill. Whit 66 C3
Hornbeam Cl. Bor 170 A4
Hornbeam La. Wild 131 F1
Hornbeam Spring. Kneb 68 C2
Hornbeam Way. Ches 147 F1
Hornbeams. Bri Wd 140 C1
Hornbeams Ave. Enf 162 B2
Hornbeams The. Harl 117 E1
Hornbeams The. Stev 51 D2
Hornets The. Watf 167 D3
Hornhill Rd. Map Cr 172 B3
Horns Cl. Hert 113 E2
Horns Mill Rd. Hert 113 E2
Hornsby Cl. Luton 46 B1
Hornsfield. Wel GC 111 E4
Horrocks Cl. Ware 93 E2
Horse Hill. Bot 150 B4
Horsecroft Rd. Heml H 124 A1
Horselers. Heml H 139 D4
Horseshoe Cl. Ched 80 A4
Horseshoe Hill. Gt Ho 42 A4
Horseshoe La. Gt Ho 42 A4
Horseshoe La. N20 171 E1
Horseshoe La. Watf 154 B4
Horseshoe The. Heml H 125 E1
Horsham Cl. Luton 46 B1
Horsleys. Map Cr 172 B3
Horton Gdns. Heml H 106 D1
Hospital Rd. Arl 11 D2
Housden Cl. Whea 108 C4
House La. Ch En 11 D4
House La. Sand 108 A1
House La. St Alb 128 B4
Housewood End. Heml H 124 A3
Housman Ave. Roystn 7 E4
How Field. Harp 85 F2
How Wood. Chis 141 D2
Howard Agne Cl. Bov 137 D2
Howard Cl. Bus 168 C1
Howard Cl. Luton 45 D2
Howard Cl. St Alb 128 B1
Howard Cl. Watf 154 A1
Howard Ct. Letw 23 D2
Howard Dri. Bor 170 B3
Howard Dri. Letw 23 D2
Howard Gate. Letw 23 D2
Howard Way. Harl 117 F1
Howards Cl. Pnr 175 D1
Howards Dri. Heml H 124 A3
Howards Wood. Letw 23 D2
Howardsgate. Wel GC 110 B3
Howe Dell. Hat 130 A3
Howe Rd. Heml H 125 D1
Howfield Green. Hod 115 D1
Howicks Green. Wel GC 111 D2
Howland Garth. St Alb 141 E4
Howlands. Wel GC 110 C2
Howton Pl. Bus 168 B1
Hoylake Gdns. Sth Ox 175 E3
Hubbards Rd. Chor 164 B2
Huckleberry Cl. Luton 45 D4
Hudnall La. L Gad 102 C4
Hudson Cl. St Alb 141 E4
Hudson Cl. Watf 153 F2
Hudson Rd. Stev 51 D4
Huggins La. Wel Gr 144 B4
Hughenden Rd. St Alb 128 B3
Hull La. Gr En 55 F4
Humberstone Cl. Luton 44 C1
Humberstone Rd. Luton 44 C1
Hunsdon. Wel GC 111 E3
Hunsdon Rd. Sta Ab 116 A3
Hunsdon Rd. Widf 95 F2
Hunston Cl. Luton 44 A3
Hunt Cl. St Alb 128 B3
Hunter Cl. Bor 170 B2
Hunter Cl. Pot B 159 D3
Hunter Wlk. Bor 170 B2
Huntercrombe Gdns. St Ox 175 E3
Hunters Cl. Bov 137 D1
Hunters Cl. Stev 51 E4
Hunters Cl. Stot 11 F3
Hunters Cl. Tri 100 A3
Hunter's La. Watf 153 F3
Hunters Oak. Heml H 125 D4
Hunters Park. Berk 122 A2
Hunters Reach. Ches 147 F1
Hunters Ride. Bric 155 D4
Hunters Way. Roystn 7 F3
Hunters Way. Wel GC 110 C2
Hunting Gate. Heml H 124 C4
Hunting Gate. Hit 22 A2
Huntingdon Cl. Hod 148 C4
Huntingdon Rd. Stev 50 A4
Hunton Bridge Hill. Abb L 153 E3
Hunts Cl. Luton 63 E3
Hunts Meadow. Wes 24 B1
Huntsmans Cl. Dagn 81 E3
Huntsmill Rd. Heml H 123 F1
Hurlock Way. Luton 44 B3
Hurst Cl. Bal 13 D1
Hurst Cl. Wel GC 111 E3
Hurst Dri. Ches 162 B3
Hurst Way. Luton 44 C3
Hutton Cl. Hertng 113 D3
Hutton Gdns. Har 176 B2
Hutton La. Har 176 B2
Hutton Wlk. Har 176 B2
Hyatt Industrial Estate. Stev 50 A3
Hyburn Cl. Bri Wd 140 C1
Hyburn Cl. Heml H 125 D1
Hyde Ave. Pot B 159 D3
Hyde Ave. Stot 11 F3
Hyde Cl. Barn 171 F3
Hyde Cl. Harp 86 A2
Hyde Green. Stev 51 D2
Hyde La. Bed 139 E3
Hyde La. Bov 137 D2
Hyde La. Chis 141 E2
Hyde La. Fro 141 E2
Hyde La. Pet Gr 65 E1

Hyde Mead. Lo Naz 149 F4
Hyde Meadows. Bov 137 D2
Hyde Rd. Cad 62 C2
Hyde Rd. Watf 167 D4
Hyde The. Stev 51 E2
Hyde The. Ware 93 D1
Hyde View Rd. Harp 86 A2
Hyde Vlly. Wel GC 110 C2
Hyde Way. Wel GC 110 C3
Hydean Way. Stev 51 D2
Hyperion Ct. Heml H 124 C3
Hyver Hill. NW7 170 B1

Ibberson Way. Hit 35 D4
Ickleford Rd. Hit 34 C4
Ickley Cl. Luton 44 A3
Icknield Cl. Ick 21 F2
Icknield Cl. St Alb 126 C1
Icknield Cres. Tri 100 A3
Icknield Green. Letw 22 C3
Icknield Rd. Luton 44 C2
Icknield Way. Bal 12 C1
Icknield Way. Dra B 99 E2
Icknield Way. Letw 22 C3
Icknield Way. Luton 45 D4
Icknield Way. Tri 99 F2
Icknield Way E. Bal 12 C1
Icknield Wlk. Roystn 7 F4
Ilford Cl. Luton 46 B2
Ilkley Rd. Sth Ox 175 E3
Imberfield. Luton 44 B2
Imperial Way. Watf 167 E4
Indells. Hat 129 F2
Industrial Park. Bor 170 B4
Ingelheim Ct. Stev 50 B4
Ingersoll Rd. Enf 162 B1
Inglefield. Pot B 145 D1
Ingles. Wel GC 89 F1
Ingleside Dri. Stev 36 A1
Inkerman Rd. St Alb 127 F1
Inkerman St. Luton 63 E4
Innes Ct. Heml H 138 B4
Inn's Cl. Stev 50 B3
Inskip Cres. Stev 50 C3
Ionian Way. Heml H 124 C3
Iredale View. Bal 13 D1
Iron Dri. Hert 114 A4
Irving Cl. Bis St 76 B2
Irving Cres. Ched 80 A4
Isenburg Way. Heml H 124 B4
Isherwood Cl. Roystn 7 E4
Itch La. Gravnd 57 E4
Iveagh Cl. Norwd 174 A1
Iveagh Ct. Heml H 124 B2
Ivel Ct. Letw 23 E2
Ivel Rd. Stev 50 B4
Ivel Way. Bal 24 A3
Ivel Way. Stot 11 F4
Ives Rd. Hert 113 D4
Ivinghoe Cl. St Alb 128 B4
Ivinghoe Cl. Watf 154 B2
Ivinghoe Rd. Bus 168 B1
Ivinghoe Rd. Ric 165 D1
Ivy House La. Berk 122 C2
Ivy House La. Pot En 122 C3
Ivy Rd. Luton 63 E4
Ivy Terr. Hod 135 E4
Ivy Wlk. Norwd 174 C1
Ivybridge. Hod 135 D2

Jackdaws. Wel GC 111 E3
Jackets La. Norwd 174 A2
Jacketts Field. Abb L 153 F4
Jackman's Pl. Letw 23 D3
Jackson Sq. Bis St 76 C4
Jackson St. Bal 12 C1
Jacksons Dri. Ches 148 A2
Jackson's La. Reed 16 C3
James Bedford Cl. Pnr 175 E1
James Cl. Bus 167 F2
James Way. Stev 50 B4
Jameson Ct. St Alb 127 F2
Jameson Rd. Harp 86 A2
Jarden. Letw 23 E2
Jarman Cl. Heml H 124 C1
Jarvis Cl. Barn 171 E2
Jarvis Cleys. Ham St 147 F3
Jasmine Gdns. Hat 130 A4
Jasons Hill. Bot 136 A1
Jasper Cl. Enf 162 B1
Jaywood. Luton 46 B3
Jeans Way. Dun 44 A1
Jeffrey Cl. Roystn 7 E4
Jeffries Rd. Ware 93 F1
Jellicoe Gdns. Stan 176 C2
Jenkins Ave. Bri Wd 140 C1
Jenkins La. Bis St 77 E3
Jenkins La. St Le 119 F2
Jenning Wood. Wl Gr 89 F4
Jennings Cl. Stev 50 C2
Jennings Rd. St Alb 128 A2
Jennings Way. Barn 171 E3
Jepps La. Roystn 7 E3
Jerome Dri. St Alb 127 D1
Jersey Cl. Hod 135 D4
Jersey La. St Alb 128 A3
Jersey Rd. Luton 44 A2
Jervis Ave. Enf 162 C2
Jervis Rd. Bis St 76 C3
Jessop Rd. Stev 37 D1
Jeves Cl. Bal 13 D1
Jillifer Rd. Luton 44 A1
Jinnings The. Wel GC 111 D2
Jocelyns. Harl 118 B2
Jocketts Hill. Heml H 123 F2
Jocketts Rd. Heml H 123 F1
Joel St. Norwd 175 D1
John Barker Pl. Hit 21 E1
John Ct. Hod 115 D1
John St. Luton 63 F4
John St. Roystn 7 E3
Johnby Cl. Enf 162 C1
Johns La. Ash Gr 121 F1
Johns Rd. Bis St 59 D1
Johnson Ct. Heml H 124 C1
Joiner's Cl. Bot 136 A1
Joint The. Bark 17 D3
Joint The. Reed 16 C3
Jones Rd. Gofs O 147 D1
Jordan Cl. Watf 153 F2
Jordans. Wel GC 111 E4
Jordan's Way. Bri Wd 140 C1
Joyce Ct. Wa Aby 163 E3
Jubilee Ave. Lon C 142 B3
Jubilee Ave. Ware 93 F1
Jubilee Cl. Pnr 175 E1
Jubilee Cotts. Bun 40 B3
Jubilee Cres. Arl 11 D1
Jubilee Ct. Hat 130 A4
Jubilee Ct. Wa Aby 163 F3
Jubilee Memorial Ave. Stev 50 B4
Jubilee Rd. Letw 23 E4
Jubilee Rd. Stev 50 A4
Jubilee Rd. Watf 154 A1
Jubilee St. Luton 45 F1
Judge St. Watf 154 A1
Judge's Hill. Nort 145 F1
Julian's Ct. Stev 50 B4
Julian's Rd. Stev 50 A4
Julius Gdns. Luton 44 C4
Juniper Ave. Bric 155 D4
Juniper Cl. Hod 148 C3
Juniper Cl. Luton 44 C1
Juniper Gate. Ric 173 E4
Juniper Gdns. Wl Gr 89 F4
Juniper Gr. Watf 154 A1
Juniper Green. Heml H 123 F2
Juno Rd. Heml H 124 C3
Jupiter Dri. Heml H 124 C3
Juxon Cl. Har 176 A1

Kardwell Cl. Hit 35 D3
Katescroft. Wel GC 110 C1
Katherine Cl. Heml H 138 C4
Katrine Sq. Heml H 124 B4
Keats Cl. Heml H 105 D1
Keats Cl. Roystn 7 E4
Keats Cl. Stev 51 E4
Keats Way. Hit 35 E4
Keble Terr. Abb L 153 F4
Kecksy's. Saw 97 F2
Keepers Cl. Luton 46 B1
Keiths Rd. Heml H 125 D1
Keiths Wood. Kneb 68 C3
Kelbys. Wel GC 111 E4
Kelling Cl. Luton 45 E4
Kelly Cl. Bor 170 B4
Kelmscott Cl. Watf 167 D2
Kelmscott Cres. Watf 167 D2
Kelshall. Watf 154 C2
Kelshall St. Kel 15 F3
Kelvin Cl. Luton 63 F3
Kelvin Cres. Har 176 C2
Kemble Cl. Pot B 159 E3
Kemp Pl. Bus 168 A2
Kempe Cl. St Alb 141 E4
Kempe Rd. Enf 162 B2
Kemprow. Aldhm 155 E2
Kemps Dri. Norwd 174 C2
Kempsey Cl. Luton 46 B1
Kendal Cl. Luton 44 B4
Kendale. Heml H 125 D1
Kendale Rd. Hit 34 C3
Kendale Rd. Luton 44 A1
Kendals Cl. Radl 155 F2
Kenerne Dri. Barn 171 F2
Kenford Cl. Watf 154 A4
Kenilworth Cl. Bor 170 B3
Kenilworth Cl. Stev 69 E4
Kenilworth Cres. Enf 161 F1
Kenilworth Ct. Watf 167 D4
Kenilworth Dri. Bor 170 B3
Kenilworth Dri. Cro Gr 166 A3
Kenilworth Gdns. Sth Ox 175 E3
Kenilworth Rd. Luton 63 E4
Kennedy Ave. Hod 134 C3
Kennedy Cl. Ches 148 C2
Kennedy Cl. Pnr 175 F2
Kennedy Rd. Dan En 71 F4
Kennelwood La. Hat 130 A3
Kenneth Gdns. Stan 176 C2
Kenneth Rd. Luton 46 A1
Kenning Rd. Hod 135 D4
Kennington Rd. Luton 45 D2
Kensington Ave. Watf 166 C3
Kensworth Rd. Stu 82 B2
Kent Cl. Bor 157 E1
Kent Cres. Bis St 76 C2
Kent Rd. Luton 62 C4
Kentish La. Bro Pk 145 E4
Kenton Gdns. St Alb 127 F1
Kenton La. Har 176 C2
Kents Ave. Heml H 138 B4
Kent's La. Stand 55 F1
Kenwood Dri. Ric 172 C4
Kenworth Cl. Ches 162 B3
Kerdistone Cl. Pot B 145 D1
Kerr Cl. Kneb 68 C3
Kerri Cl. Barn 171 E3
Kershaw Cl. Luton 45 D4
Kershaw's Hill. Hit 34 C3
Kessingland Ave. Stev 36 A1
Kestrel Cl. Berk 122 B2
Kestrel Cl. Stev 51 E1
Kestrel Cl. Watf 154 C3
Kestrel Green. Hat 130 A2
Kestrel Way. Luton 44 A3
Kestrel Wlk. Letw 23 D2
Keswick Dri. Enf 162 B2
Keswick Rd. St Alb 128 A1
Kettering Rd. Enf 162 B1
Kettle Green Rd. Had Cr 74 C1
Ketton Cl. Luton 64 A4
Kewferry Dri. Norwd 174 B3
Kewferry Rd. Norwd 174 B3
Keyfield Terr. St Alb 127 E1
Keymer Cl. Luton 46 B2
Keynton Cl. Hertng 112 C4
Keysers Rd. Lo Naz 135 D1
Kibes La. Ware 93 F1
Kilbride Ct. Heml H 124 C4
Kilby Cl. Watf 154 B2
Kildonan Cl. Watf 166 C4
Kilfillan Gdns. Berk 122 A2
Kilmarnock Rd. Sth Ox 175 E3
Kiln Ave. L Chal 150 B1
Kiln Ground. Heml H 125 D1
Kiln House Cl. Ware 93 F1
Kiln La. Bot 150 A4
Kiln Way. Norwd 174 C2
Kilncroft. Heml H 125 D1
Kilnfield. Wel GC 89 F1
Kilsmore La. Ches 148 B1
Kilvinton Dri. Enf 161 E1
Kimberley. Letw 11 F1
Kimberley Cl. Bis St 77 D3
Kimberley Rd. St Alb 127 E2
Kimble Cres. Bus 168 B1
Kimbolton Cres. Stev 69 D4
Kimbolton Green. Bor 170 B3
Kimps Way. Heml H 139 D4
Kimpton Bottom. Kim 86 C4
Kimpton Cl. Heml H 125 D4
Kimpton La. Luton 64 B4
Kimpton Pl. Watf 154 B3
Kimpton Rd. Bla En 87 D4
Kimpton Rd. Cod 88 C3
Kimpton Rd. Luton 64 A3
Kimpton Rd. Pet Gr 65 F1
Kimpton Rd. Welw 89 D3
Kimptons Cl. Pot B 158 B4
Kimptons Mead. Pot B 158 B4
Kinderscout. Heml H 125 D1
Kindersley Cl. Welw 89 E3
Kindersley Way. Abb L 153 E4
King Croft Rd. Harp 107 E4
King Ct. Berk 122 B3
King Edward Rd. Ches 162 C3
King Edward Rd. Shen 156 C3
King Edward Rd. Watf 167 F2
King Edward St. Fel 138 B4
King Edward's Rd. Ware 93 F1
King George Ave. Bus 168 A2
King George Cl. Stev 50 C3
King George Rd. Wa Aby 163 E3
King George Rd. Ware 93 F1
King Georges Ave. Watf 166 C3
King Georges Cl. Hit 21 E1
King George's Way. Whit 66 C3
King Harry La. St Alb 127 D1
King Harry St. Heml H 124 B1
King Henry's Mews. Ches 163 D1
King James' Ave. Cuf 146 C1
King James Way. Roystn 7 E3
King St. Bis St 76 C4
King St. Luton 63 F4
King St. Mark 83 F3
King St. Roystn 7 E3
King Street Mews. Bis St 76 C4
Kingfisher Cl. Norwd 174 A1
Kingfisher Cl. Whea 87 E1
Kingfisher Lure. Bed 139 D1
Kingfisher Lure. Chor 165 D3
Kingfisher Rise. Stev 51 E1
Kingfisher Way. Bis St 77 D4
Kingham Rd. Wars 94 C3
Kinghamway. Luton 45 F1
Kings Ave. Heml H 138 C4
Kings Ave. Watf 167 D3
Kings Cl. Chipf 152 A4
Kings Cl. Norwd 174 C2
Kings Cl. Watf 167 E3
Kings Court. Berk 122 B3
Kings Ct. Bis St 77 D4
Kings Farm Rd. Chor 164 B2
Kings Hedges. Hit 34 B4
King's La. Chipf 152 A4
Kings Meadow. Bed 139 D2
Kings Rd. Barn 171 E3
Kings Rd. Berk 122 A2
King's Rd. Ches 162 C3
King's Rd. Hert 114 A4
King's Rd. Hit 34 C4
King's Rd. Lon C 142 B3
King's Rd. St Alb 127 E2
King's St. Watf 167 E3
King's Walden Rd. Gt Of 33 E1
Kings Walden Rise. Stev 51 E4
Kings Wlk. Roystn 7 E3
Kingsbridge Rd. Bis St 77 D4
Kingsbury Ave. St Alb 127 E2
Kingscroft. Wel GC 111 D4
Kingsdale Rd. Berk 122 A2
Kingsdown. Hit 35 D3
Kingsdown Ave. Luton 45 E3
Kingsfield. Hod 135 D4
Kingsfield Ct. Watf 167 E1
Kingsfield Dri. Enf 162 B2
Kingsfield Rd. Dan En 71 F4
Kingsfield Rd. Watf 167 E2
Kingsfield Way. Enf 162 B2
Kingshill Ave. St Alb 128 A3
Kingshill Way. Berk 122 A1
Kingsland Rd. Heml H 124 A1
Kingsland Rd. Luton 63 F3
Kingsland Way. Ashw 4 B2
Kingsley Ave. Bor 169 F4
Kingsley Ave. Ches 148 A1
Kingsley Rd. Luton 45 D3
Kingsley Wlk. Tri 100 A2
Kingsmead. Ches 148 B2
Kingsmead. Cuf 146 C2
Kingsmead. Saw 97 F1
Kingsmead. St Alb 128 B3
Kingsmead Rd. Bis St 77 D4
Kingston Pl. Har 176 C2
Kingston Rd. Luton 45 F1
Kingston Vale. Roystn 7 F3
Kingsway. Cuf 146 C1
Kingsway. Luton 45 D1
Kingsway. Roystn 7 E4
Kingsway. Stot 11 F4
Kingsway. Ware 93 E2
Kingsway Industrial Estate. Luton 63 D4
Kingsway North Orbital Rd. Watf 154 A3
Kingswell Ride. Cuf 146 C1
Kingswood Ave. Hit 35 E4
Kingswood Rd. Watf 154 A3
Kingwell Rd. Barn 159 E1
Kinross Cres. Luton 44 B4
Kinsbourne Cl. Harp 85 E2
Kinsbourne Cres. Harp 85 E2
Kinsbourne Green La. Kin Gr 85 D2
Kipling Cl. Hit 35 E4
Kipling Gr. Heml H 105 D1
Kipling Rd. Roystn 2 C1
Kipling Way. Harp 86 A1
Kirby Cl. Norwd 174 C2
Kirby Dri. Luton 45 D4
Kirkcaldy Green. Sth Ox 175 E4
Kirkdale Rd. Harp 86 A1
Kirklands. Wel GC 89 E1
Kirkwick Ave. Harp 86 A1
Kitchener Cl. St Alb 128 A1
Kitching La. Stev 50 A3
Kite Field. Nthch 121 F4
Kite Way. Letw 22 C4
Kit's La. Wall 25 E4
Kitsbury Rd. Berk 122 A2
Kitsbury Terr. Berk 122 A2
Kitson Way. Harl 117 E1
Kitswell Way. Radl 155 F3
Kitt's End Rd. Pot B 158 C1
Knap Cl. Letw 23 E4
Knebworth Ct. Bis St 76 B3
Knebworth Path. Bor 170 B3
Kneesworth Rd. Knee 2 C4
Kneesworth St. Roystn 7 E3
Knella Green. Wel GC 111 D3
Knella Rd. Wel GC 111 D3
Knight St. Saw 97 F1
Knights Field. Luton 45 E1
Knights Templars Green. Stev 51 E4
Knightsbridge Way. Heml H 124 C2
Knightsfield. Wel GC 89 E1
Knoll Cres. Norwd 174 C1
Knoll Rise. Luton 45 F2
Knoll The. Hert 114 A4
Knolles Cres. Wel Gr 144 A4
Knolls Cl. Wing 60 A2
Knowl Way. Elst 169 F2
Knowle Dri. Harp 107 E4
Knowle The. Hod 135 D3
Knutsford Ave. Watf 154 B1
Koh-I-Noor Ave. Bus 168 A2
Kristiansand Way. Letw 23 E4
Kymswell Rd. Stev 51 E2
Kynance Cl. Luton 46 A1
Kynaston Cl. Har 176 B2
Kynaston Wood. Har 176 B2
Kyrkeby. Letw 23 E2
Kytes Dri. Watf 154 B3

Laburnum Cl. Ches 162 B4
Laburnum Cl. Luton 45 E4
Laburnum Gr. Chis 141 D3
Laburnum Gr. Luton 45 D4
Laburnum Rd. Hod 135 D4
Lachbury Cl. Luton 63 D3
Lackmore Rd. Enf 162 B2
Ladbrooke Cl. Pot B 159 D4
Ladbrooke Dri. Pot B 159 D4
Ladies Gr. St Alb 127 E3
Lady Gr. Wel GC 110 C2
Ladyhill. Luton 44 A3
Ladymeadow. Kin L 138 B2
Lady's Cl. Watf 167 E3
Ladyshot. Harl 118 A1
Ladysmith Rd. Har 176 C1
Ladysmith Rd. Ivin 80 C3
Ladysmith Rd. St Alb 127 E2
Ladywalk. Map Cr 172 C3
Ladywell Prospect. Saw 98 A1
Ladywood Cl. Chor 165 E3
Ladywood Rd. Hertng 112 C3
Laidon Sq. Heml H 124 B4
Lake Rd. Lo Naz 135 F1
Lake The. Bus 168 B1
Lake View. Pot B 159 E3
Lakeland Cl. Har 176 B2
Lakeside. Elst 170 A2
Lakeside. Tri 100 A3
Lakeside Pl. Lon C 142 B2
Lakeside Rd. Ches 148 B2
Lalleford Rd. Luton 46 B1
Lamb Cl. Hat 130 A2
Lamb La. Red 106 A3
Lamb Meadow. Arl 11 D2
Lambert Ct. Bus 167 E3
Lambourn Chase. Radl 155 F2
Lambourn Gdns. Harp 85 F2
Lambs Cl. Cuf 146 C1
Lambs Cl. Dun 44 A1
Lambton Ave. Ches 162 B3
Lamer La. Bla En 87 E2
Lamers Rd. Luton 46 A1
Lammas Mead. Hit 21 F1
Lammas Path. Stev 51 D2
Lammas Rd. Ched 80 A4
Lammas Rd. Wat St 70 B2
Lammas Rd. Watf 167 E2
Lammas Way. Letw 22 C4
Lammasmead. Hod 148 C4
Lamorna Cl. Luton 44 C3
Lamorna Cl. Radl 156 A3
Lampits. Hod 135 D3
Lamsey Rd. Heml H 124 B1
Lancaster Ave. Hit 34 C4
Lancaster Ave. Luton 45 E4
Lancaster Dri. Bov 136 C2
Lancaster Rd. Hit 34 C4
Lancaster Rd. St Alb 127 F3
Lancaster Way. Welw 89 E2
Lancastor Ave. Barn 159 E1
Lancing Rd. Luton 46 B2
Lancing Way. Cro Gr 166 A2
Landau Way. Ches 148 C3
Landford Cl. Ric 173 F4
Landmead Rd. Ches 148 C1
Lands End. Elst 169 E2
Lane End. Hat 129 F1
Lane Gdns. Bus 168 C1
Lanefield Wlk. Wel GC 110 B3
Lanercost Cl. Wl Gr 90 A4
Langbridge Cl. Hit 35 D2
Langdale Ave. Harp 86 B1
Langdale Ct. Heml H 124 C3
Langdale Gdns. Enf 162 B2
Langdon St. Tri 100 A2
Langfield Cl. Lo Naz 135 F1
Langford Dri. Luton 46 A2
Langham Cl. Luton 45 E4
Langham Cl. St Alb 128 B4
Langland Ct. Norwd 174 B2
Langland Dri. Pnr 175 F2
Langley Ave. Heml H 138 C4
Langley Cres. Kin L 139 D1
Langley Cres. St Alb 127 E3
Langley Gr. Sand 108 B1
Langley Hill. Kin L 138 C1
Langley Hill Cl. Kin L 139 D1
Langley La. Abb L 153 F4
Langley Rd. Abb L 153 F4
Langley Rd. Chipf 138 A1
Langley Rd. Watf 167 D4
Langley St. Luton 63 F3
Langley Way. Watf 166 C4
Langleybury La. Kin L 153 D2
Langmead Dri. Bus 168 B1
Langthorne Ave. Stev 50 C3
Langton Gr. Norwd 174 B3
Langton Rd. Har 176 B2
Langton Rd. Hod 134 C3
Langwood Gdns. Watf 167 D4
Lankester Rd. Roystn 7 E3
Lannock. Letw 23 E2
Lannock Hill. Wes 23 F1
Lanrick Copse. Berk 122 C3
Lansdowne Cl. Watf 154 B2
Lansdowne Rd. Luton 45 E1
Lapwing Cl. Heml H 124 C4
Lapwing Dell. Letw 23 D2
Lapwing Rd. Luton 44 A2
Larch Ave. Bri Wd 140 C1
Larch La. Wl Gr 89 F4
Larches Ave. Enf 162 B2
Larches The. Luton 45 E1
Larches The. Norwd 174 B2
Larches The. Nthch 121 E3
Larches The. Ware 93 E2
Larches The. Watf 167 F2
Larchwood. Bis St 76 B3
Larchwood Rd. Heml H 124 C3
Lark Rise. Hat 130 A2
Larke Way. Luton 44 B3
Larken Dri. Bus 168 B1
Larkens Cl. Puc 55 E2
Larkins Cl. Bal 12 C1
Larkinson. Stev 50 B4
Larksfield. Ware 93 F2
Larkswood Rise. St Alb 128 B4
Larmans Rd. Enf 162 B2
Larsen Dri. Wa Aby 163 E3
Latchmore Bank. L Hal 77 D1
Latchmore Cl. Hit 34 C3
Latimer Cl. Heml H 125 D4
Latimer Cl. Pnr 175 E1
Latimer Gdns. Pnr 175 E1
Latimer Rd. Lat 150 B1
Latimer Rd. Luton 63 F3
Lattimore Rd. St Alb 127 F2
Lattimore Rd. Whea 108 B4
Lauderdale Rd. Abb L 153 E3
Laughton Cl. Bor 170 B4
Laundry La. Lo Naz 149 F3
Laurel Ave. Pot B 158 C4
Laurel Cl. Heml H 124 C2
Laurel Park. Har 176 C2
Laurel Rd. St Alb 127 F2
Laurel Way. Ick 21 F2
Laureldene. Had Cr 74 C1
Laurels Cl. St Alb 141 D4
Laurels The. Pot En 123 E3
Lavender Cl. Ham St 147 F2
Lavender Ct. Bal 12 C1
Lavender Gdns. Enf 161 D1
Lavender Rd. Enf 161 E1
Lavender Way. Hit 34 B4
Lavender Wlk. Heml H 124 B3
Lavinia Ave. Watf 154 B3
Lavrock La. Ric 165 F1
Law Hall La. Whit 66 A4
Lawford Ave. Chor 164 B2
Lawford Cl. Chor 164 B2
Lawford Cl. Luton 63 E4

Lawn Ave. Kim 66 B1
Lawn Gdns. Luton 63 E3
Lawn La. Heml H 138 B4
Lawn The. Harl 118 A2
Lawn Vale. Pnr 175 F1
Lawns. The. Stev 51 E2
Lawns Cl. Gt Of 33 E1
Lawns Dri The. Hod 134 C1
Lawns The. Heml H 123 F2
Lawns The. Pnr 176 A2
Lawns The. St Alb 127 E2
Lawns The. Wel GC 89 E1
Lawrance Gdns. Ches 148 B2
Lawrance Rd. St Alb 127 E4
Lawrence Ave. Letw 23 D2
Lawrence Ave. Saw 97 F2
Lawrence Ave. Stev 50 C4
Lawrence Cl. Hertng 112 C4
Lawrence End Rd. Pet Gr 65 E2
Laxton Cl. Luton 46 C1
Laxton Gdns. Bal 24 A4
Layard Rd. Enf 161 F1
Laybrook Cl. St Alb 128 A4
Layham Dri. Luton 46 C1
Layston Meadow. Bun 40 C3
Layston Park. Roystn 7 E3
Lea Bushes. Watf 154 C2
Lea Cl. Bis St 59 D1
Lea Cl. Bus 168 A2
Lea Gr. Bis St 59 D1
Lea Mount. Gofs O 147 F2
Lea Rd. Harp 86 A2
Lea Rd. Hod 135 E4
Lea Rd. Luton 63 F4
Lea Rd. Wa Aby 163 D3
Lea Rd. Watf 154 A1
Lea Wlk. Harp 86 B2
Leaders Cl. Wing 60 A2
Leaf Cl. Norwd 174 B2
Leaford Cres. Watf 153 F1
Leagrave High St. Luton 44 A2
Leagrave Rd. Luton 45 D1
Leahoe Gdns. Hert 113 E3
Leamington Rd. Luton 45 D4
Leander Gdns. Watf 154 C1
Leas The. Bal 23 F4
Leas The. Bus 167 F4
Leas The. Heml H 139 D4
Leasey Bridge La. Harp 87 D1
Leat Cl. Saw 97 F2
Leathersellers Cl. Barn 171 F3
Leathwaite Cl. Luton 44 C3
Leaves Spring. Stev 51 D1
Leavesden Rd. Watf 154 A1
Leaview. Wa Aby 163 D3
Lebanon Cl. Watf 153 E2
Lectern La. St Alb 141 E4
Lecthmore Cl. Stev 50 B3
Leda Ave. Enf 162 B1
Ledgemore La. Gt Ga 103 F3
Ledwell Rd. Cad 62 C2
Lee Cl. Hert 113 E2
Lee Farm Cl. Bot 136 A1
Leeches Way. Ched 80 A4
Leecroft Rd. Barn 171 F3
Leeming Rd. Bor 169 F4
Lees Ave. Norwd 174 C1
Leeside. Barn 171 F2
Leete Pl. Roystn 7 E4
Leggatts Cl. Watf 153 F2
Leggatts Rise. Watf 154 A2
Leggatts Way. Watf 154 A2
Leggatts Wood Ave. Watf 154 A2
Leggett Gr. Stev 50 C4
Leggfield Terr. Heml H 123 F2
Leghorn Cres. Luton 44 A2
Legions Way. Bis St 77 D4
Leicester Rd. Luton 44 C1
Leigh Comm. Wel GC 110 C2
Leigh Rodd. Watf 175 F4
Leighton Buzzard Rd. Gt Ga 103 F1
Leighton Buzzard Rd. Heml H 124 B2
Leighton Buzzard Rd. Pic En 124 B3
Leighton Rd. Har 176 B1
Leighton Rd. Wing 60 B2
Lemonfield Dri. Watf 154 C3
Lemsford Ct. Bor 170 B3
Lemsford La. Wel GC 110 A2
Lemsford Rd. Hat 130 A3
Lemsford Rd. St Alb 127 F2
Lemsford Village. Lem 109 F3
Lensbury Cl. Ches 148 C2
Leonard Ct. Har 176 B1
Leonard's Cl. Wl Gr 89 F4
Leslie Cl. Stev 51 E1
Letchfield. Bot 150 A4
Letchmore Rd. Radl 156 A2
Letchmore Rd. Stev 50 B4
Letchworth Cl. Sth Ox 175 E3
Letchworth Gate. Letw 23 D2
Letchworth La. Letw 22 C2
Letchworth Rd. Bal 23 F4
Letchworth Rd. Luton 45 D2
Leven Cl. Ches 162 B3
Leven Cl. Sth Ox 175 E3
Leven Dri. Ches 162 B3
Leven Way. Heml H 124 B4
Leveret Cl. Watf 154 A3
Leverstock Green Rd. Heml H 125 D2
Leverstock Green Rd. Heml H 125 E1
Leverstock Green Way. Heml H 125 E1
Leverton Way. Wa Aby 163 E3
Lewes Way. Cro Gr 166 B3
Lewsey Rd. Luton 44 A2
Lexington Cl. Bor 170 A3
Lexington Ct. Pot B 158 B4
Lexington Way. Barn 171 E3
Ley Wlk. Wel GC 111 E3
Leyburne Cl. Men 61 E4
Leyburne Rd. Luton 45 D3
Leycroft Way. Harp 107 F4
Leyden Rd. Stev 50 B1
Leygreen Cl. Luton 64 A4
Leyhill Dri. Luton 63 D2
Leyland Ave. St Alb 127 E1
Leyland Cl. Ches 148 B1
Leys Ave. Letw 22 C3
Leys Cl. Hare 173 E1
Leys Rd. Heml H 124 C1
Leys The. St Alb 128 B3
Leys The. Tri 100 A2
Leysdown. Wel GC 111 E3
Leyton Green. Harp 86 A1
Leyton Rd. Harp 86 A1
Library Rd. Luton 63 F4
Lichfield Rd. Norwd 175 D1
Lichfield Way. Hod 134 C1
Liddel Cl. Luton 45 D2
Lidgate Cl. Luton 44 A3
Lighthorne Rise. Luton 45 D4
Lilac Cl. Ches 162 A4
Lilac Gr. Luton 44 B4
Lilac Rd. Hod 135 D4
Lilac Way. Harp 107 E3
Lilacs Ave. Enf 162 B2
Lilley Bottom. Cok Gr 47 D3
Lilley Bottom. Kin Wd 47 E2
Lilley Bottom. Lily 46 C4
Lilley Bottom Rd. Whit 66 B4
Lilleyhoo La. Lily 32 C1
Lilliard Cl. Hod 115 D1
Limberlost The. Wl Gr 89 D4
Limbrick Rd. Harp 107 D3
Limbury Rd. Luton 44 C2
Lime Ave. Bla En 87 D4
Lime Ave. Luton 44 B2
Lime Cl. Stev 51 E2
Lime Cl. Ware 93 F1
Lime Cl. Watf 167 E1
Lime Gr. N20 171 F1
Lime Gr. Roystn 7 F4
Lime Tree Pl. St Alb 127 F1
Lime Tree Wlk. Bus 176 C4
Lime Tree Wlk. Chor 165 D2
Lime Tree Wlk. Enf 161 E1
Lime Wlk. Heml H 124 C1
Limedene Cl. Pnr 175 E1
Limekiln La. Bal 23 F4
Limekiln La. Sta Mo 59 E3
Limes Cres. Bis St 77 D4
Limes Rd. Ches 162 C4
Limes The. Ch En 11 D4
Limes The. Hit 34 B3
Limes The. St Alb 127 F3
Limes The. Wel GC 111 D2
Limetree Ave. Nwml E 85 D4
Linbridge Way. Luton 46 C1
Lincoln Cl. Bis St 76 B3
Lincoln Cl. St Alb 128 B4
Lincoln Cl. Wel GC 111 E4
Lincoln Ct. Berk 122 A2
Lincoln Ct. Bor 170 B2
Lincoln Dri. Cro Gr 166 A3
Lincoln Dri. Sth Ox 175 E4
Lincoln Rd. Luton 45 D1
Lincoln Rd. Stev 37 D1
Lincoln Way. Cro Gr 166 A3
Lindbergh. Wel GC 111 E3
Linden Cres. St Alb 128 B2
Linden Ct. Harp 107 D4
Linden Glade. Heml H 124 A1
Linden Lea. Watf 154 A3
Linden Rd. Luton 44 C2
Linden Rd. Red 106 A3
Lindencroft. Letw 12 A1
Lindens The. Bis St 76 C3
Lindens The. Fel 137 F4
Lindens The. Stev 50 C2
Lindley Cl. Harp 86 A2
Lindley Ct. Harp 86 A2
Lindlings. Heml H 123 F1
Lindsay Ave. Hit 35 D3
Lindsay Cl. Roystn 2 B1
Lindsey Cl. Bis St 58 C1
Lindsey Rd. Bis St 58 C1
Lindsey Rd. Luton 46 B1
Lindum Pl. St Alb 127 D1
Lingfield Cl. Norwd 174 C2
Lingfield Rd. Roystn 7 F3
Lingfield Rd. Stev 37 E1
Lingholm Way. Barn 171 E2
Linington Ave. Bot 136 A1
Link Dri. Hat 130 A3
Link Rd. Bus 167 E4
Link Rd. Wl Gr 89 F4
Link The. Letw 12 A1
Link Way. Bis St 76 C3
Link Wlk. Hat 130 A3
Linkfield. Wel GC 110 C1
Links Ave. Hert 114 A4
Links Dri. Elst 169 F3
Links Dri. Radl 155 F3
Links The. Ches 148 B3
Links View. St Alb 127 E3
Links Way. Cro Gr 166 B3
Links Way. Luton 45 E4
Linkside Rd. Bis St 77 E3
Linksway. Norwd 174 B1
Linkway. Pnr 175 E1
Linkways E. Stev 50 C3
Linkways W. Stev 50 C3
Linley Dell. Luton 46 B1
Linnet Cl. Bus 168 B1
Linnet Cl. Letw 22 C4
Linnet Cl. Luton 44 A2
Linnet Wlk. Hat 130 A2
Linsey Cl. Heml H 139 D4
Linster Gr. Bor 170 B2
Linten Cl. Hit 35 E3
Linton Ave. Bor 169 F4
Lintott Cl. Stev 50 B3
Linwood. Saw 97 F1
Linwood Rd. Harp 107 E4
Linwood Rd. Ware 93 F2
Lion Ct. Bor 170 B4
Lion Yd. Kim 66 B1
Liphook Rd. Sth Ox 175 E3
Lippitts Hill. Luton 45 F3
Lismore. Heml H 125 E1
Lismore. Stev 51 E1
Lister Ave. Hit 34 C3
Liston Cl. Luton 44 A3
Little Acre. St Alb 127 E3
Little Acres. Gt Am 114 B4
Little Berries. Luton 44 C4
Little Bridge Rd. Berk 122 B2
Little Burrow. Wel GC 110 B2
Little Bushey La. Bus 168 B2
Little Chishill Rd. L Chis 18 B4
Little Church Rd. Luton 46 A2
Little Dell. Wel GC 110 B4
Little Ganett. Wel GC 111 E2
Little Gr. Bus 168 A3
Little Graylings. Abb L 153 F3
Little Green La. Cro Gr 166 A3
Little Hardings. Wel GC 111 E4
Little Hayes. Kin L 139 D1
Little Heath. L Hal 98 C2
Little Heath La. Pot En 123 D2
Little Hill. Chor 164 B2
Little Hoo. Tri 99 F2
Little How Croft. Abb L 153 E4
Little Hyde. Stev 51 D2
Little La. Harp 107 E3
Little La. Pirt 20 B2
Little Lake. Wel GC 111 D2
Little Ley. Wel GC 110 C2
Little Martins. Bus 168 A2
Little Mead. Hat 130 A4
Little Mollards. Wing 60 A2
Little Moss La. Pnr 175 F1
Little Mundells. Wel GC 110 C4
Little Orchard Cl. Pnr 175 F1
Little Oxhey La. Sth Ox 175 E3
Little Oxhey La. Watf 175 F3
Little Park. Bov 137 D2
Little Piper's Cl. Gofs O 147 D1
Little Potters. Bus 168 C1
Little Rd. Heml H 124 C2
Little Ridge. Wel GC 111 D3
Little Rivers. Wel GC 111 D4
Little Thistle. Wel GC 111 E2
Little Tring Rd. Tri 99 F3
Little Twye Rd. Buc Co 119 F2
Little Wade. Wel GC 110 C2
Little Widbury. Ware 93 F1
Little Widbury La. Ware 93 F1
Little Windmill Hill. Sar 151 F4
Little Wlk. Harl 117 E1
Little Wood Croft. Luton 44 C4
Little Youngs. Wel GC 110 B3
Littlebrook Gdns. Ches 148 B1
Littlecote Pl. Pnr 175 F1
Littlefield Rd. Luton 46 A1
Littlegreen La. Cad 62 C2
Liverpool Rd. Luton 63 E4
Liverpool Rd. St Alb 127 F2
Liverpool Rd. Watf 167 D2
Livingstone Link. Stev 51 D4
Livingstone Wlk. Heml H 124 C4
Lloyd Way. Kim 66 B1
Loates La. Watf 167 E3
Loates Pasture. Sta Mo 59 E4
Local Board Rd. Watf 167 E2
Locarno Ave. Luton 44 B3
Lochnell Rd. Berk 121 F3
Lockers Park La. Heml H 124 A2
Locket Rd. Har 176 C1
Lockley Cres. Hat 130 A4
Lockleys Dri. Welw 89 E3
Lodge Ave. Elst 169 F2
Lodge Cl. Hert 113 E4
Lodge Cres. Ches 162 B3
Lodge Ct. Ick 21 F2
Lodge Dri. Chor 165 E3
Lodge Dri. Hat 130 B4
Lodge End. Cro Gr 166 B3
Lodge End. Radl 156 A3
Lodge Field. Wel GC 89 F1
Lodge La. Wa Aby 163 E2
Lodge Way. Stev 51 D1
Loftus Cl. Luton 44 A2
Lombardy Cl. Heml H 125 E1
Lombardy Dri. Berk 122 B2
Lombardy Way. Bor 169 F4
Lomond Rd. Heml H 124 B4
London Rd. Bal 23 F3
London Rd. Bar 8 C1
London Rd. Bark 17 E1
London Rd. Berk 122 C2
London Rd. Bis St 77 D3
London Rd. Bun 40 C3
London Rd. Bus 167 F2
London Rd. Dra B 99 D2
London Rd. Gos 35 D2
London Rd. Gt Am 114 C4
London Rd. Harl 118 B1
London Rd. Heml H 138 B4
London Rd. Hert 113 F3
London Rd. Hert H 114 A2
London Rd. Hit 34 C3
London Rd. Kneb 69 D3
London Rd. L Alm 49 D4
London Rd. Lan 49 E3
London Rd. Luton 63 F2
London Rd. Mark 83 F3
London Rd. Nwml E 85 D3
London Rd. Pot En 123 D1
London Rd. Ric 173 F4
London Rd. Roystn 7 E3
London Rd. Saw 97 F1
London Rd. Shen 156 C3
London Rd. St Alb 127 F1
London Rd. St Ipp 35 D1
London Rd. Stev 50 C1
London Rd. Tri 100 B2
London Rd. Wl Gr 69 D1
London Row. Arl 11 D2
Londrina Terr. Berk 122 B2
Long Acre. Harl 118 A2
Long Arrotts. Heml H 124 A3
Long Barn Cl. Watf 154 A4
Long Buftlers. Harp 107 F4
Long Chaulden. Heml H 123 F2
Long Cl. Luton 46 B2
Long Croft. Sta Mo 59 E4
Long Croft. Watf 167 D1
Long Croft Dri. Ches 163 D3
Long Croft Rd. Luton 63 D4
Long Croft Rd. Map Cr 172 B3
Long Cutt. Red 106 A3
Long Elmes. Har 176 B1
Long Elms. Abb L 153 E3
Long Elms Cl. Abb L 153 E3
Long Fallow. Chis 141 D2
Long Hyde. Stev 51 D2
Long John. Heml H 124 C1
Long La. Bov 150 C4
Long La. Heron 164 B1
Long La. Stev 51 F3
Long Leaves. Stev 51 D1
Long Ley. Ched 80 A4
Long Ley. Wel GC 111 E3
Long Marston Rd. Mars 79 F2
Long Meadow. Bis St 76 B3
Long Meadow. Mark 83 F3
Long Moor. Ches 148 C1
Long Ridge. Stev 51 E1
Long View. Berk 122 A3
Long Wlk. Wa Aby 163 D4
Longacres. St Alb 128 A2
Longbridge Cl. Tri 100 A3
Longcliffe Path. Sth Ox 175 D4
Longcroft Ave. Harp 85 F1
Longcroft Green. Wel GC 110 B3
Longcroft La. Bov 137 E3
Longcroft La. Wel GC 110 B3
Longcroft Rd. Stev 50 C4
Longcrofts. Wa Aby 163 F3
Longdean Park. Heml H 139 D4
Longfield. Heml H 125 D1
Longfield Ave. Enf 162 B1
Longfield Dri. Luton 44 B1
Longfield Gdns. Tri 99 F2
Longfield La. Ches 148 A2
Longfield Rd. Harp 107 E4
Longfield Rd. Tri 99 F2
Longfields. Stev 51 E1
Longlands. Heml H 125 D2
Longlands Cl. Ches 162 B4
Longlands Rd. Wel GC 110 C3
Longmans. Brag 55 F4
Longmead. Bun 40 B4
Longmead. Hat 130 A4
Longmead. Letw 22 C4
Longmead. Wl Gr 69 D1
Longmeadow Dri. Ick 21 F3
Longmore Cl. Map Cr 172 C3
Longmore Gdns. Wel GC 110 C3
Longspring. Watf 154 A1
Longwood Rd. Hertng 112 C4
Loning The. Enf 162 B1
Lonsdale. Heml H 124 C3
Lonsdale Cl. Luton 45 D3
Lonsdale Cl. Pnr 175 F2
Lonsdale Ct. Stev 50 C4
Lonsdale Rd. Stev 50 C4
Loom La. Radl 156 A2
Loom Pl. Radl 156 A2
Loop Rd. Wa Aby 163 D4
Lorane Ct. Watf 167 D4
Lord Mead La. A St L 88 B4
Lord St. Hod 134 B3
Lord St. Watf 167 E3
Lords Meadow. Red 106 A3
Lords Wood. Wel GC 111 E3
Lordship Centre. Letw 23 D2
Lordship La. Letw 23 D2
Lordship Rd. Ches 148 A1
Lorne Rd. Har 168 C3
Lorraine Pk. Har 176 C2
Lothair Rd. Luton 46 A2
Loudwater Dri. Chor 165 E3
Loudwater Hts. Chor 165 D3
Loudwater La. Chor 165 E3
Loudwater Ridge. Chor 165 E3
Louvain Way. Watf 154 A4
Lovatts. Cro Gr 166 A3
Love La. Abb L 139 F1
Love La. Ashw 4 A2
Love La. Kin L 138 C2
Love La. Pnr 175 E1
Lovel Cl. Heml H 124 A2
Lovell Cl. Hit 35 D3
Lovell Rd. Enf 162 A2
Low Hill Rd. Roy 135 F3
Lowbell La. Lon C 142 C2
Lower Barn. Heml H 138 C4
Lower Bourne Cl. Ware 93 E2
Lower Bourne Gdns. Ware 93 E2
Lower Clabdens. Ware 93 F1
Lower Dagnall St. St Alb 127 E2
Lower Emms. Heml H 125 E4
Lower End. Wing 60 A1
Lower Gower Rd. Roystn 7 E4
Lower Green. Tewin 90 C1
Lower Harpenden Rd. Nwml E 64 B2
Lower Hatfield Rd. Hertng 113 D2
Lower Hatfield Rd. L Berk 132 C4
Lower High St. Watf 167 E2
Lower Icknield Way. Drab 99 D3
Lower Icknield Way. Mars 80 A1
Lower Icknield Way. Wils 99 E4
Lower Innings. Hit 34 B4
Lower Island Way. Wa Aby 163 D2
Lower King St. Roystn 7 E3
Lower Kings Rd. Berk 122 B3
Lower Luton Rd. Bla En 86 C1
Lower Luton Rd. Harp 86 B2
Lower Luton Rd. Whea 87 D1
Lower Mardley Hill. Wl Gr 89 F4
Lower Paddock Rd. Watf 167 F2
Lower Park Cres. Bi St 76 C3
Lower Paxton Rd. St Alb 127 F1
Lower Plantation. Chor 165 E3
Lower Rd. Bed 139 D2
Lower Rd. Bre Wd 47 F1
Lower Rd. Chor 164 B2
Lower Rd. Gt Am 114 C4
Lower Rd. Heml H 139 D3
Lower Rd. L Hal 98 B4
Lower Sales. Heml H 123 F1
Lower Sean. Stev 51 D2
Lower Shott. Ham St 147 F3
Lower St. Sta Mo 59 F4
Lower Tail. Watf 175 F4
Lower Tub. Bus 168 B1
Lower Wiggington. Wigg 120 C4
Lower Yott. Heml H 124 C1
Lowerfield. Wel GC 111 D3
Lowestoft Rd. Watf 167 D4
Lowfield. Saw 97 F1
Lowfield La. Hod 135 D3
Lowgate La. Sac Gr 72 A2
Lowlands. Hat 130 B4
Lowson Gr. Watf 167 F1
Lowswood Cl. Norwd 174 B1
Lowther Cl. Elst 169 F2
Loxley Rd. Berk 121 F3
Lucan Rd. Barn 171 F3
Lucas Ct. Wa Aby 163 F3
Lucas Gdns. Luton 45 D4
Lucas La. Ashw 4 C2
Lucas La. Hit 34 B4
Lucerne Way. Luton 45 E2
Lucks Hill. Heml H 123 F2
Ludgate. Tri 99 F2
Ludlow Ave. Luton 63 F2
Ludlow Mead. Sth Ox 175 D4
Ludlow Way. Cro Gr 166 B3
Ludwick Green. Wel GC 110 C3
Ludwick Way. Wel GC 110 C3
Lukes La. Lon M 79 E2
Lukes Lea. Mars 80 A1
Lullington Cl. Luton 46 B2
Lullington Garth. Bor 170 A2
Lulworth Ave. Gofs O 147 D1
Lumbards. Wel GC 90 A1
Lumen Rd. Roystn 7 E4
Lundin Wlk. Sth Ox 175 E3
Luring Rd. Berk 122 B2
Luton Dri The. Nwml E 64 A2
Luton La. Red 106 A4
Luton Rd. Cad 62 C2
Luton Rd. Cok Gr 46 C2
Luton Rd. Dun 44 A1
Luton Rd. Gt Of 33 D1
Luton Rd. Harp 85 F2
Luton Rd. Kim 66 A1
Luton Rd. Luton 44 A4
Luton Rd. Mark 83 F4
Luton Rd. Str 31 D3
Luton White Hill. Gt Of 33 D1
Luxembourg Cl. Luton 44 B4
Lybury La. Red 105 F4
Lycaste Cl. St Alb 128 A1
Lych Gate. Watf 154 B3
Lydia Mews. Wel Gr 144 B4
Lydon Mead. Sand 108 B1
Lye Hill. Bre Gr 65 E4
Lye La. Bri Wd 141 D1
Lye La. Chis 141 D2
Lygetun Dri. Luton 44 C4
Lygrave. Stev 69 E4
Lyles La. Wel GC 110 C4
Lyle's Row. Hit 34 C3
Lymans Rd. Arl 11 D3
Lyme Ave. Nthch 121 E4
Lymington Rd. Stev 50 A4
Lynbury Ct. Watf 167 D3
Lynch Hill. Ken Co 83 D4
Lynch The. Hod 135 D3
Lyndale. Stev 50 C2
Lyndhurst Ave. Pnr 175 D1
Lyndhurst Cl. Harp 86 B1
Lyndhurst Dri. Harp 86 B1
Lyndhurst Gdns. Pnr 175 D1
Lyndhurst Rd. Luton 63 E4
Lyndon Ave. Pnr 175 F2
Lyne Way. Heml H 123 F3
Lyneham Rd. Luton 46 B1
Lynn Cl. Har 176 B1
Lynsey Cl. Red 106 A3
Lynton Ave. Arl 11 D3
Lynton Ave. St Alb 128 B1
Lynwood Ave. Luton 46 A2
Lynwood Dri. Norwd 174 C1
Lynwood Hts. Chor 165 E2
Lyon Way. St Alb 129 D2
Lys Hill Gdns. Hert 113 D4
Lysander Cl. Bov 137 D2
Lysander Way. Wel GC 111 E4
Lytham Ave. Sth Ox 175 E3
Lytton Ave. Enf 162 C1

Lytton Ave. Letw 22 C3
Lytton Fields. Kneb 68 C3
Lytton Gdns. Wel GC 110 B3
Lytton Rd. Pnr 175 F2
Lytton Way. Stev 50 A3
Lyttons Way. Hod 115 D1

Mabbutt Cl. Bri Wd 140 C1
Mabey's Wlk. H Wy 97 D1
Macaulay Rd. Luton 44 A1
Macdonnell Gdns. Watf 153 F2
Macers Ct. Hod 148 C4
Macer's La. Hod 148 C4
Mackenzie Sq. Stev 51 D2
Mackerel Hall. Roystn 7 D3
Maddles. Letw 23 E2
Maddox Rd. Harl 117 F1
Maddox Rd. Heml H 125 D2
Made Feld. Stev 50 C3
Madgeways Cl. Gt Am 114 C3
Madgeways La. Gt Am 114 C3
Magellan Cl. Stev 51 E3
Magna Cl. Harp 107 E3
Magnaville Rd. Bis St 76 C2
Magnaville Rd. Bus 168 C1
Magpie Cres. Stev 51 E2
Magpie Hall Rd. Bus 176 C4
Magpie Wlk. Hat 130 A2
Maiden St. Wes 24 B1
Maidenhall Rd. Luton 45 D1
Maidenhead. Hert 113 E3
Maidenhead St. Hert 113 E3
Main Ave. Norwd 174 B4
Main Par. Chor 164 B3
Main Rd. Bram 91 E2
Main Road N. Dagn 81 D3
Main Road S. Dagn 81 E2
Maitland Rd. Sta Mo 59 F3
Malden Rd. Bor 170 A3
Malden Rd. Watf 167 D4
Maldon Ct. Harp 86 A1
Malham Cl. Luton 44 C2
Malins Cl. Barn 171 E2
Mall The. Chis 141 E2
Mallard Gdns. Luton 45 D3
Mallard Rd. Roystn 7 E3
Mallard Rd. Stev 51 E1
Mallard Way. Norwd 174 B2
Mallard Way. Watf 154 C2
Mallion Ct. Wa Aby 163 F3
Mallories. Harl 117 F1
Mallow Wlk. Roystn 7 F3
Malm Cl. Ric 173 E4
Malmes Croft. Heml H 125 E1
Malmsdale. Wel GC 89 E1
Malt La. Radl 156 A3
Maltby Dri. Enf 162 A1
Malthouse Ct. St Alb 127 E1
Malthouse La. Stot 12 A4
Malting La. Ald 101 E3
Malting La. Dagn 81 E3
Malting La. Gr En 55 F4
Malting La. Had Cr 74 C1
Maltings Cl. Clo 13 D1
Maltings Cl. Roystn 7 E4
Maltings Dri. Whea 108 B4
Maltings La. Gt Ch 9 F1
Maltings The. Abb L 153 E3
Maltings The. Heml H 124 B2
Maltings The. Wal 52 A4
Malus Cl. Heml H 125 D2
Malvern Cl. Hat 129 F3
Malvern Cl. St Alb 128 B4
Malvern Rd. Enf 162 C1
Malvern Rd. Luton 63 D4
Malvern Way. Cro Gr 166 A2
Malvern Way. Heml H 124 C3
Malzeard Rd. Luton 45 E1
Manan Cl. Heml H 125 E1
Manchester St. Luton 63 F4
Mancroft Rd. Cad 62 C1
Mandela Ave. Harl 117 F1
Mandelyns. Nthch 121 F4
Mandeville. Stev 69 E4
Mandeville Cl. Hert 113 E2
Mandeville Cl. Hod 134 C2
Mandeville Cl. Watf 153 F1
Mandeville Dri. St Alb 141 E4
Mandeville Rd. Enf 162 C2
Mandeville Rd. Hert 113 E2
Mandeville Rd. Pot B 159 E4
Mandeville Rise. Wel GC 110 B4
Mangrove Dri. Hert 113 F2
Mangrove La. Bric 133 F4
Mangrove La. Hert 113 F2
Mangrove Rd. Hert 113 F2
Mangrove Rd. Luton 46 B1
Mangrove Rd. Man Gr 46 C2
Manland Ave. Harp 86 B1
Manland Way. Harp 86 B2
Manley Rd. Heml H 124 C2
Manly Dixon Dri. Enf 162 C1
Mannicotts. Wel GC 110 A3
Manor Ave. Heml H 138 B4
Manor Cl. Barn 171 F3
Manor Cl. Berk 122 B2
Manor Cl. Hat 129 F4
Manor Cl. Hert 113 E4
Manor Cl. Ick 21 F2
Manor Cl. Letw 22 C2
Manor Cotts. Norwd 174 C1
Manor Cres. Hit 35 D3
Manor Ct. Cad 62 C2
Manor Ct. Enf 162 A2
Manor Ct. Pot B 158 C4
Manor Dri. Chis 141 D2
Manor Farm La. Men 61 E4
Manor Farm Rd. Enf 162 A2
Manor House Dri. Stev 51 E4
Manor House Gdns. Abb L 153 E4
Manor Links Dri. Bis St 77 E4
Manor Par. Hat 129 F4
Manor Pound Rd. Ched 80 A4
Manor Rd. Barn 171 F3
Manor Rd. Bis St 77 D4
Manor Rd. Bla En 86 C1
Manor Rd. Cad 62 C2
Manor Rd. Ched 79 F4
Manor Rd. Harl 118 B3
Manor Rd. Hat 129 F4
Manor Rd. Hod 135 D4
Manor Rd. Lon C 142 B3
Manor Rd. Luton 63 F3
Manor Rd. Pot B 159 D4
Manor Rd. St Alb 127 F2
Manor Rd. Sta Mo 59 F3
Manor Rd. Tri 100 A3
Manor Rd. Wa Aby 163 E3
Manor Rd. Watf 167 D4
Manor St. Berk 122 B2
Manor View. Stev 51 D1
Manor Way. Bor 170 B3
Manor Way. Ches 162 B4
Manor Way. Cro Gr 166 A3
Manor Way. Letw 22 C2
Manor Way. Pot B 145 D1
Manorside. Barn 171 F3
Manorville Rd. Fel 138 B4
Mansard Cl. Tri 100 A2
Manscroft Rd. Heml H 124 A3
Mansdale Rd. Red 105 F2
Manse Ct. Mark 83 F3
Mansfield. H Wy 97 D1
Mansfield Gdns. Hert 113 E4
Mansfield Rd. Bal 23 F4
Mansfield Rd. Luton 45 D1
Mansion Dri. Tri 100 A2
Manston Cl. Ches 148 B1
Manston Dri. Bis St 77 E4
Manton Dri. Luton 45 E2
Manton Rd. Hit 35 D3
Maple Ave. Bis St 76 B4
Maple Ave. St Alb 127 E4
Maple Cl. Bis St 76 B4
Maple Cl. Bus 167 F4
Maple Cl. Hat 130 A2
Maple Gr. Bis St 76 B4
Maple Gr. Watf 167 D4
Maple Gr. Wel GC 110 C4
Maple Green. Heml H 123 F3
Maple Lodge Cl. Map Cr 172 C3
Maple Rd. Harp 85 F1
Maple Rd E. Luton 63 D4
Maple Rd W. Luton 63 D4
Maple Spring. Bis St 76 B4
Maple Way. Ken Co 82 C4
Maple Way. Roystn 7 F4
Maplecroft La. Lo Naz 135 F1
Maplefield. Chis 141 E1
Maples The. Hit 34 C3
Mapleton Cres. Enf 162 B1
Maplewood. Ware 93 E2
Maran Ave. Welw 89 E2
Mardley Ave. Wl Gr 90 A4
Mardley Dell. Wl Gr 69 D1
Mardley Hill. Wl Gr 89 F4
Mardley Hts. Wl Gr 90 A4
Mardley Wood. Wl Gr 89 F4
Mardleybury Ct. Wl Gr 69 D1
Mardleybury Rd. Wl Gr 69 D1
Mardyke Rd. Harl 118 A1
Marford Rd. Stanb 109 E3
Marford Rd. Whea 108 C4
Margaret Ave. St Alb 127 E3
Margaret Cl. Abb L 153 F4
Margaret Cl. Pot B 159 E3
Margaret Cl. Wa Aby 163 E3
Margeholes. Watf 175 F4
Margery Wood. Wel GC 90 A1
Maricas Ave. Har 176 B1
Marigold Pl. Harl 118 A2
Marina Gdns. Ches 148 B1
Mariner Way. Heml H 125 D1
Marion Cl. Bus 167 F4
Mark Hall Moors. Harl 118 A2
Mark Rd. Heml H 125 D3
Markab Rd. Norwd 175 D3
Markeston Green. Sth Ox 175 E3
Market Hill. Bun 40 C4
Market Hill. Roystn 7 E3
Market Oak La. Heml H 139 D4
Market Pl. Hat 130 A3
Market Pl. Hert 113 E3
Market Pl. Hit 34 C4
Market Pl. St Alb 127 E2
Market Pl. Watf 167 E3
Market Sq. Bis St 76 C4
Market Sq. Stev 50 B3
Market Sq. Wa Aby 163 E3
Market St. Bis St 76 C4
Market St. Harl 118 B2
Market St. Hert 113 E3
Market St. Watf 167 D3
Markfield Cl. Luton 45 E4
Markgate Rd. Cad 84 A4
Markham Rd. Luton 45 E4
Marlands. Saw 97 F2
Marlborough Cl. Bis St 76 C3
Marlborough Cl. Wl Gr 89 F4
Marlborough Gate. St Alb 127 F2
Marlborough Rd. Luton 45 E1
Marlborough Rd. Stev 51 E3
Marlborough Rd. Watf 167 D3
Marlborough Rise. Heml H 124 C3
Marley Ct. Hod 148 C4
Marley Rd. Wel GC 111 D2
Marlin Cl. Berk 121 F3
Marlin Hill. Has 120 A4
Marlin Sq. Abb L 153 F4
Marlins Cl. Chor 164 C4
Marlins The. Norwd 174 C3
Marlins Turn. Heml H 124 A3
Marlowe Cl. Stev 51 E4
Marlowes. Heml H 124 B2
Marnham Rise. Heml H 124 A3
Marple Gdns. Wa Aby 163 E4
Marquis Cl. Harp 86 B1
Marquis La. Harp 86 B1
Marrilyne Ave. Enf 162 C1
Marriott Rd. Barn 171 E3
Marriott Rd. Luton 45 D3
Marriotts Way. Heml H 124 B1
Marryat Rd. Enf 162 A2
Marschefield. Stot 11 F3
Marsden Cl. Wel GC 110 A2
Marsden Green. Wel GC 110 A2
Marsden Rd. Wel GC 110 B3
Marsh Cl. Ches 162 C3
Marsh Hill. Wa Aby 149 F2
Marsh La. Gt Am 114 C4
Marsh La. Harl 118 C3
Marsh La. Sta Ab 115 E2
Marsh Rd. Luton 44 C2
Marshall Ave. St Alb 127 F3
Marshall Rd. Luton 46 B1
Marshalls Heath La. Bla En 87 D2
Marshall's La. H Cr 72 B1
Marshall's La. Sac Gr 72 A2
Marshalls Way. Bla En 86 C1
Marshal's Dri. St Alb 127 F3
Marshalswick La. St Alb 128 A3
Marshcroft Dri. Ches 148 C1
Marshcroft La. Tri 100 B3
Marshe Cl. Pot B 159 E4
Marshgate. Stev 50 B3
Marshgate Dri. Hert 113 F4
Marshmoor Cres. Hat 130 B1
Marshmoor La. Wel Gr 144 B4
Marsom Gr. Luton 45 D4
Marston Cl. Heml H 125 D1
Marston Ct. Lon M 79 D2
Marston Gdns. Luton 45 E2
Marston Rd. Hod 135 D4
Marsworth Ave. Pnr 175 E1
Marsworth Rd. Pit 80 B2
Marten Gate. St Alb 128 A4
Martham Ct. Harp 86 B2
Marthorne Cres. Har 176 B1
Martian Ave. Heml H 124 C3
Martin Cl. Hat 130 A2
Martindale Rd. Heml H 123 F2
Martinfield. Wel GC 110 C3
Martingale Rd. Roystn 7 F3
Martins Dri. Ches 148 C2
Martins Way. Stev 36 C1
Martins Wlk. Bor 170 A3
Martlesham. Wel Gc 111 F3
Martyr Cl. St Alb 141 E4
Marwood Cl. Kin L 139 D1
Marwoods Rd. Watf 167 D3
Mary McArthur Pl. Sta Mo 59 F4
Mary Park Gdns. Bis St 76 C2
Maryland. Hat 130 A3
Marymead Ct. Stev 69 D4
Marymead Dri. Stev 69 D4
Maryport Rd. Luton 45 D1
Masefield. Hit 35 E4
Masefield Ave. Bor 170 A2
Masefield Ave. Stan 176 C3
Masefield Ct. Harp 86 A2
Masefield Rd. Harp 86 A2
Mason Cl. Bor 170 B4
Mason Way. Wa Aby 163 F3
Masons Rd. Enf 162 B2
Masons Rd. Heml H 125 D2
Masters Cl. Luton 63 D3
Matching La. Bis st 76 B4
Mathams Dr. Bis St 76 B3
Matlock Cres. Luton 44 B1
Matlock Cres. Sth Ox 175 E4
Matthew Gate. Hit 35 D3
Mattocke Rd. Hit 21 E1
Maud Jane's Cl. Ivin 80 C3
Maude Cres. Watf 154 A1
Maulden Cl. Luton 46 D1
Maxted Cl. Heml H 125 E3
Maxted Rd. Heml H 125 E3
Maxwell Cl. Ric 173 D4
Maxwell Rd. Bor 170 A3
Maxwell Rd. Norwd 174 B2
Maxwell Rd. St Alb 128 A1
Maxwell Rd. Stev 50 A3
Maxwell Rise. Watf 167 F1
Maxwell's Path. Hit 34 B4
May Cl. St Alb 127 E3
May St. Gt Ch 9 F1
May St. Luton 63 F3
Maybury Ave. Ches 148 A2
Maycock Gr. Norwd 174 C2
Maycroft. Letw 12 A1
Maycroft. Pnr 175 D1
Maycroft Rd. Ham St 147 F3
Maydencroft La. Gos 34 C2
Maydwell Lodge. Bor 169 F4
Mayes Cl. Bis St 77 E4
Mayfair Cl. St Alb 128 B4
Mayfare. Cro Gr 166 B2
Mayfield. Wa Aby 163 E3
Mayfield. Wel GC 89 E1
Mayfield Cl. Harl 118 C2
Mayfield Cl. Harp 85 F2
Mayfield Park. Bis St 76 B2
Mayfield Rd. Luton 46 A2
Mayflower Ave. Heml H 124 B2
Mayflower Cl. Hertng 112 C2
Mayflower Cl. Lo Naz 135 F1
Mayflower Rd. Chis 141 D2
Mayhill Rd. Barn 171 F2
Maylands Ave. Heml H 125 D3
Maylands Rd. Sth Ox 175 E3
Maylin Cl. Hit 35 E4
Maylins Dri. Saw 97 E1
Maynard Ct. Wa Aby 163 F3
Maynard Dri. St Alb 141 E4
Maynard Pl. Cuf 146 C1
Maynard Rd. Heml H 124 B1
Mayne Ave. Luton 44 B2
Mayne Ave. St Alb 126 C1
Mayo Cl. Ches 148 B2
Mays La. Barn 171 E2
Mayshades Cl. Wl Gr 69 D1
Maythorne Cl. Watf 166 C3
Maytree Cres. Watf 153 F2
Maytree La. Stan 176 C2
Maytrees. Hit 35 D3
Maze Green Rd. Bis St 76 B4
Mazoe Cl. Bis St 76 C3
Mazoe Rd. Bis St 76 C3
Mc Adam Cl. Hod 135 D4
McGredy. Ches 148 A1
McKellar Cl. Bus 176 B4
Mckenzie Rd. Hod 135 D2
Mead Cl. Har 176 B1
Mead Cl. Stev 50 C3
Mead Ct. Sta Mo 59 E4
Mead Ct. Wa Aby 163 D3
Mead La. Hert 113 F4
Mead Pl. Ric 165 D1
Mead Rd. Shen 157 D3
Mead The. Ches 148 B1
Mead The. Hit 21 F1
Mead The. Watf 175 F4
Mead View. Sto P 43 F3
Mead Way. Bus 167 F4
Meadgate. Lo Naz 135 E2
Meadow Cl. Barn 171 F2
Meadow Cl. Berk 122 A1
Meadow Cl. Bri Wd 141 D1
Meadow Cl. Dat 69 E1
Meadow Cl. Enf 162 C1
Meadow Cl. Lon C 142 B2
Meadow Cl. St Alb 128 B3
Meadow Cl. Tri 100 A2
Meadow Cl. Wel Gr 144 B4
Meadow Croft. Hat 129 F3
Meadow Dell. Hat 129 F3
Meadow Green. Wel GC 110 B3
Meadow La. Pit 80 C2
Meadow Rd. Berk 122 A3
Meadow Rd. Bor 170 A4
Meadow Rd. Bus 168 A2
Meadow Rd. Heml H 139 D4
Meadow Rd. Luton 45 D2
Meadow Rd. Watf 154 A3
Meadow The. Wel GC 111 E4
Meadow Way. Bed 139 F2
Meadow Way. Cad 62 C2
Meadow Way. Chor 165 E1
Meadow Way. Cod 67 F1
Meadow Way. Gt Of 33 E2
Meadow Way. Heml H 138 A4
Meadow Way. Hit 34 B3
Meadow Way. Kin L 139 D1
Meadow Way. Letw 22 C3
Meadow Way. Pot B 159 D3
Meadow Way. Saw 98 A1
Meadow Way. Stev 50 C3
Meadow Way. Stot 11 F3
Meadow Way. Ther 16 A3
Meadow Way The. Har 176 C1
Meadow Wlk. Harp 107 E4
Meadow Wlk. Stand 55 F1
Meadowbank. Hit 35 D4
Meadowbank. Kin L 139 D1
Meadowbank. Watf 167 E1
Meadowbrook. Tri 100 A3
Meadowcroft. St Alb 142 A4
Meadowcroft. Sta Mo 59 F4
Meadowcross. Wa Aby 163 F3
Meadowlands. Bis St 59 D1
Meadows The. Bre Wd 47 F1
Meads La. Whea 87 E1
Meads The. Bri Wd 140 C1
Meads The. Letw 22 C3
Meads The. Luton 45 D2
Meads The. Nthch 121 F3
Meads The. Tri 100 A2
Meadview Rd. Gt Am 114 A4
Meadway. Barn 171 F3
Meadway. Berk 122 A2
Meadway. Coln H 143 E4
Meadway. Enf 162 B2
Meadway. Harp 107 F4
Meadway. Hod 135 D2
Meadway. Kneb 68 C2
Meadway. Stev 50 A3
Meadway. Wel GC 110 C2
Meadway Cl. Pnr 176 A2
Meadway The. Cuf 146 C1
Meautys. St Alb 127 D1
Medalls Link. Stev 51 D2
Medalls Path. Stev 51 D2
Medcalf Rd. Enf 162 C1
Medina Rd. Luton 45 D1
Medlows. Harp 85 F1
Medow Mead. Radl 155 F3
Medway Cl. Watf 154 B3
Medway Rd. Heml H 124 C4
Medwick Mews. Heml H 125 D4
Medworth Ave. Ches 162 B3
Mees Cl. Luton 31 D1
Meeting Alley. Watf 167 E3
Meeting House La. Bal 12 C1
Megg La. Chipf 138 A1
Melbourn Cl. Stot 11 F3
Melbourn Rd. Roystn 7 E4
Melbourn St. Roystn 7 E3
Melbourne Cl. St Alb 127 F4
Melbourne Ct. Wel GC 110 A3
Melbourne Rd. Bus 168 A2
Melford Cl. Luton 46 B1
Melings The. Heml H 125 D4
Melne Rd. Stev 69 D4
Melrose Ave. Bor 170 A2
Melrose Ave. Pot B 159 D4
Melrose Pl. Watf 153 F1
Melson St. Luton 63 F4
Melsted Rd. Heml H 124 A2
Melville Ct. Norwd 174 B2
Memorial Rd. Luton 44 C2
Mendip Cl. St Alb 128 B4
Mendip Rd. Bus 168 B2
Mendip Way. Heml H 124 C3
Mendip Way. Luton 44 B4
Mentley La. Gt Mu 54 C2
Mentley La E. Brag 55 E2
Mentley La W. Puc 55 E2
Mentmore Rd. Ched 79 F4
Mentmore Rd. St Alb 127 F1
Mentmore View. Tri 99 F3
Mepham Cres. Har 176 B2
Mepham Gdns. Har 176 B2
Mercer Pl. Pnr 175 E1
Mercers. Heml H 124 C3
Mercers Row. St Alb 127 E1
Merchant Dri. Hert 113 F4
Merchants Wlk. Bal 13 D1
Mercia Rd. Bal 24 A4
Mercury Wlk. Heml H 124 C3
Meredith Cl. Pnr 175 E2
Meredith Rd. Stev 51 D4
Meriden Way. Watf 154 C1
Merle Ave. Hare 173 E1
Merling Croft. Nthch 121 F4
Merritt Wlk. Wel Gr 144 A4
Merrow Dri. Heml H 123 F2
Merrows Cl. Norwd 174 B2
Merry Hill Mount. Bus 168 A1
Merry Hill Rd. Bus 168 A1
Merryfield Cl. Bor 169 F4
Merryfields. St Alb 128 C2
Mersey Pl. Heml H 124 C4
Mersey Pl. Luton 63 E4
Merton Rd. Enf 161 E1
Merton Rd. Watf 167 D3
Metropolitan Station App. Watf 166 C3
Meux Cl. Ches 162 A4
Meyer Green. Enf 162 A1
Meyrick Ave. Luton 63 E3
Mezen Cl. Norwd 174 B3
Michaels Rd. Bis St 59 D1
Micklefield Rd. Heml H 125 E2
Micklefield Way. Bor 156 C1
Micklem Dri. Heml H 123 F2
Midcot Way. Berk 121 F3
Middle Drift. Roystn 7 E3
Middle Furlong. Bus 168 A3
Middle La. Bov 137 D1
Middle Ope. Watf 154 A1
Middle Rd. Berk 122 A2
Middle Rd. Wa Aby 163 D4
Middle Row. Bis St 76 C3
Middle St. Lo Naz 149 F4
Middle Way. Watf 154 A1
Middle Way The. Har 176 C1
Middlefield. Hat 130 A3
Middlefield. Wel GC 110 C2
Middlefield Ave. Hod 135 D4
Middlefield Cl. St Alb 128 B3
Middlefield Rd. Hod 135 D4
Middlefields. Letw 11 F1
Middlehill. Heml H 123 F2
Middleknights Mill. Heml H 124 A3
Middleton Rd. Luton 46 B2
Middleton Rd. Ric 165 D1
Midhurst. Letw 22 C4
Midhurst Gdns. Luton 45 E3
Midland Cotts. Hit 22 A1
Midland Rd. Heml H 124 B2
Midland Rd. Luton 63 F4
Midway. St Alb 141 D4
Milburn Cl. Luton 31 D1
Mildmay Rd. Stev 37 D1
Mildred Ave. Bor 170 A3
Mildred Ave. Watf 167 D3
Mile Cl. Wa Aby 163 E3
Mile House Cl. St Alb 142 A4
Mile House La. St Alb 142 A4
Milestone Cl. Ast 51 E2
Milestone Rd. Hit 21 E1
Milestone Rd. Kneb 69 D3
Milford Cl. St Alb 128 B4
Milford Mill. Harp 86 B2
Milksey La. Gra 36 B3
Mill Bridge. Barn 171 F2
Mill Bridge. Hert 113 E3
Mill Cl. Heml H 139 D3
Mill Cl. Hit 35 E4
Mill Cl. Lem 110 A3
Mill Cl. Wing 60 A2
Mill Cnr. Barn 171 F4
Mill Farm Cl. Pnr 175 E1
Mill Field. Harl 118 B2
Mill Gdns. Tri 100 A2
Mill Green La. Wel GC 110 B1
Mill Green Rd. Wel GC 110 C3
Mill Hill. Roystn 7 F2
Mill La. Ches 148 C2
Mill La. Clap 57 E3
Mill La. Fla 84 A1
Mill La. Gos 34 C2
Mill La. Harl 118 C2
Mill La. Henlw 10 C2
Mill La. Hex 19 E2
Mill La. Hod 134 C1

Mill La. Kin L 139 D1
Mill La. L Hal 98 C2
Mill La. Mee 30 A3
Mill La. Saw 97 F2
Mill La. Stot 12 A3
Mill La. Ther 15 F4
Mill La. Wat St 70 C3
Mill La. Welw 89 E3
Mill La. Wes 24 B1
Mill La. Wing 60 B1
Mill Lane Cl. Hod 134 C1
Mill Race. Sta Ab 115 E2
Mill Rd. Gos 35 D2
Mill Rd. Hert 113 E3
Mill Rd. Roystn 7 E4
Mill Side. Sta Mo 59 F3
Mill St. Ashw 4 B2
Mill St. Berk 122 B2
Mill St. Bis St 77 D3
Mill St. Heml H 138 B4
Mill St. Luton 63 E4
Mill View Rd. Tri 99 F2
Mill Way. Bus 167 F4
Mill Way. Ric 164 C1
Millacres. Ware 93 E1
Millard Way. Hit 22 B1
Millbrook Rd. Bus 167 F4
Millcrest Rd. Gofs O 147 D2
Millcroft. Bis St 59 D1
Miller Cl. Pnr 175 E1
Millers Ct. Hert 113 E3
Millers La. Sta Ab 115 E2
Millers Yard. Hert 113 E3
Millfield. Berk 122 B3
Millfield. Wad 93 F4
Millfield. Wel GC 111 E4
Millfield La. Cad 62 B1
Millfield La. Gos 34 C2
Millfield Rd. Luton 45 D2
Millfield Way. Cad 62 B2
Millfield Wlk. Heml H 125 D1
Millfields. Saw 97 F2
Millfields. Sta Mo 59 F3
Millhoo Ct. Wa Aby 163 F3
Millhouse La. Bed 140 A2
Millstream Cl. Hert 113 D3
Millstream Cl. Hit 22 A1
Millthorne Cl. Cro Gr 165 F2
Millwards. Hat 130 A1
Millway. Bre Wd 47 E1
Milne Cl. Letw 23 D2
Milne Field. Pnr 176 A2
Milner Cl. Watf 154 A3
Milner Ct. Bus 168 A2
Milneway. Hare 173 D1
Milton Ave. Barn 171 F2
Milton Cl. Roystn 2 B1
Milton Ct. Ham St 147 F3
Milton Ct. Wa Aby 163 E3
Milton Dri. Bor 170 A2
Milton Rd. Harp 86 A1
Milton Rd. Luton 63 E3
Milton Rd. Ware 93 E1
Milton St. Wa Aby 163 E3
Milton St. Watf 167 D4
Milton View. Hit 35 E4
Milverton Green. Luton 45 D4
Mimas Rd. Heml H 124 C3
Mimms Hall Rd. Pot B 158 B4
Mimms La. Ridge 157 E4
Mimms La. Shen 157 E3
Mimram Rd. Hert 113 D3
Mimram Rd. Welw 89 E3
Mimram Wlk. Welw 89 E3
Minchen Rd. Harl 118 A1
Minehead Way. Stev 50 A4
Minerva Dri. Watf 153 F2
Minorca Way. Luton 44 A2
Minsden Rd. Stev 51 E2
Minster Cl. Hat 130 A2
Minster Rd. Roystn 7 E4
Missden Dri. Heml H 125 E1
Mistletoe Hill. Luton 64 B4
Mistley Rd. Harl 118 A1
Miswell La. Tri 99 F2
Mitchell Cl. Bov 136 C2
Mitchell Cl. St Alb 141 E4
Mitchell Cl. Wel GC 111 E3
Mixes Hill Rd. Luton 45 F2
Mixies The. Stot 11 F3
Moakes The. Luton 44 C4
Moat Cl. Bus 168 A2
Moat La. Luton 45 D2
Moat La. Wing 60 A1
Moat The. Puc 55 E2
Moatfield Rd. Bus 168 A2
Moatside. Ans 29 D4
Moatwood Green. Wel GC 110 C3
Mobbsbury Way. Stev 51 D4
Mobley Green. Luton 46 A2
Moffats Cl. Bro Pk 145 D3
Moffats La. Bro Pk 144 C3
Moira Cl. Luton 44 B4
Moles La. Wyd 28 A2
Molescroft. Harp 85 E2
Molesworth. Hod 115 D1
Molewood Rd. Hert 113 D4
Mollison Ave. Enf 162 C1
Molteno Rd. Watf 167 D4
Momples Rd. Harl 118 A1
Monarch's Way. Ches 162 C3
Monastery Cl. St Alb 127 E2
Money Hill Rd. Ric 165 E1
Money Hole La. Wel GC 111 E3
Monica Cl. Watf 167 E4
Monklands. Letw 22 B3
Monks Cl. Hod 135 D2
Monks Cl. Letw 22 B3
Monks Cl. Red 106 A3
Monks Cl. St Alb 127 F1
Monks Horton Way. St Alb 128 A2
Monks Rise. Wel GC 89 E1
Monks View. Stev 50 C1
Monks Wlk. Bun 40 C4
Monks Wlk. Wel GC 89 E1
Monksmead. Bor 170 B3
Monkswick Rd. Harl 117 F1
Monkswood. Wel GC 89 E1
Monkswood Ave. Wa Aby 163 E3
Monkswood Gdns. Bor 170 B3
Monkswood Way. Stev 50 C2
Monmouth Rd. Watf 167 D3
Monro Gdns. Har 176 C2
Mons Ave. Bal 23 F3
Mons Cl. Harp 107 E3
Monson Rd. Hod 134 C2
Montacute Rd. Bus 168 C1
Montague Ave. Luton 44 B3
Montague Rd. Berk 122 A2
Montayne Rd. Ches 162 B4
Montesole Ct. Pnr 175 E1
Montfitchet Wlk. Stev 51 E4
Montgomerie Cl. Berk 122 A3
Montgomery Ave. Heml H 125 D2
Montgomery Dri. Ches 148 C2
Monton Cl. Luton 44 C3
Montrose Ave. Luton 45 E2
Montrose Rd. Har 176 C1
Moon La. Barn 171 F3
Moor End Rd. Heml H 124 B1
Moor Hall Rd. Harl 118 C2
Moor La. Ric 174 A4
Moor La. Sar 151 F2
Moor Lane Crossing. Watf 166 B1
Moor Mill La. Fro 141 F1
Moor Park Rd. Norwd 174 B2
Moor St. Luton 63 E4
Moor View. Watf 167 D2
Moore Rd. Berk 121 F3
Moorend. Wel GC 111 D2
Moorhurst Ave. Gofs O 147 D1
Moorland Gdns. Luton 63 E4
Moorland Rd. Harp 86 A2
Moorland Rd. Heml H 124 A1
Moorlands. Fro 141 F2
Moorlands. Wel GC 111 D2
Moormead Cl. Hit 34 B3
Moormead Hill. Hit 34 B3
Moors Ley. Wal 38 A1
Moors The. Wel GC 111 D4
Moors Wlk. Wel GC 111 E4
Moorside. Wel GC 111 D2
Moortown Rd. Sth Ox 175 E3
Morefields. Tri 100 A3
Moremead. Wa Aby 163 E3
Moreton Ave. Harp 85 F1
Moreton Cl. Ches 148 A2
Moreton End Cl. Harp 85 F1
Moreton End La. Harp 85 F1
Moreton Pl. Harp 85 F2
Moreton Rd. Luton 46 A1
Morgan Cl. Norwd 174 C2
Morgan Cl. Stev 36 B1
Morgans Cl. Hert 113 E2
Morgan's Rd. Hert 113 E2
Morgan's Wlk. Hert 113 E2
Morice Rd. Hod 134 C4
Morland Way. Ches 148 C2
Morley Gr. Harl 117 E1
Morley Hill. Enf 161 E1
Mornington. Har Gr 90 A2
Mornington Rd. Radl 156 A3
Morpeth Ave. Bor 156 C1
Morrell Cl. Luton 45 D4
Morris Cl. Henlw 10 B3
Morris Cl. Luton 44 C4
Morris Ct. Wa Aby 163 F3
Morris Way. Lon C 142 B3
Morriston Cl. Sth Ox 175 E3
Mortimer Cl. Bus 168 A2
Mortimer Cl. Luton 62 C4
Mortimer Hill. Tri 100 A2
Mortimer Rd. Roystn 7 F4
Mortimer Rise. Tri 100 A2
Morton Cl. Ivin 80 B2
Morton St. Roystn 7 E4
Morven Cl. P Bar 159 E4
Moss Cl. Pnr 175 F1
Moss Cl. Ric 173 E4
Moss Green. Wel GC 110 C2
Moss La. Pnr 175 F1
Moss Rd. Watf 154 A3
Moss Side. Bri Wd 140 C1
Moss Way. Hit 21 E1
Mossbank Ave. Luton 64 B4
Mossendew Cl. Hare 173 E1
Mostyn Rd. Bus 168 B2
Mostyn Rd. Luton 44 C2
Mott St. Wa Aby 163 E1
Motts Cl. Wat St 70 B2
Moulton Rise. Luton 63 F4
Mount Cl. Heml H 123 F2
Mount Dri. Pk St 141 E3
Mount Dri. Sta Mo 59 F3
Mount Garrison. Hit 34 C4
Mount Grace Rd. Luton 46 B3
Mount Grace Rd. Pot B 159 D4
Mount Pleasant. Hare 173 D1
Mount Pleasant. Hert H 114 B2
Mount Pleasant. Hit 34 B3
Mount Pleasant. St Alb 127 E2
Mount Pleasant Cl. Hat 130 B4
Mount Pleasant La. Bri Wd 140 C1
Mount Pleasant La. Hat 130 B4
Mount Pleasant Rd. Luton 44 C3
Mount Rd. Hertng 113 D3
Mount Rd. Whea 87 E1
Mount The. Bar 8 C1
Mount The. Chor 165 E2
Mount The. Ham St 147 E3
Mount The. Pot B 145 D1
Mount View. Enf 160 C1
Mount View. Lon C 142 C2
Mount View. Ric 165 D1
Mount Way. Wel GC 110 C2
Mountbatten Cl. St Alb 142 A4
Mounteagle. Roystn 7 E3
Mountfield Rd. Heml H 124 C2
Mountfield Rd. Luton 45 F1
Mountfitchet Rd. Sta Mo 59 F3
Mountjoy. Hit 22 B1
Mountside. Stan 176 C1
Mountview. Norwd 174 C2
Mountview Rd. Ham St 147 F3
Mountway. Pot B 145 D1
Mountway Cl. Wel GC 110 C2
Mowbray Cres. Stot 11 F4
Mowbray Gdns. Hit 35 D3
Mowbray Rd. Harl 118 A2
Moxes Wood. Luton 44 C4
Moxon St. Barn 171 F3
Mozart Ct. Stev 50 B3
Mud La. Harp 107 F3
Muddy La. Letw 22 C2
Muirfield Cl. Sth Ox 175 E3
Muirfield Green. Sth Ox 175 E3
Muirfield Rd. Sth Ox 175 E3
Muirhead Way. Kneb 68 C3
Mulberry Cl. Chis 141 D2
Mulberry Cl. Hod 148 C4
Mulberry Cl. Tri 100 A3
Mulberry Ct. Bis St 77 D3
Mulberry Ct. Heml H 124 B2
Mulberry Green. Harl 118 B2
Mulberry Terr. Harl 118 A2
Mullion Cl. Har 176 A1
Mullion Cl. Luton 46 A3
Mullion Wlk. Sth Ox 175 E3
Mullway. Letw 22 B3
Mundells. Wel GC 111 D4
Mundells Ct. Wel GC 110 C4
Munden Gr. Watf 154 B1
Munden Rd. Dan En 71 F4
Munden View. Watf 154 B2
Mundesley Cl. Stev 36 A1
Mundesly Cl. Sth Ox 175 E3
Mungo-Park Cl. Bus 176 B4
Munro Rd. Bus 168 A2
Muntings The. Stev 51 D2
Murchison Rd. Hod 115 D1
Muriel Ave. Watf 167 E2
Murray Cres. Pnr 175 E1
Murray Rd. Berk 122 A3
Murray Rd. Norwd 174 C2
Murrell La. Stot 12 A3
Murton Ct. St Alb 127 F2
Musk Hill. Heml H 123 F1
Muskalls Cl. Ham St 148 A2
Muskham Rd. Harl 118 A2
Musleigh Manor. Ware 93 F1
Musley Hill. Ware 93 F1
Musley La. Ware 93 F1
Muswell Cl. Luton 45 D3
Mutchetts Cl. Watf 154 C3
Mutford Croft. Luton 46 B1
Mutton La. Pot B 158 C4
Myddelton Ave. Enf 161 F1
Myddelton Path. Ches 162 A4
Myddleton Rd. Ware 114 B4
Mymms Dri. Bro Pk 145 D2
Myrtle Gr. Enf 161 E1
Myrtle Green. Heml H 123 F2
Myrtleside Cl. Norwd 174 B2

N Luton Industrial Estate. Luton 44 A4
Nails La. Bis St 76 C4
Nairn Cl. Harp 107 E3
Nairn Green. Sth Ox 175 D4
Nan Aires. Wing 60 A2
Nancy Downs. Watf 167 E1
Nap The. Kin L 139 D1
Napier Ct. Ches 148 A2
Napier Dri. Bus 167 F3
Napier Rd. Luton 63 E4
Nappsbury Rd. Luton 44 B3
Napsbury Ave. Lon C 142 B3
Napsbury La. St Alb 142 A4
Narrowbox La. Stev 51 E4
Nascot Pl. Watf 167 D4
Nascot Rd. Watf 167 D4
Nascot St. Watf 167 D4
Nascot Wood Rd. Watf 153 F1
Naseby Rd. Luton 63 D4
Nash Cl. Elst 169 F3
Nash Cl. Stev 51 D3
Nash Cl. Wel GC 144 B4
Nash Green. Heml H 139 D3
Nash Mills La. Heml H 138 C3
Nash Rd. Roystn 7 E3
Nathaniel Wlk. Tri 100 A3
Nathans Cl. Welw 89 E3
Nayland Cl. Luton 46 C1
Nazeing New Rd. Hod 135 D1
Nazeing Rd. Lo Naz 135 E1
Neagle Cl. Bor 170 B4
Neal Cl. Norwd 175 D1
Neal Ct. Wa Aby 163 F3
Neal St. Watf 167 E2
Necton Rd. Whea 108 C4
Needham Rd. Luton 44 A3
Nelson Ave. St Alb 142 A4
Nelson Rd. Bis St 77 D3
Nelson Rd. Dagn 81 E3
Nelson St. Hert 113 D4
Nene Rd. Henlw 10 A2
Neptune Dri. Heml H 124 C3
Neston Rd. Watf 154 B1
Nether St. Widf 95 F2
Netherby Cl. Tri 100 B3
Nethercott Cl. Luton 46 B1
Netherfield La. Sta Ab 115 E2
Netherfield Rd. Harp 107 D2
Netherhall Rd. Roy 135 F3
Netherstones. Stot 11 F4
Netherway. St Alb 141 D4
Netley Dell. Letw 23 D2
Netteswell Cross. Harl 117 F1
Netteswell Rd. Harl 117 F2
Nettlecroft. Heml H 124 A1
Nettlecroft. Wel GC 111 D4
Nettleden Rd. Gt Ga 103 F1
Nettleden Rd. L Gad 102 C3
Nettleden Rd. Net 103 D1
Nettleden Rd. Pot En 123 D4
Nevell's Green. Letw 22 C4
Nevell's Rd. Letw 22 C3
Nevill Gr. Watf 167 D4
Neville Cl. Pot B 158 C4
Neville Rd. Luton 45 D3
New Barn La. Gt Ha 77 E1
New Barn La. L Hal 77 D1
New Barnes Ave. St Alb 142 A4
New Barns La. Muc H 74 C2
New Bedford Rd. Luton 45 E3
New Cl. Kneb 68 C3
New England St. St Alb 127 E2
New Farm La. Norwd 174 C1
New Ford Rd. Ches 162 C3
New Forge Pl. Red 106 A3
New Greens Ave. St Alb 127 E4
New House Park. St Alb 142 A4
New Inn Rd. Hin 3 E3
New Kent Rd. St Alb 127 E2
New Par. Chor 164 B3
New Park Dri. Heml H 125 D2
New Park Rd. Hare 173 E1
New Park Rd. New St 146 B4
New Path. Bis St 76 C3
New Pl. Welw 89 D2
New Rd. Aldhm 168 C4
New Rd. Berk 122 B3
New Rd. Chipf 137 F1
New Rd. Cro Gr 166 A2
New Rd. Elst 169 E2
New Rd. Gt Ch 9 E3
New Rd. Har Gr 89 F2
New Rd. Harl 118 B2
New Rd. Henlw 10 A4
New Rd. Hert 113 E4
New Rd. Hod 135 D2
New Rd. L Had 75 D4
New Rd. Nthch 121 F4
New Rd. Radl 155 F1
New Rd. Sar 151 F1
New Rd. Shen 157 D3
New Rd. Stanb 110 A2
New Rd. Tri 100 A3
New Rd. Ware 93 E1
New Rd. Watf 167 E3
New Rd. Wils 99 E4
New Rd. Wl Gr 69 D1
New River Ave. Sta Ab 115 D2
New River Cl. Hod 135 D4
New St. Berk 122 B2
New St. Cad 63 E1
New St. Ched 79 F4
New St. Luton 63 E3
New St. Saw 97 F2
New St. Watf 167 E3
New Town. Cod 67 F1
New Town Rd. Luton 63 F3
New Town St. Luton 63 F3
New Wood. Wel GC 111 E4
Newark Cl. Roystn 7 E4
Newark Green. Bor 170 B3
Newark Rd. Luton 45 D1
Newberries Ave. Radl 156 A2
Newberries Par. Radl 156 A2
Newbiggin Path. Sth Ox 175 E3
Newbold Rd. Luton 45 E2
Newbolt Rd. Stan 176 C3
Newbury Ave. Enf 162 C1
Newbury Cl. Bis St 76 C4
Newbury Cl. Luton 44 C1
Newcombe Path. Shen 157 D3
Newcombe Rd. Luton 63 E4
Newcome Rd. Shen 157 D3
Newdigate Green. Hare 173 E1
Newdigate Rd. Hare 173 E1
Newdigate Rd E. Hare 173 E1
Newell La. Luf 38 B4
Newell Rd. Heml H 138 C4
Newells. Letw 23 E2
Newells Hedge. Ivin 80 B3
Newfield La. Heml H 124 C2
Newfields. Wel GC 110 A3
Newford Cl. Heml H 125 D2
Newgate. Stev 51 D2
Newgate Cl. St Alb 128 B3
Newgate St. New St 146 B4
Newgate Street Village. New St 146 C3
Newgatestreet Rd. Gofs O 147 E2
Newgatestreet Rd. Ham St 147 D3
Newground Rd. Ald 101 D2
Newhall Cl. Bov 137 D2
Newhall Ct. Wa Aby 163 F3
Newhouse Cres. Watf 154 A4
Newhouse Rd. Bov 137 D3
Newland Cl. Pnr 175 F2
Newland Cl. St Alb 142 A4
Newlands. Letw 23 D2
Newlands Ave. Radl 155 F3
Newlands Cl E. Hit 34 C2
Newlands Cl W. Hit 34 C2
Newlands La. Hit 34 C2
Newlands Pl. Barn 171 E2
Newlands Rd. Heml H 123 F2
Newlands Rd. Luton 63 E1
Newlands Rd. Nwml E 63 F1
Newlands Way. Pot B 145 D1
Newlands Wlk. Watf 154 B3
Newlyn Cl. Bri Wd 140 C1
Newlyn Cl. Stev 50 A3
Newlyn Rd. Barn 171 F3
Newman Ave. Roystn 7 F3
Newmans Dri. Harp 85 F1
Newmarket Rd. Roystn 7 F3
Newnham Cl. Luton 46 B1
Newnham Rd. Newn 12 C3
Newnham Way. Ashw 4 A1
Newport Cl. Enf 162 C1
Newport Mead. Sth Ox 175 E3
Newports. Saw 97 E1
Newquay Gdns. Sth Ox 175 D4
Newstead. Hat 129 F1
Newteswell Dri. Wa Aby 163 E4
Newton Cl. Harp 107 E3
Newton Cl. Hod 115 D1
Newton Dri. Saw 97 E1
Newton Rd. Har 176 C1
Newton Rd. Stev 51 D3
Newtons Way. Hit 34 C3
Newtown Rd. Bis St 76 C3
Niagara Cl. Ches 148 B1
Nicholas Cl. St Alb 127 E4
Nicholas Cl. Watf 154 A1
Nicholas La. Hert 113 E3
Nicholas Pl. Stev 36 B1
Nicholas Rd. Elst 169 F2
Nicholas Way. Heml H 124 C3
Nicholas Way. Norwd 174 B1
Nicholls Cl. Red 105 F3
Nichols Cl. Luton 46 B1
Nicola Cl. Har 176 B1
Nicoll Way. Bor 170 B3
Nicolson Dri. Bus 176 B4
Nidderdale. Heml H 124 C3
Nightingale Ave. Knee 2 A3
Nightingale Cl. Luton 46 B3
Nightingale La. St Alb 142 B4
Nightingale Pl. Ric 165 E1
Nightingale Rd. Bus 168 A2
Nightingale Rd. Chor 165 E1
Nightingale Rd. Hit 34 C4
Nightingale Way. Bal 23 F3
Nightingale Wlk. Heml H 105 E1
Nightingale Wlk. Stev 51 E3
Nightingales. Wa Aby 163 F3
Nimmo Dri. Bus 168 B1
Ninefields. Wa Aby 163 F3
Ninesprings Way. Hit 35 D3
Ninian Rd. Heml H 124 C4
Ninning's La. Wl Gr 68 C1
Ninth Ave. Luton 44 B4
Niton Cl. Barn 171 E2
Nobles The. Bis St 76 B3
Nodes Dri. Stev 51 D1
Noke La. Chis 140 C2
Noke Shot. Harp 86 B2
Noke Side. Pk St 141 D2
Noke The. Stev 69 D4
Nokes The. Heml H 124 A3
Nokeside. Stev 69 D4
Norfolk Ave. Watf 154 B1
Norfolk Gdns. Bor 170 B3
Norfolk Rd. Bun 40 C4
Norfolk Rd. Luton 64 A4
Norfolk Rd. Ric 165 F1
Norfolk Way. Bis St 76 C3
Norman Ave. Bis St 76 B3
Norman Cl. Wa Aby 163 E3
Norman Cres. Pnr 175 E1
Norman Ct. Pot B 145 E1
Norman Ct. Sta Mo 59 F4
Norman Rd. Luton 45 D1
Norman Rd. Welw 89 D2
Normandy Ave. Barn 171 F3
Normandy Dri. Berk 122 A3
Normandy Rd. St Alb 127 E2
Normans Cl. Letw 11 F1
Norman's La. Roystn 7 E3
Normans La. Wl Gr 68 C1
Norman's Way. Sta Mo 59 F4
Normansfield Cl. Bus 168 A1
Norris Cl. Bis St 77 E4
Norris Gr. Hod 134 C2
Norris Rd. Hod 135 D3
Norris Rise. Hod 134 C4
North App. Norwd 174 B4
North App. Watf 154 A3
North Ave. Letw 23 D4
North Ave. Shen 156 C4
North Barn. Lo Naz 135 D1
North Bridge Rd. Berk 122 A3
North Cl. Barn 171 E2
North Cl. Chis 141 D3
North Cl. Roystn 7 E4
North Common Rd. Red 106 A2
North Cotts. Lon C 142 A3
North Dri. H Cr 72 C1
North Dri. St Alb 128 C3
North Drift Way. Luton 63 D3
North Gate. Harl 117 E1
North Hill. Chor 164 C4
North Orbital Rd. Abb L 154 B4
North Orbital Rd. Bri Wd 140 C1
North Orbital Rd. Chis 141 D3
North Orbital Rd. St Alb 129 E1
North Orbital Rd. St Alb 141 F3
North Orbital Rd. Tyt 142 C4
North Pl. Hit 21 E1
North Pl. Wa Aby 163 D3
North Rd. Bal 12 C1
North Rd. Berk 122 A2
North Rd. Ches 162 C3

North Rd. Chor 164 B2
North Rd. Hertng 113 D4
North Rd. Hod 135 D4
North Rd. Stev 36 B1
North Ride. Welw 89 E3
North Riding. Bri Wd 141 D1
North Road Ave. Hertng 113 D4
North Road Gdns. Hert 113 D3
North St. Bis St 76 C4
North St. Lo Naz 135 F1
North St. Luton 45 F1
North Terr. Bis St 76 C4
North Way South Letw 23 D3
North Western Ave. Bus 188 D3
North Western Ave. Elst 169 D1
North Western Ave. Watf 154 B2
Northam Rd E. Nort 146 C1
Northaw Cl. Heml H 125 D4
Northaw Rd W. Nort 160 A4
Northbrook Dri. Norwd 174 C2
Northbrook Rd. Barn 171 F2
Northcliffe Dri. N20 171 F1
Northcote. Pnr 175 D1
Northdown Rd. Hat 130 A1
Northend. Heml H 125 E1
Northern Ave. Henlw 10 B2
Northfield. Brag 55 F4
Northfield. Hat 130 A4
Northfield Gdns. Watf 154 B1
Northfield Rd. Ashw 1 B1
Northfield Rd. Bor 170 A4
Northfield Rd. Ches 162 C4
Northfield Rd. Harp 86 B2
Northfield Rd. Saw 97 F2
Northfields. Letw 11 F1
Northgate. Norwd 174 B2
Northgate End. Bis St 76 C4
Northgate Path. Bor 156 C1
Northlands. P Bar 159 E4
Northolt Ave. Bis St 59 D1
Northridge Way. Heml H 124 A2
Northview Rd. Luton 45 F1
Northway. Ric 165 F1
Northway. Wel GC 89 F1
Northwell Dri. Luton 44 C4
Northwick Rd. Sth Ox 175 E3
Northwood. Wel GC 111 E3
Northwood Hills Cir. Norwd 175 D1
Northwood Rd. Ric 173 F2
Northwood Way. Hare 173 E1
Northwood Way. Norwd 175 D1
Norton Bury La. Letw 12 B2
Norton Cres. Bal 23 F4
Norton Green Rd. Stev 50 B2
Norton Mill La. Letw 12 B2
Norton Rd. Bal 12 B1
Norton Rd. Letw 12 B1
Norton Rd. Luton 44 C2
Norton Rd. Stev 50 B2
Norton Rd. Stot 12 A2
Norton Way N. Letw 23 D4
Nortonstreet La. St P W 67 D4
Norvic Rd. Mars 80 A1
Norwich Cl. Stev 37 D1
Norwich Way. Cro Gr 166 A3
Norwood Cl. Hertng 112 C4
Nottingham Cl. Watf 154 A3
Nottingham Rd. Heron 164 B1
Nugents Ct. Pnr 175 F1
Nugent's Park. Pnr 175 F1
Nunfield. Chipf 152 A4
Nunnery Cl. St Alb 127 F1
Nunnery La. Luton 45 D3
Nunnery Stables. St Alb 127 E1
Nun's Cl. Hit 34 C4
Nuns La. St Alb 141 F4
Nunsbury Dri. Ches 148 C3
Nup End Cl. Wing 60 A2
Nup End La. Wing 60 A2
Nupton Dri. Barn 171 E2
Nurseries Rd. Whea 108 C4
Nursery Cl. Bis St 76 C3
Nursery Cl. Stev 69 D4
Nursery Gdns. Tri 100 A2
Nursery Gdns. Ware 93 F1
Nursery Gdns. Wel GC 89 F1
Nursery Hill. Wel GC 89 F1
Nursery Rd. Bis St 76 C3
Nursery Rd. Ches 148 C3
Nursery Rd. Hod 115 D1
Nursery Rd. Lo Naz 135 E1
Nursery Rd. Luton 44 C3
Nursery Row. Barn 171 F3
Nut Gr. Wel GC 89 E1
Nut Slip. Bun 40 C3
Nutcroft. Dat 69 E1
Nutfield. Wel GC 90 A1
Nutleigh Gr. Hit 21 E1
Nye Way. Bov 137 D2
Nymans Cl. Luton 46 B2

Oak Ave. Bri Wd 141 D1
Oak Ave. Enf 160 C1
Oak Cl. Heml H 138 C4
Oak Cl. Wa Aby 163 E3
Oak Ct. Norwd 174 B2
Oak Dri. Berk 122 B2
Oak Dri. Saw 118 B4
Oak Farm. Bor 170 B2
Oak Glade. Norwd 174 A1
Oak Gr. Hat 129 F3
Oak Gr. Hert 113 F2
Oak Green. Abb L 153 F4
Oak Green Way. Abb L 153 F4
Oak La. Buc Co 120 A1
Oak La. Cuf 146 C2
Oak La. Gra 36 B2
Oak Path. Bus 168 A2
Oak Piece. Wl Gr 89 F4
Oak Rd. Luton 63 E4
Oak Rd. Wl Gr 69 D1
Oak St. Bis St 76 C3
Oak St. Heml H 138 C4
Oak Tree Cl. Hat 130 A3
Oak Tree Cl. Hert H 114 B2
Oak Tree Ct. Elst 169 E2
Oak Way. Harp 107 D3
Oak Wood. Berk 121 F2
Oakbank. Radl 156 A2
Oakcroft Cl. Pnr 175 D1
Oakdale. Wel GC 89 E1
Oakdale Ave. Norwd 175 D1
Oakdale Cl. Sth Ox 175 E3
Oakdale Rd. Sth Ox 175 E3
Oakdene. Ches 148 C1
Oakdene Cl. Pnr 175 F2
Oakdene Rd. Heml H 138 C4
Oakdene Rd. Watf 154 A2
Oakdene Way. St Alb 128 B2
Oaken Gr. Wel GC 110 C2
Oakfield. Chor 165 D2
Oakfield Ave. Hit 35 D3
Oakfield Rd. Harp 107 D3
Oakfields. Stev 51 E1
Oakfields Ave. Kneb 69 D3
Oakfields Cl. Stev 51 E1
Oakfields Rd. Kneb 69 D3
Oakford Dri. Tri 99 F2
Oakhill. Letw 23 E2
Oakhill Ave. Pnr 175 F1
Oakhill Dri. Welw 89 D3
Oakhill Rd. Map Cr 172 C3
Oakhurst Ave. Harp 107 D3
Oakhurst Rd. Enf 162 B2
Oakington. Wel GC 111 E3
Oaklands Ave. Bro Pk 144 C2
Oaklands Ave. Watf 167 D1
Oaklands Cl. Bis St 59 D1
Oaklands Ct. Watf 167 D4
Oaklands Dri. Bis St 59 D1
Oaklands Gate. Norwd 174 C2
Oaklands La. Barn 171 D3
Oaklands La. St Alb 129 D2
Oaklands Park. Bis St 59 D1
Oaklands Rd. Ham St 147 F3
Oaklands Rd. N20 171 F1
Oaklands Rise. Wl Gr 89 F4
Oaklea. Wl Gr 89 F4
Oaklea Cl. Wl Gr 89 F4
Oaklea Wood. Wl Gr 89 F4
Oakleigh Ct. Bis St 76 B4
Oakleigh Dri. Cro Gr 166 B2
Oakleigh Rd. Pnr 176 A2
Oakley Cl. Luton 44 B2
Oakley Rd. Harp 107 E4
Oakley Rd. Luton 44 C2
Oakmeade. Pnr 176 A2
Oakmere Ave. Pot B 159 E3
Oakmere Cl. Pot B 159 E4
Oakmere La. Pot B 159 E4
Oakridge. Bri Wd 140 C1
Oakridge Ave. Radl 155 F3
Oakridge La. Aldhm 155 E3
Oakroyd Ave. Pot B 158 C3
Oakroyd Cl. Pot B 158 C3
Oaks Cl. Hit 34 C3
Oaks Cl. Radl 155 F2
Oaks Cross. Stev 51 D1
Oaks The. Berk 122 A2
Oaktree Cl. Gofs O 147 E2
Oaktree Garth. Wel GC 110 C3
Oakview Cl. Ches 148 A2
Oakway. Stu 82 A4
Oakwell Cl. Stev 69 E4
Oakwood. Wa Aby 163 F3
Oakwood Ave. Bor 170 A3
Oakwood Cl. Stev 51 E1
Oakwood Dri. Luton 44 B4
Oakwood Dri. St Alb 128 B2
Oakwood Rd. Bri Wd 140 C1
Oakwood Rd. Pnr 175 D1
Occupation Rd. Watf 167 D2
Ochard House La. St Alb 127 E1
Oddfellows Ct. Hert 113 E3
Oddy Hill. Tri 100 B2
Odessey Rd. Bor 170 A4
Offa Rd. St Alb 127 E2
Offas Way. Whea 108 B4
Offley Hill. Gt Of 33 E2
Offley Rd. Hit 34 B3
Ogard Rd. Hod 135 E4
Okeley La. Tri 99 F2
Old Barn La. Cro Gr 165 F2
Old Bedford Rd. Luton 45 E3
Old Brewery Pl. Kim 66 B1
Old Charlton Rd. Hit 34 C3
Old Church La. Wad 93 F4
Old Cross. Hert 113 E3
Old Dean. Bov 137 D2
Old Drive The. Wel GC 110 A3
Old Farm. Ivin 80 B2
Old Fishery La. Heml H 123 F1
Old Fold Cl. Barn 171 F4
Old Fold La. Barn 171 F4
Old Fold View. Barn 171 E3
Old Forge Cl. Watf 154 A3
Old Forge Cl. Wel GC 89 F1
Old Forge Rd. Enf 161 F1
Old French Horn La. Hat 130 A3
Old Gammon Cl. Nort 174 B3
Old Garden Ct. St Alb 127 E2
Old Hale Way. Hit 21 F1
Old Hall Cl. Pnr 175 F1
Old Hall Dri. Pnr 175 F1
Old Harpenden Rd. St Alb 127 F3
Old Herns La. Wel GC 111 E4
Old Hertford Rd. Hat 130 B4
Old Highway. Hod 135 E4
Old House Ct. Heml H 124 C2
Old House La. Lo Naz 149 F4
Old House Rd. Heml H 124 C2
Old Knebworth La. Old K 68 B4
Old La. Kneb 69 D3
Old Leys. Hat 130 A1
Old London Rd. Hert 113 F3
Old London Rd. St Alb 127 F1
Old Maple. Heml H 104 C1
Old Mill Gdns. Berk 122 B2
Old Mill La. L Hal 98 A3
Old Mill Rd. Abb L 153 E3
Old Nazeing Rd. Lo Naz 135 D1
Old North Rd. Knee 2 A2
Old North Rd. Roystn 7 E4
Old Oak Cl. Ch En 11 D4
Old Oaks. Wa Aby 163 F4
Old Orch. Pk St 141 E3
Old Orchard. Luton 63 E3
Old Orchard Mews. Berk 122 B2
Old Park Rd. Hit 34 C4
Old Parkbury La. Col St 141 F1
Old Rd. Harl 118 B3
Old Rectory Cl. Harp 86 A1
Old Rectory Dri. Hat 130 A3
Old Rectory Gdns. Whea 87 E1
Old Redding. Har 176 B3
Old School Cl. Cod 67 F1
Old School Green. Benn 52 C3
Old School Wlk. Arl 11 D2
Old School Wlk. Cad 63 E1
Old Shire La. Chor 164 A2
Old Sopwell Gdns. St Alb 127 F1
Old Uxbridge Rd. Map Cr 172 C2
Old Vicarage Gdns. Mark 83 E3
Old Watford Rd. Bri Wd 140 C1
Olden Mead. Letw 23 D2
Oldfield Cl. Ches 148 C2
Oldfield Dri. Ches 148 C2
Oldfield Farm Rd. Henlw 10 A2
Oldfield Rd. Heml H 123 F1
Oldfield Rd. Lon C 142 B3
Oldfield Rise. Whit 66 C4
Oldhall St. Hert 113 E3
Oldhouse Croft. Harl 117 F1
Oldhouse La. Kin L 152 C2
Oldings Cnr. Stanb 110 A1
Oldpark Ride. Ches 161 E4
Old's App. Watf 166 B1
Old's Cl. Watf 166 B1
Oldwood. Wl Gr 89 E4
Olive Taylor Ct. Heml H 124 C4
Oliver Cl. Heml H 138 C4
Oliver Cl. Pk St 141 E2
Oliver Rd. Heml H 138 C4
Oliver Rise. Heml H 138 C4
Oliver's Cl. Heml H 123 E4
Oliver's La. Stot 11 F4
Olleberrie La. Sar 151 E4
Olwen Mews. Pnr 175 E1
Olympus Rd. Henlw 10 A2
Onslow Cl. Hat 130 A3
Onslow Cl. Hit 21 E1
Onslow Rd. Luton 44 B3
On-The-Hill. Watf 175 F4
Opening The. Cod 88 C4
Openshaw Way. Letw 22 C3
Orbital Cres. Watf 153 F2
Orchard Ave. Berk 122 A2
Orchard Ave. Harp 85 F1
Orchard Ave. Watf 154 A4
Orchard Cl. Bor 169 F3
Orchard Cl. Bus 168 B1
Orchard Cl. Chor 164 B3
Orchard Cl. Cuf 146 C2
Orchard Cl. Gos 34 C2
Orchard Cl. Heml H 124 C3
Orchard Cl. L Berk 132 B2
Orchard Cl. Letw 22 C4
Orchard Cl. Radl 155 F2
Orchard Cl. St Alb 127 F1
Orchard Cl. Sta Ab 115 E2
Orchard Cl. Ware 93 E1
Orchard Cl. Watf 166 C4
Orchard Cl. Wing 60 A1
Orchard Cres. Stev 50 B4
Orchard Croft. Harl 118 A1
Orchard Dri. Chis 141 D3
Orchard Dri. Chor 164 B3
Orchard Dri. Watf 166 C4
Orchard Gdns. Wa Aby 163 E3
Orchard Mead. Hat 129 F3
Orchard Rd. Bal 12 C1
Orchard Rd. Barn 171 F3
Orchard Rd. Bis St 59 D1
Orchard Rd. Hit 22 A1
Orchard Rd. Roystn 7 D4
Orchard Rd. Stev 50 B4
Orchard Rd. Tewin 90 B2
Orchard Rd. Welw 89 E3
Orchard Sq. Hod 148 C4
Orchard St. Heml H 138 B4
Orchard St. St Alb 127 E1
Orchard The. Bal 23 F4
Orchard The. Hert 92 B1
Orchard The. Kin L 139 D1
Orchard The. Tonw 92 C4
Orchard The. Wel GC 110 B4
Orchard Way. Bov 137 D2
Orchard Way. Bre Wd 47 F1
Orchard Way. Gofs O 147 D2
Orchard Way. Ivin 80 C3
Orchard Way. Kneb 68 C3
Orchard Way. Letw 22 C4
Orchard Way. Luton 44 B2
Orchard Way. Pot B 145 D2
Orchard Way. Ric 165 D1
Orchard Way. Roystn 7 E4
Orchards The. Saw 97 F2
Orchards The. Tri 99 F2
Ordelmere. Letw 11 F1
Ordnance Rd. Enf 162 C1
Oregon Way. Luton 45 D4
Organ Hall Rd. Bor 169 F4
Orion Way. Norwd 174 C3
Orlando Cl. Hit 35 D3
Ormesby Dri. Pot B 158 B4
Ormonde Rd. Norwd 174 B3
Ormsby Cl. Luton 63 F3
Ormskirk Rd. Sth Ox 175 E3
Oronsay. Heml H 125 D1
Orphanage Rd. Watf 167 E4
Orpington Cl. Luton 44 A2
Orton Cl. St Alb 128 A4
Orwell View. Bal 13 D1
Osborne Gdns. Pot B 145 D1
Osborne Rd. Ches 148 C2
Osborne Rd. Hod 135 D2
Osborne Rd. Luton 63 F3
Osborne Rd. Pot B 145 D1
Osborne Rd. Watf 154 B1
Osborne Way. Wigg 100 B1
Osbourne Ave. Kin L 138 C2
Osmington Cl. Tri 99 F2
Osprey Gdns. Stev 51 E1
Osprey Wlk. Luton 44 A3
Oster St. St Alb 127 E2
Osterley Cl. Stev 69 E4
Oswald Rd. St Alb 127 F1
Otley Way. Sth Ox 175 E4
Otter Gdns. Hat 130 A2
Otterspool La. Bus 154 C1
Otterspool Way. Bus 168 A4
Ottoman Terr. Watf 167 E3
Ottway Wlk. Welw 89 E2
Otways Cl. Pot B 159 D3
Oudle La. Muc H 74 C1
Oughton Cl. Hit 34 B4
Oughton Head Way. Hit 34 B4
Oughtonhead La. Hit 34 B4
Oulton Cres. Pot B 158 B4
Oulton Rise. Harp 86 B2
Oulton Way. Watf 175 F3
Oundle Ave. Bus 168 B2
Oundle Ct. Stev 69 E4
Oundle Path. Stev 69 E4
Oundle The. Stev 69 E4
Ousden Cl. Ches 148 C1
Ousden Dri. Ches 148 C1
Oval The. Henlw 10 B2
Oval The. Hod 148 C4
Oval The. Stev 37 D1
Overfield Rd. Luton 46 B1
Overstone Rd. Harp 86 B1
Overstone Rd. Luton 44 B1
Overstream. Chor 165 D3
Oving Cl. Luton 46 B1
Owen Jones Cl. Henlw 10 B3
Owens Way. Cro Gr 166 A3
Owles La. Bun 40 C3
Ox La. Harp 86 A2
Oxcroft. Bis St 76 C2
Oxen Rd. Luton 45 F1
Oxendon Dri. Hod 135 D3
Oxfield Cl. Berk 122 A2
Oxford Ave. St Alb 128 B1
Oxford Cl. Ches 148 B1
Oxford Cl. Knee 2 A4
Oxford Rd. Bre Wd 47 F1
Oxford Rd. Luton 63 F3
Oxford St. Watf 167 D2
Oxhey Ave. Watf 167 E1
Oxhey Dr. Sth Ox 175 D4
Oxhey La. Pnr 176 A2
Oxhey La. Watf 175 D4
Oxhey Rd. Watf 167 E1
Oxhey Ridge Cl. Norwd 175 D3
Oxlease Dri. Hat 130 A2
Oxleys Rd. Stev 51 E2
Oxleys The. Harl 118 C2

Packhorse Cl. St Alb 128 B3
Packhorse La. Ridge 157 E4
Paddick Cl. Hod 134 C4
Paddock Cl. Hun 95 E1
Paddock Cl. Letw 23 D3
Paddock Rd. Bun 40 C4
Paddock The. Bis St 76 B2
Paddock The. Hat 130 A3
Paddock The. Hit 35 D3
Paddock The. Hod 135 D2
Paddock Way. Heml H 123 F2
Paddock Wood. Harp 107 F4
Paddocks Cl. Stev 51 D2
Paddocks The. Cod 67 F1
Paddocks The. Stev 51 D2
Paddocks The. Wel GC 111 D4
Padgets The. Wa Aby 163 F3
Page Cl. Bal 23 F3
Page Rd. Hert 114 A3
Pageant Rd. St Alb 127 E1
Pages Cl. Bis St 76 B3
Pages Croft. Berk 122 A3
Paine's La. Pnr 175 F1
Paines Orch. Ched 80 A4
Painters La. Enf 162 C2
Palace Cl. Kin L 139 D1
Palace Gdns. Roystn 7 E3
Palfrey Cl. St Alb 127 E3
Pallas Rd. Heml H 124 C3
Palmer Ave. Bus 168 A2
Palmer Cl. Hert 113 E4
Palmer Gdns. Barn 171 E2
Palmer Rd. Hert 113 E4
Palmers Gr. Lo Naz 135 F1
Palmers La. Bis St 76 C4
Palmers Rd. Bor 170 A4
Palmers Way. Ches 148 C1
Palmerston Cl. Wel GC 110 B3
Pamela Ave. Heml H 138 C4
Pamela Gdns. Bis St 76 C2
Pams La. Kim 66 B1
Pancake La. Heml H 125 E1
Pankhurst Cres. Stev 51 E3
Panshanger Dri. Wel GC 111 D3
Pantiles The. Bus 168 B1
Panxworth Rd. Heml H 124 B1
Paper Mill La. Stand 55 F1
Parade Ct. Tri 100 A2
Parade The. Radl 156 A2
Parade The. Sth Ox 175 E4
Parade The. Watf 167 D3
Paradise. Heml H 124 B1
Paradise Cl. Ches 148 A2
Paradise Rd. Wa Aby 163 E3
Parishes Mead. Stev 51 E2
Park Ave. Bis St 76 C2
Park Ave. Bus 167 F4
Park Ave. Chor 165 D3
Park Ave. Luton 44 B4
Park Ave. Pot B 159 E3
Park Ave. Radl 156 A3
Park Ave. St Alb 128 A2
Park Ave. Watf 167 D3
Park Ave N. Harp 85 F1
Park Ave S. Harp 85 F1
Park Ave Trading Estate. Luton 44 B4
Park Cl. Bal 23 F4
Park Cl. Bro Pk 145 D3
Park Cl. Bus 167 E3
Park Cl. Har 176 B1
Park Cl. Hat 130 B3
Park Cl. Mark 83 E3
Park Cl. Ric 174 B3
Park Cl. Stev 51 D1
Park Cres. Bal 23 F4
Park Cres. Bor 169 F3
Park Cres. Har 176 B1
Park Ct. Harl 117 E1
Park Dri. Bal 23 F4
Park Dri. Har 176 B2
Park Dri. Pot B 159 D4
Park Dri. Puc 55 E2
Park Farm La. Nut 18 B1
Park Gate. Hit 34 C3
Park Gdns. Bal 23 F4
Park Hill. Harl 118 A2
Park Hill. Harp 85 F1
Park Hill Rd. Heml H 124 A2
Park La. Bis St 76 C2
Park La. Ches 148 A2
Park La. Ches 162 B3
Park La. Coln H 129 E1
Park La. Hare 173 D1
Park La. Harl 117 E1
Park La. Heml H 124 B1
Park La. Hod 134 C2
Park La. Kim 66 B1
Park La. Kneb 68 C3
Park La. Old K 68 B3
Park La. Puc 55 E2
Park Lane Paradise. Ham St 148 A3
Park Mead. Harl 117 D1
Park Meadow. Hat 130 B3
Park Mews. Hat 130 B3
Park Mount. Harp 85 F2
Park Nook Gdns. Enf 161 E1
Park Pl. Hare 173 E1
Park Pl. Pk St 141 E2
Park Pl. Stev 50 B3
Park Rd. Barn 171 F3
Park Rd. Bus 168 A2
Park Rd. Ches 162 B3
Park Rd. Enf 162 C2
Park Rd. Heml H 124 B1
Park Rd. Hert 113 F3
Park Rd. Hod 135 D3
Park Rd. Nort 146 A1
Park Rd. Radl 156 A2
Park Rd. Ric 165 F1
Park Rd. Sta Mo 59 F3
Park Rd. Tri 100 A2
Park Rd. Ware 93 D1
Park Rd. Watf 167 D4
Park Rise. Har 176 C1
Park Rise. Harp 85 F2
Park Rise. Nthch 121 F3
Park Rise Cl. Harp 85 F2
Park Sq. Luton 63 F4
Park St. Bal 23 F4
Park St. Berk 122 A3
Park St. Hat 130 B3
Park St. Hit 34 C3
Park St. Luton 63 F3
Park St. Pk La 141 E2
Park St. Tri 100 A2
Park St W. Luton 63 F4
Park Street La. Bri Wd 141 D1
Park Street La. Chis 141 E2
Park Street La. Pk St 141 E2
Park The. Red 106 A3
Park The. St Alb 128 A3
Park Viaduct. Luton 63 F3
Park View. Hat 130 B4
Park View. Hod 135 D3
Park View. Pnr 175 F1
Park View. Pot B 159 E3
Park View. Stev 51 D1
Park View Cl. Luton 44 B3
Park View Dr. Mark 83 E3
Park View Rd. Berk 122 A2
Park View Rd. Pnr 175 D2
Park Way. Hit 34 C3
Park Way. Ric 165 E1
Parker Ave. Hert 113 E4
Parker Cl. Letw 22 C2
Parker St. Watf 167 D4

Parkers Field. Stev 51 E2
Parkfield. Chor 164 C3
Parkfield. Letw 23 E2
Parkfield Ave. Har 176 B1
Parkfield Cres. Har 176 B1
Parkfield Cres. Kim 66 B1
Parkfield Rd. Mark 83 E3
Parkfields. Wel GC 110 B3
Parkgate Rd. Watf 154 B1
Parkhurst Pl. Watf 167 E4
Parkhurst Rd. Hert 113 D4
Parkinson Cl. Whea 108 B4
Parkland Cl. Hod 115 D1
Parkland Dri. Luton 63 E3
Parklands. Roystn 7 F3
Parklands. Wa Aby 163 E4
Parkside. Bun 27 E1
Parkside. Welw 89 E3
Parkside Dri. Watf 166 C4
Parkside Rd. Norwd 174 C3
Parkway. Saw 97 F1
Parkway. Stev 51 D1
Parkway. Wel GC 110 B3
Parkway Cl. Wel GC 110 B3
Parkway Ct. St Alb 142 A4
Parkwood Cl. Hod 134 C2
Parkwood Dri. Heml H 123 F2
Parliament Sq. Hert 113 E3
Parndon Mill La. Harl 117 D2
Parnel Rd. Ware 93 F1
Parnell Cl. Abb L 130 F1
Parr Cres. Heml H 125 D4
Parrotts Cl. Cro Gr 166 A3
Parrott's La. Buc Co 120 A2
Parsonage Cl. Abb L 139 F1
Parsonage Cl. Tri 100 A2
Parsonage Ct. Tri 100 A2
Parsonage La. Alb 57 D3
Parsonage La. Birhr 59 F2
Parsonage La. Bis St 77 E4
Parsonage La. Wel Gr 144 A4
Parsonage Pl. Tri 100 A2
Parsonage Rd. Ric 165 E1
Parsonage Rd. Wel Gr 144 A4
Parson's Cl. Fla 84 A1
Parsons Green Estate. Stev 37 E1
Parthia Cl. Roystn 7 F3
Partridge Cl. Bus 168 B1
Partridge Hill. Ashw 4 B2
Partridge Rd. St Alb 127 E4
Parva Cl. Harp 107 E3
Parvills. Wa Aby 163 E4
Parys Rd. Luton 45 D3
Pascal Way. Letw 23 D4
Pasfield. Wa Aby 163 E3
Passingham Ave. Hit 35 D3
Paston Rd. Heml H 124 C3
Pasture Cl. Bus 168 B1
Pasture La. Bre Gr 65 F4
Pasture Rd. Letw 22 C2
Pastures The. Chis 141 D4
Pastures The. Hat 130 A2
Pastures The. N20 171 F1
Pastures The. Stev 51 E4
Pastures The. Ware 93 E2
Pastures The. Watf 167 E1
Pastures The. Wel GC 111 D2
Pastures Way. Luton 44 A2
Paternoster Cl. Wa Aby 163 F3
Paternoster Hill. Wa Aby 163 F4
Pathway The. Watf 167 E1
Patmore Cl. Bis St 76 B4
Patmore Link Rd. Heml H 125 E1
Patmore Rd. Wa Aby 163 F3
Patricia Gdns. Bis St 76 C3
Paul's Green. Ches 162 C3
Pauls La. Hod 135 D3
Paxton Rd. Berk 122 B2
Paxton Rd. St Alb 127 F1
Payne End. San 15 D1
Paynes Cl. Letw 12 A1
Paynes La. Lo Naz 149 E4
Payne's Pk. Hit 34 C4
Paynesfield Rd. Bus 168 C1
Pea La. Nthch 121 E4
Peace Gr. Wl Gr 90 A4
Peakes La. Ham St 147 F2
Peakes Way. Ham St 147 F2
Pear Tree Dell. Letw 23 D2
Pear Tree Wlk. Ham St 147 F3
Pearces Wlk. St Alb 127 E1
Pearman Dri. Dan En 71 F4
Pearson Ave. Hert 113 E2
Pearson Cl. Hert 113 E2
Peartree Cl. Heml H 124 A2
Peartree Cl. Wel GC 110 C3
Peartree Ct. Wel GC 110 C3
Peartree La. Wel GC 110 C3
Peartree Rd. Heml H 124 A2
Peartree Rd. Luton 46 B2
Peartree Way. Stev 51 D2
Peascroft Rd. Heml H 125 D1
Peasecroft. Cotrd 39 E4
Pecham Ct. Wel GC 111 E3
Peck's Hill. Lo Naz 135 F1
Pedlars La. Ther 15 F4
Pedley Hill. Stu 103 D4
Peel Cres. Hert 113 E4
Peel Pl. Luton 63 E4
Peel St. Luton 63 E4
Pegmire La. Bus 168 B4
Peg's La. Hert 113 E3
Pegs La. Widf 95 E3
Pegsdon Cl. Luton 45 D4
Pegsdon Way. Pegs 19 F1
Peitley Hill. Fla 84 A1
Pelham Ct. Heml H 125 E2
Pelham Rd. Brag 55 F4
Pelhams The. Watf 154 B2
Pelican Way. Letw 11 F1
Pemberton Cl. St Alb 141 E4
Pembridge Chase. Bov 137 D2
Pembridge Cl. Bov 137 D2
Pembridge La. Bric 133 F1
Pembridge Rd. Bov 137 D2
Pembroke Ave. Enf 162 A1
Pembroke Ave. Luton 44 C2
Pembroke Cl. Hod 148 C4
Pembroke Dri. Gofs O 147 D1
Pembroke Rd. Bal 23 F4
Pembroke Rd. Norwd 174 B4
Pemsel Ct. Heml H 138 B4
Penda Cl. Luton 44 C4
Pendennis Ct. Harp 107 E4
Pengelly Cl. Ches 148 A1
Penhill. Luton 44 B3
Penman Cl. Chis 141 D2
Penn Cl. Chor 164 B2
Penn Rd. Chis 141 E2
Penn Rd. Ric 165 D1
Penn Rd. Stev 50 C2
Penn Way. Chor 164 B2
Penn Way. Letw 23 E2
Pennine Ave. Luton 44 B4
Pennine Way. Heml H 124 C3
Pennington La. Sta Mo 59 E4
Penningtons. Bis St 76 B3
Penny Croft. Harp 107 D2
Pennyfathers La. Hai Gr 90 A2
Pennymead. Harl 118 A1
Penrose Ave. Watf 175 F4
Penrose Ct. Heml H 124 C4
Penscroft Gdns. Bor 170 B3
Penshurst. Harl 118 B2
Penshurst Cl. Harp 85 E2
Penshurst Rd. Pot B 159 E4
Pentland. Heml H 124 C3
Pentland Rd. Bus 168 B2
Pentley Cl. Wel GC 89 E1
Pentley Park. Wel GC 110 B4
Penton Dri. Ches 148 B1
Pentrich Ave. Enf 162 A1
Penzance Cl. Hare 173 E1
Peplins Cl. Bro Pk 144 C3
Peplins Way. Bro Pk 144 C3
Pepper Alley. Bal 23 F4
Pepper Hill. Gt Am 115 D2
Pepper Hill. Hert H 114 C3
Peppett's Green. Chol 120 A1
Pepsal End. Stev 69 D4
Pepsal End Rd. Fla 84 B4
Pepys Cres. Barn 171 E2
Pepys Way. Bal 23 F4
Percheron Dri. Luton 44 A2
Percheron Rd. Bor 170 B2
Percival Way. Luton 64 B4
Percy Rd. Watf 167 D3
Peregrine Cl. Watf 154 C3
Peregrine Rd. Luton 44 A2
Perimeter Rd. Hat 129 F4
Perivale Gdns. Watf 154 A3
Periwinkle Cl. Bark 17 E3
Periwinkle La. Hit 21 F1
Perowne Way. Stand 55 F2
Perram Cl. Ches 148 C3
Perriors Cl. Ham St 148 A2
Perry Dri. Roystn 7 F4
Perry Hill. Lo Naz 149 F4
Perry Mead. Bus 168 B2
Perrysfield Rd. Ches 148 C2
Perrywood La. Bram 91 D3
Perrywood La. Wat St 91 D4
Peterlee Ct. Heml H 124 C4
Peters Ave. Lon C 142 B3
Peter's Pl. Nthch 121 F3
Peters Way. Kneb 68 C3
Peters Wood Hill. Gt Am 114 B4
Petworth Cl. Stev 69 E4
Pevensey Cl. Luton 46 B2
Pheasant Cl. Berk 122 B2
Pheasant Cl. Tri 100 A3
Pheasants Way. Ric 165 D1
Phillimore Pl. Radl 155 F2
Phillipers. Watf 154 C2
Phillips Ave. Roystn 7 E4
Phipps Hatch La. Enf 161 E1
Phoebe Rd. Heml H 124 C3
Phoenix Cl. Norwd 174 C3
Piccotts End. Pic En 124 B3
Piccotts End La. Heml H 124 B4
Piccotts End La. Pic En 124 B3
Piccotts End Rd. Pic En 124 A4
Pick Hill. Wa Aby 163 F4
Pickets Cl. Bus 168 C1
Picketts. Wel GC 89 F1
Pickford Hill. Harp 86 B2
Pickford Rd. Mark 83 E3
Picknage Rd. Bar 9 D1
Pie Cnr. Fla 84 A1
Pie Gdn. Fla 84 B1
Pig La. Bis St 77 D2
Pigeonwick. Harp 86 A2
Piggotts La. Luton 44 B2
Piggotts Way. Bis St 76 C3
Piggottshill La. Harp 107 E4
Pightle Cl. Roystn 7 E4
Pig's Nose. Bun 40 C4
Pilgrim Cl. Chis 141 E2
Pilgrim Cl. Watf 154 B3
Pilgrims Way. Stev 37 D1
Piltdown Rd. Sth Ox 175 E3
Pinchfield. Map Cr 172 C3
Pindar Rd. Hod 135 E4
Pine Cl. Ches 148 B2
Pine Cl. Norwd 174 C2
Pine Gr. Bis St 77 D3
Pine Gr. Bri Wd 140 C1
Pine Gr. Bro Pk 145 D3
Pine Gr. Bus 167 F4
Pine Gr. N20 171 F1
Pine Tree Cl. Heml H 124 B2
Pinecroft. Heml H 138 C4
Pinelands. Bis St 58 C1
Pines Ave. Enf 162 A2
Pines Hill. Sta Mo 59 E3
Pinewood. Wel GC 110 C2
Pinewood Ave. Pnr 176 A2
Pinewood Cl. Bor 170 B4
Pinewood Cl. Pnr 176 A2
Pinewood Cl. St Alb 128 B2
Pinewood Gdns. Heml H 124 A2
Pinfold Rd. Bus 167 F4
Pinford Dell. Luton 46 B1
Pinnacles. Wa Aby 163 F3
Pinnate Pl. Wel GC 110 C1
Pinner Green. Pnr 175 E1
Pinner Hill. Pnr 175 D2
Pinner Hill Rd. Pnr 175 E1
Pinner Park Ave. Har 176 B1
Pinner Park Gdns. Har 176 B1
Pinner Rd. Norwd 175 D1
Pinner Rd. Pnr 175 D1
Pinner Rd. Watf 167 F1
Pinnocks Cl. Bal 23 F4
Pinnocks La. Bal 23 F4
Pinto Cl. Bor 170 B2
Pipers Ave. Harp 107 E4
Pipers Cl. Red 106 A3
Piper's Hill. Gt Ga 103 E2
Pipers Hill. Net 103 E1
Pipers La. Cad 62 C1
Pipers La. Harp 107 F4
Pippens. Wel GC 89 F1
Pirton Cl. Hit 34 B3
Pirton Cl. St Alb 128 B4
Pirton Rd. Hit 34 B3
Pirton Rd. Hol 21 D4
Pirton Rd. Luton 44 B3
Pishiobury Dri. Saw 118 B4
Pishiobury Mews. Saw 118 B4
Pitsfield. Wel GC 89 E1
Pitstone Cl. St Alb 128 B4
Pittman's Field. Harl 117 F1
Pix Farm La. Heml H 123 E1
Pix Rd. Letw 23 D3
Pix Rd. Stot 11 F3
Pixies Hill Cres. Heml H 123 F1
Pixies Hill Rd. Heml H 123 F1
Pixmore Ave. Letw 23 D3
Pixmore Way. Letw 23 D3
Plaiston Way. Gt Ch 9 F1
Plaiters Cl. Tri 100 A2
Plaitford Cl. Ric 173 F4
Plantation Rd. Luton 44 B4
Plantation Wlk. Heml H 124 A3
Plash Dri. Stev 50 C3
Plashes Cl. Stand 55 E1
Plashets. Saw 98 B1
Plaw Hatch Cl. Bis St 77 D4
Pleasance The. Harp 85 E2
Pleasant Rd. Bis St 76 C4
Pleasant Rise. Hat 130 B4
Plewes Cl. Ken Co 82 C4
Plough Hill. Cuf 146 C1
Plough La. Chipf 152 A3
Plough La. Kin Wd 48 A3
Plough La. Pot En 123 D4
Ploughmans End. Wel GC 111 E3
Plover Cl. Berk 122 B2
Plummers La. Pet Gr 65 E1
Plumpton Cl. Luton 46 B2
Plumpton Rd. Hod 135 E4
Pluto Rise. Heml H 124 C3
Poets Green. Luton 44 A1
Polayn Garth. Wel GC 110 B4
Polegate. Luton 46 B1
Polehanger La. Heml H 123 F3
Poles Hill. Sar 151 F3
Poles La. Thun 93 E3
Police Row. Ther 15 F4
Police Station La. Bus 168 A1
Pollard Gdns. Stev 50 C4
Pollards. Map Cr 172 B3
Pollards Cl. Gofs O 147 E1
Pollards Way. Pirt 20 B2
Pollicott Cl. St Alb 128 B4
Pollywick Rd. Wigg 100 B2
Polzeath Cl. Luton 64 B4
Pomeroy Cres. Watf 154 A2
Pomeroy Gr. Luton 45 F3
Pomfret Ave. Luton 63 F4
Pond Cl. Hare 173 E1
Pond Cl. Luton 44 A3
Pond Cl. Tri 100 A2
Pond Croft. Hat 129 F3
Pond La. Bal 23 F4
Pond Rd. Heml H 139 D3
Pondcroft. Wel GC 110 C3
Pondcroft Rd. Kneb 69 D2
Pondfield Cres. St Alb 128 A4
Pondside. Gra 36 B2
Pondsmeade. Red 106 A3
Pondwick Rd. Harp 85 F1
Pondwicks Cl. St Alb 127 E1
Pondwicks Rd. Luton 63 F4
Pooleys La. Wel Gr 144 B4
Popes La. Watf 154 A1
Pope's Rd. Abb L 153 F4
Popes Row. Ware 93 E2
Poplar Ave. Hat 129 E3
Poplar Ave. Luton 45 E4
Poplar Cl. H Cr 72 C1
Poplar Cl. Hit 35 D3
Poplar Cl. Pnr 175 E1
Poplar Cl. Roystn 7 F4
Poplar Dri. Roystn 7 F4
Poplar Rd. Ken Co 82 C4
Poplar Shaw. Wa Aby 163 F3
Poplars. Wel GC 111 D4
Poplars Cl. Hat 129 E3
Poplars Cl. Luton 46 A2
Poplars Cl. Watf 154 A4
Poplars The. Ch En 11 D4
Poplars The. Heml H 124 A1
Poplars The. Ick 21 F3
Poplars The. St Alb 142 A4
Popple Way. Stev 50 C3
Poppy Mead. Stev 50 C2
Poppyfields. Wel GC 111 E3
Porlock Dri. Luton 46 B1
Port Hill. Hert 113 E4
Port La. L Hal 77 D1
Port Vale. Hert 113 E3
Porters Cl. Bun 40 C4
Porters Hill. Harp 86 B2
Porters Wood. St Alb 127 F4
Portland Dri. Ches 162 A4
Portland Pl. Bis St 76 C4
Portland Pl. Hert H 114 B2
Portland Rd. Bis St 76 C4
Portland Rd. Luton 45 D1
Portland St. St Alb 127 E2
Portman Cl. Hit 21 E1
Portman Cl. St Alb 128 B4
Portmill La. Hit 34 C4
Post Office Rd. Harl 117 E1
Post Wood Rd. Gt Am 114 C4
Postfield. Wel GC 90 A1
Postwood Green. Hert H 114 B2
Potash La. Lon M 79 D3
Potten End Hill. Gt Ga 103 F1
Potter Heights Cl. Pnr 175 D2
Potter St. Bis St 76 C4
Potter St. Norwd 175 D1
Potter St. Pnr 175 D1
Potter Street Hill. Pnr 175 D2
Potters Field. St Alb 127 F4
Potters La. Bor 170 B4
Potters La. Stev 50 A2
Potterscrouch La. Chis 140 C4
Pottersheath Rd. Wl Gr 68 B1
Pottery Cl. Luton 44 C4
Potton Rd. Gu M 1 C3
Pouchen End La. Heml H 123 E2
Poulteney Rd. Sta Mo 59 F4
Pound Ave. Stev 50 B3
Pound Cl. Lo Naz 149 F4
Pound Field. Watf 153 F2
Pound Green. Gu M 1 C3
Pound La. Shen 156 C3
Poundwell. Wel GC 111 D3
Powdermill La. Wa Aby 163 D3
Powdermill Way. Wa Aby 163 D3
Power Ct. Luton 63 F4
Powis Ct. Pot B 159 E3
Poynders Hill. Heml H 125 E2
Poynders Meadow. Cod 88 C4
Poynings Cl. Harp 107 F4
Poynters Rd. Dun 44 A1
Prae Cl. St Alb 127 D2
Praetorian Ct. St Alb 141 E4
Prescot Hill. Heml H 124 A3
Prescott Rd. Ches 148 C2
Presdales Dri. Gt Am 114 C4
President Way. Luton 64 B4
Preston Gdns. Enf 162 C1
Preston Gdns. Luton 45 F1
Preston Path. Luton 45 F1
Preston Rd. Gos 34 C1
Preston Rd. Pres 48 C4
Prestwick Cl. Luton 45 F3
Prestwick Dri. Bis St 59 D1
Prestwick Rd. Sth Ox 175 E3
Pretoria Rd. Watf 167 D3
Pretty Cnr. Norwd 175 D3
Priestleys. Luton 63 D4
Primary La. Saw 98 B1
Primary Way. Arl 11 D2
Primett Rd. Stev 50 B4
Primrose Cl. Arl 11 D2
Primrose Cl. Hat 130 A2
Primrose Gdns. Bus 168 A1
Primrose Hill. Bed 139 D2
Primrose Hill Rd. Stev 50 B4
Primrose La. Arl 11 D2
Primrose Path. Ches 162 A4
Primrose View. Roystn 7 F3
Prince Andrew's Cl. Roystn 7 E3
Prince Edward St. Berk 122 B2
Prince Park. Heml H 124 A1
Prince St. Watf 167 E3
Prince Way. Luton 64 B4
Princes Ave. Enf 162 C2
Princes Ave. Watf 167 D3
Princes Cl. Berk 122 A3
Princes Ct. Bis St 76 B4
Princes Gate. Bis St 76 B4
Princes Mews. Roystn 7 E3
Prince's St. Stot 11 F4
Princes St. Ware 93 E1
Princess St. Luton 63 E4
Printers Way. Harl 118 A3
Priors Cl. Hert H 114 A2
Priors Hill. Pirt 20 B2
Priors Wood Rd. Hert H 114 B2
Priory Ave. Harl 118 B3
Priory Cl. Hod 148 C4
Priory Cl. Hod 135 D3
Priory Cl. N20 171 F1
Priory Cl. Roystn 7 F3
Priory Cl. Stan 176 C4
Priory Ct. Berk 122 B2
Priory Dell. Stev 50 C3
Priory Dri. Sta Mo 59 F3
Priory Dri. Stan 176 C4
Priory End. Hit 34 C3
Priory Gdns. Berk 122 B2
Priory Gdns. Luton 45 E2
Priory La. L Wym 35 F2
Priory La. Roystn 7 E3
Priory Orch. Fla 84 A1
Priory St. Hert 113 E3
Priory St. Ware 93 E1
Priory View. Bus 168 C1
Priory View. L Wym 35 F2
Priory Way. Hit 34 C2
Priory Wlk. St Alb 141 F4
Proctor Way. Luton 64 B4
Proctors Way. Bis St 77 D2
Progress Way. Luton 44 A4
Prospect La. Harp 107 D2
Prospect Pl. Welw 89 E3
Prospect Rd. Ches 148 B1
Prospect Rd. St Alb 127 E1
Protea Way. Letw 23 D3
Providence Gr. Stev 50 C4
Providence Way. Bal 23 F4
Prowse Ave. Bus 176 B4
Pryor Cl. Abb L 153 F4
Pryor Rd. Bal 23 F4
Pryor Way. Letw 23 E3
Pryors Cl. Bis St 77 D3
Puddephat's La. Fla 104 C4
Pudding La. Bar 9 D1
Pudding La. Heml H 124 A3
Pudgell The. Gt Ch 9 F1
Puller Rd. Barn 171 F3
Puller Rd. Heml H 124 A1
Pulleys Cl. Heml H 123 F2
Pulleys La. Heml H 123 F2
Pulter's Way. Hit 35 D3
Pumphill. Bre P 30 A1
Punch Bowl La. Heml H 125 E3
Punch Bowl La. Red 126 A4
Purbrock Ave. Watf 154 B2
Purcell Cl. Bor 169 E4
Purcell Cl. Brn Gr 90 C3
Purkiss Rd. Hert 113 E2
Purlings Rd. Bus 168 A2
Pursley Gdns. Bor 157 D1
Purway Cl. Luton 44 C4
Purwell La. Hit 35 E4
Putney Rd. Enf 162 B2
Puttenham Cl. Sth Ox 175 E4
Putteridge Rd. Luton 46 B2
Putterills The. Harp 86 A1
Putters Croft. Heml H 124 C4
Puttocks Cl. Wel Gr 144 B4
Puttocks Dri. Wel Gr 144 B4
Pyghtle The. Bun 40 B4
Pyghtle The. Luton 63 D4
Pyms Cl. Letw 23 D4
Pynchbek. Bis St 76 C2
Pynchon Paddocks. L Hal 98 B4
Pytchley Cl. Luton 45 F3

Quadrangle The. Wel GC 110 B4
Quadrant The. Letw 22 C3
Quadrant The. St Alb 128 A3
Quadrant The. Stev 50 B2
Quaker La. Wa Aby 163 E3
Quaker Rd. Ware 93 F2
Quakers La. P Bar 159 E4
Quantock Cl. Luton 45 D4
Quantock Cl. St Alb 128 B4
Quantock Rise. Luton 45 D4
Quantocks. Heml H 124 C3
Quartermass Cl. Heml H 124 A2
Quartermass Rd. Heml H 124 A2
Queen Anne's Cl. Stot 12 A3
Queen Hoo La. Dat 90 C3
Queen Mary's Ave. Watf 166 C3
Queen St. Chipf 152 A4
Queen St. Hit 34 C4
Queen St. Pit 80 B2
Queen St. St Alb 127 E2
Queen St. Stot 12 A3
Queen St. Tri 100 A2
Queens Ave. Watf 166 C2
Queen's Cl. Saw 97 F2
Queens Cl. Sta Mo 59 F4
Queens Cres. Bis St 76 C3
QUEENS Cres. St Alb 128 A3
Queens Ct. Hert 113 E3
Queen's Ct. St Alb 128 A2
Queens Dri. Abb L 153 F4
Queen's Dri. Ches 163 D3
Queen's Dri The. Ric 164 C1
Queens Head Wlk. Hod 148 C4
Queen's Pl. Watf 167 E3
Queens Rd. Barn 171 E3
Queens Rd. Berk 122 A3
Queen's Rd. Ches 162 C3
Queen's Rd. Harp 107 D4
Queen's Rd. Hert 113 E3
Queens Rd. Roystn 7 E4
Queens Rd. Ware 93 F1
Queen's Rd. Watf 167 E3
Queen's Sq The. Heml H 124 C2
Queens Way. Ches 162 C3
Queens Way. Shen 156 C4
Queensway. Hat 130 A3
Queensway. Heml H 124 C2
Queensway. Roystn 7 E4
Queensway. Stev 50 B3
Queensway Cres. Watf 154 A3
Queenswood Dri. Hit 22 B1
Quendon Dri. Wa Aby 163 E3
Quickbeams. Wel GC 90 A1
Quickley Brow. Chor 164 A1
Quickley La. Chor 164 B2
Quickley Rise. Chor 164 B2
Quickmoor La. Sar 152 B3
Quickswood. Luton 45 D4
Quickwood Cl. Chor 165 D2

Quills. Letw 23 E2
Quinces Croft. Heml H 124 A3
Quincey Rd. Ware 93 E2
Quinta Dri. Barn 171 E2
Quinton Way. Wa Aby 163 E2

Raans Rd. L Chal 150 A1
Raban Cl. Stev 51 E1
Rabley Heath Rd. Cod 68 A1
Radburn Way. Letw 23 E2
Radcliffe Rd. Hit 35 D4
Radlett La. Shen 156 C3
Radlett Park Rd. Radl 156 A2
Radlett Rd. Aldhm 155 E1
Radlett Rd. Col St 141 F1
Radlett Rd. Fro 141 F1
Radlett Rd. Watf 167 E4
Radstone Pl. Luton 46 C1
Radwell La. Radw 12 B2
Raebarn Gdns. Barn 171 D2
Raffin Cl. Dat 69 E2
Raffin Green La. Dat 69 F2
Raffin Park. Dat 69 F2
Ragged Hall La. Chis 140 C4
Raglan Ave. Ches 162 B3
Raglan Gdns. Watf 167 D1
Rags La. Ham St 147 F2
Railway Pl. Hert 113 F3
Railway Rd. Ches 162 C3
Railway St. Hert 113 E3
Railway Terr. Bed 139 D2
Rainbow Ct. Watf 167 E2
Rainier Cl. Ches 148 B1
Rainsford Rd. Sta Mo 59 F4
Raleigh Cres. Stev 51 D4
Raleigh Gr. Luton 44 B1
Rally The. Ch En 11 D4
Ralston Way. Sth Ox 175 E4
Ram Gorse. Harl 117 D1
Ramblers Way. Wel GC 111 E3
Rambling Way. Pot En 123 E3
Ramney Dri. Enf 162 C1
Ramparts The. St Alb 127 D1
Ramridge Rd. Luton 46 A1
Ramsay Cl. Hod 134 C1
Ramsbury Rd. St Alb 127 F1
Ramsdell. Stev 50 C3
Ramsey Cl. Bro Pk 145 E2
Ramsey Cl. St Alb 128 A1
Ramson Rise. Heml H 123 F1
Randalls Ride. Heml H 124 C3
Randals Hill. Stev 51 E2
Randon Cl. Har 176 A1
Rand's Cl. Hol 21 D4
Rand's Meadow. Hol 21 D4
Ranelagh Rd. Heml H 125 D2
Ranleigh Wlk. Harp 107 E3
Rannoch Wlk. Heml H 124 B4
Ranock Cl. Luton 44 B4
Ranskill Rd. Bor 170 A4
Ransom Cl. Hit 34 C2
Rant Meadow. Heml H 125 D1
Ranworth Ave. Hod 115 D1
Ranworth Ave. Stev 69 E4
Ranworth Cl. Heml H 124 B1
Raphael Dri. Watf 167 E4
Rasehill Cl. Chor 165 E2
Rathlyn. Heml H 139 D4
Ratty's La. Hod 135 E3
Raven Cl. Ric 165 E1
Raven Ct. Hat 130 A2
Ravenbank Rd. Luton 46 B3
Ravenhill Way. Luton 44 A2
Ravens La. Berk 122 B2
Ravens Wharf. Berk 122 B2
Ravenscroft. Harp 107 E3
Ravenscroft. Watf 154 C3
Ravenscroft Park. Barn 171 E3
Ravensdell. Heml H 123 F2
Ravensthorpe. Luton 46 A2
Ravenswood Park. Norwd 175 D2
Rawdon Dri. Hod 135 D3
Rayburn Rd. Heml H 124 A3
Raydon Rd. Ches 162 B4
Rayfield. Wel GC 89 E1
Raymer Cl. St Alb 127 F2
Raymond Cl. Abb L 153 E4
Raymonds Cl. Wel GC 110 C2
Raymonds Plain. Wel GC 110 C2
Raynham Rd. Bis St 77 E4
Raynham St. Hert 113 F3
Raynham Way. Luton 46 B1
Raynsford Rd. Ware 93 F1
Raynton Rd. Enf 162 B1
Ray's Hill. Chol 120 B1
Recreation Ground. Sta Mo 59 F3
Rectory Cl. Ess 131 F3
Rectory Cl. Hun 116 B4
Rectory Cl. Thor 76 B2
Rectory Gdns. Hat 130 A3
Rectory La. Berk 122 B2
Rectory La. Dat 69 E1
Rectory La. Far 58 B3
Rectory La. Kin L 139 D2
Rectory La. Ric 165 E1
Rectory La. Shen 157 D4
Rectory La. Stev 36 B1
Rectory La. Wat St 70 B2
Rectory Rd. Ric 165 E1
Rectory Rd. Wel GC 89 D1
Rectory Wood. Harl 117 E1
Red House Cl. Gt Am 114 C4
Red Lion Ct. Bis St 77 D4
Red Lion La. Heml H 139 D3
Red Lodge Gdns. Berk 122 A2
Red Rails. Luton 63 E3
Red Rd. Bor 169 F4
Red White and Blue Rd. Bis St 59 D1
Redan Rd. Ware 93 F2
Redbourn La. Harp 106 C3
Redbourn Rd. Heml H 125 D4
Redbourn Rd. Red 106 B1
Redbourn Rd. St Alb 126 C3
Redbournbury La. Red 106 B1
Redcar Dri. Stev 50 A3
Redding La. Red 105 F4
Reddings. Heml H 125 D1
Reddings. Wel GC 110 B4
Reddings Ave. Bus 168 A2
Reddings The. Bor 169 F3
Redferns Cl. Luton 63 D3
Redgrave Gdns. Luton 44 C4
Redhall Cl. Hat 129 F1
Redhall Dri. Hat 129 F1
Redhall La. Cha Cr 165 F4
Redhall La. Hat 129 F1
Redheath Cl. Watf 153 F2
Redhill Rd. Hit 34 B4
Redhoods Way E. Letw 22 C4
Redhoods Way W. Letw 22 C3
Redlands Rd. Enf 162 C1
Redmire Cl. Luton 44 A3
Redrick La. H Wy 117 F3
Redricks La. Saw 118 A4
Redvers Cl. Bis St 59 D1
Redwood Cl. Sth Ox 175 E3
Redwood Dri. Heml H 124 C1
Redwood Dri. Luton 44 B4
Redwood Rise. Bor 157 D1
Redwood Way. Barn 171 E2
Redwoods. Hert 113 E4
Redwoods. Wel GC 89 E2
Redwoods. Wl Gr 89 F4
Reedham Cl. Bri Wd 141 D1
Reedings Way. Saw 97 F2
Reedsdale. Luton 46 C1
Reeves Ave. Luton 45 D2
Regal Ct. Tri 100 A2
Regency Cl. Bis St 76 C4
Regency Ct. Hod 148 C4
Regent Cl. St Alb 128 B4
Regent Ct. Stot 11 F4
Regent St. Luton 63 F4
Regent St. Stot 11 F4
Regent St. Watf 154 A1
Regents Cl. Radl 156 A3
Regina Cl. Barn 171 E3
Reginald Rd. Norwd 174 C2
Reginald St. Luton 45 F1
Rendlesham Ave. Radl 155 F1
Rendlesham Cl. Ware 93 D1
Rendlesham Rd. Enf 161 E1
Rendlesham Way. Chor 164 B2
Renshaw Cl. Luton 46 C1
Repton Cl. Luton 44 C3
Repton Green. St Alb 127 E3
Repton Way. Cro Gr 166 A2
Reson Way. Heml H 124 A1
Reston Cl. Bor 157 D1
Reston Path. Bor 157 D1
Retford Cl. Bor 157 D1
Retreat The. Abb L 153 E4
Revels Rd. Hert 113 E4
Reynards Rd. Wl Gr 89 D4
Reynard's Way. Bri Wd 140 C1
Reynolds Cl. Heml H 124 A2
Reynolds Cres. Sand 128 A4
Rhee Spring. Bal 13 D1
Rhodes Ave. Bis St 76 C3
Rhodes Way. Watf 167 E4
Rib Vale. Hert 92 B1
Ribbledale. Lon C 142 C2
Ribblesdale. Heml H 124 C3
Ribocon Way. Luton 44 A4
Rice Cl. Heml H 124 C2
Richard Stagg Cl. St Alb 128 B1
Richards Cl. Bus 168 B1
Richards Cl. Luton 63 D3
Richardson Cl. Lon C 142 C2
Richfield Rd. Bus 168 B1
Richmond Cl. Ches 148 B1
Richmond Cl. Ware 93 D2
Richmond Ct. Hod 134 C2
Richmond Ct. Luton 45 F1
Richmond Ct. P Bar 159 E4
Richmond Dri. Watf 166 C4
Richmond Gdns. Har 176 C2
Richmond Hill. Luton 45 F1
Richmond Rd. P Bar 159 E4
Richmond Way. Cro Gr 166 B3
Richmond Wlk. St Alb 128 B4
Rickfield Cl. Hat 130 A2
Rickmansworth La. C St P 172 A3
Rickmansworth Rd. Chor 164 C3
Rickmansworth Rd. Hare 173 E2
Rickmansworth Rd. Norwd 174 B2
Rickmansworth Rd. Pnr 175 D1
Rickmansworth Rd. Watf 166 C3
Rickyard Cl. Luton 46 A2
Rickyard Meadow. Red 106 A3
Rickyard The. Ashwell 4 B2
Riddy Hill Cl. Hit 35 D3
Riddy La. Hit 35 D3
Riddy La. Luton 45 E3
Riddy The. Cod 88 C4
Ridge Ave. Harp 85 F2
Ridge Ave. Letw 23 D3
Ridge La. Watf 153 F1
Ridge Lea. Heml H 123 F2
Ridge Rd. Letw 23 D3
Ridge St. Watf 154 A1
Ridge The. Barn 171 F2
Ridge The. Norwd 174 C2
Ridgedown. Red 106 A3
Ridgehurst Ave. Watf 153 F3
Ridgeview Cl. Barn 171 E2
Ridgeway. Berk 121 F2
Ridgeway. Harp 85 F2
Ridgeway. Ken Co 82 C4
Ridgeway. L Had 57 D1
Ridgeway. Ric 165 D1
Ridgeway. Stev 50 C3
Ridgeway. Wel GC 111 D3
Ridgeway Cl. Heml H 138 C3
Ridgeway Ct. Pnr 176 A2
Ridgeway The. Cod 67 F1
Ridgeway The. Cuf 146 B2
Ridgeway The. Enf 160 B2
Ridgeway The. Hertng 112 C4
Ridgeway The. Hit 34 B3
Ridgeway The. Radl 155 F1
Ridgeway The. St Alb 128 B4
Ridgeway The. Ware 93 E2
Ridgeway The. Watf 153 F1
Ridgewood Dri. Harp 85 F2
Ridgewood Gdns. Harp 85 F2
Ridgmont Rd. St Alb 127 F1
Ridgway Rd. Luton 45 F1
Ridings The. Bis St 76 B2
Ridings The. Hertng 113 D3
Ridings The. Lat 150 B2
Ridings The. Mark 83 F3
Ridings The. Stev 51 D2
Ridler Rd. Enf 161 F1
Ridlins End. Stev 51 E1
Riley Rd. Enf 162 B1
Ringshall Dri. Rin 102 A4
Ringshall Rd. Dagn 81 D2
Ringshall Rd. Rin 81 D1
Ringtail Pl. Clo 13 D1
Ringway Rd. Chis 141 D2
Ringwood Rd. Luton 45 E3
Ripley Rd. Enf 161 E1
Ripley Rd. Luton 44 B1
Ripley Way. Ches 148 A1
Ripley Way. Heml H 123 F2
Ripon Rd. Stev 37 D1
Ripon Way. St Alb 128 B4
Rise The. Bal 23 F4
Rise The. Elst 169 F2
Rise The. Pk St 141 E3
Risedale Cl. Heml H 138 C4
Risedale Hill. Heml H 138 C4
Risedale Rd. Heml H 138 C4
Rising Hill Cl. Norwd 174 B2
Risingholme Cl. Bus 168 A1
Risingholme Cl. Har 176 C1
Risingholme Rd. Har 176 C1
Ritcroft Cl. Heml H 125 D1
Ritcroft Dri. Heml H 125 D1
Ritcroft St. Heml H 125 D1
Ritz Ct. Pot B 159 D4
Rivenhall End. Wel GC 111 E3
River Ave. Hod 135 D4
River Cl. Ches 163 D3
River Ct. Ick 21 F2
River Hill. Fla 84 A1
River Mead. Hit 21 E1
River Meads. Sta Ab 115 E2
River Park. Heml H 124 A1
River Park Industrial Estate. 122 A3
River St. Ware 93 F1
River View. Wel GC 89 F1
River Way. Harl 118 A3
River Way. Luton 44 C3
Riverfield La. Saw 97 F2
Riverford Cl. Harp 86 A2
Rivermill. Harl 117 E1
Riversend Rd. Heml H 138 B4
Rivershill. Wat St 70 C2
Riverside. Bis St 76 C4
Riverside. Bun 40 C4
Riverside Ave. Lo Naz 135 D1
Riverside Cl. Kin L 139 D1
Riverside Cl. St Alb 127 F1
Riverside Cotts. Sta Ab 115 E2
Riverside Dri. Ric 165 E1
Riverside Gdns. Berk 122 A3
Riverside Path. Ches 148 B1
Riverside Rd. Luton 45 D3
Riverside Rd. St Alb 127 F1
Riverside Rd. Watf 167 D2
Riverside Wlk. Bis St 76 C4
Riversmead. Hod 135 D3
Riversmeet. Hert 113 D3
Rivett Cl. Bal 13 D1
Roan Wlk. Roystn 7 F3
Robbery Bottom La. Wl Gr 90 A4
Robbs Cl. Heml H 124 A3
Robe End. Heml H 123 F3
Robert Ave. St Alb 141 E4
Robert Cl. Pot B 158 C3
Robert Wallace Cl. Bis St 58 C1
Roberts Rd. Watf 167 E2
Roberts Way. Hat 129 F2
Roberts Wood Dri. C St P 172 A3
Robertson Cl. Ches 148 C3
Robin Hill. Berk 122 B2
Robin Hood Dri. Bus 167 F4
Robin Hood Dri. Har 176 C2
Robin Hood La. Hat 130 A3
Robin Hood Meadow. Heml H 124 C4
Robin Mead. Wel GC 90 A1
Robin Way. Cuf 146 C2
Robins Nest Hill. L Berk 132 B3
Robins Rd. Heml H 125 D1
Robins Way. Hat 129 F1
Robinsfield. Heml H 124 A2
Robinson Ave. Gofs O 147 D2
Robinson Cl. Bis St 76 C3
Robinson Cres. Bus 168 B1
Robinsway. Wa Aby 163 F3
Robinswood. Luton 45 F3
Robsons Cl. Ches 148 B1
Rochester Ave. Luton 46 B2
Rochester Way. Cro Gr 166 A3
Rochford Ave. Wa Aby 163 E3
Rochford Cl. Ches 148 C3
Rochford Dri. Luton 46 C1
Rochford Rd. Bis St 59 E1
Rock Rd. Roystn 7 E4
Rockfield Ave. Ware 93 E2
Rockingham Way. Stev 50 C2
Rockley Rd. Luton 63 D4
Rockliffe Ave. Kin L 139 D1
Rockways. Barn 170 C2
Rode Heath. Luton 44 B2
Roden Cl. Harl 118 C2
Rodgers Cl. Elst 169 E2
Rodney Avenue. St Alb 128 A1
Rodney Cres. Hod 135 D4
Roe Cl. Stot 11 F3
Roe End La. Mark 83 D2
Roe Green Cl. Hat 129 F2
Roe Green La. Hat 129 F3
Roe Hill Cl. Hat 129 F2
Roebuck Cl. Luton 63 D3
Roebuck Gate. Stev 50 C1
Roebuck Retail Park. Stev 50 C1
Roedean Ave. Enf 162 B1
Roedean Cl. Luton 46 B2
Roefields Cl. Fel 138 A4
Roehyde Way. Hat 129 F1
Roestock Gdns. Coln H 129 F1
Rofant Rd. Norwd 174 C2
Rogate Rd. Luton 46 B3
Roger's La. Ans 29 D3
Rogers Ruff. Norwd 174 B1
Roland St. St Alb 128 A1
Rolleston Cl. Ware 93 E2
Rollswood. Wel GC 110 C2
Rollswood Rd. Wl Gr 89 D4
Rollys La. Ashw 4 B2
Roman Cl. Hare 173 D1
Roman Gdns. Abb L 139 D1
Roman La. Clo 24 A4
Roman Rd. Luton 44 C2
Roman Rd. Welw 89 E3
Roman St. Hod 135 D4
Roman Vale. Harl 118 B3
Roman Way. Mark 83 F3
Roman Way. Puc 55 E2
Roman Way. Welw 89 E3
Romany Cl. Letw 22 B3
Romeland. St Alb 127 E2
Romeland. Wa Aby 163 E3
Romeland Hill. St Alb 127 E2
Romilly Dri. Watf 175 F3
Rondini Ave. Luton 45 D2
Rook Tree Cl. Stot 12 A3
Rook Tree La. Stot 12 A3
Rookery The. Sta M 59 F4
Rooke's Alley. Hert 113 F3
Rookes Cl. Letw 23 D2
Rooks Hill. Chor 165 E3
Rooks Hill. Wel GC 110 B3
Rooks Nest La. Ther 16 A3
Rookwood Dri. Stev 51 D1
Rosary Ct. Pot B 145 D1
Rose Gdns. Watf 167 D2
Rose La. Whea 87 E1
Rose Lawn. Bus 168 B1
Rose Mead. Pot B 145 E1
Rose Meadow. Hay St 41 F2
Rose Vale. Hod 135 D3
Rose Wlk. Radl 156 A2
Rose Wlk. St Alb 128 B3
Rose Wood Cl. Luton 45 F1
Roseacre Gdns. Wel GC 111 E3
Roseacres. Saw 97 E2
Rosebank. Wa Aby 163 F3
Roseberry Ct. Watf 167 D4
Roseberry Way. Tri 100 A3
Rosebery. Bis St 77 E3
Rosebery Ave. Harp 85 F1
Rosebery Rd. Bus 168 A1
Rosebriar Wlk. Watf 153 F2
Rosecroft Dri. Watf 153 F2
Rosecroft La. Wl Gr 90 A4
Rosedale. Wel GC 89 F1
Rosedale Ave. Ches 147 F1
Rosedale Cl. Bri Wd 140 C1
Rosedale Cl. Luton 44 B4
Rosedale Way. Ches 148 A2
Roseheath. Heml H 123 F2
Rosehill Cl. Hod 134 C3
Rosehill Gdns. Abb L 153 E4
Roselands Ave. Hod 114 C1
Rosemary Cl. Harl 118 B2
Rosewood Ct. Heml H 123 F2
Rosewood Dri. Enf 161 D2
Roslyn Cl. Hod 134 C1
Ross Cl. Har 176 B2
Ross Cl. Hat 130 A4
Ross Cl. Luton 63 D3
Ross Cres. Watf 154 A2
Ross Way. Norwd 174 C3
Rossfold Rd. Luton 44 B4
Rossgate. Heml H 124 A3
Rossington Ave. Bor 156 C1
Rosslyn Cres. Luton 45 E3
Rosslyn Rd. Watf 167 D3
Rossway. Cad 63 D1
Rossway Dri. Bus 168 B2
Rossway La. Wigg 121 D4
Roswell Cl. Ches 148 C1
Rothampstead Ave. Harp 86 A1
Rother Cl. Watf 154 B3
Rother Field. Luton 46 B2
Rotheram Ave. Luton 63 D3
Rotherfield. Enf 162 B1
Rothesay Rd. Luton 63 E4
Rotten End Hill. Pot En 123 F4
Roughdown Ave. Heml H 138 A4
Roughdown Rd. Heml H 138 A4
Roughdown Villas Rd. Heml H 138 A4
Roughs The. Norwd 174 C4
Roughwood Cl. Watf 153 F1
Round Mead. Stev 51 E2
Round Wood. Kin L 138 C2
Roundabout La. Wl Gr 89 F4
Roundcroft. Ham St 147 F3
Roundfield Ave. Harp 86 B2
Roundhaye. Puc 55 E2
Roundhedge Way. Enf 160 C1
Roundhills. Wa Aby 163 F3
Roundings The. Hert H 114 B1
Roundmoor Dri. Ches 148 C1
Roundway The. Watf 166 C2
Roundwood Cl. Hit 22 B1
Roundwood Cl. Wl Gr 89 E4
Roundwood Dri. Wel GC 110 B4
Roundwood Gdns. Harp 85 F1
Roundwood La. Harp 85 E2
Roundwood Park. Harp 85 F2
Rounton Dri. Watf 153 F1
Rounton Rd. Wa Aby 163 F3
Rousebarn La. Cro Gr 166 B3
Rowan Cl. Bric 155 D4
Rowan Cl. Luton 63 D4
Rowan Cl. St Alb 128 C2
Rowan Cl. Wes 37 D4
Rowan Cres. Letw 22 C4
Rowan Cres. Stev 50 C4
Rowan Dri. Hod 148 C4
Rowan Way. Harp 107 E4
Rowan Wlk. Hat 130 A1
Rowans. Wel GC 90 A1
Rowans The. Bal 23 F4
Rowans The. Heml H 124 A2
Rowcroft. Heml H 123 F1
Rowel Field. Luton 46 B1
Rowington Cl. Luton 46 C1
Rowland Pl. Norwd 174 C2
Rowland Rd. Stev 50 C2
Rowland Way. Letw 22 C3
Rowlands Ave. Pnr 176 A2
Rowlands Cl. Ches 148 B1
Rowlatt Dri. St Alb 127 D1
Rowley Cl. Watf 167 F2
Rowley Green Rd. Barn 171 D2
Rowley La. Bor 170 C3
Rowley's Rd. Hert 113 F4
Rowney Gdns. Saw 118 B4
Rowney La. Sac Gr 72 A3
Rowney Wood. Saw 97 E1
Roy Rd. Norwd 174 C2
Royal Ave. Ches 162 C3
Royal Ct. Heml H 138 C4
Royal Ct. Tri 101 D3
Royal Oak Cl. Chipp 27 E3
Royal Oak La. Pirt 20 B2
Royal Rd. St Alb 128 A2
Royce Cl. Hod 134 C1
Roydon Ct. Heml H 105 D1
Roydon Lodge Chalet Estate. Roy 116 B1
Roydon Rd. Harl 116 C1
Roydon Rd. Sta Ab 115 F2
Royse Gr. Roystn 7 E2
Royston Cl. Hert 113 D3
Royston Gr. Pnr 176 A2
Royston Park Rd. Pnr 176 A3
Royston Rd. Ashw 14 A3
Royston Rd. Bal 12 C1
Royston Rd. Bar 8 C2
Royston Rd. Bark 17 E3
Royston Rd. Byg 13 E1
Royston Rd. St Alb 128 A1
Rucklers La. Chipf 138 A2
Rucklers La. Kin L 138 B2
Ruckles Cl. Stev 50 C3
Rudd Cl. Stev 51 D2
Rudham Gr. Letw 23 E2
Rudolph Rd. Bus 168 A2
Rudyard Cl. Luton 44 B2
Rue De St Lawrence. Wa Aby 163 E3
Rueley Dell Rd. Lily 32 B1
Rugby Way. Cro Gr 166 A2
Ruins The. Red 106 A3
Rumballs Cl. Heml H 139 D4
Rumballs Rd. Heml H 139 D4
Rumbold Rd. Hod 135 E4
Runcie Cl. St Alb 128 A4
Runcorn Cres. Heml H 124 C4
Rundells. Letw 23 E2
Runfold Ave. Luton 45 D3
Runham Cl. Luton 44 A2
Runham Rd. Heml H 124 C1
Runley Rd. Luton 62 C4
Runnalow. Letw 22 C4
Runsley. Wel GC 90 A1
Ruscombe Dri. Chis 141 E3
Rushall Green. Luton 46 B1
Rushby Mead. Letw 23 D3
Rushby Pl. Letw 23 D3
Rushby Wlk. Letw 23 D3
Rushden Rd. Ro Gr 26 A4
Rushen Dri. Hert H 114 B2
Rushendon Furlong. Ivin 80 C3
Rushes Ct. Bis St 77 D3
Rushfield. Pot B 158 B3
Rushfield. Saw 97 F1
Rushfield Rd. Ware 93 F2
Rushleigh Ave. Ches 148 B1
Rushleigh Green. Bis St 76 B2
Rushmere La. Ash Gr 136 A2
Rushmoor Cl. Ric 173 E4
Rushton Ave. Watf 154 A2
Ruskin Ave. Wa Aby 163 F3
Ruskin Cl. Ham St 147 F3
Ruskin La. Hit 35 E4
Rusper Green. Luton 46 B2
Russell Ave. St Alb 127 E2
Russell Cl. Ken Co 82 C4
Russell Cl. Stev 51 D1

Russell Cres. Watf 153 F2
Russell Ct. Bri Wd 141 D1
Russell La. Watf 153 E2
Russell Pl. Heml H 138 A4
Russell Rd. Enf 161 F1
Russell Rd. Norwd 174 B3
Russell Rise. Luton 63 E3
Russell St. Hert 113 E3
Russell St. Luton 63 E3
Russellcroft Rd. Wel GC 110 B4
Russell's Ride. Ches 162 C4
Russell's Slip. Hit 34 C3
Russettwood. Wel GC 111 E3
Rutherford Cl. Stev 50 A3
Rutherford Way. Bus 168 C1
Ruthin Cl. Luton 63 E3
Ruthven Ave. Ches 162 B3
Rutland Cres. Luton 64 A4
Rutland Gdns. Heml H 124 C2
Rutts The. Bus 168 B1
Rydal Way. Luton 44 C3
Ryde The. Hat 130 B4
Ryder Ave. Ick 21 E2
Ryder Cl. Bov 137 D2
Ryder Cl. Bus 168 A2
Ryder Way. Ick 21 E2
Ryders Ave. Coln H 129 F2
Rye Cl. Harp 86 A2
Rye Gdns. Bal 13 D1
Rye Hill. Harp 86 A2
Rye Rd. Hod 135 E4
Rye Rd. Sta Ab 115 E1
Rye St. Bis St 58 C1
Ryecroft. Hat 129 F2
Ryecroft. Stev 50 C4
Ryecroft Cl. Heml H 125 E1
Ryecroft Cres. Barn 171 D2
Ryecroft Ct. St Alb 128 C2
Ryecroft Way. Luton 46 A2
Ryefeld Cl. Hod 115 D1
Ryefield. Luton 31 D1
Ryefield Cres. Norwd 175 D1
Ryelands. Wel GC 110 C2
Ryelands Heath. Luton 46 C1
Ryley Cl. Henlw 10 A2
Ryman Ct. Chor 164 B2
Rymill Cl. Bov 137 D2
Ryton Cl. Luton 63 D4

Saberton Cl. Red 105 F2
Sacombe Green Rd. Sac 71 F2
Sacombe Pound. Sac 71 F2
Sacombe Rd. Cha En 92 A2
Sacombe Rd. Heml H 123 F3
Sacombe Rd. Hert 92 B1
Sacombs Ash La. H Wy 96 C4
Saddlers Cl. Bal 23 F4
Saddlers Cl. Bor 170 B2
Saddlers Cl. Pnr 176 A2
Saddlers Path. Bor 170 B2
Sadleir Rd. St Alb 127 F1
Sadlers Way. Hertng 113 D3
Sadlier Rd. Stand 55 F1
Saffron Cl. Hod 134 C4
Saffron Hill. Letw 22 C3
Saffron La. Heml H 124 A2
Saffron St. Roystn 7 F3
Sainfoin End. Heml H 125 D3
St. Clare Ct. Wal 52 A4
St Agnells Ct. Heml H 125 D4
St Agnells La. Heml H 125 D4
St Albans Dri. Stev 36 C1
St Albans Hill. Heml H 124 C1
St Albans La. Bed 140 A3
St Albans Rd. Abb L 154 B4
St Albans Rd. Barn 171 F4
St Albans Rd. Cod 88 C4
St Albans Rd. Harp 107 D4
St Albans Rd. Heml H 124 C1
St Albans Rd. Pot B 158 B2
St Albans Rd. Red 106 B2
St Albans Rd. Sand 128 A4
St Albans Rd. Watf 154 B2
St Albans Rd East. Hat 130 A3
St Albans Rd W. Hat 129 E3
St Andrew St. Hert 113 E3
St Andrew's Ave. Harp 85 F1
St Andrew's Cl. Cad 63 D1
St Andrew's Pl. Hit 34 C4
St Andrew's Rd. Fel 138 B4
St Andrews Rd. Sth Ox 175 E4
St Andrews Wlk. Cad 63 E1
St Anne's Cl. Ham St 147 F2
St Annes Cl. Sth Ox 175 E3
St Anne's Rd. Hit 34 C4
St Anne's Rd. Lon C 142 B2
St Ann's Rd. Luton 63 F4
St Anthonys Ave. Heml H 125 D1
St Audreys Cl. Hat 130 A1
St Audreys Green. Wel GC 110 C3
St Augustine Ave. Luton 45 E2
St Augustine Cl. Hit 34 C4
St Augustines Cl. Hod 134 C2
St Augustines Dri. Hod 134 C2
St Bernards Cl. Luton 45 E2
St Bernard's Rd. St Alb 127 F2
St Brelades Pl. St Alb 128 B4
St Catharine's Rd. Hod 135 D2
St Catherines Ave. Luton 45 D2
St Catherine's Ct. Hod 135 D2
St Cross Ct. Hod 135 D2
St Cuthberts Gdns. Pnr 175 F2
St Cuthbert's Rd. Hod 115 E1
St David's Cl. Heml H 125 E1
St David's Dri. Hod 134 C2
St Dunstan's Rd. Hun 116 B4
St Edmunds. Berk 122 B2
St Edmund's Way. Harl 118 B2
St Ethelbert Ave. Luton 45 E2
St Etheldreda's Dri. Hat 130 B3
St Faiths Cl. Hit 22 A1
St Francis Cl. Pot B 159 E3
St Francis Cl. Watf 167 D1
St George's Drive. Watf 175 F3
St George's Rd. Enf 161 F1
St George's Rd. Fel 138 B4
St George's Rd. Watf 154 A1
St George's Way. Stev 50 B3
St Giles' Ave. Pot B 158 A3
St Giles Rd. Cod 67 F1
St Helen's Cl. Whea 108 B4
St Heliers Rd. Sand 128 A4
St Ives Cl. Har Gr 89 F2
St Ives Cl. Luton 45 D2
St James' Ave. Luton 45 D2
St James Rd. Harp 86 A2
St James Rd. Watf 167 D2
St James's Rd. Gofs O 147 E2
St John Cl. Luton 63 D3
St Johns. Stand 55 F2
St John's Ave. Harl 118 B2
St John's Cl. Pot B 159 E3
St Johns Cl. Welw 89 E3
St John's Cres. Sta Mo 59 F4
St John's Ct. Harp 107 E4
St John's Ct. Hert 113 E3
St Johns Ct. St Alb 128 A3
St John's La. Sta Mo 59 F4
St John's Path. Hit 34 C3
St John's Rd. Arl 11 D2
St John's Rd. Harp 107 E4
St John's Rd. Heml H 124 A1
St John's Rd. Hit 34 C3
St John's Rd. Sta Mo 59 F4
St John's Rd. Watf 167 D4
St John's St. Hert 113 E3
St John's Terr. Enf 161 E1
St John's Well Ct. Berk 122 A3
St John's Well La. Berk 122 A3
St Johns Wlk. Harl 118 B2
St Josephs Cl. Luton 45 D2
St Julian's Rd. St Alb 127 E1
St Katherines Cl. Ick 21 E2
St Katherines Way. Berk 122 A3
St Laurence Dri. Hod 148 C4
St Lawrence Cl. Abb L 139 F1
St Lawrence Cl. Bov 137 D2
St Lawrence Way. Bri Wd 140 C1
St Lawrences Ave. Luton 45 E2
St Leonards Cl. Bus 167 F3
St Leonards Cl. Hert 113 F4
St Leonards Cres. Sand 108 B1
St Leonards Ct. Sand 108 B1
St Leonard's Rd. Hert 113 E4
St Leonards Rd. Lo Naz 149 F4
St Luke's Ave. Enf 161 E1
St Luke's Cl. Luton 44 C1
St Margarets. Stev 50 C1
St Margarets Ave. Luton 45 D2
St Margaret's Cl. Berk 122 B2
St Margarets Cl. Str 31 D3
St Margaret's Rd. Hod 115 D1
St Margarets Way. Heml H 125 E2
St Mark's Cl. Coln H 129 D1
St Mark's Cl. Hit 21 E1
St Martin's Ave. Luton 45 F1
St Martins Cl. Harp 86 B2
St Martins Cl. Sth Ox 175 E3
St Martin's Rd. Kneb 69 D3
St Mary's Ave. Norwd 174 C3
St Mary's Ave. Nthch 121 E3
St Mary's Ave. Stot 11 F3
St Marys Cl. Heml H 124 B2
St Mary's Cl. Letw 22 C1
St Mary's Cl. Pirt 20 B2
St Mary's Cl. Stev 51 F1
St Marys Cl. Welw 89 E3
St Mary's Ct. Heml H 124 B2
St Mary's Ct. Welw 89 E2
St Mary's Dri. Sta Mo 59 F3
St Mary's La. Hertng 112 C2
St Mary's La. Red 106 A2
St Mary's Rd. Ches 148 B1
St Mary's Rd. Heml H 124 B2
St Mary's Rd. Luton 63 F4
St Mary's Rd. Stand 55 E1
St Mary's Rd. Watf 167 D3
St Mary's Rise. Bre Wd 47 E1
St Mary's Sq. Hit 34 C4
St Mary's Way. Bal 23 F3
St Marys Wlk. St Alb 128 A4
St Matthews Cl. Luton 63 F4
St Matthews Cl. Watf 167 E2
St Michaels Ave. Heml H 125 D1
St Michaels Cl. Harp 107 E4
St Michael's Cres. Luton 45 E2
St Michael's Ct. St Alb 127 D2
St Michael's Mount. Hit 35 D4
St Michaels Rd. Hit 35 D4
St Michael's Rd. Hod 135 D2
St Michael's St. St Alb 127 D2
St Michaels Way. Pot B 145 D1
St Mildred's Ave. Luton 45 D2
St Monicas Ave. Luton 45 D2
St Neots Cl. Bor 157 D1
St Nicholas Cl. Elst 169 E2
St Nicholas Mount. Heml H 123 F2
St Olam's Cl. Luton 45 D3
St Olives. Stot 11 F3
St Pauls Pl. St Alb 128 A2
St Paul's Rd. Heml H 124 C2
St Paul's Rd. Luton 63 F3
St Pauls Way. Wa Aby 163 E3
St Pauls Way. Watf 167 E4
St Peter's Ave. Ch En 11 D4
St Peter's Cl. Barn 171 D2
St Peter's Cl. Bus 168 B1
St Peters Cl. Hat 130 A3
St Peter's Cl. Ric 165 D1
St Peter's Cl. St Alb 127 E2
St Peters Hill. Tri 100 A2
St Peters Rd. Luton 63 D4
St Peter's Rd. St Alb 127 F2
St Peter's St. St Alb 127 E2
St Peters Way. Chor 164 A3
St Rowans Cl. Barn 159 E1
St Saviour's Cres. Luton 63 E3
St Stephen's Ave. St Alb 141 D4
St Stephen's Cl. St Alb 141 D4
St Stephen's Hill. St Alb 127 E1
St Stephens Rd. Barn 171 E2
St Stephen's Rd. Enf 162 B1
St Thomas Dri. Pnr 175 F1
St Thomas Pl. Whea 108 B4
St Thomas's Rd. Luton 46 A2
St Vincent Dri. St Alb 128 A1
St Vincent's Way. Pot B 159 E3
St Winifreds Ave. Luton 45 E2
St Yon Cl. St Alb 128 C2
Sale Dri. Bal 13 D1
Salisbury Ave. Harp 85 F1
Salisbury Ave. St Alb 128 A2
Salisbury Cl. Bis St 76 C3
Salisbury Cl. Pot B 159 E4
Salisbury Cres. Ches 162 D4
Salisbury Gdns. Wel GC 110 C3
Salisbury Rd. Bal 12 C1
Salisbury Rd. Barn 171 F3
Salisbury Rd. Enf 162 C1
Salisbury Rd. Harp 86 B2
Salisbury Rd. Hod 135 E4
Salisbury Rd. Luton 63 E3
Salisbury Rd. Stev 37 D1
Salisbury Rd. Watf 154 A1
Salisbury Rd. Wel GC 111 D3
Salisbury Sq. Hat 130 B3
Salisbury Sq. Hert 113 E3
Sally Deards La. Cod 68 A2
Salmon Meadow
Footpath. Heml H 138 C4
Salmons Cl. Ware 93 E2
Saltars Way. Luton 44 B2
Saltdean Cl. Luton 46 B2
Salter's Cl. Berk 121 F3
Salters Gdns. Watf 167 D4
Saltfield Cres. Luton 44 B2
Salusbury La. Gt Of 33 E1
Salwey Cres. Hod 134 C2
Samian Gate. St Alb 126 C1
Sampson Ave. Barn 171 E2
Sancroft Rd. Har 176 C1
Sanctuary Cl. Hare 173 E2
Sandalwood Cl. Luton 45 D4
Sanday Cl. Heml H 125 D1
Sandbrook La. Wils 79 E1
Sanderling Cl. Letw 22 C4
Sanders Cl. Heml H 138 C4
Sanders Cl. Lon C 142 B2
Sanders Rd. Heml H 139 D4
Sandfield Rd. St Alb 128 A2
Sandgate Rd. Luton 44 B1
Sandhurst Ct. Harp 107 E3
Sandifield. Hat 130 A1
Sandle Rd. Bis St 77 D4
Sandmere Cl. Heml H 125 D1
Sandon Cl. Tri 99 F2
Sandon Rd. Ches 148 B1
Sandover Cl. Hit 35 D3
Sandown Rd. Stev 37 E1
Sandown Rd. Watf 154 B1
Sandpit La. St Alb 128 B3
Sandpit Rd. Wel GC 110 C2
Sandridge Cl. Heml H 105 D1
Sandridge Rd. St Alb 127 F3
Sandridgebury La. Sand 108 A1
Sandringham Cres. St Alb 128 B4
Sandringham Rd. Pot B 145 D1
Sandringham Rd. Watf 154 B1
Sandringham Way. Ches 162 B3
Sandy Cl. Hertng 113 D3
Sandy Gr. Hit 34 C3
Sandy La. Bus 168 B3
Sandy La. Norwd 175 D3
Sandy Lodge Ct. Norwd 174 C3
Sandy Lodge La. Norwd 174 C4
Sandy Lodge Rd. Ric 174 B4
Sandy Lodge Way. Norwd 174 C3
Sandycroft Rd. L Chal 150 B1
Sanfoin Rd. Luton 44 A2
Sanfoine Cl. Hit 35 E4
Santers La. Pot B 158 C3
Santingfield N. Luton 63 D3
Santingfield S. Luton 63 D3
Saottfield Cl. Sand 108 B1
Sappers Cl. Saw 97 F1
Saracens Head. Heml H 125 D2
Sarratt La. Chor 165 E3
Sarratt Rd. Sar 165 F4
Sarum Pl. Heml H 124 C4
Sarum Rd. Luton 44 C2
Saturn Way. Heml H 124 C3
Sauncey Ave. Harp 86 A1
Sauncey Wood. Kim 86 B2
Sauncey Wood La. Kim 86 C3
Saunders Cl. Letw 23 E4
Savoy Cl. Hare 173 E1
Sawbridgeworth Rd. Saw 98 C2
Sawells. Hod 134 C1
Sawtry Cl. Luton 45 D3
Sawtry Way. Bor 157 D1
Sawyers La. Pot B 158 B3
Sawyers Way. Heml H 124 C2
Saxon Ave. Stot 11 F4
Saxon Cl. Harp 86 B2
Saxon Cl. Letw 11 F1
Saxon Ct. Bor 169 F4
Saxon Rd. Luton 45 E1
Saxon Rd. Welw 89 D2
Saxon Rd. Whea 108 B4
Saxon Way. Bal 13 D1
Saxon Way. Wa Aby 163 E3
Saxtead Cl. Luton 46 B1
Sayer Way. Kneb 68 C2
Sayers Gdns. Berk 122 A3
Sayes Gdns. Saw 97 F1
Sayesbury Ave. Saw 97 F2
Sayesbury Rd. Saw 97 F1
Saywell Rd. Luton 46 A1
Scarborough Ave. Stev 50 A4
Scatterdells La. Chipf 138 A1
Scholar's Hill. Wars 95 D2
Scholars Wlk. Hat 130 A1
School Cl. Stev 51 D2
School Gdns. Pot En 123 D3
School La. Ast 51 F1
School La. Bar 9 D1
School La. Bric 155 D4
School La. Bus 168 A1
School La. Ess 131 F3
School La. Gt Of 33 E2
School La. Harl 117 F1
School La. Hat 130 B3
School La. Luton 44 B2
School La. Pres 48 C3
School La. Tewin 90 C1
School La. Wat St 70 C2
School La. Welw 89 D2
School Mead. Abb L 153 E4
School Rd. Pot B 145 E1
School Row. Heml H 123 F1
School Wlk. Letw 23 D3
Schubert Rd. Elst 169 E2
Scot Gr. Pnr 175 F2
Scots Hill. Cro Gr 165 F2
Scots Hill Cl. Cro Gr 165 F2
Scots Mill La. Cro Gr 165 F2
Scott Ave. Sta Ab 115 D2
Scott Cl. Roystn 2 B1
Scott Rd. Bis St 76 C3
Scott Rd. Stev 51 D3
Scotts Cl. Gt Am 114 B4
Scott's Rd. Gt Am 114 B4
Scottswood Cl. Bus 167 F4
Scottswood Rd. Bus 167 F4
Scrubbitts Park Rd. Radl 156 A2
Scrubbitts Sq. Radl 156 A2
Seabrook. Luton 44 B2
Seabrook Rd. Bed 139 E2
Seacroft Gdns. Sth Ox 175 E4
Seaford Cl. Luton 46 B2
Seaforth Dri. Ches 162 B3
Seaman Cl. Pk St 141 E3
Searches La. Bed 140 B2
Seaton Rd. Heml H 124 C1
Seaton Rd. Lon C 142 B3
Seaton Rd. Luton 44 C2
Sebright Rd. Barn 171 E3
Sebright Rd. Heml H 124 A1
Sebright Rd. Mark 83 F3
Secker Cres. Har 176 B1
Second Ave. Letw 23 E3
Second Ave. Watf 154 B2
Sedbury Cl. Luton 45 D3
Sedge Green. Lo Naz 135 F2
Sedge Green. Roy 135 F2
Sedgwick Rd. Luton 44 A3
Seebohm Cl. Hit 21 E1
Seeleys. Harl 118 B2
Sefton Ave. Har 176 B1
Sefton Cl. St Alb 127 F2
Sefton Rd. Stev 37 D1
Selbourne Rd. Luton 45 D1
Selby Ave. St Alb 127 E2
Selden Hill. Heml H 124 B1
Sele Rd. Hert 113 D3
Selina Cl. Luton 44 B4
Sells Rd. Ware 93 F1
Sellwood Dri. Barn 171 E2
Selsey Dri. Luton 46 B2
Selwyn Ave. Hat 129 F2
Selwyn Cres. Hat 129 F3
Selwyn Dri. Hat 129 F3
Sempill Rd. Heml H 138 C4
Senate Pl. Stev 37 D1
Sequoia Cl. Bus 168 B1
Sequoia Park. Pnr 176 A2
Serby Ave. Roystn 7 E4
Sergehill La. Bed 140 A3
Service Rd The. Pot B 159 D4
Seven Acres. Norwd 175 D2
Sevenoaks Ct. Norwd 174 B2
Severalls The. Luton 46 A2
Severn Dri. Enf 162 A1
Severn Way. Watf 154 B3
Severnmead. Heml H 124 C3
Severnvale. Lon C 142 C2
Sewardstone Rd. Wa Aby 163 E2
Sewardstone Way. Wa Aby 163 E2
Sewell Cl. St Alb 128 C2
Sewell Harris Cl. Harl 118 A1
Sewells. Wel GC 89 F1
Seymour Ave. Luton 63 F3
Seymour Cl. Pnr 175 F1
Seymour Cres. Heml H 124 C2
Seymour Mews. Saw 118 C4
Seymour Rd. Luton 63 F3
Seymour Rd. Nthch 121 F3
Seymour Rd. St Alb 127 F3
Shackledell. Stev 50 C1
Shacklegate La. Whit 66 C3
Shackleton Spring. Stev 51 D2
Shackleton Way. Wel GC 111 E3
Shady Bush Cl. Bus 168 B1
Shady La. Watf 167 D4
Shaftenhoe End Rd. Bar 9 D1
Shaftesbury Ct. Stev 50 C2
Shaftesbury Rd. Luton 45 D1
Shaftesbury Rd. Watf 167 E3
Shaftesbury Way. Bed 139 E2
Shaftesbury Way. Roystn 7 F3
Shakespeare. Roystn 7 E4
Shakespeare Rd. Harp 86 A1
Shakespeare Rd. Luton 44 A1
Shakespeare St. Watf 154 A1
Shalcross Dri. Ches 148 C1
Shallcross Cres. Hat 130 A1
Shangani Rd. Bis St 76 C3
Shanklin Cl. Ches 147 F1
Shanklin Cl. Luton 45 D4
Shanklin Gdns. Sth Ox 175 E3
Shantock Hall La. Bov 136 C1
Shantock La. Bov 136 C1
Sharmans Cl. Har Gr 89 F2
Sharpenhoe Rd. Str 31 D3
Sharpes La. Heml H 123 D1
Sharples Green. Luton 45 D4
Shaw Cl. Bus 176 C4
Shaw Cl. Ches 148 B2
Shaws The. Wel GC 111 E3
Sheepcot Dri. Watf 154 B3
Sheepcot La. Watf 154 A3
Sheepcote. Wel GC 111 D2
Sheepcote La. Whea 87 F1
Sheepcote Rd. Heml H 124 C2
Sheepcroft Hill. Stev 51 E2
Sheephouse Rd. Heml H 124 C1
Sheering Dri. Harl 118 C2
Sheering Lower Rd. Harl 118 C4
Sheering Lower Rd. Saw 98 A1
Sheering Mill La. Saw 97 F1
Sheering Rd. Harl 118 C3
Sheethanger La. Fel 138 A4
Shefton Rise. Norwd 175 D2
Sheldon Cl. Ham St 147 F3
Shelford Rd. Barn 171 E2
Shelley Cl. Norwd 174 C3
Shelley Cl. Roystn 2 B1
Shelley Ct. Harp 86 A1
Shelley Rd. Luton 44 A1
Shelly Cl. Hit 35 E4
Shelton Way. Luton 46 A2
Shenley Ct. Heml H 125 D4
Shenley Hill. Radl 156 A2
Shenley La. Lon C 142 B2
Shenley Rd. Bor 170 A3
Shenley Rd. Heml H 125 E4
Shenleybury. Shen 142 C1
Shenleybury Cotts. Shen 156 C4
Shenstone Hill. Berk 122 C3
Shephall Green. Stev 51 D1
Shephall Green La. Stev 51 D1
Shephall La. Stev 51 D1
Shephall View. Stev 51 D3
Shephall Way. Stev 51 E2
Shepherd Cl. Roystn 7 F3
Shepherds Ct. Hert 92 B1
Shepherds Green. Heml H 123 F1
Shepherd's La. Chor 164 B2
Shepherd's La. Ric 164 C1
Shepherds La. Stev 50 A3
Shepherds Mead. Hit 21 F1
Shepherds Rd. Watf 166 C3
Shepherds Way. Bro Pk 145 E2
Shepherds Way. Harp 85 E2
Shepherds Way. Ric 165 D1
Shepley Mews. Ches 163 D1
Sheppard Cl. Enf 162 A1
Sheppards Cl. St Alb 127 F3
Shepperton Cl. Bor 170 B4
Sheppey's La. Abb L 139 E1
Sheraton Cl. Elst 169 F2
Sherborne Ave. Luton 45 E3
Sherborne Way. Cro Gr 166 A3
Sherd Cl. Luton 44 C4
Sheredes Dri. Hod 134 C2
Sherfield Ave. Ric 173 F4
Sheridan Rd. Luton 45 E1
Sheridan Rd. Watf 167 E1
Sheriff Way. Watf 154 A3
Sheringham Ave. Stev 50 A4
Sheringham Cl. Luton 45 E4
Sherington Ave. Pnr 176 A2
Shernbroke Rd. Wa Aby 163 F3
Sherrardspark Rd. Wel GC 110 B4
Sherwood. Letw 22 C4
Sherwood Ave. Pot B 158 C4
Sherwood Ave. St Alb 128 A3
Sherwood Rd. Luton 45 D1
Sherwoods Rd. Watf 167 F1
Sherwoods Rise. Harp 107 E4
Shetland Cl. Bor 170 B2
Shillington Rd. Aps En 19 F3
Shillington Rd. Pirt 20 A3
Shillitoe Ave. Pot B 158 C4
Shingle Cl. Luton 45 D4
Shire Cl. Ches 148 C3
Shire La. Buc Co 120 A3
Shire La. C St P 172 A3
Shire La. Chor 164 B2
Shire La. Has 119 F4
Shiremeade. Elst 169 F2
Shires The. Luton 45 E1
Shires The. Roystn 7 F3
Shirley Cl. Ches 148 B1
Shirley Cl. Hod 148 C4
Shirley Cl. Stev 51 E4
Shirley Rd. Abb L 153 F4
Shirley Rd. Luton 63 E4
Shirley Rd. St Alb 127 F1
Shooters Dri. Lo Naz 135 F1
Shootersway. Berk 121 F2
Shootersway La. Berk 121 F2
Shootersway Park. Berk 121 F2
Shoplands. Wel GC 89 E1
Shoreham Cl. Stev 50 A4

Short La. Ast 51 F2
Short La. Bri Wd 140 C1
Shortcroft. Bis St 77 E4
Shortlands Green. Wel GC 110 C3
Shortmead Dri. Ches 162 C4
Shothanger Way. Fel 137 E3
Shott La. Letw 23 D3
Shrub Hill Rd. Heml H 123 F1
Shrubbery Gr. Roystn 7 E2
Shrubbery The. Heml H 123 F2
Shrublands. Bro Pk 145 D3
Shrublands Ave. Berk 122 A2
Shrublands Rd. Berk 122 A3
Shrublands The. Pot B 158 C3
Shrubs Rd. Ric 173 F2
Shugars Green. Tri 100 A3
Sibley Ave. Harp 107 F4
Sibley Cl. Luton 46 A2
Sibthorpe Rd. Wel Gr 144 B4
Siccut Rd. L Wym 35 F2
Sicklefield Cl. Ham St 147 F3
Siddons Rd. Stev 51 E3
Sidford Cl. Heml H 123 F2
Sidings The. Hat 129 F2
Sidmouth Cl. Sth Ox 175 D4
Sidney Terr. Bis St 76 C3
Silam Rd. Stev 50 C3
Silecroft Rd. Luton 64 A4
Silk Mill Ct. Watf 167 D1
Silk Mill Rd. Watf 167 D1
Silk Mill Way. Tri 100 A3
Silver Cl. Har 176 B2
Silver Dell. Watf 153 F2
Silver Hill. Shen 157 E2
Silver St. Ans 29 D3
Silver St. Ashw 4 B2
Silver St. Ches 147 E1
Silver St. Gu M 1 C2
Silver St. Luton 63 F4
Silver St. Sta Mo 59 E3
Silver St. Wa Aby 163 E3
Silver Trees. Bri Wd 140 C1
Silverbirch Ave. Stot 11 F4
Silverdale Rd. Bus 167 F2
Silverfield. Hod 134 C1
Silverthorn Dri. Heml H 139 D4
Silverwood Cl. Norwd 174 B1
Simmonds Rise. Heml H 124 B1
Simon Dean. Bov 137 D2
Simpson Dri. Bal 23 F4
Simpsons Ct. Bal 23 F4
Sinderby Cl. Bor 169 F4
Sinfield Cl. Stev 51 D3
Singlets La. Fla 84 B1
Sir Herbert James Village The. Luton 44 B2
Sir Peter's Way. Stu 81 F3
Sirita Cl. Har 176 B1
Sirus Rd. Norwd 175 D3
Sish Cl. Stev 50 B3
Sish La. Stev 50 B3
Siskin Cl. Bor 170 A3
Sisson Cl. Stev 51 E1
Sitwell Gr. Stan 176 C3
Six Acres. Heml H 139 D4
Six Hills Way. Stev 50 B2
Sixth Ave. Watf 154 B2
Skegness Rd. Stev 50 A4
Skegsbury La. Pet Gr 65 F1
Skidmore Way. Ric 165 F1
Skimpans Cl. Wel Gr 144 B4
Skimpton Rd. Luton 44 A1
Skipton Cl. Stev 68 C4
Skua Cl. Luton 44 A3
Skys Wood Rd. St Alb 128 A4
Sleaford Green. Sth Ox 175 E4
Sleapcross Gdns. St Alb 129 E1
Sleaps Hyde. Stev 51 E1
Sleapshyde La. St Alb 129 E1
Sleddale. Heml H 124 C3
Sleets End. Heml H 124 A3
Slimmons Dri. St Alb 128 A4
Slip La. St P W 68 A3
Slipe La. Hod 148 C4
Slipe The. Ched 80 A4
Sloansway. Wel GC 90 A1
Slype The. Bla En 87 D3
Small Acre. Heml H 123 F2
Smallcroft. Wel GC 111 D4
Smallford La. St Alb 129 D1
Smallwood Cl. Whea 108 C4
Smarts Green. Ham St 147 F3
Smith St. Watf 167 E3
Smith's End La. Bar 8 C1
Smiths La. Ham St 147 E3
Smiths La Mall. Luton 63 F4
Smithy The. L Had 57 D1
Smug Oak La. Bri Wd 141 E1
Smug Oak La. Fro 141 F1
Snailswell La. Ick 21 F3
Snatchup. Red 106 A3
Snells Mead. Bun 40 C4
Snipe The. Wes 24 A1
Snowford Cl. Luton 45 D4
Snowley Par. Bis St 59 D1
Soham Rd. Enf 162 C1
Solesbridge Cl. Chor 164 C3
Solesbridge La. Chor 165 D4
Sollershott E. Letw 22 C2
Sollershott W. Letw 22 C2
Solomon's Hill. Ric 165 E1
Solway. Heml H 124 C3
Solway Rd. Luton 45 D2
Solway Rd S. Luton 45 D2
Somerby Cl. Hod 135 D1
Someries Rd. Harp 86 B2
Someries Rd. Heml H 123 F3
Somers Rd. Wel Gr 144 B4
Somers Sq. Wel Gr 144 B4
Somers Way. Bus 168 B1
Somersby Cl. Luton 63 F3
Somerset Ave. Luton 46 A1
Somerset Rd. Enf 163 D1
Somersham. Wel GC 111 E3
Soothouse Spring. St Alb 127 F4
Sopers Rd. Cuf 146 C1
Sopwell La. St Alb 127 E1
Sorrel Cl. Luton 45 D4
Sorrel Cl. Roystn 7 F3
Sorrel Garth. Hit 35 D3
Sotheron Rd. Watf 167 E3
Souberie Ave. Letw 22 C3
Souldern St. Watf 167 D2
South App. Norwd 174 B4
South Bank Rd. Nthch 121 F3
South Cl. Bal 23 F4
South Cl. Barn 171 F3
South Cl. Chis 141 D3
South Cl. Pnr 175 E1
South Cl. Roystn 7 D4
South Cottage Dri. Chor 164 C2
South Cottage Gdns. Chor 164 C2
South Dri. Cuf 146 C1
South Dri. St Alb 128 C2
South Drift Way. Luton 63 D3
South Hill Cl. Hit 35 D3
South Hill Rd. Heml H 124 B2
South Ley. Wel GC 110 C2
South Mimms By-Ps. Pot B 157 F4
South Par. Wa Aby 163 E3
South Park Ave. Chor 164 C2
South Park Gdns. Berk 122 A3
South Pl. Harl 118 A2
South Pl. Hit 34 B4
South Rd. Bal 23 F4
South Rd. Bis St 77 D3
South Rd. Chor 164 B2
South Rd. Harl 118 A2
South Rd. Hat 130 A1
South Rd. Luton 63 E3
South Rd. Stand 55 F1
South Riding. Bri Wd 141 D1
South St. Bis St 76 C3
South St. Hert 113 E3
South St. Sta Ab 115 E2
South View. Letw 22 C3
South View Rd. Pnr 175 D2
South Way. Abb L 153 F3
South Way. Wa Aby 163 E2
South Weald Dri. Wa Aby 163 E3
Southacre Way. Pnr 175 E1
Southall Cl. Ware 93 E1
Southbrook. Saw 97 F1
Southbrook Dri. Ches 148 B2
Southdown Ct. Hat 130 A1
Southdown Ind Est. Harp 107 E4
Southdown Rd. Harp 107 D4
Southdown Rd. Hat 130 A1
Southend Cl. Stev 50 B4
Southern Ave. Henlw 10 B2
Southern Rise. Nwml E 85 F4
Southern Way. Letw 22 C4
Southernwood Cl. Heml H 125 D2
Southfield. Barn 171 E2
Southfield. Brag 55 F4
Southfield. Wel GC 110 B2
Southfield Ave. Watf 154 B1
Southfield Rd. Ches 162 C4
Southfield Rd. Hod 135 D4
Southfield Way. St Alb 128 B3
Southfields. Letw 11 F1
Southfields. Stand 55 F1
Southgate. Stev 50 B2
Southgate Rd. Pot B 159 E3
Southmead Cres. Ches 148 C1
Southmill Rd. Bis St 77 D3
Southsea Ave. Watf 167 D3
Southsea Rd. Stev 50 A4
Southview Cl. Ham St 147 F3
Southview Rd. Harp 86 B2
Southwark Cl. Stev 37 D1
Southwold Rd. Watf 154 B1
Soval Ct. Norwd 174 B2
Sowerby Ave. Luton 46 B2
Sparhawke. Letw 12 A1
Sparrow Cl. Luton 44 A2
Sparrows Herne. Bus 168 B1
Sparrowswick Ride. St Alb 127 E4
Spayne Cl. Luton 45 D4
Spear Cl. Luton 44 C3
Speedwell Cl. Luton 45 D4
Speke Cl. Stev 51 E3
Spellbrook La E. Spel 97 F4
Spellbrook La W. Spel 97 F4
Spellbrooke. Hit 34 B4
Spencer Ave. Ham St 147 F3
Spencer Cl. Sta Mo 59 E3
Spencer Gate. St Alb 127 F3
Spencer Pl. Sand 108 B1
Spencer Rd. Har 176 C1
Spencer Rd. Luton 45 E1
Spencer St. Hert 113 F4
Spencer St. St Alb 127 E2
Spencer Way. Heml H 124 A3
Spencer Wlk. Chor 165 E2
Spenser Cl. Roystn 2 B1
Spenser Rd. Harp 86 B1
Sperberry Hill. St Ipp 35 D1
Sphere Industrial Estate The. St 128 A1
Spicer St. St Alb 127 E2
Spicers La. Harl 118 B2
Spicersfield. Ham St 148 A2
Spinney Cl. Hit 35 D3
Spinney La. Wl Gr 68 B1
Spinney Rd. Luton 44 B4
Spinney St. Hert 114 A3
Spinney The. Bal 23 F4
Spinney The. Harp 85 F2
Spinney The. Hert 113 F3
Spinney The. Hod 134 C2
Spinney The. Pot B 159 E4
Spinney The. Stev 51 E4
Spinney The. Watf 167 D4
Spinney The. Wel GC 110 C3
Spittlesea Rd. Luton 64 B3
Spooners Dri. Chis 141 E2
Spratts La. Ken Co 82 C4
Spreckley Cl. Henlw 10 A3
Spring Cl. Bor 170 A4
Spring Cl. Hare 173 E1
Spring Cl. Lat 150 B2
Spring Court Rd. Enf 161 D1
Spring Crofts. Bus 168 B3
Spring Dri. Stev 69 D4
Spring Field Rd. Berk 122 A3
Spring Gdns. Watf 154 B2
Spring Hills. Harl 117 D1
Spring La. Cotrd 39 E3
Spring La. Heml H 124 A2
Spring Pl. Luton 63 E3
Spring Rd. Kin Gr 85 D2
Spring Rd. Letw 22 C3
Spring View Rd. Gt Am 114 A4
Spring Wlk. Hod 134 B1
Springfield. Bus 168 B1
Springfield. St Alb 129 D2
Springfield Cl. Cro Gr 166 A2
Springfield Cl. Pot B 159 E4
Springfield Cres. Harp 86 A2
Springfield Rd. Ches 162 C4
Springfield Rd. Heml H 124 C2
Springfield Rd. Luton 45 E3
Springfield Rd. St Alb 128 A1
Springfield Rd. Watf 154 A3
Springfields. Hod 134 C2
Springfields. Wa Aby 163 F3
Springfields. Wel GC 110 A2
Springfields House. Wel GC 110 B2
Springhall La. Saw 97 F1
Springhall Rd. Saw 97 F1
Springhead. Ashw 4 B2
Springle La. Hod 114 C1
Springs The. Hod 148 C3
Springshott. Letw 22 C3
Springwell Ave. Ric 173 D4
Springwell La. Hare 173 D3
Springwood. Ham St 148 A3
Springwood Cl. Hare 173 E1
Springwood Wlk. St Alb 128 B3
Spruce Way. Chis 141 D2
Spur Cl. Abb L 153 E3
Spur The. Ches 148 B2
Spur The. Stev 50 C2
Spurrs Cl. Hit 35 D4
Square The. Brag 55 F4
Square The. Chipp 27 E3
Square The. Heml H 124 B2
Square The. Hod 148 C4
Square The. Red 105 F3
Square The. Saw 97 F1
Square The. Watf 154 A1
Squires Ride. Heml H 104 C1
Squirrels Cl. Bis St 76 C4
Squirrels The. Bus 168 B2
Stackfield. Harl 118 A2
Stacklands. Wel GC 110 A2
Staddles. L Hal 98 A4
Stafford Cl. Ches 148 A1
Stafford Dri. Hod 135 D2
Stafford Rd. Har 176 B2
Staffords. Harl 118 C2
Stag Green Ave. Hat 130 B4
Stag La. Chor 164 B2
Stagg Hill. Barn 159 F2
Stainer Rd. Bor 169 E4
Stains Cl. Ches 148 C2
Stake Piece Rd. Roystn 7 E3
Stakers Ct. Harp 86 A1
Stamford Ave. Roystn 7 E4
Stamford Cl. Har 176 C2
Stamford Cl. Pot B 159 E4
Stamford Rd. Watf 167 D4
Stanborough Ave. Bor 157 D1
Stanborough Cl. Wel GC 110 B3
Stanborough Green. Wel GC 110 B2
Stanborough La. Wel GC 110 B2
Stanborough Rd. Wel GC 110 B2
Stanborough Villas. Watf 154 A2
Stanbury Ave. Watf 153 F1
Standard Rd. Enf 162 C1
Standfield. Abb L 139 F1
Standhill Cl. Hit 34 C3
Standhill Rd. Hit 34 C3
Standon Hill. Stand 55 E1
Standon Rd. L Had 56 C2
Standring Rise. Heml H 138 A4
Stane Cl. Bis St 58 C1
Stane Field. Letw 23 D2
Stanelow Cres. Stand 55 E1
Stanford Rd. Luton 46 A1
Stangate Cres. Bor 170 C2
Stanhope Ave. Har 176 B1
Stanhope Rd. Barn 171 E2
Stanhope Rd. St Alb 127 F2
Stanier Rise. Nthch 121 F4
Stanley Ave. Chis 141 D3
Stanley Gdns. Bor 169 F4
Stanley Gdns. Tri 99 F2
Stanley Rd. Hert 113 F3
Stanley Rd. Norwd 175 D1
Stanley Rd. Stev 51 D4
Stanley Rd. Str 31 D3
Stanley Rd. Watf 167 E3
Stanley St. Luton 63 E3
Stanmore Cres. Luton 44 C2
Stanmore Rd. Stev 50 B4
Stanmore Rd. Watf 167 D4
Stanmount Rd. Chis 141 D3
Stannington Path. Bor 170 A4
Stanstead Dri. Hod 135 D4
Stanstead Rd. Hert 114 A3
Stanstead Rd. Hert H 114 C3
Stanstead Rd. Hod 115 D1
Stansted Hill. Gr Ty 75 D1
Stansted Rd. Birhr 59 E2
Stansted Rd. Bis St 59 D1
Stanton Cl. St Alb 128 B4
Stanton Rd. Luton 44 B1
Staplefield Cl. Pnr 175 F2
Stapleford. Wel GC 111 E3
Stapleford Rd. Luton 46 B2
Stapleton Cl. Pot B 159 E4
Stapleton Rd. Bor 157 D1
Stapley Rd. St Alb 127 E2
Stapylton Rd. Barn 171 F3
Star St. Ware 93 F1
Starling La. Cuf 146 C2
Statam Cl. Luton 31 D1
Station App. Ches 162 C3
Station App. Chor 164 B3
Station App. Harp 86 A1
Station App. Hit 35 D4
Station App. Kneb 68 C3
Station App. Norwd 174 C2
Station App. Radl 156 A2
Station App. Sth Ox 175 E4
Station Cl. Bro Pk 144 C3
Station Cl. Pot B 158 C4
Station Mews. Pot B 159 D4
Station Pl. Letw 22 C3
Station Rd. Abb L 139 D1
Station Rd. Ald 101 D3
Station Rd. Arl 11 D2
Station Rd. Bal 12 C1
Station Rd. Berk 122 A3
Station Rd. Bis St 77 D4
Station Rd. Bor 170 A3
Station Rd. Bric 155 D4
Station Rd. Bun 40 C4
Station Rd. Ched 79 F4
Station Rd. Cuf 146 C1
Station Rd. Had Cr 74 C1
Station Rd. Har Gr 89 F2
Station Rd. Harl 118 B2
Station Rd. Harl 117 E2
Station Rd. Harp 86 B1
Station Rd. Heml H 124 B1
Station Rd. Henlw 10 A2
Station Rd. Hod 135 D2
Station Rd. Ivin 80 C3
Station Rd. Kneb 69 D3
Station Rd. Let Gr 112 A1
Station Rd. Letw 22 C3
Station Rd. Lon M 79 D2
Station Rd. Luton 44 C3
Station Rd. Luton 63 F4
Station Rd. Odsey 5 E1
Station Rd. Puc 55 E2
Station Rd. Radl 156 A2
Station Rd. Ric 165 E1
Station Rd. Saw 97 F2
Station Rd. St Alb 129 D2
Station Rd. Sta Ab 115 E2
Station Rd. Sta Mo 59 F3
Station Rd. Stand 55 F1
Station Rd. Ste Mo 5 D4
Station Rd. Tri 100 B2
Station Rd. Ware 93 F1
Station Rd. Wat St 70 B2
Station Rd. Watf 167 D4
Station Rd. Wel Gr 144 B3
Station Rd. Whea 87 E1
Station Way. Letw 22 C3
Staveley Rd. Luton 44 B1
Steeplands. Bus 168 A1
Steeple View. Bis St 76 C4
Stephens Cl. Luton 46 A2
Stephens Way. Red 105 F3
Stepnells. Mars 80 A1
Sterling Ave. Ches 162 B3
Sterling Rd. Enf 161 E1
Stevenage Cres. Bor 169 F4
Stevenage Rd. Hit 35 D3
Stevenage Rd. Kneb 68 C4
Stevenage Rd. L Wym 35 E2
Stevenage Rd. St Ipp 35 D2
Stevenage Rd. Wal 51 F4
Stevenage Rise. Heml H 124 C4
Stevens Green. Bus 168 B1
Steward Cl. Ches 148 C1
Stewardstone St. Wa Aby 163 E3
Stewart Cl. Abb L 153 F4
Stewart Rd. Harp 86 A1
Stewarts The. Bis St 76 C3
Stile Plntn. Roystn 7 F3
Stilton Path. Bor 157 D1
Stirling Cl. Stev 69 E4
Stirling Cnr. Barn 170 B2
Stirling Way. Bor 170 B2
Stirling Way. Wel GC 111 F3
Stobart Cl. Kneb 68 C3
Stock La. News 8 B1
Stockbreach Cl. Hat 130 A3
Stockbreach Rd. Hat 130 A3
Stockens Dell. Kneb 68 C2
Stockens Green. Kneb 68 C2
Stockers Farm Rd. Ric 173 E4
Stockfield Ave. Hod 135 D4
Stockholm Way. Luton 44 C4
Stocking La. Nut 18 B1
Stockings La. L Berk 132 B3
Stockingstone Rd. Luton 45 F2
Stockport Rd. Heron 164 B1
Stocks Rd. Ald 101 E4
Stockwell Cl. Ches 148 A2
Stockwell La. Ches 148 A2
Stockwood Cres. Luton 63 E3
Stone Cross. Harl 117 E1
Stonecroft. Kneb 68 C3
Stonecross. St Alb 127 F2
Stonecross Cl. St Alb 127 F2
Stonecross Rd. Hat 130 A4
Stonehills. Wel GC 110 B4
Stonelea Rd. Heml H 138 C4
Stoneleigh. Saw 97 E2
Stoneleigh Ave. Enf 162 A1
Stoneleigh Cl. Ches 162 B3
Stoneleigh Cl. Luton 45 D4
Stoneley. Letw 11 F1
Stonemead. Wel GC 89 E2
Stones Alley. Watf 167 D3
Stoneways Cl. Luton 44 B3
Stoney Common. Sta Mo 59 F3
Stoney Common Rd. Sta Mo 59 E3
Stoney Croft. Ald 101 E3
Stoney La. Bov 137 E3
Stoney La. Chipf 137 F1
Stoneycroft. Heml H 124 A2
Stoneycroft. Wel GC 111 D4
Stoneyfield Dri. Sta Mo 59 F3
Stoneygate Rd. Luton 44 B2
Stonleigh Dri. Hod 115 D1
Stonnells Cl. Letw 22 C4
Stony Croft. Stev 50 C3
Stony Hills. Cha En 92 B4
Stony La. Chen 150 C1
Stony La. T Gr 47 E2
Stonyshotts. Wa Aby 163 F3
Stookslade. Wing 60 A2
Stopsley Way. Luton 46 A2
Storehouse La. Hit 34 C3
Storey St. Heml H 138 B4
Stormont Rd. Hit 21 F1
Stornoway. Heml H 125 D1
Stort Lodge. Bis St 76 B4
Stort Mill. Harl 118 A3
Stort Rd. Bis St 76 C3
Stortford Hall Park. Bis St 77 D4
Stortford La. Stand 55 F1
Stortford Rd. Hod 135 E4
Stortford Rd. L Had 57 E1
Stortford Rd. L Hal 98 C2
Stotfold Rd. Cal 3 E1
Stotfold Rd. Ch En 11 D4
Stotfold Rd. Letw 22 B2
Stotfold Rd. Radw 12 B4
Stow The. Harl 117 F1
Stox Mead. Har 176 B1
Strafford Cl. Pot B 159 D4
Strafford Ct. Kneb 69 D3
Strafford Gate. Pot B 159 D4
Strafford Rd. Barn 171 F3
Straits The. Wa Aby 163 D4
Strangers Way. Luton 44 B2
Strangeways. Watf 153 F2
Stratfield Dri. Hod 134 C2
Stratfield Rd. Bor 170 A4
Stratford Rd. Luton 45 D1
Stratford Rd. Watf 167 D4
Stratford Way. Heml H 138 A4
Stratford Way. Watf 167 D4
Strathmore Ave. Hit 21 F1
Strathmore Ave. Luton 63 F3
Strathmore Rd. Whit 66 C3
Strathmore Wlk. Luton 63 F3
Stratton Ave. Enf 161 E1
Stratton Gdns. Luton 45 E2
Strawberry Field. Hat 130 A1
Strawberry Field. Luton 44 C4
Strawfields. Wel GC 111 D4
Strawmead. Hat 130 A4
Strawplait Way. Arl 11 D2
Strayfield Rd. Enf 161 D1
Street The. Brag 55 F4
Street The. Chipf 152 A4
Street The. Fur P 43 D2
Street The. Hault 53 F2
Street The. Saw 98 C1
Street The. Wall 25 E4
Stretton Way. Bor 156 C1
Stringers La. Ast 51 F1
Stroma Cl. Heml H 125 E1
Stronsay. Heml H 125 E1
Stuart Ct. Elst 169 E2
Stuart Dri. Hit 35 D4
Stuart Dri. Roystn 7 E4
Stuart Pl. Luton 63 E4
Stuart Rd. Welw 89 D2
Stuart St. Luton 63 E4
Stuart Way. Ches 162 A4
Stuarts Cl. Heml H 124 B1
Stud Green. Watf 154 A4
Studham La. Dagn 81 E2
Studham La. Stu 82 A4
Studio Way. Bor 170 B4
Studios The. Bus 168 A2
Studlands Rise. Roystn 7 F3
Studley Rd. Luton 45 E1
Sturgeon's Way. Hit 22 A1
Sturlas Way. Ches 162 B3
Styles Cl. Luton 46 B1
Such Cl. Letw 23 D4
Sudbury Rd. Luton 44 A3
Suffolk Cl. Bor 170 B2
Suffolk Cl. Lon C 142 B3
Suffolk Cl. Luton 44 A2
Suffolk Rd. Pot B 158 C4
Suffolk Rd. Roystn 7 F3
Sugar La. Heml H 123 D1
Sulgrave Cres. Tri 100 B3
Sullivan Cres. Hare 173 E1
Sullivan Way. Elst 169 E2
Summer Ct. Heml H 124 B3
Summer Dale. Wel GC 89 E1
Summer Gr. Elst 169 E2

Summer Hill. Elst 170 A2
Summer St. Cad 63 E1
Summer Wlk. Mark 83 F3
Summerfield. Hat 130 A1
Summerfield Cl. Lon C 142 B3
Summerfield Rd. Luton 62 C4
Summerfield Rd. Watf 154 A2
Summerhouse La. Bus 168 B4
Summerhouse La. Hare 173 D2
Summerhouse Way. Abb L 139 F1
Summerlands Rd. St Alb 128 B4
Summers Rd. Luton 46 B1
Summerswood La. Ridge 157 F2
Summit Rd. Pot B 144 C1
Sumpter Yd. St Alb 127 E1
Sun Hill. Roystn 7 E3
Sun La. Harp 86 A1
Sun St. Bal 23 F4
Sun St. Hit 34 C3
Sun St. Saw 98 A1
Sun St. Wa Aby 163 E3
Sunderland Ave. St Alb 128 A2
Sundon Park Rd. Luton 44 B4
Sunmead Rd. Heml H 124 B3
Sunningdale. Bis St 76 C3
Sunningdale. Luton 45 F2
Sunny Bank. Ched 79 F4
Sunny Hill. Bun 40 C4
Sunnybank Rd. Pot B 159 D3
Sunnydell. Chis 141 D3
Sunnyfield. Hat 130 B4
Sunnyhill Rd. Heml H 124 A2
Sunnyhill Rd. Map Cr 172 B2
Sunnyside. Sta Mo 59 F3
Sunnyside Rd. Hit 35 D3
Sunridge Ave. Luton 45 F1
Sunrise Cres. Heml H 138 C4
Sunset Dri. Luton 45 F2
Sunset View. Barn 171 F4
Surrey Pl. Tri 100 A2
Sursham Ct. Mark 83 F3
Sussex Cl. Hod 135 D4
Sussex Pl. Luton 46 B1
Sussex Rd. Watf 154 A1
Sutcliffe Cl. Bus 168 B3
Sutcliffe Cl. Stev 51 D4
Sutherland Ave. Cuf 146 B2
Sutherland Cl. Barn 171 F3
Sutherland Ct. Wel GC 110 C4
Sutherland Pl. Luton 63 E3
Sutherland Way. Cuf 146 C2
Sutton Acres. L Hal 98 B4
Sutton Cl. Hod 134 C2
Sutton Cl. Tri 100 A3
Sutton Cres. Barn 171 E2
Sutton Gdns. Luton 44 B3
Sutton Path. Bor 170 A4
Sutton Rd. St Alb 128 A2
Sutton Rd. Watf 167 E3
Swallow Cl. Bus 168 B1
Swallow Cl. Chor 165 E1
Swallow Cl. Luton 44 A2
Swallow End. Wel GC 110 C3
Swallow Gdns. Hat 130 A2
Swallow La. St Alb 142 A4
Swallowdale La. Heml H 125 D3
Swallowfields. Wel GC 110 C3
Swallows. Harl 118 B2
Swallows The. Wel GC 89 F1
Swan La. Gu M 1 C2
Swan Pike Rd. Enf 163 D1
Swan St. Ashw 4 B2
Swanfield Rd. Ches 162 C3
Swangley's La. Kneb 69 D2
Swanhill. Wel GC 90 A1
Swanland Rd. Pot B 158 A4
Swanland Rd. Wa En 144 A2
Swanley Bar La. Pot B 145 D2
Swanley Cres. Pot B 145 D1
Swanmead. Luton 44 A3
Swannells Wood. Stu 82 B2
Swans Cl. St Alb 128 C1
Swanstand. Letw 23 E2
Swanston Path. Sth Ox 175 E4
Swasedale Rd. Luton 45 D3
Sweet Briar. Wel GC 111 D3
Sweetbriar Cl. Heml H 124 A3
Sweyns Mead. Stev 51 E4
Swift Cl. Letw 22 C4
Swift Cl. Roystn 2 B1
Swifts Green Cl. Luton 46 A3
Swifts Green Rd. Luton 46 A3
Swinburne Ave. Hit 21 E1
Swinburne Cl. Roystn 2 B1
Swing Gate La. Berk 122 B1
Swingate. Stev 50 B3
Swinnell Cl. Knee 2 A3
Swiss Ave. Watf 166 C3
Swiss Cl. Watf 166 C3
Sycamore Ave. Hat 130 A2
Sycamore Cl. Bus 167 F4
Sycamore Dri. Pk St 141 E2
Sycamore Dri. Tri 100 A2
Sycamore Rd. Cro Gr 166 B2
Sycamore Rise. Berk 122 B2
Sycamores The. Bal 23 F4
Sycamores The. Bis St 77 D3
Sycamores The. Fel 137 F4
Sydney Rd. Watf 166 C2
Sylam Cl. Luton 44 C4
Sylvan Cl. Heml H 125 D1
Sylvan Way. Wel GC 111 E3
Sylvandale. Wel GC 111 E3
Sylvia Ave. Pnr 175 F2
Symonds Green La. Stev 50 A3
Symonds Green Rd. Stev 50 A4

Tabbs Cl. Letw 23 D4
Takeley Cl. Wa Aby 163 E3
Talbot Ave. Watf 167 F1
Talbot Ct. Heml H 124 B1
Talbot Rd. Har 176 C1
Talbot Rd. Hat 130 A4
Talbot Rd. Luton 45 F1
Talbot Rd. Ric 165 F1
Talbot St. Hert 113 F3
Talbot Way. Letw 12 B1
Tall Trees. Roystn 7 F3
Tallack Cl. Har 176 C2
Tallents Cres. Harp 86 B2
Tallis Way. Bor 169 F4
Tamar Green. Heml H 124 C4
Tamarisk Cl. St Alb 127 F4
Tamworth Rd. Hert 113 F4
Tancred Rd. Luton 46 A2
Tanfield Cl. Ham St 148 A2
Tanfield Green. Luton 46 C1
Tanglewood. Wl Gr 90 A4
Tanglewood Cl. Stan 176 C4
Tanners Cres. Hert 113 E2
Tanners Hill. Abb L 154 A4
Tanners Way. Hun 116 B4
Tanners Wood La. Abb L 153 F4
Tannery Cl. Roystn 7 E3
Tannery Drift. Roystn 7 E3
Tannery The. Bun 40 C4
Tannsfield Dri. Heml H 124 C3
Tannsmore Cl. Heml H 124 C3
Tansycroft. Wel GC 111 D4
Tanworth Cl. Norwd 174 B2
Tanworth Gdns. Pnr 175 E1
Tanyard La. A St L 88 A4
Tany's Dell. Harl 118 A2
Tapster St. Barn 171 F3
Taransey. Heml H 125 D1
Tarpan Way. Ches 148 C3
Tarrant Dri. Harp 107 E4
Tassell Hall. Red 105 F3
Tatlers La. Ast 51 F2
Tatsfield Ave. Lo Naz 149 E4
Tattershall Dri. Heml H 105 D1
Tattle Hill. Bram 91 F1
Tattlers Hill. Wing 60 A2
Taunton Ave. Luton 46 A1
Taverners. Heml H 124 C3
Tavistock Ave. St Alb 141 E4
Tavistock Cl. Pot B 159 E4
Tavistock Cl. St Alb 141 E4
Tavistock Cres. Luton 63 F3
Tavistock Rd. Watf 167 E4
Tavistock St. Luton 63 F3
Taylor Cl. St Alb 128 A4
Taylor St. Luton 63 F4
Taylors Ave. Hod 135 D3
Taylor's Hill. Hit 34 C3
Taylors La. Barn 171 F4
Taylor's Rd. Stot 3 D1
Taylor's Rd. Stot 11 F4
Taywood Cl. Stev 51 D1
Teasdale Cl. Roystn 2 B1
Teasel Cl. Roystn 7 F3
Tedder Ave. Henlw 10 A3
Tedder Rd. Heml H 125 D2
Tee Side. Hert 114 A4
Teesdale. Heml H 124 C3
Telford Ave. Stev 51 D3
Telford Cl. Watf 154 B2
Telford Ct. St Alb 127 F1
Telford Rd. Lon C 142 B2
Telford Way. Luton 63 E4
Telmere Industrial Estate. Luton 63 F3
Telscombe Way. Luton 46 B2
Temperance St. St Alb 127 E2
Tempest Ave. Pot B 159 E4
Templar Ave. Bal 23 F3
Templars Dri. Har 176 B2
Templars La. Pres 48 B3
Temple Cl. Ches 162 A4
Temple Cl. Hit 34 B2
Temple Cl. Watf 166 C4
Temple Ct. Hert 92 B1
Temple Fields. Hert 92 B1
Temple Gdns. Ric 174 A3
Temple La. Tonw 92 C4
Temple Mead. Heml H 124 B3
Temple Mead. Roy 116 A1
Templepan La. Cha Cr 152 C1
Templewood. Wel GC 89 F1
Tempsford. Wel GC 111 E3
Tempsford Ave. Bor 170 B3
Temsford Cl. Har 176 B1
Tenby Dri. Luton 44 C2
Tene The. Bal 23 F4
Tennand Cl. Ham St 147 F3
Tennison Ave. Bor 170 A2
Tennyson Ave. Hit 35 E4
Tennyson Ave. Wa Aby 163 F3
Tennyson Cl. Roystn 2 B1
Tennyson Rd. Chis 141 D3
Tennyson Rd. Harp 86 A2
Tennyson Rd. Luton 63 F3
Tenth Ave. Luton 44 B4
Tenzing Gr. Luton 63 E3
Tenzing Rd. Heml H 125 D2
Teresa Gdns. Ches 162 B3
Terminus St. Harl 117 E1
Terrace Gdns. Watf 167 D4
Terrace The. Tri 100 A2
Tethys Rd. Heml H 124 C3
Tewin Cl. St Alb 128 B4
Tewin Cl. Tewin 90 B3
Tewin Ct. Wel GC 110 C4
Tewin Hill. Tewin 90 C2
Tewin Rd. Heml H 125 E2
Tewin Rd. Wel GC 110 C4
Thackeray Cl. Roystn 2 B1
Thames Ave. Heml H 124 C4
Thames Ct. Luton 45 D2
Thamesdale. Lon C 142 C2
Thatchers Croft. Heml H 124 C4
Thatchers End. Hit 35 E4
Thaxted Way. Wa Aby 163 E3
Thaynesfield. P Bar 159 E4
Thelby Cl. Luton 44 C3
Thele Ave. Sta Ab 115 E2
Thele Estate. Sta Ab 115 F2
Theobald Cres. Har 176 B1
Theobald St. Bor 169 F4
Theobald's Cl. Cuf 146 C1
Theobald's La. Ches 162 B4
Theobalds Park Rd. Enf 161 D2
Theobald's Rd. Cuf 146 C1
Therfield Rd. St Alb 127 E3
Thieves' La. Hertng 112 C3
Thieves' La. Hertng 112 C4
Third Ave. Letw 23 E4
Third Ave. Luton 44 B4
Third Ave. Watf 154 B2
Thirlestone. St Alb 127 F2
Thirlestone Rd. Luton 44 B1
Thirlmere Dri. St Alb 128 A1
Thirlmere Gdns. Norwd 174 B2
Thirsk Rd. Bor 157 D1
Thirston Path. Bor 170 A4
Thistle Cl. Heml H 123 F1
Thistle Gr. Wel GC 111 E2
Thistle Rd. Luton 63 F4
Thistlecroft. Heml H 124 A1
Thistles The. Heml H 124 A2
Thistley La. Gos 34 C1
Thomas Rochford Way. Ches 148 C3
Thompsons Cl. Harp 86 A1
Thorley High. Thor 76 C1
Thorley Hill. Bis St 76 C3
Thorley La. Bis St 76 C2
Thorley La. Thor 76 B2
Thorley Park Rd. Bis St 76 C2
Thorn Ave. Bus 168 B1
Thorn Gr. Bis St 77 D3
Thornage Cl. Luton 45 E4
Thornbera Cl. Bis St 76 C2
Thornbera Gdns. Bis St 76 C2
Thornbera Rd. Bis St 76 C2
Thornbury. Harp 86 B1
Thornbury Cl. Hod 115 D1
Thornbury Cl. Stev 69 D4
Thornbury Gdns. Bor 170 B3
Thorncroft. Heml H 125 D1
Thorndyke Ct. Pnr 175 F2
Thornfield Rd. Bis St 76 C4
Thornhill Rd. Luton 44 C1
Thornhill Rd. Norwd 174 B3
Thornton Gr. Pnr 176 A2
Thornton Rd. Barn 171 F3
Thornton Rd. Pot B 145 E1
Thornton St. Hert 113 E3
Thornton St. St Alb 127 E2
Thorpe Cres. Watf 167 E1
Thorpe Rd. St Alb 127 E1
Thorpefield Cl. St Alb 128 B3
Thrales Cl. Luton 44 C4
Three Cherry Trees La. Heml H 125 E4
Three Close La. Berk 122 B2
Three Corners. Heml H 125 D1
Three Houses La. Lan 67 F3
Three Stiles. Benn 52 C2
Thricknells Cl. Luton 44 C4
Thrift Farm La. Bor 170 B4
Thrimley La. Far 58 A3
Thristers Cl. Letw 23 D2
Thrums. Watf 154 A1
Thrush Ave. Hat 130 A2
Thrush Gr. Chor 165 E1
Thrush La. Cuf 146 C2
Thumbswood. Wel GC 111 D2
Thumpers. Heml H 124 C3
Thundercourt. Ware 93 E1
Thundridge Cl. Wel GC 111 E3
Thurgood Rd. Hod 135 D4
Thurlow Cl. Stev 36 B1
Thurnall Ave. Roystn 7 E3
Thurnall Cl. Bal 23 F4
Tibbles Cl. Watf 154 C2
Tibbs Hill Rd. Abb L 139 F1
Tiberius Rd. Luton 44 C3
Tichborne. Map Cr 172 B3
Tile Kiln Cl. Heml H 125 D1
Tile Kiln Cres. Heml H 125 D1
Tile Kiln La. Heml H 125 D1
Tilecroft. Wel GC 89 E1
Tilehouse Cl. Bor 169 F3
Tilehouse La. Map Cr 172 C1
Tilehouse St. Hit 34 C3
Tilgate. Luton 46 B2
Tillers Link. Stev 51 D1
Tillotson Rd. Har 176 A2
Tilsworth Wlk. St Alb 128 B4
Timber Orch. Wat 92 A1
Timber Ridge. Chor 165 E3
Timbercroft. Wel GC 89 F1
Timbers Ct. Harp 85 F1
Times Cl. Hit 21 E1
Timplings Row. Heml H 124 A3
Timworth Cl. Luton 46 B1
Tingeys Cl. Red 106 A3
Tinkers La. Wigg 121 D3
Tintagel Cl. Heml H 124 B4
Tintagle Cl. Luton 45 D2
Tintern Cl. Harp 85 E2
Tintern Cl. Stev 69 D4
Tippendell La. Chis 141 E3
Tippet Ct. Stev 50 B2
Tiree Cl. Heml H 125 D1
Titan Rd. Heml H 124 C3
Titchfield Rd. Enf 162 C1
Tithe Barn Cl. St Alb 141 E4
Tithe Cl. Cod 67 F1
Titian Ave. Bus 168 C1
Titmus Cl. Stev 50 C3
Tiverton Ct. Harp 107 F3
Tiverton Rd. Enf 159 F4
Toddington Rd. Luton 44 B3
Toland Cl. Luton 44 B1
Tolcarne Dri. Pnr 175 D1
Tollgate Cl. Chor 164 C3
Tollgate Rd. Coln H 143 F4
Tollgate Rd. Enf 162 B2
Tollpit End. Heml H 124 A3
Tolmers Ave. Cuf 146 C2
Tolmers Gdns. Cuf 146 C1
Tolmers Rd. Cuf 146 C2
Tolpits Cl. Watf 166 C2
Tolpits La. Watf 166 C1
Tomkins Cl. Bor 169 E4
Toms Croft. Heml H 124 C1
Toms Field. Hat 129 F2
Tom's Hill. Cha Cr 152 C1
Toms Hill Rd. Ald 101 E3
Tom's La. Bed 139 E2
Tooke Cl. Pnr 175 F1
Toorack Rd. Har 176 B1
Tooveys Mill Cl. Kin L 139 D2
Topstreet Way. Harp 107 E4
Torquay Cres. Stev 50 A4
Torquay Dri. Luton 44 B2
Torridge Wlk. Heml H 124 C4
Torrington Dri. Pot B 159 E4
Torrington Rd. Berk 122 A2
Torwood Cl. Berk 121 F2
Torworth Rd. Bor 157 D1
Tot La. Birhr 59 E2
Totteridge Comm. N20 171 E1
Totteridge La. N20 171 E1
Totteridge Rd. Enf 162 B1
Totteridge Village. N20 171 F1
Totts La. Wal 38 B1
Toulmin Dri. St Alb 127 E4
Tounshend St. Hert 113 F3
Tovey Ave. Hod 135 D4
Tovey Cl. Lo Naz 149 F4
Tower Cl. Berk 122 A2
Tower Cl. L Wym 35 F2
Tower Hill. Chipf 137 F1
Tower Hill. Muc H 74 C1
Tower Hill La. Sand 108 C2
Tower Rd. Cod 67 F1
Tower Rd. Luton 64 A4
Tower Rd. Ware 93 F1
Tower St. Hert 113 E4
Tower Way. Luton 64 A4
Towers Rd. Heml H 124 C2
Towers Rd. Pnr 175 F1
Towers Rd. Stev 50 B2
Town Centre. Hat 130 A3
Town Farm Cres. Stand 55 F1
Town Fields. Hat 130 A3
Town La. Benn 52 C2
Town Mead Rd. Wa Aby 163 E3
Towne Rd. Roystn 7 E3
Townfield. Chor 165 E1
Townley. Letw 23 E2
Townsend. Heml H 124 B3
Townsend Ave. St Alb 127 F2
Townsend Cl. Bark 17 E2
Townsend Cl. Harp 85 F1
Townsend Dri. St Alb 127 E3
Townsend La. Harp 85 F1
Townsend Rd. Harp 86 A1
Townsend Way. Norwd 174 C2
Townsley Cl. Luton 63 F3
Trafalgar Ave. Hod 134 C1
Trafford Cl. Stev 36 C1
Traherne Cl. Hit 34 C3
Trapstyle Rd. Ware 93 D1
Travellers Cl. Wel Gr 144 B4
Travellers La. Hat 130 A2
Treacle La. Rus 25 F2
Treacy Cl. Bus 176 B4
Trebellan Dri. Heml H 124 C2
Treehanger Cl. Tri 100 A2
Treetops Cl. Norwd 174 B3
Trefoil Cl. Luton 44 A2
Trefusis Wlk. Watf 166 C4
Tregelles Rd. Hod 135 D4
Tremaine Gr. Heml H 124 C4
Trent Cl. Stev 50 C4
Trent Rd. Luton 45 D2
Tresco Rd. Berk 121 F3
Tresilian Sq. Heml H 124 C4
Trevalga Way. Heml H 124 C4
Trevellance Way. Watf 154 B3
Trevelyan Way. Berk 122 A3
Trevor Cl. Stan 176 C2
Trevor Rd. Hit 35 D4
Trevose Way. Sth Ox 175 E4
Trewenna Dri. Pot B 159 E4
Triangle The. Hit 34 C3
Trident Rd. Watf 153 F3
Triggs Way. Cok Gr 46 C2
Trimley Cl. Luton 44 A3
Trinder Rd. Barn 171 E2
Tring Ford Rd. Tri 100 A4
Tring Hill. Dra B 99 E2
Tring Rd. Lon M 79 E2
Tring Rd. Nthch 121 E4
Tring Rd. Wils 79 E1
Tring Rd. Wing 60 B1
Trinity Cl. Bis St 76 C3
Trinity Cl. Hert H 114 B2
Trinity Cl. Norwd 174 C2
Trinity Gr. Hert 113 E4
Trinity Hall Cl. Watf 167 E4
Trinity La. Ches 162 C4
Trinity Mens. Heml H 125 E1
Trinity Pl. Stev 50 B3
Trinity Rd. Hert H 114 B2
Trinity Rd. Luton 45 D2
Trinity Rd. Stev 50 B3
Trinity Rd. Stot 11 F4
Trinity Rd. Ware 93 F1
Trinity St. Bis St 76 C3
Trinity Way. Bis St 76 C3
Tristram Rd. Hit 22 A1
Triton Way. Heml H 124 C3
Trooper Rd. Ald 101 E3
Trotters Bottom. Pot B 158 A1
Trotter's Gap. Sta Ab 115 F2
Trout Rise. Chor 165 D3
Troutstream Way. Chor 165 D3
Trowbridge Gdns. Luton 45 F2
Trowley Bottom. Fla 105 D4
Trowley Hill Rd. Fla 84 A1
Trowley Rise. Abb L 153 F4
Truemans Rd. Hit 21 E1
Trumper Rd. Stev 36 C1
Trumpington Dri. St Alb 141 E4
Trundlers Way. Bus 168 C1
Truro Gdns. Luton 45 D3
Trust Rd. Ches 162 C3
Tucker St. Watf 167 E2
Tucker's Row. Bis St 76 C3
Tudor Ave. Ches 162 A4
Tudor Ave. Watf 154 B1
Tudor Cl. Ches 162 A4
Tudor Cl. Hat 129 F1
Tudor Cl. Hun 116 B4
Tudor Cl. Stev 36 B1
Tudor Cres. Enf 161 E1
Tudor Ct. Bor 169 F
Tudor Ct. Hit 34 B3
Tudor Dri. Watf 154 B1
Tudor Hill. Heml H 124 B1
Tudor Manor Gdns. Watf 154 B4
Tudor Parade. Ric 165 D1
Tudor Rd. Har 176 B1
Tudor Rd. Luton 45 D1
Tudor Rd. Pnr 175 E1
Tudor Rd. St Alb 127 F4
Tudor Rd. Welw 89 D2
Tudor Rd. Whea 108 C4
Tudor Rise. Hod 134 C1
Tudor Way. Hertng 113 D4
Tudor Way. Ric 165 D1
Tudor Way. Wa Aby 163 E3
Tudor Wlk. Watf 154 B1
Tuffnells Way. Harp 85 E2
Tunnel Wood Cl. Watf 153 F1
Tunnel Wood Rd. Watf 153 F1
Tunnmeade. Harl 118 A1
Turf La. Gra 36 A2
Turkey St. Enf 162 B1
Turmore Dale. Wel GC 110 B3
Turnberry Ct. Sth Ox 175 E4
Turnberry Dr. Bri Wd 140 C1
Turner Cl. Stev 36 B1
Turner Rd. Bus 168 B3
Turners Cl. Bram 91 E2
Turners Cl. Harp 86 B2
Turner's Hill. Ches 148 B1
Turners Hill. Heml H 124 C1
Turners Rd N. Luton 46 A1
Turners Rd S. Luton 46 A1
Turnpike Dri. Luton 31 E1
Turnpike La. Ick 21 F2
Turnstones The. Watf 154 C2
Turpins Chase. Wl Gr 89 F4
Turpins Cl. Hertng 112 C3
Turpin's Ride. Roystn 7 E3
Turpins Ride. Wl Gr 89 F4
Turpin's Rise. Stev 50 C1
Turpin's Way. Bal 23 F4
Tuxford Cl. Bor 156 C1
Tweed Cl. Berk 122 A3
Twelve Acres. Wel GC 110 C2
Twelve Leys. Wing 60 A2
Twickenham Gdns. Har 176 C2
Twigden Ct. Luton 44 C3
Twinwoods. Stev 50 C2
Twist The. Wigg 100 B1
Twitchell The. Bal 23 F4
Two Acres. Wel GC 110 C2
Two Beeches. Heml H 124 C4
Two Dells La. Ash Gr 136 A3
Two Oaks Dri. Brn Gr 90 B3
Two Waters Rd. Heml H 124 B1
Twyford Bury La. Bis St 77 D2
Twyford Business Centre The. Bis St 77 D2
Twyford Cl. Bis St 77 D3
Twyford Dri. Luton 46 B1
Twyford Gdns. Bis St 76 C2
Twyford Rd. Bis St 77 D3
Twyford Rd. St Alb 128 B4
Tye End. Stev 69 D4
Tyfield Cl. Ches 148 B1
Tylers. Harp 86 B1
Tylers Cl. Kin L 138 C2
Tylers Cswy. New St 132 B1
Tylers Hill Rd. Bot 150 A4
Tylers Mead. Luton 45 F3
Tylers Way. Bus 168 C2
Tylersfield. Abb L 154 A4
Tynedale. Lon C 142 C2
Tynemouth Dri. Enf 162 A1
Tynfield Rd. Hod 115 D
Tysoe Ave. Enf 162 C
Tythe Rd. Luton 44 B3
Tyttenhanger Green. Tyt 142 C4

Uckfield Rd. Enf 162 B
Ufford Cl. Har 176 A
Ufford Rd. Har 176 A
Ullswater Rd. Heml H 125 E
Underacres Cl. Heml H 125 D
Underwood Rd. Stev 36 B

Union Green. Heml H 124 B3
Union St. Barn 171 F3
Union St. Luton 63 F3
Union Terr. Bun 40 C4
Unity Rd. Enf 162 B1
University Cl. Bus 168 A3
Unwin Cl. Letw 22 C2
Unwin Pl. Stev 51 E2
Unwin Rd. Stev 51 E2
Updale Cl. Pot B 158 C3
Uplands. Brag 55 F3
Uplands. Cro Gr 165 F2
Uplands. Luton 44 B4
Uplands. Stev 51 E4
Uplands. Ware 93 F1
Uplands. Wel GC 89 E1
Uplands Ave. Hit 35 D3
Uplands Dri. Bro Pk 145 D3
Uplands The. Bri Wd 140 C1
Uplands The. Harp 107 D2
Upper Ashlyns Rd. Berk 122 A2
Upper Barn. Heml H 138 C4
Upper Clabdens. Ware 93 F1
Upper Culver Rd. St Alb 127 F3
Upper Dagnall St. St Alb 127 E2
Upper Ditch. Watf 167 F1
Upper George St. Luton 63 E4
Upper Green. Tewin 90 B2
Upper Green Rd. Tewin 90 C1
Upper Hall Park. Berk 122 C1
Upper Heath Rd. St Alb 127 F3
Upper Highway. Abb L 153 E3
Upper Hill Rise. Ric 165 D2
Upper Icknield Way. Dra B 99 D2
Upper Icknield Way. Pit 80 C1
Upper Icknield Way. Tri 100 B4
Upper Lattimore Rd. St Alb 127 F2
Upper Marlborough Rd. St Alb 127 F2
Upper Marsh La. Hod 135 D3
Upper Maylins. Letw 23 E2
Upper Paddock Rd. Watf 167 F2
Upper Park. Harl 117 D1
Upper Sales. Heml H 123 F1
Upper Sean. Stev 51 D2
Upper Shot. Wel GC 111 D4
Upper Shott. Ham St 147 F3
Upper Station Rd. Radl 156 A2
Upper Tail. Watf 175 F4
Upper Tilehouse St. Hit 34 B4
Upperfield Rd. Wel GC 110 C3
Upshire Rd. Wa Aby 163 F4
Upton Ave. St Alb 127 E2
Upton Cl. Luton 45 E3
Upton Cl. Pk St 141 E3
Upton Lodge Cl. Bus 168 B1
Upton Rd. Watf 167 D3
Upwell Rd. Luton 46 A1
Uranus Rd. Heml H 124 C3
Urban Rd. Bis St 77 D4
Uxbridge Rd. Har 176 B2
Uxbridge Rd. Pnr 176 A2
Uxbridge Rd. Ric 173 D4
Uxbridge Rd (Hatch End). Pnr 175 F2
Uxbridge Rd (Pinner). Pnr 175 E1

Vadis Cl. Luton 44 C4
Vale Ave. Bor 170 A2
Vale Cl. Harp 85 E2
Vale Ct. Whea 108 B4
Vale Dri. Barn 171 F3
Vale Rd. Bus 167 F2
Valence Dri. Ches 148 A2
Valency Cl. Norwd 174 C3
Valerie Cl. St Alb 128 A2
Valeside. Hertng 113 D3
Vallans Cl. Ware 93 E2
Vallansgate. Stev 51 D1
Valley Cl. Hert 113 E3
Valley Cl. Pnr 175 D1
Valley Cl. Stu 82 A2
Valley Cl. Wa Aby 163 E4
Valley Cl. Ware 93 D1
Valley Green. Heml H 105 D1
Valley Green The. Wel GC 110 B4
Valley La. Fla 83 F1
Valley Rd. Berk 121 F3
Valley Rd. Chor 165 D2
Valley Rd. Cod 67 F1
Valley Rd. Letw 22 B4
Valley Rd. St Alb 127 F4
Valley Rd. Stu 82 A2
Valley Rd. Wel GC 110 A3
Valley Rise. Bla En 86 C1
Valley Rise. Roystn 7 F3
Valley Rise. Watf 154 A3
Valley The. Whit 66 C4
Valley View. Barn 171 F2
Valley View. Gofs O 147 E1
Valley Way. Stev 51 D2
Valley Wlk. Cro Gr 166 B2
Valleyside. Heml H 123 F2
Vanda Cres. St Alb 127 F1
Vantorts Cl. Saw 97 F1
Vantorts Rd. Saw 97 F1
Vardon Rd. Stev 50 C4
Varna Cl. Luton 45 D2
Varney Cl. Ches 148 A2
Varney Cl. Heml H 123 F2
Varney Rd. Heml H 123 F2
Vaughan Rd. Harp 86 A1
Vaughan Mead. Red 106 A2
Vaughan Rd. Stot 11 F4
Vauxhall Rd. Heml H 125 D2
Vauxhall Rd. Luton 64 A3
Vauxhall Way. Luton 46 A1
Vega Cres. Norwd 174 C3
Vega Rd. Bus 168 B1
Velizy Ave. Harl 117 E1
Venetia Rd. Luton 46 A2
Ventnor Gdns. Luton 45 D4
Venus Hill. Bov 151 D4
Ver Rd. Red 106 B3
Ver Rd. St Alb 127 E2
Vera Ct. Watf 167 E1
Verdure Cl. Watf 154 C4
Verity Way. Stev 51 D4
Veritys. Hat 130 A3
Verney Cl. Berk 121 F3
Verney Cl. Tri 100 B3
Vernon Ave. Enf 162 C2
Vernon Dri. Hare 173 E1
Vernon Rd. Bus 167 F2
Vernon Rd. Luton 63 E4
Vernon's Cl. St Alb 127 F1
Verulam Cl. Wel GC 110 C3
Verulam Gdns. Luton 44 C3
Verulam Pas. Watf 167 D1
Verulam Rd. Hit 34 C4
Verulam Rd. St Alb 127 E2
Verwood Rd. Har 176 B1
Vespers Cl. Luton 44 A1
Vesta Ave. St Alb 141 E4
Vesta Rd. Heml H 124 C3
Viaduct Rd. Gt Am 114 C4
Viaduct Way. Wel GC 89 F1
Vian Ave. Enf 162 C2
Vicarage Cl. Ch En 11 D4
Vicarage Cl. Heml H 124 B1
Vicarage Cl. Nort 145 F1
Vicarage Cl. St Alb 141 E4
Vicarage Cl. Stand 55 F1
Vicarage Cswy. Hert H 114 A2
Vicarage Gdns. Fla 84 A1
Vicarage Gdns. Mars 80 A1
Vicarage Gdns. Pot En 123 D4
Vicarage La. Bov 137 D2
Vicarage La. Ivin 80 C3
Vicarage La. Kin L 138 C1
Vicarage La. Wat 92 A2
Vicarage Rd. Bun 40 C4
Vicarage Rd. Mars 80 A1
Vicarage Rd. Pit 80 C2
Vicarage Rd. Pot En 123 D4
Vicarage Rd. Ware 93 F1
Vicarage Rd. Watf 167 D2
Vicarage Rd. Wigg 100 B1
Vicarage Rd Prec. Watf 167 D3
Vicarage St. Luton 63 F4
Vicarage Wood. Harl 118 A1
Victoria Cl. Ric 165 E1
Victoria Cl. Stev 50 B4
Victoria Cres. Roystn 7 E4
Victoria La. Barn 171 F3
Victoria Pas. Watf 167 D3
Victoria Rd. Berk 122 B2
Victoria Rd. Bus 168 A1
Victoria Rd. Harp 86 A1
Victoria Rd. Hit 34 B4
Victoria Rd. Wa Aby 163 E3
Victoria Rd. Watf 154 A1
Victoria St. Luton 63 F3
Victoria St. St Alb 127 F2
Victory Rd. Berk 122 A3
View Rd. Pot B 159 E4
Vigors Croft. Hat 129 F2
Villa Rd. Luton 63 E4
Village St. Lan 49 F1
Villiers Cres. St Alb 128 B3
Villiers Rd. Watf 167 F2
Villiers St. Hert 113 F3
Villiers-Sur-Marne Ave. Bis St 76 B3
Vincent. Letw 23 E2
Vincent Cl. Ches 148 C2
Vincent Ct. Norwd 174 C1
Vincent Rd. Luton 44 B3
Vincenzo Cl. Wel Gr 144 B4
Vine Cl. Wel GC 110 C4
Vine Gr. H Wy 117 F3
Vineyard Hill. Nort 146 A1
Vineyard The. Ware 94 A1
Vineyard The. Wel GC 89 F1
Vineyards Rd. Nort 146 A1
Vineyards The. Ware 94 A1
Vinters Ave. Stev 50 C3
Violet Ave. Enf 161 E1
Violet Way. Chor 165 E3
Violets La. Fur P 43 D3
Virgil Dri. Hod 148 C4
Viscount Cl. Luton 45 D3
Vivian Cl. Watf 167 D1
Vivian Gdns. Watf 167 D1
Vyse Cl. Barn 171 E3

Wacketts. Ham St 148 A2
Waddesdon Cl. Luton 46 B1
Waddington Rd. St Alb 127 E2
Wade The. Wel GC 111 D2
Wades The. Hat 130 A1
Wadesmill Rd. Cha En 92 B2
Wadesmill Rd. Hert 92 B1
Wadesmill Rd. Ware 93 E1
Wadham Rd. Abb L 153 F4
Wadhurst Ave. Luton 45 E2
Wadley Cl. Heml H 124 C1
Wadnall Way. Kneb 68 C2
Waggon Rd. Barn 159 E1
Waggon Rd. Pot B 159 D2
Wagon Way. Chor 165 E3
Wain Cl. Pot B 145 D1
Wakefields Wlk. Ches 162 B4
Walcot Ave. Luton 46 A1
Waldeck Rd. Luton 63 E4
Waldegrave Park. Harp 86 B1
Walden End. Stev 50 C2
Walden Pl. Wel GC 110 B4
Walden Rd. Wel GC 110 B4
Waleran Cl. Stan 176 C3
Waleys Cl. Luton 44 C4
Walfords Cl. Harl 118 B2
Walk The. Hertng 113 D3
Walk The. Pot B 159 D4
Walkern Rd. Benn 70 A4
Walkern Rd. Stev 50 B4
Walkern Rd. Stev 51 E4
Walkern Rd. Wal 52 B3
Walkern Rd. Wat St 70 B3
Walkers Cl. Harp 107 E4
Walkers Rd. Harp 107 D4
Wallace Way. Letw 22 A1
Waller Ave. Luton 44 C2
Waller Dr. Norwd 175 D1
Waller St Mall. Luton 63 F4
Waller's Cl. Gt Ch 9 F1
Wallers Way. Hod 115 D1
Wallingford Wlk. St Alb 141 E4
Wallington Rd. Clo 13 E1
Wallington Rd. Wall 14 A1
Walmar Cl. Barn 159 E1
Walnut Ave. Bal 24 A4
Walnut Cl. Chis 141 D2
Walnut Cl. Hit 35 D3
Walnut Cl. Luton 46 A2
Walnut Cl. Stot 11 F3
Walnut Ct. Wel GC 110 C2
Walnut Dri. Bis St 76 B2
Walnut Gr. Heml H 124 B2
Walnut Gr. Wel GC 110 C2
Walnut Green. Bus 167 F4
Walnut Tree Ave. Saw 97 F2
Walnut Tree Cl. Ches 162 B4
Walnut Tree Cl. Hod 135 D3
Walnut Tree Cl. Stev 51 E2
Walnut Tree Cres. Saw 97 F2
Walnut Tree Rd. Pirt 20 B2
Walnut Tree Wlk. Gt Am 114 C3
Walnut Way. Ick 21 F2
Walpole Cl. Pnr 176 A2
Walsh Cl. Hit 34 B4
Walsham Cl. Stev 69 E4
Walshford Way. Bor 157 D1
Walsingham Cl. Hat 129 F4
Walsingham Cl. Luton 45 E4
Walsingham Way. Lon C 142 B2
Waltham Gdns. Enf 162 B1
Waltham Rd. Hit 34 C3
Waltham Rd. Lo Naz 149 F3
Walton Gdns. Wa Aby 163 D3
Walton Rd. Bus 167 E3
Walton Rd. Gt Am 114 B4
Walton Rd. Hod 135 E4
Walton St. St Alb 127 F3
Walverns Cl. Watf 167 E2
Wandon Cl. Luton 46 B2
Wannions Cl. Bot 136 A1
Wansford Park. Bor 170 C3
Warburton Cl. Har 176 B2
Ward Cl. Ham St 148 A2
Ward Cl. Ware 93 E1
Ward Cres. Bis St 76 C3
Warden Hill Cl. Luton 45 E4
Warden Hill Gdns. Luton 45 E4
Warden Hill Rd. Luton 45 E4
Wardown Cres. Luton 45 F1
Ware Park Rd. Hert 113 F4
Ware Rd. Gt Am 115 D1
Ware Rd. Hert 113 F3
Ware Rd. Hod 135 D4
Ware Rd. Sac 71 E1
Ware Rd. Tonw 92 C4
Ware Rd. Wat St 71 D2
Ware Rd. Widf 95 E2
Wareham's La. Hert 113 E3
Warenford Way. Bor 170 A4
Wareside. Heml H 105 D1
Wareside Cl. Wel GC 111 D3
Warham Rd. Har 176 C1
Warmark Rd. Heml H 123 F3
Warneford Pl. Watf 167 F2
Warner Rd. Gt Am 114 B4
Warners Ave. Hod 134 C2
Warners Cl. Stev 51 E2
Warners End Rd. Heml H 124 A2
Warren Cl. Hat 130 A4
Warren Cl. Letw 22 B4
Warren Dale. Wel GC 89 E1
Warren Dri The. Nwml E 64 B1
Warren Gr. Bor 170 B3
Warren Green. Hat 130 A4
Warren La. Clo 24 B4
Warren La. Stan 176 C4
Warren Park Rd. Hert 113 E4
Warren Rd. Bus 168 B1
Warren Rd. Luton 62 C4
Warren Rd. St Alb 141 E4
Warren Terr. Hert 113 E4
Warren The. Harp 107 D3
Warren The. Radl 156 A3
Warren The. Roystn 7 E3
Warren Way. Har Gr 89 F2
Warrenfield Cl. Ches 162 A4
Warrengate La. Pot B 144 B1
Warrengate Rd. Wa En 144 B2
Warrensgreen La. Wa Gr 37 E3
Warton Green. Luton 46 C1
Warwick Ave. Cuf 146 B2
Warwick Cl. Bus 168 C1
Warwick Cl. Cuf 146 B2
Warwick Cl. Hert 113 E2
Warwick Dri. Ches 148 B2
Warwick Gdns. Pot B 158 C1
Warwick Rd. Bis St 77 D3
Warwick Rd. Bor 170 B3
Warwick Rd. Enf 162 C1
Warwick Rd. St Alb 127 F3
Warwick Rd. Stev 51 E3
Warwick Rd E. Luton 63 D4
Warwick Rd W. Luton 63 D4
Warwick Way. Cro Gr 166 B3
Wash La. Pot B 158 B3
Wash The. Hert 113 E3
Wash The. Sto P 43 D3
Washington Ave. Heml H 124 C4
Watchlytes. Wel GC 111 E3
Watchmead. Wel GC 111 D3
Water End Rd. Heml H 123 E4
Water La. Bed 139 D1
Water La. Berk 122 B2
Water La. Bis St 76 C4
Water La. Bov 137 D1
Water La. Hert 113 E3
Water La. Hit 21 F1
Water La. Sta Mo 59 F3
Water La. Watf 167 E3
Water Row. Ware 93 E1
Waterbeach. Wel GC 111 E3
Watercroft Cl. Stev 51 E3
Waterdale. Hert 113 E2
Waterdell La. Gos 35 D1
Waterend La. A St P 88 B1
Waterend La. Red 106 A3
Waterend La. Whea 109 E4
Waterfield. Wel GC 111 D4
Waterford Comm. Wat 92 A1
Waterford Green. Wel GC 111 D3
Watergate The. Watf 175 E4
Waterhouse St. Heml H 124 B1
Waterloo La. Hol 21 D3
Waterman Cl. Watf 167 D2
Waterman's Yd. Watf 167 E3
Watermead Rd. Luton 44 C3
Watermill Estate. Bun 40 C3
Watermill La. Hert 113 E4
Waters Dri. Ric 165 F1
Waterside. Berk 122 B2
Waterside. Kin L 139 D1
Waterside. Lon C 142 C2
Waterside. Sta Mo 59 F3
Waterside. Wel GC 90 A1
Waterslade Green. Luton 45 D3
Watery La. Fla 84 C2
Watery La. Hat 129 F2
Watery La. Lon C 142 B2
Watery La. Mars 79 F1
Watford By-Ps. Elst 169 D1
Watford Field Rd. Watf 167 E2
Watford Heath. Watf 167 E1
Watford Rd. Abb L 153 E3
Watford Rd. Chis 141 D3
Watford Rd. Cro Gr 166 A2
Watford Rd. Elst 169 E2
Watford Rd. Kin L 153 D4
Watford Rd. Radl 155 F2
Watford Rd. St Alb 141 D4
Watling Cl. Heml H 124 C3
Watling Knoll. Radl 155 F3
Watling St. Pk St 141 E3
Watling St. St Alb 141 E4
Watling View. St Alb 141 E4
Watlington Rd. Harl 118 B2
Watson Ave. St Alb 127 F3
Watson's Walk. St Alb 127 F1
Watton Rd. Dat 69 F1
Watton Rd. Kneb 69 D3
Watton Rd. Ware 93 E1
Watton Rd. Wat St 70 A1
Watts Cl. L Had 57 E1
Wauluds Bank Dri. Luton 44 C4
Wavell Cl. Ches 148 C2
Waveney. Heml H 124 C4
Waveney Rd. Harp 86 B2
Waverley Cl. Stev 69 D4
Waverley Gdns. Norwd 175 D1
Waverley Rd. St Alb 127 E3
Waxhouse Gate. St Alb 127 E2
Waxwell Cl. Pnr 175 E1
Waxwell La. Pnr 175 E1
Wayre St. Harl 118 B2
Wayre The. Harl 118 B2
Waysbrook. Letw 23 D2
Wayside. Chipf 138 A1
Wayside. Pot B 159 E3
Wayside Ave. Bus 168 B2
Wayside The. Heml H 125 E1
Waysmeet. Letw 23 D2
Waytemore Rd. Bis St 76 C3
Weald La. Har 176 B1
Weald Rise. Har 176 C1
Wealdwood Gdns. Pnr 176 A2
Weall Green. Watf 154 A4
Weatherby Rd. Luton 44 B1
Weavers Rd. Tri 99 F2
Webb Rise. Stev 51 D4
Webber Cl. Elst 169 E2
Wedgewood Cl. Norwd 174 B2
Wedgewood Ct. Stev 37 E1
Wedgewood Way. Stev 37 D1
Wedmore Rd. Hit 35 D3
Wedon Way. Byg 4 B2
Weedon Cl. Henlw 10 B3
Weighton Rd. Har 176 B1
Welbeck Cl. Bor 170 A3
Welbeck Rd. Luton 63 F4
Welbeck Rise. Harp 107 E3
Welbury Ave. Luton 45 E4
Welch Pl. Pnr 175 E1
Welclose St. St Alb 127 E2
Welham Cl. Wel Gr 144 B4
Welham Manor. Wel Gr 144 B4
Well App. Barn 171 E2
Well Croft. Heml H 124 A2
Well End Rd. Shen 157 E1
Well Garth. Wel GC 110 C3
Well Green. Bram 91 E2
Well La. Cra 61 D4
Well La. Harl 117 D1
Well Rd. Barn 171 E2
Well Rd. Nort 145 F1
Wellands. Hat 130 A4
Wellbury Terr. Heml H 125 E2
Wellcroft. Ivin 80 C3
Wellcroft Cl. Wel GC 111 D2
Wellcroft Rd. Wel GC 111 D2
Wellen Rise. Heml H 138 C4
Wellers Gr. Ches 148 A2
Wellesley Ave. Norwd 174 C3
Wellesley Cres. Pot B 158 C3
Wellfield Ave. Luton 44 B4
Wellfield Cl. Hat 130 A3
Wellfield Rd. Hat 130 A3
Wellgate Rd. Luton 44 B1
Wellhouse Cl. Luton 63 D4
Wellhouse La. Barn 171 E3
Wellingham Ave. Hit 21 E1
Wellington Ave. Pnr 175 F1
Wellington Dri. Wel GC 111 E3
Wellington Pl. Knee 2 A3
Wellington Rd. Lon C 142 B3
Wellington Rd. Pnr 175 F1
Wellington Rd. St Alb 128 A1
Wellington Rd. Stev 51 E3
Wellington Rd. Watf 167 D4
Wellington St. Hert 113 D4
Wellington St. Luton 63 E3
Well-Row. Bay 132 C3
Wells Cl. Harp 85 F2
Wells Yard. Watf 167 D3
Wellside Cl. Barn 171 E3
Wellstones. Watf 167 D3
Wellswood Cl. Heml H 125 D2
Welsummer Way. Ches 148 B2
Weltmore Rd. Luton 44 C3
Welwyn By Pass Rd. Welw 89 E2
Welwyn Ct. Heml H 124 C4
Welwyn Rd. Hertng 112 C4
Wendover Cl. Harp 86 B1
Wendover Cl. St Alb 128 B4
Wendover Dri. Welw 89 E3
Wendover Way. Bus 168 B2
Wendover Way. Luton 45 F2
Wengeo La. Ware 93 D1
Wenlock St. Luton 63 F4
Wensley Cl. Harp 107 E3
Wensley Dale. Luton 45 F1
Wensleydale. Heml H 124 C3
Wensum Way. Ric 165 E1
Wentbridge Path. Bor 157 D1
Wentworth Ave. Elst 169 F2
Wentworth Ave. Luton 44 B3
Wentworth Cl. Pot B 159 D4
Wentworth Cl. Watf 153 F1
Wentworth Cotts. Hod 134 C1
Wentworth Dri. Bis St 76 B3
Wentworth Rd. Barn 171 E3
Wentworth Rd. Hert 113 E2
Wenwell Cl. Dra B 99 D2
Wesley Ave. Hert 113 E3
Wesley Cl. Arl 11 D2
Wesley Cl. Gofs O 147 E2
Wesley Rd. Mark 83 F3
Wessex Dri. Pnr 175 F2
West Alley. Hit 34 C4
West Ave. Bal 23 F4
West Ave. Chis 141 D3
West Burrowfield. Wel GC 110 B2
West Chantry. Har 176 A1
West Cl. Barn 171 D2
West Cl. Hit 22 A1
West Cl. Hod 135 D4
West Cl. Stev 50 C3
West Comm. Harp 107 D3
West Common Cl. Harp 107 D3
West Common Gr. Harp 107 D3
West Common Way. Harp 107 D3
West Dene. Gt Ga 104 A4
West Dri. Arl 11 D2
West Dri. Har 176 B2
West Dri. Watf 154 A2
West Drive Gdns. Har 176 B2
West End. Ashw 4 B2
West End La. Barn 171 E3
West End Rd. Bric 147 F4
West End Rd. Ched 79 F4
West Gate. Harl 117 E1
West Hill. Hit 34 B4
West Hill Rd. Hod 135 D4
West Hill Rd. Luton 63 F3
West Hyde La. C St P 172 A2
West La. Gt Of 33 E1
West La. Pirt 20 B3
West Leith. Tri 99 F1
West Mead. Wel GC 111 D2
West Rd. Berk 122 A3
West Rd. Bis St 76 C3
West Rd. Harl 118 A2
West Rd. Saw 97 E2
West Rd. Sta Mo 59 F3
West Reach. Stev 50 C1
West Riding. Bri Wd 140 C1
West Riding. Tewin 90 B3
West Side. Hod 148 C3
West Side Centre. Luton 63 E4
West Sq. Harl 117 E1
West St. Hert 113 E3
West St. Lily 32 B1
West St. Ware 93 E1
West Valley Rd. Fel 138 B4
West View. Hat 130 A4
West View. Letw 22 C3
West View Gdns. Elst 169 E2
West View Rd. St Alb 127 E2
West Way. Harp 86 B1
West Way. Ric 165 D1
West Way. Wa Aby 163 D1
Westall Cl. Hert 113 E3
Westall Mews. Hert 113 E3

Westbourne Rd. Luton 45 D1
Westbury Cl. Hit 34 B4
Westbury Gdns. Luton 45 F2
Westbury Pl. Letw 22 C3
Westbury Rd. Norwd 174 C4
Westbury Rd. Watf 167 D2
Westbush Cl. Hod 114 C1
Westcott. Wel GC 111 E4
Westcroft Cl. Enf 162 B1
Westcroft Ct. Hod 135 D2
Westell Cl. Bal 24 A4
Westerdale. Heml H 124 C3
Westerdale. Luton 44 A3
Western Ave. Henlw 10 A2
Western Cl. Letw 11 F1
Western Rd. Lo Naz 135 F1
Western Rd. Luton 63 E3
Western Rd. Tri 99 F2
Western Way. Letw 11 F1
Westfield. Wel GC 111 D4
Westfield Ave. Harp 86 A2
Westfield Ave. Watf 154 B1
Westfield Cl. Bis St 76 C4
Westfield Cl. Ches 162 C4
Westfield Cl. Hit 34 B4
Westfield Ct. St Alb 128 B3
Westfield Dri. Harp 86 A2
Westfield La. Hit 34 B4
Westfield Park. Pnr 175 F2
Westfield Pl. Harp 86 A2
Westfield Rd. Berk 121 F3
Westfield Rd. Bis St 76 C4
Westfield Rd. Harp 86 A2
Westfield Rd. Hert 113 E4
Westfield Rd. Hod 134 C4
Westfield Wlk. Ches 162 C4
Westfields. St Alb 141 D4
Westgate. Stev 50 B3
Westholm. Letw 22 C4
Westland Dri. Bro Pk 144 C2
Westland Rd. Kneb 69 D3
Westland Rd. Watf 167 D4
Westlea Ave. Watf 154 C1
Westlea Cl. Hod 148 C4
Westlea Rd. Hod 148 C4
Westlecote Gdns. Luton 45 E2
Westly Wood. Wel GC 111 D4
Westmeade Cl. Ches 148 A1
Westmill La. Ick 21 E1
Westmill Rd. Hit 21 E1
Westmill Rd. Thun 93 D2
Westminster Ct. St Alb 127 E1
Westmorland Ave. Luton 44 C3
Weston Ave. Roystn 7 E4
Weston Rd. Stev 36 C1
Weston Way. Bal 23 F4
Westray. Heml H 125 E1
Westridge Cl. Heml H 123 F2
Westview Ct. Elst 169 E2
Westview Rise. Heml H 124 B2
Westway. Luton 46 B2
Westwick Cl. Heml H 125 E1
Westwick Row. Heml H 125 F1
Westwood Ave. Hit 35 D3
Westwood Cl. Pot B 145 D1
Wetherby Rd. Bor 169 F4
Wetherby Rd. Enf 161 E1
Wetherfield. Sta Mo 59 E4
Wetherne Link. Luton 44 B3
Wexham Cl. Luton 44 C4
Weybourne Cl. Harp 86 B1
Weybourne Dri. Luton 45 E4
Weymouth St. Heml H 138 B4
Whaley Rd. Pot B 159 E3
Wharf La. Nthch 121 E4
Wharf La. Ric 165 F1
Wharf Rd. Bis St 76 C3
Wharf Rd. Heml H 124 A1
Wharf Rd. Hod 148 C4
Wharfedale. Heml H 124 C3
Wheat Cl. St Alb 128 A4
Wheat Croft. Bis St 76 C2
Wheat Hill. Letw 22 C4
Wheatbarn. Wel GC 111 D4
Wheatcotes. Dat 69 E1
Wheatcroft. Ches 148 A2
Wheatfield. Hat 130 A3
Wheatfield Ave. Harp 107 D3
Wheatfield Cres. Roystn 7 F3
Wheatfield Rd. Harp 107 D2
Wheathampstead Pl. Whea 87 E1
Wheathampstead Rd. Harp 107 F4
Wheatlands. Stev 51 E4
Wheatley Cl. Saw 97 E1
Wheatley Cl. Wel GC 111 D2
Wheatley Rd. Wel GC 111 D2
Wheatleys. St Alb 128 B3
Wheatlock Mead. Red 106 A3
Wheatsheaf Dri. Ware 93 D2
Wheatsheaf Rd. Hun 95 E1
Wheelers Cl. Lo Naz 135 F1
Wheelers La. Heml H 124 C1
Wheelright Cl. Bus 168 A2
Whempstead La. Wat St 71 D3
Whempstead Rd. Heb En 52 C1
Whetstone Cl. Wl Gr 89 F4
Whinbush Gr. Hit 34 C4
Whinbush Rd. Hit 34 C4
Whippendell Hill. Chipf 138 B1
Whippendell Rd. Watf 166 C2
Whipperley Ring. Luton 63 D3
Whipperley Way. Luton 63 E3
Whisper Wood. Chor 165 D3
Whitby Rd. Luton 45 E1
White Bear. Sta Mo 59 F4
White Crofts. Stot 11 F3
White Gate Gdns. Har 176 C2
White Hart Cl. Bun 40 C4
White Hart Dri. Heml H 124 C1
White Hart Rd. Heml H 125 D1
White Hedge Dri. St Alb 127 E3
White Hill. Ash Gr 136 B4
White Hill. Fla 105 D4
White Hill. Heml H 123 F1
White Hill. Ric 174 A2
White Hill. Wal 38 B1
White Hill. Welw 89 D2
White Horse La. Brn Gr 90 B4
White Horse La. Lon C 142 C3
White Horse La. Wl Gr 69 D1
White La. L Alm 49 E4
White Lion St. Heml H 138 B4
White Orchs. N20 171 F1
White Post Field. Saw 97 E1
White Shack La. Cha Cr 152 C1
White Stubbs La. Bay 133 D1
White Stubbs La. Bric 133 E1
White Stubbs La. Hod 134 B1
White Way The. Stev 51 E4
Whitebarns. Fur P 43 D3
Whitebarns La. Fur P 43 D3
Whitebeams. Chis 141 E2
Whitebeams. Hat 130 A1
Whitebroom Rd. Heml H 123 F3
Whitechurch Cl. Luton 46 B1
Whitechurch Gdns. Letw 23 E2
Whitecroft. St Alb 142 A4
Whitecroft Rd. Luton 64 A4
Whitefield Ave. Luton 44 B4
Whitefields Rd. Ches 148 B2
Whitefriars Ave. Har 176 C1
Whitefriars Dri. Har 176 C1
Whitefriars Trading Estate. Har 176 B1
Whitegale Cl. Hit 35 D3
Whitegates Cl. Cro Gr 166 A3
Whitehall Cl. Lo Naz 135 F1
Whitehall La. Bis St 58 C1
Whitehall Rd. Bis St 58 C1
Whitehands Cl. Hod 134 C3
Whitehart Cross. Bov 136 C2
Whitehicks. Letw 12 A1
Whitehill. Berk 122 B3
Whitehill Ave. Luton 63 E3
Whitehill Ct. Berk 122 B3
Whitehill Rd. Hit 35 D3
Whitehorn Way. Luton 63 D3
Whitehorse St. Bal 12 C1
Whitehorse Vale. Luton 45 D4
Whitehouse Ave. Bor 170 A3
Whitehouse La. Bed 140 B2
Whitehurst Ave. Hit 21 F1
Whitelands Ave. Chor 164 B3
Whiteleaf Rd. Heml H 138 B4
Whiteley Cl. Dan En 71 F4
Whiteley La. Buck 27 E4
Whitesmead Rd. Stev 50 C4
Whitestone Wlk. Heml H 124 A3
Whitethorn. Wel GC 111 D3
Whitethorn La. Letw 23 D2
Whitewaites. Harl 117 F1
Whiteway. Letw 23 E2
Whitewaybottom La. Pet Gr 66 A2
Whitewebbs La. Enf 161 F2
Whitewebbs Rd. Enf 161 E2
Whitewood Rd. Berk 122 A2
Whitfield Way. Ric 164 C1
Whitings Cl. Harp 86 B2
Whitings Rd. Barn 171 E2
Whitlars Dri. Kin L 138 C2
Whitley Rd. Hod 135 D4
Whitney Dri. Stev 36 B1
Whittingham Cl. Luton 46 C1
Whittingstall Rd. Hod 135 D4
Whittington La. Stev 50 C2
Whittington Way. Bis St 76 C2
Whittle Cl. Henlw 10 A2
Whittlesea Cl. Har 176 B2
Whittlesea Path. Har 176 B1
Whittlesea Rd. Har 176 B1
Whitwell Cl. Luton 45 D4
Whitwell Rd. Watf 154 B2
Whitworth Jones Ave. Henlw 10 B3
Whitworth Rd. Stev 37 D2
Whomerley Rd. Stev 50 C2
Whydale Rd. Roystn 7 F3
Whytingham Rd. Tri 100 B2
Wick Ave. Whea 108 B4
Wick Hill. Ken Co 82 C4
Wick Rd. Wigg 120 B4
Wick The. Hert 92 B1
Wicken Fields. Ware 93 E2
Wickets The. Luton 45 E4
Wickfield Cl. Wl Gr 69 D1
Wickham Cl. Hare 173 E1
Wickham Rd. Har 176 B1
Wicklands Rd. Hun 116 B4
Wickmere Cl. Luton 45 E4
Wickstead Ave. Luton 44 C2
Wickwood Ct. St Alb 128 A2
Widbury Gdns. Ware 93 F1
Widbury Hill. Ware 94 A1
Widford Rd. Had Cr 95 F4
Widford Rd. Hun 95 E1
Widford Rd. Wel GC 111 D3
Widford Terr. Heml H 105 D1
Widgeon Way. Watf 154 C2
Widmore Dri. Heml H 125 D3
Wieland Rd. Norwd 175 D2
Wiggenhall Rd. Watf 167 E2
Wigmore La. Luton 46 B1
Wigmores N. Wel GC 110 B4
Wigmores S. Wel GC 110 B3
Wigram Way. Stev 51 D2
Wilbury Cl. Letw 22 B4
Wilbury Hills Rd. Letw 22 B3
Wilbury Rd. Letw 22 C4
Wilbury Way. Hit 22 A1
Wilcot Ave. Watf 167 F1
Wilcox Cl. Bor 170 B4
Wild Cherry Dri. Luton 63 E3
Wild Oaks Cl. Norwd 174 C2
Wilderness. Berk 122 B2
Wildwood. Norwd 174 B2
Wildwood Ave. Bri Wd 140 C1
Wildwood La. Stev 50 C2
Wilford Cl. Norwd 174 B2
Wilga Rd. Welw 89 D3
Wilkin's Green La. St Alb 129 E2
Willenhall Cl. Luton 45 D4
William Covell Cl. Enf 160 C1
William Pl. Stev 51 D2
William St. Berk 122 B2
William St. Bus 167 E3
William St. Luton 45 F1
William St. Mark 83 F3
Williams Way. Radl 156 B2
Williamson St. Luton 63 F4
Willian Church Rd. Will 23 D1
Willian Rd. Hit 22 C1
Willian Rd. Will 23 D1
Willian Way. Bal 23 F3
Willian Way. Letw 23 D2
Willinghall Cl. Wa Aby 163 E4
Williton Rd. Luton 46 B1
Willoughby Cl. Hod 134 C1
Willoughby Rd. Harp 86 A2
Willoughby Way. Hit 35 D3
Willow Cl. Bis St 76 C4
Willow Cl. Gt Ho 42 A4
Willow Cl. Ham St 147 F3
Willow Cl. Reed 16 B3
Willow Cres. St Alb 128 B2
Willow Dene. Bus 168 C1
Willow Dene. Pnr 175 E1
Willow Dri. Barn 171 F3
Willow Edge. Kin L 139 D1
Willow Gr. Wel GC 89 E2
Willow Green. Bor 170 B2
Willow La. Hit 34 B3
Willow La. Watf 167 D2
Willow Mead. Saw 97 F1
Willow Path. Wa Aby 163 F3
Willow Way. Chis 141 D2
Willow Way. Harp 86 B2
Willow Way. Hat 129 F1
Willow Way. Heml H 124 A3
Willow Way. Luton 44 C3
Willow Way. Pot B 159 D3
Willow Way. Radl 155 F2
Willow Wlk. Wl Gr 89 E4
Willowby Ct. Lon C 142 B3
Willowdene. Ches 148 C2
Willowgate Trading Estate. Luton 44 A4
Willowmead. Hertng 113 D3
Willows Cl. Pnr 175 E1
Willows Link. Stev 51 D1
Willows The. Hit 35 D3
Willows The. Ric 173 D4
Willows The. St Alb 142 A4
Willows The. Stev 51 D1
Willows The. Watf 167 D1
Willowside. Lon C 142 C2
Willowside Way. Roystn 7 E4
Wilsden Ave. Luton 63 E3
Wilshere Ave. St Alb 127 E1
Wilshere Cres. Hit 35 E4
Wilshere Rd. Welw 89 D2
Wilsmere Dri. Har 176 C2
Wilsons Cl. Stev 36 B1
Wilsons La. Ashw 4 B2
Wilstone Dri. St Alb 128 B4
Wilton Cl. Bis St 77 D4
Wilton Cres. Hert 113 E2
Wilton Rd. Hit 21 F1
Wilton Way. Hert 113 E2
Wiltshire Rd. Stev 51 D2
Wimborne Cl. Saw 97 E1
Wimborne Gr. Watf 153 F1
Wimborne Rd. Luton 63 E4
Wimple Rd. Luton 44 A1
Winch Cl. Cod 88 C4
Winch St. Luton 45 F1
Winchdells. Heml H 139 D4
Winches Farm Dri. St Alb 128 B2
Winchester Cl. Bis St 76 B2
Winchester Cl. Stev 37 D1
Winchester Rd. Norwd 174 C1
Winchester Way. Cro Gr 166 A2
Winchfield Way. Chor 165 E1
Windermere Ave. St Alb 128 A1
Windermere Cl. Chor 164 B2
Windermere Cl. Heml H 125 E1
Windermere Cres. Luton 44 C3
Windhill. Bis St 76 C4
Windhill. Wel GC 111 D4
Windhill Fields. Bis St 76 C4
Windhill Old Rd. Bis St 76 C4
Winding Hill. Muc H 75 D2
Winding Shot. Heml H 124 A2
Winding Shott. Bram 91 E2
Windmill Ave. St Alb 128 B4
Windmill Cl. Bark 17 E3
Windmill Cl. Ivin 80 C3
Windmill Cl. Wa Aby 163 F3
Windmill Dri. Cro Gr 165 F2
Windmill Field. Gt Am 114 B4
Windmill Fields. Harl 118 C2
Windmill Hill. Chipf 151 F4
Windmill Hill. Sar 151 F4
Windmill La. Barn 170 C2
Windmill La. Bus 168 C1
Windmill La. Ches 148 C1
Windmill Rd. Bre Wd 47 E1
Windmill Rd. Heml H 124 C1
Windmill Rd. Luton 63 F4
Windmill Rd. Mark 84 A3
Windmill St. Bus 168 C1
Windmill Way. Had Cr 74 C1
Windmill Way. Tri 99 F2
Windmore Ave. Pot B 158 B4
Windridge Cl. St Alb 127 D1
Winds End Cl. Heml H 125 D3
Windsor Cl. Bor 170 A4
Windsor Cl. Bov 137 D2
Windsor Cl. Ches 148 A1
Windsor Cl. Norwd 175 D1
Windsor Cl. Stev 69 D4
Windsor Cl. Welw 89 D2
Windsor Dri. Hertng 112 C4
Windsor Rd. Barn 171 E2
Windsor Rd. Enf 162 B2
Windsor Rd. Har 176 B1
Windsor Rd. Roystn 7 F3
Windsor Rd. Watf 154 B1
Windsor Rd. Welw 89 D2
Windsor St. Luton 63 E3
Windsor Way. Ric 165 D1
Windward Cl. Enf 162 B2
Windy Rise. Dan En 71 F4
Winford Dri. Hod 134 C1
Wingate Gdns. Welw 89 D3
Wingate Rd. Luton 44 C1
Wingate Way. St Alb 128 A1
Wingrave Rd. Lon M 79 E1
Wingrave Rd. Tri 100 A3
Winifred Rd. Heml H 138 B4
Winkfield Cl. Luton 44 A1
Winkwell. Heml H 123 E1
Winnington Rd. Enf 162 B1
Winsdon Hill. Luton 63 E3
Winsdon Rd. Luton 63 E3
Winslow Cl. Luton 45 E2
Winslow Rd. Wing 60 A2
Winston Cl. Hit 34 B4
Winston Cl. Stan 176 C2
Winston Ct. Har 176 A2
Winston Gdns. Berk 121 F2
Winston Way. Pot B 159 D3
Winstre Rd. Bor 170 A4
Winters La. Wal 38 B1
Winterscroft Rd. Hod 134 C4
Winton App. Cro Gr 166 B2
Winton Cl. Letw 23 E4
Winton Cl. Luton 45 E3
Winton Cres. Cro Gr 166 A2
Winton Dri. Ches 148 C1
Winton Dri. Cro Gr 166 B2
Winton Rd. Ware 93 F1
Wisden Rd. Stev 36 C1
Wisemans Gdns. Saw 97 E1
Wistlea Cres. Coln H 129 D1
Wistow Rd. Luton 45 D3
Witchford. Wel GC 111 E3
Withy Cl. Luton 44 A2
Witney Cl. Pnr 175 F2
Witter Ave. Ick 21 F2
Wiveton Cl. Luton 45 E4
Woburn Cl. Bus 168 B2
Woburn Cl. Stev 69 E4
Wodecroft Rd. Luton 45 D3
Wolsey Ave. Ches 147 F1
Wolsey Rd. Heml H 124 B1
Wolsey Rd. Norwd 174 B4
Wolston Cl. Luton 63 E4
Wolves Mere. Wl Gr 69 D1
Wood Cl. Hat 130 A3
Wood Common. Hat 130 A4
Wood Cres. Heml H 124 C1
Wood Dri. Stev 51 D1
Wood End. Chis 141 E2
Wood End Hill. Harp 85 E2
Wood End La. Fla 104 C4
Wood End Rd. Harp 85 E2
Wood Farm Rd. Heml H 124 C1
Wood Green Cl. Luton 46 A3
Wood Green Rd. Luton 46 B3
Wood La. Heml H 124 B1
Wood Lane End. Heml H 125 D2
Wood St. Barn 171 E3
Wood St. Luton 63 F3
Wood Vale. Hat 130 A3
Wood View. Cuf 146 C2
Wood View. Heml H 124 A3
Woodacre Dri. Wl Gr 90 A4
Woodbine Gr. Enf 161 E1
Woodbridge Cl. Luton 44 C2
Woodbrook Gdns. Wa Aby 163 F3
Woodbury Hill. Luton 45 F1
Woodbury Hill Path. Luton 45 F1
Woodcock Hill. Ric 173 F3
Woodcock Hill. Sand 108 C1
Woodcock Rd. Luton 63 D4
Woodcock Rd. Stev 51 E1
Woodcote Cl. Ches 148 B1
Woodcroft Ave. Sta Ab 115 E2
Woodfall Ave. Barn 171 F2
Woodfield Ave. Norwd 174 C3
Woodfield Cl. Sta Mo 59 F3
Woodfield Dri. Heml H 125 E1
Woodfield Gdns. Heml H 125 E1
Woodfield La. New St 145 F4
Woodfield Rd. Radl 156 A2
Woodfield Rd. Stev 36 B1
Woodfield Rd. Wel GC 110 C3
Woodfield Rise. Bus 168 B1
Woodfield Terr. Sta Mo 59 F3
Woodfield Way. St Alb 128 B3
Woodfields. Sta Mo 59 F3
Woodford Cres. Pnr 175 D1
Woodford Rd. Watf 167 E4
Woodforde Cl. Ashw 4 C2
Woodgate. Watf 154 A3
Woodgate Cres. Norwd 175 D2
Woodgreen Way. Ches 162 C4
Woodhall Ave. Pnr 175 F1
Woodhall Cl. Hert 113 E4
Woodhall Ct. Wel GC 110 C3
Woodhall Dri. Pnr 175 F1
Woodhall Gate. Pnr 175 E2
Woodhall Gr. Bis St 76 B3
Woodhall La. Heml H 124 C3
Woodhall La. Shen 156 C2
Woodhall La. Sth Ox 175 E3
Woodhall La. Wel GC 110 C2
Woodham Way. Sta Ab 115 E2
Woodhouse Eaves. Norwd 175 D3
Woodhurst. Letw 22 C4
Woodhurst Ave. Watf 154 B2
Woodland Ave. Heml H 124 A1
Woodland Ave. Luton 45 D2
Woodland Cl. Heml H 124 A1
Woodland Cl. Tri 99 F1
Woodland Dri. St Alb 128 B2
Woodland Dri. Watf 166 C4
Woodland La. Chor 164 B3
Woodland Mount. Hert 113 F3
Woodland Pl. Heml H 124 A1
Woodland Rd. Hert H 114 B2
Woodland Rd. Map Cr 172 B3
Woodland Rise. Stu 82 A4
Woodland Rise. Wel GC 110 B4
Woodland Way. Bal 23 F3
Woodland Way. Gofs O 147 D2
Woodland Way. Stev 51 D1
Woodland Way. Wl Gr 89 F4
Woodlands. Bis St 77 E4
Woodlands. Bro Pk 145 D3
Woodlands. Harp 85 F2
Woodlands. Radl 156 A3
Woodlands. Roystn 7 F3
Woodlands Ave. Berk 122 B2
Woodlands Cl. Bor 170 A3
Woodlands Cl. Hod 135 D3
Woodlands Dri. Bed 139 E2
Woodlands Dri. Hod 135 D2
Woodlands Dri. Stan 176 C2
Woodlands Meade. Wes 37 D4
Woodlands Rd. Bed 139 D2
Woodlands Rd. Bus 167 F2
Woodlands Rd. Enf 161 E1
Woodlands Rd. Hert 113 F3
Woodlands Rd. Thun 93 E3
Woodlea Gr. Norwd 174 B2
Woodley Rd. Ware 93 F1
Woodman Rd. Heml H 124 C1
Woodmans Yd. Watf 167 E3
Woodmere. Luton 31 D1
Woodmere Ave. Watf 154 C1
Woodmill Mews. Hod 135 D4
Woodpecker Cl. Bus 168 B1
Woodridge Way. Norwd 174 C2
Woodridings Ave. Pnr 175 F1
Woodridings Cl. Pnr 175 F2
Woods Ave. Hat 130 A3
Woods The. Norwd 175 D3
Woodshots Meadow. Watf 166 B2
Woodside. Bis St 77 E4
Woodside. Elst 169 F3
Woodside. Hert H 114 B1
Woodside. Watf 154 A2
Woodside Rd. Abb L 154 A4
Woodside Rd. Bri Wd 140 C1
Woodside Rd. Cad 63 D2
Woodside Rd. Har Gr 89 F2
Woodside Rd. Norwd 174 C2
Woodstock Cl. Hert H 114 A2
Woodstock Rd. Bus 168 C1
Woodstock Rd. Hod 134 C2
Woodstock Rd N. St Alb 128 A2
Woodstock Rd S. St Alb 128 A2
Woodville Ct. Watf 167 D4
Woodward Gdns. Stan 176 C2
Woodwaye. Watf 167 E1
Woodwicks. Map Cr 172 B3
Woolands. Chis 141 E2
Woolgrove Rd. Letw 22 A1
Woollam Cres. St Alb 127 E4
Woollard St. Wa Aby 163 E3
Woolmans Cl. Hod 134 C1
Woolmer Dri. Heml H 125 E2
Woolmers La. Let Gr 112 A1
Woolners Way. Stev 50 B3
Woolston Ave. Letw 23 D2
Wootton Cl. Luton 45 D4
Wootton Dri. Heml H 124 C4
Worcester Rd. Hat 129 F3
Worcesters Ave. Enf 162 A1
Wordsworth Cl. Roystn 2 B1
Wordsworth Rd. Harp 86 A2
Wordsworth Rd. Luton 44 A1
Works Rd. Letw 23 E4
Worley Rd. St Alb 127 E2
Wormley Lodge Cl. Hod 148 C4
Worsted La. H St H 41 F4
Wortham Rd. Roystn 7 F2
Wortham Way. Stev 51 D2
Wratten Cl. Hit 34 C3
Wratten Rd E. Hit 34 C3
Wratten Rd W. Hit 34 C3
Wrayfields. Stot 12 A4
Wren Cl. Kim 66 A1
Wren Cl. Luton 46 B3
Wren Cl. Stev 51 D3
Wren Cres. Bus 168 B1
Wren Wood. Wel GC 111 D4
Wrenbrook Rd. Bis St 76 C3
Wrensfield. Heml H 124 A2
Wrestlers Cl. Hat 130 B4
Wrexham Terr. Roystn 7 E4
Wright Cl. Whea 108 C4
Wright's Buildings. Watf 167 D4
Wright's Green La. L Hal 98 B4
Wrights Meadow. Wal 52 A4
Wrights Orch. Ast 51 F1
Wrotham Rd. Barn 171 F4